T0330346

Principles of Financial Modelling

Founded in 1807, John Wiley & Sons is the oldest independent publishing company in the United States. With offices in North America, Europe, Australia and Asia, Wiley is globally committed to developing and marketing print and electronic products and services for our customers' professional and personal knowledge and understanding.

The Wiley Finance series contains books written specifically for finance and investment professionals as well as sophisticated individual investors and their financial advisors. Book topics range from portfolio management to e-commerce, risk management, financial engineering, valuation and financial instrument analysis, as well as much more.

For a list of available titles, visit our Web site at `www.WileyFinance.com`.

Principles of Financial Modelling

Model Design and Best Practices using Excel and VBA

MICHAEL REES

WILEY

This edition first published 2018

Registered office
John Wiley & Sons Ltd, The Atrium, Southern Gate, Chichester, West Sussex, PO19 8SQ, United Kingdom

For details of our global editorial offices, for customer services and for information about how to apply for permission to reuse the copyright material in this book please see our website at www.wiley.com.

Library of Congress Cataloging-in-Publication Data is Available:

ISBN 978-1-118-90401-5 (hardback) ISBN 978-1-118-90400-8 (ePub)

ISBN 978-1-118-90394-0 (ePDF)

Cover Design: Wiley
Cover Images: © AmbientShoot/Shutterstock;
© whiteMocca/Shutterstock

Set in 10/12pt Sabon by SPi Global, Chennai, India

Printed in Great Britain by TJ International Ltd, Padstow, Cornwall, UK

10 9 8 7 6 5 4 3 2 1

"To my mother, father and
the Godsall and Rees families"

Contents

Preface xxv

About the Author xxvii

About the Website xxix

PART ONE

Introduction to Modelling, Core Themes and Best Practices 1

CHAPTER 1
Models of Models 3
Introduction 3
Context and Objectives 3
The Stages of Modelling 3
Backward Thinking and Forward Calculation Processes 4

CHAPTER 2
Using Models in Decision Support 7
Introduction 7
Benefits of Using Models 7
Providing Numerical Information 7
Capturing Influencing Factors and Relationships 7
Generating Insight and Forming Hypotheses 8
Decision Levers, Scenarios, Uncertainties, Optimisation, Risk Mitigation and Project Design 8
Improving Working Processes, Enhanced Communications and Precise Data Requirements 9
Challenges in Using Models 9
The Nature of Model Error 9
Inherent Ambiguity and Circularity of Reasoning 10
Inconsistent Scope or Alignment of Decision and Model 10
The Presence on Biases, Imperfect Testing, False Positives and Negatives 11
Balancing Intuition with Rationality 11
Lack of Data or Insufficient Understanding of a Situation 12
Overcoming Challenges: Awareness, Actions and Best Practices 13

CHAPTER 3
Core Competencies and Best Practices: Meta-themes **15**
Introduction 15
Key Themes 15
Decision-support Role, Objectives, Outputs and Communication 16
Application Knowledge and Understanding 17
Skills with Implementation Platform 17
Defining Sensitivity and Flexibility Requirements 18
Designing Appropriate Layout, Input Data Structures and Flow 20
Ensuring Transparency and Creating a User-friendly Model 20
Integrated Problem-solving Skills 21

PART TWO

Model Design and Planning **23**

CHAPTER 4
Defining Sensitivity and Flexibility Requirements **25**
Introduction 25
Key Issues for Consideration 25
Creating a Focus on Objectives and Their Implications 26
Sensitivity Concepts in the Backward Thought and Forward Calculation Processes 26
Time Granularity 30
Level of Detail on Input Variables 30
Sensitising Absolute Values or Variations from Base Cases 31
Scenarios Versus Sensitivities 32
Uncertain Versus Decision Variables 33
Increasing Model Validity Using Formulae 34

CHAPTER 5
Database Versus Formulae-driven Approaches **37**
Introduction 37
Key Issues for Consideration 37
Separating the Data, Analysis and Presentation (Reporting) Layers 37
The Nature of Changes to Data Sets and Structures 39
Focus on Data or Formulae? 40
Practical Example 42

CHAPTER 6
Designing the Workbook Structure **47**
Introduction 47
Designing Workbook Models with Multiple Worksheets 47
Linked Workbooks 47
Multiple Worksheets: Advantages and Disadvantages 48

Generic Best Practice Structures 49
The Role of Multiple Worksheets in Best Practice Structures 49
Type I: Single Worksheet Models 50
Type II: Single Main Formulae Worksheet, and Several Data Worksheets 50
Type III: Single Main Formulae Worksheet, and Several Data and Local Analysis Worksheets 51
Further Comparative Comments 51
Using Information from Multiple Worksheets: Choice (Exclusion) and Consolidation (Inclusion) Processes 52
Multi-sheet or "Three Dimensional" Formulae 53
Using Excel's Data/Consolidation Functionality 54
Consolidating from Several Sheets into a Database Using a Macro 55
User-defined Functions 56

PART THREE

Model Building, Testing and Auditing **57**

CHAPTER 7

Creating Transparency: Formula Structure, Flow and Format **59**

Introduction 59
Approaches to Identifying the Drivers of Complexity 59
Taking the Place of a Model Auditor 59
Example: Creating Complexity in a Simple Model 60
Core Elements of Transparent Models 61
Optimising Audit Paths 62
Creating Short Audit Paths Using Modular Approaches 63
Creating Short Audit Paths Using Formulae Structure and Placement 67
Optimising Logical Flow and the Direction of the Audit Paths 68
Identifying Inputs, Calculations and Outputs: Structure and Formatting 69
The Role of Formatting 70
Colour-coding of Inputs and Outputs 70
Basic Formatting Operations 73
Conditional Formatting 73
Custom Formatting 75
Creating Documentation, Comments and Hyperlinks 76

CHAPTER 8

Building Robust and Transparent Formulae **79**

Introduction 79
General Causes of Mistakes 79
Insufficient Use of General Best Practices Relating to Flow, Formatting, Audit Paths 79

Insufficient Consideration Given to Auditability and Other Potential Users 79
Overconfidence, Lack of Checking and Time Constraints 80
Sub-optimal Choice of Functions 80
Inappropriate Use or Poor Implementation of Named Ranges, Circular References or Macros 80
Examples of Common Mistakes 80
Referring to Incorrect Ranges or To Blank Cells 80
Non-transparent Assumptions, Hidden Inputs and Labels 82
Overlooking the Nature of Some Excel Function Values 82
Using Formulae Which are Inconsistent Within a Range 83
Overriding Unforeseen Errors with IFERROR 84
Models Which are Correct in Base Case but Not in Others 85
Incorrect Modifications when Working with Poor Models 85
The Use of Named Ranges 85
Mechanics and Implementation 86
Disadvantages of Using Named Ranges 86
Advantages and Key Uses of Named Ranges 90
Approaches to Building Formulae, to Testing, Error Detection and Management 91
Checking Behaviour and Detecting Errors Using Sensitivity Testing 91
Using Individual Logic Steps 93
Building and Splitting Compound Formulae 94
Using Absolute Cell Referencing Only Where Necessary 96
Limiting Repeated or Unused Logic 96
Using Breaks to Test Calculation Paths 97
Using Excel Error Checking Rules 97
Building Error-checking Formulae 98
Handling Calculation Errors Robustly 100
Restricting Input Values Using Data Validation 100
Protecting Ranges 101
Dealing with Structural Limitations: Formulae and Documentation 102

CHAPTER 9
Choosing Excel Functions for Transparency, Flexibility and Efficiency 105
Introduction 105
Key Considerations 105
Direct Arithmetic or Functions, and Individual Cells or Ranges? 105
IF Versus MIN/MAX 107
Embedded IF Statements 109
Short Forms of Functions 111
Text Versus Numerical Fields 112
SUMIFS with One Criterion 112
Including Only Specific Items in a Summation 113

AGGREGATE and SUBTOTAL Versus Individual Functions 114
Array Functions or VBA User-defined Functions? 115
Volatile Functions 115
Effective Choice of Lookup Functions 116

CHAPTER 10
Dealing with Circularity **117**
Introduction 117
The Drivers and Nature of Circularities 117
Circular (Equilibrium or Self-regulating) Inherent Logic 117
Circular Formulae (Circular References) 118
Generic Types of Circularities 119
Resolving Circular Formulae 119
Correcting Mistakes that Result in Circular Formulae 120
Avoiding a Logical Circularity by Modifying the Model Specification 120
Eliminating Circular Formulae by Using Algebraic (Mathematical) Manipulation 121
Resolving a Circularity Using Iterative Methods 122
Iterative Methods in Practice 123
Excel's Iterative Method 123
Creating a Broken Circular Path: Key Steps 125
Repeatedly Iterating a Broken Circular Path Manually and Using a VBA Macro 126
Practical Example 128
Using Excel Iterations to Resolve Circular References 129
Using a Macro to Resolve a Broken Circular Path 129
Algebraic Manipulation: Elimination of Circular References 130
Altered Model 1: No Circularity in Logic or in Formulae 130
Altered Model 2: No Circularity in Logic in Formulae 131
Selection of Approach to Dealing with Circularities: Key Criteria 131
Model Accuracy and Validity 132
Complexity and Transparency 133
Non-convergent Circularities 134
Potential for Broken Formulae 138
Calculation Speed 140
Ease of Sensitivity Analysis 140
Conclusions 141

CHAPTER 11
Model Review, Auditing and Validation **143**
Introduction 143
Objectives 143
(Pure) Audit 143
Validation 144
Improvement, Restructuring or Rebuild 145

Processes, Tools and Techniques 146
Avoiding Unintentional Changes 146
Developing a General Overview and Then Understanding the Details 147
Testing and Checking the Formulae 151
Using a Watch Window and Other Ways to Track Values 151

PART FOUR

Sensitivity and Scenario Analysis, Simulation and Optimisation 153

CHAPTER 12
Sensitivity and Scenario Analysis: Core Techniques 155
Introduction 155
Overview of Sensitivity-related Techniques 155
DataTables 156
Overview 156
Implementation 157
Limitations and Tips 157
Practical Applications 160
Example: Sensitivity of Net Present Value to Growth Rates 160
Example: Implementing Scenario Analysis 160

CHAPTER 13
Using GoalSeek and Solver 163
Introduction 163
Overview of GoalSeek and Solver 163
Links to Sensitivity Analysis 163
Tips, Tricks and Limitations 163
Practical Applications 164
Example: Breakeven Analysis of a Business 165
Example: Threshold Investment Amounts 166
Example: Implied Volatility of an Option 167
Example: Minimising Capital Gains Tax Liability 167
Example: Non-linear Curve Fitting 169

CHAPTER 14
Using VBA Macros to Conduct Sensitivity and Scenario Analyses 171
Introduction 171
Practical Applications 172
Example: Running Sensitivity Analysis Using a Macro 172
Example: Running Scenarios Using a Macro 173
Example: Using a Macro to Run Breakeven Analysis with GoalSeek 173
Example: Using Solver Within a Macro to Create a Frontier of Optimum Solutions 175

CHAPTER 15
Introduction to Simulation and Optimisation 177
Introduction 177
The Links Between Sensitivity and Scenario Analysis, Simulation and Optimisation 177
The Combinatorial Effects of Multiple Possible Input Values 177
Controllable Versus Non-controllable: Choice Versus Uncertainty of Input Values 178
Practical Example: A Portfolio of Projects 179
Description 179
Optimisation Context 180
Risk or Uncertainty Context Using Simulation 180
Further Aspects of Optimisation Modelling 182
Structural Choices 182
Uncertainty 183
Integrated Approaches to Optimisation 183
Modelling Issues and Tools 184

CHAPTER 16
The Modelling of Risk and Uncertainty, and Using Simulation 187
Introduction 187
The Meaning, Origins and Uses of Monte Carlo Simulation 187
Definition and Origin 187
Limitations of Sensitivity and Scenario Approaches 188
Key Benefits of Uncertainty and Risk Modelling and the Questions Addressable 189
The Nature of Model Outputs 190
The Applicability of Simulation Methods 190
Key Process and Modelling Steps in Risk Modelling 191
Risk Identification 191
Risk Mapping and the Role of the Distribution of Input Values 191
The Modelling Context and the Meaning of Input Distributions 192
The Effect of Dependencies Between Inputs 192
Random Numbers and the Required Number of Recalculations or Iterations 193
Using Excel and VBA to Implement Risk and Simulation Models 194
Generation of Random Samples 194
Repeated Recalculations and Results Storage 195
Example: Cost Estimation with Uncertainty and Event Risks Using Excel/VBA 196
Using Add-ins to Implement Risk and Simulation Models 196
Benefits of Add-ins 196
Example: Cost Estimation with Uncertainty and Event Risks Using @RISK 197

PART FIVE

Excel Functions and Functionality **199**

CHAPTER 17
Core Arithmetic and Logical Functions **201**
Introduction 201
Practical Applications 201
Example: IF, AND, OR, NOT 202
Example: MIN, MAX, MINA, MAXA 204
Example: MINIFS and MAXIFS 204
Example: COUNT, COUNTA, COUNTIF and Similar Functions 205
Example: SUM, AVERAGE, AVERAGEA 206
Example: SUMIF, SUMIFS, AVERAGEIF, AVERAGEIFS 206
Example: PRODUCT 207
Example: SUMPRODUCT 209
Example: SUBTOTAL 209
Example: AGGREGATE 210
Example: IFERROR 212
Example: SWITCH 215

CHAPTER 18
Array Functions and Formulae **217**
Introduction 217
Functions and Formulae: Definitions 217
Implementation 217
Advantages and Disadvantages 218
Practical Applications: Array Functions 218
Example: Capex and Depreciation Schedules Using TRANSPOSE 218
Example: Cost Allocation Using SUMPRODUCT with TRANSPOSE 218
Example: Cost Allocation Using Matrix Multiplication Using MMULT 219
Example: Activity-based Costing and Resource Forecasting Using Multiple Driving Factors 220
Example: Summing Powers of Integers from 1 Onwards 222
Practical Applications: Array Formulae 225
Example: Finding First Positive Item in a List 225
Example: Find a Conditional Maximum 226
Example: Find a Conditional Maximum Using AGGREGATE as an Array Formula 227

CHAPTER 19
Mathematical Functions **229**
Introduction 229
Practical Applications 229
Example: EXP and LN 229
Example: ABS and SIGN 232

Example: INT, ROUNDDOWN, ROUNDUP, ROUND and TRUNC 233
Example: MROUND, CEILING.MATH and FLOOR.MATH 235
Example: MOD 236
Example: SQRT and POWER 236
Example: FACT and COMBIN 237
Example: RAND() 238
Example: SINE, ASIN, DEGREES and PI() 239
Example: BASE and DECIMAL 241

CHAPTER 20
Financial Functions 243
Introduction 243
Practical Applications 243
Example: FVSCHEDULE 244
Example: FV and PV 244
Example: PMT, IPMT, PPMT, CUMIPMT, CUMPRINC and NPER 246
Example: NPV and IRR for a Buy or Lease Decision 248
Example: SLN, DDB and VDB 250
Example: YIELD 252
Example: Duration of Cash Flows 252
Example: DURATION and MDURATION 253
Example: PDURATION and RRI 254
Other Financial Functions 255

CHAPTER 21
Statistical Functions 257
Introduction 257
Practical Applications: Position, Ranking and Central Values 258
Example: Calculating Mean and Mode 258
Example: Dynamic Sorting of Data Using LARGE 260
Example: RANK.EQ 261
Example: RANK.AVG 262
Example: Calculating Percentiles 262
Example: PERCENTRANK-type Functions 263
Practical Applications: Spread and Shape 264
Example: Generating a Histogram of Returns Using FREQUENCY 265
Example: Variance, Standard Deviation and Volatility 267
Example: Skewness and Kurtosis 271
Example: One-sided Volatility (Semi-deviation) 272
Practical Applications: Co-relationships and Dependencies 273
Example: Scatter Plots (*X–Y* Charts) and Measuring Correlation 274
Example: More on Correlation Coefficients and Rank Correlation 275
Example: Measuring Co-variances 277

Example: Covariance Matrices, Portfolio Volatility and Volatility Time Scaling 277
Practical Applications: Probability Distributions 280
Example: Likelihood of a Given Number of Successes of an Oil Exploration Process 282
Example: Frequency of Outcomes Within One or Two Standard Deviations 283
Example: Creating Random Samples from Probability Distributions 283
Example: User-defined Inverse Functions for Random Sampling 284
Example: Values Associated with Probabilities for a Binomial Process 285
Example: Confidence Intervals for the Mean Using Student (T) and Normal Distributions 285
Example: the CONFIDENCE.T and CONFIDENCE.NORM Functions 287
Example: Confidence Intervals for the Standard Deviation Using Chi-squared 289
Example: Confidence Interval for the Slope of Regression Line (or Beta) 289
Practical Applications: More on Regression Analysis and Forecasting 291
Example: Using LINEST to Calculate Confidence Intervals for the Slope (or Beta) 291
Example: Using LINEST to Perform Multiple Regression 292
Example: Using LOGEST to Find Exponential Fits 293
Example: Using TREND and GROWTH to Forecast Linear and Exponential Trends 294
Example: Linear Forecasting Using FORECAST.LINEAR 295
Example: Forecasting Using the FORECAST.ETS Set of Functions 296

CHAPTER 22
Information Functions **299**
Introduction 299
Practical Applications 300
Example: In-formula Comments Using ISTEXT, ISNUMBER or N 300
Example: Building a Forecast Model that Can Be Updated with Actual Reported Figures 300
Example: Detecting Consistency of Data in a Database 301
Example: Consistent use of “N/A” in Models 301
Example: Applications of the INFO and CELL Functions: An Overview 303
Example: Creating Updating Labels that Refer to Data or Formulae 303

Example: Showing the User Which Recalculation Mode the File Is On 305
Example: Finding the Excel Version Used and Creating Backward Compatible Formulae 305
Example: File Location and Structural Information Using CELL, INFO, SHEET and SHEETS 306

CHAPTER 23
Date and Time Functions **307**
Introduction 307
Practical Applications 308
Example: Task Durations, Resource and Cost Estimation 308
Example: Keeping Track of Bookings, Reservations or Other Activities 308
Example: Creating Precise Time Axes 309
Example: Calculating the Year and Month of a Date 309
Example: Calculating the Quarter in Which a Date Occurs 310
Example: Creating Time-based Reports and Models from Data Sets 311
Example: Finding Out on What Day of the Week You Were Born 311
Example: Calculating the Date of the Last Friday of Every Month 311
Example: the DATEDIF Function and Completed Time Periods 312

CHAPTER 24
Text Functions and Functionality **313**
Introduction 313
Practical Applications 314
Example: Joining Text Using CONCAT and TEXTJOIN 314
Example: Splitting Data Using the Text-to-columns Wizard 315
Example: Converting Numerical Text to Numbers 316
Example: Dynamic Splitting Text into Components I 316
Example: Dynamic Splitting Text into Components II 317
Example: Comparing LEFT, RIGHT, MID and LEN 317
Example: Dynamic Splitting Text into Components III 318
Example: Comparing FIND and SEARCH 319
Example: the UPPER and LOWER Functions 319
Example: the PROPER Function 319
Example: the EXACT Function 320
Example: Comparing REPLACE with SUBSTITUTE 320
Example: the REPT Function 320
Example: the CLEAN and TRIM Functions 321
Example: Updating Model Labels and Graph Titles 322
Example: Creating Unique Identifiers or Keys for Data Matching 323

CHAPTER 25
Lookup and Reference Functions **325**
Introduction 325
Practical Applications: Basic Referencing Processes 326
Example: the ROW and COLUMN Functions 326
Example: the ROWS and COLUMNS Functions 327
Example: Use of the ADDRESS Function and the Comparison with CELL 327
Practical Applications: Further Referencing Processes 328
Example: Creating Scenarios Using INDEX, OFFSET or CHOOSE 328
Example: Charts that Can Use Multiple or Flexible Data Sources 330
Example: Reversing and Transposing Data Using INDEX or OFFSET 331
Example: Shifting Cash Flows or Other Items over Time 334
Example: Depreciation Schedules with Triangle Calculations 334
Practical Applications: Combining Matching and Reference Processes 335
Example: Finding the Period in Which a Condition is Met Using MATCH 335
Example: Finding Non-contiguous Scenario Data Using Matching Keys 336
Example: Creating and Finding Matching Text Fields or Keys 336
Example: Combining INDEX with MATCH 337
Example: Comparing INDEX-MATCH with V- and HLOOKUP 338
Example: Comparing INDEX-MATCH with LOOKUP 343
Example: Finding the Closest Matching Value Using Array and Other Function Combinations 344
Practical Applications: More on the OFFSET Function and Dynamic Ranges 345
Example: Flexible Ranges Using OFFSET (I) 345
Example: Flexible Ranges Using OFFSET (II) 346
Example: Flexible Ranges Using OFFSET (III) 347
Example: Flexible Ranges Using OFFSET (IV) 347
Practical Applications: The INDIRECT Function and Flexible Workbook or Data Structures 349
Example: Simple Examples of Using INDIRECT to Refer to Cells and Other Worksheets 349
Example: Incorporating Data from Multiple Worksheet Models and Flexible Scenario Modelling 351
Example: Other Uses of INDIRECT – Cascading Drop-down Lists 352
Practical Examples: Use of Hyperlinks to Navigate a Model, and Other Links to Data Sets 352
Example: Model Navigation Using Named Ranges and Hyperlinks 353

CHAPTER 26
Filters, Database Functions and PivotTables 355
Introduction 355
Issues Common to Working with Sets of Data 356
Cleaning and Manipulating Source Data 356
Static or Dynamic Queries 356
Creation of New Fields or Complex Filters? 357
Excel Databases and Tables 357
Automation Using Macros 359
Practical Applications: Filters 359
Example: Applying Filters and Inspecting Data for Errors or Possible Corrections 359
Example: Identification of Unique Items and Unique Combinations 362
Example: Using Filters to Remove Blanks or Other Specified Items 363
Example: Extraction of Data Using Filters 365
Example: Adding Criteria Calculations to the Data Set 365
Example: Use of Tables 366
Example: Extraction of Data Using Advanced Filters 369
Practical Applications: Database Functions 370
Example: Calculating Conditional Sums and Maxima Using DSUM and DMAX 370
Example: Implementing a Between Query 371
Example: Implementing Multiple Queries 371
Practical Applications: PivotTables 373
Example: Exploring Summary Values of Data Sets 373
Example: Exploring Underlying Elements of the Summary Items 376
Example: Adding Slicers 376
Example: Timeline Slicers 378
Example: Generating Reports Which Ignore Errors or Other Specified Items 380
Example: Using the GETPIVOTDATA Functions 380
Example: Creating PivotCharts 382
Example: Using the Excel Data Model to Link Tables 383

CHAPTER 27
Selected Short-cuts and Other Features 387
Introduction 387
Key Short-cuts and Their Uses 387
Entering and Modifying Data and Formulae 388
Formatting 390
Auditing, Navigation and Other Items 391
Excel KeyTips 393
Other Useful Excel Tools and Features 393
Sparklines 393
The Camera Tool 393

PART SIX

Foundations of VBA and Macros **395**

CHAPTER 28
Getting Started **397**
Introduction 397
Main Uses of VBA 397
Task Automation 398
Creating User-defined Functions 398
Detecting and Reacting to Model Events 398
Enhancing or Managing the User Interface 399
Application Development 399
Core Operations 399
Adding the Developer Tab to Excel's Toolbar 399
The Visual Basic Editor 399
Recording Macros 401
Typical Adaptations Required When Using Recorded Code 402
Writing Code 403
Running Code 404
Debugging Techniques 405
Simple Examples 406
Example: Using Excel Cell Values in VBA 406
Example: Using Named Excel Ranges for Robustness and Flexibility 407
Example: Placing a Value from VBA Code into an Excel Range 408
Example: Replacing Copy/Paste with an Assignment 409
Example: A Simple User-defined Function 409
Example: Displaying a Message when a Workbook is Opened 410

CHAPTER 29
Working with Objects and Ranges **413**
Introduction 413
Overview of the Object Model 413
Objects, Properties, Methods and Events 413
Object Hierarchies and Collections 414
Using Set. . .=. . . . 415
Using the With. . .End With Construct 415
Finding Alternatives to the Selection or Activation of Ranges and Objects 416
Working with Range Objects: Some Key Elements 416
Basic Syntax Possibilities and Using Named Ranges 416
Named Ranges and Named Variables 417
The CurrentRegion Property 417
The xlCellTypeLastCell Property 418
Worksheet Names and Code Names 419
The UsedRange Property 419

The Cells Property 420
The Offset Property 421
The Union Method 421
InputBox and MsgBox 421
Application.InputBox 422
Defining Multi-cell Ranges 422
Using Target to React to Worksheet Events 422
Using Target to React to Workbook Events 423

CHAPTER 30
Controlling Execution **425**
Introduction 425
Core Topics in Overview 425
Input Boxes and Message Boxes 425
For. . .Next Loops 425
For Each. . . In. . .Next 426
If. . .Then 427
Select Case. . .End Select 427
GoTo 428
Do. . .While/Until. . .Loop 428
Calculation and Calculate 429
Screen Updating 432
Measuring Run Time 432
Displaying Alerts 433
Accessing Excel Worksheet Functions 433
Executing Procedures Within Procedures 434
Accessing Add-ins 435
Practical Applications 435
Example: Numerical Looping 435
Example: Listing the Names of All Worksheets in a Workbook 436
Example: Adding a New Worksheet to a Workbook 437
Example: Deleting Specific Worksheets from a Workbook 437
Example: Refreshing PivotTables, Modifying Charts and Working Through Other Object Collections 438

CHAPTER 31
Writing Robust Code **441**
Introduction 441
Key Principles 441
From the Specific to the General 441
Adapting Recorded Code for Robustness 442
Event Code 442
Comments and Indented Text 442
Modular Code 443
Passing Arguments ByVal or ByRef 443
Full Referencing 445

Using Worksheet Code Numbers 447
Assignment Statements, and Manipulating Objects Rather Than Selecting or Activating Them 447
Working with Ranges Instead of Individual Cells 448
Data Types and Variable Declaration 448
Choice of Names 449
Working with Arrays in VBA 450
Understanding Error Codes: An Introduction 451
Further Approaches to Testing, Debugging and Error-handling 452
General Techniques 452
Debugging Functions 453
Implementing Error-handling Procedures 454

CHAPTER 32
Manipulation and Analysis of Data Sets with VBA **455**
Introduction 455
Practical Applications 455
Example: Working Out the Size of a Range 455
Example: Defining the Data Set at Run Time Based on User Input 457
Example: Working Out the Position of a Data Set Automatically 457
Example: Reversing Rows (or Columns) of Data I: Placement in a New Range 459
Example: Reversing Rows (or Columns) of Data II: In Place 460
Example: Automation of Other Data-related Excel Procedures 461
Example: Deleting Rows Containing Blank Cells 462
Example: Deleting Blank Rows 463
Example: Automating the Use of Filters to Remove Blanks or Other Specified Items 464
Example: Performing Multiple Database Queries 468
Example: Consolidating Data Sets That Are Split Across Various Worksheets or Workbooks 469

CHAPTER 33
User-defined Functions **473**
Introduction 473
Benefits of Creating User-defined Functions 473
Syntax and Implementation 474
Practical Applications 475
Example: Accessing VBA Functions for Data Manipulation: Val, StrReverse and Split 476
Example: A Wrapper to Access the Latest Excel Function Version 477
Example: Replication of IFERROR for Compatibility with Excel 2003 478

Example: Sum of Absolute Errors 479
Example: Replacing General Excel Calculation Tables or Ranges 480
Example: Using Application.Caller to Generate a Time Axis as an Array Function 480
Example: User-defined Array Functions in Rows and Columns 482
Example: Replacing Larger Sets of Excel Calculations: Depreciation Triangles 484
Example: Sheet Reference Functions 485
Example: Statistical Moments when Frequencies Are Known 487
Example: Rank Order Correlation 489
Example: Semi-deviation of a Data Set 491

Index **493**

Preface

This text aims to address key topics in the design and building of financial models, so that such models are appropriate to decision support, are transparent and flexible. It aims to address the issues that are generally applicable in many applications, highlighting several core themes:

- Building models that meet their decision-support role.
- Designing models so that sensitivity analysis can be conducted as relevant, and which meet core requirements for flexibility.
- Minimising the complexity, subject to the model meeting the core requirements.
- Structuring models to have an effective layout and flow, with audit (dependency) paths as short as possible.
- Focusing on the creation of transparency.
- Using Excel functions and functionality (and perhaps VBA/macros) in the most effective and appropriate way (requiring one to have a good knowledge of the possibilities and options available).
- Employing problem-solving skills in an integrated way.

The work is structured into six Parts:

- Part I presents a framework to describe modelling processes, discusses the role of models in decision support and summarises some key themes and best practices.
- Part II discusses model design, focusing on sensitivity and flexibility requirements, and the optimisation of data structures and layout.
- Part III covers the process of building models, focusing on maximising transparency, using the appropriate Excel functions, and creating models which are error-free and easy to audit.
- Part IV covers sensitivity and scenario analysis, simulation and optimisation.
- Part V provides practical examples of the use of Excel functions and functionality in financial modelling.
- Part VI covers an introduction to VBA and its key areas of application within financial modelling.

Note that Part V and Part VI are relevant on a stand-alone basis and could be read before the other Parts. This allows the earlier Parts of the text to focus on the general issues relating to model design, build and use, even as, on occasion, they refer to the later Parts.

This text builds on some key principles that were also a core aspect of the author's earlier work *Financial Modelling in Practice: A Concise Guide for Intermediate and Advanced Level* (John Wiley & Sons, 2008), especially that of using sensitivity thought processes as a model design tool. However, the discussion here is more extensive and detailed, reflecting the author's enhanced view of these topics that has been gained through the decade since the publication of the earlier work. Indeed, this text is approximately three times the length of that of the corresponding elements of the earlier work (i.e. of Chapters 1, 2 and 6 in that work). Note that, unlike the earlier work, this text does not aim to treat specific applications in depth (such as financial statements, valuation, options and real options). Further, the topic of risk, uncertainty and simulation modelling is covered only briefly, since the author's *Business Risk Modelling in Practice: Using Excel, VBA and @RISK* (John Wiley & Sons, 2015) provides a detailed treatment of this topic.

The website associated with this text contains approximately 235 Excel files (screen-clips of most of which are shown in the text). These are an integral part of this work, and it will generally be necessary to refer to these files in order to gain the maximum benefit from reading this text.

About the Author

Michael Rees has a Doctorate in Mathematical Modelling and Numerical Algorithms and a B.A. with First Class Honours in Mathematics, both from Oxford University. He has an MBA with Distinction from INSEAD in France. In addition, he studied for the Wilmott Certificate of Quantitative Finance, where he graduated in first place for coursework and received the Wilmott Award for the highest final exam mark.

Since 2002, he has worked as an independent expert in quantitative decision support, financial modelling, economic, risk and valuation modelling, providing training, model-building and advisory services to a wide range of corporations, consulting firms, private equity businesses and training companies.

Prior to becoming independent, Michael was employed at J.P. Morgan, where he conducted valuation and research work, and prior to that he was a Partner with strategy consultants Mercer Management Consulting, both in the U.K. and in Germany. His earlier career was spent at Braxton Associates (a boutique strategy consulting firm that became part of Deloitte and Touche), where he worked both in the UK and as a founding member of the start-up team in Germany.

Michael is a dual UK/Canadian citizen. He is fluent in French and German, and has wide experience of working internationally and with clients from diverse cultural backgrounds. In additional to this text, he is the author of *Financial Modelling in Practice: A Concise Guide to Intermediate and Advanced Level* (John Wiley & Sons, 2008), *Business Risk and Simulation Modelling in Practice* (John Wiley & Sons, 2015), a contributing author to *The Strategic CFO: Creating Value in a Dynamic Market Environment* (Springer, 2012) and has also contributed articles to the Wilmott Magazine.

About the Website

This book is accompanied by a companion website which can be accessed at www.principlesoffinancialmodelling.com (Password hint: The last word in Chapter 5).

The website includes:

- 237 PFM models (screen-clips of most of which are shown in the text), which demonstrate key principles in modelling, as well as providing many examples of the use of Excel functions and VBA macros.

  These facilitate learning and have a strong emphasis on practical solutions and direct real-world application.

PART One

Introduction to Modelling, Core Themes and Best Practices

CHAPTER 1

Models of Models

INTRODUCTION

This chapter provides an overview of financial modelling, including its objectives, stages and processes. The discussion sets the context and frameworks that are used in much of the subsequent text.

CONTEXT AND OBJECTIVES

A model is a numerical or mathematical representation of a real-life situation. A financial model is one which relates to business and finance contexts. The typical objectives of financial modelling include to support decisions relating to business plans and forecasts, to the design, evaluation and selection of projects, to resource allocation and portfolio optimisation, to value corporations, assets, contracts and financial instruments, and to support financing decisions.

In fact, there is no generally accepted (standardised) definition of financial modelling. For some, it is a highly pragmatic set of activities, essentially consisting of the building of Excel worksheets. For others, it is a mainly conceptual activity, whose focus is on the use of mathematical equations to express the relationships between the variables in a system, and for which the platform (e.g. Excel) that is used to solve such equations is not of relevance. In this text, we aim to integrate theory and practice as much as possible.

THE STAGES OF MODELLING

The modelling process can be considered as consisting of several stages, as shown in Figure 1.1.

The key characteristics of each stage include:

- Specification: This involves describing the real-life situation, either qualitatively or as a set of equations. In any case, at this stage one should also consider the overall objectives and decision-making needs, and capture the core elements of

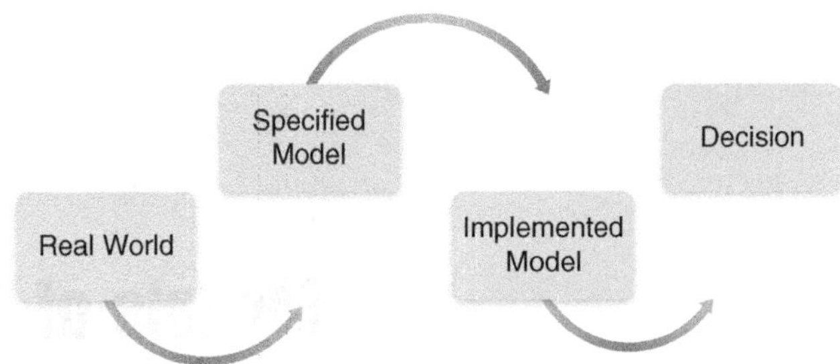

FIGURE 1.1 A Generic Framework for Stages of the Modelling Process

the behaviour of the real-world situation. One should also address issues relating to the desired scope of model validity, the level of accuracy required and the trade-offs that are acceptable to avoid excessive complexity whilst providing an adequate basis for decision support.
- Implementation: This is the process to translate the specification into numerical values, by conducting calculations based on assumed input values. For the purposes of this text, the calculations are assumed to be in Excel, perhaps also using additional compatible functionality (such as VBA macros, Excel add-ins, optimisation algorithms, links to external databases and so on).
- Decision support: A model should appropriately support the decision. However, as a simplification of the real-life situation, a model by itself is almost never sufficient. A key challenge in building and using models to greatest effect is to ensure that the process and outputs provide a value-added decision-support guide (not least by providing insight, reducing biases or correcting invalid assumptions that may be inherent in less-rigorous decision processes), whilst recognising the limitations of the model and the modelling process.

Note that in many practical cases, no explicit specification step is conducted; rather, knowledge of a situation is used to build an Excel workbook directly. Since Excel does not calculate incorrectly, such a model can never truly be "(externally) validated": the model specification is the model itself (i.e. as captured within the formulae used in Excel). Although such "self-validation" is in principle a significant weakness of these pragmatic approaches, the use of a highly formalised specification stage is often not practical (especially if one is working under tight deadlines, or one believes that the situation is generally well-understood). Some of the techniques discussed in this text (such as sensitivity-driven model design and the following of other best practices) are particularly important to support robust modelling processes, even where little or no documented specification has taken place or is practically possible.

BACKWARD THINKING AND FORWARD CALCULATION PROCESSES

The modelling process is essentially two-directional (see Figure 1.2):

- A "backward thought process", in which one considers a variable of interest (the model output) and defines its underlying, or causal, factors. This is a qualitative process, corresponding to reading Figure 1.2 from left to right. For example, cash flow may be represented as being determined from revenue and cost, each of which may be determined by their own causal factors (e.g. revenue is determined by price and volume). As a qualitative process, at this stage, the precise the nature of the relationships may not yet be made clear: only that the relationships exist.

- A "forward-calculation process", in which one which starts with the assumed values of the final set of causal factors (the "model inputs") and builds the required calculations to determine the values of the intermediate variables and final outputs. This is a numerical process corresponding to reading Figure 1.2 from right to left. It involves defining the nature of the relationships sufficiently precisely that they can be implemented in quantitative formulae. That is, inputs are used to calculate the intermediate variables, which are used to calculate the outputs. For example, revenue would be calculated (from an assumed price and volume), and cost (based on fixed and variable costs and volume), with the cash flow as the final output.

Note that the process is likely to contain several iterations: items that may initially be numerical inputs may be chosen to be replaced by calculations (which are determined from new numerical inputs), thus creating a model with more input variables and detail. For example, rather than being a single figure, volume could be split by product group. In principle, one may continue the process indefinitely (i.e. repeatedly replacing hard-coded numerical inputs with intermediate calculations). Of course, the potential process of creating more and more detail must stop at some point:

- For the simple reason of practicality.
- To ensure accuracy. Although the creation of more detail would lead one to expect to have a more accurate model, this is not always the case: a detailed model will require more information to calibrate correctly (for example, to estimate the values of all the inputs). Further, the capturing of the relationships between these inputs will become progressively more complex as more detail is added.

The "optimal" level of detail at which a model should be built is not a trivial question, but is discussed further in Chapter 4.

It may be of interest to note that this framework is slightly simplified (albeit covering the large majority of cases in typical Excel contexts):

- In some applications (notably sequential optimisation of a time series, and decision trees), the calculations are required to be conducted both forward and backward,

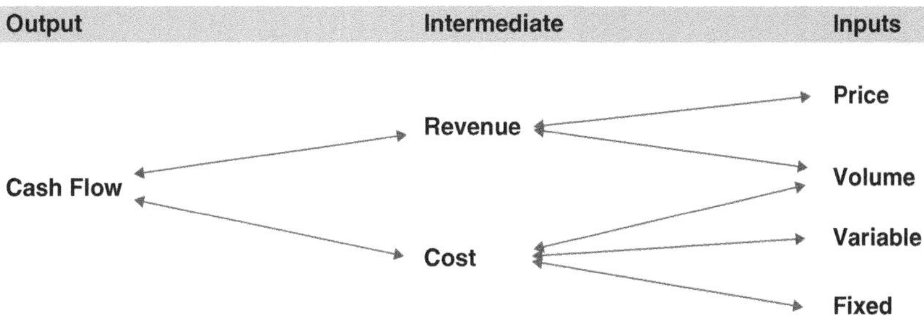

FIGURE 1.2 Modelling as a Combination of a Backward Thought Process and a Forward Calculation Process

as the optimal behaviour at an earlier time depends on considering all the future consequences of each potential decision.
- In econometrics, some equations may be of an equilibrium nature, i.e. they contain the same variable(s) on both sides of an equation(s). In such cases, the logic flow is not directional, and will potentially give rise to circular references in the implemented models.

CHAPTER 2

Using Models in Decision Support

INTRODUCTION

This chapter summarises the main benefits and challenges of using models in decision support. Where significant amounts of money are at stake, or the choice of the most appropriate decision option is important for some other reason, it is often taken as a given that the building of a model would be useful. However, it is important to understand the specific sources of benefits, and the challenges and potential weaknesses of modelling processes. Doing so will help to support a more robust basis for decision-making, and reduce the likelihood that the outputs are misinterpreted, misused, or assumed to apply to a context for which the model was not designed.

BENEFITS OF USING MODELS

This section highlights the key benefits potentially achievable by the use of models.

Providing Numerical Information

A model calculates the possible values of variables that are considered important in the context of the decision at hand. Of course, this information is often of paramount importance, especially when committing resources, budgeting and so on.

Nevertheless, the calculation of the numerical values of key variables is not the only reason to build models; the modelling process often has an important exploratory and insight-generating aspect (see later in this section). In fact, many insights can often be generated early in the overall process, whereas numerical values tend to be of most use later on.

Capturing Influencing Factors and Relationships

The process of building a model should force a consideration of which factors influence the situation, including which are most important. Whilst such reflections may be of an intuitive or qualitative nature (at the early stages), much insight can be gained through the use of a quantitative process. The quantification of the relationships requires one to consider the nature of the relationships in a very precise way (e.g. whether a change in one would impact another and by how much, whether such a change is linear or non-linear, whether other variables are also affected, or whether there are (partially) common causal factors between variables, and so on).

Generating Insight and Forming Hypotheses

The modelling process should highlight areas where one's knowledge is incomplete, what further actions could be taken to improve this, as well as what data is needed. This can be valuable in its own right. In fact, a model is effectively an explicit record of the assumptions and of the (hypothesised) relationships between items (which may change as further knowledge is developed). The process therefore provides a structured approach to develop a better understanding. It often uncovers many assumptions that are being made implicitly (and which may be imprecisely understood or incorrect), as well as identifying the assumptions that are required and appropriate. As such, both the qualitative and the quantitative aspects of the process should provide new insights and identify issues for further exploration.

The overlooking or underestimation of these exploratory aspects is one of the main inefficiencies in many modelling processes, which are often delegated to junior staff who are competent in "doing the numbers", but who may not have the experience, or lack sufficient project exposure, authority, or the credibility to identify and report many of the key insights, especially those that may challenge current assumptions. Thus, many possible insights are either lost or are simply never generated in the first place. Where a model produces results that are not readily explained intuitively, there are two generic cases:

- It is over-simplified, highly inaccurate or wrong in some important way. For example, key variables may have been left out, dependencies not correctly captured, or the assumptions used for the values of variables may be wrong or poorly estimated.
- It is essentially correct, but provides results which are not intuitive. In such situations, the modelling process can be used to adapt, explore and generate new insights, so that ultimately both the intuition and the model's outputs become aligned. This can be a value-added process, particularly if it highlights areas where one's initial intuition may be lacking.

In this context, the following well-known quotes come to mind:

- "Plans are useless, but planning is everything" (Eisenhower).
- "Every model is wrong, some are useful" (Box).
- "Perfection is the enemy of the good" (Voltaire).

Decision Levers, Scenarios, Uncertainties, Optimisation, Risk Mitigation and Project Design

When conducted rigorously, the modelling process distinguishes factors which are controllable from those which are not. It may also highlight that some items are partially controllable, but require further actions that may not (currently) be reflected in the planning nor in the model (e.g. the introduction of risk mitigation actions). Ultimately, controllable items correspond to potential decisions that should be taken in an optimal way, and non-controllable items are those which are risky or subject to uncertainty. The use of sensitivity, scenario and risk techniques can also provide insight into the extent of possible exposure if a decision were to proceed as planned, lead to modifications to the project or decision design, and allow one to find an optimal decision or project structure.

Improving Working Processes, Enhanced Communications and Precise Data Requirements

A model provides a structured framework to take information from subject matter specialists or experts. It can help to define precisely the information requirements, which improves the effectiveness of the research and collection process to obtain such information. The overall process and results should also help to improve communications, due to the insights and transparency generated, as well as creating a clear structure for common working and co-ordination.

CHALLENGES IN USING MODELS

This section highlights the key challenges faced when using models in decision support.

The Nature of Model Error

Models are, by nature, simplifications of (and approximations to) the real-world. Errors can be introduced at each stage (as presented in Figure 1.1):

- Specification error. This is the difference between the behaviour of the real-world situation and that captured within the specification or intentions of the model (sometimes this individual part is referred to as "model risk" or "model error"). Although one may often be able to provide a reasonable intuitive assessment of the nature of some such errors, it is extremely challenging to provide a robust quantification, simply because the nature of the real world is not fully known. (By definition, the ability to precisely define and calculate model error would only arise if such error were fully understood, in which case, it could essentially be captured in a revised model, with error then having been eliminated.) Further, whilst one may be aware of some simplifications that the model contains compared to the real-life situation, there are almost certainly possible behaviours of the real-life situation that are not known about. In a sense, one must essentially "hope" that the model is a sufficiently accurate representation for the purposes at hand. Of course, a good intuition, repeated empirical observations and large data sets can increase the likelihood that a conceptual model is correct (and improve one's confidence in it), but ultimately there will be some residual uncertainty ("black swans" or "unknown unknowns", for example).

- Implementation error. This is the difference between the specified model (as conceived or intended) and the model as implemented. Such errors could result by mistake (calculation error) or due to subtler issues, such as the use of a discrete time axis in Excel (when events in fact materialise in continuous time), or of a finite time axis (instead of an unlimited one). Errors also arise frequently in which a model calculates correctly in the base case, but not in other cases (due to mistakes, or overlooking key aspects of the behaviour of the situation).
- Decision error. This is the idea that a decision that is made based on the results of a model could be inappropriate. It captures the (lack of) effectiveness of the decision-making process, including a lack of understanding of a model and its limitations. Note that a poor outcome following a decision does not necessarily imply that the decision was poor, nor does a good outcome imply that the decision was the correct choice.

Some types of model error relate to multiple process stages (rather than a single one), including where insufficient attention is given to scenarios, risk and uncertainties.

Inherent Ambiguity and Circularity of Reasoning

The modelling process is inherently ambiguous: in order to specify or build a model, one must already understand the situation reasonably well. However, the model and modelling process can provide benefit only to the extent that the initial understanding is imperfect. (By definition, were a perfect understanding to exist even before a model is built, then no model would be required, since there would be no way to improve the understanding further!)

This ambiguity also creates potentially uncertainty around the meaning of the model outputs: indeed, in the first instance, the outputs provides information only about the model (rather than the real-life situation). It may also create a circularity in the reasoning: when conducting sensitivity analysis, one may conclude that a specific variable is important, whereas the importance of a variable (e.g. as determined from running sensitivity analysis) directly reflects the assumptions used and the implicit logic that is embedded within the model.

Inconsistent Scope or Alignment of Decision and Model

Every model has a limited scope of validity. Typically, assumptions about the context have been made that are implicit or not well documented. Such implicit assumptions are easy to overlook, which may result in a model being invalid, or becoming so when it is applied to a different situation. For example, an estimate of the construction cost for a project may use the implicit assumption about the geographic location of the project. If such assumptions are insufficiently documented (or are implicit and not at all documented), then the use of the model in a subsequent project in a new geographic location may be invalid, for it is likely that that new line items or other structural changes are necessary, yet some or all of these may be overlooked.

The Presence on Biases, Imperfect Testing, False Positives and Negatives

Decisions (or input assumptions and model formulae) may be biased in ways that favours a particular outcome or ignore important factors or risks. Biases may have several generic forms:

- Motivational or political. These are where one has some incentive to deliberately bias a process, a set of results, or assumptions used.
- Cognitive. These are inherent to the human psyche, and often believed to have arisen for evolutionary reasons. They include the bias toward optimism, anchoring to an initial view, or making a different decision if the information is presented in terms of making gains versus avoiding losses.
- Structural. These relate to situation in which the modelling approach, methodology or implementation platform inherently creates biases. For example, the use of fixed input values to drive calculations can be regarded as an approach that is typically structurally biased (for the purposes of economic analysis and decision-making): where model inputs are set at their most likely values, the output will generally not show its true most likely value. Further, the mean (average) of the output is generally the single most important quantity for financial decision-making, yet this can typically not be shown as a valid model case. A detailed discussion of such topics is beyond the scope of this text, but is contained in the author's *Business Risk and Simulation Modelling in Practice* (John Wiley & Sons, 2015).

One may consider that the use of a model to support a decision is rather like performing any other form of test. A perfect test would be one which results not only in genuinely good projects being (always) indicated as good, but also in genuinely bad ones (always) being indicated as bad. In practice, modelling processes seem to have a high false-negative rate (i.e. projects which are in fact bad are not detected as such), so that such projects are not ruled out or stopped sufficiently early. False positives are also rare (that is, where there is a good project, but the model indicates that it is a bad one).

Balancing Intuition with Rationality

Most decisions are made using a combination of intuition and rational considerations, with varying degrees of balance between these.

Intuitive approaches are typically characterised by:

- Gut feel, experience and biases.
- Rapid decision-making, with a bias to reinforce initial conclusions and reject counter-narratives.
- Ignoring or discounting items that are complex or not understood well.
- Little (formalised) thinking about risks, uncertainties and unknowns.
- Little (formalised) decision processes or governance procedures.
- Lack of transparency into decision criteria and the importance placed on various items.
- Seeking input from only a small set of people, rather than from a diverse group.

At its best, intuitive decision-making can be powerful and effective, i.e. a low investment nevertheless resulting in a good decision.

By contrast, rational approaches are characterised by:

- Non-reliance on personal biases.
- Strong reliance on analysis, models and frameworks.
- Objective, holistic and considered thinking.
- Self-critical: ongoing attempts to look for flaws and possible improvements in the process and the analysis.
- Openness to independent review and discussion.
- Formalised processes and decision governance.
- Setting objectives and creating higher levels of transparency into explicit decision criteria.
- A desire to consider all factors that may be relevant, to incorporate alternative viewpoints and the needs of different stakeholders and to achieve diverse input from various sources.
- Explicitly searching out more information and a wide variety of diverse inputs, and the collection of data or expert judgement.
- Openness to use alternative tools and techniques where they may be appropriate.
- Willingness to invest more in time, processes, tools and communication.
- Exposing, challenging, overcoming or minimising biases that are often present in situations where insufficient reflection or analysis has taken place.
- (Usually) with some quantification and prioritisation.
- (Ideally) with an appropriate consideration of factors that may lead to goals being compromised (risks and uncertainties).

It is probably fair to say that intuition is generally the dominant force in terms of how decisions are made in practice: a course of action that "feels wrong" to a decision-maker (but is apparently supported by rational analysis) is unlikely to be accepted. Similarly, a course of action that "feels right" to a decision-maker will rarely be rejected, even if the analysis would recommend doing so. Where the rational and intuitive approaches diverge in their initial recommendations, one may either find areas where the decision-makers' intuition may be incorrect, or where the rational analysis is incomplete, or is based on incorrect assumptions about the decision-maker's preferences or the decision context. Ideally such items would be incorporated in a revised analysis, creating an alignment between the rational analysis and the intuition. Where this results in a change (or improvement) to the intuitive understanding of a situation, such a process will have been of high value added.

Lack of Data or Insufficient Understanding of a Situation

The absence of sufficient data is often stated as a barrier to building models. If there is no data, no way to create expert estimates or use judgements and there are no proxy measures available, then it may be difficult to build a model. However, even in some such cases, models that capture behaviours and interactions can be built, and populated with generic numbers. This can help to structure the thought process, generate insight and identify where more understanding, data or research is required.

Of course, there may be situations where useful models cannot be built, such as:

- Where the objectives are not defined in a meaningful way. For example, doing one's best to "build a model of the moon" might not result in anything useful, at least without further clarification. However, the requirement to build a model which calculates the variation in the temperature of the surface of the moon may be sufficient to provide a reasonable starting point for modelling activities.
- Where basic structural elements or other key factors that drive the behaviour of the situation are not known or have not been decided upon. For example, it could prove to be a challenge to try to model the costs of building a new manufacturing facility in a new but unknown country, and which will produce new products that need still to be defined and developed, in accordance with regulations that have not yet been released, using technology that has not yet specified.

Thus, whilst in some cases models may not initially be able to be built, very often such cases can be used to clarify objectives, to highlight where further understanding needs to be generated, there are the additional data requirements and so on. Models which generate insight can then be built, resulting in an iterative process in which the quality of a model is gradually improved.

Overcoming Challenges: Awareness, Actions and Best Practices

Best practices in modelling partly concern themselves with reducing the sources of total error, whether they relate to model specification, implementation, decision-making processes, or other factors. The range of approaches to doing this includes topics of a technical nature, and those that relate to organisational behaviour and processes. Such themes include:

- Being aware of biases.
- Asking for examples of why an analysis could be wrong, or why outcomes could be significantly different to the ones expected or considered so far.
- Explicitly seeking and supporting dissension and alternate opinions.
- Being aware of model error: as noted earlier, in the first instance, the results of a model say something about the model, not the real-life situation!
- Being open to rejecting projects, even when some organisational effort, personal capital or investment has already been made in them (and focusing only future benefits, not sunk costs).
- Ensuring that models are designed and implemented in accordance with best practice principles. These include the use of flexibility and sensitivity techniques (as mentioned earlier, and discussed in more detail later in the text).
- Using risk modelling approaches (rather than static approaches based only on sensitivity or scenario analysis). In particular, this can help to overcome many of the biases mentioned earlier.
- Not using the lack of data as an excuse to do nothing! Even with imperfect data, the modelling process can often provide a framework to generate insight into a situation, even where the numerical output (for a given set of assumptions) may have a high degree of uncertainty associated with it.

CHAPTER 3

Core Competencies and Best Practices: Meta-themes

INTRODUCTION

This chapter discusses the foundation of modelling best practices and the core competencies required to build good models. The discussion here is at a high level, since the rest of this text is essentially a more detailed discussion of these topics.

KEY THEMES

It is probably fair to say that many models built in practice are of mediocre quality, especially larger ones. Typical weakness that often arise include:

- They are hard to understand, to audit or validate. They require an over-dependence on the original modeller to use, maintain or modify, with even minor changes requiring significant rework.
- They are either excessively complex for a given functionality, or lack key functionality. For example, it may be cumbersome to run sensitivity or scenario analysis for important cases (such as changing multiple items simultaneously, or delaying the start date of part of a project), the granularity of the data or time axis may be inappropriate, and it may be cumbersome to include new data, or replace forecasted items with actual figures as they become available, and so on. Additionally, the choice of functions used in Excel may limit the ability to modify the model, or be computationally inefficient.
- They are likely to contain errors, or assumptions which are implicit but which may have unintended consequences (such as being invalid in certain circumstances, and which are overlooked even when such circumstances arise). This is often due to excessive complexity and lack of transparency, as well as due to the use of poor structures and excessively complex formulae which have not been fully tested through a wide range of scenarios.

We consider that seven key areas form the core competencies and foundation of best practices:

1. Gaining a good understanding of the objective, and the role of analysis in the decision process.
2. Having a sufficient understanding of the specific application.
3. Having sufficient knowledge of the implementation platform (e.g. Excel and VBA), not only to implement the models in the most effective way, but also to foster creativity to consider alternative possible modelling approaches.
4. Designing models that meet the requirements for flexibility and sensitivities.
5. Designing models that have the appropriate data structures, layout and flow.
6. Ensuring transparency and user-friendliness.
7. Employing integrated problem-solving skills.

The rest of this chapter provides an overview of these, whilst the purpose of most of the rest of the text is to address many of these issues in detail.

Decision-support Role, Objectives, Outputs and Communication

It is important for a modelling process to remain focused on the overall objective(s), including its decision-support role, as well as the wider context, organisational processes, management culture and so on. Some specific points are worth addressing early in the process, including:

- What are the key business decisions that one wishes to take?
- What are the outputs that are required?
- What type of sensitivity, scenario or risk analysis will be needed? (This is likely to affect choice of variables, model data structures and overall design, amongst other items.)
- Are there optimisation issues that need to be captured (e.g. to distinguish explicitly the effect of controllable items (i.e. decisions) from that of non-controllable one, and to design the model so that additional optimisation algorithms can be applied most efficiently)?
- What types of variables should be included?
- What level of detail is required for the variables and for the time axis (e.g. by product or product group, and whether daily, weekly, monthly, quarterly, or annually. . .)?
- What should be the logical flow, in terms of which variables are inputs, calculated (dependent) variables and outputs?
- What data is available?
- How often will the model need to be updated?
- What other processes or models do the results need to be consistent with?
- What is required to make the model "as simple as possible, but no simpler"?

Establishing the answer to such questions early on will help to ensure that a model is appropriately adapted to reflect the key business issues, the effect of specific possible decisions and the communication needs of decision-makers.

Application Knowledge and Understanding

In general, a modeller will need to have a sufficient understanding of the situation to be able to express it using logical relationships and assumptions. In some situations, high accuracy is required, whereas in others, cruder approximations may be sufficient. For example:

- The building of a forecast of a company's financial statements generally requires only a minimal knowledge of basic arithmetic operations in Excel (such as to add, subtract, multiply, divide and to use the IF or MAX/MIN functions). Yet it does require a reasonable knowledge of the meaning of the main financial statements (income statement, balance sheet, cash flow statement) and how they relate to each other. Without sufficient knowledge, the building of a model would be a significant challenge.
- The implementation of a discounted flow valuation model in Excel may be very straightforward for someone who has a good understanding of valuation theory, whereas acquiring the knowledge about this theory may be harder in the first instance.
- In financial derivatives, the Black–Scholes closed-form formulae for the value of a European vanilla option are relatively straightforward to implement in Excel. Yet one would generally need to have a good knowledge of the theory concerning the valuation of derivatives (i.e. of risk-neutral or arbitrage-free methods) to understand and apply the results appropriately, or to be able to develop analogous approaches that would be valid in other applications.

In practice, a modelling analyst will often be required to build a bespoke customised representation of a decision situation or project for which there may be little in the way of pre-existing guidelines, publications, templates, or underlying established (theoretical) basis. One can broadly distinguish two generic contexts:

- Where the area of application is essentially standardised. In this case, the design and implementation process is typically straightforward if one is familiar with the standard knowledge.
- Where the area of application is non-standard or may require innovation. In such cases, the modelling process has (or should have) a stronger "problem-solving" component that relates to hypothesis-testing, experimentation and discovery. In a sense, dealing with these is essentially the core of what may be considered as "advanced" modelling.

Therefore, many modelling situations require a sufficient knowledge of the underlying situation, as well as the ability to reflect bespoke needs. Problem-solving skills are required in order to design and integrate various components together in an efficient and appropriate way (see later in this chapter).

Skills with Implementation Platform

The modeller must have sufficient skill with whichever platform has been chosen (e.g. Excel), including the ability to creatively consider a variety of options and to choose the one which is most appropriate overall. Often, models are implemented in ways that are either insufficiently flexible, or are flexible but are unnecessarily complicated. In this latter case, the reasons that complexity has not been reduced are usually a combination of:

- Insufficient reflection and/or knowledge of the possibilities that are available within Excel/VBA. Most frequently, an inappropriate function choice is used (or VBA macros are not used when their use would in fact be highly effective).
- Insufficient consideration (or implementation) of issues concerning layout, data structures, formatting and other transparency-related topics.
- A lack of advanced problem-solving skills.
- Lack of discipline (or time) to implement better solutions, even when their existence is known or hypothesised.

Defining Sensitivity and Flexibility Requirements

The topic of clearly defining the sensitivity requirements is perhaps the single most important area in model design; once these are adequately defined, the appropriate approach to many other aspects of the modelling also become clear. In fact, we use the term "flexibility requirements" to emphasise the wider applicability of this concept, which includes:

- Standard sensitivity analysis, i.e. of the ability to change input values and see the effect on calculations and outputs.
- The use of "sensitivity thought processes" to validly implement the "backward thought process" described in Chapter 1, whilst ensuring that such a process terminates at an appropriate point.
- The ability to include new data sets and/or remove old ones (or update data that is linked to an external source), whilst having to make minimum changes when doing so. For example, at each month end, new data may need to be introduced into the model, which then automatically reports the prior three-month aggregate figures (including the most recently added data). If such a requirement is not incorporated as a fundamental part of a model's design, then one will spend much time each month in manipulating the data in less efficient ways. Such functionality may not be considered as a standard sensitivity requirement, but falls within the scope of "flexibility requirements".
- Being able to update a forecast model with realised figures as they become available, without having to conduct inordinate modelling (re-)work to do so; the creation of such functionality would need to form a fundamental part of the model design process, as it generally cannot be added as an afterthought.
- The inclusion of (the ability to create or run) multiple scenarios, and to distinguish between decision variables (whose value is to be chosen optimally) and uncertainty/risk variables.
- Increasing the scope of validity of a model by turning contextual assumptions (or limitations) into input assumptions. For example, a model may list as an "assumption" that the start date is (say) 1 January 2018, yet does not adapt appropriately if this date were to be changed (e.g. sales volume may need to be shifted in time, even as the price achievable is not shifted, as it may relate to external market variables).

In other words, the start date is a limitation (or a contextual assumption), not an input assumption. In fact, it can be challenging to create a model so that its calculations are correct as the start date is altered, but if this were done, then the contextual limitation has become a genuine input assumption.

Clearly, a model which has more flexibility will in principle also be more complex; typically, it may be larger, and use more advanced formulae and functions, as well as VBA macros or user-defined functions. To some extent, an increase in complexity is therefore potentially unavoidable as flexibility is increased. On the other hand, many models are built with insufficient focus on reducing their complexity, even as there are typically many ways to do so (whilst retaining the flexibility features).

We consider that the core of modelling "best practices" is the creation of models that lie on (or close to) the "best practice frontier", shown schematically in Figure 3.1. In this framework, the core to modelling best practices is:

- Defining the nature of the flexibilities required.
- Building a model that has the minimum complexity that can be achieved whilst capturing these flexibilities: for every level of flexibility requirement, many possible models can be built, but only some of these have the lowest possible complexity.

Note that the flexibility features that are required should be limited to those that are genuinely necessary, since:

- Model complexity increases disproportionally to flexibility.
- The process to simplify a complex model is often more cumbersome than the process to add flexibility to a well-built model.

Note that many specific topics that are often considered to constitute best practices in fact simply follow as a direct result of applying this generic framework, including: the need for overall transparency, for a clear layout, for borders around key areas, of using formatting and colour-coding, the judicious choice of functions, the selected and appropriate use of VBA, and so on. In a sense, this can also be captured through the guiding principle: "Everything should be made as simple as possible, but no simpler" (Einstein).

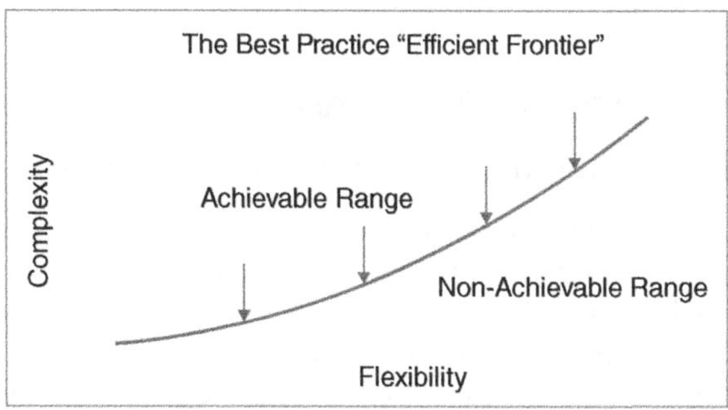

FIGURE 3.1 The Best Practice Efficient Frontier: Minimising Complexity for Given Flexibility

Designing Appropriate Layout, Input Data Structures and Flow

A key aspect of model implementation in Excel is the choice of an appropriate layout, which includes the structure of the input data (or data sets). Not only does an appropriate layout facilitate the transparency (through the creation of a clear flow to the logic), but also the use of appropriate input data structures is critical in circumstances in which there is a requirement to introduce new data sets regularly, as well as in cases where the volume of data significantly dominates the number of formulae.

To some extent, the role of achieving a good layout is to compensate for the lack of (visual) influence-diagrams in Excel. In other words, the Excel environment is not per se one in which the logic structure (or the relationships between inputs and calculations) is clear by default, since it is contained within the formulae. (For example, the Excel representation of Figure 1.2 would simply be some numbers contained in cells and some calculations, with the labels in other cells.) Generally, techniques to improve transparency – such as the use of borders around input and calculation areas – are partial proxies for influence diagrams, since they use visual techniques as a rapid way to enhance transparency and understanding.

The overall design (in terms of layout and data structures) also has a major influence on the extent to which a model can be used flexibly. For example:

- A model built in a single worksheet can be copied easily (by copying the whole sheet), whereas one built in multiple worksheets cannot (without copying the whole workbook as a new file). A template model in one worksheet can be used to create a multi-sheet workbook, in which each worksheet contains a model (e.g. that represents a business unit), whose figures are consolidated within the same workbook. Such "modular structures" can be very beneficial, as discussed later in the text.
- Where new data sets need to be regularly introduced (such as the latest month's reported figures), a structure which allows this to be done easily will be important. Once again, this may involve using separate worksheets for each month's data, or using a single consolidated database (or a mixture of the two).
- Specific applications may be dominated by data and reports or queries of this data, with the number of calculations being limited. In this case, the Excel "model" becomes a database application and should be structured as such. An important point is to make a clear distinction between "data-dominated" situations and "formula-dominated" situations ("traditional" models), as discussed in Chapter 5.

Ensuring Transparency and Creating a User-friendly Model

The creation of models which are transparent (easy to understand) has several purposes:

- A transparent (clear) model is a direct reflection of a transparent (clear) thought process. If the model is not clear, then it is most likely that the underlying logical process is also unclear, and also likely to be incomplete or wrong in some way.
- There are less likely to be errors of calculation.
- It is a more effective use of resources, as it will take less time for a user or new team member to understand it, and it allows the team to share, roles to change and staff to be deployed flexibly.

Transparency is not an absolute requirement for a model to be "correct", but a way to work efficiently, gain confidence that the overall process is robust, and reduce the chance of errors or invalid assumptions.

Note that some models have sophisticated user-interfaces, which guide (and limit) the user as to the data entry that should be provided. Whilst such models may be considered "easy to use", and may help to ensure integrity of the inputs provided, they also tend to be of a black-box nature, so that the transparency (of the model's logic) may be lacking. Thus, when considering the use of such approaches, one needs careful reflection as to the appropriate method to use.

Integrated Problem-solving Skills

When modelling a standard application, there is little problem-solving involved. For example, for the underlying theory, one can simply refer to a standard text on corporate finance or accounting, whilst the Excel aspects are generally straightforward in terms of the functions and operations required. On the other hand, when dealing with a one-off or bespoke situation, one cannot rely on standard texts or previous, so that there is potentially a significant aspect that involves problem-solving. In a sense, such skills are arguably the essential component of "advanced" modelling.

In fact, in practice, many apparently standardised situations may (or should) also potentially have a "problem-solving" component. Typically – except in the simplest cases – there may be additional issues or questions that may arise, which the model should be designed to address. These could include the need to have functionality to:

- Easily run multiple scenarios.
- Update the model over time with actuals in place of forecasts (without excessive rework).
- Bring in new underlying data sets, whose consolidated data form the main values of some of the input assumptions.
- Run optimisation routines, or simulation techniques that see the distribution of outcomes as inputs varying simultaneously across probabilistic ranges.

Problem-solving skills have many components and facets. In relation to financial modelling, it involves the ability to find appropriate ways to design and implement bespoke models that identify and address all requirements for flexibility, whilst being "as simple as possible, but no simpler", transparent and computationally effective. This is determined from a combination of acquirable knowledge (such as that about Excel, VBA and best practice principles), innate underlying ability, a particular mindset, inherent discipline and willingness to question and explore different approaches, amongst other factors. In a sense, the entirety of this text forms the building blocks that should help to simplify modelling and promote problem-solving, whilst acknowledging that some key aspects of problem-solving remain elusive, and are difficult to teach or communicate in a systematic or highly structured way.

PART

Two

Model Design and Planning

CHAPTER 4

Defining Sensitivity and Flexibility Requirements

INTRODUCTION

This chapter discusses what is perhaps the single most important area to consider when planning and designing models. This concerns ensuring that one clearly defines (early in the processes) the nature of the sensitivity analysis that will be used in decision support, and using this as the fundamental driver in model design. As in the author's earlier work *Financial Modelling in Practice*, we use the term "sensitivity-analysis thinking" ("SAT") to describe this, and to emphasise the conceptual nature of this approach to model design (and to contrast it with quantitative sensitivity analysis that may be used later in the process).

In fact, a generalisation of the SAT concept is that in which the focus is on the "flexibility requirements" of the model. This covers functionality beyond standard sensitivities, such as the ability to update a forecasting model with realised figures as they occur, or the facility to be able to introduce new data or data sets without having to perform undue structural modifications.

In the subsequent text, we will still use the term "SAT" to refer to this general concept of "flexibility and sensitivity thinking". This chapter focuses on a discussion of the (generalised) SAT concept, whilst Chapter 5 and Chapter 6 discuss design issues relating to model flexibility, especially those which are linked to the design of the data sets and the workbook and worksheet structures.

KEY ISSUES FOR CONSIDERATION

Some form of sensitivity-related techniques is relevant at all stages of the modelling process: at the model design stage, the focus is of a conceptual (qualitative) nature and seeks to define precisely the sensitivity and flexibility requirements. As the model is being built, sensitivity analysis can be used to test it for the absence of logical errors, to ensure that more complex formulae are implemented correctly, and that the relationships between the variables are correctly captured. Once the model is built, sensitivity analysis can be used in the traditional sense, i.e. to better understand the range of possible variation around a point forecast.

Creating a Focus on Objectives and Their Implications

In Chapter 1, we noted the importance of focusing on the overall objective(s) of a modelling process, which is usually to support a decision in some way. We also mentioned some core questions that one may need to ask, such as those relating to the nature of the business decision, and the information requirements that are necessary to provide appropriate decision support.

In fact, a more precise structure and clearer focus can be brought to the process of defining objectives by focusing explicitly on the sensitivity and flexibility requirements that will be needed once the model is built (i.e. by using SAT). Indeed, once these requirements are adequately defined, the appropriate approach to many other aspects of the modelling process typically also becomes clear (such as the nature of the required formulae and the overall layout and structure of the model).

Thus, where time is very limited (such as in the proverbial 30-second elevator ride with the CEO), one may find that focusing on this subject alone is sufficient to define almost all aspects required in order to be able to start to build an effective model.

Sensitivity Concepts in the Backward Thought and Forward Calculation Processes

The use of SAT is key to ensuring that both the backward and the forward processes described in Chapter 1 (Figure 1.2) are implemented appropriately. Note that the backward process by itself is not sufficient to fully determine the nature of an appropriate model:

- There are typically many ways of breaking down an item into subcomponents. For example, a sales figure could be conceived as:
  - Sales = volume multiplied by price.
  - Sales = market size multiplied by market share.
  - Sales = sum of the sales per customer.
  - Sales = sum of sales per product group.
  - . . .
- It is not clear at what level of detail to work with (i.e. at what point in the backward thought process to stop). For example, in the latter case above, the sales for each product group could be broken into:
  - Sales per product group = Sum of sales of individual products.
  - Sales per product group = Sum of sales of product sub-groups.
  - . . .

The use of SAT will help to clarify which approach is appropriate, especially relating to the choice of variables that are used for inputs and intermediate calculations, and the level of detail that makes sense (since one can run sensitivity analysis only on a model input). Further, its use will also help to ensure that the forward calculations correctly reflect dependencies between the items (general dependencies or specific common drivers of variability), since sensitivity analysis will be truly valid only if such dependencies are captured. Simply put, many aspects of the appropriate model design generally become clear by using the SAT process. It is surprising how often this fundamental approach is overlooked or insufficiently considered, resulting in models that are ineffective at addressing key questions and inefficient or cumbersome to use.

The file Ch4.1.BFDesign.xlsx contains an example of such processes, as shown in the sequence of screen-clips (Figures 4.1 to Figure 4.5). The aim is to calculate the labour cost associated with a project to renovate a house. In the first instance, a backward thought process is applied to consider possible ways of breaking down the total cost into components. As described above, there may be various ways to do this. Figure 4.1 represents the initial method used, based on a hypothesis that the items shown are the underlying drivers of the total (with the value of each item perhaps taken from a supplier quote).

On further reflection of the nature of the sensitivities, one may conclude that (since all costs are labour-related), it would not make sense to change the value only of an individual item, since if a different labour cost changes the value of one item, then (in real life) the others would also change. This would need to be reflected in the model's logic for this type of sensitivity analysis to make sense.

Figure 4.2 shows an example of a modified model, in which the backward path has been extended to include an hourly labour rate, and the forward calculation path is based on using new underlying base figures (derived so that the new totals for each are the same as the original values).

	A	B	C
1			
2		**Description**	Base Cost
3		Remove old kitchen	1500
4		Redo electrics	2000
5		Install kitchen	2500
6		New plumbing	1500
7		Paint and decorate	3000
8		Final finishings	5000
9		Install security system	1000
10		Plaster	5000
11		New floor	1800
12		Legal and architectural fees	3000
13		**Total**	**26300**

FIGURE 4.1 Initial Approach to Labour Cost Breakdown

	A	B	C	D	E
1					
2				Base	
3		Unit labour cost		10	
4					
5		**Description**	Base Cost/unit	Cost	
6		Remove old kitchen	150	1500	=C6*$D$3
7		Redo electrics	200	2000	=C7*$D$3
8		Install kitchen	250	2500	=C8*$D$3
9		New plumbing	150	1500	=C9*$D$3
10		Paint and decorate	300	3000	=C10*$D$3
11		Final finishings	500	5000	=C11*$D$3
12		Install security system	100	1000	=C12*$D$3
13		Plaster	500	5000	=C13*$D$3
14		New floor	180	1800	=C14*$D$3
15		Legal and architectural fees	300	3000	=C15*$D$3
16		**Total**		**26300**	

FIGURE 4.2 Modified Approach Based on a Possible Sensitivity Driver with Absolute Variation

In addition, one may desire to be able to vary the figures using a percentage variation (as an alternative, or in addition, to varying absolute figures). Figure 4.3 shows an example of how this may be implemented.

In a more general case, there may be several underlying factors (or different categories of labour), with some individual items driven by one of these, and other items by another. Figure 4.4 shows an example of this.

	A	B	C	D	E	F
1						
2				Base	Variation	
3		Unit labour cost		10	10%	
4						
5		**Description**	Base Cost/unit	Cost	Variation	Final Result
6		Remove old kitchen	150	1500	10%	1650
7		Redo electrics	200	2000	10%	2200
8		Install kitchen	250	2500	10%	2750
9		New plumbing	150	1500	10%	1650
10		Paint and decorate	300	3000	10%	3300
11		Final finishings	500	5000	10%	5500
12		Install security system	100	1000	10%	1100
13		Plaster	500	5000	10%	5500
14		New floor	180	1800	10%	1980
15		Legal and architectural fees	300	3000	10%	3300
16		**Total**		**26300**		**28930**
17						

FIGURE 4.3 Modified Approach Based on a Possible Sensitivity Driver with Absolute and Percentage Variation

	A	B	C	D	E	F	G
1							
2		Unit labour cost categories			Base	Variation	
3		A			10	5%	
4		B			8	10%	
5		C			12	20%	
6							
7		**Description**	Category	Base Cost/unit	Cost	Variation	Final Result
8		Remove old kitchen	A	150	1500	5%	1575
9		Redo electrics	A	200	2000	5%	2100
10		Install kitchen	A	250	2500	5%	2625
11		New plumbing	B	188	1500	10%	1650
12		Paint and decorate	B	375	3000	10%	3300
13		Final finishings	B	625	5000	10%	5500
14		Install security system	B	125	1000	10%	1100
15		Plaster	C	417	5000	20%	6000
16		New floor	C	150	1800	20%	2160
17		Legal and architectural fees	C	250	3000	20%	3600
18		**Total**			**26300**		**29610**

FIGURE 4.4 Approach Sensitivity Driver Categories

	A	B	C	D	E	F	G
1							
2		Unit labour cost categories			Base	Variation	Final Result
3		A			10	5%	6300
4		B			8	10%	11550
5		C			12	20%	11760
6		**Total**					29610
7							
8		**Description**	Category	Base Cost/unit	Cost	Variation	Final Result
9		Remove old kitchen	A	150	1500	5.0%	1575
10		Redo electrics	A	200	2000	5.0%	2100
11		New plumbing	B	188	1500	10.0%	1650
12		Plaster	C	417	5000	20.0%	6000
13		Paint and decorate	B	375	3000	10.0%	3300
14		New floor	C	150	1800	20.0%	2160
15		Install kitchen	A	250	2500	5.0%	2625
16		Final finishings	B	625	5000	10.0%	5500
17		Install security system	B	125	1000	10.0%	1100
18		Legal and architectural fees	C	250	3000	20.0%	3600
19		**Total**			**26300**		29610

FIGURE 4.5 Sensitivity Driver Categories with Flexible Data Entry

Finally, in general when items fall into categories, it may be preferable to build a model which is not structurally constrained by the categories; in other words, one in which the items can be entered in any order (rather than having to be entered by category). This is simple to do by using functions such as INDEX, MATCH and SUMIFS. Figure 4.5 shows an example (the reader may inspect the formulae in the file, if desired).

Of course, the above demonstrates only one example of the use of such principles, which essentially apply in all model design situations.

Another important case is that of models with a time axis (perhaps to forecast items such as volumes, prices, revenues or cost), where an important question is whether the assumptions used for the forecast (e.g. for the growth rate in revenues) should be individual to each time period, or common to several time periods: a separate assumption in each period can be cumbersome and inhibit sensitivity analysis, whereas a single assumption that applies to all future periods may be too crude (and unrealistic), resulting in an excessively high sensitivity of the output to the input value. A compromise approach, in which there are several growth rates, each applied to several periods, is often the most appropriate. This can also be considered as a "parameter reduction", i.e. the number of inputs is reduced to a more manageable level, whilst aiming to retain sufficient accuracy (in terms of its reflecting reality reasonably well).

The file Ch4.2.TimeDesign.xlsx provides an example, shown in Figure 4.6, in which there is a single assumption for revenue growth in each of years 1–3, a single assumption for each of years 4–5 and a single assumption for each of years 6–10.

	A	B	C	D	E	F	G	H	I	J	K	L	M	N
1														
2			2016	2017	2018	2019	2020	2021	2022	2023	2024	2025	2026	2027
3		Actual or Forecast? (A or F)	A	A	F	F	F	F	F	F	F	F	F	F
4		Revenues	400	408	431	452	488	537	577	606	636	668	702	737
5		% Growth		2.0%	2.0%	2.0%	2.0%	3.0%	3.0%	4.0%	4.0%	4.0%	4.0%	4.0%
6														

FIGURE 4.6 Parameter Reduction to Aid Sensitivity Analysis

Time Granularity

Where models have a time component (such as each column representing a time period), it is important to consider the granularity of the time axis (such as whether a column is to represent a day, a month, a quarter or a year, and so on). It is generally better to build the model so that the granularity of the time axis is at least as detailed as that required for the purposes of development of the formulae and results analysis. For example, if one may wish to delay some cash flows by a month, then a monthly model should be considered. Similarly, if the refinancing conditions for a bank or project loan are to be verified quarterly (in accordance with some agreed contract), then a model which forecasts whether such conditions will be met should generally be built to be at least quarterly.

The benefits of increasing granularity potentially include:

- Models with a very granular (detailed) time axis can be used to give the relevant figures for longer periods (by summation).
- It is harder to validly allocate aggregate figures (i.e. for a period of a year) into the components (such as monthly figures), since the effect of growth or other factors would lead to non-equal values in the component periods.

The disadvantages of increasing granularity include:

- Models with a very detailed time axis become large and cumbersome to maintain, whilst not necessarily offering sufficient additional accuracy.
- It may be hard to calibrate the model by finding or estimating input data that is itself required to be very granular.
- One may be required to forecast the time allocation of items that may be difficult to assess at that level of detail. For example, in a model for a manufacturing business that produces a low volume of high-value bespoke engineering products with a long lead-time between a customer order and the fulfilment of the order, it may be cumbersome to produce a full forecast based on a weekly time axis: the allocation of orders to precise weeks may be a difficult and low value-added process (from a financial forecasting perspective), but the allocation into quarterly periods may be much easier and more sensible.

Level of Detail on Input Variables

Just as there is likely to be an optimal level of detail for the granularity of the time axis, the same applies to input variables. The appropriate level of detail will closely relate to the nature of the sensitivities to be conducted, as well as to the data requirements and sources.

	A	B	C	D	E
1					
2			Cost	Variation	Final Result
3		A	6000	5%	6300
4		B	10500	10%	11550
5		C	9800	20%	11760
6		Total	26300		29610
7					

FIGURE 4.7 Model Built Using Category Totals as Direct Inputs

As an example, with respect to Figure 4.4, since the sensitivity analysis will in principle be conducted at the category level (i.e. using the percentage variation figures in cells F3:F5), one could have considered building the model using category totals only (see Figure 4.7, which is also contained in the example file referred to earlier).

Note, however, that this more aggregate model does not allow for an easy calibration based on the more granular information provided (such as the cost of removing the old kitchen, or of redoing the electrics), as this information is used only implicitly when determining the base category totals (in Column C).

Thus, the appropriate level of granularity may be one that uses the detailed information explicitly (as shown in Figure 4.4): this reflects not only the sensitivities required, but also the nature of the data available. In other words, data may be input at a granular level, but the sensitivities are designed to be conducted at the category level (even as one could in theory conduct a sensitivity to an individual item, even if this may not be logically consistent with the real-life situation).

A model that is more detailed may not have a better predictive power than a less detailed one:

- When there are more variables, the number of possible dependencies between them becomes large (in proportion to the square of the number), whilst the formulae required to capture such dependencies will become complex or may simply be overlooked. The sensitivity analysis of the results would be inaccurate, and the predicted ranges of variation would be incorrect (either too wide or too narrow).
- It may be hard to calibrate the input values, simply because data (or the ability to judge or make estimates) is not available at that level of detail.

Thus, the appropriate level of detail – whilst non-trivial to answer definitely – is closely related both to the nature of the sensitivities to be conducted, and to the nature and availability of data that will be used to populate it.

Sensitising Absolute Values or Variations from Base Cases

At the model design stage, it is useful to consider explicitly whether sensitivity analysis will be performed on an absolute or on a variation (change) basis. In the first approach, the value of a model's output is shown, as an input takes each of a pre-defined set of values. In the second approach, the output is shown for a set of input values corresponding to a variation from the base case (the variation can itself either be absolute percentages variations).

	9	10	11	12	15
26300	23670	26300	28930	31560	39450

	-15%	-10%	0%	10%	20%
26300	22355	23670	**26300**	28930	31560

FIGURE 4.8 Absolute and Percentage Sensitivities

The advantage of the variation approach is that the position of the base case within the sensitivity table is fixed (even if its underlying value has been updated), so that sensitivity tables can be formatted to highlight the base case. For example, Figure 4.8 shows two sensitivity tables in the context of the earlier labour-cost model. In the latter approach (which uses a percentage variation), the base case position is fixed (at 0% variation), even if other assumption values were updated (such as the base unit labour-cost).

When using the variation approach (whether absolute or percentages), the variation is an additional model input, which must be used together with the original absolute input figure within the calculations. Therefore, at the model design stage, it is useful to reflect on which approach to sensitivity analysis will be used, since significant rework may otherwise be required to adapt the model's formulae appropriately.

The percentage-variation approach has particular appeal, as it may correspond closely to how many decision-makers think. Its main disadvantages include the potential for error and/or confusion in cases where the base case values are percentage figures (so that it becomes less clear whether the percentage variation applied is a relative or an absolute figure, e.g. whether a 5% variation around a base of 10% represents the range 9.5–10.5% or rather 5–15%), and where base case values may themselves be zero (so that a percentage variation results in the same value).

Scenarios Versus Sensitivities

At the model design stage, it is also worth reflecting on whether the sensitivity analysis will be conducted using scenarios or not. Scenarios are used most typically where it is desired to vary three or more input values simultaneously. Another use of scenarios is to reflect possible dependencies between two or more inputs. This can be useful where the relationship between the variables is not well understood and cannot be represented with simple formulae. For example, it may be difficult to express the volume of a product that might be sold for every possible value of the price, but market research could be used to establish this at several price points, with each volume-price combination forming a possible scenario.

When scenarios are used, tables of data to define the scenarios will be required, and their placement will affect the model design, layout and construction. If the need for scenarios (and their nature, such as whether the number of scenarios is known or may vary) is not considered early in the process, then the model may later require significant rework, or indeed be structured in an inappropriate way. For example, in Chapter 25 and in Chapter 33, we show methods that can be used to use separate worksheets to contain (scenario) data that needs to be brought into the model (or deleted from it), in such a way that the model would need only minimal adjustment: these are also discussed in the context of model flexibility and workbook structure in Chapter 6.

Uncertain Versus Decision Variables

It is quite frequent that no consideration is given as to whether any change in the values of input variables corresponds to something (in the real-life situation) over which one would have control or not. For example, the price at which to launch a new product is something that one can control (or choose), whereas the price that one pays for oil is (generally) not. Thus, two generic types of input variables include:

- Those which represent items that one can control (i.e. ones for which there is a choice), with a resulting issue being how to choose them in an optimal way.
- Those which represent items that one cannot control, and are therefore uncertain or associated with risk.

It is important to reflect which category each input belongs to:

- The process to explicitly consider the distinction between the role of the variables will help to ensure that one develops additional insight into the situation, and into the levers that may be used to affect a decision.
- It would often affect the best way to layout the model so that items of the similar type (optimisation versus uncertain variables) are grouped together if possible, or are perhaps formatted differently. This will generally not only aid transparency, but also affect the ease with which additional tools can be applied:
  - The methods used to capture the effect of several sources of uncertainty will in practice often involve using simulation to evaluate many possible (non-controllable) scenarios or input combinations. Typically, inputs may need to be replaced by probability distributions, and the parameters of such distributions (e.g. mean and standard deviation, or minimum, most likely and maximum) would need to be explicitly placed somewhere in the model. Where VBA is used to generate random samples and to run simulations, it can be helpful if all such inputs are grouped into a single contiguous range.
  - The algorithms that are typically used to find an optimal set of input values (such as Solver) are usually most easily implemented if the inputs that are to be optimised (as well as data relating to any constraints that are to be respected) are grouped into a single range.
- The logic within the model may need to be adapted, potentially quite significantly. For example, if it is desired to find the price at which to sell a product in order to maximise revenues, one will need to capture (in the logic of the model) the mechanism by which volume decreases as price is increased (generally resulting in an inverted-U curve for revenue as a function of price, when implemented correctly). Achieving this can be a significant challenge, and potentially requiring one to develop a more detailed understanding of the underlying behaviour (e.g. demand-curve modelling). Where an optimum value is determined purely by constraints, such issues may be less challenging.

Increasing Model Validity Using Formulae

A model is valid only within an implicit context (that is often not documented at all, or perhaps done so insufficiently, and therefore not known by another user). Examples of assumed contexts include:

- The geographic location of a construction project.
- The timing of the start of production relative to that of the construction phase of a project.
- The timing of one set of cash flows relative to another (for example, of tax payments relative to taxable earnings).
- The composition of items which determine the cost structure.
- The range of profitability of a business. Many models use formulae to calculate tax charges that are valid only when taxable profit is positive, and are not valid where it is negative.
- The interest rate earned on cash balances. In some models, a periodic interest rate of 200% or more would result in a divergent set of calculations, and resulting errors (see Chapter 10).
- The model is to be applied only to decisions relating to the planet Earth (for example, although undocumented, the model would be incorrect if used to conduct the financial planning of a trip to Mars, where the Martian year is of approximately 687 Earth days in duration).

In fact, even where an effort is made to document a model, frequently no distinction is made between items which are *within* the model ("model assumptions") and those which are *about* the model ("contextual assumptions"):

- Model assumptions are numerical values typically (sometimes text fields also act as inputs), which the model's calculations should update correctly (i.e. reflect the reality of the real-life situation) if these values are altered (e.g. to conduct a sensitivity analysis).
- Contextual assumptions are those which limit the validity of a model, and so cannot be validly changed within the existing model.

The creation of flexibility in a model often involves increasing its validity by adapting it so that contextual (fixed or implicit) assumptions are replaced by genuine numerical ones. In such cases, the (fixed) context of the original model is generally simply a special case (possible scenario) within the new model. For example:

- If one is evaluating the economics of a construction project, using detailed assumptions for a specific project, but is also considering several locations for the project, it may be that each location has some specific characteristics; one may also require new road infrastructure to be built, whilst the other may not. Thus, instead of having a separate model for each location, a more general approach would be one in which a common model structure is developed, which includes every line item for every location (e.g. road infrastructure for each), but in which the corresponding figures are set to zero (where no such infrastructure is needed), with a scenario approach used to run the desired case.
- Methods to alter the timing (whether absolute or relative) of the occurrence of items (such as the start dates of project phases or of cash flows, and general

time-shifting) are discussed in various places later in the text. Note that one issue to consider is that a delay may affect items in different ways. For example, whereas the volume produced and sold may be fully shifted in time, the price level achieved per unit may not be shifted at all, as it may be determined from external market prices. Similarly, whilst variable costs may be shifted in time, some fixed overhead costs may remain even during the pre-start-up period. Thus, such models can become more complex.

- A model of the total payroll costs could be built by explicitly listing only all those employees who are currently on the payroll (and their salaries and other relevant benefits). On the other hand, a more general model could include a longer list of employees (including former staff and potential future staff, as well as possibly making a distinction between status: contractor, or full/part-time etc.), and use either indicator flags (e.g. 1 for current employees, 0 for others) or database-type queries to create calculations which reflect only the relevant staff. The latter approach would typically be more flexible for day-to-day working, albeit with increased complexity (again, typically using the techniques discussed later in the text).
- If building a model that is to apply when taxable income is negative, one may need to capture the reporting and cash flow effect of tax-loss carry-forwards; doing so would require a modification to the original formulae.

In fact, the creation of models with insufficient flexibility in their formulae arises most often due to inadequate consideration, a lack of knowledge, or a lack of capability in several areas, including of:

- How structural (contextual) limitations may be replaced by appropriate numerical assumptions.
- The sensitivities that decision-makers would like to see.
- How variations in multiple items may interact.
- How to implement the formulae or create model flexibility using Excel or VBA.

Thus, the discussion within this overall text is aimed at ensuring that models are built with the appropriate level of flexibility, and in ways that are efficient and which manage complexity.

CHAPTER 5

Database Versus Formulae-driven Approaches

INTRODUCTION

This chapter provides an overview of the main issues that need consideration with respect to the appropriate structure of a model's input data, focusing on two main areas: the nature of any changes that will be made to the data when the model is built, and whether the overall situation is dominated by calculations or by data.

KEY ISSUES FOR CONSIDERATION

In this section, we discuss the key issues that typically should be considered when designing a model's overall architecture. In the next, we provide a practical example which demonstrates some of these principles. In the next chapter, we discuss possibilities for specific workbook and worksheet structures.

Separating the Data, Analysis and Presentation (Reporting) Layers

One important principle is to separate the data (inputs) from the way that the data is used (calculations). This is also known as separating the data and analysis "layers" (and applies to general technical applications). In principle, such separation allows for each layer to be modified or updated independently. It is especially important in many real-life applications: for example, it would be highly inconvenient if, in order to implement a version update to software that contains a database of customer contacts, all existing contacts needed to be deleted. This framework can be extended to include an additional presentation (or reporting) layer, such as graphs that are populated using the output of a model.

The translation of this into Excel modelling contexts is fairly clear, albeit with some potential caveats:

- (Data) Inputs should be shown separately to calculations. Every cell should contain either a pure number or a pure formula or a text field. For example, a "mixed"

formula, such as =10*C6, should not be used, as there are several disadvantages in doing so:
- Lack of transparency; the input assumption (here: 10) is not directly visible in the normal view of a worksheet.
- Sensitivity analysis to the value (here: 10) is not easy to conduct (and cannot be automated); generally, the value of the number is harder to modify when it is embedded within a calculation rather than being separate.
- If such a formula is used in a range of cells (such as for a time series) so that the value (10) is repeated several times, one may overlook that the real-world behaviour of this value may have a time trend (e.g. a growth profile).

- Inputs should be clearly identifiable, and organised so that they can be updated easily. In the author's view, this does not mean that all inputs need to be grouped together (e.g. at the beginning of the model or in a separate worksheet). Rather, when using modular structures, the inputs relevant to a specific module (i.e. area of the worksheet) can be local to that area, with inputs that are of global relevance placed separately (see Chapter 6).
- In practice, the presentation layer may contain charts, sensitivity or scenario tables, or other items that require linking to the output in some way (or directly to the input, such as with PivotTables). One can argue that, rather than linking directly to the calculations, a better method is to create a separate output area, which contains direct cell references to the calculation of the outputs, and link any charts or presentation tools to this additional output area. In this way, the presentation layer is formally separated from the model. On the other hand, in practice, doing so may be cumbersome. First, it increases the size of the model (although this is a relatively small additional increase in larger models in which the volume of intermediate calculations is much larger than that of the outputs). Second, since DataTables (see Chapter 12) need to reside on the same worksheet as the inputs that are being varied, the data and presentation layers may need to be on the same worksheet. Third, some structures (such as PivotTables, or tables built with SUMIFS queries of a data set) can be considered as belonging both to the analysis and presentation layer. A strict separation would often not make sense, or would require significant duplication.
- The analysis layer is essentially the formulae in the model, although strictly speaking the presentation layer may contain some formula links to the calculated outputs (as described above).

It is worth noting that although mixed formulae (such as =10*C6) should be avoided in principle, in practice they may arguably be acceptable in some situations, including:

- Growth formulae, such as D6=C6*(1+D5), where D5 is a percentage growth rate. This standard formula could instead be written D6=C6+C6*D5, but this latter formulation may be less familiar (for example, when compared to formulae in many textbooks). Further, it repeats the use of the cell reference C6, which should be avoided in principle.
- Where Text functions are used to add comments to input values, thus creating formulae, such as D6=9.8*ISTEXT("Updated Value from Nov 2017").

- In models with conversion factors (e.g. years to months) or other parameters (i.e. constants that should not be changed), it may be clearer to include such constants within the formulae, rather than treating them as inputs in a separate cell (i.e. dividing by 12 in each cell may be a reasonable alternative to having all formulae link to a central cell containing the value of 12).

The Nature of Changes to Data Sets and Structures

In model design and implementation, it is important to consider:

- The frequency with which data will be changed or updated once the model is built (if at all).
- The nature of any changes that will be required.

Of course, if it is known in advance that the data would never change in any way, then the main design issues would revolve around building the model in the most efficient way possible (generally the quickest and simplest), whilst ensuring that it is reasonably transparent (for example, by highlighting which elements are inputs and which are calculations using colour-coding or other clear identifiers).

On the other hand, for the overwhelming majority of models, the data will need to be changed on several occasions after the model is built (or during the building process): at the simplest level, better estimates may arise for the value of some inputs, and/or traditional sensitivity analysis may need to be conducted. Beyond these, other changes that may be required to the data include:

- Creating additional scenarios for the values of some of the inputs.
- Updating a forecast model by incorporating the values of reported actuals as they become available (month, year etc.).
- Extending the number of time periods in a forecast.
- Adding data about a newly purchased business unit or asset into a model that consolidates the information for all units or assets into summary figures.
- Updating data that is linked to another workbook or to another external data source (for example, a website that contains market prices of commodities, exchange rates or other financial instruments).

Note that many models are built with the (often implicit) assumption that the numbers and sizes of the data ranges are fixed, whereas in fact this is not the case (leading to a model that it inefficient and cumbersome to use). For example, if it is known that a forecast model will need to be updated with actual figures as they become available during the forecast period, then the true nature of the data set is one that will contain two types of values (i.e. assumptions about future forecasts, and the actual values that were realised up until some point within the forecast period). However, if the model is built to include only the forecast assumptions, then there will be no any easy mechanism to update it as actual figures become available.

Where changes to the data will likely be required, the design process should ensure that an efficient mechanism will be needed to add, delete, update or change the data. In order to plan an appropriate mechanism, a further key distinction regarding the nature of the data ranges (i.e. model inputs) is fundamental:

- Their number and size are fixed. In this case, the number of data ranges, and the size of each, are known at the design stage, in principle. Many traditional models fall into this category; changes to the data result only due to modification of the values of base case assumptions or when conducting a traditional sensitivity analysis. The main requirements to being able to update a model easily are essentially that:
  - The inputs are contained in stand-alone cells (and are not embedded within formulae).
  - The inputs can be easily found and identified.
  - The model contains error-checks or other validation tools to cover the cases where invalid values are attempted to be used as inputs.
- Their number and size are not fixed. Such cases may occur where the maximum number of scenarios that one may wish to run is not known, or where an unknown number of new business units or other assets are likely to be purchased or sold. More sophisticated approaches to the design and accessing of the data will be appropriate. For example:
  - Where there is a single data range whose size is not known, database approaches (including the use of Excel Tables) can allow for flexible-sized ranges. (As an alternative, the OFFSET function within the "refers to" dialog of the Name Manager can be used to define a range whose size varies dynamically according to the size of the data set.)
  - Where new data sets are required to be added or deleted with relative ease and only minimal model adjustment, techniques to consolidate and/or select values from data that is contained in multiple worksheets can be applied. These are discussed in Chapter 6, Chapter 25 and Chapter 33.

Focus on Data or Formulae?

The consideration of whether the overall modelling context is one that needs to be dominated by formulae or by data is an important one during the design stage:

- Traditional (or classical) Excel models, such as those used in corporate finance or cash flow valuation, often have a small set of numerical assumptions, from which large tables of calculations are performed. Certainly, where a single value is used for an assumption across multiple time periods (such as a single growth rate in revenues that applies to all future time periods), arbitrarily large tables of calculations may be generated simply by extending the time axis sufficiently, even as the number of inputs remains fixed. Such modelling approaches are "formulae-focused (or dominated)". The modelling emphasis will be on highlighting the (relatively small number) of inputs, and on ensuring a clear logical flow. The way that input data is structured will not generally be an issue of significance, as long as basic care is taken, such as ensuring that inputs are clearly identifiable and are in stand-alone cells.
- In many other situations, there is a large volume of data that is required. For example, a model may calculate the annual profit by aggregating the daily revenue

figures from the daily cost figures and subtracting the two. In such cases, the appropriate modelling approach is typically a "data-focused" one, using database concepts, functionality or data-oriented architectures and modular structures. These include the structuring of data sets into (perhaps several) contiguous ranges, using a column (field)-based approach for the model's variables (with well-structured field identifiers, disciplined naming conventions, and so on). There could also be multiple data sets, each situated on separate worksheet. In addition, functions such as SUMIFS or Database functions may be used to query the data sets, and there is also likely to be a need for Lookup and other advanced functions.

- In many (more complex) real-life cases, there may be large data sets and also potentially many formulae, and it may not be clear (without further reflection) as to whether one should consider the situation to be formulae-dominated or data-dominated.

Figure 5.1 illustrates the various cases. Note that the diagonal line in the top right-hand quadrant aims to highlight that:

- A model that is built for a "formulae-dominated" situation typically cannot readily be adapted into one that would apply to "data-dominated" situation.
- A model which is structured using database-type approaches may not be the best adapted to situations where there is only limited data, but many formulae are required.

Therefore, at the design stage, the reflection on the appropriate approach is fundamental: an inappropriate choice can lead to a model that is inflexible, cumbersome and not fit for purpose.

It is also worth noting that:

- The formula-dominated approach is typically the default approach of many modellers (especially those with a corporate finance or accounting heritage).
- Many situations that one may initially consider as needing to be formulae-dominated are not necessarily best considered as such; the number of unique formulae required may in fact be quite low, even as such formulae may be copied to many cells. Thus, database approaches often have a wider applicability than is often first considered.

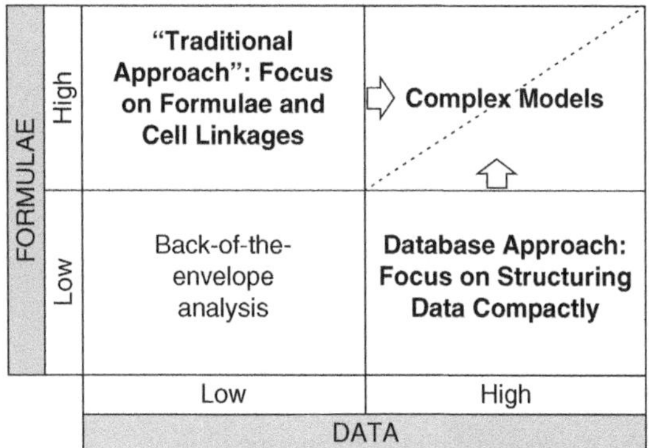

FIGURE 5.1 Classification of Modelling Situations According to the Focus on Data or on Formulae

- There is a frequent overlap between situations which are data-dominated and those in which the number and size of data sets is not fixed (for example, where new data needs to be introduced regularly, typically the amount of data is usually also dominant). Thus, as a general observation, it is typically the case that insufficient thought is given to the use of data-driven approaches, just as the issue of the nature of the data ranges is often overlooked.
- Database approaches may often be preferable to traditional approaches where there is a detailed time-axis (such as monthly or daily). The use of a time axis which develops across columns (as in many traditional forecasting models) works well for models which have only a few time periods (such as a 10-year annual forecast). However, where the time axis is more detailed (so that the volume of information becomes large, even as the number of unique formulae may be small), a database approach – in which the time axis generally develops downwards within a column – may be more appropriate. Typically, such a database may contain operational data, whereas financial data (such as interest expenses or taxes) may need to be calculated separately based on summary data, not the individual line items. Note that we use the term "database approach" (rather than pure databases) since some items are nevertheless calculated within contiguous, multiple-column ranges. In addition, unlike pure databases, in which each row is independent of the others, in such models there may be time-dependency between the item in the rows of a column.

PRACTICAL EXAMPLE

The file Ch5.1.DataStr.Horses.1.FormulaCellLinks.xlsx contains an example of the traditional formula driven approach. The Reports worksheet (see Figure 5.2) shows a summary cost figure for each horse for each month, using (see the Formula Bar)

D4 =Feb!C20

	A	B	C	D	E	F
1						
2		HORSE	Jan	Feb	March	....
3		MYSTERY RIDER	497	447	447	
4		MOCHOCINO	440	457	487	
5		FABLED STORY	318	346	349	
6		SUPER HERO	558	711	456	
7		MONTHY PYTHON	513	463	492	
8		FLYING CIRCUS	407	363	548	
9		NO JOKING	347	284	404	
10		WHEELIE BIN	323	399	377	
11		YOU CAN'T MAKE IT UP	512	524	588	
12						
13		**TOTAL**	**3914**	**3992**	**4147**	

FIGURE 5.2 The Reports Worksheet Linking to Specific Cells

	A	B	C	D	E	F	G	H
1								
2								
3		Horse Name	MYSTERY RIDER		Horse Name	SUPER HERO		Horse Nam
4		Item	Amount ($)		Item	Amount ($)		Item
5		Stables	193		Stables	81		Stables
6		Food	113		Food	167		Food
7		Transport	16		Transport	209		Transport
8		Veterinary	63		Veterinary	110		Veterinary
9		Other	62		Other	146		Other
10		**Total**	**447**		**Total**	**711**		**Total**
11								
12								
13		Horse Name	MOCHOCINO		Horse Name	MONTHY PYTHON		Horse Nam
14		Item	Amount ($)		Item	Amount ($)		Item
15		Stables	97		Stables	126		Stables
16		Food	208		Food	54		Food
17		Transport	38		Transport	213		Transport
18		Veterinary	82		Veterinary	45		Veterinary
19		Other	31		Other	24		Other
20		**Total**	**457**		**Total**	**463**		**Total**
21								
22								
23		Horse Name	FABLED STORY		Horse Name	FLYING CIRCUS		Horse Nam
24		Item	Amount ($)		Item	Amount ($)		Item

FIGURE 5.3 The Feb Data Worksheet, Containing Cost Data for February

a direct cell reference to the relevant specific cell of the applicable monthly worksheet (see Figure 5.3), i.e. Cell D4 links to the Feb data sheet, containing the data for February.

The use of such approaches is frequently seen, and presumably is favoured due to the intuitive appeal of using direct cell references, as well as out of lack of awareness (or consideration) of alternative approaches. However, this approach to generating the summary figures is generally unsatisfactory:

- The addition of data for a new month will require that many new formulae and cell links be added to the Reports sheet (which is time-consuming and has the potential for error).
- The approach is not flexible if the set of horses may change (e.g. due to new acquisitions or sales).
- The approach does not readily allow for additional types of cost items to be introduced.
- It is not easy to produce other forms of reports, such as the total expenditure by cost category (e.g. total stables cost).

The file Ch5.2.DataStr.Horses.2.Database.xlsx shows an example of the data-driven approach, resulting from recognising that the situation is dominated by the volume of data, and also that the size of the data sets is not fixed. In this case (Figure 5.4) the underlying elements are recorded as a database (whose rows may be presented in any order, of course), so that the month, horse name and item

Month	Horse Name	Item	Amount ($)
Jan	MYSTERY RIDER	Stables	152
Jan	MYSTERY RIDER	Food	160
Jan	MYSTERY RIDER	Transport	12
Jan	MYSTERY RIDER	Veterinary	55
Jan	MYSTERY RIDER	Other	118
Jan	MOCHOCINO	Stables	87
Jan	MOCHOCINO	Food	160
Jan	MOCHOCINO	Transport	31
Jan	MOCHOCINO	Veterinary	128
Jan	MOCHOCINO	Other	33
Jan	FABLED STORY	Stables	68
Jan	FABLED STORY	Food	128
Jan	FABLED STORY	Transport	82
Jan	FABLED STORY	Veterinary	16
Jan	FABLED STORY	Other	24
Jan	SUPER HERO	Stables	58
Jan	SUPER HERO	Food	117

FIGURE 5.4 Underlying Data Set as a Single Database

SUMIFS				
General	Horse	Mont	Item	Total
	MOCHOCINO	Feb	Tran:	38
HORSE	Jan	Feb	Mar	....
MYSTERY RIDER	497	447	447	
MOCHOCINO	440	457	487	
FABLED STORY	318	346	349	
SUPER HERO	558	711	456	
MONTHY PYTHON	513	463	492	
FLYING CIRCUS	407	363	548	
NO JOKING	347	284	404	
WHEELIE BIN	323	399	377	
YOU CAN'T MAKE IT UP	512	524	588	
TOTAL	**3914**	**3992**	**4147**	
DataBase	Horse Name	Mont	Item	DSUM
	MOCHOCINO	Feb	Tran:	38.2

FIGURE 5.5 The Reports Worksheet Using SUMIFS, Database Functions or a PivotTable

description become database fields which can be used to generate various reports. The Reports worksheet (shown partly in Figure 5.5) then creates the desired reports using either the SUMIFS function, or Database functions or a PivotTable (as desired).

Note also that in many more-complex applications, the query stage (shown as the reporting stage in the above example) would be linked to further additional (global) assumptions that would drive further calculations. For example, one may wish to see the aggregate effect of a percentage variation in all stables' costs.

CHAPTER 6

Designing the Workbook Structure

INTRODUCTION

This chapter discusses issues relating to the design of the overall workbook structure. These include the use of linked workbooks, the number of worksheets, the role of each worksheet and the data structures used. It is probably fair to say that insufficient attention is generally paid to such issues. We present a set of generic base practice structures in terms of the placement of data and calculations, as well as tools and techniques to select or consolidate data that is used across multiple worksheets.

Designing Workbook Models with Multiple Worksheets

This section presents some general principles relating to overall model structure, especially the use of linked workbooks, and the role of each worksheet in models with multiple worksheets.

Linked Workbooks

In principle, models should be self-contained within a single workbook, and not have links to other workbooks. The main reason is to avoid potential errors that can otherwise easily arise, yet be hard to detect:

- If structural changes are made to a source workbook (e.g. the addition/deletion of rows or columns, renaming of the workbook or of a worksheet) when the destination workbook is not open, then such changes will generally not be reflected in the formulae in the (closed) destination workbook. For example, the link may be altered to refer to last month's oil price rather than this month's. As a result, one cannot know a priori whether the linked cells in a destination workbook are linked to the correct cells in the source workbook or not. Thus, such models are inherently prone to errors. In principle, an "audit" would be required every time the model is used. Clearly, this is not only impractical but also highly unsatisfactory if one wishes to have reliable and efficient models.
- If numerical changes are made (such as to run sensitivity analysis) within linked workbook structures, the results may be incorrect unless all workbooks are open at the same time.

In practice, it may not always be possible to avoid linking workbooks. Frequently, there is a need to access a centralised data set in another workbook (such as that of a company's standard oil price forecast). Similarly, the output of a set of individual analysts' work may need to be collected into a central reference workbook. When linked workbooks cannot be avoided, there are two main ways to improve robustness:

- Using "mirror" worksheets. These are worksheets which are identical in structure, and are placed in each of the source and destination workbook. The objective is to create indirect links, so that the owner of each workbook can work independently without having to consider other workbooks:
  - The mirror sheet in the source workbook is populated from cells within the same workbook by using direct references to the relevant cells within it (i.e. taking data from that workbook).
  - The mirror sheet in the destination workbook is populated by referencing the corresponding cells in the mirror sheet of the source workbook (thus creating the links between the workbooks). Note that once the sheets are placed in each workbook, they should not be changed structurally.
  - The mirror sheet in the destination workbook is used to populate the main calculations of the destination workbook by using cell references.
- Using named ranges in the source workbook for the data that is to be linked, and referring to such data (from the destination workbook) using these names. In this way, the correct references will apply even if the cells in the source workbook have been moved when the destination workbook is not open.

The use of mirror sheets has the advantage that it isolates the linking process in a very explicit and transparent way. In principle, one can use both methods together (i.e. in which named ranges are used within mirror sheets). However, once mirror sheets have been implemented, the additional benefit of the named ranges is only marginal (whereas using only the named range approach does not isolate the linking process, nor does it create the same level of transparency about the existence of the linkages).

Multiple Worksheets: Advantages and Disadvantages

Many traditional models are structured over several worksheets. Reasons often cited for using multiple worksheets include:

- To devote a worksheet to each main item or concept. For example, one may have a dedicated worksheet for each of revenues, variable costs, capital investments, depreciation, net asset values, tax, dividends, financing, the income statement, balance sheet and cash flow statement, and so on.
- To ease model navigation or printing (this can also be facilitated using named ranges, rather than using multiple worksheets).
- As a result of the development of a model over time by various analysts. Sometimes, additional parts of the model are simply started in another worksheet to avoid changing the existing structure or to keep one's work separate from that of someone else's.
- It just seemed like a good idea!

However, there are some key disadvantages of using an excessive number of worksheets:

- Auditing the model is much more cumbersome, time-consuming and error-prone than it is for a model built in a single worksheet:
  - The audit paths are three-dimensional and diagonal, with even the following of basic logical paths requiring one to move between worksheets. On the other hand, in a single worksheet model, the dependency paths are almost always either horizontal or vertical (not diagonal). Thus, the complexity, time taken and potential for errors become significantly larger when multiple worksheets are involved.
  - The formulae are larger and look more complex, not least due to the explicit presence of worksheet names within them.
  - There are often many repeated formulae and cell references, as items are transferred from one sheet to another.
- There is a higher risk of unforeseen errors, such as the creation of circular references.
- The detection and correction of errors by modifying formulae and their linkages is much harder and cumbersome in multi-sheet calculations.
- A single worksheet model generally may be used quite readily as a template. For example, a model that is developed in a single worksheet could be copied several times within the same workbook (for example, with each worksheet representing a business unit, and a consolidation sheet used to aggregate these).

The author's overall experience is that most models have too many worksheets, with insufficient attention paid to the appropriate role of each. This is discussed in detail in the next section.

GENERIC BEST PRACTICE STRUCTURES

In this section, we present the author's view of some best practice model structures, especially with respect to the workbook structure and role of each worksheet.

The Role of Multiple Worksheets in Best Practice Structures

In the author's opinion, the most legitimate uses of using multiple worksheets are:

- To create modularised structures. There may be several components (such as business units, scenarios, months etc.) with identical structures (at least at the summary level) and which need to be used individually within an overall model.
- To allow for the easy entry or deletion of data sets (see later).
- Where several separate (single sheets) or analyses are to be consolidated. For example, the sales department may provide a revenue forecast, whereas the engineering team may provide cost analysis, with the main model using both sets of data to calculate profit. It would often make sense for the components to be in separate worksheets (and to have an additional consolidation worksheet) to allow for each group to update their own models, with each acting as an input to the overall consolidated model.

- When the structure of the calculations changes significantly between model areas. For example, the main model may contain a time axis that develops across columns, whereas some input values may be determined from a statistical analysis of a database, in which the time axis develops in the rows. In such case, it would often make sense to have the analysis and the main model on separate worksheets.
- To create robust links to another workbook using mirror sheets (see above), or to link to an external data source using a dedicated linking worksheet.
- Where it is desired to hide confidential data (by hiding the worksheet and applying the appropriate password-protection to the workbook structure); this is not a very robust approach for highly confidential data, but may be considered in less important cases.

In Figure 6.1, we show some key generic best practice model structures, which are described in the following text.

Type I: Single Worksheet Models

In single worksheet models, the input data and the calculations are built into a single sheet. Generally, there will be a presentation, reporting or summary area within the sheet as well. The author believes that, as a default approach, models should be built in this way (a view which contrasts with many models observed in practice). Single-sheet models (if reasonably well-built), will generally have easy (horizontal/vertical) audit paths, and can also be used as a template for larger models that are constructed by copying this sheet several times in the same workbook (and can form the basis for Type III models).

Type II: Single Main Formulae Worksheet, and Several Data Worksheets

In this case, data sheets contain "local" inputs (e.g. that describe data for a business unit, or a scenario or a month). In principle, these sheets have the same structure as each other. The overall model will typically require "global" inputs (such as the oil price that is applicable to all business units); such global inputs may be contained within the main formula worksheet (so that this main sheet is rather like a Type I model, albeit also requiring external inputs from the data sheets).

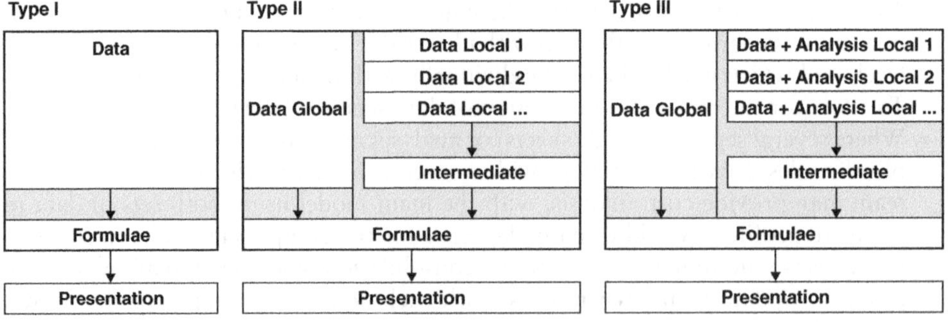

FIGURE 6.1 Generic Best Practice Model Structures

Type III: Single Main Formulae Worksheet, and Several Data and Local Analysis Worksheets

This is similar to Type II models, except that "data" sheets also contain some calculations which drive the information or values that are ultimately passed to the main model's calculations. In the following, we shall continue to refer to such sheets as data sheets, even as they also contain some calculations. In general, the calculations in each data sheet may be different to each other: for example, each sheet may represent a country, with the calculations determining the taxes payable in that country according to country-specific calculations. However, each sheet would contain a summary area (generally placed at the top of the sheet), which is structured in the same way across all sheets, and which contains the information that needs to be passed to the Intermediate sheet.

Further Comparative Comments

The following additional points are worth noting when comparing the generic structures:

- For simplicity of presentation, Figure 6.1 does not explicitly show additional worksheets that would be required to link to other workbooks (i.e. the mirror sheets). Such worksheets would simply be extra worksheets that would link into the local data worksheets or the main model sheet.
- Although Type II and Type III are typically the appropriate generic structures for multi-sheet models, they can also be considered as describing possible variations of the single sheet (Type I) model, i.e. one in which there is a modular structure, with formulae placed closed to the data which is required within the calculations. A discussion and an example of this are provided in Chapter 7.
- The models of Type II and Type III each contain an Intermediate worksheet which links into the main formula sheet. This Intermediate sheet contains the result of a structured query of the data sheets: either using the information on only one of the data sheets (i.e. an exclusive/selection process) or the information on several of the sheets at the same time (i.e. a consolidation process, in the general sense). The final model's calculations in the main formula sheet are built by referencing this Intermediate sheet (rather than referencing the individual data sheets). Although such an intermediate step is not always strictly necessary, generally it allows for more flexibility in the construction of the main model; the cell links between the main formula sheet and the Intermediate sheet can be created in any way that is appropriate for the structure of the main model, whilst the formulae within the Intermediate sheet would be required to follow the same structure as that of the data sheets.
- When the structures in Type II and Type III are used, the data sheets within each should generally have the same structure as each other. This facilitates the processes to populate the Intermediate sheet. Nevertheless, their structures do not need to be identical in all cases. For example, in Type II, each data sheet may contain a database which has the same column (field) structure as in the other data sheets, even as the number of rows within each may be different. For example, the Intermediate sheet may be constructed from these using a VBA macro to consolidate the data sets one underneath the other.

- When working with Type II or Type III structures, one may also have a template sheet (contained within the model or held separately) that contains the generic data sheet structure (Type II) or the generic data and calculations (Type III). This template can be used to add a new sheet to the model when required (it will generally be more robust to do this than to copy an existing data sheet, especially if a macro is used to add it).
- The presentation or reporting area may often be an implicit part of the main model (formula sheet), rather than a separate sheet. In particular, if one wishes to use a DataTable to show sensitivity analysis (see Chapter 12), then this needs to be on the same worksheet as the inputs that are varied.

USING INFORMATION FROM MULTIPLE WORKSHEETS: CHOICE (EXCLUSION) AND CONSOLIDATION (INCLUSION) PROCESSES

In this section, we cover techniques that can be used to access the individual data sheets, i.e. formulae and processes that can be used in the Intermediate sheet. Some of the techniques are mentioned only at a summary level here, as they are described later in more detail in Part V and Part VI. Those methods that relate to Excel functionality (rather than to its functions or to VBA) are shown with examples in this section.

It is necessary to distinguish:

- Exclusive processes, where data from only one of the sheets needs to be accessed at any one time (such as with scenario data). The data can be brought onto the Intermediate worksheet (and subsequently into main model calculations) by:
  - Using a CHOOSE function (Chapter 25) to directly reference each data sheet. This is appropriate when the number of data sheets is fixed.
  - Using the INDIRECT function (Chapter 25) where the number of data sheets may change (as new sheets are added or deleted). Similar functionality can also be obtained using VBA user-defined functions (Chapter 33).
- Consolidation processes, where data from several of the sheets needs to be accessed simultaneously (such as to add the revenues of several business units). The data can be brought onto the Intermediate worksheet (and subsequently into main model calculations) by:
  - Using direct cell (or range) references to the data sheets. This is usually straightforward, so is not discussed further, other than to note that it is most applicable and efficient only when the number of data sheets is fixed.
  - Use formulae that perform calculations across sheets, or which consolidate values across several sheets in some way. This is most appropriate where the number of data sheets may vary. Such approaches include using:
    - Multi-sheet ("3-dimensional") formulae.
    - Excel's Data/Consolidation functionality.
    - A VBA macro to create a consolidated data set.
    - User-defined functions that sum (or perform other operations) on the values in a set of data sheets, with this set (or a range which defines them) being an input parameter to the user-defined function (see Chapter 33).

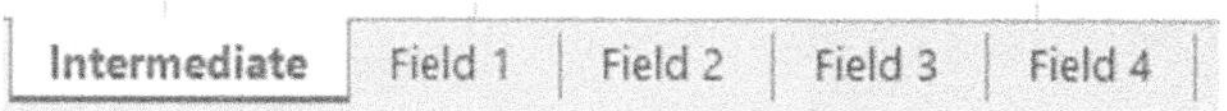

FIGURE 6.2 Structure of Worksheets in the Workbook

	A	B	C
1			
2		Month	Production
3		Jan	75
4		Feb	75
5		Mar	75
6		April	75
7		May	75
8		June	75
9		July	75
10		August	75
11		September	75
12		October	75
13		November	75
14		December	75

FIGURE 6.3 A Typical Data Sheet for the Summing Across Worksheets Example

Multi-sheet or "Three Dimensional" Formulae

The file Ch6.1.Consolidate.SumAcrossSheets.1.xlsx contains an example of multi-sheet formulae.

Figure 6.2 shows the overall worksheet structure of the workbook, which consists of several data sheets (Field1, Field2 etc.), one of which is shown in Figure 6.3 (that of Field2).

In Figure 6.4, we show the consolidation formulae used in the Intermediate sheet, which calculates the sum of the values in the corresponding cells of the data sheets.

Note that the formula is entered in the summary (Intermediate) sheet by:

- Typing "=SUM(" within the cell at which one wishes to place the formula.
- Selecting the cell in the first sheet that is desired to be included in the sum, so that the formula then reads (for example) "=SUM('Field 1'!C3".
- Holding down the Shift key.
- Clicking on the tab name of the last sheet to include (such as Field4).
- Within the Formula Bar, adding the closing bracket and pressing Enter.

It is very important to note that the worksheets included within the sum are determined by their physical placement in the model (not by their number), so that in the example file, if the data sheet Field3 were moved to be to the right of Field4, then the data for Field3 would not be included in the summation.

Note also that functions such as AVERAGE and COUNT can be used in the same way.

	A	B	C	D
1				
2		Month	Production	
3		Jan	675	=SUM('Field 1:Field 4'!C3)
4		Feb	675	=SUM('Field 1:Field 4'!C4)
5		Mar	675	=SUM('Field 1:Field 4'!C5)
6		April	675	=SUM('Field 1:Field 4'!C6)
7		May	675	=SUM('Field 1:Field 4'!C7)
8		June	675	=SUM('Field 1:Field 4'!C8)
9		July	675	=SUM('Field 1:Field 4'!C9)
10		August	675	=SUM('Field 1:Field 4'!C10)
11		September	675	=SUM('Field 1:Field 4'!C11)
12		October	675	=SUM('Field 1:Field 4'!C12)
13		November	675	=SUM('Field 1:Field 4'!C13)
14		December	675	=SUM('Field 1:Field 4'!C14)
15				

FIGURE 6.4 Summing Across Ranges of Worksheets

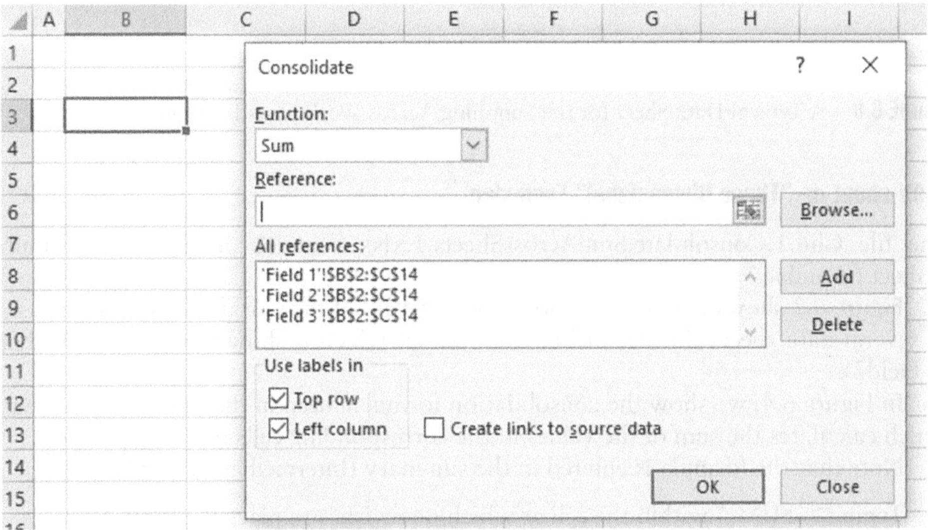

FIGURE 6.5 Using Excel's Data/Consolidation Feature

Using Excel's Data/Consolidation Functionality

The Consolidation icon on the Data tab can be used to consolidate data, either by using their values (by not retaining the links to the original data sets), or by creating direct formula links to the data sets (which would be cumbersome to create otherwise).

The file Ch6.2.Consolidation.Data.SameStructure.xlsx contains an example. Multiple tables of data with the same structure can be consolidated (using Data/Consolidation), with an example dialogue shown in Figure 6.5. In the dialogue box as shown,

	A	B	C	D
1				
2				
3			Production	
4		Jan	300	
5		Feb	300	
6		Mar	300	
7		April	300	
8		May	300	
9		June	300	
10		July	300	
11		August	300	
12		September	300	
13		October	300	
14		November	300	
15		December	300	
16				

FIGURE 6.6 Results of Consolidating Without Links to Source Data

the option to link to the source data has not been used, resulting in a consolidation as shown in Figure 6.6.

Figure 6.7 shows the results that would be produced if the "Create links to source data" option had instead been selected (see Figure 6.5). Note that in this case, the process produces grouped rows in this case. This approach retains live links to the data sets (so that the underlying values can be changed), but would only generally be appropriate if the number of data sets and their size is fixed (otherwise the process would need to be repeated, and overwrite the original formulae links, and so on).

Consolidating from Several Sheets into a Database Using a Macro

The above approaches have consolidated the values in the data sets in the sense of (generally) adding the values together. In some cases, a consolidation of the data sets may be desired in which the values of individual data are retained when transferred to the Intermediate sheet (i.e. without any calculations being performed). One way to create a single database of the data sets in the Intermediate sheet is by using a macro to sequentially assign the values in one data sheet into the Intermediate sheet, placing the data sets one under the other (see Chapter 32). Such an approach is essentially identical, irrespective of whether the number of data sheets is fixed or is variable. Note that where (especially for Type III) the data sheets are not identically structured to each other, only the (identically structured) summary part of each sheet should be copied. In such a structure, the main calculations (formulae sheet) will contain queries that refer to the Intermediate sheet (such as using SUMIFS, Database or other functions).

One potential disadvantage of this approach is the lack of live-linking from the data sets to the final calculations. Thus, a direct sensitivity analysis (in which values of items in the data sheets are varied) could not be conducted. On the other hand, whereas

	A	B	C	D
1				
2			Production	
3			100	='Field 1'!$C$3
4			75	='Field 2'!$C$3
5			125	='Field 3'!$C$3
6		Jan	300	=SUM(C3:C5)
7			100	='Field 1'!$C$4
8			75	='Field 2'!$C$4
9			125	='Field 3'!$C$4
10		Feb	300	=SUM(C7:C9)
14		Mar	300	=SUM(C11:C13)
18		April	300	=SUM(C15:C17)
22		May	300	=SUM(C19:C21)
26		June	300	=SUM(C23:C25)
30		July	300	=SUM(C27:C29)
34		August	300	=SUM(C31:C33)
38		September	300	=SUM(C35:C37)
42		October	300	=SUM(C39:C41)
46		November	300	=SUM(C43:C45)
50		December	300	=SUM(C47:C49)
51				

FIGURE 6.7 Results of Consolidating with Links to Source Data

such sensitivity could be conducted with macros (see Chapter 14), in many cases the items that would be varied would not be the individual detailed items in the data sets, but those that result from the intermediate queries.

User-defined Functions

User-defined functions (udfs) can be written which use a sheet name (or the names of multiple sheets) as an input parameter(s). They can be created to perform essentially any operation on the underlying data sets (and placed within the Intermediate sheet, or perhaps directly in the main model calculations, as appropriate). For example:

- To select the values in the same cell of a data sheet, where the name of the data sheet is an input parameter to the udf.
- To perform operations on the data within a single data sheet, where the name of the data sheet is an input parameter to the udf.
- To perform operations on the data within multiple sheets (such as add up the values in the same cell reference of several sheets), where a range of cells containing the names of the data sheets is an input parameter to the udf.

These basic elements of these approaches are covered in Chapter 33.

PART Three

Model Building, Testing and Auditing

CHAPTER 7

Creating Transparency: Formula Structure, Flow and Format

INTRODUCTION

This chapter covers some key ways to enhance the transparency of a model. This represents an important aspect of best practices, since it is one of the major approaches to reducing the complexity of a model. The main themes relate to:

- Putting oneself in the place of an auditor, since doing so helps one to understand the causes of complexity, and hence to determine characteristics of better (less complex) models.
- Drawing clear attention to the location of inputs, calculations and outputs.
- Ensuring that audit paths are clear, and are as short as possible. (Achieving this is also linked to the discussion of workbook structure in Chapter 6.)
- The appropriate use of formatting, comments and other documentation.

APPROACHES TO IDENTIFYING THE DRIVERS OF COMPLEXITY

Taking the Place of a Model Auditor

Perhaps the best way to gain an understanding of what is required to maximise transparency is to do one (ideally both) of the following:

- Review large models that have been built by someone else. When doing so, one is almost invariably struck by their complexity, and the difficulty in understanding their detailed mechanics. It seems that there is unlimited creativity when it comes to building complicated models! Especially by reviewing several models from different contexts, one can start to establish common themes which add complexity unnecessarily. Indeed, many of the themes in this chapter were determined in this way through the author's experience.

- Restructure a clear and transparent model (perhaps built by oneself), with the deliberate aim of making it as hard to follow and as complex as possible, yet leaving the calculated values unchanged (i.e. to create a model which is numerically correct but difficult to follow). It is usually possible (with only a few steps) to turn a small and simple model into one which produces the same result, but with a level of complexity that is overwhelming, and renders the model essentially incomprehensible. This approach is a particularly powerful method to highlight how excessive complexity may develop, and therefore what can be done to avoid it.

The "principle of entropy" applies to models: the natural state of a system is one of disorder, and most actions tend to increase this. Crudely speaking, there are many ways to form a pile of bricks, but the creation of a stable wall, with solid foundations that are sufficient to support the weight above it, requires proper planning and design, the right selection from a range of possible materials, and robust implementation processes. Analogous comments apply to Excel models and their components: the creation of clear and transparent models requires planning, structure, discipline, focus and explicit effort, whereas poor models can be built in a multitude of ways.

Example: Creating Complexity in a Simple Model

Following the discussion in Chapter 3, any action which increases complexity without adding required functionality or flexibility is the antithesis of "best practice"; the use of such complexity-increasing actions is therefore a simple way to highlight both the causes of complexity as well as identifying approaches to reducing it.

As a simple example, Figure 7.1 shows a small model whose key output is the profit for a business, based on using input assumptions for price, volume and costs. The model should be almost immediately understandable to most readers without further explanation.

This model could provide the same results, with a lot less transparency if one were to:

- Remove the formatting from the cells (Figure 7.2).

	A	B	C
1			
2		**Data/Assumptions**	
3		Price	10
4		Volume	1000
5		Cost	8000
6			
7		**Calculations**	
8		Revenues	10000
9		Profit	2000
10			
11		**Output**	
12		Profit	**2000**

FIGURE 7.1 An Initial Simple and Transparent Model

- Remove the labels around the main calculation areas (Figure 7.3).
- Move the inputs, calculations and outputs to different areas of the Excel workbook (Figure 7.4). Although it is not shown as an additional explicit Figure, one can imagine an even more complex case, in which items were moved to other worksheets or indeed to other workbooks that are linked. Indeed, although one may consider that the presentation of items in Figure 7.4 looks unrealistic, it is a microcosm of the type of structures that are often inherent in models in which calculations are structured over multiple worksheets.

Core Elements of Transparent Models

The key points that can be established by reference to the above example concern the techniques that could be applied in reverse, i.e. to start with a model such as in Figure 7.4 (or perhaps the more complex version with some of the items contained in other worksheets or in linked workbooks), and to can transform it into a clear

	A	B	C
1			
2		**Data/Assumptions**	
3		Price	10
4		Volume	1000
5		Cost	8000
6			
7		**Calculations**	
8		Revenues	10000
9		Profit	2000
10			
11		**Output**	
12		Profit	2000

FIGURE 7.2 Initial Model Without Formatting

	A	B	C
1			
2			
3		Price	10
4		Volume	1000
5		Cost	8000
6			
7			
8		Revenues	10000
9		Profit	2000
10			
11			
12		Profit	2000

FIGURE 7.3 Initial Model Without Formatting and Some Labels

	A	B	C	D	E	F	G	H
1								
2		Revenues	10000					
3						Cost	8000	
4								
5								
6							Price	10
7								
8					Volume	1000		
9								
10								
11		Profit	2000					
12		Profit	2000					
13								
14								

FIGURE 7.4 Restructured Model with Moved Items

model (i.e. as shown in Figure 7.1). This would require a few core elements, that also encompass many elements of general best practices:

- Using as few worksheets (and workbooks) as possible (see Chapter 6 for a detailed discussion of this).
- Grouping together inputs, as well as calculated items that are related to each other.
- Ensuring that audit paths are generally horizontal and/or vertical, and are as short as possible subject to this.
- Creating a clear direction of logical flow within each worksheet.
- Clearly distinguishing inputs, calculations and outputs, and overall logic and flow (by use of their positioning, format and labels).

These issues (and other related points) are discussed in detail in the rest of this chapter.

OPTIMISING AUDIT PATHS

A core principle to the creation of transparency (and a reduction in complexity) is to minimise the total length of all audit paths. Essentially, if one were to trace the dependency and precedence paths of each input or calculation, and sum these for all inputs, the total length should be minimised. Clearly, a model with this property is likely to be easier to audit and understand than one in which there are much longer dependency paths.

Another core principle is to ensure that audit paths are generally horizontal and vertical, with a top-to-bottom and left-to-right flow.

These principles are discussed in this section. We note that the principles are generally aligned with each other (although may conflict in some specific circumstances), and that there may also be cases where a strict following of the principle may not maximise transparency, with the "meta-principle" of creating transparency usually needing to be dominant, in case of conflicts between the general principles.

Creating Short Audit Paths Using Modular Approaches

An initial discussion of modular approaches was covered to some extent in cover in Chapter 6. In fact, although that discussion was presented within the context of the overall workbook structure, the generic structures presented in Figure 6.1 are more widely applicable (including at the worksheet level); indeed, Figure 6.1 is intended to represent model structures in general.

In this section, we discuss the use of modularised structures within workbook calculation areas. We use a simple example to demonstrate how such structures are often more flexible, transparent and have shorter audit paths than the alternatives.

The file Ch7.1.InputsAndStructures.xlsx contains several worksheets which demonstrate various possible approaches to the structure and layout of the inputs and calculations of a simple model. Despite its simplicity, the example is sufficient to highlight many of the core principles above.

Figure 7.5 shows SheetA1 of the file, which creates a forecast based on applying an assumed growth rate in each period, and with the input assumptions (cells C3:D3) held in a central area, with the calculations based on these being in Row 8 and Row 9.

This is a structure that is frequently observed, and indeed it conforms to best practices in the sense that the inputs are held separately and are clearly marked. However, one can also observe some potential disadvantages:

- The audit paths are diagonal (not purely horizontal or vertical).
- It would not be possible to copy the calculation area, were it desired to add another model component with the same logic (such as a revenue for an additional product, or a cost item). Figure 7.6 shows the incorrect formulae that would result if a copying process were to be conducted (Sheet A2 of the file). (This is because the cell references in the assumptions area and those in the new copied range are not positioned relative to each other appropriately, a problem which cannot be corrected by the use of absolute cell referencing, except in cases where assumptions are of a global nature to be used throughout the model.)

Of course, the formulae in Row 11 and Row 12 can be corrected or rebuilt, resulting in a model shown in Figure 7.7 (and in SheetA3 of the file).

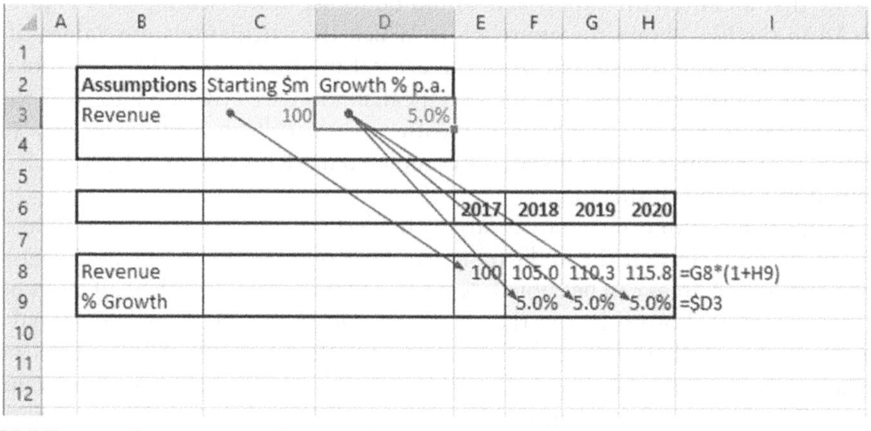

	A	B	C	D	E	F	G	H	I
1									
2		Assumptions	Starting $m	Growth % p.a.					
3		Revenue	100	5.0%					
4									
5									
6					2017	2018	2019	2020	
7									
8		Revenue			100	105.0	110.3	115.8	=G8*(1+H9)
9		% Growth				5.0%	5.0%	5.0%	=$D3
10									
11									
12									

FIGURE 7.5 Simple Forecast with Centralised Assumptions

	A	B	C	D	E	F	G	H	I
1									
2		Assumptions	Starting $m	Growth % p.a.					
3		Revenue	100	5.0%					
4		Cost	80	3.0%					
5									
6					2017	2018	2019	2020	
7									
8		Revenue			100	105.0	110.3	115.8	=G8*(1+H9)
9		% Growth				5.0%	5.0%	5.0%	=$D3
10									
11		Cost			0	0.0	0.0	0.0	=G11*(1+H12)
12		% Growth				0.0%	0.0%	0.0%	=$D6

FIGURE 7.6 Centralised Assumptions May Inhibit Copying and Re-using Model Logic

	A	B	C	D	E	F	G	H	I
1									
2		Assumptions	Starting $m	Growth % p.a.					
3		Revenue	100	5.0%					
4		Cost	80	3.0%					
5									
6					2017	2018	2019	2020	
7									
8		Revenue			100	105.0	110.3	115.8	=G8*(1+H9)
9		% Growth				5.0%	5.0%	5.0%	=$D3
10									
11		Cost			80	82.4	84.9	87.4	=G11*(1+H12)
12		% Growth				3.0%	3.0%	3.0%	=$D4

FIGURE 7.7 The Corrected Model and Its Audit Paths for the Centralised Structure

Note that an alternative approach would be to use "localised inputs". Figure 7.8 (SheetA4 in the file) shows the approach in which the calculations use values of the inputs that have been transferred from the central input area into the corresponding rows of the calculations. Note that the initial calculation area (Row 8 and Row 9) can then be copied (to Row 11 and Row 12), with only the cells in the transfer area (cells C11 and D12) needing to be relinked; the completed model is shown in Figure 7.9 (and contained in SheetA5 of the file).

The approach with transfer areas largely overcomes many of the disadvantages of the original model, in that the audit paths are horizontal and vertical (not diagonal), and the calculation areas can be copied. Note also that the total length of all audit paths in this approach is shorter than in the original model: although a single diagonal line has a shorter length than that of the sum of the two horizontal and vertical lines that arrive at the same point, the original model has more such diagonal lines: for example, in Figure 7.7, there are three diagonal lines from cell C3, whereas in Figure 7.8, these are replaced by a single vertical line and three shorter horizontal lines.

	A	B	C	D	E	F	G	H	I
1									
2		Assumptions	Starting $m	Growth % p.a.					
3		Revenue	100	5.0%					
4		Cost	80	3.0%					
5									
6					2017	2018	2019	2020	
7									
8		Revenue	100		100	105.0	110.3	115.8	=G8*(1+H9)
9		% Growth		5.0%		5.0%	5.0%	5.0%	=$D9
10									
11		Cost			0	0.0	0.0	0.0	=G11*(1+H12)
12		% Growth				0.0%	0.0%	0.0%	=$D12

FIGURE 7.8 Centralised Inputs with Transfer Areas to Create Modular Structures

	A	B	C	D	E	F	G	H	I
1									
2			Starting $m	Growth % p.a.	2017	2018	2019	2020	
3									
4		Revenue	100		100	105.0	110.3	115.8	=G4*(1+H5)
5		% Growth		5.0%		5.0%	5.0%	5.0%	=$D5
6					2017	2018	2019	2020	
7									
8		Revenue	100		100	105.0	110.3	115.8	=G8*(1+H9)
9		% Growth		5.0%		5.0%	5.0%	5.0%	=$D9
10									
11		Cost	80		80	82.4	84.9	87.4	=G11*(1+H12)
12		% Growth		3.0%		3.0%	3.0%	3.0%	=$D12

FIGURE 7.9 Audit Paths for Final Model with Centralised Inputs, Transfer Areas and Modular Structures

It is also worthwhile noting that, whilst diagonal audit paths can be easy to follow in very small models, they are very hard to follow in larger models, due to the difficulty of scrolling diagonally. Hence the importance of having only horizontal and vertical paths as far as possible.

The above approach, using modularised structures and transfer areas for the centralised assumptions, has the potential advantage that all inputs are shown in a single place. It also has some disadvantages (albeit less significant than in the original model):

- The risk of incorrectly linking the cells in the transfer area to the appropriate inputs.
- The audit paths from the centralised input area to the transfer area may be long (in large models).
- There is a duplication of input values, with those in the transfer area being "quasi inputs" or "calculated inputs", or "false formulae" (and thus having a slightly ambiguous role, i.e. as to whether they are inputs or calculations).

An alternative approach is therefore to use fully modularised structures from the beginning. Figure 7.10 (SheetB1 in the file) shows the use of a fully modularised structure for the original (revenue only) model.

Figure 7.11 (Sheet B2 in the file) shows that the original module can easily be copied and the input values altered as appropriate. It also shows the simple flow of the audit paths, and that they are very short.

It is also worth noting that the length of the audit paths in this approach is in proportion to the number of modules (since each module is self-contained), whereas in the approach shown in Figure 7.9, the audit paths are not only longer, but also have a total length which would increase according to the square of the number of modules (when in the same worksheet): the audit path from the central area to any new module has a length which includes all previous modules. Therefore in a larger model such as one would typically have in real life, the modular approach affords much better scalability.

In terms of linking this discussion to the structure presented in Chapter 6, we noted that the generic best practices structures (Figure 6.1) may apply at the worksheet level as well as at the workbook level. Thus, the fully modularised structure represents part of a Type III structure (in which only the local data and calculations have been completed, but these have not yet been brought together through the intermediate calculations, such as that of profit as the difference between revenue and cost, nor linked to other global assumptions (such as an exchange rate) that may be relevant in general contexts).

Note that, the placement of "local" inputs within their own modules does mean that not all the model's inputs are grouped together (with only the globally applicable inputs held centrally). However, this should pose no significant issue, providing that the inputs are clearly formatted, and the existence of the modularised structure is clear.

	A	B	C	D	E	F	G	H	I
1									
2			Starting $m	Growth % p.a.	2017	2018	2019	2020	
3									
4		Revenue	100		100	105.0	110.3	115.8	=G4*(1+H5)
5		% Growth		5.0%		5.0%	5.0%	5.0%	=$D5

FIGURE 7.10 Fully Modular Structure with Localised Assumptions

	A	B	C	D	E	F	G	H	I
1									
2			Starting $m	Growth % p.a.	2017	2018	2019	2020	
3									
4		Revenue	100		100	105.0	110.3	115.8	=G4*(1+H5)
5		% Growth		5.0%		5.0%	5.0%	5.0%	=$D5
6									
7		Cost	80		80	83.2	86.5	90.0	=G7*(1+H8)
8		% Growth		4.0%		4.0%	4.0%	4.0%	=$D8

FIGURE 7.11 Reuseable Logic and Short Audit Paths in the Modular Structure

Creating Short Audit Paths Using Formulae Structure and Placement

The creation of short audit paths is not only driven by workbook and worksheet structure, but also by the way that formulae are structured. Generally speaking, the paths used within formulae should be short, with any required longer paths being outside the formulae (and using simple cell references as much as possible), i.e. "short paths within formulae, long paths to link formulae".

For example, instead of using a formula such as:

$$H18 = SUM(A1:A15,\ C1:C15,\ E1:E15)$$

one could split the calculations:

$$A18 = SUM(A1:A15)$$
$$C18 = SUM(C1:C15)$$
$$E18 = SUM(E1:E15)$$
$$H18 = A18 + C18 + E18.$$

In a sense, doing the latter is rather like using a modular approach in which the ranges A1:A15, C1:C15 and E1:E15 are each input areas to the calculations of each module (with each module's calculations simply being the SUM function), and where the final formulae (in cell H18) is used to bring the calculations in the modules together.

Note once again that the latter approach has shorter total audit paths, and also that it is much easy to audit, since the interim summation calculations are shown explicitly and so are easy to check (whereas to detect a source of error in the original approach would be more complex).

Such issues become much more important in models with multiple worksheets. For example, instead of using a formula (say in the Model sheet) such as:

$$B18 = SUM(Data1!A1:A15,\ Data2!A1:A15,\ Data3!A1:A15)$$

the alternative is to build the summation into each of the worksheets Data1, Data2 and Data3:

$$A18 = SUM(A1:A15)$$

and in the Models worksheet, use:

$$B18 = Data1!A18 + Data2!A18 + Data3!A18.$$

This example highlights the fact that, where dependent formulae may potentially be placed at some distance from their inputs, it is often better to restructure the calculations so that the components required in the formula are calculated as closely as possible to the inputs, with the components then brought together in the final calculation.

Note that, in addition to the general reduction in the total length of audit paths that arise from using this approach, it also less error-prone and sometimes more computationally efficient. For example, when using the original approach (in which the formula sums a range that is on a different sheet), it is more likely that changes may be made to the range (e.g. to Data1!A1:A15), such as adding a new data point at the end of the range (i.e. in Cell A of Data1), or cutting out some rows from the range, or introducing an additional row within the range. Each of these may have unintended consequences, since unless one inspects all dependents of the range before making such changes, errors may be introduced. Where the range has many dependent formula, this can be cumbersome. Further, it may be that a summation of the range is required several times within the model. To calculate it each time (embedded in separate formulae), is not only computationally inefficient, but also leads to the range having many dependents, which can hinder the process of checking whether changes can be made to the range (e.g. adding a new data point) without causing errors.

Finally, note also that when working with multi-worksheet models, it can also be helpful to use structured "transfer" areas in the sheets (to take and pass information to other sheets), with these areas containing (as far as possible) only cell references (not formulae). These are rather like the mirror sheets to link workbooks, as discussed in Chapter 6, but are of course only ranges in the worksheets, rather than being whole worksheets. In particular, cross-worksheet references should generally only be conducted on individual cells (or ranges) and not within formulae.

Optimising Logical Flow and the Direction of the Audit Paths

The way in which logic flows should be clear and intuitive. In principle, this means that generally, the logic should follow a left-to-right and top-to-bottom flow (the "model as you read" principle). This is equivalent to saying that the audit paths (dependence or precedence arrows) would also follow these directions. If there is a mixed logical flow (e.g. most items at the bottom depending on those at the top, but a few items at the top depending on those at the bottom), then the logic is hard to follow, the model is difficult to adapt, and there is also a higher likelihood of creating unintentional circular references.

In fact, there are cases where the strict interpretation of the "model as you read" principle may not be optimal. For example, in forecast models where historic information is used to calibrate assumptions, the flow may often be reversed at some points in the model. Figure 7.12 shows an example of a frequently used structure in which the historic growth rate (Cell D4) is calculated in a "model as you read" manner, whereas the forecast assumptions (in cells E4:G4) are subsequently used in a bottom-to-top flow.

Note that the strict adherence to the "top-to-bottom" principle can be achieved. Figure 7.13 shows such a case, which uses historic data (for 2015 and 2016) as well as forecast assumptions. (The formula is analogous to when updating with actuals, as discussed in Chapter 22, using the functions such as ISBLANK.) Thus, whilst the principle has been fully respected, the model is larger and more complex.

The flow may also need to be compromised where summary calculations are shown at the top of the model, or toward the left-hand side. For example, in a 30-year forecast, in

	A	B	C	D	E	F	G
1							
2		Model 1: Some bottom-to-top flow	2015	2016	2017	2018	2019
3		Revenues	400.0	410.0	430.5	452.0	488.2
4		% growth		2.5%	5.0%	5.0%	8.0%

FIGURE 7.12 A Frequent (Often Acceptable) Violation of the "Model as You Read" Principle

Model 2: Only top-to-bottom flow	2015	2016	2017	2018	2019
Revenues - historic	400.0	410.0	420.0		
% growth - historic	NA	2.5%	2.4%		
% growth - future	NA	NA	5.0%	5.0%	8.0%
% growth - to use	NA	2.5%	2.4%	5.0%	8.0%
Revenues - to use	**400.0**	**410.0**	**420.0**	**441.0**	**476.3**

FIGURE 7.13 Strict Adherence to the "Model as You Read" Principle May Not Always Be Best from the Perspective of Simplicity and Transparency

	A	B	C	D	E	F	G	H	I	J	K	L	M	N	O	P	Q	R	S
1																			
2			Starting $m	Growth % p.a.	Total 2018-20	Total 2021-25	2017	2018	2019	2020	2021	2022	2023	2024	2025	2026	2027	2028	2029
3																			
4		Revenue	100		331.0	671.6	100	105.0	110.3	115.8	121.6	127.6	134.0	140.7	147.7	155.1	162.9	171.0	179.6
5		% Growth		5.0%				5.0%	5.0%	5.0%	5.0%	5.0%	5.0%	5.0%	5.0%	5.0%	5.0%	5.0%	5.0%
6																			
7		Cost	80		259.7	506.9	80	83.2	86.5	90.0	93.6	97.3	101.2	105.3	109.5	113.9	118.4	123.2	128.1
8		% Growth		4.0%				4.0%	4.0%	4.0%	4.0%	4.0%	4.0%	4.0%	4.0%	4.0%	4.0%	4.0%	4.0%

FIGURE 7.14 The Optimal Placement of Summary Information May Compromise the Flow Principle

which each column represents a year, one may wish to show summary data (such as total revenues for the first 10 years) toward the left of the model (such as after the revenue label) (see Figure 7.14). Note that the summation calculations (in Column E and Column F) refer to items to their right, and therefore violates the principle. The advantages of doing so include not only the visual convenience of being able to see key summary information toward the left (or the top) of the model, but also that respecting the principle would mean that the summary calculations are placed 30 columns to the right, i.e. in a part of the model that is likely not to be viewed, and which may be overwritten inadvertently (e.g. if adjustments are made to the model's calculations and copied across the columns).

The flow principle also typically needs to be compromised in financial statement modelling, since the interrelationships between items often mean that trying to achieve a strict top-to-bottom flow would require repetitions of many items, resulting in a larger model. For example, when calculating operating profit, the depreciation charge would need to refer to the fixed asset calculations, whereas the capital expenditure items may be related to the sales level. A pure top-to-bottom flow would therefore not be able to create the financial statements directly; rather, the statements would be created towards the end of the modelling process by referring to individual items that have already been calculated. On the other hand, a smaller model may be possible, in which the statements are determined more directly, but which would require a less clear flow.

IDENTIFYING INPUTS, CALCULATIONS AND OUTPUTS: STRUCTURE AND FORMATTING

It is important to highlight the identity, role and location of the various components of the model. Clearly, some of this can be done through structural methods: for example, in a simple model, one may hold all inputs in a single area, so that their location is clear without much other effort being required. In more complex cases, inputs may be held in several areas (global inputs and those for each module), and so on.

The Role of Formatting

Formatting of cells and ranges has several important roles:

- To highlight the structure, main components and logic flow. Especially the use of borders around input and calculation blocks (and modules) can create more transparency and assist a user's understanding. In that sense, this compensates for the lack of "influence diagrams" in Excel.
- To highlight inputs (see below for a detailed discussion).
- To highlight outputs. Whilst many modellers pay some attention to the formatting of inputs, the benefit of doing so for outputs is often overlooked.
- To draw attention to the occurrence of specific conditions (generally using Conditional Formatting):
  - To highlight an error, for example, as detected by an error-checking calculation when the difference between two quantities is not zero.
  - If specific criteria are met, such as if the revenue of one product becomes larger than that of another.
  - To highlight key values in a data set (such as duplicates, large values etc.); see the options within the Conditional Formatting menu.
  - In large tables of calculations in which many elements are typically zero, then it can be useful to de-emphasise cells which contain the value of zero (applications include error-checking calculations, and the triangular calculations for depreciation formulae, discussed in Chapter 18). Conditional Formatting can be used to set the font of zeros to light grey whilst non-zero values remain in the default font. Note that the use of light grey (rather than white, for example) is important to ensure that a user is not led to implicitly believe that the cells are fully blank.
- To assist in model auditing. For example, when using the F5 (GoTo) Special, as soon as one has automatically selected all cells that contain values, one can format these (at the same time) so that there is a record of these.

Colour-coding of Inputs and Outputs

The inputs to a model may in fact have different roles:

- Historical data (reported numbers that will not change, in principle).
- Conversion factors (e.g. years to months, grams to ounces, thousands to millions) or other parameters which would not be meaningful to change. (Arguably, it is acceptable to include such constants within calculations or formulae, rather than placing them in a separate cell that is then referred to by the formulae.)
- Decision variables, whose value can be chosen or selected by a decision-maker. In principle, the values are to be chosen optimally (although they may also be used in a standard sensitivity analysis).
- Uncertain variables, whose values are not directly controllable by the decision-maker (within the context of the model). Beyond standard sensitivity analysis, simulation techniques can be used to assess the range and probability of the possible outcomes.

- Text fields are inputs when they drive some calculations (such as conditional summations which are used in subsequent calculations, or to create a summary report). In such cases, one needs to make sure not only that these fields are spelled correctly, but also that the input is placed in the model only once (for otherwise, sensitivity analysis would give an incorrect result). Thus, an initial text string can be colour-coded or formatted as would be any other input, and placed only once in the model, with all subsequent uses of the text field being made by cell reference links to the unique original entry.
- Databases. In principle, any database entry which is used in a query that feeds a model or a report is an input (as are the field names where Database functions or PivotTables are used). Thus, in theory, most elements of a database should be formatted as inputs (e.g. with shading and colour-coding). In practice, this may not be the optimal way to present a database, due to the overwhelming amount of colour that may result. Further, it is usually implicitly quite clear from the context that the whole database is essentially a model input (and for this reason, this point often escapes explicit consideration entirely). Further, where an Excel Table is used, the overriding of Excel's default formatting for such objects is usually inconvenient, and may be confusing.
- "False formulae". In some cases, it can be convenient to replace input values with formulae (see Figure 7.9, for example). In such cases, in a sense, the cells containing such formulae nevertheless represent model inputs, not least because the model would be valid if the process were reversed and these formulae were replaced with hard-coded values. (This contrasts with most model contexts, in which the replacement of a calculated field by its value would generally invalidate the model, except for the single base case.)

Regarding outputs, the knowledge of which calculations represent the model's outputs (and are not simply intermediate calculations that are of no interest by themselves) is central to understanding the objectives of the model and modelling process. If the identities of the outputs are not clear, it is in fact very hard for another user to understand or use the model. For example, it would not be clear what sensitivity analysis should be conducted (if at all), or what results should be used for presentation and decision-support purposes. Generically speaking, the outputs include all of the items that are at the very end of the dependency tracing path(s), for otherwise calculations have been performed that are not required. However, outputs may also include some intermediate calculations that are not at the end of dependency paths, but are nevertheless of interest for decision-making purposes. This will be compounded if the layout is poor (especially in multi-sheet models and those with non-left-to-right flows), as the determination of the identity of items at the end of the dependency paths is a time-consuming process, and not one that is guaranteed to find all (or even the correct) the outputs. Therefore, in practice, the identity of the full set of outputs (and only the outputs) will not be clear unless specific steps are taken to highlight them.

The most basic approaches to formatting include using colour-coding and the shading of cells, using capitalised, bold, underlined or italic text, and placing borders around ranges. In principle, the inputs could be formatted according to their nature.

However, this could result in a large number of colours being used, which can be visually off-putting. In practice, it is important not to use an excessive range of colours, and not to create too many conditions, each of which would have a different format: doing so would add complexity, and therefore not be best practice. Typically, optimal formatting involves using around 3–5 colour/shading combinations as well as 2–3 border combinations (thin and thick borders, double borders and dashed borders in some cases). The author often uses the following:

- Historic data (and fixed parameters): Blue font with light grey shading.
- Forecast assumptions: There are several choices possible here, including:
  - Red font with light grey shading. This is the author's preferred approach, but is not used in cases where there is a desire to use red font for the custom formatting of negative (calculated) numbers.
  - Blue font with light yellow shading. This is an alternative that the author uses if red font is desired to be retained to be used for the custom formatting of negative numbers (and calculations).
  - Blue font with light grey shading. This is the same as for historic data, and may be appropriate in pure forecasting models in which there is no historic data (only estimates of future parameters), or if the distinction between the past and future is made in some structural (or other) way within the model (such as by using borders).
- Formulae (calculations): Calculations can typically be identified simply by following Excel's default formatting (generally black font, without cell shading), and placing borders around key calculation areas or modules. (In traditional formulae-dominated models, the use of the default formatting for the calculations will minimise the effort required to format the model.)
- "False formulae": Black font with light grey shading (the colour-code would be changed as applicable if the formula were changed into a value).
- Outputs: Key outputs can use black font with light green shading.

Some caveats about formatting are worth noting:

- The use of capitalised or bold text or numbers can be helpful to highlight key results or the names of main areas. Underlining and italics also have their roles, although their use should be much more restricted, as they can result in items that are difficult to read when in a large Excel worksheet, or when projected or printed.
- Excessive decimal places are often visually overwhelming. On the other hand, if too few decimal points are used, it may appear that a calculated quantity does not vary as some inputs are changed (e.g. where a cell containing the value 4.6% has been formatted so that it displays 5%, the cell would still show 5% if the underlying value changes to 5.2%). Thus, it is important to choose a number of decimal places based on the require figures that are significant.
- A disadvantage of Conditional and Custom Formatting is that their use is not directly visible, so that the ready understanding of the model by others (i.e. its transparency) could be partially compromised. However, cells which contain Conditional Formatting can be found using Home/Conditional Formatting/Manage Rules (where one then selects to look for all rules in This Worksheet) or selected under Home/Find and Select/Conditional Formatting or using the Go To Special (F5 Special) menu.

Basic Formatting Operations

An improvement in formatting is often relatively quick to achieve, and can dramatically improve the transparency of some models. A familiarity with some key short-cuts can be useful in this respect, including (see also Chapter 27):

- Ctrl+1 to display the main Format Cells menu.
- The Format Painter to copy the format of one cell or range to another. To apply it to multiple ranges in sequence (such as if the ranges are not contiguous in the worksheet), a double-click of the icon will keep it active (until it is deactivated by a single click).
- Using Ctrl+* (or Ctrl+Shift+Space) to select the Current Region of a cell, as a first step to placing a border around the range or to format all the cells in the same way.
- To work with borders around a range:
  - Ctrl+& to place borders.
  - Ctrl+ _ to remove borders.
- To format the text in cells or selected ranges:
  - Crtl+2 (or Ctrl+B) to apply or remove bold formatting.
  - Ctrl+3 (or Ctrl+I) to apply or remove italic formatting.
  - Ctrl+4 (or Ctrl+U) to apply or remove underlining.
- Alt+Enter to insert a line break in a cell when typing labels.
- Ctrl+Enter to copy a formula into a range without disturbing existing formats.

Conditional Formatting

Where one wishes to format a cell (or range) based on its value or content, one can use the Home/Conditional Formatting menu, for example:

- To highlight Excel errors (such as #DIV0!, #N/A!, #VALUE! etc.). This can be achieved using "Manage Rules/New Rule", then under "Format only cells that contain", setting the rule description to "Format only cells with" and selecting "errors" (and then setting the desired format using the "Format" button). Dates and blank cells can also be formatted in this way.
- To highlight cells which contain a non-zero value, such as might occur if a cross-check calculation that should evaluate to zero detects an error (non-zero) value. Such cells CAN be highlighted as above, by selecting "Cell Value is not equal to zero" (instead of "errors"). To avoid displaying very small non-zero values (e.g. that may arise from rounding errors in Excel), one can instead use the "not between" option, in which one sets the lower and upper limits to small negative and positive values respectively.
- Based on dates (using the "Dates Occurring" option on the "Format only cells with" drop-down).
- To highlight low or high values (e.g. Top 5).
- To highlight comparisons or trends using DataBars or Icon Sets.
- To detect duplicate values in a range (or detect unique values).
- To detect a specific text field or word.
- To highlight cells according to the evaluation of a formula. For example, cells which contain an error can be highlighted by using the rule type "Use a formula" to determine which cells to format and then setting the formula to be =ISERROR (cell reference). Similarly, alternate rows of a worksheet can be highlighted by setting the formula =MOD(ROW(A1),2)=1 in the data entry box.

Figure 7.15 shows an example of using Conditional Formatting to highlight dates that occurred in the last seven days. Figure 7.16 shows the use of highlighting values that are less than 1%, and Figure 7.17 shows the highlighting of the top two values only.

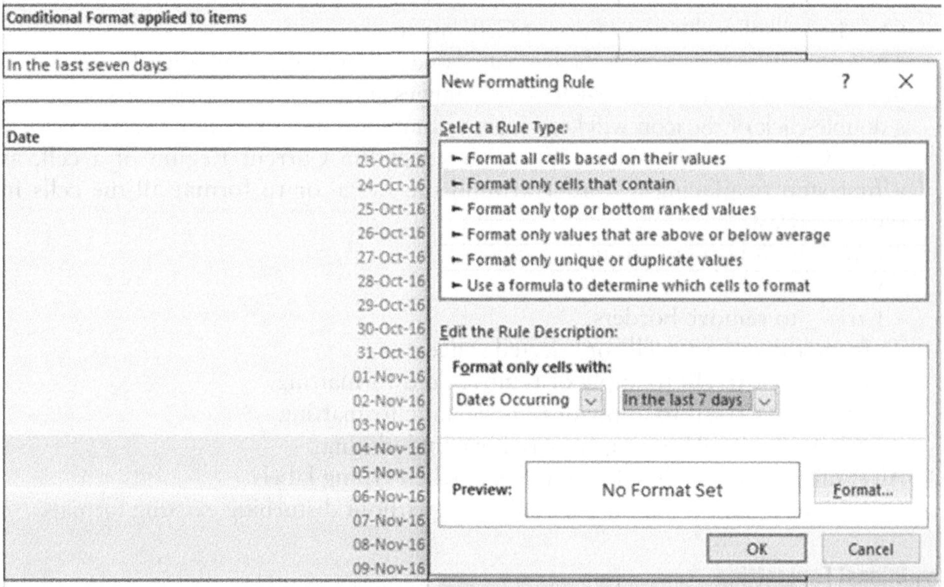

Conditional Format applied to items

In the last seven days

Date
23-Oct-16
24-Oct-16
25-Oct-16
26-Oct-16
27-Oct-16
28-Oct-16
29-Oct-16
30-Oct-16
31-Oct-16
01-Nov-16
02-Nov-16
03-Nov-16
04-Nov-16
05-Nov-16
06-Nov-16
07-Nov-16
08-Nov-16
09-Nov-16

New Formatting Rule ? ×

Select a Rule Type:

- Format all cells based on their values
- Format only cells that contain
- Format only top or bottom ranked values
- Format only values that are above or below average
- Format only unique or duplicate values
- Use a formula to determine which cells to format

Edit the Rule Description:

Format only cells with:

Dates Occurring | In the last 7 days

Preview: No Format Set | Format...

OK | Cancel

FIGURE 7.15 Example of Conditional Formatting Applied to Dates

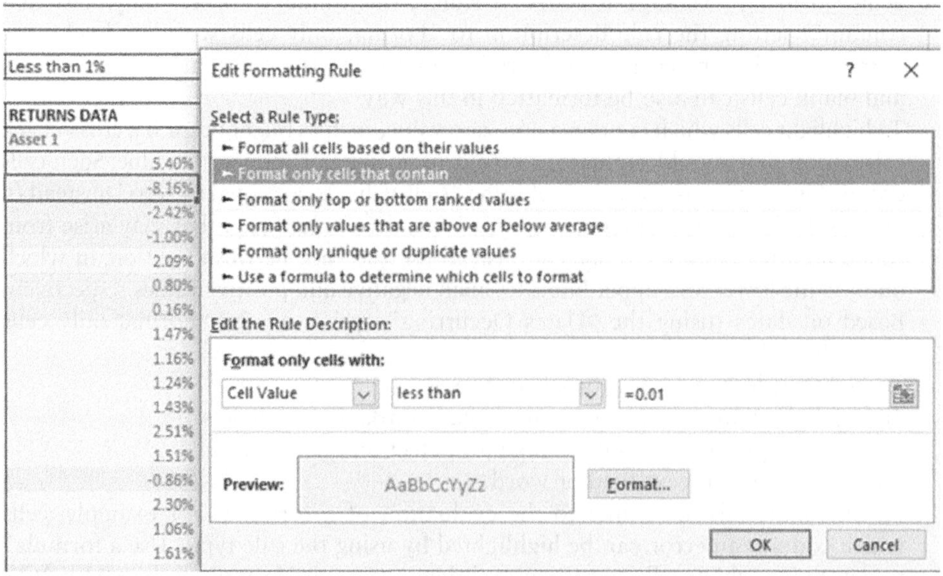

Less than 1%

RETURNS DATA
Asset 1
5.40%
-8.16%
-2.42%
-1.00%
2.09%
0.80%
0.16%
1.47%
1.16%
1.24%
1.43%
2.51%
1.51%
-0.86%
2.30%
1.06%
1.61%

Edit Formatting Rule ? ×

Select a Rule Type:

- Format all cells based on their values
- Format only cells that contain
- Format only top or bottom ranked values
- Format only values that are above or below average
- Format only unique or duplicate values
- Use a formula to determine which cells to format

Edit the Rule Description:

Format only cells with:

Cell Value | less than | =0.01

Preview: AaBbCcYyZz | Format...

OK | Cancel

FIGURE 7.16 Using Conditional Formatting to Highlight Values Less Than 1%

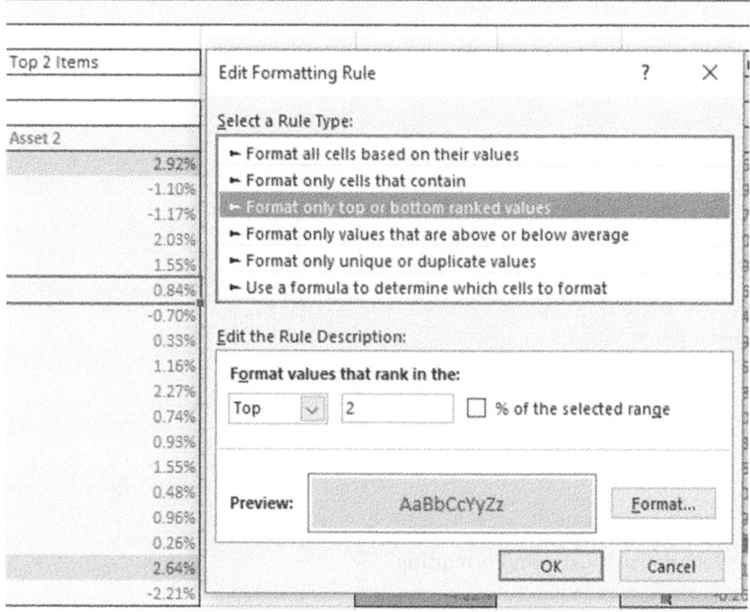

FIGURE 7.17 Using Conditional Formatting to Highlight the Top Two Values

Custom Formatting

Custom Formatting can be used to create customised (bespoke) formatting rules, for example:

- To display negative numbers with brackets.
- To use Continental Formatting, in which a space is used every three digits (in place of a comma).
- To display values in thousands (by using the letter k after the reduced-form value, rather than using actual division), and similarly for millions.
- To Format dates in a desired way (such as 01-Jan-17, if such a format is not available within the standard date options).

The menu is accessible under Home/Number (using the Show icon to bring up the Format Cells dialog and choosing the Custom category); or using the Ctrl+1 short-cut. New formats can be created by direct typing in the Type dialog box, or selecting and modifying one of the existing formats.

The file Ch7.2.CustomFormats.xlsx contains several reference examples. Figure 7.18 shows the case in which negative number are displayed in brackets. Note that the format used for positive numbers is one in which there is a blank space at the end (a blank space before the semi-colon in the format definition), so that the display of units for numbers are aligned if a positive number is displayed above a negative one (or vice versa).

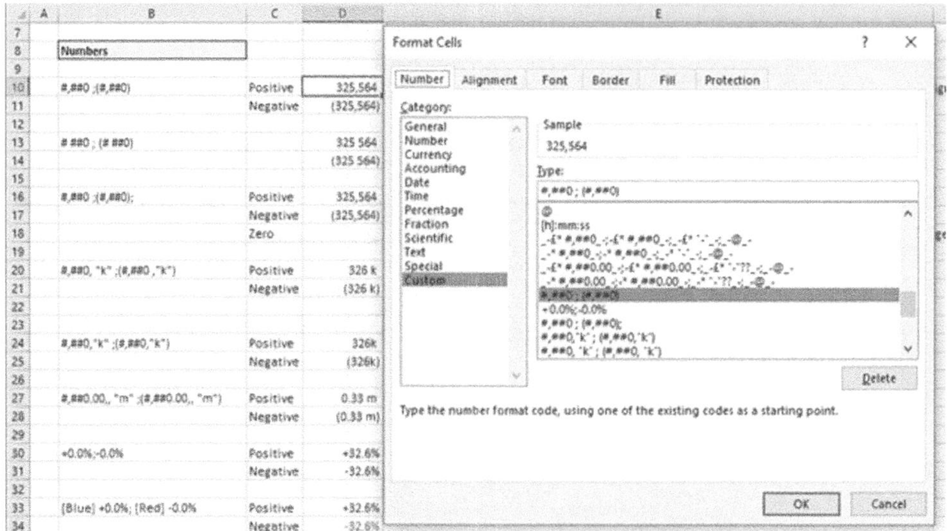

FIGURE 7.18 Examples of Custom Formatting

CREATING DOCUMENTATION, COMMENTS AND HYPERLINKS

It can be helpful to document models, whilst doing so with an emphasis on value-added points, including:

- The key objectives, contextual assumptions and structural limitations (i.e. to the validity of the model or key restrictions on the embedded logic).
- The key input assumptions, and any restrictions on how they may be used (such as requiring integer inputs or where some combinations would not represent valid scenarios).
- Any aspects that could initially appear complex or unintuitive.

Comments or other text may be created in a variety of ways, including:

- Writing general notes as regular text.
- Making a remark in a comment box of a specific cell (Review/Edit Comment menu or right-clicking on the cell to insert a comment).
- In-formula comments, such as =105*ISTEXT("data from 2017"), or similar approaches using ISNUMBER or other functions (see Chapter 22).

One of the main challenges in using comments is to ensure that they are kept up to date. It is easy to overlook the need to update them when there is a change to the formulae or the input data, or to the implicit contextual assumptions of a model. Some techniques that can help include:

- Using the Review/Show All Comments menu (or the equivalent toolbar short-cut) to show (or hide) all comment boxes, and the Reviewing Toolbar to move between them. This should be done regularly, and as a minimum as a last step before a model is finalised.

- Printing the contents of the comment boxes using Page Layout/Page Setup/Sheet and under Comments selecting whether to print comments at end of the worksheet or as they appear.
- For in-formula comments, one may have to set the model to the Formula View and inspect the comments individually. Alternatively, one may specifically search for ISTEXT, ISNUMBER or other functions and review these individually.

The use of hyperlinks can aid model navigation (and improve transparency), and be an alternative to named ranges. However, hyperlinks often become broken (not updated) as a model is changed. This is disconcerting to a user, who sees part of a model that is not working, and hence will have reduced confidence in its overall integrity. If hyperlinks are used, one should ensure (before sharing the model with others, as a minimum) that they are up to date (Chapter 25 demonstrates some simple examples).

CHAPTER 8

Building Robust and Transparent Formulae

INTRODUCTION

This chapter discusses approaches and techniques to build robust and transparent formulae. Whilst mistakes may sometimes be evident by the display of error messages, or by calculated values that are orders of magnitude different to the correct figures (or are clearly incorrect for some other reason), typically they are subtler and may therefore be overlooked.

The first section of this chapter discusses the general underlying factors which often lead to mistakes being made. The second section presents some examples of common mistakes that one often observes in models and their formulae. The third section discusses named ranges, including their advantages and disadvantages when aiming to build transparent and flexible models. The fourth section presents some key approaches that can be used to build and test formulae, and to detect, correct or manage errors.

GENERAL CAUSES OF MISTAKES

Insufficient Use of General Best Practices Relating to Flow, Formatting, Audit Paths

A key general cause of mistakes is simply the insufficient use of best practices. There is a higher risk of introducing errors into models that are excessively complex, contain unnecessary flexibility, are poorly laid out (poor flow, diagonal audit paths, too many worksheets, inconsistent structures across worksheets), have poor formatting, and so on.

Insufficient Consideration Given to Auditability and Other Potential Users

As discussed in Chapter 7, a key approach to understanding best practices and the creation of transparent models is to put oneself in the place of someone else who is tasked with auditing a model. For example, a formula that appears slightly complex as it is being built will appear to be more complex when viewed a few days later by the same model builder, and will be even more complex to a third party who reviews it subsequently. The overlooking of this key approach often leads one to build models that to the model builder may appear to be simple to follow, but in fact are not.

Overconfidence, Lack of Checking and Time Constraints

When building complex formulae, many modellers fail to test them sufficiently, and particularly may lack the discipline to find the circumstances in which the calculations would be incorrect (even as the base values may be correct). This is often compounded by an overconfidence (or optimism) in the belief that a complex formula that calculates correctly in a specific case is probably correct. Whilst practical time constraints may sometimes also play a role, this is generally a small effect and a false economy. We use the term "time-bomb" models for cases where the original model builder is aware that a formula (or a model) is correct only in a limited set of cases, but also knows that his/her responsibility for the model will soon end, and leaves these issues to a successor (with later communication about the presence of such issues being inadequate).

Sub-optimal Choice of Functions

As discussed later in more detail (see Chapter 9), although there are often many ways in which the same (and correct) figures can be calculated, model builders tend to employ either the first approach that comes to mind, or the one with which they are the most familiar. Insufficient attention is typically paid to the consideration of the possible options and the advantages or disadvantages of each, as they relate to issue of flexibility, computational effectiveness or transparency. This can lead to excessive complexity, insufficient flexibility and computational inefficiency.

Inappropriate Use or Poor Implementation of Named Ranges, Circular References or Macros

Another frequent cause of mistakes is the inappropriate use or named ranges, circular references, or macros, as well as to poor implementation of these in the cases where their use is appropriate. An extensive discussion of each of these topics is covered later (see later in the chapter for the use of named ranges, Chapter 10 for circular references and Part VI for macros). Here we simply note that an inappropriate or ineffective use of any of these will lead to reduced transparency and flexibility, resulting in an increase in the chance of errors or mistakes.

EXAMPLES OF COMMON MISTAKES

Referring to Incorrect Ranges or To Blank Cells

Models that are built in excessively complex ways are more likely to contain formulae that refer to incorrect ranges, simply because such errors will not be immediately obvious, or may be hard to detect. The checking of such formulae is cumbersome, so that such checks may not be sufficiently carried out. For example, it is awkward to audit and verify a formula that contains embedded references to multiple worksheets, such as:

B18 = SUM(Investments!C113 : C159, WorkingCapital!D81 : D109, Operations!E15 : E89)

Further, even if such formulae are built correctly for an initial application of the model, they are hard to maintain, so that subsequent versions or updates of the model may contain errors. For example, if an update to the model is made by including an additional item in the cell Investments!C160 (i.e. immediately below the original set of items in the investments sheet), then it may not be immediately clear that the formulae above (which is contained in another sheet) would need to be updated. Needless to say, such issues can largely be avoided by following the principles of best practices, particularly those discussed in Chapter 7 (for example, in which the summation of each range is first done separately in the same worksheet as the range, and cross-worksheet references are done using single cell references to these interim totals).

Similarly, models often contain formulae that refer to blank cells, which is also unsatisfactory:

- It is often not clear if the use of a blank cell is an error or not. For example, a formula such as "=SUM(D3:D20)+H9" (where H9 is blank) may arise through a simple typing error. If the user types a value, date or text into the cell (perhaps with the intention to add documentation to the model), the calculations would be incorrect, but a user may not expect such behaviour and so not be made aware of the error.
- Even if used intentionally and correctly, inputs which are blank in the default case are also often labelled poorly (as the model builder's focus is not typically drawn to the issue of labelling blank cells). This may result in a user entering incorrect values when populating these cells for the non-default case (e.g. entering 4 instead of 4% for an interest rate, or using a positive rather than a negative figure for an investment amount, and so on).
- Although Excel functions are generally designed to be robust when blank cells are used as inputs to them, the transparency of models is nevertheless often compromised by doing so. For example, MINA, MAXA and COUNTA ignore blank cells, but treat text entries as if they were zeros. Thus, a text entry entered in a cell that is initially blank could change subsequent calculations. Figure 8.1 shows an example of this (the functions are described in more detail in Chapter 17).

An important case where the deliberate use of blanks may be valuable is as place-holders for not-yet-realised figures, for example where forecast figures are used

	A	B	C	D	E	F
1						
2		34			34	
3					txt	
4		56			56	
5						
6		34	=MINA(B2:B4)		0	=MINA(E2:E4)
7		2	=COUNTA(B2:B4)		3	=COUNTA(E2:E4)
8						

FIGURE 8.1 The Behaviour of Blanks and Text Fields as Model Inputs

until actuals become available (e.g. see Chapter 22). In such models, blank cells should be formatted and placed in an input area so that it is clear that it is these that are to be populated at the appropriate point.

Non-transparent Assumptions, Hidden Inputs and Labels

There are several ways in which mistakes can arise due to lack of transparency as to which ranges represent values in a model:

- Some input values may be placed in calculation areas, even as there is a separate area (or worksheet) that has been called the "input area" (or equivalent). Note that (as per the discussion in Chapter 5, Chapter 6 and Chapter 7), best practices allow for modularised structures in which input values are not all held centrally. The issue being raised here is that in which the model is presented as one in which inputs are held centrally (or in designated areas) whereas in fact there are other areas in which input values are also held, but not clearly designated as such.
- Input values on hidden worksheets. Whilst it is generally bad practice to hide worksheets, this may be appropriate in some cases (e.g. for reasons of confidentiality or to hide old data that wishes to nevertheless be retained). However, the inclusion on hidden worksheets of input assumptions (that affect a model's calculations) is generally not appropriate; their presence will not be clear without a detailed audit, so that the model may be calculated in cases in which these inputs are set at incorrect values, rendering the resulting calculations incorrect.
- Labels as inputs. Where a text label (such as the name of a country) becomes a model input (such as the label being used in a SUMIFS function to sum within a database the revenues of the customers within that country), one typically should manage the labels carefully (see Chapter 7).
- Repeated assumptions. The repetition of input values (e.g. having a tax rate in two separate cells at different parts of the model) is clearly generally inappropriate. Not only does it render a sensitivity analysis incorrect (in which only one of the values is changed), it may also lead to subsequent mistakes or failure to update a model correctly. Nevertheless, such repetition occurs fairly often and is often overlooked. It arises most frequently where there are hidden input sheets, labels are used as assumptions, where mixed formulae are used (containing an input value embedded within a formula that is then copied), as well as in poorly structured, large multi-sheet models.
- A new category of data has been added to a database field, and this is not reflected in some of the conditional calculations. For example, a new country has been added to the list of countries within a database, whereas subsequent queries or calculations do not take this into account.

Overlooking the Nature of Some Excel Function Values

Especially when using embedded functions (which may disguise the presence of errors or incorrect values), there is a risk that one may overlook the nature of the values that some Excel functions produce. For example:

- Many financial functions (such as PMT) return negative values. Where embedded within an IF statement (e.g. to apply the result only during the life of a loan), one may overlook the default sign, and inadvertently create a formula that branches in the wrong direction.

- Inconsistent periodic interest rates. Where financial functions require the interest rate as an input (or growth or rates of return), one needs to ensure that the interest rate used is consistent with the granularity of the time period in the model (e.g. annual, quarterly or monthly). Once again, this is easy to overlook.
- Incorrect discounting: A frequent mistake when using the NPV function is to overlook that the function implicitly assumes that the value in the first cell of the range is discounted for one period, the second value is discounted for two periods, and so on. This is equivalent to assuming that all cash flows occur at the end of their periods. Thus, an investment that occurs at the very beginning of a project should generally be excluded from the function, and treated separately to calculate the total NPV.
- Overlooking the behaviour of the return values of logical statements, especially in embedded functions. For example, when embedded within a SUMPRODUCT function, a short-form statement such as =AND(E19=1, E20=1) may not evaluate as expected (i.e. not be directly equivalent to 0 or 1); see Chapter 9 for an example.
- The use of text, rather than numerical, fields as return values can also lead to the building of incorrect formulae, due to overlooking (for example) that ="TRUE" is not the same as =TRUE or =1 (see Chapter 9).
- It may be overlooked that fields that look like numbers may in fact be text. Whilst errors in direct subsequent formulae would often be obvious, mistakes in dependent embedded formulae or conditional summations will often not be so clear. The appropriate manipulation (often involving text or date functions, as discussed later in the text), may be necessary.

Using Formulae Which are Inconsistent Within a Range

The use of formulae which are inconsistent with (i.e. different to) each other is often observed. For example, if the items in a row represent a time-based forecast (such as of revenues, costs, or capital expenditures), one may find that somewhere along the row the formulae are different to those in adjacent cells in that row. There are many reasons why such inconsistencies arise:

- The first time periods have properties which are different to others. For example, the capital expenditure budget for an initial period may wish to be treated as fixed (as a specific budget has been authorised by the management), whereas the longer-term expenditure requirements would depend on the growth rate assumptions.
- A contractual provision states that an item (such as a supplier's price to the customer) is fixed for an initial period, but is to increase with inflation after that period.
- Where values are taken from another model or forecast, they may have been hard-coded (rather than using formula-links or linked workbooks).
- They are simple errors. For example, pressing F9 when working in the Formula Bar results in the formula being replaced with its value.

Of course, generally, the use of inconsistent formulae within a contiguous range is bad practice:

- The presence of the change in formulae will not normally be expected by a user, who may misuse or misinterpret the model.

- When modifying the model, extra work is created to determine whether the inconsistent formula is an error or is an intentional part of the model.
- The inconsistent formulae are likely to be overwritten when modifications are made, especially if short-cuts are used to rapidly copy formulae across a range.

On occasion, such inconsistent formulae within a range are necessary. Indeed, to some extent they happen in almost all models, as one transitions from the range containing numerical inputs to that which contains formulae. For example, in Figure 8.2 (which is a repeat of Figure 7.10, but shown here for simplicity), C4 contains an input assumption, D4 is blank, E4 is a formula which takes the value from C4, and the range F4:H4 contain growth formulae. Thus, the formulae in Row 4 are not all the same.

Where such inconsistencies are necessary, the following principles and techniques can be used to maximise transparency, and to reduce the risk of misinterpretation or subsequent errors:

- The use of formatting (colour-coding and borders) to distinguish one type of logic from another (e.g. different formulae within a contiguous range, or to mark the transition from numbers to formulae).
- Documentation and comments to describe the reason for such transitions.
- Cells or ranges may be protected in order to avoid such formulae being accidentally "corrected" by another user (see later in the chapter).
- Separate the formulae into ranges (generally only two), each of which contains formulae which are consistent within their own range, with a logic switch used in order to explicitly pick the formulae that are to be applied.

Note that (as discussed later), Excel error-checking procedures can be used to highlight inconsistent formulae. In addition, Formulas/Show Formulas (Ctrl+`) can be used to allow a visual inspection of the model's formulae, and to inspect for inconsistencies or errors.

Overriding Unforeseen Errors with IFERROR

Despite its ease of use, one should be cautious in the use of IFERROR. In general, it is better to adapt the formulae that should apply to specific occurrences of "valid errors". If one over-rides all errors however they arise, one may overlook other errors that in fact should be corrected. An approach using an IF statement to manage the specific expected error cases is arguably superior, rather than overriding all errors of whatever nature.

	A	B	C	D	E	F	G	H	I
1									
2			Starting $m	Growth % p.a.	2017	2018	2019	2020	
3									
4		Revenue	100		100	105.0	110.3	115.8	=G4*(1+H5)
5		% Growth		5.0%		5.0%	5.0%	5.0%	=$D5

FIGURE 8.2 Standard Modelling Approaches Often Use Inconsistent Formulae

Models Which are Correct in Base Case but Not in Others

A frequent mistake is for models to calculate correctly in the base case (and perhaps in a small set of other cases), but not in other cases. This can arise for many reasons:

- When a calculation has been overwritten by a hard-coded figure.
- Where the model has structural limitations which only become apparent in some cases. For example, where the range required for a lookup function exceeds that for which the model is built (such as a model containing 50 columns, but the lookup function needs to find the value in column 53 when an unexpected but valid set of inputs is used).
- When using interest calculations that involve circular references; these may diverge if the periodic interest rate that is used is 200% or more (a case that would rarely arise in practice, but nevertheless does in some cases).
- Where some formulae become invalid only where specific combinations of several input values are varied simultaneously, but not if only one or two are varied.
- Where a time-shifting mechanism may have been built in (even though the base case corresponds to a shift of zero), and this may fail if a non-integer (or negative) number of model periods is attempted to be used for the shifting.

Incorrect Modifications when Working with Poor Models

Mistakes can also arise when changes are made to models which are complex or poorly built. In principle, this can occur for many general reasons, as well as being driven by many of reasons cited elsewhere, such as:

- Where excessive absolute cell referencing is used, other formulae that have been created by copying are more likely to refer to the incorrect cells.
- Models which use hard-coded column or row numbers with VLOOKUP or HLOOKUP functions may become incorrect when a new column or row is introduced (see Chapter 25).
- Where formulae are used that refer to range on multiple sheets (see earlier).
- Where there are inconsistent formulae in a contiguous range, some of which may be incorrectly overwritten as one formula within the range is updated or corrected.
- Where macros have been written poorly written (e.g. using cell references rather than named ranges).

THE USE OF NAMED RANGES

The use of named ranges is a topic for which there is a wide range of opinions amongst Excel modellers. Some consider that their intensive use in almost all situations should be considered as best practice, whereas others tend to believe that they should essentially be avoided. It is fair to say that the improved capabilities to manage named ranges from Excel 2007 onwards both eases their use and mitigates some of their potential disadvantages compared to earlier Excel versions. The author's belief is that named ranges should be used only selectively and in specific contexts. In his opinion, their use as a default modelling approach is not appropriate in most Excel modelling situations.

Mechanics and Implementation

The following points about the mechanics of using names are worth noting:

- Names can be entered, edited and deleted using Formulas/Name Manager or Ctrl+F3.
- Named ranges can have a scope which is either a worksheet or the workbook. The scope of a name is the region of the workbook in which it does not need to be qualified to use it. In general, names which are needed in calculations on more than one worksheet should have a workbook scope (if a worksheet-scoped name is required in another worksheet it needs to be referred to with the worksheet name as a qualifier, e.g. Sheet1!RangeName).
- If the Name Box is used to implement the names rather than the Formulas/Name Manager, the scope is automatically the whole workbook. Although this is a quick procedure, it should generally be avoided, as it is important to define the scope correctly, and the use of the Formulas/Name Manager reminds one more explicitly to consider this. In addition, the use of the Name Box to change a name (rename the same range) is generally not recommended, as it will result in the original name being retained.
- The list of names whose scope is either the workbook or the current worksheet can be pasted into Excel by using F3 and selecting Paste List (or Use in Formula/Paste Names). Such techniques can be useful when:
  - Creating VBA code that refers to these names (so that the names can be copied and correctly spelled into a Range("ThisName") statement in VBA for example).
  - Auditing and documenting a model.
  - Looking for links to other workbooks.
  - Trying to locate whether a range has been given multiple names, the pasted list can be sorted using the location of the name as a key (so that names with the same location will be shown next to each other, and the sorted list can be inspected as to whether consecutive elements refer to the same range).
- When creating a formula in the Formula Bar (after typing =), the F3 key (or Formulas/Use in Formula) can be used to see a list of names that can be inserted. The names shown are those whose scope is the current worksheet or the workbook, but not other worksheets (the same applies to the list of names visible when using the drop-down Name Box).
- The use of a SPACE between the names of a column and row range will return the value of the cell in which these ranges intersect (or a #NULL! error if the ranges do not intersect).
- If names have been defined after the formulae which should use them have been built, the names can be applied by rebuilding the formulae using Formulas/Define Name/Apply Names.

Disadvantages of Using Named Ranges

Potential disadvantages of using named ranges revolve around the fact that their use can lead to less flexible and more complex models, as well as that errors may arise when multi-cell ranges are used within formulae.

Concerning limitations to the flexibility to move items or modify formulae:

- Formulae built by using multi-cell ranges may create inadvertent errors if either the formulae, or the underlying named ranges, are moved in a way that is not aligned correctly. Figure 8.3 shows an example built by using a formula driven by two multi-cell named ranges, and Figure 8.4 shows the effect of moving this formula (using cut-and-paste) by two columns. Note that the behaviour of the formula is such that inadvertent errors can be created:

- Especially in multi-worksheet models, where the time axes used on one worksheet may not be readily visible on another, the values displayed in the early part of the profit range may not be those that correspond to the correct time period for one or other of the named ranges.
- In a large model with many columns, the #VALUE! fields may be overlooked.
- When defining the ranges for several multi-cell names (such as C5:Z5 for one and C8:Z8 for the other), it is usually preferable to have consistent row or column definitions (e.g. both starting at Column C and ending at Z, rather than one starting at C and the other at B). However, this can still create confusion in some modelling applications. For example, when working with financial statement models, the items on the Balance Sheet will generally have an opening balance which is taken as a carry-forward amount from the prior period ending values, whereas items on the Income Statement or Cash Flow Statement will not have such items. Thus, the named ranges for Balance Sheet items may start one cell earlier than those for Income Statement and Cash Flow items. Alternatively, if the ranges are defined to have the same size, then the formulae will not be consistent across the range, since for Balance Sheet items, the first formulae in the range will involve cell references, and the others will use the named range.

- One may wish to move items (including moving some items to new worksheets) in order to optimise the layout and structure, a process which is inhibited by multi-cell ranges. One may have to create new names for each part, delete the old names and rebuild the formulae. Especially when building a model from scratch, or when adapting an existing model to a new situation, this can be a severe limitation and encumbrance.

	A	B	C	D	E	F	G	H	I	J	K	L
1												
2		Rev1	100	110	120	130	140					Rev1TEST
3												
4		Cost1	80	80	80	80	80					Cost1TEST
5												
6		Profit	20	30	40	50	60					=Rev1TEST-Cost1TEST

FIGURE 8.3 Multi-cell Named Ranges Used to Create Formulae

	A	B	C	D	E	F	G	H	I	J
1										
2		Rev2	100	110	120	130	140			
3										
4		Cost2	80	80	80	80	80			
5										
6					Profit	50	60	#VALUE!	#VALUE!	#VALUE!

FIGURE 8.4 Errors Arising as a Formula Using Multi-cell Named Ranges is Moved

- Once the scope (whether workbook or worksheet) of a name is initially defined, it cannot easily be changed. Deleting a name that is used in a formula will result in errors, and in potential significant rebuilding work. Find/Replace techniques can be used to overcome some of these limitations (e.g. creating a new similar name with the correct scope and then modifying the formulae that used the original name, before deleting the name).

Concerning the potential for errors to arise inadvertently if names are used in formulae, this is due to complexities of their general application, which is not always fully or widely understood.

The file Ch8.1.MultiCellNames.xslx highlights the potential for unexpected results that may arise when multi-cell named ranges are used in formulae. Figure 8.5 shows a screen-clip of the file in which the range D3:I3 (the model time axis) has been given the name Dates. Note the following:

- Row 4 and Row 5 each contain an IF statement to return a flag indicator (1, if the date of the model time axis is after the specific date tested in Column C, and 0 otherwise). Note that the presence of the + sign in the formulae in Row 5 does not affect the results.
- Row 6 and Row 7 apply a similar test, but return (instead of 1) the date of the model time axis where this is larger than the test date, and otherwise (instead of 0) return the specific date tested. Note that this is equivalent to calculate the maximum of the data tested and the date of the model time axis. Once again, the presence of the + in Row 7 does not affect the results.
- Row 8 and Row 9 show the results of using the MAX function instead of the IF statement. Since the calculations in Rows 6 and 7 also calculate a maximum, one may expect the results to be the same. However, Row 8 shows that the values returned throughout the range is the single value which corresponds to the maximum of the tested data and the full set of dates within the named range, whereas in Row 9 (due to the + symbol), the calculations return values that are specific to individual cells.

In Figure 8.6, we show the results of using the MAX function applied to the Dates field in the same example, as well as the SUM function when applied to a range named Values (D16:I16).

In Figure 8.7, we show the use of the NPV function in the same context, further highlighting that potential errors may arise.

In summary, such behaviour may not be expected by many modellers or users, so that mistakes can be made inadvertently, especially when used in larger models in which the calculation paths are longer.

	A	B	C	D	E	F	G	H	I
1									
2				Dates					
3		Functions	Test Date	01/01/2017	01/01/2018	01/01/2019	01/01/2020	01/01/2021	01/01/2022
4		=IF($C4<=Dates,1,0)	09/06/2020	0	0	0	0	1	1
5		=IF($C5<=+Dates,1,0)	09/06/2020	0	0	0	0	1	1
6		=IF($C6<=Dates,Dates,$C6)	09/06/2020	09/06/2020	09/06/2020	09/06/2020	09/06/2020	01/01/2021	01/01/2022
7		=IF($C7<=+Dates,Dates,$C7)	09/06/2020	09/06/2020	09/06/2020	09/06/2020	09/06/2020	01/01/2021	01/01/2022
8		=MAX($C8,Dates)	09/06/2020	01/01/2022	01/01/2022	01/01/2022	01/01/2022	01/01/2022	01/01/2022
9		=MAX($C9,+Dates)	09/06/2020	09/06/2020	09/06/2020	09/06/2020	09/06/2020	01/01/2021	01/01/2022

FIGURE 8.5 Referring to Full Ranges or Individual Values Within a Multi-cell Named Range

10	=MAX(Dates)		01/01/2022					
11	=MAX(+Dates)		01/01/2017					
12	=MAX(Dates)	01/01/2022						
13	=MAX(+Dates)	#VALUE!						
14								
15			Values					
16			100	100	100	100	100	100
17	=SUM(Values)		600					
18	=SUM(+Values)		100					
19	=SUM(Values)	600						
20	=SUM(+Values)	#VALUE!						

FIGURE 8.6 Possible Application of MAX and SUM Functions to Multi-cell Ranges

	A	B	C	D	E	F
1						
2				**Explicit Steps**		
3				1	2	3
4		**Co./subject**		SEARCH for "("	MID=No. Days as Text	VALUE of No. Days
5		CustA (1 Day)		7	1	1
6				=SEARCH("(",B5,1)	=MID(B5,D5+1,1)	=VALUE(E5)

FIGURE 8.7 Possible Application of the NPV Function to Multi-cell Ranges

Further potential disadvantages of using named ranges include:

- Their use does not encourage the process to ensure a clear logic flow. When using cell references, one is essentially explicitly made aware of the location of the cells used in the formula (such as whether they are above, below, or to the right of the current cell, or on another sheet). However, when building a formula (such as Profit=Revenue-Cost, created by using the F3 key or by direct typing of the pre-defined names), one is not explicitly made aware of the locations of the named ranges. Thus, it is harder to identify and correct any potential flow issues (i.e. not respecting principles of top-to-bottom and left-to-right flow, with minimal connections across worksheets etc.) Of course, whilst the use of the named ranges does not prevent the creation of clear logical flow *per se*, the issue is that the modeller's attention is not drawn to this. In practice, the flow of models built in this way is often severely compromised, and they are hard to audit.
- Their use as a default modelling approach will often result in many names that are poorly defined and structured, essentially negating the potential benefits of transparency. In some cases, the appropriate structure of the names can be determined early on, with systematic naming conventions used (e.g. using the name Price.BU1.2016.US$ rather than simply Price). However, modelling processes are often exploratory and not fully definable from the outset, so that errors may arise in several ways, including:
  - When introducing a new, better structured or appropriately scoped set of names (such as Price.BU1.2016.US$ rather Price), the formulae that need to use these will require adaptation or rebuilding, which can be cumbersome, time-consuming and error-prone.

  - If a range containing formulae is given a name which initially is appropriate to the formulae used, but the calculations are subsequently modified (such as the original formulae being overwritten by new formulae that also include a reference to a currency exchange rate), then the original name would no longer be appropriate. This may create formulae which are unclear or wrong, or (if new names are introduced for the same range) result in duplicate names for the same range (which can lead to inadvertent errors).
  - Whilst good practice would suggest that redundant names should be deleted, very often this is not done, so that any formulae that inadvertently refer to the old names may look correct (i.e. produce a reasonable value, rather than an error or #REF! message), but in fact refer to incorrect ranges.
- Many modellers or clients of models are not familiar with their use, so may find it hard to understand the model.

Thus the use of named ranges can reduce flexibility, create complexity and potentially introduce inadvertent errors, especially where a model will be developed over time, or may need to be adapted for other uses, or where there is an exploratory component to the process (so that the modelling is not simply the implementation of a prescribed algorithm or known formula).

Advantages and Key Uses of Named Ranges

There are of course some important reasons to use named ranges:

- To enable rapid model navigation (using the short-cut F5, for Home/Find and Select/Go To, or the drop-down Name Box).
- When writing VBA code so that it is robust (as discussed in Part VI).
- To enhance the transparency of formulae, by using meaningful names which describe the variables in the calculations rather than using cell references, especially when using standard formulae or algorithms, so that there is no exploratory part to the modelling process, this can make sense. For example, it would make sense when implementing the Black–Scholes formula for the valuation of a European option, as all inputs are known and the calculations steps are precisely defined. In such cases, the names can be appropriately defined before the calculation is implemented, and this can be done in a way that is clear, well-structured and which will not need to be changed.
- To create several formulae that all refer to the same range, so that the range can be extended or reduced in size without having to change the formulae (i.e. by changing only the definition of the range a single time), such as SUM(DataSet), AVERAGE(DataSet), and so on.
- To create dynamic or flexible ranges that adjust automatically as data is added or deleted to an existing data set. This can also be useful when several formulae or charts use the same range as inputs; the creation of a dynamic range will avoid having to update the range definition as data is added. One way to do this is to use the OFFSET or INDIRECT functions within the "Refers To" area when defining the name (see Chapter 25 for an example in the context of cascading drop-down lists). Note that such names will not be displayed on the drop-down Name Box, unlike when using the Name Manager. In many practical cases, an easier and more powerful way is to use Excel Tables (see Chapter 26).

- To enable the rapid printing of key areas. One can use the Name Box to select a single named range, or several ranges (by holding the Ctrl key), and then using the Set Print Area command (on the Page Layout tab); if doing this several times, one would generally wish to use Clear Print Area before defining the set of named ranges to be printed.

APPROACHES TO BUILDING FORMULAE, TO TESTING, ERROR DETECTION AND MANAGEMENT

This section covers some key approaches to building and testing robust formulae, as well as to detect, and correct or manage, errors. Some of the key principles discussed include:

- Building formulae that show each logical step separately, with compound formulae to be used only sparingly and in specific circumstances.
- Testing each formula as it is built, rather than only doing more general overall checks on a completed model; if one were to test only a completed model, not only would the number of combinations of items to test be very large, but also one would have likely not have built the model in the most appropriate way to start with.
- Testing the formulae across a wide range of individual input values: base case, variations from base case, extreme (large or small) values, and the effect of changes to several inputs simultaneously.
- Building error checks into the model, as well as using error-handling procedures appropriately and not excessively.
- Correcting the formulae or model structure as appropriate: in addition to basic error-correction, this may involve extending the size of the ranges, introducing error-handling procedures, or restricting the allowed input values, or protecting the model (or ranges within it) so that formulae cannot be altered.
- Documenting any limitations to the validity of input values or combinations, as well as to the structural limitations of the model. For example, a model may sometimes return error values that are inherently related to structural assumptions (such as the use of only a finite number of forecast periods, or formulae which are only applicable within a specific time-period). In such cases, such errors may not be able to be corrected, but must be explicitly documented (and perhaps handled).

Checking Behaviour and Detecting Errors Using Sensitivity Testing

Recall that a main theme of this book is that the sensitivity-related techniques should be used at all stages of the modelling process. In Chapter 4, we discussed its use at the model design stage to identify the requirement for sensitivity analysis and model flexibility. At the model building stage, there are several potential roles:

- To help to create the correct logic in complex formulae. For example, where embedded functions, lookup functions or conditional logic are used, testing them under various scenarios will help to ensure their robustness.

- To adapt formulae as required as structural model limits are reached. For example, one may see that with some input combinations, a lookup function may return #N/A, such as when a matching value is not found within the lookup range. In such cases, the model may need to be extended to include more rows and columns, or some form of error-handling functionality may need to be built, or otherwise a structural limitation on the model should be noted clearly within its documentation.
- To check for errors or alter the model appropriately. For example, where error checks are built into a model (such as formulae that should always evaluate to zero), their values should be tested across a wide range of scenarios: this will help to ensure that calculations are still correct when inputs are varied, not just when the base case values are used.

Note that at the model building stage, the nature of the sensitivity analysis conducted generally does not need to be very formalised; the simple changing of input values and their combinations by manual methods is usually sufficient to detect most potential errors. Note that:

- In general, formulae should be tested under a wide range of input values. As a minimum, formulae should be valid across the range of values that would be applied when sensitivity analysis is used on the completed model. More generally, positive, negative and extreme values should be tested. For example, it is surprising how often formulae are built to calculate tax charges, but with the formulae valid only when taxable income is positive, and not tested for the case where losses occur.
- Formulae involving conditional statements should be tested in a way that results in all the possible conditions occurring.
- One should explicitly try to find the conditions under which a formula will break or be invalid, and adapt the model accordingly. For example, some formulae that are frequently used to calculate the total annuity value of a set of discounted cash flows may not work whenever the growth rate is equal to the cost of capital, even where alternative formulae exist that may still be valid in many of the cases (such as when the cash flow series is finite).
- The robustness of formulae as combinations of input values are changed should also be tested. Since the number of combinations is large, it can be fruitful to explicitly try to consider cases in which combinations could be invalid (rather than finding them my trial and error). One should specifically consider whether there may be implicit dependencies between inputs that are not captured within a model. For example, there may be two input dates, one for the start of construction of a manufacturing facility and the other for the start of production at the facility. Whilst a sensible user would not deliberately input the latter date to be before the former, such a possibility could arise if sensitivity analysis is automated. Thus, one may have to adapt the formulae so that production start date is calculated as the construction start date plus an additional time period (that is restricted to positive values). Note also that a truly robust check would be to use simulation to generate many input combinations, and, whilst doing so, to track the value of key items (including of error-checking calculations, which should result in a set of zero values in all cases).
- Where one wishes to validate a formula by seeing the effect of a change in an input on several calculations which relate to it, one can use the Formulas/Watch Window. An alternative is to create a single summary area which refers to the outputs

of the individual calculations. However, such an approach is more cumbersome in larger models and especially in cases where the identity of the calculations that one may wish to monitor may need to be changed.

Using Individual Logic Steps

Compound (or embedded) formulae are difficult to test, since the input parameters will not be fixed numbers or ranges that can be chosen by the model builder or tester, but will depend on the results of other calculations. Such formulae become even more complex to assess if they involve the use of lookup functions and/or references to other worksheets (as well as if the ranges referred to also create diagonal and/or multi-sheet audit paths). For example, one should avoid a formula in Sheet1 such as:

$$\text{IF(SUM(Sheet2!C5 : C11)} > \ldots$$

In fact, even without a cross-worksheet reference, compound formulae are difficult to test. For example, to assess whether the calculations are correct within the formula:

$$= \text{IF(SUM(G3 : G19)} > \text{SUM(H3 : H19), A5, B5)}$$

one would have to inspect, sum and compare (essentially using mental arithmetic) the values within each range (G3:G19, H3:H19). On the other hand, if the two SUM functions are placed explicitly in separate cells (say G20 and H20), so that the formula becomes:

$$= \text{IF(G20} > \text{H20, A5, B5)}$$

then it is much easier to see whether the formula is evaluating as expected, since the interim summations in cells G20 and H20 are shown explicitly (and do not require mental arithmetic or additional comparison formulae to be built).

Thus, in principle, multiple levels of embedding should be avoided, as it is very often difficult to assess the accuracy of, and to test, such formulae. In other words, in principle, each formula should use only a single stage of logic.

On the other hand, there are some disadvantages to using only single-stage logic:

- Models may become visually large.
- Some multi-stage logic process can be easy to understand, either because their logic is not excessively complex or because it represents a fairly standard approach, with which many modellers and users would be familiar.

Therefore, the selective use of embedded formulae can make sense in some circumstances, including:

- Using a MATCH within an INDEX function to replace a VLOOKUP (see Chapter 25; as discussed there, the MATCH function should be retained in a separate cell when its result needs to be used several times).
- Embedding a SEARCH within a TEXT function to directly extract specific string. This may be acceptable when there is a single embedding, whereas if the identity of the element that is looked for within the SEARCH function also needs to be established as the result of another function (so that there would be three logical steps), the process should generally be split (see Chapter 24 for a description of Text functions).

- A formula such as =VALUE(MID(B3,SEARCH("(",B3,1)+1,1)) may also be considered to essentially be two logical steps, for the presence of the VALUE function will not materially hinder transparency, since it returns a number from the equivalent text field without any genuine manipulation or additional calculations.

One should generally avoid using more than two embedded logical steps. In some cases it can be more robust, flexible and transparent to replace the calculations with a user-defined function (see Part VI), especially where large Excel tabular structures contain many copied formulae (or intermediate calculations) whose values are not of explicit interest, and also where a cell reference is used several times in a single formula (as for Cell B3 in the above example).

Building and Splitting Compound Formulae

Based on the above discussion, in practice there will be cases where it makes sense to build embedded formulae, and others where is makes sense to split a formula into its individual components.

In order to build robust embedded formulae (in the cases when it makes sense), it is usually most effective to build and test each logical step separately and, by copying from the Formula Bar, to combine these into a single formula (that may be copied to several calls in a range). The procedure in which one copies from the Formula Bar will ensure that the cell references remain correct, which would not generally be the case if a simple cell copy-and-paste operation were used.

Figure 8.8 shows the case (with similar examples discussed in Chapter 24), where a sequence of Text functions is used to isolate the numerical value contained in Cell B5 (i.e. the number 1).

These logic steps should first be tested, so that they work across the full range of input formats that may be placed in Cell B5, or which will be present in a larger data set to which the sequence will be applied. Once this is done, the formulae can be combined into a single formula. A robust way to do this is to work from the final result (i.e. Cell F5, containing the formula =VALUE(E5)) and substitute the cell reference(s) within it by the formula(e) that are in those cells; thus, within Cell F5, the reference to Cell E5 would be replaced by the formula =MID(B5,D5+1,1). Figure 8.9 shows how this can be done by copying the formula from the Formula Bar (one should not copy the = sign; after selecting the part to copy and using Ctrl+C, one can escape from the Formula Bar by using the X (Cancel) button).

The result of this process is that Cell F5 would contain =VALUE(MID(B5,D5+1,1)). The next step would be to replace the new cell reference(s)) with their corresponding formulae in the same way (i.e. to replace D5 with its formula), leading to a final formula that depends only on the input (Cell B5).

	A	B	C	D	E	F
1						
2				**Explicit Steps**		
3				1	2	3
4		**Co./subject**		SEARCH for "("	MID=No. Days as Text	VALUE of No. Days
5		CustA (1 Day)		7	1	1
6				=SEARCH("(",B5,1)	=MID(B5,D5+1,1)	=VALUE(E5)

FIGURE 8.8 Sequence of Text Functions Shown as Separate Steps

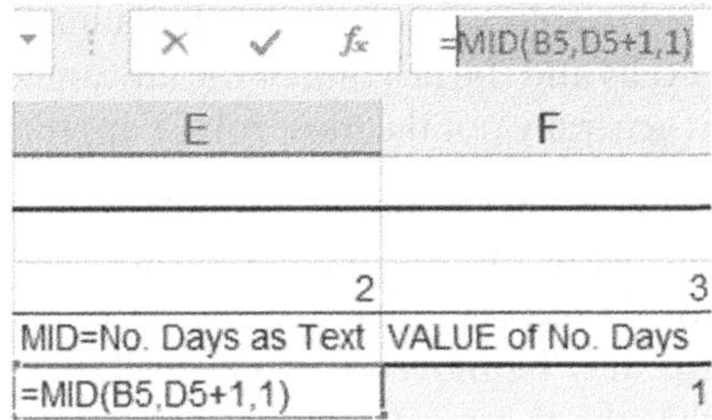

FIGURE 8.9 Sequence of Text Functions Shown as Separate Steps

D	E	F	G	H	I	J
Explicit Steps				**Building the Compound Formula in Reverse Steps**		
1	2	3		1	2	3
SEARCH for "("	MID=No. Days as Text	VALUE of No. Days				
7	1	1		1	1	1
=SEARCH("(",B5,1)	=MID(B5,D5+1,1)	=VALUE(E5)		=VALUE(E5)	=VALUE(MID(B5,D5+1,1))	=VALUE(MID(B5,SEARCH("(",B5,1)+1,1))

FIGURE 8.10 Substitution Process Using a Repeat Starting Cell

In fact, in order to do this most robustly, one should generally retain the original formulae whilst the modified formulae are built into a copy of them. Figure 8.10 shows how the process would best be conducted, in which a simple repetition of the final formula of the individual steps is used (in cell H5) as the basis to start the substitution process.

Of course, once the process is complete, one should check that the compound formula produces the same results as the individual steps (using a wide variety of possible input values), and once this is done, the individual intermediate calculations can be deleted. Figure 8.11 shows how the final formula may be used on a larger data set.

	A	B	C	D
1				
2		**Co./subject**	**No. Days**	
3		CustA (1 Day)	1	=VALUE(MID(B3,SEARCH("(",B3,1)+1,1))
4		CustomerB (2 Day)	2	=VALUE(MID(B4,SEARCH("(",B4,1)+1,1))
5		CustC (1 Day)	1	=VALUE(MID(B5,SEARCH("(",B5,1)+1,1))
6		CustoD (2 Days)	2	=VALUE(MID(B6,SEARCH("(",B6,1)+1,1))
7		CustB (2 Days)	2	=VALUE(MID(B7,SEARCH("(",B7,1)+1,1))
8		CustomerB (2 Days)	2	=VALUE(MID(B8,SEARCH("(",B8,1)+1,1))
9		CustomerE (2 Days)	2	=VALUE(MID(B9,SEARCH("(",B9,1)+1,1))
10		CustF (2 Days)	2	=VALUE(MID(B10,SEARCH("(",B10,1)+1,1))
11		CustA (2 Days)	2	=VALUE(MID(B11,SEARCH("(",B11,1)+1,1))
12		CustomG (2 Days)	2	=VALUE(MID(B12,SEARCH("(",B12,1)+1,1))
13		CustA (1 Days)	1	=VALUE(MID(B13,SEARCH("(",B13,1)+1,1))
14		CustA (2 Days)	2	=VALUE(MID(B14,SEARCH("(",B14,1)+1,1))
15		CustmG (2 Days)	2	=VALUE(MID(B15,SEARCH("(",B15,1)+1,1))
16		CusA (1 Days)	1	=VALUE(MID(B16,SEARCH("(",B16,1)+1,1))
17		CustD (2 Days)	2	=VALUE(MID(B17,SEARCH("(",B17,1)+1,1))
18		CustB (3 Days)	3	=VALUE(MID(B18,SEARCH("(",B18,1)+1,1))
19		CustomerE (2 Days)	2	=VALUE(MID(B19,SEARCH("(",B19,1)+1,1))
20		CustF (2 Days)	2	=VALUE(MID(B20,SEARCH("(",B20,1)+1,1))
21		CustA (2 Days)	2	=VALUE(MID(B21,SEARCH("(",B21,1)+1,1))

FIGURE 8.11 Applying the Compound Formula to a Larger Data Set

Where it is instead desired to split a compound formula into its components, the copying of the formula to other cells and the deleting of the unwanted items may result incorrect cell references, so this is generally not the most robust approach. Alternatives include:

- Copying the component elements from the Formula Bar into new cells.
- Using Ctrl+' in the cell below the formula (the short-cut recreates the contents of the cell directly above), and then deleting the unnecessary components. Once isolated, the component may be moved to a new cell, to clear the cell (below the original formula), so that the short-cut can be used in this cell for the next component. This allows the individual components to be isolated in turn. For example, the individual components of:

  = SUM('Finance Revenue'!P21,'Licence Fee'!P21,'Subscription Fee'!P21)

could be isolated in separate cells before being summed.

Using Absolute Cell Referencing Only Where Necessary

The ease of applying the F4 short-cut may lead to the creation of "over-dollared" formulae, i.e. ones in which the $ symbol is inserted before both the row and column references, when only one or the other is required; this will typically result in formulae that cannot be correctly copied to elsewhere. Particularly in modular structures, one may copy over-dollared formulae into a new area, and overlook that the cell references are not correct. Consideration should therefore be given as to what are the minimum requirements for absolute cell referencing.

Limiting Repeated or Unused Logic

It is perhaps surprising how often models contain calculations that are not used for the determination of the output, or which repeat calculations that are conducted elsewhere. Examples of cases that the author has observed in practice include:

- The passing of calculated values from sheet to sheet without the values being used in the intermediate steps but only at the end of the path (sometimes called "daisy chains"). This creates a long audit path. In fact, it can be acceptable to use "transfer" areas in source and destination sheets, in order to transfer values between sheets, before these are used in the calculations on the destination sheet. However, if many such transfer areas are required between many sheets in a model, it is likely that these sheets would be better combined into a single one.
- "Lazy summations", such as a cell (say D21) containing "=SUM(D3:D20)" and the next cell (D22) containing "=D21-D7". In other words, the final calculations in D22 are intended to ignore D7 and implicitly use the formula "=SUM(D3:20)-D7".

Of course, such items should ideally be improved or corrected as appropriate. This is often simple in principle, but time-consuming in practice. For example:

- Rebuilding the formulae that originally refer to the second instance of an input requires formulae to be relinked to the single intended input, and for subsequent links to this input to be deleted.

- Where (as in the example above), the Cell D7 is to be excluded from the total for some reason, one would have several possibilities to adapt it:
  - To change the model structurally, so that items that are to be excluded (i.e. Row 7 in the above example) are moved into a different range, so that only the items that are genuinely required are contained within the range (of the SUM function in this case).
  - To use flag fields (consisting of 0s and 1s, or text fields) to indicate which items are to be excluded, and use the SUMIFS function based on the full range and conditional on the flags to add up the items.

Using Breaks to Test Calculation Paths

The above discussion has emphasised the importance of testing the formulae as they are being built. The testing of formulae only within completed models is more complex, as for many formulae, their inputs are calculated values, rather than references to pure numerical values. One technique that can be used (ideally when building the model) is to break the calculation path for a specific formula. This simply means the input cell references to the formula are replaced by (a reference to) a CHOOSE function, which is used to select either the values from the main model's calculation or simply to select an alternative set of values that the user can define. For example, if Range1 is used to denote the original main range of calculations that drive the formula, and Range2 is used to denote any values that one may wish to use in its place, then one can build the model with a new range, Range3, so that:

$$\text{Range3} = \text{CHOOSE}(\text{iSwitch}, \text{Range1}, \text{Range2})$$

and link subsequent formulae to Range3 instead of to Range1.

Of course, if this method is used, one needs to take care that any use of the model for final decision and analysis purposes is based on the correct range or formulae (so that the switch should be set to choose the values in Range1 for this purpose).

Using Excel Error Checking Rules

Excel has a useful "error-checking" feature, under File/Options/Formulas (see Figure 8.12). Note that these do not (in general) check whether a calculation is accurate (since Excel calculates correctly), nor whether the calculations are appropriate within the modelling context (i.e. are in conformance to the model specification). Rather, the feature can be used to identify possible areas where formulae may lack robustness, or potentially refer to the wrong ranges, and so on (so that further investigation can be conducted, or modifications made as appropriate).

In fact, it can be distracting to have Excel's error checks active in a completed model that one knows is correct. Therefore, the options may be switched off in a completed model that has been adequately tested. On the other hand, when building (rebuilding), modifying, testing or auditing a model, it can be useful to switch the options on at various stages of these processes.

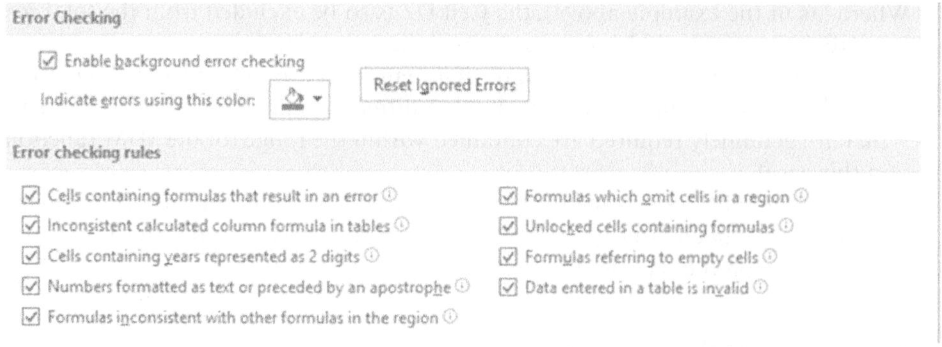

Error Checking

☑ Enable background error checking

Indicate errors using this color: Reset Ignored Errors

Error checking rules

☑ Cells containing formulas that result in an error
☑ Inconsistent calculated column formula in tables
☑ Cells containing years represented as 2 digits
☑ Numbers formatted as text or preceded by an apostrophe
☑ Formulas inconsistent with other formulas in the region
☑ Formulas which omit cells in a region
☑ Unlocked cells containing formulas
☑ Formulas referring to empty cells
☑ Data entered in a table is invalid

FIGURE 8.12 Excel's Error Checking

Building Error-checking Formulae

Error checks are formulae which calculate two paths through the model and compare the results. The most frequent implementation is where the results should be the same, so that the difference between the two calculated items should always be equal to zero. Note that:

- Since there may be various error checks used at different places in the model, a consolidated range which refers to each one could be created. A single error-check value could also be created, which sums up the values of the individual checks (absolute values of the individual items can be summed, to avoid positive and negative errors cancelling each other out). A non-zero value of this single figure would indicate that there is some error that can be investigated in more detail by referring to the individual error-checking calculations.
- Conditional Formatting can be used to highlight the occurrence of an error (e.g. using this to shade the cell contents bright yellow). This is useful, since errors may be quite rare, so that one may otherwise overlook them if there is no mechanism to draw attention to them.

It is worthwhile to focus on using "value-added" error checks. Lower value-added checks are those that that will always evaluate to zero unless truly basic errors are made. Examples include the testing, in a table of data that is summed along rows and columns using the SUM function, whether the row and column sums are the same. This is generally a low value-added check, since the sums will always be the same unless there is a very basic mistake in one of the formulae (see Figure 8.13). (Of course, basic checks on such formulae are still necessary, such as to ensure that they are linked to the full range of data and so on, but they do not need to be built permanently into a model as this increases its size and adds complexity.)

(Another low-value check is that in which one verifies that an item that is selected from a drop-down (Data/Validation menu) is genuinely contained within the list of valid items, when the list that defines the drop-down is itself defined from the same range as the list of valid items.)

An example of the type of a higher value-added error check is shown in Figure 8.14. In this case, the SUMIFS function is used (Cells H3:H7) to sum the amounts (in Column D) for each country. The error check (Cell H11) checks the difference between the sum

G	H	I	J	K
Country	<=£10000	>£10000	Total	
UK	72974	167773	**240747**	=SUM(H3:I3)
Italy	81866	161252	**243118**	=SUM(H4:I4)
Germany	38594	114097	**152691**	=SUM(H5:I5)
France	58885	121107	**179992**	=SUM(H6:I6)
Spain	43846	184902	**228748**	=SUM(H7:I7)
Total From SUMIFS	**296165**	**749131**		
	=SUM(H3:H7)	=SUM(I3:I7)		
Row sum of columns		1045296	=SUM(J3:J7)	
Column sum of rows		1045296	=SUM(H8:I8)	
Error-Check		0	=H11-H12	

FIGURE 8.13 A Lower Value-added Error Check

	A	B	C	D	E	F	G	H	I
1									
2		**Customer**	**Country**	**Amount £**	**Due Date**		**Country**	**Amounts £**	
3		Cust02	UK	12232	20-Mar-17		UK	240747	=SUMIFS($D$3:$D$102,$C$3:$C$102,$G3)
4		Cust06	Italy	4749	16-Mar-17		Italy	243118	=SUMIFS($D$3:$D$102,$C$3:$C$102,$G4)
5		Cust07	Italy	7282	12-Apr-17		Germany	160683	=SUMIFS($D$3:$D$102,$C$3:$C$102,$G5)
6		Cust03	Italy	12759	14-Jun-17		France	179992	=SUMIFS($D$3:$D$102,$C$3:$C$102,$G6)
7		Cust10	UK	12334	24-May-17		Spain	228748	=SUMIFS($D$3:$D$102,$C$3:$C$102,$G7)
8		Cust05	Italy	4283	24-Mar-17				
9		Cust06	Germany	7992	5-May-17		Total From SUMIFS	**1053288**	=SUM(H3:H8)
10		Cust06	Italy	13202	16-Apr-17		Total From Table	**1053288**	=SUM(D3:D102)
11		Cust04	Germany	12684	4-Jun-17		Error-Check	0	=H9-H10
12		Cust10	UK	11862	13-Jun-17				

FIGURE 8.14 Example of a Value-added Error Check

of these figures and the sum of all figures within the full data set. This can detect errors that are likely to occur, even as they may otherwise be overlooked, such as:

- Inclusion of a new country in the full data set, so that the list of conditional queries is not complete (overlooking the new country).
- A mistake in the spelling of a country name (in the full data set or in the query range).

The example may be extended by using Conditional Formatting in the Cell H11 to highlight the presence of an error (which is introduced here by misspelling the entry in Cell C9) (see Figure 8.15).

	A	B	C	D	E	F	G	H
1								
2		**Customer**	**Country**	**Amount £**	**Due Date**		**Country**	**Amounts £**
3		Cust02	UK	12232	20-Mar-17		UK	**240747**
4		Cust06	Italy	4749	16-Mar-17		Italy	**243118**
5		Cust07	Italy	7282	12-Apr-17		Germany	**152691**
6		Cust03	Italy	12759	14-Jun-17		France	**179992**
7		Cust10	UK	12334	24-May-17		Spain	**228748**
8		Cust05	Italy	4283	24-Mar-17			
9		Cust06	German	7992	5-May-17		Total From SUMIFS	**1045296**
10		Cust06	Italy	13202	16-Apr-17		Total From Table	**1053288**
11		Cust04	Germany	12684	4-Jun-17		Error-Check	**-7992**

FIGURE 8.15 Conditional Formatting Highlights the Presence of an Error

Handling Calculation Errors Robustly

In many cases, there may be no way of eliminating that error values may arise. For example:

- In the above product revenue growth example, there will always be some input values for which the revenues of one product never reach those of another, so that the MATCH function used will return #NA.
- The PPMT function (see Chapter 20) produces numerical values only for those time periods which are within the time-frame of the loan, and otherwise returns #NUM!
- The IRR of a function (Chapter 20) will return #NUM! if all the input cash flows are positive.

The IFERROR function (Chapter 17) can be used to override errors and replace them with an alternative value, in particular in cases in which errors are expected and will have no consequence. For example, in the case of PPMT, the (structural) fact that there is no payment due after the end of the loan contract is equivalent to a zero amount, so that the alternative value may be set to zero for most practical cases (although in a technical or legalistic sense, the absence of an obligation may not be the same as having an obligation of amount zero).

On the other hand, one should be cautious when tempted to use an IFERROR function: by over-riding all errors, however they arise, one is not alerted to other forms of mistakes or errors which should be corrected or dealt with in some way. Thus, an approach which uses the IF statement to identify only the specific (expected) cases and handles these is arguably superior, because any other form of error that arises would then be visible and can be dealt with. For example, in the case of the PPMT function, the approach would be used to eliminate explicitly only those error cases arising from the time period being outside the loan term, rather than eliminating all errors of whatever nature.

In other cases, particularly when working with large data sets, it may be more appropriate to retain errors in the data, but to filter them or ignore them in the final analysis stage, for example using the AGGREGATE function (Chapter 18) or a filtered PivotTable (Chapter 27).

Restricting Input Values Using Data Validation

In some cases, some of the formulae may be valid only if input values are restricted to specific items. Typical examples include:

- Restricting to integers (such as 1, 2, 3) the values which define the scenario number, or which represent the (whole period) delay of the start date of a project.
- Ensuring that only values or text fields within a pre-defined list are used. For example, one may restrict the possible entries in the column of data set, so that only "Yes" or "No" can be entered. Especially where the calculations may use a function such as =COUNTIF(. . ., "Yes"), one can limit the use of invalid entries such as "Y", which would lead to an incorrect value being returned (even as such entries would be sufficient for pure visual purposes).

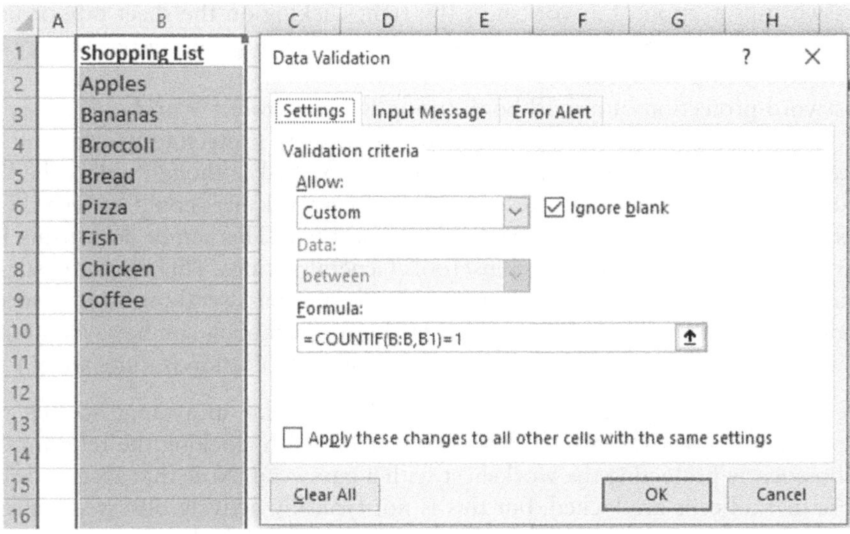

FIGURE 8.16 Custom Criteria with Data Validation

The Data/Data Validation menu can be used to restrict input values. It is largely self-explanatory, with a few points nevertheless worth emphasising:

- The Allow box on the Settings tab is used to define the nature of the restriction (e.g. whole number list). Once this is selected, a context-sensitive dialogue appears, into which the required details for that type of restriction can be entered.
- The Input Message tab can be used to create a message that is displayed when the user hovers with the cursor over the cell. This can be used to provide information, such as the role of the cell, and nature of the allowable inputs. The Error Alert tab can be used to display a message in the case that the user tries to use invalid data.
- Custom criteria on the Settings tab can be used to define a logical formula that evaluates to TRUE for valid data. This can also be used to restrict inputs where there are relationships between several inputs that must hold, for example that one input value must be larger than another.
- The use of the Circle Invalid Data option of the Data Validation menu can allow one to highlight the cells in a range that do not meet certain criteria.

Figure 8.16 shows an example in which a custom criterion is used to ensure that an item is entered at most once on a list (of course, Conditional Formatting would be an alternative approach to highlight potential duplicates).

Protecting Ranges

Excel has several tools that can be used to protect ranges, worksheets or workbooks. For example:

- Hiding a worksheet by right-clicking on the sheet tab (and selecting Hide).

- Password-protection of a worksheet (by right-clicking on the sheet tab, or using the Review/Protect Sheet menu). This can be used to stop the entire contents of a worksheet being changed.
- Password-protection of a workbook (using Review/Protect Workbook). This can be used to ensure that no worksheets are added (by protecting its structure) or to ensure that the presence of hidden sheets is masked (although unless the VBA Project is also protected, the presence of a hidden worksheet could be seen there).
- Requiring a password to open or modify a workbook. This can be done using File/Save As, then selecting MoreOptions/Tools/GeneralOptions. This menu can suggest using the workbook in read-only form (that is, not password-protected), so that accidental changes cannot be made. (A read-only workbook can be saved under a new name and then edited normally, so the level of protection is quite weak.)

Frequently, one may wish to protect only the formulae in a range so that they cannot be changed or overwritten. This can be achieved by locking the relevant cells and subsequently protecting the worksheet with a password. Note that Excel's default setting is that all cells are locked, but this is not typically actively observed, since by default worksheets are not password-protected. Therefore, to lock a range, one must:

- Unlock all cells on the worksheet. This can be done by clicking in the top-left Home box to select all worksheet cells, then using Ctrl+1 to invoke the Format Cells menu, followed by unchecking the Locked box on the Protection tab.
- Selecting the range that one wishes to protect, then using Ctrl+1 to invoke the Format Cells menu, followed by checking the Locked box on the Protection tab.
- Applying password-protection to the worksheet, as above.

The use of VBA to protect models is often very convenient. For example:

- Where hidden worksheets are used, the VBA Project can be password-protected to ensure that such sheets are not visible.
- One could write event code which shows a Disclaimer when a file is opened, or which keeps all sheets hidden until one clicks on button to accept the Disclaimer, and then exposes the worksheets.

Dealing with Structural Limitations: Formulae and Documentation

In some cases, potential errors (or unexpected values) may arise due to structural limitations of a model. Typically, the options to best deal with these include:

- Extending the size of some of the ranges, or modifying the formulae to make them more generally applicable.
- Including error-handling procedures as part of the model's formulae.
- Limiting the input values that are allowed.
- Providing documentation concerning limitations of model validity.
- Building error checks into the model.
- Using VBA code to overcome size limitations.

As an example of extending the size, Figure 8.17 shows a screen-clip of a model which calculates the time at which the revenues of one product line will exceed those of another (the file and a more detailed explanation is found in Chapter 25). Clearly, if the

	A	B	C	D	E	F	G	H	I	J	K	L	M	N	O	P
1																
2				2018	2019	2020	2021	2022	2023	2024	2025	2026	2027	2028	2029	2030
3		Product 1	100	103	106	109	113	116	119	123	127	130	134	138	143	147
4		Growth (% p.a.)	3.0%	3.0%	3.0%	3.0%	3.0%	3.0%	3.0%	3.0%	3.0%	3.0%	3.0%	3.0%	3.0%	3.0%
5		Product 2	70	74	79	83	88	94	99	105	112	118	125	133	141	149
6		Growth (% p.a.)	6.0%	6.0%	6.0%	6.0%	6.0%	6.0%	6.0%	6.0%	6.0%	6.0%	6.0%	6.0%	6.0%	6.0%
7		Test Prod2>=Prod1	13	0	0	0	0	0	0	0	0	0	0	0	0	1

FIGURE 8.17 Model with an Extended Range

assumed growth rate in revenues for Product 2 is decreased, the time at which the revenue of Product 2 overtakes that of Product 1 is pushed further into the future. To some extent, this can be dealt with by simply extending the time axis as far as necessary. In practice, in a large model, the extension of all relevant ranges can be cumbersome to do and potentially error-prone (since the formulae need adapting to ensure that the new ranges are correctly referred to). In addition, there will always be some input values for which no range is sufficiently large (for example, if the growth rate of Product 2 were the same as that of Product 1).

In some cases, VBA may be used to create models in which a limitation that would otherwise be structural simply becomes a parameter, or calculation, of a more general model. For example, the above forecast could be entirely constructed within a simple VBA loop (one pass through the loop for each year), which (for given input assumptions) is continued until the revenue conditions are met. Similarly, when using binomial (or other) tree-based methods in option valuation, rather than build a tree in Excel according to a fixed structure, the calculations implied within a tree can be captured in VBA code, with the number of branches in the tree simply being an input to a user-defined function (or subroutine).

Where a model does contain structural limitations (or contextual assumptions), these should be noted within the overall documentation, in order to ensure that the model is not used in contexts for which it is not suitable or meaningful.

CHAPTER 9

Choosing Excel Functions for Transparency, Flexibility and Efficiency

INTRODUCTION

This chapter highlights some key issues relating to the choice of which Excel function(s) or calculation method to use. Very often, although there are many ways in which the same (and correct) figures would result, model builders tend to employ either the first approach that comes to mind, or the one that is the most familiar. Insufficient attention is typically paid to the consideration of the possible options and the advantages or disadvantages of each, as they relate to issue of flexibility, computational effectiveness or transparency.

KEY CONSIDERATIONS

For the purposes of the issues discussed in this chapter, it is important to note that all methods shown will produce a correct numerical result. In other words, the result of the calculations *per se* is not a consideration; we will take the accuracy as a given (and necessary) element in all methods, and focus on issues relating to the choice of the most appropriate function or approach.

Direct Arithmetic or Functions, and Individual Cells or Ranges?

When dealing with basic arithmetic operations (i.e. addition, subtraction, multiplication, division), it is often worth considering whether either to use Excel's functions, or to perform the operations explicitly. For example, when adding together a set of items, one could:

- Use the SUM function.
- Use the + operator, referring to individual cells.

Where the items that are to be summed are laid out in a single contiguous range, the SUM formula is quick to build and can readily be adapted if a new item is added (especially by inserting/deleting a row or column within the range). However, one loses the flexibility to move items around the model. The use of the + operator would make most sense if one wishes to retain the flexibility to move data around, i.e. to cut and paste individual cells. For example, it may not be fully clear at the outset as to what the most appropriate layout is for a model. However, a major disadvantage of this approach is that it is cumbersome to add or delete data, and there is a risk of error if one forgets to update the formulae when doing so. Further, the approach is hard to audit, for it is time-consuming to check that all relevant cells have been included in the calculations (and one has not been overlooked if a row had been added, for example).

Similar comments (regarding range or individual cell references) apply not only to many other functions where simple direct arithmetic operations could be used as alternatives (including PRODUCT, COUNT, AVERAGE, SUMPRODUCT and NPV), but also to Logical functions, such as AND, OR, as well as MIN, MAX, and many others.

In Figure 9.1, an example of an OR function used with a contiguous input range is shown. Note that the function is placed close to its inputs (which is generally to be recommended, as discussed in Chapter 7). Of course, this approach would inhibit the moving of one of Row 2 or Row 3 if this were needed at some later time. For example, Inclusion Flag 1 may relate to operations, Inclusion Flag 2 to financing and it may be appropriate to place these in separate calculation areas in some models.

In Figure 9.2 we show how the alternative (individual cell) syntax would be one which would allow for the cells (i.e. in Row 2 and Row 3) to be moved to different parts of the model.

Note that when developing a larger model from a very small one, in the case of the approach used in Figure 9.1, one would likely detect that the OR function is built in a way that is inappropriate if rows are moved, so that one may change the syntax to that used in Figure 9.2 before making structural changes (e.g. moving rows). However, where such (contiguous input range) approaches are used in models with longer audit

	A	B	C	D
1				
2		Inclusion Flag 1	0	
3		Inclusion Flag 2	1	
4		Inlusion flag	TRUE	=OR(C2:C3)

FIGURE 9.1 OR Function with a Contiguous Input Range

	A	B	C	D
1				
2		Inclusion Flag 1	0	
3		Inclusion Flag 2	1	
4		Inlusion flag	TRUE	=OR(C2,C3)

FIGURE 9.2 OR Function with Separate Input Cells

	A	B	C	D
1				
2		Inclusion Flag 1	0	
3		Inclusion Flag 2	1	
4				
5				
240				
241				
242				
243		Amount before effect of inclusion flags	154	
244		Inlusion flag	TRUE	=OR(C2:C3)
245		Amount after effect of inclusion flags	154	=C243*C244

FIGURE 9.3 OR Function with a Contiguous Input Range and a Long Audit Path

paths (see Figure 9.3), during the process of moving Row 2 or Row 3, it would be easy to overlook that the formula in Row 244 would then become incorrect.

The SUM function can also be used in the multi-argument form, i.e. where it is applied to individual ranges that are separated by commas (e.g. SUM(A2, A3, A4), rather than SUM(A2:A4), and more generally SUM(A2,A3,A4,B6,B7,B8), rather than SUM(A2:A4,B6:B8)). This latter approach can make sense if one knows that the ranges may need to be moved, whilst the items within each range would not need to be separated from each other. On the other hand, in practice, the individual components, if moved, are likely not to be placed near each other, so that the audit paths may become more longer and less transparent. Thus the "mixed use" form is generally not optimal. For example, rather than:

$$\text{"B12} = \text{SUM(B10, C3 : C10)"}$$

the use of separate steps (for example):

$$\text{"C12} = \text{SUM(C3 : C10)"}$$

$$\text{"B12} = \text{B10} + \text{C12"}$$

would be more transparent (see the discussion in Chapter 7).

IF Versus MIN/MAX

In many cases, one's intuition may be to use an IF function, because the corresponding thought process is of a binary nature. However, in some cases, the name of a function can be a misleading guide as to the best or clearest choice. Indeed, the MIN or MAX functions are often more appropriate than the IF function. For example, when creating formulae to allocate an amount to various bands (or tranches, layers, bands or "buckets"), several implementations are possible. The screen-clip in Figure 9.4 shows two possibilities, of allocating the amount that is shown in Cell C2 to either the asset side or the liability side. In the first, an IF function is used, and in the second, the MIN/MAX functions are used.

	A	B	C	D	E
1					
2		**Excess Cash/(Borrowings)**	5,000		
3					
4		**Using IF,** allocation to	Result	Formulae	
5		Asset side (i.e. excess cash)	5,000	=IF(C2>=0,C2,0)	
6		Liability side (i.e. additional borrowing)	0	=-IF(C2<=0,C2,0)	
7					
8		**Using MIN, MAX,** allocation to	Result	Formulae	
9		Asset side (i.e. excess cash)	5,000	=MAX(C2,0)	
10		Liability side (i.e. additional borrowing)	0	=-MIN(C2,0)	

FIGURE 9.4 Possible Implementations of Allocating an Amount to Either Excess Cash or Additional Borrowings

	A	B	C	D
1				
2		**Taxable Income**		120000
3				
4		**Allocation to Tranche**	Layer Capacity	Allocated
5		First	10000	
6		Second	35000	
7		Third	55000	
8		Final		

FIGURE 9.5 Parameters for an Income-allocation Example

In this simple case (in which there are only two layers), the decision between the two approaches may not be so important: the only direct difference here is that whilst the IF function may be a more intuitive representation of the underlying logic (through its name), it requires three parameters (in which C2 is repeated), whereas MIN/MAX require only two parameters and have no repetition.

Whereas in simple models, there may be only one or two bands, in more general cases, there may be more (in either, or both of, the positive or negative cases). For example, when working out the income tax due based on a (positive) income figure, different tax rates may apply to parts of the income. Figure 9.5 shows an example in which it is desired to allocate the income (Cell D2) into the layers (in the range D5:D8, defined by the parameters in C5:C7), so that in subsequent calculations, a different tax rate can be applied to the income within each band.

In the author's experience, most modellers would initially try to build the required formulae using IF functions, which quickly leads one to building complex embedded IF formulae. These are not only hard to read and test, but also are very difficult to adapt appropriately if an additional band needs to be added (each additional band would involve an additional embedding within the function). This quickly becomes unwieldy and error-prone when more than two bands are needed.

Figure 9.6 shows an example of completed formulae based on the use of the MIN function, rather than embedded IF functions. In this case, the intermediate bands are all based on the same copied formula (that may also be copied if a new band is

	A	B	C	D	E	F	G
1							
2		Taxable Income		120000			
3							
4		Allocation to Tranche	Layer Capacity	Allocated	Cumulative Allocation	Formulae in col D	Formulae in col E
5		First	10000	10,000	10,000	=MIN(D$2,C5)	=SUM(D$5:D5)
6		Second	35000	35,000	45,000	=MIN(D$2-E5,C6)	=SUM(D$5:D6)
7		Third	55000	55,000	100,000	=MIN(D$2-E6,C7)	=SUM(D$5:D7)
8		Final		20,000	120,000	=D$2-E7	=SUM(D$5:D8)
9							
10		Total		120,000		=SUM(D5:D8)	
11		Error-check		0		=D2-D10	

FIGURE 9.6 Completed Income-allocation Example

	A	B	C	D	E	F	G	H	I
1									
2			2016	2017	2018	2019	2020		Formulae in Column G
3									
4		Product Line 1	100	90.0	81.0	72.9	65.6		=F4*(1+G5)
5		Growth (% p.a.)	-10.0%	-10.0%	-10.0%	-10.0%	-10.0%		=F5
6									
7		Product Line 2	50	57.5	66.1	76.0	87.5		=F7*(1+G8)
8		Growth (% p.a.)	15.0%	15.0%	15.0%	15.0%	15.0%		=F8
9									
10		PL2>PL1	0	0	0	1	1		=IF(G7>G4,1,0)
11									
12		Many Embedded IFs		0	0	1	0		=IF(G10=1,IF(F10=1,0,IF(E10=1,0,IF(D10=1,0,1))))
13		Two Embedded IFs		0	0	1	0		=IF(G10=1,IF(F10=0,1,0),0)
14		IF with AND		0	0	1	0		=IF(AND(G10=1,F10=0),1,0)

FIGURE 9.7 Core Revenue Forecast for Two Product Lines

introduced). The formulae for the first and last bands need to be adapted (for example, to reflect that the last band has unlimited capacity).

Similar situations arise in many applications, including financial statement modelling, project finance, tax calculations and production share or royalty agreements. In the case of financial statement models, the amount is initially calculated from the cash flow statement, and is needed on the balance sheet to ensure consistency, i.e. that the balance sheet indeed balances: the amount corresponds either to an additional cash balance resulting from the cash flow (when the amount is positive) or to the additional borrowing that is required (when the amount is negative).

Embedded IF Statements

The potential for embedded IF functions (i.e. the use of an IF function within another IF function) arises quite frequently, in cases that require (or appear to require) a sequential logic: that is, to check whether a first condition is met, and if not check a second condition, and, if not, whether a third condition is met, and so on.

The file Ch9.1.EmbeddedIFs.1.xlsx contains an example which forecasts the revenues of each of two product lines: one whose revenues are initially large but are in decline, and another whose revenues start smaller but grow quickly. Row 10 contains a flag field which indicates whether, in each year, the revenue for product line 2 is greater than that for product line 1. The main aim is to find out (as a calculated field) the first year in which the revenues of product line 2 are forecast to be greater than those of product line 1 (which, from Cell F19, we can see happens in 2019) (see Figure 9.7).

Of course, there are various ways to find the required information, some of which may use IF functions. Implementations of some of these are shown in Rows 12 through 14, including:

- Using a sequence of IF statements, in which each formula is self-contained and evaluates all previous columns (Row 12). Thus, the formula in the last column (G) has as many embedded levels as the number of columns up to that point. Needless to say, not only is this complex, but also it is extremely cumbersome to create or modify (as a single formula cannot be copied across columns).
- Using only two IF statements, based on using the result of the previous column (Row 13); this is an improvement over the first approach.
- Using the result of the previous column, and also the AND function, meaning that only one IF function is necessary (Row 14). This approach is probably the most transparent of the three, as it makes directly clear which conditions need to hold for the IF function to return a 1 (i.e. to indicate that a match has taken place for the first point in the sequence), whereas the second approach (Row 13) is a less direct statement of what is ultimately the same logic.

In principle, the use of one set of logical criteria that is embedded within another is often intransparent, inflexible and error-prone. In particular, the presence of inadvertent errors may arise as it can be very difficult to test the model properly: ideally, such testing involves ensuring that the calculations work correctly along all logical paths that may arise as the model inputs are varied across a wide range of values. However, without being able to see the results of the individual logical steps, it is difficult to know which paths have been activated by a specific combination of input values. Thus, there may be logical paths which are incorrect, but which become active for the first time only when another user requires a different set of input values.

In essentially all practical contexts, when there are more than two potential embedded logical functions (mostly frequently embedded IF statements), there is almost always a more convenient, transparent and flexible approach. These typically involve one of:

- Using MIN/MAX or AND/OR functions (as shown in the earlier examples).
- Using lookup functions (see Chapter 25). In the above example, the MATCH function (see Chapter 25) would generally be a better way of determining (based on the flag in Row 10) the first year in which the revenues of product line 2 are forecast to be greater than those of product line 1.

The file Ch9.2.EmbeddedIFs.2.xlsx contains an example of using lookup functions to eliminate embedded IF statements (see Figure 9.8). The file contains a table of data, showing the average temperature by time of day (Cells B2:C7). The user can input a time of day (in Cell B11 or B15) and the functions return the average temperature (Cells C11 and C15 respectively). In the first case, a sequence of embedded IF functions are used, whereas in the latter the INDEX/MATCH combination is employed. The latter is clearly easier to read, and would work immediately if a new time of day (e.g. early evening) were introduced as a new row in the data set, whereas the first approach would require significant adaptation. The embedded IFS approach has the additional disadvantage that the data would need to be placed in time-order,

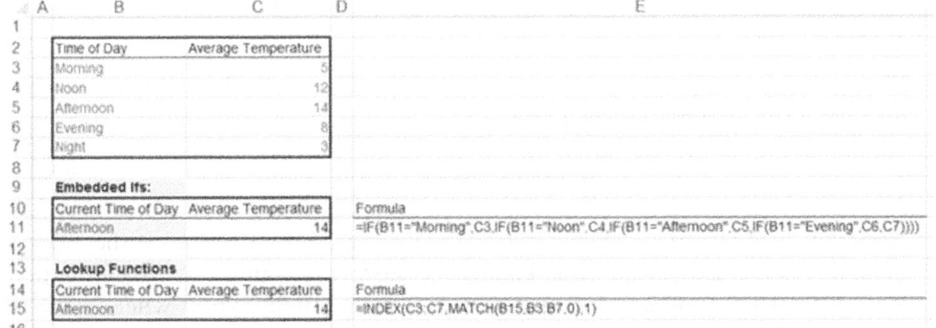

FIGURE 9.8 An Example of Using Lookup Functions in Place of Embedded IF Statements

whereas in the example, when using the lookup function approach, the data set can be in any order.

Short Forms of Functions

Generally, it is logically clearer and more transparent not to use the short forms of functions, but rather to use the slightly longer but more explicit logical expressions. This section provides a discussion of these issues.

A statement such as:

$$\text{IF}(\text{F7} > \text{F6}, 1, 0)$$

is generally clearer than simply:

$$= \text{F7} > \text{F6}$$

For, even though the second is shorter, it requires the user to explicitly consider the outcomes that result in each case.

Similarly, expressions such as =IF(G3, Value1,Value2) are unsatisfactory, since it is not explicit what aspect of G3 is being tested. In fact, it would return Value1 if cell G3 contains any non-zero number, Value2 if G3 is contains the number 0 or is blank, and #VALUE in the case of a text entry. More explicit statements of which aspect of G3 are being tested are preferable. For example, depending on the context, one may require the ISBLANK, ISNUMBER or ISTEXT functions, perhaps in combination with AND, OR or NOT.

Using full expressions, such as:

$$= \text{IF}(\text{AND}(\text{G10} = 1,\ \text{F10} = 0), 1,\ 0)$$

is arguably clearer than:

$$= \text{AND}(\text{G10} = 1,\ \text{F10} = 0)$$

for the same reason (i.e. that the consequence of results of the test are being made explicit).

Further, the fact that short-form functions often return TRUE or FALSE can lead to modelling errors:

- Many modellers may interpret the returns values as text fields, and in subsequent formula write expressions such as:

$$=\text{IF}(\text{B3}=\text{“TRUE”},\ldots.)$$

- Although such return statements are generally treated (by Excel) as if they were 0 or 1, this is not always the case. Figure 9.9 shows an example in which the pure SUMPRODUCT function does not evaluate as one might expect when its inputs are the results of short-form logic (with Cell C14 containing the value 0). To create the correct calculations, one needs to implement a modification as shown in Cell C15. However, the need to perform such modification is easy to overlook, and it also creates a more complex formula.

Text Versus Numerical Fields

As noted above, it is generally preferable to ensure that formulae in Excel evaluate to a numerical value where possible. Such a principle helps to ensure that subsequent (dependent) calculations are robust and correct. For example, a function that could be written to return the text field "TRUE" should generally rather return a 1 (and similarly for "FALSE" returning a 0). This is in addition to the points noted above (where the use of a 1 is generally preferable to the TRUE that is output by some short-form functions). Also related to this is that it is generally preferable to use the =NA() function rather than the text field "N" (or similar) in the relevant circumstances (see Chapter 22 for more details).

SUMIFS with One Criterion

For the SUMIF and AVERAGEIF functions, the range to be summed or averaged is the last parameter, whereas the range in which the condition is to be checked is the

	A	B	C	D
1				
2		Values	Include	Formula
3		1	TRUE	=B3<5
4		2	TRUE	=B4<5
5		3	TRUE	=B5<5
6		4	TRUE	=B6<5
7		5	FALSE	=B7<5
8		6	FALSE	=B8<5
9		7	FALSE	=B9<5
10		8	FALSE	=B10<5
11		9	FALSE	=B11<5
12		10	FALSE	=B12<5
13				
14			0	=SUMPRODUCT(B3:B12,C3:C12)
15			10	=SUMPRODUCT(B3:B12,C3:C12*1)

FIGURE 9.9 The SUMPRODUCT Function When Using Short-form Logic

first parameter. This is in contrast to SUMIFS and AVERAGEIFS, where the range to be summed or averaged is the first argument, with the criteria being the latter (and optional) ranges. Thus, even when a SUMIF or AVERAGEIF formula is required (i.e. with only one condition to check), often it is better to instead use a SUMIFS or AVERAGEIFS: such an approach allows additional criteria to be easily added if necessary, or for the formulae to be more easily copied or used in other formulae.

By contrast, the COUNTIF functions can be directly transformed into a COUNTIFS function if an additional criterion needs to be added. However, for the sake of a consistent approach, one may argue always to use COUNTIFS even where COUNTIF would suffice.

Including Only Specific Items in a Summation

In some cases, one may not yet know which items should be included in a final calculation. For example, one may need to choose a subset of people to form a team, whilst respecting some constraint on the total budget that is determined by adding the compensation of each person who is in the selected team. Possible desired teams can be explored by trial and error until one is found which can deliver the project whilst meeting the budget constraint.

The file Ch9.3.FlexSUM.xlsx contains an example. Figure 9.10 shows an approach which one sees frequently, in which the cost of a "trial team" has been formed by linking to direct cell references (Sheet1 in the file).

	A	B	C	D	E
1					
2			Name	Total Comp	
3			Amelia	39477	
4			Olivia	51607	
5			Emily	36457	
6			Ava	41536	
7			Isla	60284	
8			Jessica	51366	
9			Poppy	32527	
10			Isabella	84495	
11			Sophie	15000	
12			Mia	67321	
13			Ruby	15000	
14			Lily	39672	
15			Grace	87395	
16			Evie	79219	
17			Sophia	36099	
18			Ella	70585	
19			Scarlett	79436	
20			Chloe	44954	
21			Isabelle	56400	
22			Freya	45169	
23					
24			Total	1034000	=SUM(D3:D22)
25					
26					
27			Sub-Group/Team	428733	=D3+D6+D7+D10+D12+D16+D21

FIGURE 9.10 Direct Cell Reference Approach

It will no doubt be clear to many readers that a more transparent and flexible approach is to use a flag field (Column B) to explicitly define and identify the inclusion or not of someone within the team, and then to use a function to calculate the total cost of this team (Sheet2 in the file). Figure 9.11 shows that the calculation of team cost can then be achieved by using the SUMIFS function or the DSUM Database function (discussed in Chapter 26). This approach could also be the basis for the employment of optimisation techniques or tools (for example, those that find the optimum combination of 1s or 0s to achieve the objective at minimum cost).

AGGREGATE and SUBTOTAL Versus Individual Functions

The SUBTOTAL and AGGREGATE functions (see Chapter 17) have a wide variety of options, and to some extent could always be used in place of the underlying functions (for example, using AGGREGATE instead of SUM, COUNT or AVERAGE). However, such generalised approaches are often more cumbersome for a user to understand and audit; it would typically be necessary to check which function number and options are being used in a specific case (as most modellers would not remember these details).

	A	B	C	D	E
1					
2		**Incl?**	**Name**	**Total Comp**	
3		1	Amelia	39477	
4		0	Olivia	51607	
5		0	Emily	36457	
6		1	Ava	41536	
7		1	Isla	60284	
8		0	Jessica	51366	
9		0	Poppy	32527	
10		1	Isabella	84495	
11		0	Sophie	15000	
12		1	Mia	67321	
13		0	Ruby	15000	
14		0	Lily	39672	
15		0	Grace	87395	
16		1	Evie	79219	
17		0	Sophia	36099	
18		0	Ella	70585	
19		0	Scarlett	79436	
20		0	Chloe	44954	
21		1	Isabelle	56400	
22		0	Freya	45169	
23					
24			**Total**	**1034000**	=SUM(D3:D22)
25					
26			**Sub-Group/Team**		
27		1	With SUMIFS	**428733**	=SUMIFS(D3:D22,B3:B22,B27)
28					
29		Incl?	With DSUM	**428733**	=DSUM(B2:D22,D2,B29:B30)
30		1			
31					

FIGURE 9.11 Flexible Identifier Approach

Therefore, unless their use provides a unique capability (or some form of flexibility that is not available with the underlying functions), it would typically make sense to use the more specific (not generalised) function.

Cases where the generalised functions may be considered as appropriate include:

- The possibility to exclude error values from the calculations (when using AGGREGATE).
- The ability to rapidly change from one type of calculation to another (e.g. from SUM to AVERAGE or COUNT) by changing a single function argument.
- The potential to use the Wizard for the SUBTOTAL function (in order to place the function at the end of each change in the category identifier).

Array Functions or VBA User-defined Functions?

Often, there is a choice as to whether to use an (Excel) array function or a VBA user-defined function. Where such calculations return a value to a single cell (not to an array of cells), and essentially involve working with tabular data "behind the scenes", either approach is generally possible. For example, the calculation of the semi-deviation of a data set can be conducted as an array function (see Chapter 18), or as a user-defined function (see Chapter 33). Similar dual approaches could be used for some other calculations, such as of the statistical moments when frequencies are known, and the rank order correlation between two data sets (also shown in Chapter 33).

The choice between the two approaches can be finely balanced in some cases. Whilst one may wish to avoid using VBA unless it is truly necessary (or already used elsewhere in the model), array functions are more cumbersome to work with and often less flexible. For example, if the range of cells that drives the function is altered in size, it is typically slightly harder to alter the range references for an array function than it is for a user-defined function (where one can be sure – if correctly written – that each range is referred to only once).

Volatile Functions

A Volatile function is one whose value is updated at every recalculation of Excel, even when the values of its arguments have not changed. For reasons of computational efficiency, most Excel functions update only when their argument values change (i.e. they are not Volatile).

The main Volatile functions are NOW, TODAY, RAND, OFFSET, INDIRECT, CELL and INFO.

The use of Volatile functions slows down each recalculation (especially if many are used), so generally they should be used only to provide a unique functionality that cannot be replicated by other (non-Volatile) functions:

- OFFSET and INDIRECT should be favoured only when they are used to create flexible ranges or references. Where this is not necessary, other functions (such as INDEX or CHOOSE) may be sufficient (see Chapter 25).
- The ADDRESS function may be chosen in preference to the CELL function in some cases.

Effective Choice of Lookup Functions

The effective use and selection of lookup functions is a very important aspect of building flexible, transparent and efficient models. The key points are covered in detail in Chapter 25; here, we provide only a summary for consolidation purposes:

- Lookup functions should generally be considered whenever there would otherwise be logical functions embedded within others, especially embedded IF functions.
- VLOOKUP and HLOOKUP should generally be avoided, with the INDEX/MATCH combination (or perhaps LOOKUP) used instead. The reasons for this are discussed in detail in Chapter 25, but briefly include: flexibility (e.g. placement of data ranges and the ability to move parts of a range), robustness (avoiding hard-coded row or column numbers, avoiding two-dimensional ranges), auditing (reducing size of precedents and dependent ranges) and computational efficiency (avoiding repetition of multiple identical implicit matching processes, size of model due to audit paths).
- Since the SUMIF or SUMIFS functions can be used to form the conditional sum of all items in a list, they can also be used to find the value of a single item in a list that has some property. However, lookup functions should generally be used for such purposes, as they are more transparent and effective in this context.
- Where a logical statement has only two outcomes, the selection between using IF or CHOOSE may not be clear-cut: it would seem to make sense to use IF when the logical part is a result of a general branching, and to use the CHOOSE if the role of the branching process corresponds to an explicit decision that would be made.
- When building scenario input data, CHOOSE would be used for data sets which may need to be moved around (cut and paste), whereas INDEX would be used for cases where the data will always be only in a contiguous range.
- OFFSET and INDIRECT can be used to create flexible ranges and references, but as Volatile functions, they are computationally inefficient, and so should be used only where their unique functionality is employed.

CHAPTER 10

Dealing with Circularity

INTRODUCTION

This chapter discusses the issue of dealing with circularities. We make a distinction between circularities that arise as an inherent property of the real-life situation and those resulting from the presence of circular formulae within an implemented model (also called circular references). We discuss the potential advantages and disadvantages of using circular formulae, ways to deal with circular logic and methods to (where desired) retain the inherent circularity in the logic of a real-life situation whilst avoiding any circular formulae in the model.

THE DRIVERS AND NATURE OF CIRCULARITIES

This section discusses the fundamental distinction between circularities that are an inherent property of the real-life situation and those resulting from the way that formulae are implemented in Excel.

Circular (Equilibrium or Self-regulating) Inherent Logic

Many real-life situations can be described using mathematical equations. Often, such equations express some form of equilibrium or self-regulation within a system. For example, the heat generated by a thermostatically controlled radiator depends on the difference between the current room temperature and the target level. At the same time, the room temperature will be affected by (depend on) the new heat generated by the radiator. Similarly, in economics, "circular" logic may arise as a statement of some form of equilibrium within the system being modelled, characterised by the presence of a variable(s) on both sides of some equation(s).

In financial modelling contexts, examples of circular logic include:

- The bonus of senior management could depend on the net income of the company, which is itself calculated net of bonus expense. Written as formulae, one has:

$$\text{Bonus} = \text{Bonus\%.Net Income}$$

$$\text{Net Income} = \text{Net Profit Before Bonus} - \text{Bonus}$$

(For simplicity of presentation, we ignore tax; i.e. the bonus may generally be subtracted from pre-tax income.)

- The interest rate at which a company may be able to borrow will depend on the risk that the debt principal and the periodic interest payments may not be able to be met. If the interest-coverage ratio (operating profit divided by interest payment) is used as a measure of this risk, a circularity in logic is created: an increase in the assumed borrowed amount would lead to higher interest charges, a reduced coverage ratio, and hence tend to reduce the amount able to be borrowed (that was just increased). Similarly, for projects financed partially with debt, the debt capacity will depend on the ability to repay the debt, which is linked to the post-tax (and post interest) cash flows, and hence to the level of debt.
- The discount rate used to determine the value of a company (when using the discounted cash flow approach) depends on the company's debt-equity ratio (or debt-to-value ratio). However, a value determined from this approach may initially be inconsistent with the ratios assumed to determine the discount rate, for example if debt levels are regarded as fixed, so that the equity value is a residual that depends on the valuation, meaning that the new implied debt-equity ratio may not be the same as the one that was assumed to derive the value in the first place. The theoretically correct valuation is found only if all assumptions are consistent with each other, which requires an equilibrium (or circular) logic.
- A tax authority may exercise a wealth tax on individuals depending on their net worth, but the net worth is calculated after deducting the wealth taxes.

Circular Formulae (Circular References)

Circular references arise when the calculations to evaluate an Excel cell (or range) involve formulae whose value depends on the same cell or range. This may often occur through a sequence of cell references or formulae, in which the first depends on the last. Such circularities may be intentional or unintentional:

- Unintentional circularities generally result from a mistake or oversight when creating formulae, most often where a model is poorly structured, or has an unclear logical flow (e.g. does not follow the left-to-right and top-to-bottom principle, or uses multiple worksheets with complex linkages between them). A simple example would be if, in Cell B6, a formula such as "=SUM(B4:B6)" had been used in place of "=SUM(B4:B5)", so that the value in B6 refers to itself.
- Intentional circular references. In principle, these are used to reflect a circular (or equilibrium) logic that is present in the real-life situation. For example:
  - Models corresponding to any of the situations described above (i.e. management bonus, cost of debt, debt capacity, cash flow valuation, wealth tax) could potentially be implemented in ways that deliberately contain circular references.

- When calculating period-end cash balances (based on operating income and interest earned during a period), the interest earned within a period may depend on the average cash balance during that period (multiplied by the interest rate). This creates a circular reference, since the average cash balance requires the final balance to be known. In terms of equations, one has:

$$\text{Cend} = \text{Cbeg} + \text{Cop} + \text{IntRate}.(\text{Cbeg} + \text{Cend})/2$$

where Cend is the closing balance, Cbeg is the starting balance, Cop is the non-interest cash inflow and IntRate is the interest rate; the circularity is visible due to the presence of Cend on both sides of the equation.

Generic Types of Circularities

By considering possible combinations of circular logic and circular formulae, one may consider four categories of intentional modelling situations:

- NCL/NCF: No circular logic and no circular formulae. This is the situation for many traditional models: the underlying situation does not require circular logic, and the models also do not contain such logic (apart from unintended errors).
- CL/NCF: Circular logic but no circular formulae. This is where the underlying situation contains a circularity in its logic, but the model ignores this, usually for reasons of simplicity (of implementation) or transparency. Many traditional models fall into this category, such as corporate valuation models, which often ignore circular logic relating to the cost of debt.
- CL/CF: Circular logic and circular formulae. This is where circular formulae are implemented in the model to capture circularity (equilibrium) in the underlying situation. For example, the approach could be used in the contexts cited earlier.
- NCL/CF: No circular logic but circular formulae. Although this category would apparently not exist (except when unintentional circularities arise by mistake), there are cases where the original real-life situation may not be fully circular, but a slight modification to the assumed reality creates circular logic. In fact, the interest calculation described above may be considered to be such a case, since interest is usually not truly paid based on the average balance in a period, but perhaps on interim cash balances at various times throughout a period (so that the assumption that it depends on average balances is a modification to the specification of the reality, that is subsequently captured in the model). In other words, this category is effectively a CL/CF form of this modified reality.

RESOLVING CIRCULAR FORMULAE

In this section, we cover the key methods to deal with potential circular references:

- Correcting the formulae when the circularity results from a mistake or typing error.
- Ignoring the logical circularity, i.e. creating a model which provides only an approximation to, or modification of, the original situation, and in which there is no circularity within the formulae.

- Algebraic manipulation. This involves writing the equations that create the circularity as mathematical formulae, and manipulating them in order to isolate or solve for the (otherwise circular) variables on one side of an equation only. This implicitly retains the equilibrium logic that created the original circularity.
- Using iterative methods, with the aim of finding a stable set of calculations, in which all items are consistent with each other. In practice, this can be achieved by implementing one of several approaches:
  - Excel's in-built iterative calculation method, in a model with circular formulae.
  - Iterating a "broken" circular path using a VBA macro (or manually conducted copy-and-paste operations).

Correcting Mistakes that Result in Circular Formulae

Clearly, circular formulae that have been implemented by mistake should be removed or corrected. This should be done as soon as they are detected, because it is generally complex to audit completed models to find how the circularity arises: since there is no starting point for a circularity, the tracing of precedents and dependent can become time-consuming and frustrating. It may be that one will need to delete formulae on the circular path and rebuild the model in some way, as an interim step to find and correct the circularity.

Avoiding a Logical Circularity by Modifying the Model Specification

In some cases, a real-life situation may contain circular logic, but it may be possible to ignore this, yet build a model whose accuracy is regarded as sufficient. For example, many corporate valuation models simply ignore the circular logic relating to the discount rate and to the cost of debt. Similarly, for the example concerning ending cash balances, one could eliminate the circularity by assuming that interest is earned on the opening cash balance only:

$$\text{Cend} = \text{Cbeg} + \text{Cop} + \text{IntRate.Cbeg}$$

This approach is simple to implement in practice, but may not be sufficiently accurate in some cases. An improvement in accuracy can be achieved by introducing more sophistication and complexity, in which interest is earned on the total of the opening balance plus the average non-interest cash inflow:

$$\text{Cend} = \text{Cbeg} + \text{Cop} + \text{IntRate.(Cbeg} + \text{Cop)/2}$$

Of course, a reformulation will alter the value of some calculations and outputs, which may or may not be acceptable according to the context. For example, the calculation of the bonus based on pre-bonus income (rather than on post-bonus or net income) would eliminate the circularity. However, the presentation of a result in which the bonus is inconsistent with the final net income figure may not be acceptable or credible (especially since it is a figure which may attract particular attention; an inconsistency in less visible figures may be acceptable).

Eliminating Circular Formulae by Using Algebraic (Mathematical) Manipulation

From a purely mathematical perspective, a formula containing a circularity such as:

$$B6 = 1 + (1/10).B6$$

can be rearranged to give:

$$(9/10).B6 = 1$$

and then solved:

$$B6 = 10/9$$

Similarly, in the bonus example:

$$\text{Bonus} = \text{Bonus\%.Net Income}$$

i.e. Bonus = Bonus%.(Net Profit Before Bonus – Bonus)
i.e. Bonus.(1 + Bonus%) = Bonus%.Net Profit Before Bonus
i.e. Bonus = Bonus%.Net Profit Before Bonus/(1 + Bonus%)
and Net Income = Net Profit Before Bonus – Bonus.

Thus, by using the last two formulae in order, the circular references have been eliminated, whilst the underlying circularity of the logic has been retained.

In the calculation of ending cash balances, the circular equation:

$$\text{Cend} = \text{Cbeg} + \text{Cop} + \text{IntRate.(Cbeg} + \text{CEnd)}/2$$

can be re-written to isolate Cend on the left-hand side:

$$\text{Cend.}(1 - \text{IntRate}/2) = \text{Cbeg.}(1 + \text{IntRate}/2) + \text{Cop}$$

i.e. $\text{Cend} = \left(\text{Cbeg} * \left(1 + \text{IntRate}/2\right) + \text{Cop}\right) / \left(1 - \text{IntRate}/2\right)$.

Using the last formula, the ending cash balance can be calculated directly from the starting balance, the interest rate and the non-interest cash flow without creating a circularity. Once Cend is calculated, the interest income can be calculated (also without creating a circularity) as:

$$\text{Interest Income} = \text{IntRate.(Cbeg} + \text{Cend)}/2.$$

Note that when using the algebraic approach, the order of the calculation of the items can be counter-intuitive. For example, using the equations above the bonus is calculated by using the pre-bonus income, and the net income calculated once the bonus is known (which contrasts to the description and formulae at the beginning of the chapter, which defined bonus as a quantity that is determined from net income).

Similarly, in the interest calculations, using the formula from algebraic manipulation, the value of Cend is calculated before the interest income, and the interest income is calculated from CEnd, which is counter to the logic that the interest income drives the value of CEnd (or that CEnd depends on interest income).

Resolving a Circularity Using Iterative Methods

The role of a variable that is present on both sides of an equation can often be determined by an iterative solution method (whether working in Excel or more generally). This means that one starts with a trial value (such as zero) for a variable, and this is substituted into one side of the equation (and where the other side is the isolated value of this same variable). For example, with:

$$B6 = 1 + (1/10) * B6$$

using an initial value of B6 as zero on the right-hand side, the process results in the sequence 0, 1, 1.1, 1.11, 1.111. This shows that where a single and stable correct figure exists (i.e. 10/9); iterative methods generally converge very quickly to this.

In theory, an iterative sequence could be explicitly replicated in Excel by building multiple copies of a model, in which the first is populated with trial values, and the outputs of this are used to provide inputs to the second copy, and so on. For example, Figure 10.1 shows the bonus calculations (using a bonus level of 5% of net income). The net income (Cell D5) is determined after subtracting the bonus (Cell D4) from the pre-bonus income figure, and the bonus (Cell D4) itself depends on the net income (Cell D5), thus creating a circular reference. Note that when the circular formula is entered for the first time the result may evaluate to zero (Cell D4). At this point, the figures are not consistent, i.e. the bonus figure as shown is equal to 0% (not 5%) of the net income.

In Figure 10.2, we illustrate the iterative process that uses a sequence of models, where the output of each is an input to the next. The values in Row 4 (cells D4:I4) and Row 5 (cells D5:I5) rapidly converge to stable figures that are consistent with each other.

Of course, it is generally not practical to build multiple copies of a model in this way. Rather, iterative methods within the same model are required. There are several possible approaches to doing this, which are discussed in the next section.

	A	B	C	D	E
1					
2			Assumptions	Values	
3		PAT: Pre-Bonus		1000	(Assumed calculated from earlier in model)
4		Bonus (% of net income)	5.0%	0	=C4*D5
5		**Net Income**		**1000**	=D3-D4

FIGURE 10.1 Example of a Circular Reference Arising from Implementing Equilibrium Logic

	Assumptions	0	1	2	3	4	5	
PAT: Pre-Bonus		1000	1000	1000	1000	1000	1000	=H3
Bonus (% of net income)	5.0%	0	50	47.5	47.6	47.6	47.6	=$C4*H5
Net Income		**1000**	**950**	**953**	**952**	**952**	**952**	=I3-I4

FIGURE 10.2 Illustrative Iterative Process by Using Multiple Copies of a Model

ITERATIVE METHODS IN PRACTICE

In practice, iterative methods (for item(s) on a circular path) take the value of a variable at some cell, and calculate the dependent formulae in the circular path, until the original cell has been recalculated, and then the process repeats. This is rather like substituting the value into the "later" parts of the model, until such later parts (due to the circularity) meet the original cell. The general expectation is that the values that are calculated will settle (or "converge") to stable values which are consistent with each other.

This section discusses three key approaches to the implementation of iterative methods within an Excel model:

- Using Excel's default iterative calculation.
- Using manual iterations of a broken circular path.
- Automating the iterations of a broken circular path using a VBA macro.

Excel's Iterative Method

In the presence of a circular reference, Excel does not have the capability to manipulate the equations or find a correct algebraic solution. Rather, it will use its in-built iterative calculation method, in which the value of a variable at some point on the circular path is used in all dependent formulae, until the original point is reached, giving rise to a new updated value of that variable. This updated value is then used to recalculate the dependent items again, and so on.

The file Ch10.1.BonusCircRef.xlsx contains the bonus model with a circular reference. Figure 10.3 shows the model after applying Excel's iterations (producing results that are the same as in the explicit multi-model approach shown earlier).

	Assumptions	Values	
PAT: Pre-Bonus		1000	(Assumed calculated from earlier in model)
Bonus (% of net income)	5.0%	47.6	=C4*D5
Net Income		**952.4**	=D3-D4

Sheet1

Ready Calculate

FIGURE 10.3 Results of Allowing Excel to Iterate the Bonus Model Which Contains Circular References

The general presence of a circular reference will be signalled with a "Calculate" message on Excel's Status Bar (as can been seen toward the bottom of Figure 10.3). Further, the Calculation Option settings (under File/Options/Formulas) will have an effect according to the selected option:

- If (the default) Enable Iterative Calculation is switched on:
  - On (the default) Automatic calculation method:
    - No circular reference warning message will appear when the formula is created.
    - The model will directly iterate. The values that result will depend on the number of iterations and the maximum change conditions (that are defined within the calculation options, e.g. the default is to allow 100 iterations).
    - The Status Bar will show (using "Calculate") that there is a circularity present.
    - Each further use of the F9 key will result in further iterations being conducted. The model's values will change only if the earlier iterative process has not converged.
  - On the Manual recalculation method:
    - No circular reference warning message will appear when a formula containing a circular reference is first created.
    - The formula will evaluate a single time (i.e. to a context-specific, generally non-zero, value), but it will not iterate beyond this.
    - The Status Bar will show (using "Calculate") that there is a circularity present.
    - The use of the F9 key will result in the model performing iterative calculations (with the values that result depending both on the number of iterations and on the maximum change conditions defined in the calculation settings).
    - Each further use of the F9 key will result in further iterations being conducted. The model's values will change only if the iterative process has not converged.
- If Enable Iterative Calculation is switched off:
  - On the Automatic calculation method:
    - A circular reference warning message will appear when a formula containing a circular reference is first created.
    - The formula will evaluate to zero when created or re-entered.
    - The Status Bar will explicitly state the presence of a circular reference and indicate the address of one of the cells on the circular path.
    - The Excel worksheet will highlight the circularity with precedence and dependence arrows.
    - The use of the F9 key will have no further effect on the values in the model, since iterative calculation is switched off, so that the circularity cannot be attempted to be resolved.
  - On the Manual recalculation method:
    - No circular reference warning message will appear when a formula containing a circular reference is first created.
    - The formula will evaluate a single time (i.e. to a context-specific, generally non-zero, value), although the whole model will not evaluate.
    - The Status Bar will show that there is a circularity present, but these will not be immediately highlighted with explicit cell references in the Status Bar, nor with precedence and dependence arrows in the Excel worksheet.
    - The use of the F9 key will result in a message warning that there is a circular reference. At this point, the Status Bar will also explicitly state the presence of

a circular reference and indicate the address of one of the cells on the circular path. The Excel worksheet will highlight the circularity with precedence and dependence arrows. However, there will be no effect on the values in the model, since iterative calculation is switched off, so that the circularity cannot be resolved.

It is also worth noting that since Excel's default settings (i.e. when first installed) are typically the Automatic and Iterative calculation options (by default), the only indication of a possible circular reference is the presence of "Calculate" in the Status Bar. However, such a message can appear for other reasons (most notably when Excel detects that a model that is set on Manual calculation needs to be recalculated, for example due to a change in the input values used). Thus, the detection of a possible circular reference (e.g. as part of a model auditing process) will need to be done as a deliberate step.

Fortunately, it is simple to detect the presence of a circular reference: by switching off Iterative calculation, a circular reference warning will be displayed, the Status Bar will show the address of a cell on the circular path, and the dependence and precedence arrows appearing in the Excel worksheet. (In Automatic calculation, these will directly appear, whereas in Manual calculation, one will need to press the F9 key for this information to appear.)

Creating a Broken Circular Path: Key Steps

An alternative to using Excel's iterations is to "break" the circular path within the model. This is done by:

- Modifying the model to isolate in a single cell (or in a dedicated range) the value of one variable or calculation that is on the circular path.
- Adding a new cell (or range), whose role is to represent the same variable, but which contains only numbers. The new range may initially be populated with any values (such as zero).
- Relinking the formulae that depend on the original variable, so that they instead depend on the new range. This would need to be done for each formula that is dependent on the original precedent chosen, which is why it is ideal to find or create a precedent with a single dependent if possible. There would then be no more circularity, but there would be two ranges which represent the same variable: the new range (containing pure numbers) and the original range (containing calculated values). Unless the values are the same, the circularity has not been fully resolved.
- Iterate: this means recalculating the model (e.g. pressing F9) and copying the updated values (at each iteration) of the original field into the field containing only numerical values. This can be repeated until the values in each field have converged to the same figure (or the difference between them becomes very small).

The file Ch10.2.Bonus.Iterations.Manual.xlsx contains an implementation of this within the earlier bonus example (see Figure 10.4). Note the process that would have been required if one had started with the model shown in Figure 10.3: first, one would identify that Cell D4 and D5 (in Figure 10.3) are on the circular path, and that D4 has a single dependent. Second, a new range is added (i.e. Row 5 in Figure 10.4). Third, the formulae that are dependent on Cell D4 (i.e. Cell D6 in Figure 10.4, corresponding to

	A	B	C	D	E
1					
2		**Step 1**	**Assumptions**	**Values**	
3		PAT: Pre-Bonus		1000	
4		Bonus (% of net income): Calculated	5.0%	50	=C4*D6
5		Bonus (% of net income): Pasted Values		0	
6		**Net Income**		**=D3-D5**	=D3-D5

FIGURE 10.4 Creating a Broken Circular Path

Cell D5 in Figure 10.3) are relinked to depend on Cell D5. Fourth, when the model is recalculated, the values of net income (Cell D6) and the calculated bonus (Cell D4) are both updated, as they depend on the values in the new range (Cell D5), rather than on themselves (as was the case with the original circularity). Since the new range (Cell D5) contains only values, there is no longer a circularity.

Whilst the process of adapting a model in this way may seem complex at first, in fact it is easy and straightforward to implement if the model is structured in this way as it is being built.

Repeatedly Iterating a Broken Circular Path Manually and Using a VBA Macro

As noted earlier, when iterative processes are convergent, typically only a few iterations are required in order to have stable values. This means that the iterative process can be implemented in several ways:

- Manually pasting the values of the calculated bonus field (Cell D4) into the new bonus value field (Cell D5), ensuring that one recalculates the model after the paste, and repeating this process until one observes sufficient convergence between the figures.
- Implementing a VBA macro to repeatedly assign the values from D4 into D5, also ensuring that the model recalculates each time (repeating this until sufficient convergence has been achieved, which may be checked automatically by the VBA code).

For example, Figure 10.5 shows the result of conducting a single (manual) paste of the values of B4 onto B5 and letting the model recalculate once, whilst Figure 10.6

	A	B	C	D	E
1					
2			**Assumptions**	**Values**	
3		PAT: Pre-Bonus		1000	
4		Bonus (% of net income): Calculated	5.0%	47.5	=C4*D6
5		Bonus (% of net income): Pasted Values		50.0	
6		**Net Income**		**950**	=D3-D5

FIGURE 10.5 Results After One Paste of the Broken Circular Path Approach

	A	B	C	D	E
1					
2			Assumptions	Values	
3		PAT: Pre-Bonus		1000	
4		Bonus (% of net income): Calculated	5.0%	47.6	=C4*D6
5		Bonus (% of net income): Pasted Values		47.5	
6		**Net Income**		**953**	=D3-D5

FIGURE 10.6 Results After Two Pastes of the Broken Circular Path Approach

shows the results of doing this an additional time. Unsurprisingly, the sequence of results produced is the same as that shown for the first steps in Figure 10.2 (i.e. to the values 0, 50, 47.5. . . , as shown in cells D4, E4 and F4).

Of course, the manual approach may be sufficient for very simple models which are to be used in only basic ways. However, in practice there are several advantages to using a VBA macro:

- It reduces the chance of an error, especially when repeatedly pasting multi-cell ranges.
- It saves time, since the pressing of a button to run a macro will be quicker than repeatedly copying and pasting ranges, and checking for convergence.
- One is less likely to forget to update the model by recalculating the circularity (indeed, the macro could be automatically run though a workbook open or change procedure, as discussed in Part VI).
- It is easier to run sensitivity analysis, since one can integrate the circular reference macro within a single larger macro (see Chapter 14). The manual procedure would be very cumbersome, as several copy-and-paste procedures would be required each time that an input value is changed.

In Part VI, we describe a simple macro to assign values from one range into another (rather than using copy/paste) which is very straightforward. For example, a code line such as:

```
Range("BonusValue").Value = Range("BonusCalc").Value
```

will perform the assignment (where the Cell D4 has been given the range name `BonusCalc` and D5 the name `BonusValue`).

Of course, a recalculation is required after every assignment statement to ensure that the values are updated. Thus, a simple macro that would perform the assignment and recalculate the model several times (here: 10) could be:

```
Sub MRResolveCirc()
For i = 1 To 10
Range("BonusValue").Value = Range("BonusCalc").Value
Application.Calculate
Next i
End Sub
```

The file Ch10.3.CircRef.BasicMacro.xlsm contains the above macro, and a text-box button has been assigned to run it (see Figure 10.7).

	A	B	C	D	E	F	G
1							
2			Assumptions	Values			
3		PAT: Pre-Bonus		1000			
4		Bonus (% of net income): Calculated	5.0%	47.6		Resolve Circularity	
5		Bonus (% of net income): Pasted Values		47.6			
6		Net Income		952.4			

FIGURE 10.7 Resolving a Broken Circular Path Using a Macro

Note that it would be straightforward to add more capability and sophistication, such as using a preset tolerance figure (e.g. 0.00001) and iterating until the difference between the two figures is less than this tolerance, whilst allowing a higher maximum number of iterations if not:

```
Sub MRResolveCirc2()
NitsMax = 100 'Set Max no. of iterations
Tol = 0.00001 'Set tolerance
icount = 0

Do While VBA.Abs(Range("BonusValue).Value - Range("BonusCalc").
Value) >= Tol
 icount = icount + 1
 If icount <= NitsMax Then
  Range("BonusValue").Value = Range("BonusCalc").Value
  Application.Calculate
 Else
 Exit Sub
 End If
Loop
```

Further, one may display messages to the user if the circularity has not been resolved after a specific number of iterations, as well as error-handling procedures, and so on.

PRACTICAL EXAMPLE

In this section, we show each method within the context of a practical example. We assume that one wishes to forecast a final cash balance based on a starting balance, some non-interest cash flow and interest earned. We discuss the main five possible approaches, as covered earlier:

- Calculating interest income based on average cash balances. This creates a circular logic that may be implemented either with:
  - Circular references, resolved using Excel iterations.
  - Circular references, resolved using a VBA macro.
  - Elimination of the circular references using algebraic manipulation.
- Calculating interest income based on cash balances which exclude non-interest income, thus modifying the model (and its results) to eliminate both the circular logic and the circular references:
  - Using starting cash balances only to calculate interest income.

- Using starting balances and non-interest-related cash flows to calculate interest income, thus providing additional accuracy (since the results should be closer to those obtained using circular logic than if only starting cash balances were used).

Using Excel Iterations to Resolve Circular References

The file Ch10.4.1.CircRef.Res.xlsx contains a model in which interest income (Row 5) is calculated by referring to the average of the starting and ending cash balances. Figure 10.8 shows the results after using Excel iterations until the figures are stable.

Using a Macro to Resolve a Broken Circular Path

The file Ch10.4.2.CircRef.Res.xlsm contains the model with the same underlying logic (interest earned depending on average cash balances), in which a macro is used to resolve a broken circular path (see Figure 10.9). Row 7 contains the pure-values range, so that the macro (at each iteration) copies (assigns) the values from Row 6 into Row 7, until the absolute sum of the differences between the cells in Row 6 and Row 7 (calculated in Cell C8) is within the tolerance level (that is embedded within the macro).

	A	B	C	D	E	F	G	H
1								
2		**Circularity**		1	2	3		
3		Cash Flow						
4		Operating Cash Flows		100	100	100		
5		Interest Income	3.0%	3.05	6.18	9.42	=$C5*AVERAGE(F9,F11)	
6		Total Cash Flow		103.05	106.18	109.42		
7								
8		Cash Balance						
9		Starting		50.000	153.05	259.23	=E11	
10		Increase		103.05	106.18	109.42	=F6	
11		**End**	50	**153.05**	**259.23**	**368.65**	=F9+F10	

FIGURE 10.8 Using Excel's Iterative Process in a Model with Circular References

	A	B	C	D	E	F	G	H	I	J
1										
2		**Circular logic resolved using macro**		1	2	3				
3		Cash Flow						Run One Iteration		
4		Operating Cash Flows		100	100	100				
5		Interest Income	3.0%	3.05	6.18	9.42	=$C5*AVERAGE(F11,F13)			
6		Total Cash Flow Calc		103.05	106.18	109.42	=F4+F5			
7		Total Cash Flow Values		103.05	106.18	109.42		Resolve Fully		
8		*Difference (absolute terms)*	*0.00*	*0.00*	*0.00*	*0.00*				
9										
10		Cash Balance						Named Ranges used in Macros:		
11		Starting		50.00	153.05	259.23	=E13	MaxDifference	=Sheet1!$C$8	
12		Increase		103.05	106.18	109.42	=F7	TCFFormulae	=Sheet1!$D$6:$F$6	
13		**End**	50	**153.05**	**259.23**	**368.65**	=F11+F12	TCFValues	=Sheet1!$D$7:$F$7	

FIGURE 10.9 Using a Macro to Resolve Circular References

Algebraic Manipulation: Elimination of Circular References

The file Ch10.4.3.CircRef.Res.xlsx contains a model in which the formulae (derived earlier in the chapter) resulting from algebraic manipulation are used (see Figure 10.10). Note that, as well as containing no circular references (although the underlying logic remains circular), the order of the calculations is different to those in the original model: the ending cash balance is calculated before the interest income is known, with interest income calculated using the average period cash balance.

Altered Model 1: No Circularity in Logic or in Formulae

An alternative approach is to reformulate the model (and implicitly its specification, in the sense of the assumed or approximated behaviour of the real-world situation), so that there is no circularity of any form.

The file Ch10.4.4.CircRef.Res.xlsx contains the case in which interest income is determined from starting cash balances only. This removes the circularity, as interest earned no longer depends on ending cash balances (see Figure 10.11). Note that the values of the ending cash balances are different to the above examples in which circularity was retained.

	A	B	C	D	E	F	G	H	I
1									
2		**Algebraic Manipulation: No circularity**		1	2	3			
3		Cash Flow							
4		Operating Cash Flows		100	100	100			
5		Interest Income	3.0%	3.05	6.18	9.42	=$C5*AVERAGE(F9,F11)		
6		Total Cash Flow		103.05	106.18	109.42			
7									
8		Cash Balance							
9		Starting		50.000	153.05	259.23	=E11		
10		Increase		103.05	106.18	109.42	=F6		
11		**End**	50	**153.05**	**259.23**	**368.65**	=(F9*(1+$C5/2)+F4)/(1-$C5/2)		

FIGURE 10.10 Using Algebraic Manipulation to Eliminate Circular References

	A	B	C	D	E	F	G
1							
2		**Altered Model 1: No circularity**		1	2	3	
3		Cash Flow					
4		Operating Cash Flows		100	100	100	
5		Interest Income	3.0%	1.50	4.55	7.68	=$C5*F9
6		Total Cash Flow		101.50	104.55	107.68	
7							
8		Cash Balance					
9		Starting		50.000	151.50	256.05	=E11
10		Increase		101.50	104.55	107.68	=F6
11		**End**	50	**151.50**	**256.05**	**363.73**	=F9+F10

FIGURE 10.11 Altering the Model to Eliminate Circularity Using Starting Balances

Altered Model 2: No Circularity in Logic in Formulae

Another approach to reformulate the model would be to calculate interest income from starting cash balances as well as from all other (non-interest) cash sources. This would also eliminate the circularity, whilst potentially giving results that are closer to those that would be obtained if the circularity were retained.

The file Ch10.4.5.CircRef.Res.xlsx contains such a model (see Figure 10.12). Note that the values of the ending cash balances are much closer to those in the earlier examples which used circularity.

Note that in this example, the only non-interest cash flow is the single line for the operating income. In a larger model, one may wish to include all non-interest cash items (including capital investment, dividends or financing cash flows). Doing so can be a little cumbersome in practice, because one needs to create a partially complete cash flow statement, which includes all non-interest-related cash items. Sometimes a convenient compromise is to include only the major cash flow items in such a statement, where the identity of the larger items can be known in advance.

SELECTION OF APPROACH TO DEALING WITH CIRCULARITIES: KEY CRITERIA

When faced with a situation in which there is a potential for circular references, one has a choice as to which approach to use, not only in terms of their incorporation into a model, but also in the methods used to resolve them. This section discusses some key issues to consider when making such a choice.

Currently, there seems to be very little consensus or standardisation around whether and/or how to use circularities:

- Some modellers take the view that circular references should be avoided at all costs.
- Some modellers (especially some practitioners of financial statement modelling and of project finance modelling) seem to place significant value on retaining circular references in the calculations, typically for the sake of accuracy and consistency.

	A	B	C	D	E	F	G	H
1								
2		**Altered Model 2: No circularity**		1	2	3		
3		Cash Flow						
4		Operating Cash Flows		100	100	100		
5		Interest Income	3.0%	3.00	6.09	9.27	=$C5*(F9+F4/2)	
6		Total Cash Flow		103.00	106.09	109.27		
7								
8		Cash Balance						
9		Starting		50.000	153.00	259.09	=E11	
10		Increase		103.00	106.09	109.27	=F6	
11		**End**	50	**153.00**	**259.09**	**368.36**	=F9+F10	

FIGURE 10.12 Altering the Model to Eliminate Circularity Using Starting Balances and Interim Non-interest Cash Flows

- Some modellers prefer to ignore the circular logic of a situation when building models, including many valuation practitioners, as mentioned earlier in the chapter.

Although the reasons to use (or to avoid) circularities are often not addressed explicitly, there is surely some underlying rationale for many of these views, which manifests itself differently according to the context, and the modeller's experience, capabilities and biases. Indeed, there are several issues to consider when selecting an approach to deal with potential circularities:

- The accuracy and validity of the underlying logic.
- The complexity and lack of transparency of the model.
- The potential for errors due to iterative processes to not converge to a stable figure, but to diverge or float in ways that may not be evident.
- The risk of destroying calculations by the propagation of non-numerical errors along the circular path, without any easy possibility to correct them.
- The possibility that macros may be poorly written, not robust, or contain errors (especially when written by modellers with insufficient experience with VBA).
- That mistakes may be made when performing algebraic manipulation, resulting in incorrect calculations.
- That calculation speed may be compromised.
- That sensitivity analysis may be more cumbersome to conduct that in models without circularity.

These issues are discussed in detail in the remainder of the text.

Model Accuracy and Validity

Where a real-life situation involves circular (equilibrium) logic, it would seem sensible to capture this. On the other hand, although the economic concept of equilibrium is widely accepted, the notion of "circular reasoning" is generally regarded with suspicion. Thus, in some cases, one may be willing to reduce accuracy in order to retain more confidence:

- Where there is a strong need for the calculations to be as accurate as possible, and (internally) consistent, one may essentially be obliged to accept that circular logic is required. For example, typically in project finance modelling, the debt covenants or other contractual aspects may be set with reference to the figures in a model. Similarly, in the earlier bonus example, if the bonus net income figures are not consistent, then these may not be credible and are technically also wrong. In such cases, one's options are either to use algebraic manipulation (where possible) or to use iterative methods with Excel or VBA.
- Where the requirements for accuracy or consistency may be less strict, or circular logic may be distrusted *per se*, it may be sufficient (or preferable) to ignore the circular logic. The reduced accuracy may be acceptable either because the results are not materially affecting (e.g. in most interest calculations when this is only a small part of the overall cash flow) and/or simply because ignoring the circularity has become standard practice in a specific context (as is the case in some valuation work).

Note that in principle, the use of algebraic manipulation provides the best of both worlds: retaining the implicit circular logic whilst not having circular formulae. Unfortunately, there are some limitations and potential drawbacks:

- In practice, it can be used only in a limited set of specific and simple situations. Many real-life modelling situations typically contain calculations that are too complex (or impossible) to be manipulated algebraically. For example, even the relatively minor change of introducing multiple interest rates (that apply depending on the cash balance) would mean that manipulations similar to those shown earlier are no longer possible (due to the presence of IF or MIN/MAX statements in the equations).
- Even where appropriate manipulations are possible, there is generally no easy way to know if a mistake has been made when doing so. To check the results of implementing the manipulated formulae with those that would be achieved if the original formulae had been used, one would have to implement both (and the original formulae would then contain circular references which would need to be resolved by an iterative method).
- Users of a model who are not familiar with the approach may find it hard to understand. Not only would they not be explicitly aware of the underlying algebraic manipulation (unless it is made very clear in the model documentation or comments), but also the corresponding Excel formulae are generally less clear. Further, the order of the calculations is sometimes also not intuitive and confusing (e.g. ending cash balances calculated before the interest income).

Complexity and Transparency

Models with circular references are hard and time-consuming to audit (and even more so in multi-sheet models). The circular dependency path literally leads one to moving in circles when trying to understand the formulae and check their accuracy; after trying to follow the logic along a calculation path, one eventually simply returns to where one started, often without having gained any new useful information! In addition, some users may be insufficiently familiar with, and distrust, iterative processes *per se*. Finally, the potential requirement to use macros to run iterative processes can lead to further unwillingness to consider the use of circularity.

In terms of implications for choice of method, this suggests that:

- The use of circular formulae should be avoided whenever possible.
- Where circular logic (without circular formulae) is desired to be retained:
  - The use of a "broken" circular path (combined with a macro to conduct the required iterations) can be an appropriate way to retain the circular/equilibrium logic (and hence the accuracy of the model) whilst having clear dependency paths (with definite start and end points).
  - The use of algebraic manipulation (where available) is not necessarily more transparent (nor less complex) than the use of a broken circular path, since users who are not familiar with (or capable of understanding) the mathematical manipulations may find the model harder to follow.
- The use of alternative modelling approaches may overcome any complexity associated with the need to use iterative processes. However, the complexity

of the model will not be significantly reduced, since the alternative model and the broken-path model would be of similar transparency and complexity in principle. The disadvantage of using an alternative modelling approach is the reduced accuracy compared to if a broken circular path (or circular formulae) were used.

Non-convergent Circularities

The use of iterative methods can have negative consequences for the robustness of a model, and the extent to which the displayed results are meaningful and converge to the correct values.

In fact, whilst the general expectation when using iterative processes is that they will converge, this will not necessarily be the case. In fact, iterative processes may be either:

- Convergent
- Divergent
- Floating.

For example, we noted earlier that an iterative process applied to a formula such as:

$$B6 = 1 + (1/10).B6$$

converged after only a few iterations (to the true figure of 10/9).

On the other hand, whilst it is clear that the formula

$$B6 = 1 + 2.B6$$

has the true (mathematical) solution B6=–1, an iterative method (using an initial value of zero) would produce the rapidly divergent sequence: 0, 1, 3, 7, 15, 31, 63, 127, 255, 511, 1023. . . .

In fact, just as iterative processes converge quickly (where they are convergent), they also diverge quite quickly (where they are divergent). Thus, the presence of divergent circularities will typically be evident, unless only very few iterations are used.

The file Ch10.5.1.CircRef.Res.xlsx contains an example of the earlier interest-calculation model in which there is a circular reference. For ease of presentation, the file contains a second copy of the model (see Figure 10.13). In the second copy, the interest rate has been set to 200% (Cell C16). At this or any higher value, the iterative process will diverge. Since (in Excel) the number of iterations is 100 by default, the numbers shown are large, but not yet very large. Each pressing of F9 results in 100 additional iterations, so that the figures become progressively larger.

Such divergent behaviour (when the interest rate is 200% or higher) results from the circularity in the logic (not just the specific model, as implemented here): the interested reader can verify that the divergence will occur (or errors or incorrect results produced), whether a macro is used to iterate, or whether algebraic manipulation is used. The alternative models (in which interest earned is not linked to ending cash balances) do not have these properties.

	A	B	C	D	E	F	G	H
1								
2		Circularity		1	2	3		
3		Cash Flow						
4		Operating Cash Flows		100	100	100		
5		Interest Income	3.0%	3.05	6.18	9.42	=$C5*AVERAGE(F9,F11)	
6		Total Cash Flow		103.05	106.18	109.42		
7								
8		Cash Balance						
9		Starting		50.000	153.05	259.23	=E11	
10		Increase		103.05	106.18	109.42	=F6	
11		End	50	153.05	259.23	368.65	=F9+F10	
12								
13		Circularity		1	2	3		
14		Cash Flow						
15		Operating Cash Flows		100	100	100		
16		Interest Income	200.0%	20000.00	1980400.00	127518800.00	=$C16*AVERAGE(F20,F22)	
17		Total Cash Flow		20100.00	1980500.00	127518900.00		
18								
19		Cash Balance						
20		Starting		50.000	19950.00	1960650.00	=E22	
21		Increase		20100.00	1980500.00	127518900.00	=F17	
22		End	50	20150.00	2000450.00	129479550.00	=F20+F21	

FIGURE 10.13 Example of a Divergent Circular Reference

Circularities that are neither divergent nor convergent can exist; we call these "floating circularities". For example, whereas the equations:

$$x = y + 10$$
$$y = -x$$

have the solution $x = 5$, $y = -5$, an iterative process applied to the Excel cells with the formulae:

$$\text{E3} = \text{D3} + 10$$
$$\text{D3} = -\text{E3}$$

will produce a sequence of floating values for D3 and E3, i.e. they cycle through a set of values, without ever converging or diverging. The values will depend on the number of iterations used and on the assumed or implied starting values (of say D3) at the first iteration (i.e. which point in the cycle one looks at).

The file Ch10.6.1.CirRef.Floating.xlsx contains an example. The file is set to Manual recalculation, with iterative calculation on, and set to only one iteration (thus, each pressing of F9 will result in a single iteration). Figure 10.14 shows the results

	A	B	C	D	E
1					
2		Model	Constant	Calc 1	Calc 2
3			10	-1	9
4				=-E3	=C3+D3

FIGURE 10.14 The Result of One Iteration with a Floating Circularity

of conducting one iteration, Figure 10.15 shows the result of conducting two, and Figure 10.16 shows the result of conducting three. The floating nature of the circularity can be seen as the values in Figure 10.16 are the same values as those in Figure 10.14, whilst those in Figure 10.15 are different.

The non-convergent nature of the calculations (and the different results that are possible) can be seen in more detail from the lower part of the file, shown in Figure 10.17. This shows the explicit iterative steps, from an assumed value of D3 at the beginning of the iterative process (Cell D7). The user can verify that the sequence generated is different if an alternative starting value is used.

Floating circularities can arise in subtle ways, for reasons that may not be immediately apparent. For example, one may start with a calculation of all future cash sources, uses and cash balances, with the forecast showing that future balances are always positive, as shown in Figure 10.18. One may then to decide to add an additional draw-down line item, in which, at the beginning of the project, the minimum future cash balance is withdrawn (e.g. so that this cash can immediately be used for other purposes). In other words, Cell C3 is replaced by a formula which calculates the (negative of) the minimum of the range D4:H4 (see Figure 10.19, which shows both models for simplicity). This will create a "floating" circularity: as soon as cash is drawn down, the future minimum balance becomes zero, so that no future cash can be drawn down, which then resets the future minimum cash balance to a positive number, so that cash can be drawn down after all, and so on.

Floating circularities are arguably the most dangerous type:

- Since they do not diverge, the values shown may look reasonable. However, the values are not stable, and depend on the number of iterations used.
- Their cause is often subtle, so one may not be conditioned to be aware of their possible presence.
- Their presence may be overlooked, especially if intentional (convergent) circularities are also used. The main risk is that a floating circular reference will unintentionally be introduced, yet the modeller (or user) is likely to ignore any circular reference warning messages in Excel (because a circular reference was used intentionally).

	A	B	C	D	E
1					
2		Model	Constant	Calc 1	Calc 2
3			10	-9	1
4				=-E3	=C3+D3

FIGURE 10.15 The Result of Two Iterations with a Floating Circularity

	A	B	C	D	E
1					
2		Model	Constant	Calc 1	Calc 2
3			10	-1	9
4				=-E3	=C3+D3

FIGURE 10.16 The Result of Three Iterations with a Floating Circularity

	A	B	C	D	E
1					
2		Model	Constant	Calc 1	Calc 2
3			10	-1	9
4				=-E3	=C3+D3
5					
6		Iteration Number	Value of C3	Value of D3 using D3=-E3	Value of E3 using E3=C3+D3
7		0	10	-1	9
8		1	10	-9	1
9		2	10	-1	9
10		3	10	-9	1
11		4	10	-1	9
12		5	10	-9	1
13		6	10	-1	9
14		7	10	-9	1
15					

FIGURE 10.17 The Values of Each Item at Each Iteration with a Floating Circularity

	A	B	C	D	E	F	G	H	I	J
1										
2			0	1	2	3	4	5		Column C:
3		Cash flow	0	10	10	10	10	10		#N/A
4		Cumulative Cash	0	10	20	30	40	50		=C3
5			=C3	=C4+D3	=D4+E3	=E4+F3	=F4+G3	=G4+H3		

FIGURE 10.18 Initial Forecast Model

	A	B	C	D	E	F	G	H	I	J
1										
2			0	1	2	3	4	5		Column C:
3		Cash flow	0	10	10	10	10	10		#N/A
4		Cumulative Cash	0	10	20	30	40	50		=C3
5			=C3	=C4+D3	=D4+E3	=E4+F3	=F4+G3	=G4+H3		
6										
7			0	1	2	3	4	5		Column C:
8		Cash flow	2	10	10	10	10	10		=-MIN(D9:H9)
9		Cumulative Cash	2	12	22	32	42	52		=C8
10			=C8	=C9+D8	=D9+E8	=E9+F8	=F9+G8	=G9+H8		

FIGURE 10.19 Modified Forecast Model with a Floating Circularity

The main implication is that, if using Excel's iterative method, there is a risk that inadvertent floating circularities may be introduced inadvertently or be hidden by other intentional circularities. To avoid this, in principle, Excel's iterative method should not be used.

Potential for Broken Formulae

In models with circular formulae, errors may propagate along the circular path, without any easy mechanism to correct them. This can cause significant problems: in the best case, one would have to revert to a prior saved version of the file. In the worst case, one may have inadvertently saved the model with such errors in (or such errors are only propagated at the recalculation that may take place automatically when a file is saved), with the result that the model is essentially destroyed and may have to be rebuilt.

The issue arises because once a non-numerical error value (such as #DIV/0!) is introduced onto the circular path, then the iterative process will propagate it. However, if the error is corrected at only one cell on the path, the iterative process will not generally be able to recover, because some of the other cells on the path will contain non-numerical errors, so that the iterative calculation process (which requires pure numerical values as inputs) simply cannot be conducted.

Figure 10.20 shows the earlier circular calculation of interest earned (i.e. depending on average cash balances), in which the periodic interest rate had been set to 250% and the model iterated several times. Since the circularity is divergent, eventually the #NUM! error appears on cells along the circular path.

Figure 10.21 shows the result of replacing the 250% interest rate to a periodic rate of 3%, and iterating the calculations several times. One can see that the formulae on the circular path are not corrected.

In Figure 10.22, we show that even when the formulae are re-entered across Row 5, and the iterations conducted, the model remains broken. The same is true if formulae are entered in Row 6 or Row 10.

	A	B	C	D	E	F	G	H
1								
2		Circularity		1	2	3		
3		Cash Flow						
4		Operating Cash Flows		100	100	100		
5		Interest Income	250.0%	#NUM!	#NUM!	#NUM!	=$C5*AVERAGE(F9,F11)	
6		Total Cash Flow		#NUM!	#NUM!	#NUM!		
7								
8		Cash Balance						
9		Starting		50.000	#NUM!	#NUM!	=E11	
10		Increase		#NUM!	#NUM!	#NUM!	=F6	
11		End	50	#NUM!	#NUM!	#NUM!	=F9+F10	
12								

FIGURE 10.20 Initial Error Propagation due to a Divergent Circularity

	A	B	C	D	E	F	G	H
1								
2		Circularity		1	2	3		
3		Cash Flow						
4		Operating Cash Flows		100	100	100		
5		Interest Income	3.0%	#NUM!	#NUM!	#NUM!	=$C5*AVERAGE(F9,F11)	
6		Total Cash Flow		#NUM!	#NUM!	#NUM!		
7								
8		Cash Balance						
9		Starting		50.000	#NUM!	#NUM!	=E11	
10		Increase		#NUM!	#NUM!	#NUM!	=F6	
11		End	50	#NUM!	#NUM!	#NUM!	=F9+F10	
12								

FIGURE 10.21 Errors Remaining After Correction of the Cause of the Divergent Circularity

	A	B	C	D	E	F	G	H
1								
2		Circularity		1	2	3		
3		Cash Flow						
4		Operating Cash Flows		100	100	100		
5		Interest Income	3.0%	#NUM!	#NUM!	#NUM!	=$C5*AVERAGE(F9,F11)	
6		Total Cash Flow		#NUM!	#NUM!	#NUM!		
7								
8		Cash Balance						
9		Starting		50.00	#NUM!	#NUM!	=E11	
10		Increase		#NUM!	#NUM!	#NUM!	=F6	
11		End	50	#NUM!	#NUM!	#NUM!	=F9+F10	

FIGURE 10.22 Errors Remaining After Partial Rebuild of Model Formulae

In fact, only in the case in which the formulae are entered all the way to Row 11, are the formulae re-established, and then only in the first column (see Figure 10.23). Thus, to recover the model, one would need rebuild it at Row 11, progressing from left to right, one cell at a time (by re-entering the formula in each cell and then iterating or recalculating the model).

Many practical models (which are mostly larger and often do not have a strict left-to-right flow) would be essentially impossible to rebuild in this way; therefore, the potential arises to essentially destroy the model.

Note that such a problem is much simpler to deal with in a model that has been built with a broken circular path: when an error such as the above arises, the pure-values field that is used to break the circular path will be populated with the error value (e.g. #NUM!). These can be overwritten (with zero for example), in addition to correcting the input value that caused the error or divergence. Since there is no circularity in the formulae, once the contents of the values field are reset from the error value to any numerical value, the dependent formulae can all be calculated and reiterated without difficulty.

Figure 10.24 shows the earlier model with a broken circular path, iterated to the point at which the #NUM! errors occur, and Figure 10.25 shows the result of correcting in model input (periodic interest, in Cell C5), overwriting the #NUM! errors in Row 7 with zeros, and performing the iterations.

The main implication is that the use of a broken circular path is preferable to the use of Excel iterations, if one is to avoid the potential to destroy models or create significant rework.

	A	B	C	D	E	F	G	H
1								
2		Circularity		1	2	3		
3		Cash Flow						
4		Operating Cash Flows		100	100	100		
5		Interest Income	3.0%	3.05	#NUM!	#NUM!	=$C5*AVERAGE(F9,F11)	
6		Total Cash Flow		103.05	#NUM!	#NUM!		
7								
8		Cash Balance						
9		Starting		50.00	153.05	#NUM!	=E11	
10		Increase		103.05	#NUM!	#NUM!	=F6	
11		End	50	153.05	#NUM!	#NUM!	=F9+F10	

FIGURE 10.23 Successful Rebuild of One Column of the Model

	A	B	C	D	E	F	G	H	I	J
1										
2		Circular logic resolved using macro		1	2	3				
3		Cash Flow						Run One Iteration		
4		Operating Cash Flows		100	100	100				
5		Interest Income	250.0%	#NUM!	#NUM!	#NUM!	=$C$5*AVERAGE(F11,F13)			
6		Total Cash Flow Calc		#NUM!	#NUM!	#NUM!	=F4+F5			
7		Total Cash Flow Values		#NUM!	#NUM!	#NUM!		Resolve Fully		
8		*Difference (absolute terms)*	*#NUM!*	*#NUM!*	*#NUM!*	*#NUM!*				
9										
10		Cash Balance						Named Ranges used in Macros:		
11		Starting		50.00	#NUM!	#NUM!	=E13	MaxDifference	=Sheet1!$C$8	
12		Increase		#NUM!	#NUM!	#NUM!	=F7	TCFFormulae	=Sheet1!$D$6:$F$6	
13		End	50	#NUM!	#NUM!	#NUM!	=F11+F12	TCFValues	=Sheet1!$D$7:$F$7	

FIGURE 10.24 Errors in a Model with a Broken Circular Path

	A	B	C	D	E	F	G	H	I	J
1										
2		Circular logic resolved using macro		1	2	3				
3		Cash Flow						Run One Iteration		
4		Operating Cash Flows		100	100	100				
5		Interest Income	3.0%	3.05	6.18	9.42	=$C$5*AVERAGE(F11,F13)			
6		Total Cash Flow Calc		103.05	106.18	109.42	=F4+F5			
7		Total Cash Flow Values		103.05	106.18	109.42		Resolve Fully		
8		*Difference (absolute terms)*	*0.00*	*0.00*	*0.00*	*0.00*				
9										
10		Cash Balance						Named Ranges used in Macros:		
11		Starting		50.00	153.05	259.23	=E13	MaxDifference	=Sheet1!$C$8	
12		Increase		103.05	106.18	109.42	=F7	TCFFormulae	=Sheet1!$D$6:$F$6	
13		End	50	153.05	259.23	368.65	=F11+F12	TCFValues	=Sheet1!$D$7:$F$7	

FIGURE 10.25 Simple Process to Correct Errors in a Model with a Broken Circular Path

Calculation Speed

Since each iteration is a recalculation, the use of iterative processes will result in longer calculation times in similar models in which iterations are not necessary (i.e. one without circular formulae). Further, it is likely that in general, Excel iterations would be quicker than the use of a VBA macro, simply because Excel's internal calculation engine is highly optimised (and hence difficult for a general programmer to surpass in performance).

The main implication is that, from the perspective of speed, circular formulae are less efficient (so that algebraic manipulation or modified models without circular formulae would be preferred), and that, where circular formulae are required, the use of VBA macros is generally slightly less computationally efficient than the use of Excel's iterations.

Ease of Sensitivity Analysis

For models in which there is a dynamic chain of calculations between the input and outputs (whether involving circular formulae or not), Excel's DataTable sensitivity feature can be powerful (see Chapter 12). The introduction of a macro to resolve circular references will inhibit the use of this, meaning that macros would also be required to conduct sensitivity analysis in this case (see Chapter 14).

The main implication is that, from the perspective of conducting sensitivity analysis, the use of broken circular paths is more cumbersome than the use of the other methods.

Conclusions

The overall conclusions of the discussion in this section are:

Where there is circular logic that is inherent in a situation, one should consider whether it is genuinely necessary to capture this within the model (for accuracy, presentation or consistency purposes), or whether an alternative sufficiently accurate approach (which has no circular logic) can be found. In such a case, the models can be built using standard techniques (i.e. without requiring macros or iterative methods), with such models calculating quickly and allowing for standard sensitivity analysis techniques to be employed. Clearly, where this is possible, it should be the preferred approach.

Where it is necessary to capture the effect of circular logic within the model, several methods can be considered:

- Algebraic manipulation. This will avoid any circular formulae, whilst nevertheless creating a model that captures the circular logic. The model will not require iterative methods, will calculate efficiently, and allow for sensitivity analysis to be conducted (using Excel DataTables). Disadvantages include the very small number of cases where it is possible to do the required manipulations, the possibility of mistakes made during the manipulation (since to check the result would require implementing an alternative model which contains circular references), and that the transparency of the model may be slightly reduced (since the manipulations may not be clear to some users, and the order of the calculation of some items is changed and may not be intuitive).
- Excel iterations. This allows the retention of sensitivity analysis using DataTables and is more computationally efficient than using macros to iterate the circularity. The most significant disadvantages include:
  - The difficulty in auditing the model.
  - The potential for a floating circularity to not be detected, so that the model's values may be incorrect.
  - The potential to damage the model and to have to conduct significant rework.
  - The process by which Excel handles iterations may not be clear to a user, as it is neither transparent nor very explicit.
- Breaking the circularity and iterating. The advantages of this are significant, and include:
  - The model is easier to audit, as there is a (standard) dependency route (with a beginning and an end).
  - One is in explicit control of the circularity, so that inadvertent (floating) circular references (which may create incorrect model values) are easy to detect, because any indications by Excel that a circular reference is present will be a sign of a mistake in the formulae.
  - The process to correct a model after the occurrence of error values is much simpler.
- The main disadvantages compared to the use of Excel's iterative method include the need to write a macro, the slightly more cumbersome process to run a sensitivity analysis, and a slightly reduced computational efficiency.

In the author's view, the overall preference should be to avoid circularity by model reformulation if possible (where accuracy can be slightly compromised), then to explore possible algebraic approaches, and otherwise to use a macro to resolve a broken circular path. Excel's iterative method should essentially not be used.

CHAPTER 11

Model Review, Auditing and Validation

INTRODUCTION

This chapter discusses model auditing and related areas. Generally speaking, the context is that one is dealing with a model that has been built by someone else. The chapter aims to provide a structure to the definitions of possible objectives, outputs and activities of such processes.

OBJECTIVES

In model review contexts, it can useful to consider three generic types of objectives and outputs. These are presented in this section (as the author's definitions, which are not generally agreed standards).

(Pure) Audit

This involves the documentation of aspects of the model, without changing it, nor passing any direct judgement on it. The typical output is a description, including items relating to:

- Structural characteristics. These include noting the number of worksheets, the presence of links to other workbooks, and the visibility, accessibility and protection of worksheets, columns, rows or ranges.
- Layout and flow. These could include the location of input cells, the extent to which the audit paths are short or not, whether there are circular references (or circular logic) and so on. It may also be worth noting whether the outputs are clearly identifiable, and whether there is any in-built sensitivity analysis (such as using DataTables). The extent to which calculations flow between worksheets can also be noted.
- Formulae and functions. Here, one may note the functions used, the number of unique formulae, and the consistency of formulae when used in contiguous ranges (e.g. as one moves across a row), and whether formulae are implemented in accordance with best practice principles (e.g. no mixed formulae, multiple embedded

functions, the types of lookup functions used, and so on). It is also important to note whether there are named ranges, as well as the nature of their use (whether in formulae, for navigation or in VBA code).

- Whether VBA code, macros or user-defined functions are used (and whether the code is accessible or the VBA module is password-protected).
- The presence of other objects, such as PivotTables, Charts, Data Filters and Comments.
- The nature of the formatting used, such as general cell formatting, borders, italics, Conditional and Custom Formatting. One may also note whether there are merged cells, or many blank rows and columns.
- The type of calculations conducted, and (where there is no formal model specification) one may develop possible hypothesis about objective of model and its decision-support role.
- Whether there are input restrictions, such as ranges using Data Validation.
- Other contextual conditions, such as calculation settings, the author, the date of last modification.
- Whether other Excel add-ins are required to run the model.
- Possibilities to improve the model's calculations, transparency, user-friendliness, flexibility or efficiency (that would require restructuring to implement).

Note that the process (in its pure form) does not make any judgement about the validity, strengths and weaknesses of a model, does not attempt to judge its suitability to support a decision, and does not implement any improvements nor corrections. As such, the value-added created by a pure audit may often be quite limited.

Validation

Validation involves two core elements:

- The determination of whether the model is in conformance with its specification, in terms of adequately representing the real-life situation, and that it captures the decision-support requirements adequately (including flexibilities and sensitivities), and so on. Essentially, this corresponds to the first step within the process shown in Figure 1.1.
- The verification that the model's implementation as captured through the formulae and so on is correct (the second step in Figure 1.1),

In principle, a model that has been validated should be appropriate for decision support, including allowing sensitivity analysis to be conducted. However, in practice, a model which calculates correctly and which also allows for sensitivity analysis to be run, may nevertheless not be optimised from a presentational or flexibility perspective, may not be sufficiently transparent, and may not follow other general best practice principles.

Further, a genuine validation is often hindered by the fact that (in many practical situations) no sufficiently precise explicit specification has been documented. Thus, rather than being genuinely "(externally) validated", often only a more limited set of activities can be conducted, in which one looks for errors or inconsistencies, but the model largely "self-validates", i.e. its formulae and labels become an implicit specification.

Improvement, Restructuring or Rebuild

This involves conducting activities to restructure or rebuild the model to improve it, to make it match a specification more closely, to improve transparency, increase flexibility, improve its use in decision support and generally to capture best practices, as described earlier in the text.

In fact, in the author's experience, in Excel modelling contexts, it is usually this activity where there is the highest potential to create value-added (compared to pure auditing or validation activities): first, perhaps paradoxically, model review activities are often initiated in cases where a model has not been built according to best practice principles, and a user or decision-maker has found it to be complex to understand or follow (e.g. due to inappropriate data structures, poor flow, formatting and formulae etc.). Second, the detection of errors, general model testing and the running of sensitivities are time-consuming (and may not be fully possible) in a model that has been built badly. Third, once errors or mistakes are found, it becomes very difficult (essentially impossible) to check for other errors without first correcting the model (due to interactions between the errors); for example, one may hypothesise that most of a complex set of calculations is correct, yet the results shown are incorrect, due to a known error. If this error remains uncorrected, it often becomes difficult to test the formulae to detect a second error. Thus, it is often more beneficial to improve a model (after which auditing or validation of this improved model becomes much easier or largely unnecessary).

The basic objective of restructuring is to create a model which follows best practice principles, is transparent and is easier to test and validate than the original model.

Without wishing to repeat the earlier discussion of best practices, some of the key elements to do this include:

- To use appropriate workbook, worksheets and data structures.
- To reduce the number of worksheets to that which is genuinely required.
- To create a logic flow which follows a vertical (top-to-bottom) or horizontal (left-to-right) flow of logic as far as possible (not a diagonal flow), and where the total length of main audit paths is as short as possible subject to this.
- To create a clear layout, and use appropriate formatting to highlight key structural aspects. Often, the use of formatting is the single most effective way to rapidly improve transparency, because it is relatively simple to implement. (Formatting can also be a useful work-organisation tool, to act as a record to highlight any areas of the model that are not immediately changed or corrected, but which require further once other aspects of the model have been checked; such highlighting would use a separate colour to other aspects of the model, and be removed once the process is complete.) More generally, it will be necessary to move parts of the model from one area to the next.
- To ensure that it is easy to conduct relevant sensitivity analyses, for example by elimination of mixed input-calculation cells, and more generally to be able to easily test the model or run likely scenarios.
- To correct formulae, and/or make them more transparent, robust or efficient. Of course, if the original model's calculations are correct, then the two models (original and rebuilt) will produce the same results, even though they may have quite different structures and formulae. More often, one may identify and correct mistakes, at which point the results of the two models will differ.

- To reduce duplicate calculations. When consolidating calculations together that have otherwise been in separate parts of a model, one often finds repetitions that can be eliminated.

Of course, in practice the amount of effort that is worthwhile to invest in such restructuring will depend on the context and objectives.

PROCESSES, TOOLS AND TECHNIQUES

Where a model has been built in conformance with best practice principles, the process required to conduct an audit or to validate the implementation should generally be relatively straightforward. These processes can be much more complex if best practice principles were not followed.

In any case, when doing so, some specific process and techniques are worth following:

- Avoiding unintentional changes.
- Developing a general overview of the model.
- Generating a detailed understanding of the logic flow, including of the inputs and outputs.
- Testing and checking the formulae, and for items that may lead to unexpected or inadvertent errors.

In fact, when restructuring a model, similar processes may be followed, at least in the early stages. For example, when moving formulae around within a model, or consolidating calculations from several worksheets, one may wish to ensure that no changes to the calculated values arise. Only later in the process (as formulae are being corrected) may some changes in the calculated values be acceptable.

Avoiding Unintentional Changes

To avoid unintentional changes, the following principles apply:

- Work with a copy of the model.
- Do not update linked values when opening the model. Where there are links to other workbooks, further work will generally be required to ensure that a robust procedure is used to update them (such as the use of mirror sheets, as discussed earlier); in some cases, it may even be appropriate to integrate the linked workbooks into a single one.
- Do not run any macros (or press any buttons that might run macros), until one has established what they have done.
- Do not insert rows or columns until one has established whether this can be done without causing errors. Cases where rows or columns cannot be robustly inserted without further research include:
  - Where multi-cell range names are used (see Chapter 7).
  - Where lookup functions are used (especially those which involve two-dimensional ranges, mostly notably if the column or number driving the lookup process in a VLOOKUP or HLOOKUP function has been hard-coded).
  - Where a macro refers to a cell reference rather than to a named range.

- Save the work regularly as a new file (e.g. with a numbering sequence), in order to create a rapid recovery trail if one observes that unexpected or incorrect behaviours after changes have been made.
- Use cut and paste (rather than copy and paste) to retain the cell references when formulae or ranges are moved. However, ranges should not be moved until one has checked that this can be done without error. For example, the moving of parts of the range that is referred to by functions which can take range inputs (SUM, MAX, MIN, OR, AND, VLOOKUP, and many others) can be problematic. One may have to rebuild the equivalent calculations using other approaches before some parts of the ranges can be moved. For example, a SUM function may need to be replaced by its individual components, or a VLOOKUP by several INDEX/MATCH combinations. Similarly, an OR function that refers to a multi-cell contiguous range may instead be re-written to refer to individual cells.
- Document any changes that are made. For example, in some cases it may be appropriate to use in-cell comments, such as if a formula in a cell or range has been altered. Generally, one should record any other notes (on errors, potential errors, or changes made) within a separate document (such as a Word file), and to do this (i.e. record each item) in parallel with the work on the model (not afterwards). In this way, a natural by-product of the process is ready-made documentation about the original model and changes made.
- Use the methods to track the new and original values, discussed later in this section.

Developing a General Overview and Then Understanding the Details

The first main part of a review process is to gain a general overview of the model (whilst avoiding making unintentional changes, as discussed above). The main aim is to generate a broad understanding, similar to a pure audit. Once an overview has been established, it will generally be necessary to generate a very detailed understanding, especially of the logic and its flow. In a sense, this latter step is simply an extension of the first step, using similar tools and techniques, but with a more detailed focus.

Typical tools and techniques to assist in gaining a general overview include:

- Reading any documentation about the model's objectives, uses, limitations, techniques used within it, how it can be modified, and so on.
- Inspecting for protected or hidden worksheets or ranges (e.g. using the Review tab, right-clicking on a sheet tab). For example, if under Review there is an option to Unprotect Workbook, then it is possible that there are hidden worksheets which may only be accessible with a password. Clearly it is necessary to make these worksheets visible to create a full understanding of the model, especially if any formulae in the visible part of the model refer to cells in these hidden worksheets.
- Inspecting the model for macros (in a simple case, by opening the Visual Basic Editor); it is possible that a file with an xlsm extension does not contain macros, just as one with an xls extension may. One would also wish to check whether the VBA code is fully accessible or has been password-protected. Where accessible, a brief scan as to the quality and likely functionality of the code is worthwhile.
- Unfreezing any frozen panes (on the View tab).

- Inspecting the formulae to identify the types of functions and formulae used, whether there are mixed formulae, embedded functions, lookup functions, other advanced Excel functions, and so on. The use of Formulas/Show Formulas is a very quick way to get an overview of this, including observing the consistency of formulae in contiguous cells.
- Checking for circular references. By switching off Iterative calculation, a circular reference warning will be displayed, the Status Bar will show the address of a cell on the circular path, and the dependence and precedence arrows appearing in the Excel worksheet. (In Automatic calculation, these will directly appear, whereas in Manual calculation, one will need to press the F9 key for this information to appear.) Of course, where circular references are resolved using a broken path, their presence will not be detected. Typically, such models will use a macro (as discussed in Chapter 10), which can be detected as part of the macro inspection process (the presence of named ranges, with names such as MyRangeCalculated and MyRangePasted, are also an indicator of the likely presence of such logical circularities). In rare cases, the requirement to resolve circular references by manual methods as part of the modelling process would be subtle to detect.
- Checking for the use of named ranges (using the Name Manager).
- Checking for links to other workbooks. A warning about links will appear when a workbook is opened that has links to another workbook. In the first instance, such links should not be updated before an inspection of them has taken place. Data/Edit Links can be used to list the source workbooks. Links that use direct cell references have syntax such as "=[Source.xlsx]Sheet1!$D$18", and hence their location in the destination workbook can be found by searching for "[", using the Find menu (the Options sub-menu in the "Look in" box can be used to set the search area to Formulas, to avoid finding the square bracket within text labels). Where links are created through the use of named ranges, the syntax does not involve "[", being of the form "=Source.xlsx!DataToExport". Thus, one may additionally search for fields such as ".xlsx!", ".xlsm!" and ".xls!" to find further possible links.
- Conducting visual inspection about the overall structure and layout, such as the number of worksheets, and an initial assessment of the extent of the flow of calculation across sheets, the extent to which the audit paths are short, and so on (the conducting of a detailed assessment of the logic typically makes more sense only after a general overview of the whole model has been established).
- Checking for the use of multi-sheet ("three-dimensional") formulae (as described in Chapter 6), which may create inadvertent errors if sheets are added, deleted or moved.
- Identifying the inputs and their general location and assessing whether the inputs and outputs (rather than just the calculations) are clear, and whether any sensitivity analysis or other results summaries have been built in.
- Checking of some contextual conditions, such as calculation settings, the author, the date of last modification.
- Checking for the presence of objects such as PivotTables, Charts, Data Filters and Comments, and reviewing these briefly.
- Where there is no formal model specification or the documentation provided about the model is insufficient, one may develop a possible hypothesis about the objectives of the model and its decision-support role by considering the type of calculations conducted and the labels used.

- One may also identify areas where the model could be improved, especially if model restructuring activities may be needed or are desired. General areas for potential improvement could include: optimisation of the workbook structure, worksheet structure and data structures, improvements to the flow, format, transparency, modifying the functions used, correcting or improving formulae, including automated scenario and sensitivity techniques, replacing the Excel iterative method with a macro, increasing computational efficiency, and so on.

Once a general understanding has been created, a more detailed analysis of the calculations and logical flow will generally be necessary. In this respect, some tools are of particular importance (which may also be required at the more general overview stage, albeit used with less intensity and frequency):

- Following the forward and backward paths from a specific cell using the Formulas/Trace Precedents and Formulas/Trace Dependents toolbar. This has several uses:
  - Following the general logic and calculations in the model.
  - Identifying possible outputs, where this is not otherwise clear. The end-point of a sequence of forward-tracing paths should generally correspond to an output (or potential output), and the beginning to an input. Of course, not all such end points may be relevant outputs, and some intermediate calculations could also be relevant outputs, so some judgment is still likely to be required.
- Note some specific techniques to save time:
  - Double-clicking on a tracing line will allow the paths to be followed (backwards and forwards, by double-clicking on the same line again) and across worksheets.
  - Using the short-cuts Ctrl+[and Ctrl+] to go to a cell's direct precedents or dependents can save significant time.
- Using the drop-down menu under Home/Find & Select to select cells (or other objects) which meet various criteria, such as:
  - Constants (which are generally inputs to the model).
  - Ranges containing Conditional Formatting or using Data/Validation. (Ranges which contain Conditional Formatting can also be found using Home/Conditional Formatting/Manage Rule, selecting Show formatting rules for/This Worksheet.)
  - Objects.
- A more complete menu is accessible under Home/Find & Select/Go To Special or F5/Special, which includes additional options (see Figure 11.1), including:
  - Selection of errors.
  - Selection of direct (or all) precedents and dependents of a cell.
  - The last used cell.
- One can search for all cells containing mixed formula (e.g. =E4*1.3) or for fixed values arising from formulae (e.g. =5*300) by visual inspection using Formulas/Show Formulas.
- Using Excel's in-built general error checking, under File/Options/Formulas (see Figure 11.2), one can check for formulae referring to empty cells, formulae which are inconsistent in some way or formulae which contain an error.

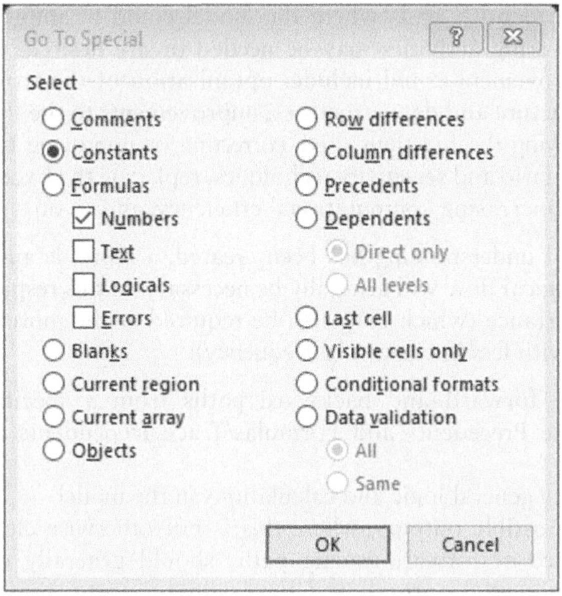

FIGURE 11.1 The Go/To Special Menu

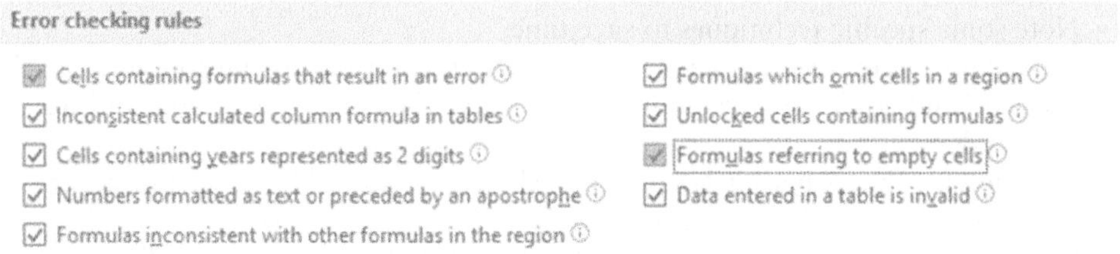

FIGURE 11.2 Excel's In-built Error-checking Options

These detailed processes will be required generally, as well as specifically before one begins to rebuild or improve a model. They will help not only to identify mistakes, but also to see possibilities to improve the calculations, transparency, user-friendliness, flexibility or efficiency. It will also help one to understand potential limitations, as well as structural changes that may need to be made in order to optimise transparency and flexibility (such as eliminating some two-dimensional lookup processes, and moving items to different places within the model).

Note also some further points about conducting changes to improve models:

- Since there is no starting point for a circularity, the tracing of precedents and dependents can become time-consuming and frustrating. It may be that one will need to delete formulae on the circular path and rebuild parts of the model.
- When removing unnecessary calculation paths or repeated references, one will generally need to work backwards from the last part of the dependency chain, to avoid deleting items that are used in subsequent calculations (which would result in #REF! errors).

- When the calculations from several worksheets are combined into one (by using cut and paste), the formulae that have been moved will contain sheet references to the sheet within which they are now placed (such as Model!. . . , when they have been moved into the Model sheet). These references are unnecessary and are simple to remove using Find/Replace to replace the sheet name and exclamation mark with nothing.
- When named ranges with worksheet-only scope are moved into different sheets, one may have to take extra care with, or rebuild, formulae which use such names, especially if the original worksheet is deleted.

Testing and Checking the Formulae

In addition to following the formula from a logical and conceptual perspective, it is almost always necessary to test complex formulae by using specific input values to ensure that they are correct and robust. In principle, the conducting of manual sensitivity analysis (changing the value of one input and observing its effect on specific calculations) is often sufficient to do this. More generally, some of the other techniques and approaches discussed elsewhere in this text (such as the simultaneous variation of multiple inputs, the use of DataTables and determining the limits of validity of formulae through using extreme values of inputs, using calculation breaks, and so on) can be helpful. Similarly, where (value-added) error checks can be introduced, the sensitivity of these to changes in input values can be tested.

Using a Watch Window and Other Ways to Track Values

When conducting general checking of formulae using sensitivity analysis, as well as when making changes to a model's structure, layout or formulae, one effective way of observing the effect of the changes is to use a Watch Window (on the Formulas tab). One may watch several variables to see the effect as changes are made or input values altered.

When using a Watch Window, one will typically be able to focus on only a few key calculations. An alternative method is to track the effect of changes on a very wide set (or all) model calculations. There are various ways to do this:

- New worksheets can be added to the model which contain copied values of the calculations in the original worksheets (i.e. by using paste values, as well as pasting the same formats). A further set of sheets can be used to create formulae which calculate the difference between the original values and those contained in the revised model. These formulae are easy to set up (by copying a single one) at the very beginning as all corresponding worksheets have the same structure. (Once structural changes are made to the workbook that is being improved, this correspondence would no longer exist.) The calculations of these differences should evaluate to zero (even as structural changes are made) at least until it is decided to correct any calculation errors.
- A more general, powerful (and more complex) approach is to use a similar method in which the various parts are kept in three separate linked workbooks (that are always kept open at the same time): the original model, the adapted model and calculations of the difference between the two. The advantage of this approach is that one can compare not only the base case values, but also the effect within each model of changing input values (in both) simultaneously.

PART Four

Sensitivity and Scenario Analysis, Simulation and Optimisation

CHAPTER 12

Sensitivity and Scenario Analysis: Core Techniques

INTRODUCTION

This chapter introduces the techniques required to conduct sensitivity and scenario analyses. At the most basic level, these can be used to answer What if? questions, and often represent an important part of providing appropriate decision support. In addition, as covered earlier, sensitivity-related techniques are a key part of all stages of the modelling process, from model design to final use. The first section of this chapter provides an overview of ways to conduct sensitivity analysis and of related tools. The second section describes one of these in detail, namely Excel's DataTable functionality. The third section shows some examples using this functionality, including the running of sensitivity and scenario analysis. The later chapters cover the details of the other approaches to sensitivity analysis.

OVERVIEW OF SENSITIVITY-RELATED TECHNIQUES

There are several simplistic ways to conduct sensitivity analysis:

- To manually change an input value and note the effect on an output. Whilst this is a very useful way to test a formula as it is being built, it would be cumbersome and inefficient to use this to conduct sensitivities on a completed model:
  - One would need to make a note of the input values used and the resulting output values, which would be cumbersome when several input values are to be changed.
  - The analysis would need to be repeated if the model is modified in any way, since there is no dynamic link between the inputs and the sensitivity results.
- To copy the model several times, and use different input values in each copy. Of course, whilst this would retain a record of the inputs used and the outputs calculated, doing so would generally be inefficient and error-prone, not least since the whole process would need to be repeated if the model subsequently needed to be modified in some way.

In this text, the focus is on more efficient and automated ways to run sensitivities and scenarios. These include methods based on:

- Using a finite number of pre-defined sensitivities or scenarios:
  - Using an Excel DataTable to capture the effect of changing one or two model inputs simultaneously. This can be combined with a lookup function to run scenario analysis, in which several inputs are changed simultaneously. These are covered in detail later in this chapter.
  - Using VBA macros to change input values and record the results for the output. This is generally required whenever other procedures also need to be run after every change in the value of model input values (for example, if circularities are resolved by macros). This is covered in Chapter 14.
- Generating many inputs combinations automatically:
  - Simulation can be used to generate combinations by random sampling of possible values. These are introduced in Chapter 15 and covered in more detail in Chapter 16.
  - Optimisation techniques search for combinations of input values so that the output equals some value, or is minimised or maximised. One may typically require that constraints (restrictions) need to apply to some input or output values in order for a particular input combination to be considered valid. In Chapter 13, we introduce Excel's GoalSeek and Solver as key tools in this respect, whilst Chapter 15 provides some further details about optimisation modelling in general contexts.

DATATABLES

This section describes the main aspects of Excel's DataTable functionality. It may be helpful to readers to refer to the example models shown later in the chapter whilst doing so.

Overview

A DataTable is an Excel functionality that shows the value of a model calculation(s) or output(s) as an input value(s) is varied through a set of pre-defined values. In other words, it recalculates the model for each of an explicitly defined set of input values and displays the results of a specific pre-selected output(s).

Some of the key uses are:

- To display the sensitivity of selected outputs to a chosen input(s). As well as being useful in its own right, it can help users who wish to see sensitivity analysis without having to become familiar with the details of the model (such as senior decision-makers). The values within the DataTable can also be used to populate graphs that show the effect of such changes.
- To create and check formulae (including detecting potential errors) by showing the values of key calculations or outputs as some inputs vary. For example, if it is seen that the values of an output are unaffected as the input values change (or are affected in an unexpected way), this is an indicator of a possible error.

A DataTable can exist in a one-way or two-way form, corresponding to the number of inputs that are varied simultaneously:

- A one-way DataTable shows the value of one or more calculations (or outputs) as the value of a single input is changed. Such tables may exist in a column form or in row form: in the column form, the set of values to be used for the input is placed in a column (and in the row form, it is placed in a row). They may track the value of several model outputs (which, in the column form, are placed in the top row of the table).
- A two-way DataTable varies two inputs, and shows the value of a single model output (or calculation). The values of the inputs to be varied are placed in the table's left column and top row, and that of the output calculation is placed in the top-left corner of the table.

Implementation

A DataTable can be implemented by:

- Creating an appropriate range of input values in a column or row (for one-way tables) or in a row and column (for two-way tables).
- Setting the outputs (or intermediate calculations) that are to be shown in the table by using a direct cell reference to the relevant calculations in the model. The output references are placed in the top row in a one-way column-form table, the left column in a one-way row-form table, and the top left cell in a two-way table.
- Selecting the whole table area (including the top row and left column), and using the Data/What-If Analysis/Data Table to link the values in the column or row to the input cells (in a one-way table, one of the cell reference entry boxes will be left blank). A frequent mistake is to use a row input for a column table or vice-versa, but the presence of such mistakes is usually clear from inspection of the values in the table.

(The reader may wish to briefly refer to Figure 12.1 and Figure 12.2 to see an illustration of these.)

Note that to be sure that the correct results are calculated, one may have to press F9 to cover the case where Excel's calculation not set to Automatic (i.e. is on the Manual setting or on the "Automatic except for data tables" setting).

Limitations and Tips

There are several limitations to DataTables, and some tips in using them most effectively:

- They can used be correctly only where there is a dynamic link between the model's inputs and the output calculations. For example, if another operation (such as GoalSeek, or the running of a macro) needs to be performed each time input values are changed, then – since the DataTable will not execute this procedure – the output values would generally be incorrect. Of course, the same issue applies to such models even if one wishes to simply alter the value of any input. An effective way to create sensitivity analysis in such a model is to use a macro to run the necessary procedure (such as GoalSeek), and another macro to run the sensitivity analysis, with this latter macro calling on the former each time the model input values are changed (see Chapter 14).

	B	C	D	E	F	G	H	I
2	Income Statement	2016	2017	2018	2019	2020	2021	2022
4	Revenues	400	410	430.5	452.0	474.6	498.4	523.3
5	% growth		2.5%	5.0%	5.0%	5.0%	5.0%	5.0%
7	Variable Costs	140	160	155.0	162.7	170.9	179.4	188.4
8	% revenues	35.0%	39.0%	36.0%	36.0%	36.0%	36.0%	36.0%
10	Fixed Costs (incl. depreciation)	70	72	73.4	74.9	76.4	77.9	79.5
11	% growth		2.9%	2.0%	2.0%	2.0%	2.0%	2.0%
13	EBIT	190	178	202	214	227	241	255
15	Total from 2018	1,140						
18	ONE -AND TWO-WAY DATATABLES							
20		1,140	=C15					
21	0.0%							
22	5.0%							
23	8.0%							

Data Table ? ×
Row input cell:
Column input cell: $E$5
OK Cancel

FIGURE 12.1 Populating a DataTable by Linking Its Values to a Model Input Cell

	B	C	D	E	F	G
18	ONE -AND TWO-WAY DATATABLES					
20		1,140	=C15			
21	0.0%	930				
22	5.0%	1140				
23	8.0%	1280				
25		202	214	227	241	255
26	0.0%	189	187	186	184	183
27	5.0%	202	214	227	241	255
28	8.0%	210	231	254	279	306
30		0.0%	5.0%	8.0%		
31	1,140	930	1140	1280		
33	1,140	34.0%	35.0%	36.0%	37.0%	38.0%
34	0.0%	971	950	930	909	889
35	5.0%	1188	1164	1140	1116	1093
36	8.0%	1332	1306	1280	1254	1228

FIGURE 12.2 Examples of One- and Two-way DataTables

- Their presence will slow down recalculation of the model, because any change to the formulae or inputs values will cause all the tables to be recalculated. Especially for large models, one may wish to switch to the "Automatic except for data tables" setting, and pressing F9 when one wishes to recalculate them. Where DataTables have been used for error checking during a model-building process, they can be deleted once the model is built.

- When testing a model, one can "re-use" a DataTable simply by changing the output reference to link to a different calculated cell or model output. In this way, one can rapidly see the effect on several calculations (including on error checks), and can avoid building unnecessarily large numbers of tables. The output reference cell of the DataTable could also contain a CHOOSE function (rather than a pure cell reference) so that it can be selected to point to one of several outputs.
- DataTables should not be used in sequence, i.e. the output of one should not be used as an input to another. The values in any tables beyond the first in the sequence can often be incorrect, since the logical order of calculations (dependency sequences) that should be applied may be ambiguous.
- The values in a table are those of an output as the selected inputs are varied, but whilst other inputs take the values to which they are currently set. In other words, the current values of the other model inputs will affect the values shown in the table. Thus, generally, one should ensure that all inputs are set to their base case values.
- It can be convenient to show the model's base case as one of outcomes within the DataTable. This can be done by formatting the cells that correspond to the base case with some form of highlighting. However, since the definition of the values that define the base case could be altered, the position of the base case output with the DataTables would also change. One approach to overcome this is to build the model so that it contains both a base value for the input, as well as a variation to be applied to that input, with the original input call being calculated from these (as discussed in Chapter 4). The DataTable sensitivity analysis can be run in which it is the variation which is altered (and not directly the base value). In this way, the physical placement of the base case within the table can always be the same (i.e. that for which the variation is zero), so that the table can also be formatted (e.g. with borders and colour-coding) to highlight this case.
- The identity of the inputs that are varied within the DataTable are not directly visible without reference to the formulae within the cells of the table. Especially when the inputs varied are of the same type (e.g. all dollar figures, or all percentages) and are of similar magnitude, it may be easy to misinterpret to which inputs the rows and columns correspond. One-way tables have the advantage that a label can be written in the top-left corner, whereas for two-way tables, the labels can be typed in the row and column immediately above and to the left.
- Since the calculation area of the table forms an array function in Excel, it is not possible to change individual cells within it. An extension of the table area can be achieved by selecting the new area and overwriting the original table (such as if an additional output reference is added to a one-way table, or if additional values are desired to be added to the set of values to be tested for a particular input). However, if a reduction in size is required, the table will need to be recreated. In practice, rather than deleting a table in its entirety, one can use Clear Contents to remove the (array) formulae within the interior of the table, and rebuild the required structures from the retained row/column inputs values.
- In principle, at most two model input values can be changed simultaneously in a table, since it has a two-dimensional structure. Where more than two changes are required, scenarios can be pre-defined and a (one-way) sensitivity analysis can be conducted, in which the input to vary is the scenario number or definition (see later in the chapter for an example).

- The table must be placed in the same worksheet as the inputs that are varied. One can overcome this in practice in several ways: by structuring a model in a single worksheet as far as possible, by moving the input's position to be in the same sheet as the DataTable, or by using lookup functions (such as INDIRECT, as discussed in Chapter 25).

PRACTICAL APPLICATIONS

Example: Sensitivity of Net Present Value to Growth Rates

The file Ch12.1.RevSensitivityDataTables.xlsx contains examples of completed one- and two-way DataTables for a model which forecasts revenues, cost and profit, based on historic data and input assumptions. Figure 12.1 shows the last step in the process, in which the cell reference to the input is being made in the dialogue box for a one-way (column form) DataTable, where the numbers in the left-hand column of the table (cells B21:B23) represent the values that the input assumption for revenue growth (Cell E5) is to take.

Figure 12.2 shows the results of doing this, as well as providing some additional examples of DataTables. Note that the second table (Rows 25 through 28) is a one-way column-form table with multiple outputs (the EBIT profile over time), the third table is a one-way row form table, and the fourth is a two-way table.

Example: Implementing Scenario Analysis

Scenario analysis involves assessing the effect on the output as several inputs (typically more than two) are changed at the same time, using explicit pre-defined combinations (each representing a logical set that could arise in practice). For example, when looking at profit scenarios, a worst case could be represented by one in which prices achieved are low, whilst volumes sold are also low, and input costs are high.

Scenario analysis has many applications, including:

- When it is considered that there are distinct (discrete) cases possible for the value of a variable, rather than a continuous range.
- To begin to explore the effect on the model's calculations where several input variables change simultaneously. This can be used both as a first step towards a full simulation, or as an optimisation method that looks for the best scenario. In particular, it can be useful to generate a better understanding of a complex situation: by first thinking of specific scenarios, and the interactions and consequences that would apply for each, one can gradually consolidate ideas and create a more comprehensive understanding.
- As a proxy tool to capture dependencies (or conditional occurrences) between variables, especially where a relationship is known to exist, but where expressing it through explicit (parameterised) formulae is not possible or is too complex. For example:
  - In the context of the relationship between the volume sold and the price charged for a product, it may be difficult to create a valid formula for the volume that would apply for any assumed price. However, it may be possible to estimate (through judgement, expert estimates or market research) what the volume would be at some specific price points. In other words, although it may not be possible to capture the whole demand curve in a parameterised fashion,

individual price-volume combinations can be treated as discrete scenarios, so that the dependency is captured implicitly.

- The relationship between the number of sales people and the productivity of each, or that of employee morale with productivity. This may be hard to establish in a functional form, whereas particular combinations may be able to be estimated.
- In macro-economic forecasting, one may wish to make assumptions for the values taken by several variables (perhaps as measured from cases that arose in historic data), but without having to define explicit parametrised relationships between them, which may be hard to do in a defensible manner.

Scenarios are generally best implemented in Excel by combining lookup functions (e.g. CHOOSE or INDEX) with a DataTable: each scenario is associated with an integer, which is used to drive a lookup function that returns the values that apply for the model input values for that scenario. The sensitivity analysis is run by varying the scenario number. (One could alternatively have named scenarios, in which the sensitivity is to the scenario name, but then a MATCH (or SWITCH) function is typically required in addition.) Note that, although Excel's Scenarios Manager (under Data/What-If Analysis) can be used to create scenarios, it has the disadvantage that the scenarios are not explicitly visible nor computationally accessible in the worksheet. (This approach is not discussed further in this text, nor generally used by the author in practice.)

The file Ch12.2.RevScenario.DataTable.xlsx contains an example (see Figure 12.3). There are three pre-defined revenue-growth scenarios (Rows 3–5), with the one that is to be used shown in Row 2, and selected by choice of the value placed in Cell A2. The original input values (Row 10) are replaced by cell references to the values that apply in that scenario. The DataTable (Row 25–28) is a one-way, column-form table, which uses the scenario number as the input.

	A	B	C	D	E	F	G	H	I	J
1										
2	2	Revenues Scenarios			5.0%	5.0%	5.0%	5.0%	5.0%	=CHOOSE($A2,I3,I4,I5)
3		Low			-2.0%	-2.0%	3.0%	4.0%	5.0%	
4		Base			5.0%	5.0%	5.0%	5.0%	5.0%	
5		High			6.0%	8.0%	8.0%	10.0%	12.5%	
6										
7		Income Statement	2016	2017	2018	2019	2020	2021	2022	
8										
9		Revenues	400	410	431	452	475	498	523	
10		% growth			5.0%	5.0%	5.0%	5.0%	5.0%	=I2
11										
12		Variable Costs	140	160	155.0	162.7	170.9	179.4	188.4	
13		% revenues	35.0%	39.0%	36.0%	36.0%	36.0%	36.0%	36.0%	
14										
15		Fixed Costs (incl. depreciation)	70	72	73.4	74.9	76.4	77.9	79.5	
16		% growth		2.9%	2.0%	2.0%	2.0%	2.0%	2.0%	
17										
18		EBIT	190	178	202	214	227	241	255	
19										
20		Total from 2018	1,140							
21										
22										
23		ONE-WAY DATATABLE								
24										
25			1,140							
26		1	940							
27		2	1140							
28		3	1279							

FIGURE 12.3 Combining a DataTable with a CHOOSE Function to Run Scenarios

CHAPTER 13

Using GoalSeek and Solver

INTRODUCTION

This chapter provides a description of Excel's GoalSeek, as well as an introduction to Solver. These can both be considered as forms of optimisation tools, in the sense that they search for the input value(s) required so that a model's output has some property or value. Solver's functionality is richer than that of GoalSeek, so that this chapter focuses only on its general application, whilst some further aspects are covered in Chapter 15.

OVERVIEW OF GOALSEEK AND SOLVER

Links to Sensitivity Analysis

Whereas the sensitivity techniques discussed in Chapter 12 can be thought of as "forward-calculating" in nature, GoalSeek and Solver are "backward" approaches:

- GoalSeek (under Data/What-If Analysis) uses an iterative search to determine the value of a single input that would be required to make an output equal to a value that the user specifies.
- Solver determines the values that are required of several inputs so that the output equals some value, or is minimised or maximised. One may also impose restrictions on the allowable value of inputs or calculated values for the set of values to be considered valid. Solver is a free Excel add-in that initially needs to be installed under Excel Options/Add-Ins, and which will then be found under Excel's Data/Analysis menu. It can also be installed (and uninstalled) using the Manage tool for add-ins under Office/Excel Options/Add-ins.

Tips, Tricks and Limitations

Whilst Goal Seek and Solver are quite user-friendly, it is almost always preferable to set up the calculations so that the target value that is to be achieved is zero (rather than some other figure that must be typed into the dialog box). To do this, one simply adds two cells to the model: one containing the desired target value (as a hard-coded figure), and the other that calculates the difference between this value and the model's current output. Thus, the objective becomes to make the value of the difference equal to zero. This setting-to-zero approach has several advantages:

- It is more transparent, since the original value is retained and shown in the model (rather than being a figure that is entered in the GoalSeek dialog box each time that it is run).
- It is more efficient, and less error-prone. If the procedures are likely to be run several times (as is usually the case, not least if other model input values are changed), then it is much easier to enter zero as the desired target value within the GoalSeek or Solver dialogs, rather than to repeatedly enter a more complex value (such as 12.75%).
- It allows for the easier adaptation and generalisation of macros which are recorded when the procedures are run.
- It allows one to use simple techniques to improve accuracy: within the cell containing the difference calculation, one can magnify the raw difference (by multiplication by a number such as 1000), and use GoalSeek to set this magnified difference to zero. This will usually increase accuracy, since the tolerance of Goal Seek's iterative method cannot otherwise be controlled. A similar approach can also be used for Solver, but is usually not necessary, due to its higher inherent accuracy.

When using Solver, some additional points are often worth bearing in mind:

- There must be only one objective, whereas multiple constraints are allowed. Thus, a real-life objective such as "to maximise profits at minimal cost" would generally have to be reformulated. Typically, all but one of the initial (multiple) objectives must be re-expressed as constraints, such as "maximise profit whilst keeping costs below $10m and delivering the project within 3 years".
- Solver (and GoalSeek) can only find a solution if one exists. Whilst this may seem obvious, a solution may not exist for several reasons: first, one may have too many constraints (or modified objectives). Second, the nature of the model's logic may not capture a true U-shaped curve as an input varies (this is often, but not always, a requirement in optimisation situations). Third, if the constraints are not appropriately formulated, then there can also be many (or infinitely many) solutions; in such cases, the algorithms may not converge, or may provide solutions which are apparently unstable. Fourth, infinitely many solutions can arise in other special cases, for example if one is asked to find the optimal portfolio that can include two assets which have identical characteristics, and so that any amount of one can be substituted for the same amount of the other.
- From a model design perspective, it is often most convenient and transparent to place all the inputs that are varied within the optimisation in a single contiguous range.

PRACTICAL APPLICATIONS

There are many possible applications of such tools, such as to determine:

- The sales volume required for a business to achieve breakeven.
- The maximum allowable investment for a project's cash flows to achieve a specified return target.

- The internal-rate-of-return of a project, i.e. the discount rate for which the net present value is zero (which could be compared to the IRR function).
- The required constant annual payment to pay down a mortgage over a certain time period (which could be compared with the PMT function).
- The mix of assets within a portfolio to sell so that the capital gains tax liability is minimised.
- The parameters to use to define a quadratic (or other) curve, so that it best fits a set of data points.
- The implied volatility of a European option, i.e. the volatility required so that the value determined by the Black–Scholes formula is equal to the observed market price.

Examples of most of these are given below.

Example: Breakeven Analysis of a Business

The file Ch13.1.GoalSeek.Breakeven.xlsx contains a simple model which calculates the profit of a business based on the price per unit sold, the number of units sold and the fixed and per unit (variable) cost. We require to determine the number of units that must be sold so that the profit is zero (i.e. the breakeven volume), and use GoalSeek to do so. (Of course, this assumes that all other inputs are unchanged.) Figure 13.1 shows the initial model (showing a profit of 1000 in Cell C11, when the number of units sold is 1200, shown in Cell C4), as well as the completed GoalSeek dialog box. The model has been set up with the difference calculation method discussed earlier, so that the target value to achieve (that is set within the dialog box) is zero.

In Figure 13.2, the results are shown (i.e. after pressing the OK button twice, once to run GoalSeek, and once to accept its results). The value required for Cell C4 is 1000 units, with Cell C11 showing a profit of zero, as desired.

	A	B	C	D
1				
2		**Inputs**		
3		Price per unit	10.0	
4		No of units	1200	
5		Fixed Cost	5000	
6		VC per unit	5	
7				
8		**Calculations**		
9		Revenue	12000	=C3*C4
10		Total Cost	11000	=C5+C4*C6
11		**Profit**	**1000**	=C9-C10
12				
13		Target Number	0	
14		Difference with Target	1000	=C11-C13

Goal Seek
Set cell: $C$14
To value: 0
By changing cell: $C$4
OK Cancel

FIGURE 13.1 Initial Model with Completed GoalSeek Dialog

	A	B	C	D
1				
2		**Inputs**		
3		Price per unit	10.0	
4		No of units	1000	
5		Fixed Cost	5000	
6		VC per unit	5	
7				
8		**Calculations**		
9		Revenue	10000	=C3*C4
10		Total Cost	10000	=C5+C4*C6
11		**Profit**	0	=C9-C10
12				
13		Target Number	0	
14		Difference with Target	0	=C11-C13

FIGURE 13.2 Results of Using Goal Seek for Breakeven Analysis

Example: Threshold Investment Amounts

The file Ch13.2.InvestmentThreshold.IRR.xlsx contains an example in which Goal-Seek is used to determine the maximum allowable investment so that the post-tax cash flow stream will have an internal rate of return of a specified value. Figure 13.3 shows the GoalSeek dialog to run this. Note that the difference calculation (Cell C12) has been scaled by 1000, in order to try to achieve a more accurate result. The reader can themselves experiment with different multiplication factors, which in principle should be as large as possible (whereas the author's practical experience has been that very large values create a less stable GoalSeek result, and are also generally unnecessary in terms of generating sufficient accuracy).

	A	B	C	D	E	F	G	H	I	J	K	L
1												
2		Period			01 Jan 18	01 Jan 19	01 Jan 20	01 Jan 21	01 Jan 22	01 Jan 23	01 Jan 24	01 Jan 25
3		EBIT				250	250	250	250	250	250	250
4		Interest charges	1000	3.0%		30.0	30.0	30.0	30.0	30.0	30.0	30.0
5		PBT			0	220.0	220.0	220.0	220.0	220.0	220.0	220.0
6		Tax	25%		0	55	55	55	55	55	55	55
7		Investment			753	0	0	0	0	0	0	0
8		Total Cash Flow			-753	165	165	165	165	165	165	165
9												
10		Target	10.00%									
11		XIRR	12.00%	=XIRR(E8:L8,E2:L2,10%)								
12		Difference (scaled)	2000.0%	=(C11-C10)*1000								
13												
14												
15												

FIGURE 13.3 Running GoalSeek with a Scaled Target Value for Improved Accuracy

Example: Implied Volatility of an Option

The file Ch13.3.GS.ImpliedVol.xlsx contains the calculation of the value of a European option using the Black–Scholes formula (with six inputs, one of which is the volatility). GoalSeek is used to find the value of the volatility that results in the Black–Scholes-based value equalling the observed market price. Figure 13.4 shows the model and results of running GoalSeek.

Example: Minimising Capital Gains Tax Liability

The file Ch13.4.Solver.AssetSale.OneStep.xlsx contains an example of the use of Solver. The objective is to find the portion of each of a set of assets that should be sold so that the total proceeds is maximised, whilst ensuring that the realised capital gain (current value less purchase value) does not exceed a threshold at which capital gains tax would start to be paid. Figure 13.5 shows the model, including the data required to calculate the proceeds and capital gains for the whole portfolio (Columns C, D, E), and the corresponding figures if only a proportion of each asset is sold (Columns E, F, G), which are currently set at 100%. Thus the complete selling of all assets in the portfolio would realise £101,000 in proceeds and £31,000 in capital gains. With a capital gain threshold of £10,500, one can see that selling 10,500/31,000 of each asset (approx. 33.9%, as shown in cell H12) would result in the capital gain that is exactly equal to the limit, whilst proceeds would be £34,210 (cell H13). This can be considered

	A	B	C	D	E	F	G	H	I	J	K
1		Black-Scholes Formula for European Call Option									
2											
3		Parameters		Variables			BS Call Value	5.00	=S*EDT*NDOne-E*ERT*NDTwo		
4		Sigma (Volatility)	21.96%	S	100						
5		Irate	5.0%	T-t (years)	0.25		Call Price (observed)	5.00			
6		D	0.0%	E	100		Difference	0.00			
7											
8		Intermediate calculations for BS Call Value:					Named Range	Cell			
9		Exp(-D(T-t))	1.000	=EXP(-D*Tminust)			D	=ImpliedVol!$C$6			
10		Exp(-r(T-t))	0.988	=EXP(-Irate*Tminust)			DOne	=ImpliedVol!$C$12			
11		SigmaRootTminust	0.110	=Sigma*SQRT(Tminust)			DTwo	=ImpliedVol!$C$13			
12		d1	0.17	=(LN(S/E)+(Irate-D+0.5*Sigma*Sigma)*Tmi			E	=ImpliedVol!$E$6			
13		d2	0.06	=(LN(S/E)+(Irate-D-0.5*Sigma*Sigma)*Tmir			EDT	=ImpliedVol!$C$9			
14		N(DOne)	0.567	=NORMSDIST(DOne)			ERT	=ImpliedVol!$C$10			
15		N(DTwo)	0.524	=NORMSDIST(DTwo)			Irate	=ImpliedVol!$C$5			

FIGURE 13.4 Using GoalSeek to Determine the Implied Volatility of a European Option

	A	B	C	D	E	F	G	H	I
1									
2			Purchase Price	Value	Capital Gain	Trial Values: % sold	Value	Gains	
3		Fund 1	16,000	27,000	11,000	100%	27,000	11,000	
4		Fund 2	18,000	25,000	7,000	100%	25,000	7,000	
5		Fund 3	8,000	7,000	-1,000	100%	7,000	-1,000	
6		Fund 4	12,000	18,000	6,000	100%	18,000	6,000	
7		Fund 5	6,000	9,000	3,000	100%	9,000	3,000	
8		Fund 6	10,000	15,000	5,000	100%	15,000	5,000	
9		Total	70,000	101,000	31,000		101,000	31,000	
10									
11		Tax payable above capital gain of:						10,500	
12		Threshold % if sold in equal proportion (to give exact capital gain)						33.9%	=H11/E9
13		Proceeds at this threshold						34210	=H12*D9
14									

FIGURE 13.5 Model for Calculation of Sales Proceeds and Capital Gains

as a first estimate (or lower limit) of the possibilities. Thus the objective is to find an alternative set of proportions in which the realised figure is higher than this, whilst respecting the capital gains limit.

The completed Solver dialog box (invoked, as described at the beginning of the chapter, on the Data tab, after installation) is shown in Figure 13.6. Note that the weights (trial values for the proportions) are constrained to be positive and less than one (i.e. one can only sell what one owns, without making additional purchases or conducting short sales). Figure 13.7 shows the completed model with new trial values once Solver has been run. Note that total proceeds realised are £45,500, and that the constraints are all satisfied, including that the capital gains amount is exactly the threshold value. Of course, the proportion of each asset sold is different to that of the first estimate, whilst the proceeds are higher (£45,500).

It is also worth noting that, since the situation is a continuous one (i.e. the inputs can be varied in a continuous way, and the model's calculations depend in a simple continuous way on these), one should expect that the optimum solution will in principle be one in which the constraints will be met exactly. (If the total portfolio value were below this threshold, this would not apply of course, as it would also not if one constrained the possible values of the inputs in some specific ways.)

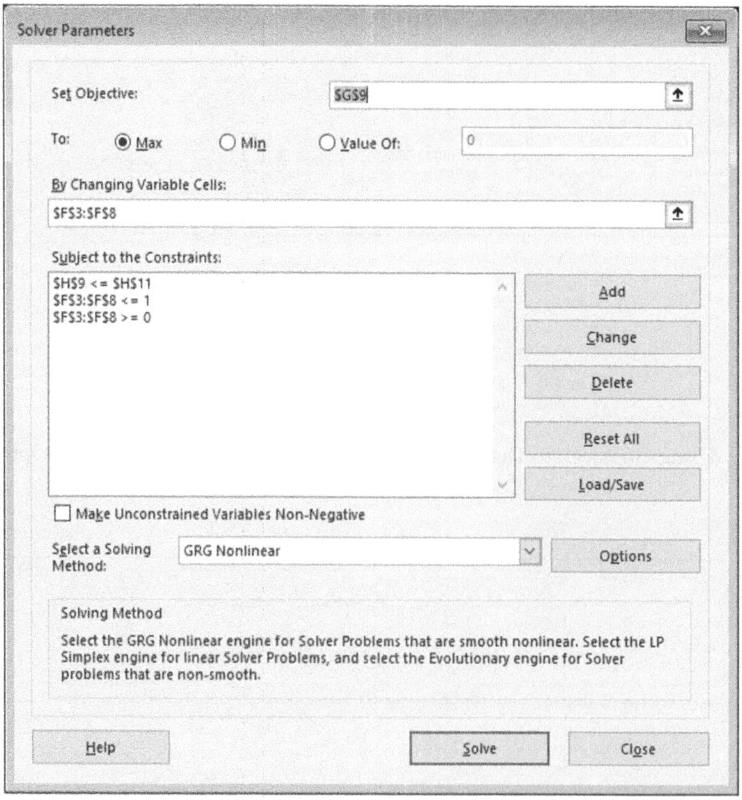

FIGURE 13.6 Application of Solver to Optimise Sales Allocation

	Purchase Price	Value	Capital Gain	Trial Values: % sold	Value	Gains	
Fund 1	16,000	27,000	11,000	0%	0	0	
Fund 2	18,000	25,000	7,000	100%	25,000	7,000	
Fund 3	8,000	7,000	-1,000	100%	7,000	-1,000	
Fund 4	12,000	18,000	6,000	19%	3,343	1,114	
Fund 5	6,000	9,000	3,000	59%	5,336	1,779	
Fund 6	10,000	15,000	5,000	32%	4,821	1,607	
Total	70,000	101,000	31,000		45,500	10,500	
Tax payable above capital gain of:						10,500	
Threshold % if sold in equal proportion (to give exact capital gain)						33.9%	=H11/E9
Proceeds at this threshold						34210	=H12*D9

FIGURE 13.7 Results of Running Solver to Determine Optimum Sales Allocation

Example: Non-linear Curve Fitting

In many situations, one may be required to create (or model) a relationship between two items for which one has data, but where the relationship is not known. One may have deduced from visual inspection that the relationship is not a linear one, and so may wish to try other functional forms. (Where this cannot be done with adequate accuracy or validity, one may instead have to use a scenario approach, in which the original data sets represent different scenarios and the relationship between the items is captured only implicitly as the scenario is varied.)

The file Ch13.5.Solver.CurveFitAsOptimisation.xlsx contains an example of the use of optimisation to fit a curve. A hypothesised relationship (in this case using a logarithmic curve) is created with trial values for each of the required parameters of the relationship. One then reforecasts the calculated values (in this case, the employee productivity) using that relationship. The parameters are determined by setting them as variables that Solver should find in order that the square of the difference between the original and the predicted values is minimised. Figure 13.8 shows the results of doing this. Note that the trial values for the parameters which describe the hypothesised

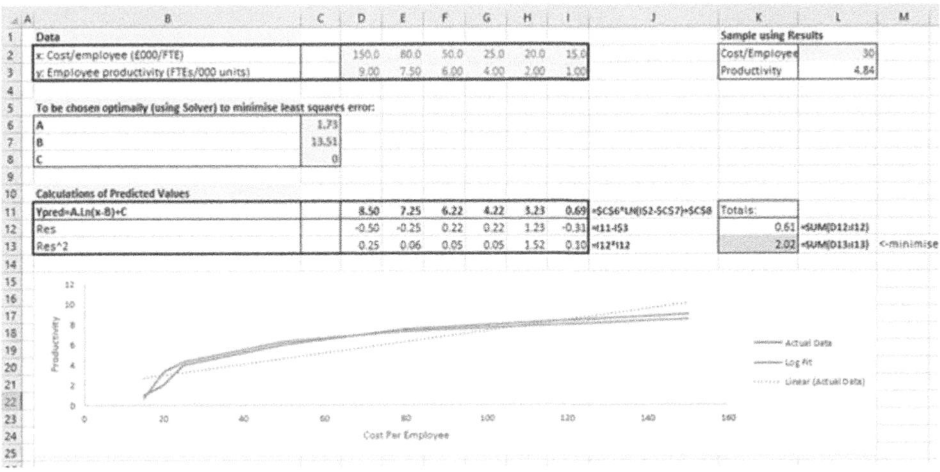

	C	D	E	F	G	H	I	J	K	L	M
Data									Sample using Results		
x: Cost/employee (£000/FTE)		150.0	80.0	50.0	25.0	20.0	15.0		Cost/Employee	30	
y: Employee productivity (FTEs/000 units)		9.00	7.50	6.00	4.00	2.00	1.00		Productivity	4.84	
To be chosen optimally (using Solver) to minimise least squares error:											
A	1.73										
B	13.51										
C	0										
Calculations of Predicted Values											
Ypred=A.Ln(x-B)+C		8.50	7.25	6.22	4.22	3.23	0.69	=$C$6*LN(I$2-$C$7)+$C$8	Totals:		
Res		-0.50	-0.25	0.22	0.22	1.23	-0.31	=I11-I$3	0.61	=SUM(D12:I12)	
Res^2		0.25	0.06	0.05	0.05	1.52	0.10	=I12*I12	2.02	=SUM(D13:I13)	<-minimise

FIGURE 13.8 Results of Using Solver to Fit a Non-linear Curve to Data

curve (called A, B, C) are in cells C6, C7 and C8 respectively, the predicted values are in Row 11 and the item to minimise (sum of squared differences) in cell K13.

It is also worth noting that other forms of relationship can be established in this way, including the determination of the parameters that define the standard least-squares (regression) method to approximate a linear relationship (instead of using the SLOPE and INTERCEPT or LINEST functions, discussed later in the text). One may also experiment with other non-linear relationships, such as one in which the productivity is related to the square root of the cost (rather than its logarithm), and so on. These are left as an exercise for the interested reader.

CHAPTER 14

Using VBA Macros to Conduct Sensitivity and Scenario Analyses

INTRODUCTION

This chapter discusses the use of VBA macros to run sensitivity and scenario analysis. This is needed in cases where any form of additional intervention or procedure is required between the changing of an input value and the calculation of the output. Examples of where such approaches may be required include:

- Where a model contains circular references that are resolved using a macro (as described in Chapter 10).
- If, after changing input values, GoalSeek or Solver needs to be run before the final output can be calculated.
- If other macros are needed to be run for any reason if input values change. For example, each scenario may require external data to be queried before the model is recalculated.

(Note that readers who are not familiar with VBA should nevertheless be able to follow the core principles of this chapter; otherwise they may choose to selectively study Part VI first.)

When using a VBA macro to run sensitivity analysis, generally two sets of procedures require automation:

- The first steps through the values to be used for the input(s) in the sensitivity or scenario analysis. This forms the outer loop of the overall process, and is a general step that essentially applies to all such approaches.
- The second applies the additional procedure that is to be performed at each step of the first loop (e.g. resolving circularities, running GoalSeek, querying the external data etc.). This forms the inner loop of the process, and is specific to each situation.

PRACTICAL APPLICATIONS

The examples covered in this section include those which:

- Demonstrate only the outer loop of the process, to run both sensitivity and scenario analysis. The objective here is to focus on the core concepts and VBA code required for the general (outer) loop.
- Describe the steps and syntax required to automate specific procedures, especially GoalSeek and Solver (the resolution of circular references using a macro was discussed in Chapter 10, so is not covered here). More generally, macros to automate other forms of procedures (e.g. querying external data sets) can be developed by using the techniques discussed in Part VI.

Example: Running Sensitivity Analysis Using a Macro

The file Ch14.1.ProfitSensitivity.xlsm contains an example of using a macro to run a sensitivity analysis, by stepping through a set of input values, recalculating the model and recording the results for the output(s). The model is similar to that used in Chapter 13, where it was used to demonstrate the application of GoalSeek to find the breakeven sales volume of a business for a given set of input assumptions, including the sales price. In this example, we are not (yet) using GoalSeek to find the breakeven volume; rather (as a first step), we aim to calculate the profit for various values of the input price (shown in cells E3:E11), and to record the resulting profit figures (in cells F3:F11). (Thus, at this stage, without the need for the additional GoalSeek procedure such analysis could be performed using a DataTable.) In order to automate the use of various input prices, the cell references that are required by the macro are given named ranges. Figure 14.1 shows the model prior to the running of the macro (including the button to run it), and Figure 14.2 shows the model once the macro has been run.

The core elements of the VBA code are:

```
N = Range("PriceHeader").CurrentRegion.Rows.Count - 1
For i = 1 To N
 Range("Price") = Range("PriceHeader").Offset(i, 0)
 Application.Calculate
 Range("ProfitHeader").Offset(i, 0) = Range("Profit")
Next i
```

	A	B	C	D	E	F	G	H	I
1									
2		Inputs			PriceHeader	ProfitHeader		Name	Range
3		Price per unit	12.0		8.0			Price	=Sheet1!$C$3
4		No of units	1000		8.5			PriceHeader	=Sheet1!$E$2
5		Fixed Cost	5000		9.0			Profit	=Sheet1!$C$11
6		VC per unit	5		9.5			ProfitHeader	=Sheet1!$F$2
7					10.0				
8		Calculations			10.5				
9		Revenue	12000		11.0			Run Sensitivity	
10		Total Cost	10000		11.5				
11		Profit	2000		12.0				
12									

FIGURE 14.1 Model Before Running the Sensitivity Analysis Macro

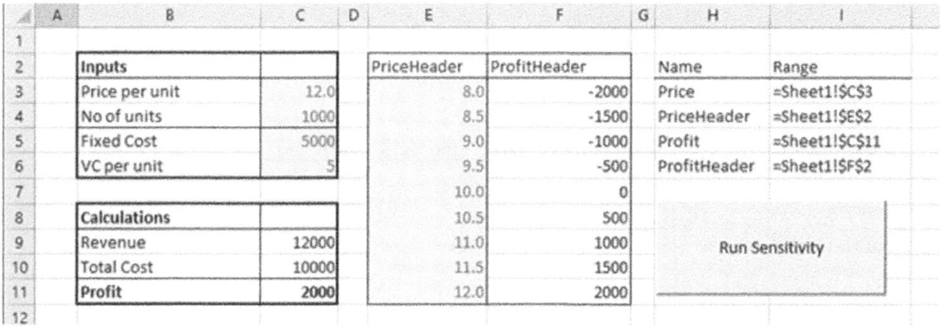

	A	B	C	D	E	F	G	H	I
1									
2		Inputs			PriceHeader	ProfitHeader		Name	Range
3		Price per unit	12.0		8.0	-2000		Price	=Sheet1!$C$3
4		No of units	1000		8.5	-1500		PriceHeader	=Sheet1!$E$2
5		Fixed Cost	5000		9.0	-1000		Profit	=Sheet1!$C$11
6		VC per unit	5		9.5	-500		ProfitHeader	=Sheet1!$F$2
7					10.0	0			
8		Calculations			10.5	500			
9		Revenue	12000		11.0	1000		Run Sensitivity	
10		Total Cost	10000		11.5	1500			
11		Profit	2000		12.0	2000			
12									

FIGURE 14.2 Model After Running the Sensitivity Analysis Macro

(As covered in Part VI, in practice more sophistication (and best practices) could be built into this procedure, including clearing the results range at the beginning of each run of the macro, and the use of full and explicit referencing. One could also track the initial state before the macro is run (i.e. the value used for the price) and reset the model to this state afterwards, as well as perhaps switching off screen-updating, and so on.)

Example: Running Scenarios Using a Macro

The file Ch14.2.RevScenario.xlsm contains an example of the use of a macro to run scenario analysis. The macro simply runs through a set of integers, and uses a lookup function (such as CHOOSE) to select the appropriate data for each scenario. All cells or ranges that need referencing from the VBA code are given Excel named ranges as part of the process of writing the macro. Figure 14.3 shows the results of running the macro, whose key elements are:

```
For i = 1 To 3
 Range("ScenarioNo") = i
 Application.Calculate
 Range("ResultsHeader").Offset(i, 0) = Range("Output")
Next i
```

Example: Using a Macro to Run Breakeven Analysis with GoalSeek

The file Ch14.3.GoalSeekMacro.Breakevenanalysis.xlsm contains an example of the automation of GoalSeek within a macro. It is similar to the first example in the chapter, with the additional step added in which (for each value of the price) GoalSeek is used to find the breakeven volume. The macro was created by simply recording the GoalSeek process once, and placing this within the loop which steps through the set of values that are to be used for the prices. Figure 14.4 shows the results of running the macro.

3	Revenues Scenarios			6.0%	8.0%	8.0%	10.0%	12.5%
	Low			-2.0%	-2.0%	3.0%	4.0%	5.0%
	Base			5.0%	5.0%	5.0%	5.0%	5.0%
	High			6.0%	8.0%	8.0%	10.0%	12.5%
	Income Statement	**2016**	**2017**	**2018**	**2019**	**2020**	**2021**	**2022**
	Revenues	400	410	435	469	507	558	627
	% growth			6.0%	8.0%	8.0%	10.0%	12.5%
	Variable Costs	140	160	156.5	169.0	182.5	200.7	225.8
	% revenues	35.0%	39.0%	36.0%	36.0%	36.0%	36.0%	36.0%
	Fixed Costs (incl. depreciation)	70	72	73.4	74.9	76.4	77.9	79.5
	% growth		2.9%	2.0%	2.0%	2.0%	2.0%	2.0%
	EBIT	190	178	205	225	248	279	322
	Total from 2018	1,279						
	SCENARIO RESULTS							
		RESULTS						
	1	940						
	2	1140						
	3	1279						

Name	Range
Output	=Model!$C$20
ResultsHeader	=Model!$C$25
ScenarioNo	=Model!$A$2

Run Scenarios

FIGURE 14.3 Using a Macro to Run Scenarios

Inputs	
Price per unit	12.0
No of units	714
Fixed Cost	5000
VC per unit	5.0

Calculations	
Revenue	8571
Total Cost	8571
Profit	0

Target Number	0
Difference with Target	0

PriceHeader	BEvenVolHeader
8.0	1667
8.5	1429
9.0	1250
9.5	1111
10.0	1000
10.5	909
11.0	833
11.5	769
12.0	714

Run Goal Seek For All Prices to Find Breakeven Volumes

Name	Range
BEvenVolHeader	=Sheet1!$F$2
DiffToTarget	=Sheet1!$C$14
Price	=Sheet1!$C$3
PriceHeader	=Sheet1!$E$2
Volume	=Sheet1!$C$4

FIGURE 14.4 Use of GoalSeek Within a Macro to Calculate the Price–Volume Breakeven Frontier

Note that we are using the setting-to-zero approach described earlier. The core aspects of the VBA code are:

```
N = Range("PriceHeader").CurrentRegion.Rows.Count - 1
For i = 1 To N
Range("Price") = Range("PriceHeader").Offset(i, 0)
```

```
Range("DiffToTarget").GoalSeek Goal:=0, Changing-
Cell:=Range("Volume")
Range("BEvenVolHeader").Offset(i, 0) = Range("Volume")
Next i
```

Example: Using Solver Within a Macro to Create a Frontier of Optimum Solutions

The use of Solver within VBA code is in many ways similar to that of GoalSeek: in principle, the most effective method is to record a macro of the process, ensure that all Excel ranges are referred to with named ranges and place the code within an appropriate loop (which is used to govern the way that input values are changed before Solver is applied). However, there are several points worth noting:

- One first needs to make a reference to the add-in within the Visual Basic Editor. This can be achieved using Tools/References and checking the relevant box for the Solver. Of course, Solver needs to be have been installed on the computer (as described in Chapter 13). This can therefore be inconvenient if the optimisation is to be run by someone who is not familiar with this process (e.g. if the file is sent to someone else by e-mail, who will need to implement this procedure).
- The recording of a macro does not capture the full syntax necessary to place the code within a loop. To automate the process requires one to add the `True` statement after `SolverSolve` in the code. This captures the closing of the message box once Solver has finished running, which is otherwise not captured by the recording process.

The file Ch14.4.SolverAssetSale.OneStep.xlsm contains the example from Chapter 13, in which the maximum sales proceeds were realised for a specific capital gains threshold. It is adapted to calculate the same figure in the case that a range of threshold values is desired to be run. The following shows the core of the required code, using the (essentially self-explanatory) named ranges created in the file, and noting the points above about referencing and the addition of the `True` statement:

```
N = Range("ResultsHeader").CurrentRegion.Rows.Count - 1

For i = 1 To N
'CHANGE CGT Threshold Values
Range("CGTThreshold").Value = Range("CGTThresholdsHeader").Offset(i, 0).Value
Application.Calculate

'RUN SOLVER
 SolverOk SetCell:=Range("ValueRealised"), MaxMinVal:=1, ValueOf:=0, _
 ByChange:=Range("TrialValues"), _
 Engine:=1, EngineDesc:="GRG Nonlinear"
 SolverSolve True

'RECORD RESULTS
 Range("ResultsHeader").Cells(1, 1).Offset(i, 0).Value = Range("ValueRealised").Value
 Range("ResultsHeader").Cells(1, 1).Offset(i, 1).Value = Range("Gains").Value
Next i
```

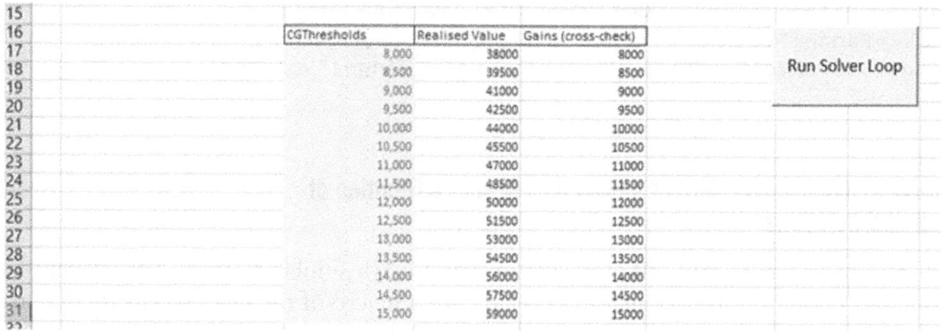

CGThresholds	Realised Value	Gains (cross-check)
8,000	38000	8000
8,500	39500	8500
9,000	41000	9000
9,500	42500	9500
10,000	44000	10000
10,500	45500	10500
11,000	47000	11000
11,500	48500	11500
12,000	50000	12000
12,500	51500	12500
13,000	53000	13000
13,500	54500	13500
14,000	56000	14000
14,500	57500	14500
15,000	59000	15000

Run Solver Loop

FIGURE 14.5 Results of Running Solver with a Macro to Determine Proceeds for Various Tax Thresholds

Figure 14.5 shows the completed model, including a table of values showing the maximum proceeds that are realisable for various capital gains tax threshold levels.

CHAPTER 15

Introduction to Simulation and Optimisation

INTRODUCTION

This chapter introduces the topics of simulation (with a more complete discussion being the subject of Chapter 16). It also extends the earlier discussion of optimisation. These are both natural extensions of sensitivity and scenario analysis. The first section discusses the link between these methods, and uses a practical example to illustrate the discussion. The latter sections of the chapter highlight some additional points that relate to general applications of optimisation modelling.

THE LINKS BETWEEN SENSITIVITY AND SCENARIO ANALYSIS, SIMULATION AND OPTIMISATION

Simulation and optimisation techniques are in effect special cases of sensitivity or scenario analysis, and can in principle be applied to any model which is built appropriately. The specific characteristics are that:

- Several inputs are varied simultaneously. As a result, combinatorial effects are important, i.e. there are many possible input combinations and corresponding output values.
- There is an explicit distinction between controllability and non-controllability of the process by which inputs vary.

These points are described in more detail below.

The Combinatorial Effects of Multiple Possible Input Values

When models contain several inputs that may each take several possible values, the number of possible input combinations generally becomes quite large (and hence so does the number of possible values for the model's output). For example, if 10 inputs could each take one of three possible values, there would be 3^{10} (or 59,049) possible combinations: the first input can take any of three values, for each of which the second can take any of three values, giving nine possible combinations of the first two inputs, 27 for the first three inputs, and so on.

In practice, one needs automated methods to calculate (a reasonably large subset of) the possible combinations. For example, whereas traditional sensitivity and scenario analysis involves pre-defining the *values* that are to be used, simulation and optimisation (generally) automate the *process* by which such values are chosen. Naturally, for simulation methods, the nature of this automation process is different to that for optimisation, as described later.

Controllable Versus Non-controllable: Choice Versus Uncertainty of Input Values

The use of traditional sensitivity and scenario analysis simply requires that the model is valid as its input values are changed in combination. This does not require one to consider (or define) whether – in the real-life situation – the process by which an input value would change is one which can be controlled or not. For example, if a company has to accept the prevailing market price for a commodity (such as if one purchases oil on the spot market), then such a price is not controllable (and hence likely to be uncertain). On the other hand, the company may be able to decide at what price to sell its own product (considering that a high price would reduce sales volume and a lower price would increase it), and hence the price-setting is a controllable process or choice. In other words, where the value of an input variable can be fully controlled, then its value is a choice, so that the question arises as to which choice is best (from the perspective of the analyst or relevant decision-maker). Where the value cannot be controlled, one is faced with uncertainty or risk. Thus, there are two generic sub-categories of sensitivity analysis:

- Optimisation context or focus, where the input values are fully controllable within that context, and should be chosen optimally.
- Risk or uncertainty context or focus, where the inputs are not controllable within any specific modelled context. (Subtly, the context in which one chooses to operate is an optimisation issue, as discussed later.)

These are illustrated in Figure 15.1.

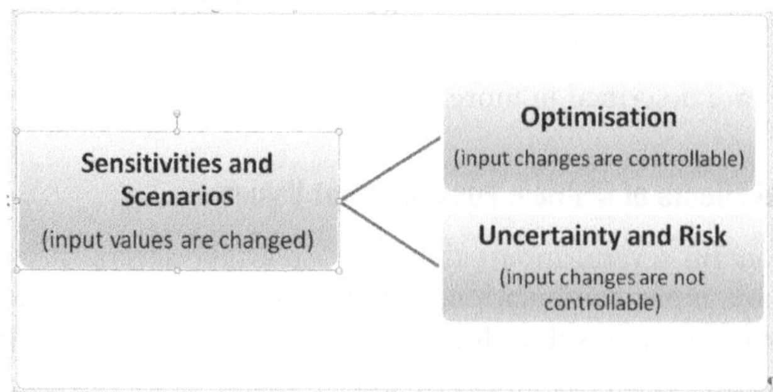

FIGURE 15.1 Basic Distinction Between Choice and Uncertainty as an Extension of Traditional Sensitivities

Of course, the distinction between whether one is faced with a situation in which there is uncertainty versus one of choice may depend one's perspective and role in a given situation. For example, it may be an individual's choice as to what time to plan to arise in the morning on a particular day, whereas from the perspective of someone else, the time at which the other person rises may be considered to be uncertain.

PRACTICAL EXAMPLE: A PORTFOLIO OF PROJECTS

Description

The file Ch15.1.TimeFlex.Risk.Opt.xlsx (see Figure 15.2) contains an example of a portfolio of 10 projects, with the cash flow profile of each being shown on a generic time axis (i.e. an investment followed by a positive cash flow from the date that each project is launched). Another grid shows the effect when each project is given a specific start date, defined in the range C15:C24, and which can be changed to be any set of integers (the model's calculations use lookup and other functions which the reader can inspect). In the case shown, all projects start in 2018, resulting in a portfolio with a net present value (NPV) of $1212m for the first 10 years' cash flows at a 10% discount rate, whilst the maximum financing requirement in any given year is $2270m (Cell D25).

As mentioned earlier, the role of the various launch dates of the projects could depend on the situation:

- An optimisation context, in which the start dates are entirely within the discretion and control of the decision-maker, and can be chosen in the way that is the most suitable from the perspective of the decision-maker.
- A risk or uncertainty context, in which each project would be launched according to some timetable that is not within the decision-scope of the users of the model. Thus, each project is subject to uncertainty on its timing, so that the future cash flow and financing profile is also uncertain.

	A	B	C	D	E	F	G	H	I	J	K	L	M
1													
2		**Generic schedule**		1	2	3	4	5	6	7	8	9	10
3		Project 1	$m	-250	67	67	67	60	54	49	44	40	36
4		Project 2	$m	-300	87	87	87	87	78	70	63	57	51
5		Project 3	$m	-160	43	43	43	43	43	39	35	32	28
6		Project 4	$m	-120	46	46	46	41	37	34	30	27	24
7		Project 5	$m	-240	97	97	97	97	87	79	71	64	57
8		Project 6	$m	-300	80	80	80	80	80	72	65	58	52
9		Project 7	$m	-160	44	44	44	40	36	32	29	26	24
10		Project 8	$m	-200	77	77	77	77	70	63	56	51	46
11		Project 9	$m	-180	72	72	72	72	72	65	58	53	47
12		Project 10	$m	-360	95	95	95	85	77	69	62	56	50
13													
14		**Specific dates**	Start date (year 1)	2018	2019	2020	2021	2022	2023	2024	2025	2026	2027
15		Project 1	2018	(250)	67	67	67	60	54	49	44	40	36
16		Project 2	2018	(300)	87	87	87	87	78	70	63	57	51
17		Project 3	2018	(160)	43	43	43	43	43	39	35	32	28
18		Project 4	2018	(120)	46	46	46	41	37	34	30	27	24
19		Project 5	2018	(240)	97	97	97	97	87	79	71	64	57
20		Project 6	2018	(300)	80	80	80	80	80	72	65	58	52
21		Project 7	2018	(160)	44	44	44	40	36	32	29	26	24
22		Project 8	2018	(200)	77	77	77	77	70	63	56	51	46
23		Project 9	2018	(180)	72	72	72	72	72	65	58	53	47
24		Project 10	2018	(360)	95	95	95	85	77	69	62	56	50
25		**Cash Flow**		**-2270**	**709**	**709**	**709**	**684**	**635**	**571**	**514**	**463**	**417**
26													
27		**Disc Cash flow yrs 1-10**	**1212**	=NPV(10%,D25:M25)									
28		**Min CF years 1-5**	**-2270**	=MIN(D25:H25)									
29		**Min acceptable**	-500										
30													

FIGURE 15.2 Variable Launch Dates for Each Project Within a Portfolio

Optimisation Context

As an optimisation issue, one may wish to maximise the NPV over the first 10 years, whilst not investing more than a specified amount in each individual year. For example, if one considers that the total cash flow in any of the first five periods (net of investment) should not drop to below (minus) $500m, then the case shown in Figure 15.2 would not be acceptable as a set of launch dates (since the cash flow in 2018 is (minus) $2,270). On the other hand, delaying some projects would reduce the investment requirement in the first period, but would also reduce NPV. Thus, a solution may be sought which optimises this trade-off.

The file Ch15.2.TimeFlex.Risk.Opt.Solver.xlsx (see Figure 15.3) contains an alternative set of launch dates, determined by applying Solver, in which some projects start later than 2018. This is an acceptable set of dates, as the value in Cell C28 is larger than that in C29. Whilst it is possible that this set of dates is the best one that could be achieved, there may be an even better set. (Note that in a continuous linear situation, an optimal solution would meet the constraints exactly, whereas in this case, the input values are discrete integers, so that the constraints would be respected, but not necessarily met exactly.)

Risk or Uncertainty Context Using Simulation

As a risk or uncertainty issue, the same model would apply if the project start dates were uncertain, driven by items that are not known or not within the control of the modeller or user.

Of course, given the large possible number of combinations for the start dates, whilst one could define and run a few scenarios, it would be more practical to have an automated way to generate all or many of the possible scenarios. Monte Carlo Simulation is an automated process to recalculate a model many times as its inputs are simultaneously randomly sampled. In the case of the example under discussion, one

	A	B	C	D	E	F	G	H	I	J	K	L	M
1													
2		Generic schedule		1	2	3	4	5	6	7	8	9	10
3		Project 1	$m	-250	67	67	67	60	54	49	44	40	36
4		Project 2	$m	-300	87	87	87	87	78	70	63	57	51
5		Project 3	$m	-160	43	43	43	43	43	39	35	32	28
6		Project 4	$m	-120	46	46	46	41	37	34	30	27	24
7		Project 5	$m	-240	97	97	97	97	87	79	71	64	57
8		Project 6	$m	-300	80	80	80	80	80	72	65	58	52
9		Project 7	$m	-160	44	44	44	40	36	32	29	26	24
10		Project 8	$m	-200	77	77	77	77	70	63	56	51	46
11		Project 9	$m	-180	72	72	72	72	72	65	58	53	47
12		Project 10	$m	-360	95	95	95	85	77	69	62	56	50
13													
14		Specific dates	Start date (year 1)	2018	2019	2020	2021	2022	2023	2024	2025	2026	2027
15		Project 1	2021	0	0	0	(250)	67	67	67	60	54	49
16		Project 2	2018	(300)	87	87	87	87	78	70	63	57	51
17		Project 3	2018	(160)	43	43	43	43	43	39	35	32	28
18		Project 4	2019	0	(120)	46	46	46	41	37	34	30	27
19		Project 5	2019	0	(240)	97	97	97	97	87	79	71	64
20		Project 6	2021	0	0	0	(300)	80	80	80	80	80	72
21		Project 7	2019	0	(160)	44	44	44	40	36	32	29	26
22		Project 8	2020	0	0	(200)	77	77	77	77	70	63	56
23		Project 9	2020	0	0	(180)	72	72	72	72	72	65	58
24		Project 10	2020	0	0	(360)	95	95	95	85	77	69	62
25		Cash Flow		-460	-390	-422	12	709	691	652	602	550	495
26													
27		Disc Cash flow yrs 1-10	820	=NPV(10%,D25:M25)									
28		Min CF years 1-5	-460	=MIN(D25:H25)									
29		Min acceptable	-500										

FIGURE 15.3 Using Solver to Determine Optimal Start Dates

could replace the start dates with values that are drawn randomly in order to sample future year numbers (as integers), do so many times and record the results.

Figure 15.4 shows an example of the part of the model concerning the time-specific cash flow profile in one random scenario. Each possible start date is chosen randomly but equally (and independently to the others) from the set 2018, 2019, 2020, 2021 and 2022.

Clearly, each random sample of input values would give a different value for the output of the model (i.e. the cash flow time profile, the investment amount and the NPV), so that the output of the simulation process is a set of values (for each model output) that could be represented as a frequency distribution. Figure 15.5 shows the results of doing this and running 5000 random samples with the Excel add-in @RISK (as discussed in Chapter 16 and Chapter 33, such calculations can also be done with VBA, but add-ins can have several advantages, including the ease with which high-quality graphs of the results can be generated).

Note that often – even if the variation of each input is uniform – the profile of an output will typically have a central tendency, simply because cases where all inputs are chosen at the high end of their range (or all are chosen at their low end) are less

14	**Specific dates**	Start date (year 1)	2018	2019	2020	2021	2022	2023	2024
15	Project 1	2022	0	0	0	0	(250)	67	67
16	Project 2	2018	(300)	87	87	87	87	78	70
17	Project 3	2021	0	0	0	(160)	43	43	43
18	Project 4	2019	0	(120)	46	46	46	41	37
19	Project 5	2020	0	0	(240)	97	97	97	97
20	Project 6	2021	0	0	0	(300)	80	80	80
21	Project 7	2021	0	0	0	(160)	44	44	44
22	Project 8	2022	0	0	0	0	(200)	77	77
23	Project 9	2019	0	(180)	72	72	72	72	72
24	Project 10	2022	0	0	0	0	(360)	95	95
25	**Cash Flow**		**-300**	**-213**	**-35**	**-318**	**-340**	**696**	**684**
26									
27	**Disc Cash flow yrs 1-10**	**611**	=NPV(10%,D25:M25)						
28	**Min CF years 1-5**	**-340**	=MIN(D25:H25)						
29	**Min acceptable**	-500							

FIGURE 15.4 A Random Scenario for Project Start Dates and its Implications for the Calculations

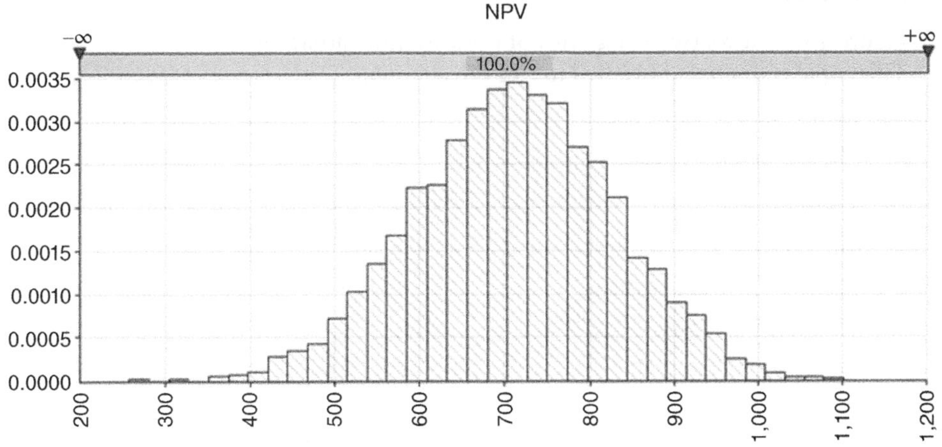

FIGURE 15.5 Distribution of NPV that Results from the Simulation

frequent than mixed cases (in which some are at the high end and others are at the low end). In other words, the need to use frequency distributions to describe the range and likelihood of output values is an inevitable result of the combinatorial effect arising due to the simultaneous variation of several inputs.

Note also that, within the earlier optimisation context, one may try to use simulation to search for the solution to the optimisation situation, by choosing the input combination that gives the best output; in practice, this is usually computationally inefficient, not least as the constraints are unlikely to be met unless a specific algorithm has been used to enforce this. This also highlights that simulation is not the same as risk modelling: simulation is a tool that may be applied to contexts of risk/uncertainty, as well as to other contexts. Similarly, there are other methods to model risks that do not involve simulation (such as using the Black–Scholes formula, binomial trees and many other numerical methods that are beyond the scope of this text).

FURTHER ASPECTS OF OPTIMISATION MODELLING

Structural Choices

Although we have presented optimisation situations as ones that are driven by large numbers of possibilities for input values, a specific objective, and constraints (i.e. combinatorial-driven optimisation), the topic also arises when one is faced with choices between structurally different situations, i.e. ones that each involve a different logic structure. For example:

- One may consider the decision as to whether to go on a luxury vacation or to buy a new car as a form of optimisation problem in which one is trying to decide on the best alternative. In such cases, there may be only a small number of choices available, but each requires a different model and a mechanism to compare them (decision trees are a frequent approach).
- The choice as to whether a business should expand organically, or through an acquisition or a joint venture, is a decision with only a few combinations (choices), but where each is of a fundamentally different (structural) nature.

Figure 15.6 shows two categories of optimisation situation.

This topic is discussed briefly later in the chapter.

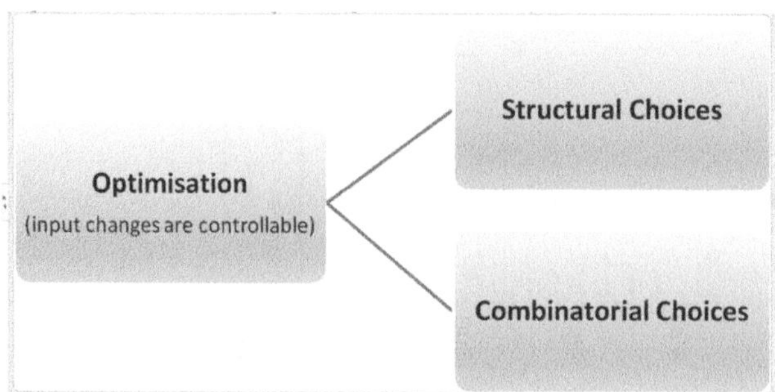

FIGURE 15.6 Structural and Combinatorial Optimisation

Uncertainty

The discussion so far has presented optimisation as the issue as to how to choose some input values whilst others are fixed. However, in some cases, these other variables may be subject to uncertainty. For example:

- One may try to find the optimum route to drive through a large town, either under the assumption that the transit time for each possible section of the route and the traffic lights and traffic conditions are known, or under the assumption that these items are uncertain. It is conceivable that the optimum route is the same, irrespective of whether uncertainty is considered. However, uncertainty can also impact risk-tolerances, so that if one needed to be sure to arrive at one's destination by a fixed time (such as to fix the time for a meeting), one may decide to choose a route that is longer on average but is less uncertain, so that a more reliable plan can be made.
- In the traditional frameworks used to describe the optimisation of financial portfolios, one is trying to choose the weights of each asset in the context in which the returns of each asset are uncertain (but with known values of the parameters that described the uncertainty, such as the mean and standard deviation of returns).

Integrated Approaches to Optimisation

From the above discussion, it is clear that in general one may have to reflect not only structural optimisation, but also (either or both of) combinatorial optimisation and uncertainty. For example:

- Faced with the structural decision as to whether either to stay at home or to meet a friend at the other side of town: if one chooses to meet the friend, there may be many possible combinations of routes that one could drive. At the same time, the length of time required to navigate each section of the route may be uncertain.
- When designing any large potential project (including when conducting risk assessment and risk management on it), one will generally have several options as to the overall structural design or technical solution. Within each, there will be design-related items that are to be optimised, as well as risks to mitigate, and residual risks or uncertainties that cannot be effectively mitigated further. Thus, the optimal project design and risk mitigation (or response) strategy will typically have elements both of structural and combinatorial optimisation, as well as uncertainty: structural optimisation about which context in which to operate (or overall technical solution to choose), combinatorial optimisation to find the best set of risk mitigation measures within that context and residual uncertainty that cannot be further reduced in an economically efficient way.
- Faced with the decision as to whether to proceed or not with a project, there may be characteristics which allow its scope to be modified after some initial information about its likely future success has been gained. For example, once initial information about a potential oil drilling (or pharmaceutical) project becomes available, the activities could be conducted as originally expected, or abandoned or expanded. Note that, although valuable, the information obtained may be imperfect, incur a cost to obtain it, and the process of doing so could delay the project (compared to deciding whether to proceed without this information). Real-life

business situations in which a decision is possible either before or after uncertainty has been resolved (decision–chance–decision structures) are often termed "real options" situations.

Modelling Issues and Tools

Some important modelling issues that arise in optimisation contexts include:

- To ensure a clear and correct distinction between controllable and non-controllable inputs.
- To capture the nature of the optimisation within the model's logic. Where the optimisation is driven mainly by constraints, this is usually straightforward. Where it is driven by the U-shaped nature (in real life) of an output as an input varies, the model must also capture this logic. For example, a model which calculates sales revenues by multiplying price with volume may be sufficient for some simple sensitivity analysis purposes, but would be meaningless if used to find the optimal price, unless volume is made to depend on price (with higher prices leading to lower volumes). Thus, models which are intended to be used for optimisation purposes may have more demanding requirements on their logic than those that are to be used for simple "what-if" analysis, or if scenario approaches are used.
- To formulate the optimisation so that it has only one objective. Most optimisation algorithms allow for only one objective, whereas most business situations involve multiple objectives (and stakeholders with their own objectives). Thus, one typically needs to reformulate all but one of these as constraints. Whilst in theory the optimal solution would be the same in each, in practice, participants could often be (or feel themselves to be) at an advantage if their own objective is the one used for the optimisation (and at a disadvantage if their objective is instead translated into one of many constraints): psychologically, an objective has positive overtones, and is something that one should strive to achieve, whereas constraints are more likely to be de-emphasised, ignored or regarded as inconvenient items that can be modified or negotiated. Thus, when one's objective becomes expressed as only one item within a set of constraints, a focus on it is likely to be lost.
- Not to overly constrain the situation. A direct translation of management's objectives (when translated into constraints) often leads to a set of demands that are impossible to meet; so that optimisation algorithms will then not find a solution. Often, it can be useful to start with less constraints, so that an optimum can be found, and then seeks to show how the application of additional constraints changes the nature of the optimum solution, or leads eventually to no solution.

There is a large range of approaches and associated numerical techniques that may be applicable depending on the situation, including:

- Core tools for combinatorial optimisation, such as Excel's Solver. Where the optimisation problem is "multi-peaked" (or has certain other complex characteristics), Solver may not be able to find a solution, and other tools or add-ins (such as Palisade's Evolver based on genetic algorithms) may have a role.

- Combining optimisation with analytic methods. For example, in traditional approaches to the optimisation of financial portfolios, matrix algebra is used to determine the volatility of a portfolio based on its components. Thus, uncertainty has been "eliminated" from the model, so that standard combinatorial optimisation algorithms can be used.
- Combining optimisation with simulation. Where uncertainty cannot be dealt with by analytic or other means, one may have to use simulation. For example, with reference to the example earlier in the chapter, if there is uncertainty in the level of the cash flows for each project after its launch, then for every possible set of dates tried as a solution of the optimisation, a simulation would need to be run to see the uncertainty profile within that situation, with the optimum solution dependent on this (e.g. one may define the optimum one as the which maximises the average of the NPV, or alternatively as the one in which the NPV is above some figure with 90% frequency etc.). Where a full simulation is required for each trial of a potential optimal solution, it is often worth considering whether the presence of the uncertainty would change the actual optimum solution in any significant way. The potential time involved in running many simulations can be significant, whereas it may not generate any significantly different solutions. For example, in practice, the optimal route to travel across a large city may (in many cases) be the same irrespective of whether one considers the travel time for each potential segment of the journey to be uncertain or fixed. The implementation of such approaches may be done with several possible tools:
  - Using VBA macros to automate the running of Solver and the simulation.
  - Using Excel add-ins. For example, the RiskOptimizer tool that is in the Industrial version of the Excel add-in @RISK allows for a simulation to be run within each optimisation trial.
- Use of decision trees and lattice methods. Decision trees are often used due to their visual nature. In fact, decision trees can have a powerful numerical role that is independent of the visual aspect. When there is a sequential decision structure (in which one decision is taken after another, possibly within uncertain events in between), the optimum behaviour today can only be established by considering the future consequence of each possible choice. Thus, tree-based methods often use backward calculation paths, in which each future scenario must first be evaluated first, before a final view on today's decision can be taken. (The same underlying logic of backward calculations can in fact be implemented in Excel.) Generalisations of decision-tree approaches include those which are based on lattice methods, such as the finite difference or finite element methods that are applied on grids of data points; these are beyond the scope of this text.
- Decision trees may also need to be combined with simulation or other methods. For example, if there are uncertain outcomes that occur in between decision points, then each decision may be based on maximising the average (or some other property) of the future values. A backward process may need to be implemented to evaluate the last decision (based on its uncertain future outcomes), and once the choice for this decision is known, the prior decision can be evaluated; such stochastic optimisation situations are beyond the scope of this text.

Despite this complexity, one nice feature of many optimisation situations (especially those defined by a U-shaped curves) is that there are often several scenarios or choices that provide similar (if slightly sub-optimal) outcomes, since (around the optimum) point any deviation has a limited effect on the value of the curve (which is flat at the optimum point). Thus, sub-optimal solutions are often sufficiently accurate for many practical cases, and this may partly explain why heuristic methods (based on intuition and judgement, rather than numerical algorithms) are often used.

CHAPTER 16

The Modelling of Risk and Uncertainty, and Using Simulation

INTRODUCTION

This chapter extends the discussion of simulation that was begun in Chapter 15. We describe the origins, uses and main benefits of simulation techniques (with a focus on risk and uncertainty modelling), and describe some key ways to implement these. We cover the basic use of VBA macros, as well as highlighting some key benefits of using Excel add-ins, such as @RISK. A few simple examples of core applications (risk registers and cost budgeting) are shown, using both Excel/VBA and @RISK. The author's *Business Risk and Simulation Modelling in Practice Using Excel, VBA and @RISK* provides a much more extensive discussion of risk assessment processes and the issues involved in the design and implementation of risk models; the interested reader is referred to that text.

THE MEANING, ORIGINS AND USES OF MONTE CARLO SIMULATION

Definition and Origin

Monte Carlo Simulation ("MCS", or simply "simulation") is the use of random sampling to automate the process to recalculate a model many times as several inputs are varied simultaneously. The creation of randomness *per se* is not an objective of simulation; rather its role is to allow for automation of the process, and to ensure that a wide set of input combinations is used.

The first large-scale use of simulation was in the 1940s by scientists working on nuclear weapons projects at the Los Alamos National Laboratory in the USA, where it was used to compute integrals numerically: the value of $\int_0^1 f(x)dx$ is equal to the average of $f(x)$ as x varies over the range 0 to 1. Hence, by calculating $f(x)$ for a set of x-values (drawn randomly and uniformly) between 0 and 1, and taking their average, one can estimate the integral. The scientists considered that the method resembled gambling, and coined the term "Monte Carlo Simulation".

Simulation is not the same as risk modelling, but rather it is a technique that can be applied to evaluate risk or other forms of models. For example, simulation could be used to try to find a solution to an optimisation problem, by generating many input combinations and looking for the one which produces the best results and meets the constraints. In such a context, the underlying probability distributions used to create the random samples would not be of great significance, and would not need to correspond to any notion of risk of the input variables. Indeed, as an optimisation problem, one assumes that such variables are not subject to risk, but are controllable.

On the other hand, in practice, the use of simulation in business applications is predominately to capture the risks, uncertainties and their impacts. In such cases, the random sampling has the additional purpose (in addition to process automation) of describing the risk (or uncertainty) that is inherent in the input values: the distributions are chosen to best match the uncertainty of the (in real life) variable that it represents. Thus, risk modelling is a much richer subject than is that of pure simulation.

Limitations of Sensitivity and Scenario Approaches

Traditional sensitivity and scenario approaches have several limitations, including:

- They show only a small set of explicitly pre-defined cases.
- The cases shown are not clearly defined, and may not be representative or relevant for decision purposes, for example:
  - The likelihood of any outcome is not known (such as the extent to which the base plan is realistically achievable or not).
  - The use of the most likely values for inputs will not generally result in the model's output being calculated at its most likely value.
  - The average outcome is not known, yet this is the most relevant single economic measure of the value of a project or of a series of cash flows.
  - Since the base case is not, in general, a well-defined case, nor are any cases which are derived from it. For example, a +/– 10% variation of inputs around their base values is also using undefined cases, and using these to form an average, or to represent (say) a worst or best case could be very misleading.
  - It is not easy to reflect risk tolerances (or contingency requirements) adequately in the decision, or to set appropriate targets or appropriate objectives.
  - It is not easy to compare one project with another when they have different degrees of uncertainty.
- They do not explicitly drive a thought process that explores true risk drivers and risk-mitigation actions, and hence may not be based on genuine scenarios that one may be exposed to.
- They do not distinguish between variables that are risky or uncertain and those that are to be optimised (chosen optimally).

Simulation can help to overcome some of these limitations by allowing one to implement risk and uncertainty modelling to determine the range and frequency of possible outcomes.

Key Benefits of Uncertainty and Risk Modelling and the Questions Addressable

The explicit consideration of risk (or uncertainty) has many benefits, both from a process and decision-making perspective:

- It highlights the possibility of multiple outcomes. The real-life outcome will almost always be different to that shown in any single scenario or base case: this difference is not necessarily the result of a poor model, but an inherent property of real life.
- It forces one to consider sources of uncertainty, and to ask more in-depth questions about the situation (such as how the uncertainty could be controlled or managed).
- It may lead to a revised model which includes a larger set of factors than in the original model, including the presence of event risks and of risk mitigation measures. The process of doing so requires one to identify which sources of risk are the most significant, to determine how the risk profile would be changed by the implementation of risk–response measures, and to determine the optimal strategy for risk mitigation.
- It is a necessity when modelling situations that are inherently stochastic (such as the movement of share prices), and also to capture certain forms of dependencies between such relationships (such as correlation).
- It allows one to determine statistics that are relevant for economic evaluation, decision-making and risk management, such as:
  - Measures of the centre of the range of possible outcomes:
    - What is the average outcome?
    - What is the most likely outcome?
    - What value is the half-way point, i.e. where we are equally likely to do better or worse?
  - Measures of the spread of the range of possible outcomes:
    - What are the worst and best cases that are realistically possible?
    - Is the risk equally balanced on each side of a base case?
    - Is there a single measure that we can use to summarise the risk?
  - The likelihood that a base or other planned case can be achieved:
    - How likely is it that the planned case will be achieved (or not)?
    - Should we proceed with the decision as it is, or should we iterate through a risk mitigation and risk response process to further modify and optimise the decision?
- It allows for the calculation of project contingencies (such as: "in order to have enough money in 95% of cases, we need to increase the project's budget by 15%"). Such information is directly available once one has established the spread of possible outcomes. For example, given the spread (distribution) of possible cost for a project, the 90th percentile will represent the total figure that would be a sufficient budget in 90% of cases; the contingency (for 90% success) would be the figure that needs to be added to the base budget to achieve this total figure (i.e. it would be the difference between this figure and the base case).
- It can help to partially correct for biases in the process. By showing the base (or reference) case in the context of the full range of outcomes, some biases may be made more explicit. These may take several forms:
  - Intentional biases. These are where deliberately optimistic or pessimistic values are used for motivational or political reasons.

- Unintentional biases. One may simply be unaware of a bias until it is pointed out or where more detailed reflections about a situation are explicitly undertaken. One important form of unintentional bias is "the fallacy of the most likely", in which it may implicitly be believed that a model that is populated with its inputs at their most likely values will show the most likely value of the output (and similarly "the fallacy of the average", for average values). In fact, such beliefs are often not justified: factors such as non-symmetries of some uncertain processes, the presence of event risks and non-linear logic within the model (e.g. MIN, MAX or IF statements, or division by an input whose value is uncertain), can mean that the results are biased.

The Nature of Model Outputs

The simulation will of course be used to capture the range of outcomes for key metrics (performance indicators), such as cost, profit, cash flow, financing needs, resource requirements, project schedule, and so on. Several points about such outputs are important to be aware of:

- The output is a set of individual data points. These represent a sample of the "true" distribution of the output, but are not a distribution function *per se*. Nevertheless, for simplicity, one often refers to a simulation as providing a "distribution".
- The data set allows one to estimate properties of the true distribution, such as its average or the value in the worst 10% of cases, or to plot it graphically (such as a histogram of the frequency distribution of the points). It also allows one to calculate relationships between variables (especially correlation coefficients between inputs and an output), and to generate X–Y scatter-plots of the values of variables (providing the relevant data is saved at each recalculation).
- The more recalculations one performs, the closer should be the estimated properties to those of the true distribution. The required number of recalculations needs to be sufficient to provide the necessary basis for decision support; in particular, it should ensure the validity and stability of any resulting decision. This will itself depend on the context, decision metrics used and accuracy requirements.
- It is generally not a valid question to ask which specific combination of inputs will lead to a specific outcome; in general, there would be many.

The Applicability of Simulation Methods

Simulation techniques have found applications in many areas. The reasons for this include:

- They can be used in almost any model, irrespective of the application or sector.
- They are conceptually quite straightforward, essentially involving repeated recalculation to generate many scenarios. They require only an understanding of specific core aspects of statistics and probability, dependency relationships and (on occasion) some additional modelling techniques; the required level of mathematical knowledge is quite specific and limited.
- They are often by far the simplest method available to assess uncertainty or risk.

- They generally provide a reasonably (and sufficiently) accurate estimate of the properties of the output distribution, even when only relatively few recalculations have been conducted.
- They can be a useful complement to analytic or closed-form approaches; especially in more complex cases, simulation can be used to create intuition about the nature and the behaviour of the underlying processes.
- They can often produce a high level of insight and value-added with little effort or investment in time or money.

KEY PROCESS AND MODELLING STEPS IN RISK MODELLING

Whereas simulation is the automation of the process to recalculate a model many times, risk modelling involves the design and building of models to reflect the effect of the risks and uncertainties in a situation. At a superficial level, the key steps in risk modelling are similar to those in general risk management: For example, it is necessary to identify key risks and uncertainties. On the other hand, the risk modelling process needs to capture the nature of the uncertainties and their effects in ways that are much more specific and precisely defined than for pure qualitative risk management processes. This section describes some key elements of the process at a high level; once again, the interested reader can refer to the author's *Business Risk and Simulation Modelling in Practice* for a detailed discussion of these.

Risk Identification

Clearly, the necessary starting point for any form of analysis is the identification of all the risks and uncertainties that may reasonably affect a situation (to an acceptable degree of tolerance). The process of risk identification will generally also lead naturally to a discussion of risk mitigation or response measures, and to the subject of the residual risk once such measures are taken. The final model will need to reflect this revised project structure as well as the costs and effect of the mitigation measures.

Risk Mapping and the Role of the Distribution of Input Values

The risk mapping process involves describing the risks or uncertainties in a form that can be built into a quantitative model. Thus, one needs to understand the nature of the risk or uncertainty (e.g. continuous or discrete, a one-time or multiple event, its time behaviour and its relationship to other items in the model).

This can be a challenging part of the process in practice: first, from a process perspective, general project participants may have a focus on risk management, rather than full risk modelling, and therefore not understand the need for detailed descriptions of the nature of the uncertainties. Second, the quantitative process is more complex than simply selecting distributions, since some processes may be composed of compound effects, or effects which develop over time, or which interact with other processes, or have other complex dependencies. These will need to be reflected in the model's logic and formulae.

The choice of input distribution is an important part of a risk mapping process, with the idea being that the distributions match the true nature of the underlying randomness in each process as closely as possible (risk, variability or uncertain variation). However, this is more complex than simply assuming that any identified risk or uncertainty can be directly captured through a single distribution.

The Modelling Context and the Meaning of Input Distributions

It is important not to overlook the (seemingly obvious) point that in a risk model a distribution represents the non-controllable aspect of the process, within the context being modelled. This point is subtler than it may appear at first; the context may be something that one may control or choose, even where the process within that context is not. For example:

- When crossing a road, one can choose how many times to look, whether to put running shoes on, and so on; once such choices are made, the actual outcome (whether one arrives safely or not on the other side) is subject to non-controllable uncertainty. (Alternatively, one may choose another context, in which one does not cross the road at all, but achieves the required objective by some other means, such as placing an online order for groceries, so that one does not have to cross the road whilst walking to the shops.)
- In the early phases of evaluating a potential construction project, the range for the cost of purchasing materials may be represented by a distribution of uncertainty. As more information becomes available (e.g. quotes are received or the project progresses), the range may narrow. Each stage represents a change of context, but at any particular stage, a distribution can be used to represent the uncertainty at that point.

Thus, an important aim is to find the optimal context in which to operate; one cannot simply use a distribution to abdicate responsibility to optimise the chosen context of operation! Indeed, one of the criticisms sometimes levelled at risk modelling activities is that they may interfere with the incentives. Certainly, if one misunderstands or incorrectly interprets the role of distributions, then there is a likelihood that such issues may arise.

The Effect of Dependencies Between Inputs

The use of probability distributions also facilitates the process of capturing possible dependencies between input processes. There are various types of possible relationships, including:

- Those of a causal or directional nature. For example, the occurrence of one event may increase the likelihood of another event occurring. Thus, the random samples (or intermediate calculations determined from these) of one process are used to determine the parameter value(s) of another random process.
- Those which are determined the way that samples from distributions are jointly drawn. The use of correlation (or "correlated sampling") is one key example.

At this point, we simply note that any dependencies between the inputs would change the distribution of the possible outcomes. For example, in a model which sums its input values, if a dependency relationship were such that a low value of one input would mean that all other inputs took low values (and similarly for high values), then the likelihood of more extreme (low or high) values would increase compared to the case where the inputs are independent of each other.

Random Numbers and the Required Number of Recalculations or Iterations

Simulation methods will in general produce a set of numbers that should approximate those of the true distribution of outcomes. The difference between a statistic produced in the simulation and that of the true distribution can be considered as the "error" associated with the simulation. Of course, the true figure is rarely known (which is the main reason to use simulation in the first place!). Nevertheless, in principle, a more accurate result will be achieved if:

- The simulation is run many times, i.e. with many recalculations of the same model.
- The algorithm used to generate the random numbers is of high quality:
  - The random numbers generated should be representative and not biased, so that (given enough samples) all combinations would be generated with their true frequency.
  - Since a computer is a finite instrument, it cannot contain every possible number. At some point any random number generation method would repeat itself, at least in theory (superior methods will have very long cycles that do not repeat in practice).

In general, for many random number algorithms used in practice, an "inverse square root law" applies: on average, the error is halved as the number of recalculation (iterations) is quadrupled. Truly accurate results are therefore only achievable with very large numbers of iterations (an extra decimal of accuracy requiring 100 times as many recalculations). At first sight, this may seem to be a major disadvantage of simulation methods. However, there are a number of points to bear in mind in this respect:

- Although many (recalculations) may be required to improve the relative error significantly, the actual calculated values are usually close to the true figures, even with small numbers of iterations; in other words, the starting point for the application of an inverse-square-root law is one in which the error (or numerator) is generally quite low.
- The number of iterations required may ultimately depend on the objectives: estimating the mean or the values of other central figures usually requires far less iterations than estimating a P99 value, for example. However, even figures such as the P90 are often reasonably accurate with small numbers of iterations.
- One must accept that the results will never be exact; the error will (generally) never be zero, however many iterations are run. In business contexts, the models are not likely to be highly accurate (due to an imperfect understanding of the processes, and the various estimates that are likely to be required); generally, it is the stability and validity *of the decision* that is of importance, not the extremely precise calculation of a figure. Thus, running "sufficient" iterations may be more important than trying to run many more. (In some cases, the use of a fixed seed for the random number algorithm in order to be able to repeat the simulation exactly is useful.) In addition, in business contexts, one is generally more interested in central values (in which we include the P90) than in cases that may only arise very rarely; such central figures can often be estimated with reasonable accuracy with relatively few recalculations.

- When one is building models, testing them, exploring hypotheses and drawing initial directional conclusions, the most effective working method can be to run relatively few iterations (typically several hundred or a few thousand). When final results are needed, the numbers of iterations can be increased (and perhaps the random number seed can be fixed, in order to allow repetition of the simulation).
- The reliance on graphical displays to communicate outputs (instead of on statistics) will generally require more iterations; when it is intuitively clear that the underlying situation is a smooth continuous process, participants will expect to see this reflected in graphical outputs. In particular, histograms for probability density curves that are created by counting the number of output data points in each of a set of pre-defined "bins" may not look smooth unless large numbers of samples are used (due to randomness, a point may be allocated to a neighbouring bin by a close margin). The use of cumulative curves and statistics can partially overcome this, but graphical displays in general will be apparently less stable than statistical measures.

USING EXCEL AND VBA TO IMPLEMENT RISK AND SIMULATION MODELS

The implementation of basic risk models using simulation methods in Excel/VBA is straightforward. At the simplest level, the RAND function can be used to generate random samples from a uniform distribution, which can be transformed into random samples from many other distributions using the inverse functions (percentiles) for those distributions. Some of these inverse functions are available directly in Excel, and some can be calculated explicitly. A VBA macro can be used to recalculate the model many times, storing the key outputs as one does so. Correlated random numbers can also be generated with some additional effort.

In this section, we demonstrate some of the core techniques in this respect. However, the subject is in fact much richer than it may first appear. For example, there are many ways in which the process can be structured. These could include using results and analysis worksheets that are separate to the model worksheet(s), generating random samples in VBA rather than in Excel, creating user-defined functions for distributions, and issues relating to computational optimisation and results presentation (e.g. automation of graphical output). Such topics are beyond the scope of this text, and generally covered more extensively in the author's text *Business Risk and Simulation Modelling in Practice*, as already referenced. At the same time, the potential richness of the topics means that the use of add-ins, such as @RISK, is often also of benefit.

The core aspects demonstrated in this section are therefore simply the use of Excel/VBA to:

- Create random samples from some distributions.
- Repeatedly calculate a model and store the results.

Generation of Random Samples

The generation of random samples from probability distributions can be achieved by first using the RAND function to sample from a uniform distribution between zero and one. The sampled value is treated as a probability value, which is used to find the associated percentile for the final distribution that is desired to be sampled. In other words, the process of finding the percentile value for a given probability value is equivalent to inverting the cumulative distribution at that probability value: if the probability samples are chosen uniformly, then the inverted values will be representative of the distribution. For example, the sampling of a uniform distribution on [0,1] would result in a random number in the range 0 to 0.1 being drawn in 10% of cases; the inverted Normal distribution for each of these values would produce a sample in the range $-\infty$ to -1.28 in those 10% of cases.

For example:

- For uniform continuous ranges:

$$\text{Value or Impact} = \text{Min} + (\text{Max} - \text{Min}) * \text{RAND}()$$

- For the occurrence of the risk events:

$$\text{Occurrence or Not} = \text{IF}(\text{RAND}() \leq \text{Prob}, 1, 0)$$

- For a standard Normal distribution

$$\text{Value} = \text{NORM.S.INV}(\text{RAND}())$$

Note that the first two examples are explicitly calculated analytically, whereas the last example uses one of the inverse functions available in Excel. Other such Excel functions include:

- BINOM.INV, to create a sample from a binomial distribution; the parameter Alpha of the function would refer to the random P.
- LOGNORM.INV to sample a Lognormal distribution (note that this function uses the logarithmic parameters, not the natural ones).
- BETA.INV to sample a Beta distribution.
- GAMMA.INV to sample a Gamma distribution.

Repeated Recalculations and Results Storage

A simple VBA loop can be used to recalculate the model and store the results. For example, the code below assumes that a model has been built containing three predefined named ranges: one to define the number of times that the simulation should be run, another for the output, and another which contains a header field for the results. The VBA code then simply recalculates the model for the desired number of times and stores the output results one under another,

```
Sub MRRunSim()
NCalcs = Range("NCalcs").Value
For i = 1 To NCalcs
 Application.Calculate
 Range("SimResultsHeader").Offset(i, 0).Value = Range("SimOutput").Value
Next i
End Sub
```

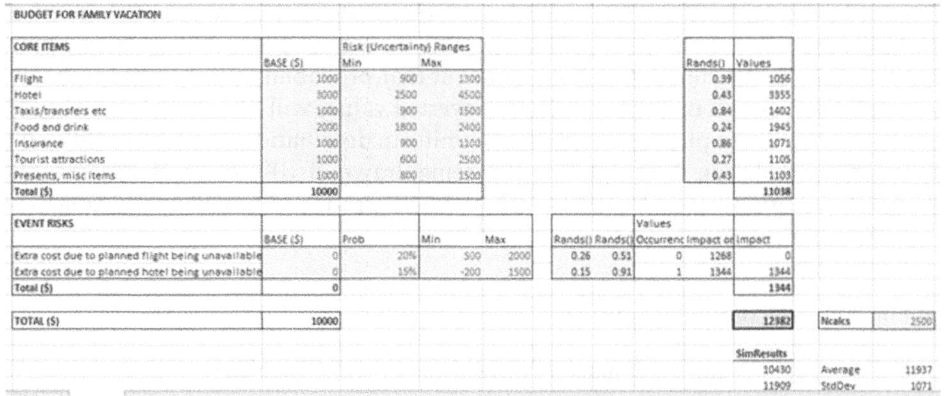

BUDGET FOR FAMILY VACATION

CORE ITEMS	BASE ($)	Risk (Uncertainty) Ranges Min	Max	Rands()	Values
Flight	1000	900	1300	0.39	1056
Hotel	3000	2500	4500	0.43	3355
Taxis/transfers etc	1000	900	1500	0.84	1402
Food and drink	2000	1800	2400	0.24	1945
Insurance	1000	900	1100	0.86	1071
Tourist attractions	1000	600	2500	0.27	1105
Presents, misc items	1000	800	1500	0.43	1103
Total ($)	10000				11038

EVENT RISKS	BASE ($)	Prob	Min	Max	Rands()	Rands()	Values Occurrenc	Impact or	Impact
Extra cost due to planned flight being unavailable	0	20%	500	2000	0.26	0.51	0	1268	0
Extra cost due to planned hotel being unavailable	0	15%	-200	1500	0.15	0.91	1	1344	1344
Total ($)	0								1344

TOTAL ($)	10000	12382	Ncalcs	2500

SimResults		
10430	Average	11937
11909	StdDev	1071

FIGURE 16.1 Simple Model that Generates Random Samples in Excel and Uses a Macro to Simulate Many Outcomes

Example: Cost Estimation with Uncertainty and Event Risks Using Excel/VBA

The file Ch16.1.CostEstimation.BasicSim.xlsm contains a simple example of a model for the costs of a family vacation, using only uniform distributions and event risks. The simulation results are shown in the file (and the simulation can be re-run using macros) (see Figure 16.1).

USING ADD-INS TO IMPLEMENT RISK AND SIMULATION MODELS

There are a number of commercial add-ins available to assist in the building of risk modelling and in the running of simulations (the main large-scale add-ins are @RISK, CrystalBall, RiskSolver and ModelRisk). This section discusses the general benefits of add-ins over the use of pure Excel/VBA approaches, and demonstrates some results using @RISK.

Benefits of Add-ins

The use of add-ins can have many benefits compared to the writing of VBA code:

- They can facilitate many aspects associated with the processes of building risk models and communicating their concepts and results. Key steps are often easier, quicker, more transparent, and more robust. This is especially due to the graphics capabilities and statistical tools, as well as the ease of creating dependency relationship, especially correlated sampling.
- There is usually a large set of distributions and parameters available. Some special distributions would also be cumbersome to replicate with Excel/VBA approaches.
- Models can generally be structured without particular consideration given to where risk distributions are placed within them, nor to whether their ranges need to be contiguous to each other.

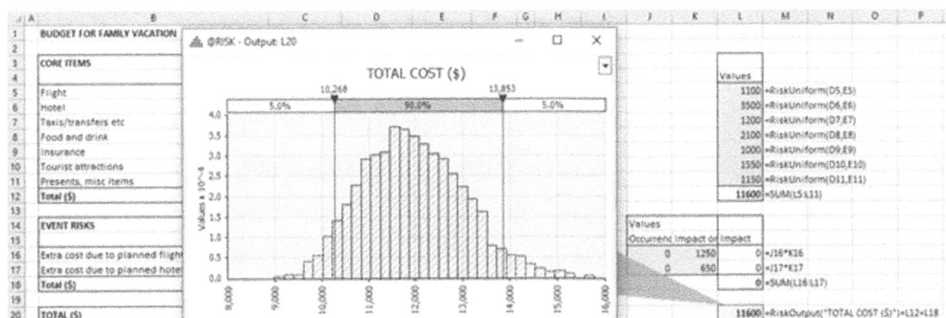

FIGURE 16.2 Using @RISK in the Simple Model

- Many aspects of the simulation and random number selection are easy to control, including the ability to repeat a simulation exactly, to conduct multiple simulations, or to select the random number generation algorithms and the sampling type. In addition, it is often straightforward to embed procedures that need to be run at each iteration of a simulation.
- There are tools to assist in the auditing of models, and to conduct enhanced results analysis.
- There is generally no VBA coding required.
- They are tried and tested applications, whereas bespoke-written VBA code is more likely to contain coding errors or not be robust.
- In summary, more time can be focused on generation of insights, solutions and recommendations, and creating value-added in a business and organisational context.

Example: Cost Estimation with Uncertainty and Event Risks Using @RISK

The file Ch16.2.CostEstimation.Basic.@RISK.xlsx contains the same simple example model used earlier, implemented with @RISK. Figure 16.2 shows a screen-clip of the model and the simulation results.

PART
Five

Excel Functions and Functionality

CHAPTER 17

Core Arithmetic and Logical Functions

INTRODUCTION

This chapter discusses a core set of functions that are required in a wide range of financial modelling applications, including revenue and cost estimation, basic statistical and data analysis, general forecasting, integrated financial statement modelling, cash flow valuation, project finance modelling, and so on. The functions are drawn from a range of Excel's categories, and include:

- IF, AND, OR and NOT.
- MIN, MAX, MINA, MAXA, MINIFS and MAXIFS.
- COUNT, COUNTA, COUNTBLANK, COUNTIF and COUNTIFS.
- SUM, AVERAGE, AVERAGEA, SUMIF, SUMIFS, AVERAGEIF and AVERAGEIFS.
- PRODUCT and SUMPRODUCT.
- AGGREGATE and SUBTOTAL.
- IFERROR.
- SWITCH.

Most of these functions are likely to be well known to many readers, and are essentially self-explanatory. Nevertheless, some specific features are worth noting, including their behaviour in special cases (such as how they treat non-numerical (text) or blank fields, or error values), as well as some issues that relate to the choice of which function to use when several are available (see also Chapter 9).

PRACTICAL APPLICATIONS

Figure 17.1 shows the data set that will be referred to in several examples in the early part of this chapter. It shows the number of visits by specific patients to a set of physicians.

	A	B	C	D	E
1					
2					
3		Family Name	First Name	Primary Physician	Annual Visits 2016
4	1	Smith	Amelia	Cooper	3
5	2	Jones	Olivia	Clarke	2
6	3	Taylor	Emily	Patel	1
7	4	Williams	Ava	Mitchell	4
8	5	Brown	Isla	Clarke	7
9	6	Davies	Jessica	James	2
10	7	Evans	Poppy	Cooper	4
11	8	Wilson	Isabella	Clarke	8
12	9	Thomas	Sophie	James	
13	10	Roberts	Mia	Cooper	12
14	11	Johnson	Ruby	Clarke	0
15	12	Lewis	Lily	James	4
16	13	Walker	Grace	Cooper	3
17	14	Robinson	Evie	Clarke	6
18	15	Wood	Sophia	Patel	3
19	16	Thompson	Ella	Patel	7
20	17	White	Scarlett	Mitchell	4
21	18	Watson	Chloe	Clarke	2
22	19	Jackson	Isabelle	Cooper	8
23	20	Wright	Freya	Cooper	4
24					

FIGURE 17.1 Data Set Used as a Basis for Several Examples in the Early Part of Chapter 17

Example: IF, AND, OR, NOT

In principle, the use of functions such as IF, AND, OR and NOT is straightforward. However, some specifics are worth noting:

- Short-forms. Many logical functions may be used in their short-forms, such as =AND(E19=1, E20=1) or =F7>F6. These implicitly involve an IF statement, which evaluates to either TRUE or FALSE. These are not text strings, but are interpreted as one or zero respectively when used in most subsequent calculations in Excel. For example, =50*(F7>F6) would return either 50 or zero. The long-form equivalent explicitly involves an IF statement, such as =IF(F7>F6,1,0). (Note also, that these are different to =IF(F7>F6,"TRUE","FALSE"), as this returns text strings, and is therefore generally inconvenient when the results of such expressions are to be used in further numerical calculations.) The results of short-form logical tests (i.e. FALSE or TRUE) may, however, act in unexpected ways (i.e. not as directly equivalent to 0 or 1) when embedded within other Excel functions (such as SUMPRODUCT, as discussed in Chapter 9). Therefore, the author's preference is to use the full logical form, which creates an explicit, more transparent and more robust set of output values.
- Tests for blanks. The statement =IF(G3,1,0) should not be used to test whether a cell is empty or not. This would return 1 if G3 contains a strictly positive (or strictly negative) value, 0 where G3 is equal to 0 or is blank, and #VALUE in the case of a text entry. In addition, it is not explicit which property of G3 is being tested by such a statement. Functions with more explicit and clear logical tests

(such as ISBLANK, ISNUMBER or ISTEXT, perhaps in combination with AND, OR or NOT) are to be preferred.

The file Ch17.1.IF.AND.OR.NOT.xlsx shows examples of some of these functions, with screen-clips shown in Figure 17.2 and Figure 17.3

D	E	F	G	H
		6	Cooper	
Primary Physician	**Annual Visits 2016**	**Threshold passed?**	**Physician Match**	**Both conditions ?**
Cooper	3	=IF(E4>F$1,1,0)	=IF(D4=G$1,1,0)	=IF(AND(F4=1,G4=1),1,0)
Clarke	2	=IF(E5>F$1,1,0)	=IF(D5=G$1,1,0)	=IF(AND(F5=1,G5=1),1,0)
Patel	1	=IF(E6>F$1,1,0)	=IF(D6=G$1,1,0)	=IF(AND(F6=1,G6=1),1,0)
Mitchell	4	=IF(E7>F$1,1,0)	=IF(D7=G$1,1,0)	=IF(AND(F7=1,G7=1),1,0)
Clarke	7	=IF(E8>F$1,1,0)	=IF(D8=G$1,1,0)	=IF(AND(F8=1,G8=1),1,0)
James	2	=IF(E9>F$1,1,0)	=IF(D9=G$1,1,0)	=IF(AND(F9=1,G9=1),1,0)
Cooper	4	=IF(E10>F$1,1,0)	=IF(D10=G$1,1,0)	=IF(AND(F10=1,G10=1),1,0)
Clarke	8	=IF(E11>F$1,1,0)	=IF(D11=G$1,1,0)	=IF(AND(F11=1,G11=1),1,0)
James		=IF(E12>F$1,1,0)	=IF(D12=G$1,1,0)	=IF(AND(F12=1,G12=1),1,0)
Cooper	12	=IF(E13>F$1,1,0)	=IF(D13=G$1,1,0)	=IF(AND(F13=1,G13=1),1,0)
Clarke	0	=IF(E14>F$1,1,0)	=IF(D14=G$1,1,0)	=IF(AND(F14=1,G14=1),1,0)
James	4	=IF(E15>F$1,1,0)	=IF(D15=G$1,1,0)	=IF(AND(F15=1,G15=1),1,0)
Cooper	3	=IF(E16>F$1,1,0)	=IF(D16=G$1,1,0)	=IF(AND(F16=1,G16=1),1,0)
Clarke	6	=IF(E17>F$1,1,0)	=IF(D17=G$1,1,0)	=IF(AND(F17=1,G17=1),1,0)
Patel	3	=IF(E18>F$1,1,0)	=IF(D18=G$1,1,0)	=IF(AND(F18=1,G18=1),1,0)
Patel	7	=IF(E19>F$1,1,0)	=IF(D19=G$1,1,0)	=IF(AND(F19=1,G19=1),1,0)
Mitchell	4	=IF(E20>F$1,1,0)	=IF(D20=G$1,1,0)	=IF(AND(F20=1,G20=1),1,0)
Clarke	2	=IF(E21>F$1,1,0)	=IF(D21=G$1,1,0)	=IF(AND(F21=1,G21=1),1,0)
Cooper	8	=IF(E22>F$1,1,0)	=IF(D22=G$1,1,0)	=IF(AND(F22=1,G22=1),1,0)
Cooper	4	=IF(E23>F$1,1,0)	=IF(D23=G$1,1,0)	=IF(AND(F23=1,G23=1),1,0)

FIGURE 17.2 Examples of the IF and AND Functions Using the Formula View

D	E	F	G	H
		6	Cooper	
Primary Physician	**Annual Visits 2016**	**Threshold passed?**	**Physician Match**	**Both conditions ?**
Cooper	3	0	1	0
Clarke	2	0	0	0
Patel	1	0	0	0
Mitchell	4	0	0	0
Clarke	7	1	0	0
James	2	0	0	0
Cooper	4	0	1	0
Clarke	8	1	0	0
James		0	0	0
Cooper	12	1	1	1
Clarke	0	0	0	0
James	4	0	0	0
Cooper	3	0	1	0
Clarke	6	0	0	0
Patel	3	0	0	0
Patel	7	1	0	0
Mitchell	4	0	0	0
Clarke	2	0	0	0
Cooper	8	1	1	1
Cooper	4	0	1	0

FIGURE 17.3 Examples of the IF and AND Functions Showing the Results

Example: MIN, MAX, MINA, MAXA

The file Ch17.2.MAX.MIN.xlsx shows examples of the MAX and MIN functions to work out the maximum and minimum of the values in a data set respectively, with a screen-clip shown in Figure 17.4. It also shows the use of the MAXA and MINA functions. It is worth noting that:

- The MIN and MAX functions ignore blank cells and text. In particular, blank cells are not treated as if they contained zeros. For example, the minimum (MIN) of a set of items which includes blanks and strictly positive (non-zero) values will be the smallest strictly positive number (not zero).
- The MINA and MAXA functions do not ignore blanks, so that MINA of a set of items which includes blanks and strictly positive (non-zero) values will be zero. Text fields are not ignored by the functions, but their presence has no effect on the returned output (this is in contrast to COUNTA, where the presence of text fields will change the result).

Example: MINIFS and MAXIFS

The file Ch17.3.MAXIFS.MINIFS.xlsx shows an example of the MAXIFS function to perform conditional queries. Figure 17.5 shows the maximum number of visits for some of the physicians.

Note that the MINIFS and MAXIFS functions were introduced into Excel in early 2016; prior to this, the closest similar functionality could have been achieved either by use of the Database functions (DMIN and DMAX), array formulae, or of the array form of the AGGREGATE function, all of which are discussed later in this text.

G	H	I
Item	Result	Formula
Maximum number of visits	12	=MAX(E4:E23)
Minimum number of visits	0	=MIN(E4:E23)
Minimum number of visits including blank cells, but with no zeros in the range	1	=MIN(D4:E12)
Minimum number of visits including blank cells, but with no zeros in the range	0	=MINA(D4:E12)

FIGURE 17.4 Examples of the MIN and MAX Functions

G	H	I
Item	Result	Formula
Maximum number of visits		
Cooper	12	=MAXIFS(E$4:E$23,D$4:D$23,G5)
Clarke	8	=MAXIFS(E$4:E$23,D$4:D$23,G6)
Patel	7	=MAXIFS(E$4:E$23,D$4:D$23,G7)
Mitchell	4	=MAXIFS(E$4:E$23,D$4:D$23,G8)

FIGURE 17.5 Example of the MAXIFS Functions

Example: COUNT, COUNTA, COUNTIF and Similar Functions

The file Ch17.4.CountAndVariants.xlsx shows examples of the COUNT-type functions including COUNT, COUNTA, COUNTBLANK, COUNTIF and COUNTIFS (see Figure 17.6).

A few points are worthy of note:

- COUNT counts the numbers in a range, ignoring blank cells, i.e. blank cells are not treated as if they contained zeros, but as if they did not exist at all (i.e. as if they were left out of the set of input cells).
- COUNTA counts both text and numbers in a range, ignoring blank cells.
- COUNTBLANK can be used to count the number of blank cells in a range, as can COUNTIF.
- COUNTIF can be used to conduct conditional calculations, and some specific cases are worth noting:
  - The application of a condition of equality (such as counting the number of items that are exactly equal to a specific figure) can be achieved by direct use of the relevant value or cell reference in the corresponding function argument.
  - Conditions of inequality require the entry of the appropriate symbol (such as >, <, >=, or <=), which are contained within inverted commas, such as “>=2”.
  - When conditions of inequality should reference cells (rather than using hard-coded values), manual editing of the function is required. For example, a criterion that is desired to refer to a cell such as “>=G24” would need editing to create “>=”&G24.
  - “Between” conditions can be created by using the COUNTIFS function and applying two sets of conditions to the same referred range (such as checking both “>=” and “<=” in the same range, using two function criteria fields).
  - Where there is a single condition, it is essentially irrelevant whether one uses COUNTIF or COUNTIFS. The latter function works when there is only one criterion, and the use of the former is easy to adapt if additional criteria are needed (by adding an “S” to the function).

G	H	I
Item	Result	Formula
Number of non-blank visit entries	19	=COUNT(E4:E23)
Number of non-blank visit entries	19	=COUNTA(E4:E23)
Number of blank visit entries	1	=COUNTBLANK(E4:E23)
Number of patients, using COUNT (incorrect for patient numbers using list of names)	0	=COUNT(B4:B23)
Number of patients, using COUNTA	20	=COUNTA(B4:B23)
Number of non-blank cells in range B11:E11	4	=COUNTA(B11:E11)
Number of non-blank cells in range B12:E12	3	=COUNTA(B12:E12)
Number of non-blank cells in range B13:E13 that contain only numbers	1	=COUNT(B13:E13)
Number of patients with blank entry	1	=COUNTIF(E4:E23,"")
Number of patients with 0 entry	1	=COUNTIF(E4:E23,0)
Number of patients with 2 visits (taken from cell G23)	3	=COUNTIF(E4:E23,G24)
Number of patients who actually visited, excluding blanks and those with 0 entry	18	=COUNTIF(E4:E23,">0")
Number of patients who visited between 2 and 4 time inclusive (blanks and those with 0 entry woul	11	=COUNTIFS(E4:E23,">=2",E4:E23,"<=4")
Using cell references (trial 1): Number of patients who visited between 2 and 4 times inclusive	0	=COUNTIFS(E4:E23,">=G24",E4:E23,"<=G25")
Using cell references (trial 2): Number of patients who visited between 2 and 4 times inclusive	11	=COUNTIFS(E4:E23,">="&G24,E4:E23,"<="&G25)

FIGURE 17.6 Examples of the COUNT, COUNTA, COUNTIF and Similar Functions

Example: SUM, AVERAGE, AVERAGEA

The file Ch17.5.Sum.Average.xlsx shows examples of the SUM and AVERAGE function, and also the explicit calculation of the average using COUNT; a screen-clip is shown in Figure 17.7. It also shows an example of AVERAGEA.

A few points are worthy of particular note:

- The SUM function will treat as zero (or ignore, which for this function are the same) cells which are either blank or which contain text.
- The AVERAGE function ignores cells which are blank or which contain text (so that such cells are not included in the count of the cells in the denominator of the calculations); the function gives the same result as using the SUM divided by the COUNT.
- The AVERAGEA function treats text as if it were zero, so that it is included within the count (for the denominator) without affecting the total (numerator), and hence potentially providing a different answer to AVERAGE. For example, when applied to a range containing only positive numbers and some text, AVERAGEA will return a lower value than would AVERAGE.

Example: SUMIF, SUMIFS, AVERAGEIF, AVERAGEIFS

The file Ch17.6.SUM.AVG.IF.IFS.xlsx shows examples of the SUMIF, SUMIFS, AVERAGEIF and AVERAGIFS functions, with a screen-clip shown in Figure 17.8. It is worth noting that:

- The COUNTIF function can be easily transformed into a COUNTIFS function by the simple inclusion of an additional criterion. However, an equivalent process is not possible if the SUMIF or AVERAGEIF functions are attempted to be adapted into SUMIFS and AVERAGEIFS; in the latter functions, the range to be summed or averaged is required to be the first argument (parameter), whereas it must be the last (and optional) parameter of the SUMIF and AVERAGEIF functions.
- In versions of Excel prior to Excel 2013, multi-criteria formulae could have been created using the Conditional Sum Wizard (a step-by-step utility); formulae created in this way are array formulae which are still compatible with later versions of Excel, but the utility itself is now essentially redundant as the "IFS"-type functions can be readily used in its place.

G	H	I
Item	Result	Formula
Number of annual visits (total)	84	=SUM(E4:E23)
Sum, including text within the range	8	=SUM(D11:E11)
Average of two cells: a zero and another number	6	=AVERAGE(E13:E14)
Average of a cell containing a number and blank cell	8	=AVERAGE(E11:E12)
Average of only numerical fields	8	=AVERAGE(D11:E11)
Average number of annual visits, including those with 0 entry	4.42	=AVERAGE(E4:E23)
Average number of annual visits, including those with 0 entry	4.42	=SUM(E4:E23)/COUNT(E4:E23)
Average of all fields	4	=AVERAGEA(D11:E11)

FIGURE 17.7 Examples of the SUM and AVERAGE Functions

G	H	I
Item	Result	Formula
Total number of visits to physician Cooper using SUMIF:		
Cooper	34	=SUMIF($D$4:$D$23,G6,$E$4:$E$23)
Total number of visits to physician Cooper using SUMIFS with one criteria:		
Cooper	34	=SUMIFS($E$4:$E$23,$D$4:$D$23,G9)
Average number of visits to physician Cooper using AVERAGEIF:		
Cooper	5.67	=AVERAGEIF($D$4:$D$23,G12,$E$4:$E$23)
Average number of visits to physician Cooper using AVERAGEIFS with one criteria:		
Cooper	5.67	=AVERAGEIFS($E$4:$E$23,$D$4:$D$23,G12)

FIGURE 17.8 Examples of the SUMIF, SUMIFS, AVERAGEIF and AVERAGIFS Functions

	A	B	C	D	E
1					
2			Probability(occur)	Probability(not occur)	Formulae
3		Event number 1	60%	40%	=1-C3
4		Event number 2	80%	20%	=1-C4
5		Event number 3	60%	40%	=1-C5
6		Event number 4	50%	50%	=1-C6
7		Event number 5	90%	10%	=1-C7
8		P(all)	13.0%	0.2%	=PRODUCT(D3:D7)
9			=PRODUCT(C3:C7)	=PRODUCT(D3:D7)	

FIGURE 17.9 Using PRODUCT to Calculate Probabilities of Occurrence and Non-occurrence

Example: PRODUCT

The file Ch17.7.PRODUCT.xlsx shows some examples of calculations using the PRODUCT function. This multiplies its arguments, which can be either a single contiguous range of cells. Of course, where only two cells are to be multiplied, one could instead use a standard multiplication operation. Thus, the function is most useful when the items in a multi-cell contiguous range are to be multiplied. In such cases, the use of the function avoids having to create a formula with many multiplication operators (such as =E5*E6*E7*E8). As well as being cumbersome to create, such a formula is error-prone in cases where one may need to insert cells later. (This is analogous to using the SUM function in place of repeated use of the addition operator that would refer to individual cells.)

An application is to probability calculations: where several independent events may each occur with a given probability, the probability that they all occur is the product of the individual probabilities. Similarly, the probability that none of them occur is the product of the probability that each of them do not occur. Figure 17.9 shows an example. Using similar calculations, one can show that in a group of 23 (or more) people, the chance that two people share the same birthday is just over 50%

G	H	I	J	K
Person Number	No. days to choose from	Prob. Different date=No. days/365	Cumulative Probability	Formulae
1	365	100.0%	100.0%	=PRODUCT(I$3:I3)
2	364	99.7%	99.7%	=PRODUCT(I$3:I4)
3	363	99.5%	99.2%	=PRODUCT(I$3:I5)
4	362	99.2%	98.4%	=PRODUCT(I$3:I6)
5	361	98.9%	97.3%	=PRODUCT(I$3:I7)
6	360	98.6%	96.0%	=PRODUCT(I$3:I8)
7	359	98.4%	94.4%	=PRODUCT(I$3:I9)
8	358	98.1%	92.6%	=PRODUCT(I$3:I10)
9	357	97.8%	90.5%	=PRODUCT(I$3:I11)
10	356	97.5%	88.3%	=PRODUCT(I$3:I12)
11	355	97.3%	85.9%	=PRODUCT(I$3:I13)
12	354	97.0%	83.3%	=PRODUCT(I$3:I14)
13	353	96.7%	80.6%	=PRODUCT(I$3:I15)
14	352	96.4%	77.7%	=PRODUCT(I$3:I16)
15	351	96.2%	74.7%	=PRODUCT(I$3:I17)
16	350	95.9%	71.6%	=PRODUCT(I$3:I18)
17	349	95.6%	68.5%	=PRODUCT(I$3:I19)
18	348	95.3%	65.3%	=PRODUCT(I$3:I20)
19	347	95.1%	62.1%	=PRODUCT(I$3:I21)
20	346	94.8%	58.9%	=PRODUCT(I$3:I22)
21	345	94.5%	55.6%	=PRODUCT(I$3:I23)
22	344	94.2%	52.4%	=PRODUCT(I$3:I24)
23	343	94.0%	49.3%	=PRODUCT(I$3:I25)

FIGURE 17.10 Using PRODUCT to Calculate Probabilities of Shared Birthdays

M	N	O	P
Period Number	Growth Rates	Value & adjustment	Formulae
0		100	
1	2.0%	102.0%	=1+N4
2	3.0%	103.0%	=1+N5
3	5.0%	105.0%	=1+N6
4	8.0%	108.0%	=1+N7
5	7.0%	107.0%	=1+N8
6	6.0%	106.0%	=1+N9
7	5.0%	105.0%	=1+N10
8	4.0%	104.0%	=1+N11
9	2.0%	102.0%	=1+N12
10	2.0%	102.0%	=1+N13
		153.5	=O$3*PRODUCT(O$4:O13)

FIGURE 17.11 Using PRODUCT to Calculate Future Values

(in other words, for there to be more than a 50% chance that two people in a group share the same birthday, the group size needs to be 23 people or more) (see Figure 17.10).

Another example of the PRODUCT function is to calculate the ending value of something that grows with rate g_1 in period 1, g_2 in period 2, and so on. The value at the end of period N is:

$$V_N = V_0(1+g_1)(1+g_2)...(1+g_N)$$

In Figure 17.11, we show the calculation of this, assuming that the field containing the 1+g items is first calculated in Excel (Column O).

	A	B	C	D	E
1					
2		Asset Number	% in Each Asset	Return (expected)	
3		1	40.0%	10%	
4		2	25.0%	15%	
5		3	20.0%	18%	
6		4	15.0%	20%	
7		Total	100%	14.4%	
8			=SUM(C3:C6)	=SUMPRODUCT(C3:C6,D3:D6)	

FIGURE 17.12 Portfolio Returns Using the SUMPRODUCT

	A	B	C	D	E	F	G	H	I	J	K	L	M	N
1														
2		Years		2015	2016	2017	2018	2019	2020					
3		Capex		100	105	120	80	50	100					
4														
5		Generic Periods		1	2	3	4	5						
6		Depreciation Schedule	100%	30%	25%	20%	15%	10%						
7														
8		Depreciation		2015	2016	2017	2018	2019	2020	2021	2022	2023	2024	
9		2015	100	30%	25%	20%	15%	10%						
10		2016	105		30%	25%	20%	15%	10%					
11		2017	120			30%	25%	20%	15%	10%				
12		2018	80				30%	25%	20%	15%	10%			
13		2019	50					30%	25%	20%	15%	10%		
14		2020	100						30%	25%	20%	15%	10%	
15		Total		30.0	56.5	82.3	=SUMPRO	84.8	87.0	59.0	35.5	20.0	10.0	=SUMPRODUCT($C9:$C14,M9:M14)
16														

FIGURE 17.13 Depreciation Calculations Using SUMPRODUCT

Example: SUMPRODUCT

The SUMPRODUCT function works with a set of row or column ranges of equal size (and which are either all in columns or all in rows), and multiplies the first elements in each range, the second elements in each range, and so on, and then adds these up. Although it can be applied when there are several ranges, the most frequent use is where there are just two. (Where one wishes to multiply row with column data, one can use array functions, such as TRANSPOSE or MMULT, as discussed in Chapter 18.)

The file Ch17.8.SUMPRODUCT.1.xlsx shows an example in portfolio analytics, where the function is used to calculate the return of a portfolio based on the weighted average of its individual components (assets) (see Figure 17.12).

Similarly, the file Ch17.9.SUMPRODUCT.2.xlsx shows an example in which a "triangle-type" structure is used to calculate the total depreciation profile when the capital expenditure profile is known and the generic depreciation schedule is given (see Figure 17.13).

Example: SUBTOTAL

The SUBTOTAL function allows a variety of summary calculations to be performed on a set of data that is arranged in columns (not rows). It ignores other SUBTOTAL functions within its range, so that double-counting (and circular references) are avoided. It also allows one to specify how hidden rows are to be treated.

Function	FunctionNumber	
	To include hidden values	To ignore hidden values
AVERAGE	1	101
COUNT	2	102
COUNTA	3	103
MAX	4	104
MIN	5	105
PRODUCT	6	106
STDEV	7	107
STDEVP	8	108
SUM	9	109
VAR	10	110
VARP	11	111

FIGURE 17.14 Function Numbers When Using SUBTOTAL

The file Ch17.10.SUBTOTAL.1.xlsx shows a summary of the different calculation possibilities for the function, including how to treat data that is hidden, defined using the first parameter of the function; these are also shown in Figure 17.14.

Note that one needs to take extra care when using hidden areas and Excel filters at the same time (see Chapter 26).

The function can be entered either:

- By direct insertion into a cell. This could make sense, for example in a financial statement model, where the total assets may be calculated from the (subtotal) of the fixed and current assets, which may themselves each be the subtotals of more detailed calculations (such as of equipment, working capital etc.).
- Using the Subtotal Wizard on Excel's Data tab. The use of the Wizard is particularly powerful when applied to a set of data in which one of the columns contains a category variable that has been sorted (using Data/Sort, for example) so that all items within the category are in contiguous rows; in this case, the Wizard can be used to create subtotals by category.

The file Ch17.11.SUBTOTAL.2.xlsx shows an example of the first approach, in which the function has been inserted manually into several rows, in order to calculate the total number of pages of a book, whilst also showing the number of pages in the individual parts (see Figure 17.15).

The file Ch17.12.SUBTOTAL.3.Wizard.xlsx shows an example of the second approach, in which the function Wizard is used. In the first step, the data set is sorted per desired category variable for which subtotal calculations are required (using the Sort menu on the Data tab); this is shown in the screen-clip in Figure 17.16, in which a sort by Customer is conducted.

In the second step, the Wizard (on the Data tab, within the Outline category) is used to create subtotals of the amounts by customer identity (see Figure 17.17).

In Figure 17.18, we show the result when the Wizard process has been completed.

Example: AGGREGATE

The AGGREGATE function (in Excel 2013 onwards), like SUBTOTAL, is designed for columns (not rows) of data. Although in its basic form it will generally work with data arranged in rows, one may get unexpected results if columns are hidden.

	A	B	C	D
1				
2			Pages	Formulae
3		PART I	80	=SUBTOTAL(9,C4:C6)
4		Chapter 1	25	
5		Chapter 2	20	
6		Chapter 3	35	
7		PART II	100	=SUBTOTAL(9,C8:C12)
8		Chapter 4	15	
9		Chapter 5	20	
10		Chapter 6	30	
11		Chapter 7	20	
12		Chapter 8	15	
13		PART III	55	=SUBTOTAL(9,C14:C15)
14		Chapter 8	25	
15		Chapter 9	30	
16		PART IV	100	=SUBTOTAL(9,C17:C18)
17		Chapter 10	75	
18		Chapter 11	25	
19		Total	=SUBTOTAL(	=SUBTOTAL(9,C3:C18)

FIGURE 17.15 Use of SUBTOTAL by Direct Insertion

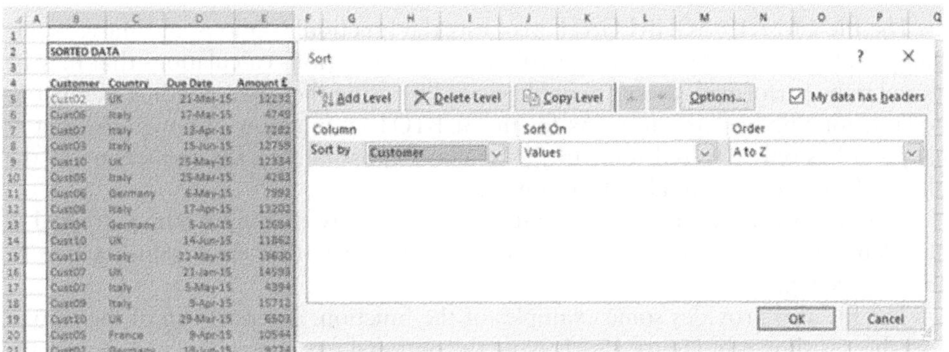

FIGURE 17.16 Insertion of SUBTOTAL Functions by Category Using the Wizard

The main comparison with the SUBTOTAL function is:

- The AGGREGATE function has more options as to how data is to be treated, including to ignore error values. This is a key point; most all Excel functions require that there be no errors within the data set (e.g. SUM, MAX, SUBTOTAL). This property is used in Chapter 18 to show how the array form of the function can be used to replicate conditional calculations.
- There is a slightly larger set of possibilities for the underlying functions.
- The function is not affected by the application of a filter in Excel.
- There is no Wizard to facilitate its insertion at various places within a data set.

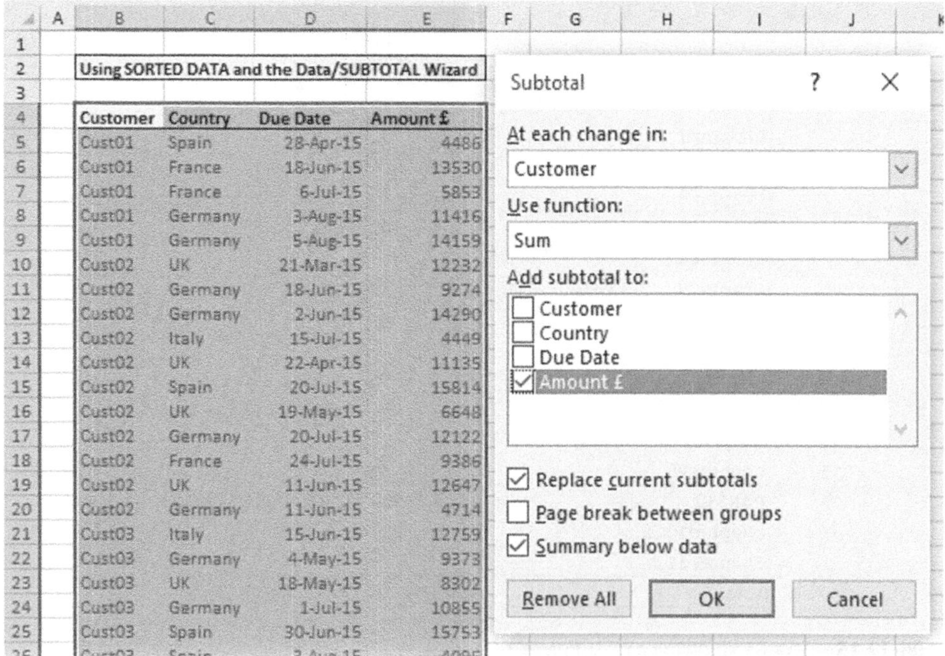

Using SORTED DATA and the Data/SUBTOTAL Wizard

Customer	Country	Due Date	Amount £
Cust01	Spain	28-Apr-15	4486
Cust01	France	18-Jun-15	13530
Cust01	France	6-Jul-15	5853
Cust01	Germany	3-Aug-15	11416
Cust01	Germany	5-Aug-15	14159
Cust02	UK	21-Mar-15	12232
Cust02	Germany	18-Jun-15	9274
Cust02	Germany	2-Jun-15	14290
Cust02	Italy	15-Jul-15	4449
Cust02	UK	22-Apr-15	11135
Cust02	Spain	20-Jul-15	15814
Cust02	UK	19-May-15	6648
Cust02	Germany	20-Jul-15	12122
Cust02	France	24-Jul-15	9386
Cust02	UK	11-Jun-15	12647
Cust02	Germany	11-Jun-15	4714
Cust03	Italy	15-Jun-15	12759
Cust03	Germany	4-May-15	9373
Cust03	UK	18-May-15	8302
Cust03	Germany	1-Jul-15	10855
Cust03	Spain	30-Jun-15	15753

FIGURE 17.17 Insertion of SUBTOTAL Functions by Category Using the Wizard

The file Ch17.13.AGGREGATE.xlsx lists the function's options and shows some examples. Figure 17.19 shows the possibilities for the various calculations that may be desired to be performed; these are implemented by using the corresponding number as the FunctionNumber argument. As for the SUBTOTAL function, although the text at this point has only covered some of the function's possibilities, the application to the full set of functions should be clear in principle.

The file also shows the options that relate to the way that input data is treated in the calculations. For example, option number 6 instructs that error values are to be ignored (see Figure 17.20).

The file also provides some examples of the function. A screen-clip of the second worksheet is shown in Figure 17.21. Note the optional parameter, k, which represents the additional parameter, requires the function numbers 14 through 19.

Example: IFERROR

The IFERROR function is contained within Excel's Logical category. It allows for an alternative value to be output in the case that the default set of calculations returns an error.

The file Ch17.14.IFERROR.xlsx shows an example (see Figure 17.22). This is based on the fact that the PPMT function (which calculates the principal part of a fixed payment required to repay a loan over several periods – see Chapter 7 for details) produces valid numerical values only for those periods which are within the time-frame of the loan. Beyond the time period in which the loan applies, the function returns a

	A	B	C	D	E	F	G
1							
2		**Using SORTED DATA and the Data/SUBTOTAL Wizard**					
3							
4		**Customer**	**Country**	**Due Date**	**Amount £**		
5		Cust01	Spain	28-Apr-15	4486		
6		Cust01	France	18-Jun-15	13530		
7		Cust01	France	6-Jul-15	5853		
8		Cust01	Germany	3-Aug-15	11416		
9		Cust01	Germany	5-Aug-15	14159		
10		**Cust01 Total**			49444		
11		Cust02	UK	21-Mar-15	12232		
12		Cust02	Germany	18-Jun-15	9274		
13		Cust02	Germany	2-Jun-15	14290		
14		Cust02	Italy	15-Jul-15	4449		
15		Cust02	UK	22-Apr-15	11135		
16		Cust02	Spain	20-Jul-15	15814		
17		Cust02	UK	19-May-15	6648		
18		Cust02	Germany	20-Jul-15	12122		
19		Cust02	France	24-Jul-15	9386		
20		Cust02	UK	11-Jun-15	12647		
21		Cust02	Germany	11-Jun-15	4714		
22		**Cust02 Total**			112711		
23		Cust03	Italy	15-Jun-15	12759		
24		Cust03	Germany	4-May-15	9373		
25		Cust03	UK	18-May-15	8302		
26		Cust03	Germany	1-Jul-15	10855		
27		Cust03	Spain	30-Jun-15	15753		
28		Cust03	Spain	3-Aug-15	4095		
29		Cust03	UK	6-Aug-15	12737		
30		Cust03	UK	22-Jul-15	8814		
31		Cust03	Spain	4-Aug-15	13064		

FIGURE 17.18 Final Result After Insertion of SUBTOTAL Functions Using the Wizard

#NUM! error (even though by this time the loan has been repaid). In this example, the model has been set to have 10 periods, although the loan length is only of seven periods. Hence the principal part of the repayments for years 8, 9 and 10 (cells K8:M8) is returned as #NUM! For most practical or calculation purposes, the (structural) fact that there is no payment due after the end of the loan contract is equivalent to a payment amount of zero. Of course, in a technical or legalistic sense, the absence of an obligation may not be the same has having an obligation of amount zero (this latter case is the one that the function's calculations most closely resemble). Therefore, it is often most practical to consider that the error values are really zeros, particularly if these values are required to be used in further model calculations or graphical displays. In Row 9, this has been achieved by using an IF statement, which returns alternative values for the payment (i.e. zero) if the time period is beyond that of the validity of the loan. Note that the IF function is not detecting directly whether the PPMT function has returned an error; rather, it is dealing with a specific case in which it is known in

Function	FunctionNumber
AVERAGE	1
COUNT	2
COUNTA	3
MAX	4
MIN	5
PRODUCT	6
STDEV.S	7
STDEV.P	8
SUM	9
VAR.S	10
VAR.P	11
MEDIAN	12
MODE.SNGL	13
LARGE(array,k)	14
SMALL(array,k)	15
PERCENTILE.INC(array,k)	16
QUARTILE.INC(array,quart)	17
PERCENTILE.EXC(array,k)	18
QUARTILE.EXC(array,quart)	19

FIGURE 17.19 Possibilities for the Calculations to be Performed by the AGGREGATE Function

Values to ignore	OptionNumber
Ignore nested SUBTOTAL and AGGREGATE functions	0 or omitted
Ignore hidden rows, nested SUBTOTAL and AGGREGATE functions	1
Ignore error values, nested SUBTOTAL and AGGREGATE functions	2
Ignore hidden rows, error values, nested SUBTOTAL and AGGREGATE functions	3
Ignore nothing	4
Ignore hidden rows	5
Ignore error values	6
Ignore hidden rows and error values	7

FIGURE 17.20 Possibilities for Ignoring Input Data when the AGGREGATE Function Evaluates

Array or Ref1	Ref2 for Reference Form
678	488
993	110
5	581
59	738
#DIV/0!	227
1199	1230
347	1026
#NUM!	804
363	408
416	1770
11	1733

Array Form: (FunctionNumber, Options, Array, [k or quart])					
FunctionNumber	OptionNumber	k or quart	Result	Formula	Comments
4	6	NA	1199	=AGGREGATE(B17, C17, $B$3:$B$13)	Largest value, ignoring errors
12	6	NA	363	=AGGREGATE(B18, C18, $B$3:$B$13)	Calculated median, ignoring errors
15	6	2	11	=AGGREGATE(B19, C19, $B$3:$B$13,D19)	2nd smallest, ignoring errors

Reference Form: (FunctionNumber, Options, Ref1, [Ref2, ...])					
FunctionNumber	OptionNumber	Ref2	Result	Formula	Comments
12	6		534.5	=AGGREGATE(B23, C23, $B$3:$B$13,$C$3:$C$13)	Calculated median of all data sets, ignoring errors
12	6	NA	534.5	=AGGREGATE(B24, C24, $B$3:$C$13)	Calculated median, ignoring errors

FIGURE 17.21 Examples of the Application of the AGGREGATE Function

	B	C	D	E	F	G	H	I	J	K	L	M	N
2	Periodic interest rate	5.0%											
3	Periods to end of term	7											
4	Principal amount ($)	1,000											
6	Principal by period	Sum	1	2	3	4	5	6	7	8	9	10	Formula
8	Principal repayment using PPMT	#NUM!	123	129	135	142	149	157	165	#NUM!	#NUM!	#NUM!	=-PPMT($C2,M6,$C3,$C4)
9	Principal repayment using PPMT (with IF)	1,000	123	129	135	142	149	157	165	0	0	0	=IF(M6<=$C$3,M8,0)
11	Principal repayment using PPMT (with IFERROR)	1,000	123	129	135	142	149	157	165	0	0	0	=IFERROR(-PPMT($C2,M6,$C3,$C4),0)

FIGURE 17.22 Example of the IFERROR Function

advance that the function would produce an error. As an alternative, one may use the IFERROR function directly (Row 11) to simply replace any values of the PPMT that would be an error with zeros.

Note also that prior to Excel 2007, the equivalent functionality to IFFERROR could have been achieved by embedding an ISERROR (Information) function within an IF statement.

Despite its ease of use, one should be cautious in the use of IFERROR. In general, it is better to adapt the formulae that should apply to specific occurrences of "valid errors". If one overrides all errors however they arise, one may overlook other errors that in fact should be corrected. Thus, in the example above, the approach using the IF statement is arguably superior, as it is used to eliminate explicitly only those error cases arising from the loan term, rather than eliminating all errors of whatever nature.

Example: SWITCH

The SWITCH function can be used to avoid embedded IF statements, and in this sense is similar to many lookup functions (see Chapter 25).

The file Ch17.15.SWITCH.1.xlsx shows an example (see Figure 17.23).

	B	C	D
2	**Month**	**Main Activity**	
3	January	Work	
4	February	Work	
5	March	Work	
6	April	Vacation	
7	May	Work	
8	June	Work	
9	July	Vacation	
10	August	Vacation	
11	September	Work	
12	October	Work	
13	November	Work	
14	December	Vacation	
16	**Month**	**Main Activity**	
17	April	Vacation	=SWITCH(B17,B3,C3,B4,C4,B5,C5,B6,C6,B7,

FIGURE 17.23 General Example of the SWITCH Function

	A	B	C	D
1				
2		**Revenues Scenarios**		
3		Low	1	
4		Base	2	
5		High	3	
6				
7		Base	2	=SWITCH($B$7,B3,C3,B4,C4,B5,C5)
8				

FIGURE 17.24 Using SWITCH to Change a Text Description into a Number

The file Ch17.16.SWITCH.2.xlsx uses the SWITCH function to transition from a text description of a scenario to a numbered one (see Figure 17.24). (In a real-life example, the numerical scenario value would generally be used in a subsequent calculation that looks up the values of model inputs in that scenario and which drives the final model calculations; see Chapter 25.)

CHAPTER 18

Array Functions and Formulae

INTRODUCTION

This chapter presents a general discussion of array functions and formulae. It is worth treating these before presenting many other Excel functions: not only are array functions present in several Excel function categories, but also essentially any Excel function can be used as part of an array formula. The chapter covers the core principles, which are used at various places elsewhere in the text.

Functions and Formulae: Definitions

The essential feature of array functions and formulae is that "behind the scenes" they perform calculations that would otherwise be required to be conducted in several ranges or multi-cell tables. The output (return statement) of an array function generally extends over a range of multiple contiguous cells; however, some return values only to a single cell.

The distinction between functions and formulae is:

- Array functions are in-built Excel functions which inherently require the use of a contiguous array in their calculations or output form. They are a type of function, not a separate function category. Examples include TRANSPOSE (Lookup and Reference category), MMULT, MINVERSE (Math&Trig category) and FREQUENCY and LINEST (Statistical category). Some user-defined functions that are created using VBA macros may also be written to be array functions.
- Array formulae use standard Excel functions or operations (such as SUM, MIN or IF), but are written so that intermediate calculation steps are performed inherently "behind the scenes", rather than explicitly calculated in multi-cell Excel ranges.

Implementation

Array functions or formulae must be entered by placing the cursor within the Formula Bar and pressing Ctrl+Shift+ENTER. The cell range over which they are to be entered can be selected immediately before the formula is built, or after it has been built within the first cell of the range (in which case Ctrl+Shift+ENTER needs to be used again).

Advantages and Disadvantages

In some specific contexts, array functions are almost unavoidable, as the alternatives are much less efficient (the examples provided later in this chapter and in the subsequent text should make this clear). On the other hand, the use of array formulae is generally a choice. Possible benefits include:

- To create more transparent models, in which the explicitly visible part focuses on displaying inputs, key outputs and summary calculations, whereas tables of intermediate calculations (whose individual values are of no specific interest) are conducted behind the scenes.
- To create formulae which are more flexible if there are changes to the size of the data range or the time axis.
- To avoid having to implement some types of calculation as VBA user-defined functions.

There are several disadvantages in using array functions and formulae:

- Entering the formula incorrectly (e.g. by using just ENTER instead of Ctrl+Shift+ENTER) could result in an incorrect value (such as zero) appearing in the cell; the main danger is that such values may not obviously be wrong, and so may be overlooked (in contrast to the cases where a #VALUE message appears). Thus, inadvertent errors may arise.
- Many users are not familiar with them, which may result in the model being harder for others to understand or interpret (or where the user may accidentally edit a formula and return ENTER).
- In some cases, their presence can slow down the calculation of a workbook.

PRACTICAL APPLICATIONS: ARRAY FUNCTIONS

Example: Capex and Depreciation Schedules Using TRANSPOSE

The TRANSPOSE function can be used to turn data or calculations that are in a row into a column, and vice versa. Such a transposition can be performed explicitly within an Excel range, or embedded within a formula.

The file Ch18.1.SUMPRODUCT.TRANSPOSE.1.xlsx shows an example of each approach within the context of "triangle-type" calculations for depreciation expenses (as presented in Chapter 17).

On the "Range" worksheet, the TRANSPOSE function is used to explicitly create a range which contains the capex data in a column (cells C9:C14), so that this data set can be multiplied with the column data of depreciation percentages using the SUMPRODUCT function (see Figure 18.1).

On the "Formula" worksheet, the transposed capex data is not entered explicitly in Excel; rather it is implicitly embedded as an array, by using TRANSPOSE within the SUMPRODUCT formula (see Figure 18.2).

Example: Cost Allocation Using SUMPRODUCT with TRANSPOSE

The file Ch18.2.SUMPRODUCT.TRANSPOSE.2.xlsx shows an application to the allocation of the projected costs of a set of central overhead departments to business units, based on an allocation matrix; a screen-clip of the file is shown in Figure 18.3.

	A	B	C	D	E	F	G	H	I	J
1										
2		Years		2015	2016	2017	2018	2019	2020	
3		Capex		100	105	120	80	50	100	
4										
5		Generic Periods		1	2	3	4	5		
6		Depreciation Schedule	100%	30%	25%	20%	15%	10%		
7										
8		Depreciation		2015	2016	2017	2018	2019	2020	202
9		2015	100	30%	25%	20%	15%	10%		
10		2016	105		30%	25%	20%	15%	10%	
11		2017	120			30%	25%	20%	15%	10'
12		2018	80				30%	25%	20%	15'
13		2019	50					30%	25%	20'
14		2020	100						30%	25'
15		Total, using direct reference from Row 3		30.0	56.5	82.3	=SUMPRODUCT($C9:$C14,G9:G14)			

FIGURE 18.1 Using TRANSPOSE to Transpose a Data Range

	A	B	C	D	E	F	G	H	I	J	K
1											
2		Years		2015	2016	2017	2018	2019	2020		
3		Capex		100	105	120	80	50	100		
4											
5		Generic Periods		1	2	3	4	5			
6		Depreciation Schedule	100%	30%	25%	20%	15%	10%			
7											
8		Depreciation		2015	2016	2017	2018	2019	2020	2021	2
9		2015		30%	25%	20%	15%	10%			
10		2016			30%	25%	20%	15%	10%		
11		2017				30%	25%	20%	15%	10%	
12		2018					30%	25%	20%	15%	
13		2019						30%	25%	20%	
14		2020							30%	25%	
15		Total, using direct reference from Row 3		30.0	56.5	82.3	=SUMPRODUCT(TRANSPOSE($D3:$I3),G9:G14)				

FIGURE 18.2 Using TRANSPOSE Embedded Within a Formula

Once again, the TRANSPOSE function is used within SUMPRODUCT to ensure that the data sets being multiplied are implicitly both row (or both column) data; the alternative would be to explicitly transpose all the data in one of the two input data ranges.

Example: Cost Allocation Using Matrix Multiplication Using MMULT

Excel has several array functions that relate to mathematically oriented approaches. In fact, the cost allocation example shown in Figure 18.3 can also be considered as a matrix multiplication in which a single row vector and a single column vector are multiplied together using MMULT. Note that when doing so, per standard mathematical convention, the row vector must be the first of the two function-argument entries, and no transposition of the data is required.

The file Ch18.3.MMULT.1.xlsx shows an implementation of this in the cost allocation example used above; a screen-clip is shown in Figure 18.4.

Example 1: Using Array functions

Indirect Expenses	2017	2018	2019	2020	2021
Development	6,000	6,300	6,615	6,946	7,293
Research	25,000	26,250	27,563	28,941	30,388
Supply Chain	7,000	7,350	7,718	8,103	8,509
Group IT	12,000	12,600	13,230	13,892	14,586
Sales & Marketing	25,000	26,250	27,563	28,941	30,388
Group Support	8,000	8,400	8,820	9,261	9,724
Total ($k)	83,000	87,150	91,508	96,083	100,887

Business Units	Development	Research	Supply Chain	Group IT	Sales & Marketing	Group Support
BU1	35%	20%	20%	25%	30%	25%
BU2	20%	25%	35%	20%	20%	20%
BU3	30%	35%	25%	25%	20%	35%
BU4	15%	20%	20%	30%	30%	20%
Total	100%	100%	100%	100%	100%	100%

Business Units	2017	2018	2019	2020	2021
BU1	21,000	22,050	23,153	24,310	25,526
BU2	18,900	19,845	=SUMPRODUCT(E$5:E$10,TRANSPOSE($C15:$H15))		
BU3	23,100	24,255	25,468	26,741	28,078
BU4	20,000	21,000	22,050	23,153	24,310
Total ($k)	83,000	87,150	91,508	96,083	100,887

FIGURE 18.3 Use of TRANSPOSE with SUMPRODUCT in Cost Allocation

Example 1: Using Array functions

Indirect Expenses	2017	2018	2019	2020	2021
Development	6,000	6,300	6,615	6,946	7,293
Research	25,000	26,250	27,563	28,941	30,388
Supply Chain	7,000	7,350	7,718	8,103	8,509
Group IT	12,000	12,600	13,230	13,892	14,586
Sales & Marketing	25,000	26,250	27,563	28,941	30,388
Group Support	8,000	8,400	8,820	9,261	9,724
Total ($k)	83,000	87,150	91,508	96,083	100,887

Business Units	Development	Research	Supply Chain	Group IT	Sales & Marketing	Group Support
BU1	35%	20%	20%	25%	30%	25%
BU2	20%	25%	35%	20%	20%	20%
BU3	30%	35%	25%	25%	20%	35%
BU4	15%	20%	20%	30%	30%	20%
Total	100%	100%	100%	100%	100%	100%

Business Units	2017	2018	2019	2020	2021
BU1	21,000	22,050	23,153	24,310	25,526
BU2	18,900	19,845	=MMULT($C15:$H15,E$5:E$10)		22,973
BU3	23,100	24,255	25,468	26,741	28,078
BU4	20,000	21,000	22,050	23,153	24,310
Total ($k)	83,000	87,150	91,508	96,083	100,887

FIGURE 18.4 Use of MMULT in Cost Allocation

Example: Activity-based Costing and Resource Forecasting Using Multiple Driving Factors

When building a model to forecast the resources required to be able to achieve and deliver a desired revenue profile, one may have some resources whose activities are determined by several underlying factors. One may have a few examples, or be able to make estimates of possible scenarios in terms of the resource level required for different levels of activity drivers; from these, one can determine the scaling coefficients (under the assumption of a linear scaling from activity levels to resource requirements).

For example, if a resource (staff) level of 30 is observed to serve 25 customers spread over 150 sites, whereas 35 staff are needed to serve 20 customers over 200 sites, one may write this in terms of activity coefficients:

$$R = A_0 S + A_1 C$$

where R denotes the resource level, S the number of sites and C the number of customers. If the equations corresponding to the two specific cases are written in full, then matrix algebra can be used to solve for the coefficients A_0 and A_1.

The file Ch18.4.CostDriverForecasting.xlsx contains an implementation of this (see Figure 18.5). Note that if the coefficients A_0 and A_1 are considered as the components of a column vector, they are the solution to the equation:

$$R^T = D^T A$$

where R is the set of resources used (cells C5:D5), D is the detailed data of sites and customers (cells C3:D4), and T represents the transpose operation. Therefore, A can be found by inverting the transpose of D and multiplying by the resource vector:

$$A = (D^T)^{-1} R^T$$

	A	B	C	D	E
1					
2			BU1	BU2	
3		No of sites	150	200	
4		No of customers	25	20	
5		Staff Level	30	35	Staff=A0.Sites+A1.Customers
6					
7		Transpose	150	25	{=TRANSPOSE(C3:D4)}
8			200	20	
9					
10		Inverse	-0.01	0.01	{=MINVERSE(C7:D8)}
11			0.10	-0.08	
12					
13		Transpose	30		{=TRANSPOSE(C5:D5)}
14			35		
15					
16		Coefficients			
17		A0	0.14		{=MMULT(C10:D11,C13:C14)}
18		A1	0.38		
19					
20		Example			
21		No of sites	320		
22		No of customers	40		
23		Staff Level	59		=SUMPRODUCT(C17:C18,C21:C22)

FIGURE 18.5 Using Array Functions for Matrix Calculations to Calculate Cost Driver Coefficients

Rows 7 through Row 18 shows the individual steps of this operation (which could be combined into a single column range if desired, rather than broken out as individual steps). Once the components are determined, they can be applied to a new case (or cases) that would arise in a forecast model (in which the number of customers and sites is forecast, and this part of the model also determines the resource requirements), as shown in cells C21 to C23. The array functions used are TRANSPOSE, MINVERSE and MMULT.

Example: Summing Powers of Integers from 1 Onwards

The MINVERSE array function finds the inverse of a square matrix (mathematically inclined readers may also wish to use MDETERM to check that its determinant is non-zero, and hence that an inverse can be found). Although the function has several uses in more advanced financial applications (such as optimisation of portfolios of financial assets, and in determining risk-neutral state prices, amongst others), at this point in the text we will use it to find the solution to a general numerical problem.

For example, it is well known that the sum of the integers from 1 to N is given by:

$$1+2+3+\ldots+N=\frac{N(N+1)}{2}$$

or:

$$S_N^1=\frac{N(N+1)}{2}$$

As is commonly known, this formula can be derived simply by writing out the set of integers twice, once in the natural order and once in reverse order: this creates N pairs of integers, each of which sums to $N+1$.

In order to more clearly relate this to the discussion below, we note that:

$$S_N^1=\frac{1}{2}N^2+\frac{1}{2}N^1+0N^0$$

In a next step, one may wish to find an expression for the sum of a power of each of the integers from 1 to any number N (e.g. sum of the squares of each integer, or sum of the cubes of each integer). In order words, for a chosen power, p, we aim to find an expression for:

$$S_N^p=1^p+2^p+3^p+\ldots+N^p$$

Since there are N terms and the power is p, we can hypothesise that the desired expression is of the form:

$$S_N^p=C_{p+1}N^{p+1}+C_pN^p+\ldots+C_1N^1+C_0N^0$$

For example, in the case that $p=2$, we may hypothesise that

$$S_N^2=C_3N^3+C_2N^2+C_1N^1+C_0N^0$$

with the coefficients C_i still to be determined (for i=0 to 3).
If the sum of the squares is evaluated for each integer (i) from 0 to 3, we obtain:

$$S_0^2 = 0^2 = 0$$

$$S_1^2 = 1^2 = 1$$

$$S_2^2 = 1^2 + 2^2 = 5$$

$$S_3^2 = 1^2 + 2^2 + 3^2 = 14$$

Thus:

$$0 = S_0^2 = C_0$$

$$1 = S_1^2 = C_3 + C_2 + C_1$$

$$5 = S_2^2 = C_3 2^3 + C_2 2^2 + C_1 2^1$$

$$14 = S_3^2 = C_3 3^3 + C_2 3^2 + C_1 3^1$$

One can immediately see that $C_0 = 0$ (and that this would be the case for any power of p); this coefficient is therefore left out of the future discussion.

One way to find the value of the remaining coefficients is to solve by repeated substitution (first a forward pass, and then a backward pass): for the forward pass, first, C_1 is eliminated by using the second equation to write:

$$C_1 = 1 - C_3 - C_2$$

The third equation then becomes:

$$5 = C_3 2^3 + C_2 2^2 + (1 - C_3 - C_2) 2^1$$

This can be rearranged to express C_2 in terms of C_3:

$$C_2 = \left(\frac{3 - 6C_3}{2}\right)$$

The fourth equation can then be written entirely in terms of C_3, by substituting the terms involving C_1 for C_2, and then similarly C_2 for C_3, to arrive at an equation that involves only C_3 i.e:

$$14 = C_3 3^3 + \left(\frac{3 - 6C_3}{2}\right) 3^2 + \left(1 - C_3 - \left(\frac{3 - 6C_3}{2}\right)\right) 3^1$$

This gives:

$$C_3 = \frac{1}{3}$$

The backward pass then calculates C_2 from C_3 (to give $C_2 = \frac{1}{2}$), and then C_1 from C_3 and C_2 (to give $C_1 = \frac{1}{6}$), so that:

$$S_N^2 = \frac{1}{3}N^3 + \frac{1}{2}N^2 + \frac{1}{6}N$$

On the other hand, instead of explicitly solving the equations in this way, one could use matrix algebra to express the last three equations (since the first equation has solution $C_0 = 0$) as:

$$\begin{pmatrix} 1 & 1 & 1 \\ 8 & 4 & 2 \\ 27 & 9 & 3 \end{pmatrix} \begin{pmatrix} C_3 \\ C_2 \\ C_1 \end{pmatrix} = \begin{pmatrix} 1 \\ 5 \\ 14 \end{pmatrix}$$

Therefore, the vector of C_i can be found by matrix inversion:

$$\begin{pmatrix} C_3 \\ C_2 \\ C_1 \end{pmatrix} = \begin{pmatrix} 1 & 1 & 1 \\ 8 & 4 & 2 \\ 27 & 9 & 3 \end{pmatrix}^{-1} \begin{pmatrix} 1 \\ 5 \\ 14 \end{pmatrix}$$

This can be readily calculated in Excel using the MINVERSE function.

The file Ch18.5.MINV.SumofPowers.xlsx shows these calculations, as well as the coefficients that result for the first, second, third, fourth and fifth powers. Note that the results are formatted using Excel's Fraction formatting option; Figure 18.6 shows a screen-clip.

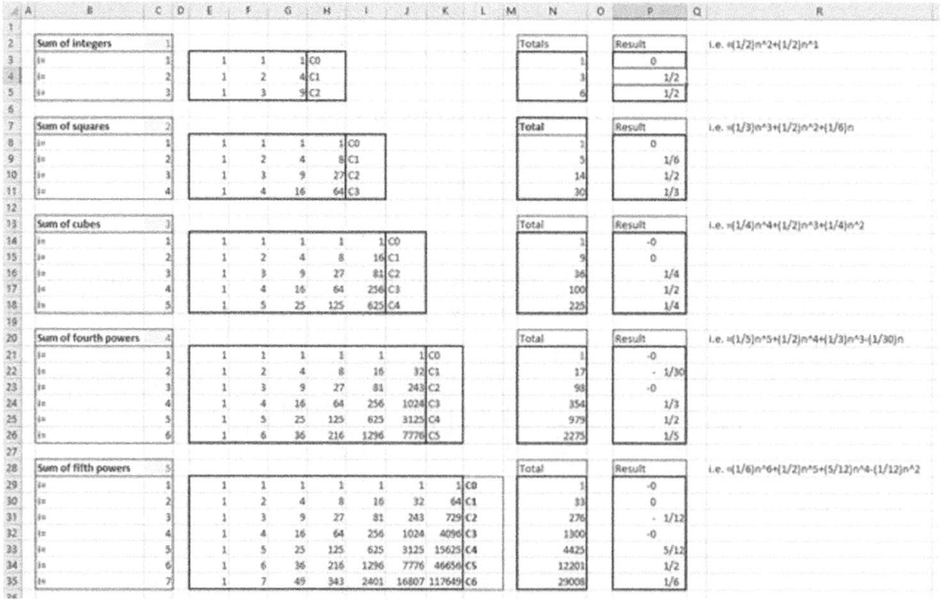

FIGURE 18.6 Calculation of Sums of the Powers of Integers Using MINVERSE

From the results, we see:

$$S_N^1 = \frac{1}{2}N^2 + \frac{1}{2}N$$

$$S_N^2 = \frac{1}{3}N^3 + \frac{1}{2}N^2 + \frac{1}{6}N$$

$$S_N^3 = \frac{1}{4}N^4 + \frac{1}{2}N^3 + \frac{1}{2}N^2$$

$$S_N^4 = \frac{1}{5}N^5 + \frac{1}{2}N^4 + \frac{1}{3}N^3 - \frac{1}{30}N$$

$$S_N^5 = \frac{1}{6}N^6 + \frac{1}{2}N^5 + \frac{5}{12}N^4 - \frac{1}{12}N^2$$

Of course, the equations for higher powers may also readily be derived by extending the procedure.

PRACTICAL APPLICATIONS: ARRAY FORMULAE

Example: Finding First Positive Item in a List

In Chapter 17, we noted that the "MAXIF" or "MAXIFS" functions were introduced into Excel in 2016. Prior to this (and hence in some models built before this time), the functionality could have been achieved by combining the MAX (or MIN) and IF functions in an array formula.

The file Ch18.6.MAXIF.MINIF.FirstCashFlow.xlsx shows an example, used in the context of finding the date of the first negative and first positive values in a time series (note that other approaches, such as lookup functions, can also be used; see Chapter 25); Figure 18.7 shows a screen-clip.

The array formulae embed an IF statement within a MIN function to find the minimum (in a set of numeric dates) for which a condition is met (either that the cash flow is positive or that it is negative). For example, the formula in Cell C7 is:

$$C7 = \{MIN(IF(E7:BL7 < 0, E2:BL2))\}$$

	A	B	C	D	E	F	G	H	I	J	K	L	M
1													
2			Period Start		1-Jan-16	1-Apr-16	1-Jul-16	1-Oct-16	1-Jan-17	1-Apr-17	1-Jul-17	1-Oct-17	1-Jan-18
3			Period End		31-Mar-16	30-Jun-16	30-Sep-16	31-Dec-16	31-Mar-17	30-Jun-17	30-Sep-17	31-Dec-17	31-Mar-18
4													
5			First Negative Cash Flow	First Positive Cash Flow	Cash Flows								
6		Project 1	1-Jul-16	1-Apr-17	-	-	(200)	(80)	(30)	20	30	45	45
7		Project 2	1-Jan-17	1-Jan-18	-	-	-	-	(100)	(50)	(45)	(40)	50
8		Project 3	1-Jan-16	1-Oct-16	(400)	(300)	(200)	50	80	110	130	150	170
9													
10		Project 1	First Negative Cash Flow	Formula									
11		Correct	1-Jul-16	{=MIN(IF(E6:BL6<0,$E$2:$BL$2))}									
12		Incorrect	0-Jan-00	{=MIN(IF(E6:BL6<0,1,0)*($E$2:$BL$2))}	Returns zeros due to zeros being the default multiplier when the condition is not met								
13													
14		Using MINIFS	First Negative Cash Flow	First Positive Cash Flow									
15		Project 1	1-Jul-16	1-Apr-17									
16		Project 2	1-Jan-17	1-Jan-18									
17		Project 3	1-Jan-16	1-Oct-16									
18													

FIGURE 18.7 Combining the MIN and IF in an Array Formula to Find Dates of First Cash Flows

Note the syntax of the IF function within the formulae: there is no explicit statement as to the treatment of cases where the condition (such as E7:Bl7<0) has not been met; the formulae explicitly refer to the date range only for cases in which the condition is met. One may try to make such cases more explicit, for example by using a formula such as:

$$C7 = \{MIN(IF(E7 : BL7 < 0,1,0) * (E2 : BL2))\}$$

However, the result would be a minimum of zero (in this case), as whenever the condition is not met, the result of the IF statement will evaluate to zero, which would then be multiplied by the corresponding numerical (positive) date, to give a set of data which is either positive or zero (and thus has a minimum of zero). The fact that the treatment of cases in which the condition is not met is not shown explicitly does reduce transparency, since one must know (or may have to pause to consider or test) how the array formula is treating such cases. This may be a reason to be cautious of using such approaches if other alternatives are available.

The file also shows the equivalent calculations using the MAXIFS and MINIFS functions (which are not shown in the screen-clip, but can be referred to by the interested reader).

Example: Find a Conditional Maximum

One may generalise the method in the prior example to find conditional maxima or minima, subject to the application of multiple criteria.

The file Ch18.7.MAXIF.MAXIFS.DataSet.xlsx shows an example in which one wishes to find the maximum of the "Amount £" field, both for a customer or country, and for a customer–country combination. Figure 18.8 shows a screen-clip, with the file containing formulae IF statements such as:

$$C5 = \{MAX(IF(B7 : B106 = B3, IF(C7 : C106 = C3, E7 : E106)))\}$$

$$C6 = \{MIN(IF(B7 : B106 = B3, IF(C7 : C106 = C3, E7 : E106)))\}$$

	A	B	C	D	E	F	G	H	I
1									
2		Customer	Country				Item	As array formulae	Formula
3		Cust10	UK				Maximum amount: Cust10	14647	{=MAX(IF((B7:B106=B3),E7:E106))}
4							Minimum amount: Cust10	-11862	{=MIN(IF((B7:B106=B3),E7:E106))}
5							Maximum amount: Cust10 and UK	14001	{=MAX(IF(B7:B106=B3,IF(C7:C106=C3,E7:E106)))}
6		Customer	Country	Due Date	Amount £		Minimum amount: Cust10 and UK	-11862	{=MIN(IF(B7:B106=B3,IF(C7:C106=C3,E7:E106)))}
7		Cust02	UK	21-Mar-15	12232				
8		Cust06	Italy	17-Mar-15	4749				
9		Cust07	Italy	13-Apr-15	7282		Incorrect:		
10		Cust03	Italy	15-Jun-15	12759		Minimum amount: Cust10 and UK	0	{=MIN(IF(AND(B7:B106=B3,C7:C106=C3),1,0)*E7:E106)}
11		Cust10	UK	25-May-15	12334		Non-embedded conditions	15851	{=MAX(IF(B7:B106=B3,C7:C106=C3),E7:E106)}
12		Cust05	Italy	25-Mar-15	4283				
13		Cust06	Germany	6-May-15	7992				
14		Cust06	Italy	17-Apr-15	13202				
15		Cust04	Germany	5-Jun-15	12684				
16		Cust10	UK	14-Jun-15	-11862				

FIGURE 18.8 Application of Multiple Criteria Using Array Formulae to Calculate Conditional Maxima and Minima

Note that, as shown in cells G10 and G11:

- Once again, attempting to make more explicit the case where the criteria are not met (cell G10) is likely to result in incorrect calculations (the minimum appears to be zero, due to the conditional not being met, rather than the true minimum, which is a -11862 in Cell E16).
- Using a single (non-embedded) IF function would also not be correct.

Example: Find a Conditional Maximum Using AGGREGATE as an Array Formula

The above examples have shown that although one can use array formulae to calculate conditional maxima and minima, there are some disadvantages, including that the treatment of cases where the condition is not met is not very explicit, and that the application of multiple criteria will often require embedded IF statements.

The AGGREGATE function (Excel 2013 onwards) could be used as an alternative. One advantage is that the nature of the calculation could rapidly be changed or copied (i.e. instead of a maximum or minimum, one could switch to the average) using the wide set of function types possible (as shown in Chapter 17, Figure 17.19).

To use the function in the context of a conditional query, one creates a calculation which results in an error when the condition is not met, and uses the function in the form in which it ignore errors (Option 6).

As we are using an array formula, the array form (not the reference form) of the AGGREGATE function should be used; that is, for the maximum, we use the LARGE function (not MAX) and for the minimum we use SMALL (not MIN). In both cases, the (non-optional) k-parameter is set to 1.

The file Ch18.8.MAXIFS.AGGREGATE.xlsx shows an example (see Figure 18.9).

Columns J through M of the same file show how the calculations can also be performed directly using the non-array form of the AGGREGATE function, so long as the

	A	B	C	D	E	F	G	H
1								
2		Customer	Country				As array function	Formula
3		Cust10	UK				14001	{=AGGREGATE(14,6,((E7:E106)/((B7:B106=B$3)*(C7:C106=C$3))),1)}
4								
5								
6		Customer	Country	Due Date	Amount £			
7		Cust02	UK	21-Mar-15	12232			
8		Cust06	Italy	17-Mar-15	4749			
9		Cust07	Italy	13-Apr-15	7282			
10		Cust03	Italy	15-Jun-15	12759			
11		Cust10	UK	25-May-15	12334			
12		Cust05	Italy	25-Mar-15	4283			
13		Cust06	Germany	6-May-15	7992			
14		Cust06	Italy	17-Apr-15	13202			
15		Cust04	Germany	5-Jun-15	12684			
16		Cust10	UK	14-Jun-15	11862			
17		Cust10	Italy	22-May-15	13630			
18		Cust07	UK	21-Jan-15	14593			
19		Cust07	Italy	5-May-15	4394			

FIGURE 18.9 Example of Using an Array Formula with AGGREGATE to Calculate the Conditional Maximum of a Data Set

J	K	L	M	N
Without an Array Formula	**Result**	**Formula**		
Conditional Maximum using MAX	14001	=AGGREGATE(4,6,K7:K106)		
Conditional Maximum using LARGE	14001	=AGGREGATE(14,6,K7:K106,1)		
CriteriaMet (1 or #DIV/0!)	**New Amount**	**Column J**	**Column K**	
#DIV/0!	#DIV/0!	=IF(AND(B7=B$3,C7=C$3),1,1/0)	=E7*J7	
#DIV/0!	#DIV/0!	=IF(AND(B8=B$3,C8=C$3),1,1/0)	=E8*J8	
#DIV/0!	#DIV/0!	=IF(AND(B9=B$3,C9=C$3),1,1/0)	=E9*J9	
#DIV/0!	#DIV/0!	=IF(AND(B10=B$3,C10=C$3),1,1/0)	=E10*J10	
1	12334	=IF(AND(B11=B$3,C11=C$3),1,1/0)	=E11*J11	
#DIV/0!	#DIV/0!	=IF(AND(B12=B$3,C12=C$3),1,1/0)	=E12*J12	
#DIV/0!	#DIV/0!	=IF(AND(B13=B$3,C13=C$3),1,1/0)	=E13*J13	
#DIV/0!	#DIV/0!	=IF(AND(B14=B$3,C14=C$3),1,1/0)	=E14*J14	
#DIV/0!	#DIV/0!	=IF(AND(B15=B$3,C15=C$3),1,1/0)	=E15*J15	
1	11862	=IF(AND(B16=B$3,C16=C$3),1,1/0)	=E16*J16	
#DIV/0!	#DIV/0!	=IF(AND(B17=B$3,C17=C$3),1,1/0)	=E17*J17	
#DIV/0!	#DIV/0!	=IF(AND(B18=B$3,C18=C$3),1,1/0)	=E18*J18	
#DIV/0!	#DIV/0!	=IF(AND(B19=B$3,C19=C$3),1,1/0)	=E19*J19	
#DIV/0!	#DIV/0!	=IF(AND(B20=B$3,C20=C$3),1,1/0)	=E20*J20	
1	6503	=IF(AND(B21=B$3,C21=C$3),1,1/0)	=E21*J21	
#DIV/0!	#DIV/0!	=IF(AND(B22=B$3,C22=C$3),1,1/0)	=E22*J22	
#DIV/0!	#DIV/0!	=IF(AND(B23=B$3,C23=C$3),1,1/0)	=E23*J23	
#DIV/0!	#DIV/0!	=IF(AND(B24=B$3,C24=C$3),1,1/0)	=E24*J24	
#DIV/0!	#DIV/0!	=IF(AND(B25=B$3,C25=C$3),1,1/0)	=E25*J25	
#DIV/0!	#DIV/0!	=IF(AND(B26=B$3,C26=C$3),1,1/0)	=E26*J26	
#DIV/0!	#DIV/0!	=IF(AND(B27=B$3,C27=C$3),1,1/0)	=E27*J27	
#DIV/0!	#DIV/0!	=IF(AND(B28=B$3,C28=C$3),1,1/0)	=E28*J28	
#DIV/0!	#DIV/0!	=IF(AND(B29=B$3,C29=C$3),1,1/0)	=E29*J29	
1	14001	=IF(AND(B30=B$3,C30=C$3),1,1/0)	=E30*J30	
#DIV/0!	#DIV/0!	=IF(AND(B31=B$3,C31=C$3),1,1/0)	=E31*J31	

FIGURE 18.10 Using the Non-array Form of the AGGREGATE Function Based on Explicit Individual Calculations

calculations that are implicit (behind the scenes) for the array formula are conducted explicitly in Excel (see Figure 18.10). Thus, the array formula can save a lot of space and may be easier to modify in some cases (e.g. as the size of the data set is altered). Note that the equivalent calculations could not be performed with the MIN or MAX functions, as these are not allowed to have errors in their data sets.

CHAPTER 19

Mathematical Functions

INTRODUCTION

This chapter covers a wide set of Excel functions that relate to arithmetic and mathematical calculations. We focus on those that are in Excel's Math&Trig category, which are generally the most frequently used in practical financial modelling applications. (We do not repeat the discussion for those functions covered in Chapter 17.) We also mention a few other functions, to give a hint of the types of possibilities that exist more generally; readers may choose to review the full set of functions within this category to identify whether others may be useful to them in their own contexts.

The examples provided include uses of:

- LN, EXP.
- ABS, SIGN.
- INT, ROUND, ROUNDUP, ROUNDDOWN, TRUNC.
- MROUND, CEILING.MATH, FLOOR.MATH.
- MOD.
- SQRT, POWER.
- FACT, COMBIN.
- SINE, ASIN, COS, ACOS, TAN, ATAN.
- DEGREES, PI, SQRTPI.
- BASE, DECIMAL.
- ARABIC, ROMAN.

PRACTICAL APPLICATIONS

Example: EXP and LN

The EXP function calculates the natural exponent of any number, i.e. for any input x it calculates y, where:

$$y = e^x$$

The LN function is the inverse to this, i.e. it calculates the natural logarithm of a number, y, which is the x-value that would solve the above equation for x when y is the input value, so that x=LN(y).

Note that the logarithm of the product of two numbers is the sum of their individual logarithms. That is:

$$LN(y_1 y_2) = LN(y_1) + LN(y_2)$$

This can be seen easily, for if

$$y_1 = e^{x_1} \text{ and } y_2 = e^{x_2}$$

$$(\text{i.e. } x_1 = LN(y_1) \text{ and } x_2 = LN(y_2))$$

then

$$y_1 y_2 = e^{x_1} e^{x_2} = e^{x_1 + x_2}$$

so that (taking logarithms of both sides for the first equality in the following equation, and using the definition of the x's in terms of the y's for the second):

$$LN(y_1 y_2) = x_1 + x_2 = LN(y_1) + LN(y_2).$$

An important use of these is in the calculation or calibration of time series. One measure of the returns (or changes or growth rate) in the value of an asset (or other positive items, such as revenue) is found by taking the logarithm of the ratios of the values:

$$\text{Return, change or growth rate} = \text{LN(EndingValue / StartingValue)}.$$

Then, due to the additive property of logarithms, if one has a set of returns data for individual time periods (daily, monthly, annually), one can calculate the return for any subset of the data (such as the total return between month 3 and 7), by simply adding up the individual periodic returns.

This contrasts with many "traditional" or "corporate finance" applications, where one often measures the return (or change, or growth rate) as:

$$\text{Return, change or growth rate} = \text{(EndingValue / StartingValue)} - 1.$$

In this latter approach, the additive property of the returns is lost, so that – when given only returns (growth or price change) data – one would generally need to apply an additional calculation step to reconstruct the absolute asset price to calculate the returns for a multi-period subset of the data.

The file Ch19.1.LN.EXP.Returns.xlsx shows both types of calculations. In the worksheet named "LNEXP", one starts from a set of periodic asset prices, and calculates the periodic returns using the LN function. As if working backwards from given asset returns, the SUM function is used to cumulative the total returns to any point in time, from which the price series is recreated using the EXP function; a screen-clip is shown in Figure 19.1.

	B	D	F	G	I	J	K	M	N
1									
2	Period No.	Prices at Period End	Returns Calculations	Formula	Cumulative Return	Formula	Comments	Prices Calculated using Additive Returns	Formula
3	0	100.00					Formulae do NOT rely on prior period calculation of cumulative return	100.00	
4	1	105.55	5.40%	=LN(D4/D3)	5.40%	=SUM(F$4:F4)	"	105.55	=M$3*EXP(I4)
5	2	97.28	-8.16%	=LN(D5/D4)	-2.76%	=SUM(F$4:F5)	"	97.28	=M$3*EXP(I5)
6	3	94.95	-2.42%	=LN(D6/D5)	-5.18%	=SUM(F$4:F6)	"	94.95	=M$3*EXP(I6)
7	4	94.01	-1.00%	=LN(D7/D6)	-6.18%	=SUM(F$4:F7)	"	94.01	=M$3*EXP(I7)
8	5	95.99	2.09%	=LN(D8/D7)	-4.09%	=SUM(F$4:F8)	"	95.99	=M$3*EXP(I8)
9	6	96.76	0.80%	=LN(D9/D8)	-3.29%	=SUM(F$4:F9)	"	96.76	=M$3*EXP(I9)
10	7	96.92	0.16%	=LN(D10/D9)	-3.13%	=SUM(F$4:F10)	"	96.92	=M$3*EXP(I10)
11	8	98.35	1.47%	=LN(D11/D10)	-1.67%	=SUM(F$4:F11)	"	98.35	=M$3*EXP(I11)
12	9	99.49	1.16%	=LN(D12/D11)	-0.51%	=SUM(F$4:F12)	"	99.49	=M$3*EXP(I12)

FIGURE 19.1 Periodic Returns and Reforecast Prices Using LN and EXP

In the worksheet named "OnePlus" of the same file, one starts from the same set of periodic asset prices, but calculates the periodic returns using the traditional corporate finance approach. One sees that when working backwards to reconstitute asset prices from such data, the formula for the cumulative returns at a particular period requires one to know the cumulative return at the immediate prior period (rather than just the raw return figure, as in the logarithmic returns method). Thus, an extra calculation step is required (equivalently or alternatively, one must know the prior period reforecast ending asset value in order to reforecast the current period's value using the periodic return figure); this is shown in the screen-clip of Figure 19.2.

Note also the following:

- Of course, the reforecast asset values are the same in each case, if one uses each approach correctly and consistently. Also, if the volatility of periodic changes is relatively small, then the returns profiles are similar whether the LN function is applied to the ratios, or whether the change is measured using the traditional corporate finance approach.
- When using the traditional (non-logarithmic) returns definition, the calculation of returns for sub-periods directly from the periodic returns data (i.e. without explicitly forecasting each period's values) can in fact be achieved by use of the FVSCHEDULE function, discussed in Chapter 20.

	B	D	F	G	I	J	K	M	N
1									
2	Period No.	Prices at Period End	Returns Calculations (Logarithmic)	Formula	Cumulative Return	Formula	Comments	Prices Calculated using Additive Returns	Formula
3	0	100.00					Formulae DO rely on prior period calculation of cumulative return	100.00	
4	1	105.55	5.55%	=D4/D3-1	5.55%			105.55	=M$3*(1+I4)
5	2	97.28	-7.83%	=D5/D4-1	-2.72%	=(1+F5)*(1+I4)-1	"	97.28	=M$3*(1+I5)
6	3	94.95	-2.39%	=D6/D5-1	-5.05%	=(1+F6)*(1+I5)-1	"	94.95	=M$3*(1+I6)
7	4	94.01	-0.99%	=D7/D6-1	-5.99%	=(1+F7)*(1+I6)-1	"	94.01	=M$3*(1+I7)
8	5	95.99	2.11%	=D8/D7-1	-4.01%	=(1+F8)*(1+I7)-1	"	95.99	=M$3*(1+I8)
9	6	96.76	0.80%	=D9/D8-1	-3.24%	=(1+F9)*(1+I8)-1	"	96.76	=M$3*(1+I9)
10	7	96.92	0.16%	=D10/D9-1	-3.08%	=(1+F10)*(1+I9)-1	"	96.92	=M$3*(1+I10)
11	8	98.35	1.48%	=D11/D10-1	-1.65%	=(1+F11)*(1+I10)-1	"	98.35	=M$3*(1+I11)
12	9	99.49	1.16%	=D12/D11-1	-0.51%	=(1+F12)*(1+I11)-1	"	99.49	=M$3*(1+I12)

FIGURE 19.2 Periodic Returns and Reforecast Prices Using Traditional Corporate Finance Approach

Because of their role in calculations involving continuous time, the EXP and LN functions are also useful in many areas, such as operational, breakdown and maintenance optimisation modelling.

Example: ABS and SIGN

The ABS function gives the absolute value of a number. That is, it returns the number when it is positive, and it's negative when it is negative. The SIGN function returns the sign of a number (1 for positive numbers, -1 for negative numbers and 0 for zero).

One important modelling application of the ABS function is to build robust error-checking formulae; these compare the values of a single variable, calculated using two (or more) calculation routes in a model. In most cases, it is convenient to calculate the difference between the two values, which should always be zero (even as sensitivity analysis is conducted).

Especially when building many error checks at various places into large models, it can be useful to have a single global check, which is the sum of all the individual error checks (and which also should always also be zero). In such cases, the ABS function can be applied to each individual error-check value, before these are used to calculate global summary values. The use of the absolute values will help to avoid cases where errors in the detailed calculation would cancel out at a global level (due to some being negative and others being positive, such as may be the case when dealing with a non-balancing balance sheet in a financial statement model).

Note also that the functions ABS, SIGN, IF, MAX, MIN are interrelated in many ways. For example:

$$ABS(N) = IF(N >= 0, N, -N)$$

$$ABS(N) = MAX(N,0) - MIN(N,0)$$

$$N = SIGN(N) * ABS(N)$$

The file Ch19.2.SIGN.ABS.xlsx contains an example of such formulae; Figure 19.3 shows a screen-clip which shows that part of the file in which the IF and MAX/MIN functions are compared with ABS.

In Figure 19.4, we show a screen-clip of another part of the file, which uses the SIGN and ABS functions to conduct individual error checks and sum these into a global total (the error check in this case is to verify that the IF formula gives the same figure as the MAX–MIN approach).

	A	B	C	D	E	F	G	H	I	J	K
1											
2		Number		ABS	Formulae		IF	Formulae		MAX-MIN	Formulae
3		93.270		93.270	=ABS(B3)		93.270	=IF(B3>=0,B3,-B3)		93.270	=MAX(B3,0)-MIN(B3,0)
4		62.430		62.430	=ABS(B4)		62.430	=IF(B4>=0,B4,-B4)		62.430	=MAX(B4,0)-MIN(B4,0)
5		-83.200		83.200	=ABS(B5)		83.200	=IF(B5>=0,B5,-B5)		83.200	=MAX(B5,0)-MIN(B5,0)
6		-81.000		81.000	=ABS(B6)		81.000	=IF(B6>=0,B6,-B6)		81.000	=MAX(B6,0)-MIN(B6,0)
7		76.501		76.501	=ABS(B7)		76.501	=IF(B7>=0,B7,-B7)		76.501	=MAX(B7,0)-MIN(B7,0)
8		-4.326		4.326	=ABS(B8)		4.326	=IF(B8>=0,B8,-B8)		4.326	=MAX(B8,0)-MIN(B8,0)
9		-7.700		7.700	=ABS(B9)		7.700	=IF(B9>=0,B9,-B9)		7.700	=MAX(B9,0)-MIN(B9,0)
10		0.000		0.000	=ABS(B10)		0.000	=IF(B10>=0,B10,-B10)		0.000	=MAX(B10,0)-MIN(B10,0)
11											

FIGURE 19.3 Calculating Absolute Values Using ABS, IF, MAX and MIN

L	M	N	O	P	Q	R	S	T
	SIGN	Formulae		ABS*SIGN	Formulae		Error checking	Formulae
	1	=SIGN(B3)		93.270	=ABS(B3)*SIGN(B3)		0.000	=ABS(G3-J3)
	1	=SIGN(B4)		62.430	=ABS(B4)*SIGN(B4)		0.000	=ABS(G4-J4)
	-1	=SIGN(B5)		-83.200	=ABS(B5)*SIGN(B5)		0.000	=ABS(G5-J5)
	-1	=SIGN(B6)		-81.000	=ABS(B6)*SIGN(B6)		0.000	=ABS(G6-J6)
	1	=SIGN(B7)		76.501	=ABS(B7)*SIGN(B7)		0.000	=ABS(G7-J7)
	-1	=SIGN(B8)		-4.326	=ABS(B8)*SIGN(B8)		0.000	=ABS(G8-J8)
	-1	=SIGN(B9)		-7.700	=ABS(B9)*SIGN(B9)		0.000	=ABS(G9-J9)
	0	=SIGN(B10)		0.000	=ABS(B10)*SIGN(B10)		0.000	=ABS(G10-J10)
							Global Error Check	
							0.000	=SUM(S3:S11)

FIGURE 19.4 Using the SIGN Function, and Global Error Checking Using ABS

Example: INT, ROUNDDOWN, ROUNDUP, ROUND and TRUNC

The INT, ROUNDDOWN, ROUNDUP and ROUND functions provide a variety of ways to perform rounding of numbers:

- The INT function rounds down to the nearest integer, so that a negative input value (such as –4.2) would be at least as small, or even smaller (such as –5). In other words, it rounds to the left.
- Other related functions include ROUNDDOWN, ROUNDUP, ROUND and TRUNC. Each has an argument that corresponds to the number of digits to which one rounds.
- ROUNDDOWN rounds towards zero: a positive input figure will result in a number that is the same or smaller, whereas a negative input figure will result in a number that is at least as large (i.e. not smaller than its input); in other words, it rounds towards zero. By contrast, ROUNDUP rounds away from zero. TRUNC and ROUNDDOWN are very similar functions; however, the number of digits is a required argument in ROUNDDOWN, but is optional in TRUNC (and equal to zero if omitted).
- ROUND rounds the number according to the number of required digits, so that the direction of rounding depends on whether the number is positive or negative, as well as the value of the number itself (e.g. –4.324 rounds at two digits to –4.32, i.e. upwards, whereas –4.326 rounds to –4.33, i.e. downwards.)

The file Ch19.3.INT.ROUND.1.xlsx contains an example of these functions; Figure 19.5 shows a screen-clip.

There are many possible uses of these in financial modelling. One is to use the numerical value for a month (e.g. April is month 4) to calculate the relevant quarter (quarter 1 being January to March, quarter 2 being April to June, and so on). Any of these functions can be used to turn a month number into a quarter (a lookup table could also be used).

The file Ch19.4.INT.ROUND.2.Quarters.xlsx shows an example; Figure 19.6 shows a screenshot.

	A	B	C	D	E	F	G
1							
2		Number, #	INT	ROUNDDOWN(#,0)	ROUNDUP(#,0)	ROUND(#,2)	TRUNC(#,0)
3		98.730	98.000	98.000	99.000	98.730	98.000
4		76.501	76.000	76.000	77.000	76.500	76.000
5		63.326	63.000	63.000	64.000	63.330	63.000
6		-4.324	-5.000	-4.000	-5.000	-4.320	-4.000
7		-4.326	-5.000	-4.000	-5.000	-4.330	-4.000
8		-7.700	-8.000	-7.000	-8.000	-7.700	-7.000

FIGURE 19.5 Examples of INT and Various ROUND-type Functions for Positive and Negative Inputs

	A	B	C	D	E	F	G	H	I	J
1										
2			Calculations of Quarter							
3		Month Number	INT	Formula	Using ROUNDDOWN	Formula	Using ROUNDUP	Formula	Using ROUND	Formula
4		1	1	=INT((B4-1)/3)+1	1	=ROUNDDOWN((B4-1)/3,0)+1	1	=ROUNDUP((B4-3)/3+1,0)	1	=ROUND((B4+1)/3,0)
5		2	1	=INT((B5-1)/3)+1	1	=ROUNDDOWN((B5-1)/3,0)+1	1	=ROUNDUP((B5-3)/3+1,0)	1	=ROUND((B5+1)/3,0)
6		3	1	=INT((B6-1)/3)+1	1	=ROUNDDOWN((B6-1)/3,0)+1	1	=ROUNDUP((B6-3)/3+1,0)	1	=ROUND((B6+1)/3,0)
7		4	2	=INT((B7-1)/3)+1	2	=ROUNDDOWN((B7-1)/3,0)+1	2	=ROUNDUP((B7-3)/3+1,0)	2	=ROUND((B7+1)/3,0)
8		5	2	=INT((B8-1)/3)+1	2	=ROUNDDOWN((B8-1)/3,0)+1	2	=ROUNDUP((B8-3)/3+1,0)	2	=ROUND((B8+1)/3,0)
9		6	2	=INT((B9-1)/3)+1	2	=ROUNDDOWN((B9-1)/3,0)+1	2	=ROUNDUP((B9-3)/3+1,0)	2	=ROUND((B9+1)/3,0)
10		7	3	=INT((B10-1)/3)+1	3	=ROUNDDOWN((B10-1)/3,0)+1	3	=ROUNDUP((B10-3)/3+1,0)	3	=ROUND((B10+1)/3,0)
11		8	3	=INT((B11-1)/3)+1	3	=ROUNDDOWN((B11-1)/3,0)+1	3	=ROUNDUP((B11-3)/3+1,0)	3	=ROUND((B11+1)/3,0)
12		9	3	=INT((B12-1)/3)+1	3	=ROUNDDOWN((B12-1)/3,0)+1	3	=ROUNDUP((B12-3)/3+1,0)	3	=ROUND((B12+1)/3,0)
13		10	4	=INT((B13-1)/3)+1	4	=ROUNDDOWN((B13-1)/3,0)+1	4	=ROUNDUP((B13-3)/3+1,0)	4	=ROUND((B13+1)/3,0)
14		11	4	=INT((B14-1)/3)+1	4	=ROUNDDOWN((B14-1)/3,0)+1	4	=ROUNDUP((B14-3)/3+1,0)	4	=ROUND((B14+1)/3,0)
15		12	4	=INT((B15-1)/3)+1	4	=ROUNDDOWN((B15-1)/3,0)+1	4	=ROUNDUP((B15-3)/3+1,0)	4	=ROUND((B15+1)/3,0)

FIGURE 19.6 Examples of Using INT and Various ROUND-type Functions to Calculate Quarters

The respective formulae are:

$$\text{Quarter using INT} = \text{INT}((\text{Month} - 1) / 3) + 1$$

$$\text{Quarter using ROUNDDOWN} = \text{ROUNDDOWN}((\text{Month} - 1) / 3, 0) + 1$$

$$\text{Quarter using ROUNDUP} = \text{ROUNDUP}((\text{Month} - 3) / 3 + 1, 0)$$

$$\text{Quarter using ROUND} = \text{ROUND}((\text{Month} + 1) / 3, 0).$$

Month numbers can be determined from a date, using the MONTH function (Chapter 23).

Note also that:

- Half-year periods (first and second half) can similarly be created by division by 6 instead of by 3.
- If one wished to alter the definition of the first quarter of the year (such as that the first quarter starts in April, as in the UK financial year), one could adapt the above formulae appropriately.

Example: MROUND, CEILING.MATH and FLOOR.MATH

The MROUND function rounds an input to the nearest value of a chosen multiple. For example, a company may calculate the annual bonus for each employee using an exact formula derived from a variety of input metrics, but determine the final value to be paid by rounding this the nearest $100 (for example, so that an initial exact calculation of bonus entitlement of, say, $1365.23 would become $1400).

The file Ch19.5.MROUND.xlsx shows an example of the MROUND function for various values of the numerical input field and the desired multiple. Note that, at the time of writing, the function works only if the input number and the multiple are of the same sign. One can create a workaround for this, using ABS to turn both the number and the multiple into positive figures, and using the SIGN function to return a result that is of the same sign as the original numerical input; see the screen-clip in Figure 19.7.

The CEILING.MATH function (an extension of the legacy CEILING function) rounds a number up to the nearest chosen multiple (this rounding up is in contrast to MROUND, which rounds in either direction). The function has an additional optional parameter which allows one to round away from zero (so that for negative numbers, the rounding up process actually makes the result no greater than original number).

The file Ch19.6.CEILING.xlsx shows an example, including the comparison with MROUND; a screen-clip is shown in Figure 19.8.

Similarly, the FLOOR.MATH function (and its legacy FLOOR function) rounds a number downwards to the nearest chosen multiple.

Number, #	Multiple	MROUND(#, 5)	Formulae	Adaptation	Formulae
93.270	5	95	=MROUND(B3, C3)	95	=MROUND(ABS(B3), ABS(C3))*SIGN(B3)
62.430	5	60	=MROUND(B4, C4)	60	=MROUND(ABS(B4), ABS(C4))*SIGN(B4)
-83.200	-5	-85	=MROUND(B5, C5)	-85	=MROUND(ABS(B5), ABS(C5))*SIGN(B5)
-81.000	-5	-80	=MROUND(B6, C6)	-80	=MROUND(ABS(B6), ABS(C6))*SIGN(B6)
76.501	-5	#NUM!	=MROUND(B7, C7)	75	=MROUND(ABS(B7), ABS(C7))*SIGN(B7)
-4.326	5	#NUM!	=MROUND(B8, C8)	-5	=MROUND(ABS(B8), ABS(C8))*SIGN(B8)
-7.700	5	#NUM!	=MROUND(B9, C9)	-10	=MROUND(ABS(B9), ABS(C9))*SIGN(B9)

FIGURE 19.7 Using MROUND to Round to Nearest Multiples, and Adapting the Calculations Using ABS and SIGN

Number, #	Multiple	MROUND(#, 5)	Adapted MROUND	CEILING.MATH(#,multiple,0)	CEILING.MATH(#,multiple,1)
93.270	5	95	95	95	95
62.430	5	60	60	65	65
-83.200	-5	-85	-85	-80	-85
-81.000	-5	-80	-80	-80	-85
76.501	-5	#NUM!	75	80	80
-4.326	5	#NUM!	-5	0	-5
-7.700	5	#NUM!	-10	-5	-10

FIGURE 19.8 Examples of the CELING.MATH Function

Example: MOD

The MOD function provides the modulus of a number with a specified divisor (that is, the remainder when the divisor is repeatedly subtracted from the number until no more full subtractions are possible). For example, using a divisor of five, the modulus of the number 1 is 1, of the number 2 is 2, whilst the modulus of 5 is 0, that of 6 is 1, that of 7 is 2, and that of 10 is zero, and so on.

One application is the allocation of items into groups, in which one cycles through the available groups in sequence (more specifically, this could relate to the allocation of patients to clinical trials, of customers to service centres and so on).

The file Ch19.7.MOD.xlsx shows an example in which there are five groups (the number of groups acts as the divisor) and the items are allocated to these based on their ordered arrival number (or time). As the MOD function returns zero when the number is a multiple of the divisor, the formula has been adapted to reflect that the group numbers are 1,2,3,4,5 (i.e. that there is no group number 0) by the subtraction and addition of the number 1 at the appropriate calculation steps; a screen-clip is shown in Figure 19.9.

Example: SQRT and POWER

In Excel, one can calculate powers and roots of numbers either using direct arithmetic operations or using the POWER function. In the case of wishing to calculate square roots, one can also use the SQRT function.

The file Ch19.8.POWER.SQRT.xlsx gives an example of these. One (arguable) advantage of the POWER function over general arithmetic approaches is that the formula is moderately easier to read in some cases; a screen-clip is shown in Figure 19.10.

	A	B	C	D
1				
2		# Groups to Allocate To	5	
3				
4		Item Number	Group Allocation	Formula
5		1	1	=MOD(B5-1,C$2)+1
6		2	2	=MOD(B6-1,C$2)+1
7		3	3	=MOD(B7-1,C$2)+1
8		4	4	=MOD(B8-1,C$2)+1
9		5	5	=MOD(B9-1,C$2)+1
10		6	1	=MOD(B10-1,C$2)+1
11		7	2	=MOD(B11-1,C$2)+1
12		8	3	=MOD(B12-1,C$2)+1
13		9	4	=MOD(B13-1,C$2)+1
14		10	5	=MOD(B14-1,C$2)+1
15		11	1	=MOD(B15-1,C$2)+1
16		12	2	=MOD(B16-1,C$2)+1
17		13	3	=MOD(B17-1,C$2)+1
18		14	4	=MOD(B18-1,C$2)+1
19		15	5	=MOD(B19-1,C$2)+1
20		16	1	=MOD(B20-1,C$2)+1
21		17	2	=MOD(B21-1,C$2)+1
22		18	3	=MOD(B22-1,C$2)+1

FIGURE 19.9 Using MOD to Allocate Items to Groups

Example	Formulae
729	=POWER(9,3)
9	=729^(1/3)
9	=POWER(729,1/3)
1.414	=2^(1/2)
1.414	=POWER(2,0.5)
1.414	=SQRT(2)

FIGURE 19.10 Examples of the POWER and SQRT Functions and Comparison with Direct Arithmetic

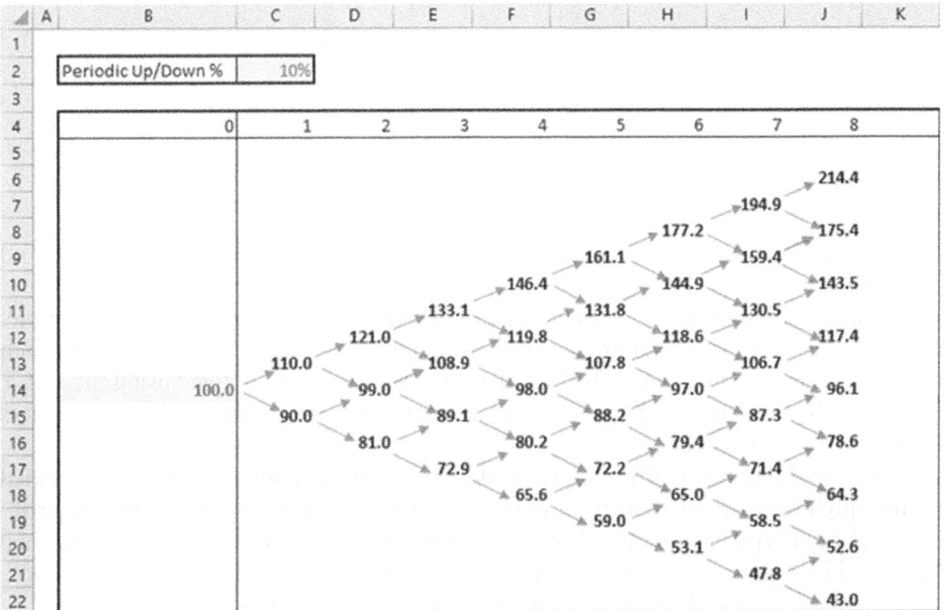

FIGURE 19.11 A Recombining Tree Using Simple Absolute Periodic Price Changes of 10%

Example: FACT and COMBIN

The COMBIN and FACT functions are useful in some probabilistic and statistical contexts. For example, if the value of an asset, or the price of a commodity, is modelled as an uncertain process in which the price changes every period in either a percentage up or down movement (each with a specified probability), one could use these functions to work out the number of possible ways of reaching each point in the tree (as well as the likelihood of that outcome).

The file Ch19.9.COMBIN.FACT.xlsx contains an example; Figure 19.11 shows a screen-clip taken from the worksheet "RecombiningTreeSimple", in which there is an assumed possible 10% upward or downward movement.

For additional reference, in the same file, the worksheet "RecombiningTreeLN" (not shown in the screen-clip) contains a similar tree in which the 10% price change is

8	# Up	# Down	# Paths	Formula	Using FACT	Formula
214.4	8	0	1	=COMBIN(8,L6)	1	=FACT(8)/(FACT(L6)*FACT(M6))
175.4	7	1	8	=COMBIN(8,L8)	8	=FACT(8)/(FACT(L8)*FACT(M8))
143.5	6	2	28	=COMBIN(8,L10)	28	=FACT(8)/(FACT(L10)*FACT(M10))
117.4	5	3	56	=COMBIN(8,L12)	56	=FACT(8)/(FACT(L12)*FACT(M12))
96.1	4	4	70	=COMBIN(8,L14)	70	=FACT(8)/(FACT(L14)*FACT(M14))
78.6	3	5	56	=COMBIN(8,L16)	56	=FACT(8)/(FACT(L16)*FACT(M16))
64.3	2	6	28	=COMBIN(8,L18)	28	=FACT(8)/(FACT(L18)*FACT(M18))
52.6	1	7	8	=COMBIN(8,L20)	8	=FACT(8)/(FACT(L20)*FACT(M20))
43.0	0	8	1	=COMBIN(8,L22)	1	=FACT(8)/(FACT(L22)*FACT(M22))

FIGURE 19.12 Number of Possibilities to Achieve Each Outcome in the Binomial Tree

a logarithmic one, so that the upward and downward values scale by EXP(10%) and EXP(-10%) in each period.

Figure 19.12 shows a screen-clip taken from the file in which the COMBIN function is used to work out the number of ways of achieving (at the end of period 8) each of the nine possible outcomes. The formula for this can also be derived using the FACT function (which calculates the factorial of a number, i.e. the product of all the integers from 1 up to this number).

The actual frequency (probability or likelihood) of each outcome would be formed by multiplying the number of total outcomes that each state represents by the probability of each type of outcome. If p is the probability of an upward movement, then the probability of occurrence of any specific path that leads to i outcomes is $p^i(1-p)^{8-i}$, with the number of such paths being given by the COMBIN function.

Thus, the probability of i upwards movements in total is:

$$p(i) = p^i(1-p)^{8-i}\text{COMBIN}(8, i)$$

(with the required adaptation for trees with other than eight periods being fairly clear).

These are shown in Figure 19.13 for an assumed upward probability movement of 60%.

Example: RAND()

The RAND() function generates a random sample between 0 and 1 from a uniform continuous distribution. It will resample whenever F9 is pressed, i.e. whenever the workbook is recalculated. (Note that RANDBETWEEN provides only a sample of integer values, not continuous ranges.) By treating the random values as if they were probabilities, one can derive random samples from other distributions:

J	K	L	M	N	O	P	Q	R	S	T	U
										60%	p
										40%	=1-T2
8		# Up	# Down	# Paths	Formula		Using FACT	Formula		Direct Calc	Formula
214.4		8	0	1	=COMBIN(8,L6)		1	=FACT(8)/(FACT(L6)*FACT(M6))		1.68%	=($T$2^L6)*($T$3^M6)*N6
175.4		7	1	8	=COMBIN(8,L8)		8	=FACT(8)/(FACT(L8)*FACT(M8))		8.96%	=($T$2^L8)*($T$3^M8)*N8
143.5		6	2	28	=COMBIN(8,L10)		28	=FACT(8)/(FACT(L10)*FACT(M10))		20.90%	=($T$2^L10)*($T$3^M10)*N10
117.4		5	3	56	=COMBIN(8,L12)		56	=FACT(8)/(FACT(L12)*FACT(M12))		27.87%	=($T$2^L12)*($T$3^M12)*N12
96.1		4	4	70	=COMBIN(8,L14)		70	=FACT(8)/(FACT(L14)*FACT(M14))		23.22%	=($T$2^L14)*($T$3^M14)*N14
78.6		3	5	56	=COMBIN(8,L16)		56	=FACT(8)/(FACT(L16)*FACT(M16))		12.39%	=($T$2^L16)*($T$3^M16)*N16
64.3		2	6	28	=COMBIN(8,L18)		28	=FACT(8)/(FACT(L18)*FACT(M18))		4.13%	=($T$2^L18)*($T$3^M18)*N18
52.6		1	7	8	=COMBIN(8,L20)		8	=FACT(8)/(FACT(L20)*FACT(M20))		0.79%	=($T$2^L20)*($T$3^M20)*N20
43.0		0	8	1	=COMBIN(8,L22)		1	=FACT(8)/(FACT(L22)*FACT(M22))		0.07%	=($T$2^L22)*($T$3^M22)*N22
										100.00%	

FIGURE 19.13 Final Probability of Each Ending State

For uniform continuous ranges:

$$\text{Sample} = \text{Min} + (\text{max} - \text{Min}) * \text{RAND}()$$

For the occurrence of event risks (Bernoulli processes):

$$\text{Occurrence or Not} = \text{IF}(\text{RAND}() \leq \text{Prob}, 1, 0)$$

Samples from many other distributions can also be created by using the RAND() function as input into the inversion of the cumulative distribution for that function (a few further sampling examples are shown later in the book, and the author's *Business Risk and Simulation Modelling in Practice* provides much more detail on this point).

The file Ch19.10.RAND.xlsx shows an example in which the RAND() function is used in each period of a model to determine whether the price of an asset moves up or down, assuming a probability of 60% of an upward movement. The possible percentage change in price (10%) each period is interpreted here as a logarithmic figure, with the price each period calculated from the prior period's price depending on the outcome of the RAND() function within that period. The paths shown in this model therefore essentially correspond to the individual paths that exist in the recombining tree in the earlier example; Figure 19.14 shows a screen-clip of the file.

In practice, the determination, and recording, of all possible scenarios usually requires a VBA macro, in order to repeatedly recalculate the workbook and store the results (see Chapter 16).

Example: SINE, ASIN, DEGREES and PI()

There is a wide set of trigonometric and similar functions which are occasionally useful in financial modelling. For example, when considering the capital expenditure necessary to build a cellphone relay station with sufficient coverage of a particular area, one

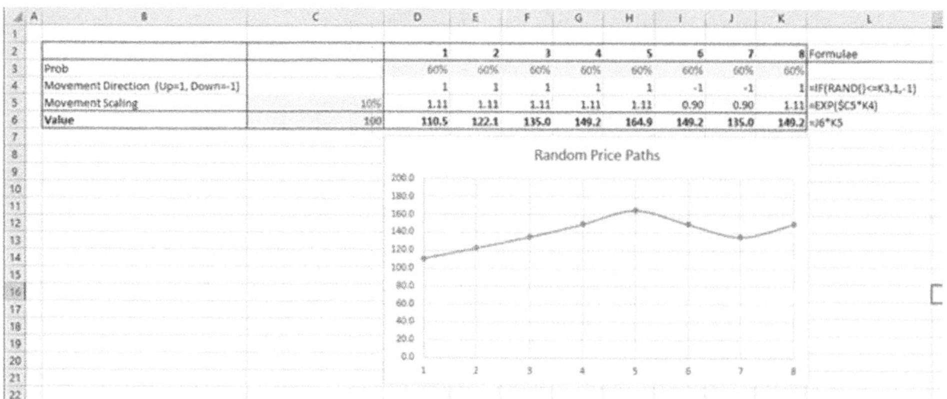

FIGURE 19.14 Random Possible Price Paths Using RAND()

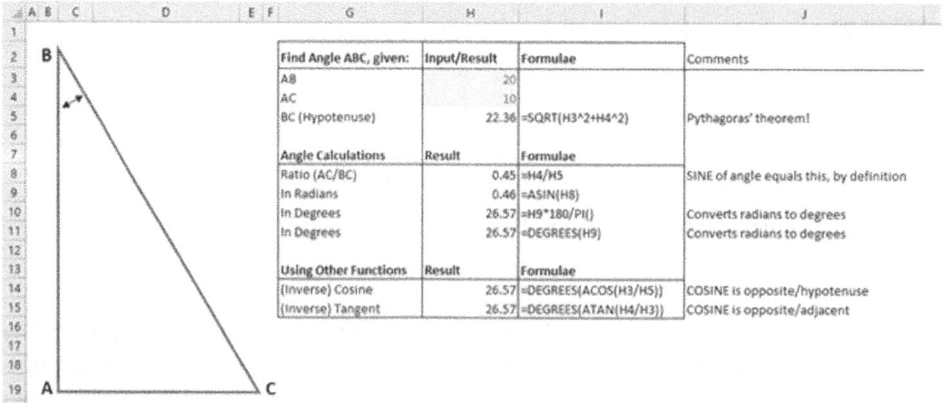

FIGURE 19.15 Using ASIN to Find the Angle Within a Triangle

may need to be able to calculate angles relating to the propagation of electromagnetic radiation between the station and centres of population. Thus, functions which calculate the lengths of the sides of right-angled triangles given another particular angle (i.e. sines, cosines or tangents) can be useful, as can those which calculate the angles of the triangle when the lengths of its sides are known (i.e. the inverse functions).

The file Ch19.11.SINE.ASIN.xlsx shows an example of the SINE, ASIN, COS, ACOS, TAN and ATAN functions to perform such calculations. Figure 19.15 shows a screen-clip of the file. One can see that the ASIN function is used to calculate that the angle ABC is approximately 26.57 degrees (i.e. when a right-angled triangle has edge lengths 10 and 20, the two non-right-angled angles are approximately 26.57 and 63.43 degrees).

By default, Excel works in radians; the conversion to degrees can be done using the DEGREES function, or directly by multiplying by $\frac{180}{\pi}$. One can use the PI() function (accurate to about 15 decimal places) rather than having to type π (3.141592653589793. . .).

	A	B	C	D	E
1					
2		Decimal number	Radix (Base)	Result	Formulae
3		215	2	11010111	=BASE(B3,C3)
4					
5		Text	Radix (Base)	Result	Formulae
6		11010111	2	215	=DECIMAL(B6,C6)

FIGURE 19.16 Conversion Between Decimals and Equivalents in Other Numerical Bases Example: ARABIC and ROMAN

	A	B	C	D
1				
2		Roman Number	Result	Formulae
3		MCMLXXXIV	1984	=ARABIC(B3)
4				
5		Arabic Number	Result	Formulae
6		1984	MCMLXXXIV	=ROMAN(B6)

FIGURE 19.17 Conversion Between Arabic and Roman Equivalents

The function SQRTPI() gives the square root of π as a pre-calculated figure (that is sometimes required in statistical applications and related fields).

Note also that it is the inverse functions that are of importance in this example (to convert from lengths to angles); if one were aware of the SINE function, but not of ASIN, then a similar inversion procedure could be set up using GoalSeek (see Chapter 13); however, this is less efficient than using an in-built function procedure where one exists.

Example: BASE and DECIMAL

Occasionally one may need to convert numbers from one base (or "radix") to another. This could arise in some data manipulation contexts, where data has arisen from other computerised or binary sources. The BASE and DECIMAL functions allow conversion between number bases, whereby the non-decimal numbers are expressed as text fields.

The file Ch19.12.BASE.DECIMAL.xlsx contains an example, which is shown in the screen-clip in Figure 19.16.

One may occasionally (once again, most likely in the field of text or data manipulation) need to convert Roman (text) numbers to Arabic and vice versa.

The file Ch19.13.ARABIC.ROMAN.xlsx contains an example using the ARABIC and ROMAN functions, and is shown in the screen-clip in Figure 19.17.

CHAPTER 20

Financial Functions

INTRODUCTION

This chapter focuses on providing examples of a wide set of functions within Excel's Financial category, relating to:

- Annuity and general growth or discounting calculations.
- Mortgage and capital repayment calculations.
- General investment valuation and analysis.
- Depreciation calculations.
- Yields, bond, general securities and specific financial calculations.

PRACTICAL APPLICATIONS

Several points are worth bearing in mind:

- Many of the functions return negative figures by default, especially those that relate to calculating required payments or cash outflows. One needs to be particularly careful in their use, especially when they are embedded in logical statements such as those involving IF, MIN or MAX formulae.
- The use of an IF or IFERROR statement around such functions is frequently required. For example, some functions will return error values for a time period that is outside a valid limit (such as the lifetime of a mortgage). As covered in Chapter 17, it is generally better to exclude specific conditions in which error values are known to occur but are valid (by using an IF statement applied to this specific situation), rather than over-riding all errors by using IFERROR.
- Many of the functions are formatted in the local currency (i.e. that of the Excel version being used), which is sometimes inconvenient, especially when working on international projects; one may find it more convenient to switch to a general format.
- Where the functions require the use of interest rates (or growth or rates of return), one needs to ensure that the interest rate used is consistent with the periods of the model (e.g. annual, quarterly or monthly).

Example: FVSCHEDULE

FVSCHEDULE gives the future value of a quantity after applying a series of growth rates to it. The required inputs to the function are:

- The original value (or "principal").
- A schedule of growth, return or interest rates.

The file Ch20.1.FVSCHEDULE.xlsx contains an example of various applications of the function, both to situations with constant growth rates and to time-varying growth rates (see Figure 20.1).

One application is to work out the total (and average) compounded growth rate for a multi-period model or data set, where the rate in each period is different, and is measured using the traditional corporate finance method (see Chapter 19). By setting the original (principal) value to 1, the function returns the product of "1 plus the growth rate" in each period, so that subtracting 1 from this product gives the total growth, and taking the appropriate root gives the average annual compound figure (e.g. the square root for the annualised average over a two-year period).

The file Ch20.2.FVSCHEDULE.Returns.xlsx contains an example. The context is that one is given a set of traditional return figures (or growth rates) and wishes to work out the average return (or growth rate) between two periods directly from this data (without having to explicitly calculate the actual asset values in each period, nor the explicit cumulative compounded growth rate for each period). Figure 20.2 shows a screen-clip of the calculation of the total return between period 5 and 15 directly from the returns data. On the right-hand side of the file (rightwards from Column I, not shown in the screen-clip) are the explicit calculations that would otherwise be required.

Example: FV and PV

The FV function calculates the total value of a set of cash payments that grow constantly over a finite time period, based on an initial payment. It also has optional parameters that allow for the present value of a lump-sum future payment to be included, and to treat cash flows as occurring at the beginning (rather than the end) of each period. The PV function is similar, but discounts the periodic payment (instead of growing it).

	B	C	D	E	F	G	H	J	K
2	Using the FVSCHEDULE Function								
4			1	2	3	4	5		
5	Principal	100						Result	Formula
6	Schedule 1		5.0%	5.0%	5.0%	5.0%	5.0%	127.6	=FVSCHEDULE($C$5,D6:H6)
7	Schedule 2		0.0%	0.0%	0.0%	0.0%	0.0%	100.0	=FVSCHEDULE($C$5,D7:H7)
8	Schedule 3		2.0%	3.0%	4.0%	5.0%	6.0%	121.6	=FVSCHEDULE($C$5,D8:H8)
10	EXPLICIT CALCS: For Schedule 3								
12	Cumulative Rate		102.0%	105.1%	109.3%	114.7%	121.6%		
13	Periodic Value		102.0	105.1	109.3	114.7	121.6		

FIGURE 20.1 Examples of the FVSCHEDULE Function

	A	B	C	D	E	F	G
1							
2		Period No.				Using FVSCHEDULE to Calculate Return Between Periods 5 and 15	
3		0		Returns		Total	Average
4		1		5.55%		12.41%	1.18%
5		2		-7.83%		=FVSCHEDULE(1,D9:D18)-1	=(FVSCHEDULE(1,D9:D18))^(1/10)-1
6		3		-2.39%			
7		4		-0.99%			
8		5		2.11%			
9		6		0.80%			
10		7		0.16%			
11		8		1.48%			
12		9		1.16%			
13		10		1.24%			
14		11		1.44%			
15		12		2.54%			
16		13		1.52%			
17		14		-0.85%			
18		15		2.32%			

FIGURE 20.2 Use of FVSCHEDULE to Calculate Total and Average Growth Rates

	B	C	D	F	G	H	J	K
1								
2	Using the FV Function							
3								
4		Ex 1	Ex 2	Ex 3			Ex 4	Ex 5
5	Rate	5.0%	5.0%	5.0%			5.0%	5.0%
6	Nper	1	10	10			1	10
7	Pmt	-100	-100	-100			-100	-100
8	[pv]			500			0	0
9	[type]						1	1
10	Result	100	1258	443			105	1321
11	Formula	=FV(C5,C6,C7)	=FV(D5,D6,D7)	=FV(F5,F6,F7,F8)			=FV(J5,J6,J7,J8,J9)	=FV(K5,K6,K7,K8,K9)
12								
13	EXPLICIT CALCS							
14								
15		Inflated	Cumulative	Future Payment	Inflated Future Payment	Total	Discounted/Inflated	Cumulative
16	1	100	100				105	105
17	2	105	205				110	215
18	3	110	315				116	331
19	4	116	431				122	453
20	5	122	553				128	580
21	6	128	680				134	714
22	7	134	814				141	855
23	8	141	955				148	1003
24	9	148	1103				155	1158
25	10	155	1258	-500	-814	443	163	1321
26		=-C$7*(1+C$5)^($B25-1)	=SUM(C$16:C25)	=-F8	=F25*(1+$C$5)^$B25	=D25+G25	=-C$7*(1+C$5)^$B25	=SUM(J$16:J25)

FIGURE 20.3 Examples of the FV Function

The file Ch20.3.FV&PV.xlsx shows examples (each function is shown on a separate worksheet, with the corresponding name); see also the screen-clips in Figure 20.3 and Figure 20.4. The file also shows the equivalent results when the calculations are done explicitly in Excel.

The mathematically inclined reader will note that such values can be derived by direct mathematical manipulation, for example with:

$$S = 1 + (1+g) + \ldots + (1+g)^{N-1}$$

By multiplying each side by $(1+g)$:

$$S(1+g) = (1+g) + (1+g)^2 + \ldots + (1+g)^N$$

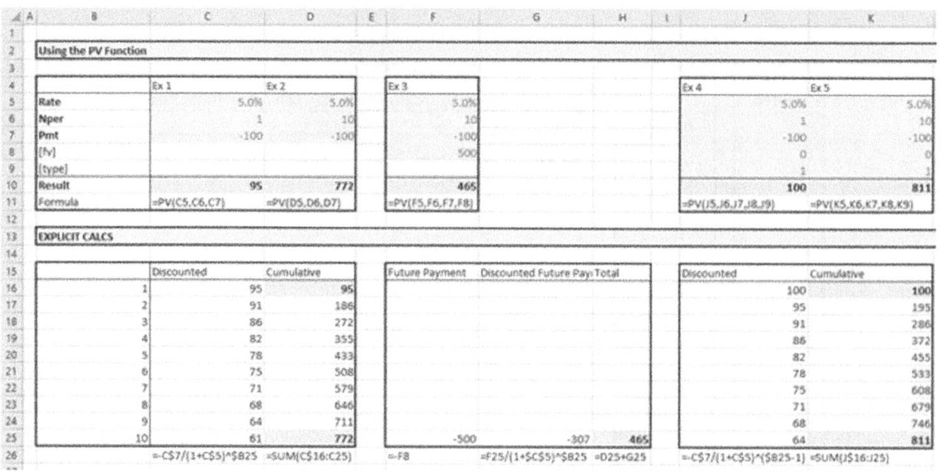

FIGURE 20.4 Examples of the PV Function

Subtracting the first equation from the second, and dividing by g, gives:

$$S = \frac{(1+g)^N - 1}{g}$$

Similarly, with:

$$T = 1 + \frac{1}{1+d} + \ldots + \frac{1}{(1+d)^N}$$

one has

$$T = \frac{(1+d)^N - 1}{d(1+d)^N}$$

These formulae are implemented in the Excel file (Row 29, not shown in the screen-clip).

Example: PMT, IPMT, PPMT, CUMIPMT, CUMPRINC and NPER

Several functions relate to the calculation of loan and mortgage repayments:

- PMT calculates the fixed-level repayment level that is required to be made in each period so that a loan (subject to a fixed interest rate) is paid off by the end of its life. This single figure implicitly comprises a component for interest repayment and one for capital repayment. Since capital is gradually being paid off, the interest amount in each period is reducing, so that the capital repayment portion is increasing from one period to the next.

- IPMT and PPMT calculate the interest and principal components explicitly; since these change in each time period, the functions have an extra parameter (compared to PMT) to indicate which period is being referred to.
- CUMIPMT and CUMPRINC calculate the cumulative interest and principal paid between two specified time periods.
- NPER calculates the number of period required to pay off a loan given a constant payment amount.

The file Ch20.4.PMT.PPMT&CUM.xlsx shows an example of these (see the worksheet "PMT" for all the functions, except for NPER, which is shown in the "NPER" worksheet). The file also contains the corresponding calculations that would be required if done explicitly in Excel, i.e. without using the functions. Note that for the explicit calculations, the repayment amount is an assumed hard-coded figure equal to that produced by the PMT function; if the functions were not available, this figure could be determined by manual experimentation or more efficiently by Excel's Goal-Seek or Solver. Figure 20.5 and Figure 20.6 show screen-clips of the example.

	A	B	C	D	E	F	G
1							
2		**Periodic interest rate**	5.0%				
3		**Periods to end of term**	15		Needs to be <=15 if using the		
4		**Principal amount ($)**	100,000				
5		FV	0		Optional argument (not used i		
6		Type	0		Optional for some of the functi		
7							
8		**For CUM functions**					
9		First period	2				
10		Last period	3				
11							
12		**Using PMT, CUMIPMT, CUMPRINC, IPMT and PPMT**					
13							
14		Total Constant Payment using PMT	-9,634	=PMT(C2,C3,C4)			
15							
16		Period by period Split into interst and principal		1	2	3	4
17		Interest part of total, using IPMT	-44,513	-5,000	-4,768	-4,525	-4,270
18		Principal part of total, using PPMT	-100,000	-4,634	-4,866	-5,109	-5,365
19							
20		Cumulative interest between periods using CUMIPMT	-9,293	=CUMIPMT(C2,C3,C4,C9,C10,C6)			
21		Cumulative principal between periods using CUMPRINC	-9,975	=CUMPRINC(C2,C3,C4,C9,C10,C6)			
22							
23		**Explicit Calculation**					
24							
25		Periodic payment assumed	9,634		Set so that ending balance is		
26		Ending balance at end of term	0		Cross-check, or for use with G		
27							
28		**Direct calculation of interest and principal by period**		1	2	3	4
29		Starting balance		100,000	95,366	90,500	85,391
30		(+) Interest (=balance * interest rate)	9,293	5,000	4,768	4,525	4,270
31		(-) Principal repayment (=assumed payment-interest)	9,975	4,634	4,866	5,109	5,365
32		Ending balance		95,366	90,500	85,391	80,026
33							

FIGURE 20.5 Examples of Uses of PMT, IPMT, PPMT, CUMIPMT and CUMPRINC Functions

	A	B	C	D
1				
2		Rate	5.0%	
3		PMT	-9634	
4		PV	100000	
5		FV	0	
6		Type	0	
7		**NPER**	**15.0**	=NPER(C2,C3,C4,C5,C6)

FIGURE 20.6 Example of the NPER Function

Example: NPV and IRR for a Buy or Lease Decision

The NPV and IRR functions are widely used in general investment evaluation and analysis. For equally spaced cash flows, NPV calculates their net present value at a specified discount rate, and IRR calculates their internal rate-of-return (i.e. the discount rate that would make the net present value equal to zero).

The use of the NPV function to calculate the discounted value of a set of cash flows is essentially straightforward (provided one is familiar with the concept of discounting). A frequent mistake is to overlook that the function implicitly assumes that the value in the first cell of the range is discounted for one period, the second value is discounted for two periods, and so on. This is equivalent to assuming that all cash flows occur at the end of their periods. Some adjustments may be required if the timing is expected to be different: for example, investments made at the initiation of a project should not be discounted, and so should be excluded as an input to the NPV function, but added to (or subtracted from) its result.

The file Ch20.5.NPV.IRR.1.Leasing.xlsx provides an example in the context of a decision either to lease or to buy an asset. It shows the calculation of the cash flows in each case and the differential cash flows between the two options. The IRR and NPV functions are used, and the calculation of the net present value of the differential cash flows (discounted at the post-tax interest rate) is created, in a way that the initial cash outflow associated with the purchase of the asset is not discounted. The file also shows that the net present value is zero if the IRR is used as the discount rate (see Figure 20.7).

The IRR function can also be used to calculate yields of bonds.

The use of IRR as a measure of project performance has some drawbacks, including:

- It only exists if there is at least one change of sign in the cash flows. For example, the discounted value of purely positive cash flows will always be positive, however large the discount rate.
- If cash flows change sign multiple times during the forecast period, there are as many possible IRR values as there are changes in sign of the cash flows. Thus, for a project with an initial investment, a cash-producing period and subsequent decommissioning costs, there are at least two possible values of the IRR. The function will return a single value, corresponding to one of the two, but one cannot a priori know which of the two is returned and whether it is an appropriate measure.
- As it is a percentage measure, it does not allow for easy comparison of projects whose orders of magnitude are different.

Asset cost	1,000,000												
Asset life	10												
Annual depreciation	100,000												
Interest rate (pre-tax)	6.0%												
Tax rate	30.0%												
Interest rate (post-tax)	4.2%												
Lease rental payment	125,000		(Could also use Goal Seek on this figure to set NPV to zero to find maximum acceptable to pay)										
Cash flows		0	1	2	3	4	5	6	7	8	9	10	
If Leasing													
Lease expense: Pre-tax	-125,000												
Lease expense: Post-tax	**-87,500**		-87,500	-87,500	-87,500	-87,500	-87,500	-87,500	-87,500	-87,500	-87,500	-87,500	
If Buying													
Asset cost	-1,000,000	-1,000,000	0	0	0	0	0	0	0	0	0	0	
Tax shield from depreciation	30,000		30,000	30,000	30,000	30,000	30,000	30,000	30,000	30,000	30,000	30,000	
Net cash flow		-1,000,000	30,000	30,000	30,000	30,000	30,000	30,000	30,000	30,000	30,000	30,000	
Differential cash flow		-1,000,000	117,500	117,500	117,500	117,500	117,500	117,500	117,500	117,500	117,500	117,500	
IRR of differential		3.05%	=IRR(D18:N18,10%)										
NPV of differential (at after-tax interest rate)	4.20%	-56388	=D18+NPV(C21,E18:N18)										
NPV of differential (at IRR)	3.05%	0	=D18+NPV(C23,E18:N18)										

FIGURE 20.7 Use of NPV and IRR for a Buy-versus-lease Decision

- It is not clear how risks can be taken into account in the project decision. Two projects may have the same IRR but have very different risk profiles. By contrast, the NPV approach more explicitly chooses a discount rate that should be appropriate for the risk of the cash flows being considered.
- The behaviour of the IRR in relation to timing effects may lead to ineffective or inappropriate decisions.

Some of these issues are illustrated in the following examples.

The file Ch20.6.NPV.IRR.2.CFSigns.xlsx shows the effect of trying to calculate NPV and IRR for various sets of cash flows, including those that are only positive (see Figure 20.8). The first cash flow profile is purely positive, so that the IRR does not exist at all. The second profile has up-front investments and subsequent decommissioning costs. Note that the IRR of the future cash flows exists in some years, but does not always provide a good indicator of future value generation. For example, in Column G (year 2022), the NPV of the future cash flows is positive, whereas the IRR is negative.

The file Ch20.7.NPV.IRR.3.DelayEvaluation.xlsx shows the effect on IRR and NPV of various scenarios for delaying the cash inflow of a project after an investment has been made (see Figure 20.9):

- In the first example, a single investment is made and the same amount is returned either one period later or 10 periods later. Note that the IRR is zero in both cases,

	2018	2019	2020	2021	2022	2023	2024	2025	2026	2027	2028	2029	2030	Formulae in column F
Cash Profile 1	50	300	500	400	300	250	150	100	75	50	0	0	0	
Future NPV @10%	1,444	1,539	1,393	1,032	735	509	310	190	110	45	0	0	0	=NPV(10%,F4:$O4)
Future IRR	#NUM!	#NUM!	#NUM!	#NUM!	#NUM!	#NUM!	#NUM!	#NUM!	#NUM!	#NUM!	#NUM!	#NUM!	#NUM!	=IRR(F4:$O4,10%)
Cash Profile 2	-300	-100	100	250	300	250	150	100	75	50	-50	-100	0	
Future NPV @10%	343	678	845	830	663	429	222	94	4	-71	-128	-91	0	=NPV(10%,F8:$O8)
Future IRR	32%	160%	#NUM!	#NUM!	-32%	-29%	-23%	-13%	8%	100%	#NUM!	#NUM!	#NUM!	=IRR(F8:$O8,10%)

FIGURE 20.8 Results of IRR Function for Some Non-standard Cash Flow Profiles

	A	B	C	D	E	F	G	H	I	J	K	L	M	N
1														
2		NPV @10%	IRR	0	1	2	3	4	5	6	7	8	9	10
3														
4		-41	0.0%	-500	500	0	0	0	0	0	0	0	0	0
5		-279	0.0%	-500	0	0	0	0	0	0	0	0	0	500
6														
7		69	13.7%	-500	100	100	100	100	100	100	100	100	100	0
8		21	11.0%	-500	0	100	100	100	100	100	100	100	100	100

FIGURE 20.9 Comparison of NPV and IRR When There is a Possibility of Delayed Cash Inflows

whereas the NPV is lower in the case of a delay; this provides some intuition as to the lower potential sensitivity of IRR to project delays (especially for projects whose IRR is low in the first place).

- In the second example, a project is delayed by one period after the initial investment has been made; the change to NPV is proportionally much larger than the change to the IRR; once again, the effect is generally strongest for projects whose NPV is only slightly positive.

The key point from this example is that, when using IRR only, one may underestimate the (effect of) the risk of delay to projects, especially those that are borderline positive. This may lead decision-makers to believing that delaying a project has little consequence, and hence to giving it insufficient priority or attention.

The file Ch20.8.NPV.IRR.SalesTiming.xlsx shows another example of how IRR may potentially lead to sub-optimal decision-making. It is based on the idea that there is a set of cash flows over time, and at any time the right to obtaining the future cash flows can be waived in exchange for the present value of those future cash flows. The graph shows the resulting IRR that would arise, depending on the year in which a project is sold (see Figure 20.10). The use of IRR as a performance measure may (arguably) encourage short-term thinking by incentivising an early sale of such projects.

Variations on the NPV and IRR functions that are sometimes useful include:

- XNPV and XIRR are analogous to NPV and IRR but where the timing of the cash flows is specified (i.e. generally, the cash flows are not equally spaced).
- MIRR function can be used to calculate the internal rate of return in the case that positive and negative cash flows are financed at different rates.

Example: SLN, DDB and VDB

Excel has various functions to assist in depreciation calculations, including:

- DB and DDB calculate the depreciation of an asset for a specified period by using the fixed-declining and double-declining balance methods.
- SLN calculates the straight-line depreciation of an asset for one period.
- VDB calculates the depreciation of an asset for a specified or partial period by using a choice of declining balance methods.
- SYD calculates the sum-of-years' digits depreciation of an asset for a specified period.

The file Ch20.9.VDB.Depreciation.SingleYear.xlsx contains examples of the use of the SLN, DDB and VDB functions (see Figure 20.11).

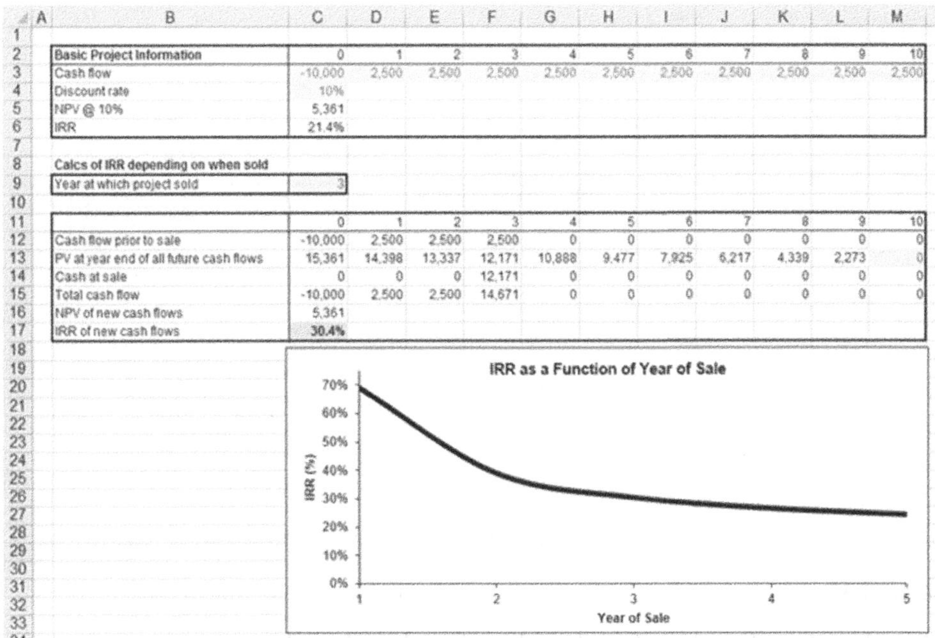

Basic Project Information	0	1	2	3	4	5	6	7	8	9	10
Cash flow	-10,000	2,500	2,500	2,500	2,500	2,500	2,500	2,500	2,500	2,500	2,500
Discount rate	10%										
NPV @ 10%	5,361										
IRR	21.4%										

Calcs of IRR depending on when sold

Year at which project sold	3

	0	1	2	3	4	5	6	7	8	9	10
Cash flow prior to sale	-10,000	2,500	2,500	2,500	0	0	0	0	0	0	0
PV at year end of all future cash flows	15,361	14,398	13,337	12,171	10,888	9,477	7,925	6,217	4,339	2,273	0
Cash at sale	0	0	0	12,171	0	0	0	0	0	0	0
Total cash flow	-10,000	2,500	2,500	14,671	0	0	0	0	0	0	0
NPV of new cash flows	5,361										
IRR of new cash flows	30.4%										

FIGURE 20.10 IRR as Function of the Year of Sale of a Positive NPV Project

Use of VDB function to calculate depreciation for a single year

	SLN	DDB: Ex 1	DDB: Ex 2	VBD
Asset Cost	10,000	10,000	10,000	10,000
% value at end of life	0.0%	0.0%	0.0%	0.0%
Life of assets	10	10	10	10
Start period (or period for DDB)	NA	1	1	5
End period	NA	NA	NA	6
Factor for VDB method	NA	1	2	2
No_Switch	NA	NA	NA	0
Function Results	1,000	1,000	2,000	655
	=SLN(D4,D4*D5,D6)	=DDB(F4,F4*F5,F6,F7,F9)	=DDB(G4,G4*G5,G6,G7,G9)	=VDB(I4,I4*I5,I6,I7,I8,I9,I10)

FIGURE 20.11 Examples of the SLN, DDB and VBB Functions

Of course, in practice, the functions may be required to calculate the depreciation profile based on an input set of capital expenditure (CapEx) data, or where CapEx figures are calculated from other assumptions.

The file Ch20.10.VDB.Depreciation.Triangle.xlsx contains examples of this. The depreciation results from a "triangle-type" calculation, as covered earlier in the text (also using the TRANSPOSE function to transpose the original date and CapEx ranges) and the VDB function is embedded within an error-checking statement (using IF and AND functions to ensure that errors are not shown in a year in which prior CapEx has already been depreciated fully) (see Figure 20.12).

	A	B	C	D	E	F	G	H	I	J	K	L	M	N
1		Use of VDB function to calculate depreciation schedule from a given capex schedule												
2														
3		Depreciation policy												
4		Life of assets	7											
5		% value at end of life	10.0%											
6		Factor for VDB method	2		E.g. 1=st. line when no residual value, 2=double declining balance etc.									
7														
8				2018	2019	2020	2021	2022	2023	2024	2025	2026	2027	2028
9														
10		Capex (£k)		8,000	10,000	12,000	15,000	12,000	10,000	8,000	6,000	5,000	5,000	5,000
11														
12			Capex	2018	2019	2020	2021	2022	2023	2024	2025	2026	2027	2028
13		2018	8,000	2,286	1,633	1,166	833	595	425	262	0	0	0	0
14		2019	10,000	0	2,857	2,041	1,458	1,041	744	531	328	0	0	0
15		2020	12,000	0	0	3,429	2,449	1,749	1,249	892	637	394	0	0
16		2021	15,000	0	0	0	4,286	3,061	2,187	1,562	1,116	797	492	0
17		2022	12,000	0	0	0	0	3,429	2,449	1,749	1,249	892	637	394
18		2023	10,000	0	0	0	0	0	2,857	2,041	1,458	1,041	744	531
19		2024	8,000	0	0	0	0	0	0	2,286	1,633	1,166	833	595
20		2025	6,000	0	0	0	0	0	0	0	1,714	1,224	875	625
21		2026	5,000	0	0	0	0	0	0	0	0	1,429	1,020	729
22		2027	5,000	0	0	0	0	0	0	0	0	0	1,429	1,020
23														
24		Depreciation total		2,286	4,490	6,636	9,025	9,875	9,911	9,324	8,135	6,944	6,030	3,894

FIGURE 20.12 Calculation of a Full Depreciation Profile Based on a CapEx Profile

Example: YIELD

The YIELD function calculates the yield on a security that pays periodic interest. It is similar in many ways to IRR, except that maturity and settlements dates are explicitly required as arguments, and that no explicit (period-by-period) cash flow profile needs to be created (unlike for IRR). The application is specific to bond-type situations, so that there is a single purchase or cash outflow event followed by cash inflows, whereas the IRR could be applied when the initial cash outflows are all negative for several periods.

The file Ch20.11.YIELD.IRR.xlsx shows an example of the use of the YIELD function, as well as the explicit calculation of the yield using the IRR for the corresponding situation (see Figure 20.13).

Other functions relating to yield include YIELDDISC, YIELDMAT, TBILLYIELD, ODDFYIELD and ODDLYIELD.

Example: Duration of Cash Flows

When considering any set of cash flows, one may develop several possible measures of their average timing:

- The time-weighted average nominal (non-discounted) cash flows.
- The time-weighted average discounted cash flows (with some assumed discount rate).
- Other modified measures that may serve for standardisation purposes.

The non-discounted time-weighted value may be considered as the "duration" of the cash flows, with the time-weighted average of the discounted cash flows often

Calculation of bond yield from market price using YIELD function

Bond price	95	
Face value ($)	100	
Annual coupon rate (%)	4.0%	
Settlement	01/01/2018	
Maturity	01/01/2028	
Frequency	1	
Yield to maturity using YIELD	4.636%	=YIELD(C7,C8,C6,C4,C5,1)

Calculation of bond yield from market price using IRR function

Bond price	95
Face value ($)	100
Annual coupon rate (%)	4.0%

Period Number	0	1	2	3	4	5	6	7	8	9	10	Total
Cash flow	-95.0	4.0	4.0	4.0	4.0	4.0	4.0	4.0	4.0	4.0	104.0	45.0

Yield to maturity using IRR	4.636%	=IRR(D20:N20,5%)

FIGURE 20.13 Use of YIELD Function and Comparison with IRR

known as the "Macaulay duration". When the Macaulay duration is modified by further discounting, this is known as the "modified duration".

The file Ch20.12.CashDuration.xlsx shows an example of the calculation of such measures for a general cash flow profile (see Figure 20.14).

Example: DURATION and MDURATION

In the specific context of bond calculations, given the relevant information about a bond (price, coupon, settlement and maturity dates etc.), one can calculate the duration figures directly (without having to perform the explicit cash flow forecast). Note that the DURATION function calculates the Macaulay duration (i.e. based on cash flows discounted at the yield rate), and MDURATION calculates the modification of this Macaulay duration. Thus, the "raw" or non-discounted figure (i.e. the "duration") is not available through a specific Excel function, although it can be calculated by using SUMPRODUCT.

General Cash Flows

		1	2	3	4	5	6	7	8	9	10	Total	Time Average	
Cash Flow		10.0	10.0	10.0	10.0	10.0	10.0	10.0	10.0	10.0	10.0	100.0	5.50	=SUMPRODUCT(D$4:M$4,D5:M5)/N5
Periodic Discount Factor	8.0%	8.0%	8.0%	8.0%	8.0%	8.0%	8.0%	8.0%	8.0%	8.0%	8.0%			
Cumulative Discount Factor		92.6%	85.7%	79.4%	73.5%	68.1%	63.0%	58.3%	54.0%	50.0%	46.3%			
Discounted Cash Flow		9.26	8.57	7.94	7.35	6.81	6.30	5.83	5.40	5.00	4.63	67.1	4.87	=SUMPRODUCT(D$4:M$4,D8:M8)/N8
													4.51	=O8/(1+C6)

FIGURE 20.14 Calculations of Duration, Macaulay Duration and Modified Duration of Cash Flows

The file Ch20.13.BondDuration.xlsx shows an example (see Figure 20.15). Note that the YIELD function is required as an input to the calculations (to find the rate at which to discount). The equivalent calculations are also shown directly in Excel as if the explicit cash flows were forecast.

Example: PDURATION and RRI

The PDURATION function is not directly related to bond calculations, nor to the other duration functions discussed above; instead, it calculates the number of periods required for an investment to reach a specified value, assuming a periodic growth rate. In other words, it finds n so that:

$$FV = PV(1+g)^n$$

Of course, instead of using the function, one could solve this equation directly (to find n):

$$n = \frac{LN\left(\frac{FV}{PV}\right)}{LN(1+g)}$$

Similarly, the RRI function provides the value that could be found by solving for g:

$$g = EXP\left(LN\left(\frac{FV}{PV}\right)/n\right) - 1$$

(RRI may be thought of as the "rate-of-return-implied" if g considered as a rate-of-return rather than a growth rate.)

The file Ch20.14.PDURATION.RRI.xlsx provides an example of these functions (see Figure 20.16).

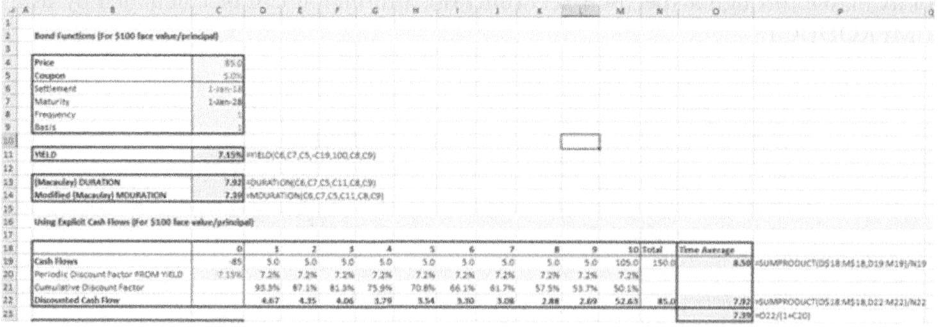

Bond Functions (For $100 face value/principal)

Price	85.0	
Coupon	5.0%	
Settlement	1-Jan-18	
Maturity	1-Jan-28	
Frequency	1	
Basis	1	
YIELD	7.15%	=YIELD(C6,C7,C5,-C19,100,C8,C9)
(Macauley) DURATION	7.92	=DURATION(C6,C7,C5,C11,C8,C9)
Modified (Macauley) MDURATION	7.39	=MDURATION(C6,C7,C5,C11,C8,C9)

Using Explicit Cash Flows (For $100 face value/principal)

	0	1	2	3	4	5	6	7	8	9	10	Total	Time Average	
Cash Flows	-85	5.0	5.0	5.0	5.0	5.0	5.0	5.0	5.0	5.0	105.0	150.0	8.50	=SUMPRODUCT(D$18:M$18,D19:M19)/N19
Periodic Discount Factor FROM YIELD	7.15%	7.2%	7.2%	7.2%	7.2%	7.2%	7.2%	7.2%	7.2%	7.2%	7.2%			
Cumulative Discount Factor		93.3%	87.1%	81.3%	75.9%	70.8%	66.1%	61.7%	57.5%	53.7%	50.1%			
Discounted Cash Flow		4.67	4.35	4.06	3.79	3.54	3.30	3.08	2.88	2.69	52.63	85.0	7.92	=SUMPRODUCT(D$18:M$18,D22:M22)/N22
													7.39	=O22/(1+C20)

FIGURE 20.15 Use of DURATION and MDURATION and Comparison with Explicit Calculations

	A	B	C	D	E	F	G	H	I
1									
2		Rate	10%			NPER	7.27		
3		PV	100			PV	100		
4		FV	200			FV	200		
5		**PDURATION**	**7.27**	=PDURATION(C2,C3,C4)		**RRI**	**10.0%**	=RRI(G2,G3,G4)	
6		**Direct calculation**	**7.27**	=LN(C4/C3)/LN(1+C2)		**Direct calculation**	**10.0%**	=EXP(LN(G4/G3)/G2)-1	

FIGURE 20.16 Example of PDURATION and Its Equivalent Calculated Directly

OTHER FINANCIAL FUNCTIONS

The other functions in Excel's Financial category mostly relate to interest rates and bonds:

- ACCRINT and ACCRINTM calculate the accrued interest for a security that pays interest periodically or at maturity respectively.
- COUPDAYBS, COUPDAYS, COUPDAYSNC, COUPNCD, COUPNUM and COUPPCD perform a variety of calculations about dates, numbers and amounts of coupons payable.
- DISC calculates the discount rate for a security.
- DOLLARDE and DOLLARFR convert dollar prices expressed as a fraction to those expressed as decimal numbers and vice versa.
- EFFECT and NOMINAL calculate effective and nominal interest rates when interest can be compounded several times per period.
- INTRATE calculates the interest rate for a fully invested security.
- RATE calculates the interest rate per period of an annuity.
- ODDFPRICE (ODDLPRICE) calculate the price per $100 face value of a security with an odd first (last) period.
- PRICE calculates the value of a security that pays periodic interest.
- PRICEDISC calculates the value of a discounted security.
- PRICEMAT calculates the value of a security that pays interest at maturity.
- RECEIVED calculates the amount received at maturity for a fully invested security.
- TBILLEQ calculates the bond-equivalent yield for a Treasury bill.
- TBILLPRICE calculates the value of a Treasury bill.

The reader can explore these in more depth where they are of potential relevance.

CHAPTER 21

Statistical Functions

INTRODUCTION

This chapter provides examples of many of the functions in Excel's Statistical category. These are often required to conduct data analysis, investigate relationships between variables, and to estimate or calibrate model inputs or results. Most of the calculations concern:

- The position, ranking, spread and shape of a data set.
- Probability distributions (X-to-P and P-to-X calculations).
- Co-relationships and regression analysis.
- Forecasting and other statistical calculations.

Since Excel 2010, the category has undergone significant changes, which were introduced for several reasons:

- To provide clearer definitions, for example as to whether the calculations are based on samples of data or on full population statistics.
- To allow additional function possibilities and user-options, such as whether probability distributions are expressed in their cumulative or density form.
- To create new types of calculations that previously may not have existed, such as those within the FORECAST-related suite of functions.

In order to create backward compatibility with earlier versions of Excel, many of the changes have been introduced by naming the new functions with a ".", such as MODE.SNGL, or RANK.EQ or STDEV.S.

Note that Excel's function categories are in some cases slightly arbitrary constructs, with the result that some functions are not necessarily in the category that one might expect. In particular, the distinction between Statistical and Math&Trig functions is not totally clear-cut. For example, SUMIFS, COMBIN and RAND are classified within the Math&Trig category, whereas AVERAGEIFS, PERMUT, NORM.DIST, NORM.IN and PROBE are within the Statistical category. Note that this chapter provides no further specific treatment of functions that have already been covered earlier (such as AVERAGE, AVERAGEA, AVERAGEIF, AVERAGEIFS, MAXIFS, MINIFS, COUNT, COUNTA, COUNTBLANK, COUNTIF, COUNTIFS, MAX, MAXA, MIN, MINA).

PRACTICAL APPLICATIONS: POSITION, RANKING AND CENTRAL VALUES

In general, when presented with a set of data, one may wish to calculate summary information, such as:

- The average, minimum and maximum values.
- The most likely value (mode or most frequently occurring).
- The median point, i.e. where 50% of items are higher/lower than this value.
- The value which is exceeded in 10% of cases, or for which 10% of the items in the data set are below this value.
- Measures of dispersion, range or the spread of the data.

The main functions relating to such information are:

- MODE.SNGL calculates the most common (most frequent) value in a data set, as long as a unique value exists. MODE.MULT calculates a vertical array of the most frequently occurring in a range of data, including repetitive values. MODE is a legacy version of the MODE.SNGL function.
- GEOMEAN and HARMEAN calculate the geometric and harmonic means of a set of data, and TRIMMEAN calculates the mean of the interior of a data set.
- LARGE and SMALL calculate the specified largest or smallest values in a data set (e.g. first, second, third largest or smallest etc.)
- RANK.EQ (RANK in earlier versions of Excel) calculates the rank of a number in a list of numbers, with RANK.AVG giving the average rank in the case of tied values.
- PERCENTILE.EXC and PERCENTILE.INC (and its legacy PERCENTILE) calculate a specified percentile of the values in a range, exclusive and inclusive respectively. The QUARTILE.EXC and QUARTILE.INC functions (QUARTILE in earlier versions) calculate percentiles for specific 25th percentage multiples. MEDIAN calculates the median of the given numbers, i.e. the 50th percentile.
- PERCENTRANK.INC (PERCENTRANK in earlier versions) and PERCENTRANK.EXC calculate the percentage rank of a value in a data set, inclusive and exclusive respectively.

Example: Calculating Mean and Mode

The average of a set of data can be calculated by summing the individual values and dividing by the number of items. In Excel, it can be calculated directly using the AVERAGE function or by dividing the result of using SUM and COUNT.

In relation to the average, note that:

- The average as calculated from the full (raw) set of individual data points is also called the "weighted-average". This because every value will automatically be included in the calculations in the total according to the frequency with which it occurs in the data set.
- In mathematics, the (weighted) average is also called the "mean" or the "Expected Value (EV)". At the time of writing, there is no "MEAN" or "WEIGHTEDAVERAGE" function in Excel. However, in the case where the full data set of individual items (including repeated values) is not provided, but rather the values and the frequency of each value is given, the SUMPRODUCT function can be used to calculate the (weighted) average.

- In order to calculate the frequency of each item in a data set, one can use either COUNTIFS-type functions (see Chapter 17), or the FREQUENCY array function (covered in Chapter 18). An important application is to count the frequency in which points in a data set fall within ranges ("buckets" or "bins").
- Other conditional calculations may also be required: for example, AVERAGEIFS, MINIFS and MAXIFs (and array functions relating to these) can be used to calculate the corresponding figures for a subset of the data according to specified criteria. These were covered in Chapter 17 and Chapter 18, and so are not discussed further.

The most likely (or most frequently occurring) value in a data set is known as the mode (or modal value). Some of its key properties include:

- It may be thought of as a "best estimate", or indeed as the value that one might "expect" to occur; to expect anything else would be to expect something that is less likely. Therefore, it is often the value that would be chosen as the base case value for a model input, especially where such values are set using judgment or expert estimates.
- It is not the same as the mathematical definition of "Expected Value", which is the (weighted) average (or mean); generally, these two "expectations" will be different, unless the data set is symmetric.
- It exists only if one value occurs more frequently than others. Thus, for a simple sample of data from a process (in which each measurement occurs just once), the mode would not exist, and the functions would return and error message.

The file Ch21.1.MODE.xlsx shows examples of the MODE and MODE.SNGL functions, as well as of the MODE.MULT array function (see Figure 21.1). One can see that the MODE.MULT function will report multiple values when there are several that are equally likely (the last three items in the data set are repetitions of other values, and there are three modes; the last field returns #N/A as the function has been entered to return up to four values).

	A	B	C	D
1				
2		Data 1		
3		1.59	1.59	=MODE(B3:B15)
4		-1.78	1.59	=MODE.SNGL(B3:B15)
5		1.12	1.59	{=MODE.MULT(B3:B15)}
6		1.56	-1.78	{=MODE.MULT(B3:B15)}
7		0.59	1.56	{=MODE.MULT(B3:B15)}
8		-0.34	#N/A	{=MODE.MULT(B3:B15)}
9		1.03		
10		1.06		
11		1.05		
12		0.80		
13		1.56		
14		1.59		
15		-1.78		
16				

FIGURE 21.1 Use of the MODE-type Functions

E	F	G	H
	Data 2		
	1.59	#N/A	=MODE(F3:F102)
	-1.78	#N/A	=MODE.SNGL(F3:F102)
	1.12	#N/A	{=MODE.MULT(F3:F102)}
	1.56		
	0.59		
	-0.34		
	1.03		
	1.06		
	1.05		
	0.80		
	0.61		
	0.87		
	-0.22		
	2.40		
	0.46		
	2.10		
	0.40		

FIGURE 21.2 Use of MODE-type Functions in Situation Containing Only Unique Values

The same file also shows that these functions will return #N/A when each value in a data set occurs only once (see Figure 21.2).

Note that although there is no simple "MEAN" function in Excel, the functions TRIMMEAN, GEOMEAN and HARMEAN do exist:

- TRIMMEAN calculates the average after excluding a specified number of the largest and smallest items (the number excluded is the same at both the high end and low end, and so the function calculates the required number to exclude based on the user's input percentage value; therefore, one needs to be careful when using the function to ensure that the number of exclusions corresponds to the desired figure).
- GEOMEAN calculates the geometric mean of a set of n positive numbers; this is the n-th root of the product of these numbers.
- HARMEAN calculates the harmonic mean of a set of positive numbers, which is the reciprocal of the average of the reciprocals of the individual values.

The file Ch21.2.MEANS.xlsx shows some examples of these (see Figure 21.3).

Example: Dynamic Sorting of Data Using LARGE

Although the sorting of data can be achieved using the tools on Excel's Data tab, this is a process that must be done manually (or using a VBA macro that runs the sorting procedure). An alternative is to use the LARGE function to calculate the data in sorted order. This is especially useful in models that need to be dynamic (either if new data will be brought in regularly, or if a sensitivity analysis of the output needs to be run). Of course, the function can also be used to find only the largest, or second or third largest, item of

	A	B	C	D
1				
2		**Data 1**		
3		1.59	0.668	=AVERAGE(B3:B12)
4		-1.78	0.668	=TRIMMEAN(B3:B12,0%)
5		1.12	0.668	=TRIMMEAN(B3:B12,10%)
6		1.56	0.859	=TRIMMEAN(B3:B12,30%)
7		0.59		
8		-0.34	1.010	=GEOMEAN(B5:B7)
9		1.03	1.010	=PRODUCT(B5:B7)^(1/COUNT(B5:B7))
10		1.06		
11		1.05	0.931	=HARMEAN(B5:B7)
12		0.80	0.931	=1/((1/3)*(1/B5+1/B6+1/B7))

FIGURE 21.3 Examples of TRIMMEAN, GEOMEAN and HARMEAN

	A	B	C	D	E	F	G	H
1								
2		**Data 1**		**Largest 11**			**Smallest 11**	
3	1	1.59		3.30	=LARGE(B$3:B$102,$A3)		-1.78	=SMALL($B$3:$B$102,$A3)
4	2	-1.78		2.78	=LARGE(B$3:B$102,$A4)		-1.62	=SMALL($B$3:$B$102,$A4)
5	3	1.12		2.66	=LARGE(B$3:B$102,$A5)		-1.20	=SMALL($B$3:$B$102,$A5)
6	4	1.56		2.41	=LARGE(B$3:B$102,$A6)		-0.77	=SMALL($B$3:$B$102,$A6)
7	5	0.59		2.40	=LARGE(B$3:B$102,$A7)		-0.57	=SMALL($B$3:$B$102,$A7)
8	6	-0.34		2.39	=LARGE(B$3:B$102,$A8)		-0.54	=SMALL($B$3:$B$102,$A8)
9	7	1.03		2.39	=LARGE(B$3:B$102,$A9)		-0.51	=SMALL($B$3:$B$102,$A9)
10	8	1.06		2.30	=LARGE(B$3:B$102,$A10)		-0.47	=SMALL($B$3:$B$102,$A10)
11	9	1.05		2.25	=LARGE(B$3:B$102,$A11)		-0.46	=SMALL($B$3:$B$102,$A11)
12	10	0.80		2.21	=LARGE(B$3:B$102,$A12)		-0.36	=SMALL($B$3:$B$102,$A12)
13	11	0.61		2.20	=LARGE(B$3:B$102,$A13)		-0.34	=SMALL($B$3:$B$102,$A13)
14	12	0.87		2.10				
15	13	-0.22		2.10				
16	14	2.40		2.09				
17	15	0.46		2.08				
18	16	2.10		2.07				

FIGURE 21.4 Using LARGE and SMALL to Sort and Manipulate Data

data, and there is no requirement to have to place all of the original data set in order. The SMALL function is analogous, returning the smallest values first. (Of course, if one is interested only in the largest or smallest value, one can simply use MAX or MIN.)

The file Ch21.3.LARGE.SMALL.xlsx provides an example (see Figure 21.4). The LARGE and SMALL functions are used to list the 11 largest and smallest items in a data set of 100 items.

Example: RANK.EQ

The rank of an item within its data set is its ordered position; that is, the largest number has rank 1 (or the smallest does, depending on the preferred definition), the second largest (or smallest) has rank 2, and so on. The ranking is closely linked to the LARGE

	A	B	C	D	E	F	G	H
1								
2		Data		Rank Order Descending		Rank Order Ascending		
3		1.59		29	=RANK.EQ(B3,B$3:B$102)	72	=RANK.EQ(B3,B$3:B$102,1)	
4		-1.78		100	=RANK.EQ(B4,B$3:B$102)	1	=RANK.EQ(B4,B$3:B$102,1)	
5		1.12		44	=RANK.EQ(B5,B$3:B$102)	57	=RANK.EQ(B5,B$3:B$102,1)	
6		1.56		30	=RANK.EQ(B6,B$3:B$102)	71	=RANK.EQ(B6,B$3:B$102,1)	
7		0.59		68	=RANK.EQ(B7,B$3:B$102)	33	=RANK.EQ(B7,B$3:B$102,1)	
8		-0.34		90	=RANK.EQ(B8,B$3:B$102)	11	=RANK.EQ(B8,B$3:B$102,1)	
9		1.03		50	=RANK.EQ(B9,B$3:B$102)	51	=RANK.EQ(B9,B$3:B$102,1)	
10		1.06		48	=RANK.EQ(B10,B$3:B$102)	53	=RANK.EQ(B10,B$3:B$102,1)	

FIGURE 21.5 Examples of the RANK.EQ Function

and SMALL functions, essentially as inverse processes (e.g. the rank of a number is its ordered position as if the data set were sorted, whereas the LARGE function returns the actual number for a given ordered position).

The ranking of items is sometimes required in financial modelling, such as for reporting on how important an item is. It is also required in calculation of rank (Spearman) correlation coefficients when analysing relationships between multiple data sets, as discussed later in this chapter.

The file Ch21.4.RANKEQ.xlsx shows examples of the RANK.EQ function applied to a data set of 100 unique values, showing both the cases where the optional parameter is omitted and where it is included (to provide the descending or ascending rank order respectively) (see Figure 21.5). The legacy function RANK is also shown in the file (but not in the screenshot).

Example: RANK.AVG

The file Ch21.5.RANKAVG.xlsx (see Figure 21.6) shows a data set containing duplicate values (such as in cells B5 and B16), so that there is a tied ranking. The RANK.EQ function provides an equal rank for each tie and skips over the ordered position (e.g. there is no item with rank of 4). The RANK.AVG value instead provides the average value of the items (that is 3.5, as the average of 3 and 4 in this example).

Example: Calculating Percentiles

Another important statistic is the percentile (sometimes called centile). This shows – for any assumed percentage figure – the x-value below which that percentage of outcomes lie. For example, the 10th percentile (or P10) is the value below which 10% of the outcomes lie, and the P90 would be the value below which 90% of occurrences lie. Note that the minimum and maximum are the 0th and 100th percentile respectively. Another important special case is the 50th percentile (P50), i.e. the point where 50% of items are higher/lower than this value. This is known as the median.

Functions such as PERCENTILE, PERCENTILE.INC and PERCENTILE.EXC can be used to calculate percentiles of data sets, depending on the Excel version used (with the special cases P0, P100 and P50 also able to be captured through the MIN, MAX and MEDIAN functions as an alternative).

	A	B	C	D	E	F
1						
2		Data	Rank Order Descending		Rank Order Descending	
3		1.59	1	=RANK.EQ(B3,B$3:B$16)	1	=RANK.AVG(B3,B$3:B$16)
4		-1.78	14	=RANK.EQ(B4,B$3:B$16)	14	=RANK.AVG(B4,B$3:B$16)
5		1.12	3	=RANK.EQ(B5,B$3:B$16)	3.5	=RANK.AVG(B5,B$3:B$16)
6		1.56	2	=RANK.EQ(B6,B$3:B$16)	2	=RANK.AVG(B6,B$3:B$16)
7		0.59	11	=RANK.EQ(B7,B$3:B$16)	11	=RANK.AVG(B7,B$3:B$16)
8		-0.34	13	=RANK.EQ(B8,B$3:B$16)	13	=RANK.AVG(B8,B$3:B$16)
9		1.03	7	=RANK.EQ(B9,B$3:B$16)	7	=RANK.AVG(B9,B$3:B$16)
10		1.06	5	=RANK.EQ(B10,B$3:B$16)	5	=RANK.AVG(B10,B$3:B$16)
11		1.05	6	=RANK.EQ(B11,B$3:B$16)	6	=RANK.AVG(B11,B$3:B$16)
12		0.80	9	=RANK.EQ(B12,B$3:B$16)	9	=RANK.AVG(B12,B$3:B$16)
13		0.61	10	=RANK.EQ(B13,B$3:B$16)	10	=RANK.AVG(B13,B$3:B$16)
14		0.87	8	=RANK.EQ(B14,B$3:B$16)	8	=RANK.AVG(B14,B$3:B$16)
15		-0.22	12	=RANK.EQ(B15,B$3:B$16)	12	=RANK.AVG(B15,B$3:B$16)
16		1.12	3	=RANK.EQ(B16,B$3:B$16)	3.5	=RANK.AVG(B16,B$3:B$16)

FIGURE 21.6 RANK.EQ and RANK.AVG in the Case of Tied Items

Whereas these statistical properties are in theory generally clearly defined only for continuous (infinite) data sets, in practice they would be applied in many contexts to finite (discrete) data. In this regard, one needs to be careful to apply them correctly, as well as understanding the results that are returned: the PERCENTILE-type functions will generally need to interpolate between values to find an approximation to the true figure (an implicit assumption is that the underlying process that produces the data is a continuous one). For example, the value of PERCENTILE.INC({1,2,3,4,5},10%) is returned as 1.4, and PERCENTILE.INC({1,2,3,4,5},20%) is returned as 1.8.

The file Ch21.6.PERCENTILES.xlsx shows some implementations of the PERCENTILE-type functions. Note that, whereas PERCENTILE.INC and the legacy PERCENTILE functions can be applied with any percentage value (including 0% or 100%), the PERCENTILE.EXC function will only work where the input percentage is between $1/n$ and $1-1/n$, where n is the number of points in the data set. Within this range, its interpolation procedure may provide a more accurate estimate of the underlying percentile value; this can partly be seen from the file with respect to the P10 calculations (the right-hand side of the file shows the data in sorted order, using the LARGE function, in order to see the more accurate value produced by PERCENTILE.EXC) (see Figure 21.7). (Later in the chapter, we provide a further example of where this latter function is also more accurate, although our general testing indicates that it may not always be so.)

Example: PERCENTRANK-type Functions

The file Ch21.7.PERCENTRANK.xlsx (see Figure 21.8) contains examples of some PERCENTRANK-type functions; these calculate the percentage rank of a value in a data set. The PERCENTRANK.INC (inclusive) function corresponds to the legacy PERCENTRANK function, whereas the PERCENTRANK.EXC (exclusive) provides a new set of calculations.

	A	B	C	D	E	F	G	H
1								
2		Data 2						
3		1.59	2.203	=PERCENTILE(B3:B102,90%)		1	3.302	=LARGE(B$3:B$102,$F3)
4		-1.78	2.203	=PERCENTILE.INC(B3:B102,90%)		2	2.78	=LARGE(B$3:B$102,$F4)
5		1.12	2.212	=PERCENTILE.EXC(B3:B102,90%)		3	2.66	=LARGE(B$3:B$102,$F5)
6		1.56				4	2.41	=LARGE(B$3:B$102,$F6)
7		0.59	3.044	=PERCENTILE(B3:B102,99.5%)		5	2.40	=LARGE(B$3:B$102,$F7)
8		-0.34	3.044	=PERCENTILE.INC(B3:B102,99.5%)		6	2.39	=LARGE(B$3:B$102,$F8)
9		1.03	#NUM!	=PERCENTILE.EXC(B3:B102,99.5%)		7	2.39	=LARGE(B$3:B$102,$F9)
10		1.06				8	2.30	=LARGE(B$3:B$102,$F10)
11		1.05	3.302	=PERCENTILE(B3:B102,100%)		9	2.25	=LARGE(B$3:B$102,$F11)
12		0.80	3.302	=PERCENTILE.INC(B3:B102,100%)		10	2.213	=LARGE(B$3:B$102,$F12)
13		0.61	#NUM!	=PERCENTILE.EXC(B3:B102,100%)		11	2.202	=LARGE(B$3:B$102,$F13)
14		0.87				12	2.10	
15		-0.22				13	2.10	

FIGURE 21.7 Use of the PERCENTILE-type and MEDIAN Functions

	A	B	C	D	E	F	G	H	I
1									
2		Data		Rank Order Ascending		PERCENTRANK.INC		PERCENTRANK.EXC	
3		1.59		72	=RANK.EQ(B3,B$3:B$102,1)	72%	=PERCENTRANK.INC(B$3:B$102,B3)	71%	=PERCENTRANK.EXC(B$3:B$102,B3)
4		-1.78		1	=RANK.EQ(B4,B$3:B$102,1)	0%	=PERCENTRANK.INC(B$3:B$102,B4)	1%	=PERCENTRANK.EXC(B$3:B$102,B4)
5		1.12		57	=RANK.EQ(B5,B$3:B$102,1)	57%	=PERCENTRANK.INC(B$3:B$102,B5)	56%	=PERCENTRANK.EXC(B$3:B$102,B5)
6		1.56		71	=RANK.EQ(B6,B$3:B$102,1)	71%	=PERCENTRANK.INC(B$3:B$102,B6)	70%	=PERCENTRANK.EXC(B$3:B$102,B6)
7		0.59		33	=RANK.EQ(B7,B$3:B$102,1)	32%	=PERCENTRANK.INC(B$3:B$102,B7)	33%	=PERCENTRANK.EXC(B$3:B$102,B7)
8		-0.34		11	=RANK.EQ(B8,B$3:B$102,1)	10%	=PERCENTRANK.INC(B$3:B$102,B8)	11%	=PERCENTRANK.EXC(B$3:B$102,B8)
9		1.03		51	=RANK.EQ(B9,B$3:B$102,1)	51%	=PERCENTRANK.INC(B$3:B$102,B9)	50%	=PERCENTRANK.EXC(B$3:B$102,B9)
10		1.06		53	=RANK.EQ(B10,B$3:B$102,1)	53%	=PERCENTRANK.INC(B$3:B$102,B10)	52%	=PERCENTRANK.EXC(B$3:B$102,B10)
11		1.05		52	=RANK.EQ(B11,B$3:B$102,1)	52%	=PERCENTRANK.INC(B$3:B$102,B11)	51%	=PERCENTRANK.EXC(B$3:B$102,B11)
12		0.80		43	=RANK.EQ(B12,B$3:B$102,1)	42%	=PERCENTRANK.INC(B$3:B$102,B12)	43%	=PERCENTRANK.EXC(B$3:B$102,B12)
13		0.61		35	=RANK.EQ(B13,B$3:B$102,1)	34%	=PERCENTRANK.INC(B$3:B$102,B13)	35%	=PERCENTRANK.EXC(B$3:B$102,B13)

FIGURE 21.8 Examples of PERCENTRANK Functions

Note that, whereas the default settings for the RANK.EQ, RANK.AVG and RANK functions are to show the descending rank order (i.e. when the optional parameter is omitted), for the PERCENTRANK-type functions the implicit ranking is ascending.

PRACTICAL APPLICATIONS: SPREAD AND SHAPE

The spread and overall "shape" of the points are also key aspects of a data set, providing aggregate indications, rather than those associated with individual data points.

Some key measures associated with the shape include:

- FREQUENCY is an array function that counts the number of times that points within a data set lie within each of a set of pre-defined ranges (or bins), i.e. the frequency distribution.
- The symmetry of the data set. In Excel, SKEW.P (Excel 2013 onwards) calculates the skewness of a full population of data, and SKEW estimates the skewness of the population based on a sample (SKEW.S does not exist at the time of writing).

- The extent to which data points are within the tails (towards the minimum or maximum extremes) versus being of a more central nature. KURT estimates (excess) kurtosis of a population for a data set that represents a sample (KURT.P and KURT.S do not exist at the time of writing).

Some key measures of the dispersion of points in a range include:

- The total width of the range (the maximum value less the minimum value), or the difference between two percentiles (P90 less P10). The MIN, MAX, PERCENTILE-type and other related functions could be used in this respect (see earlier in the chapter).
- The standard deviation, or other measures of deviation, such as the semi-deviation. At the time of writing, there are many functions related to the calculation of the standard deviation and the variance of data sets. However, there is no function for the semi-deviation (see later in this chapter for calculation methods, and also Chapter 33 for its implementation as a user-defined function using VBA):
  - VAR.P (VARP in earlier versions) calculates the population variance of a set of data, i.e. the average of the squares of the deviations of the points from the mean, assuming that the data representing the entire population. Similarly, VAR.S (VAR in earlier versions) estimates the population variance based on the assumption that the data set represents a sample from the population (so that a correction term for biases is required to be used within the formula).
  - STDEV.P (STDEVP in earlier versions) and STDEV.S (STDEV in earlier versions) calculate or estimate the standard deviations associated with the population, based on population or sample data respectively. Such standard deviations are the square root of the corresponding variances.
  - AVEDEV calculates the average of the absolute deviations of data points from their mean (the average deviation from the mean is of course zero).

Other related functions include:

- VARPA, STDEVPA, VARA and STDEVA calculate the population and sample-based statistics, including numbers, text and logical values in the calculations.
- DEVSQ calculates the sum of squares of deviations from the mean for a data set.
- STANDARDIZE calculates the number of deviations that the input value is from an assumed figure, and with an assumed standardised deviation factor.

It is worthwhile noting that in most cases such functions assume that the data set given is a listing of individual occurrences of a sample or population. Thus they do not allow one to use explicitly any data on the frequency of occurrences. (An exception is the use of SUMPRODUCT in which the frequency is one of the input fields.)

Example: Generating a Histogram of Returns Using FREQUENCY

FREQUENCY counts the number of data points that lie within each of a set of pre-defined ranges (or bins). It can be used to create the data to produce a bar chart (histogram) of the data set. Note that it is an array function that must be entered in a vertical (not horizontal) range.

	A	B	C	D	E	F	G
1							
2		Period	Returns		Xbins	FREQUENCY	
3		1	5.40%		-10.0%	0	{=FREQUENCY(C3:C202,E3:E23)}
4		2	-8.16%		-9.00%	0	{=FREQUENCY(C3:C202,E3:E23)}
5		3	-2.42%		-8.00%	1	{=FREQUENCY(C3:C202,E3:E23)}
6		4	-1.00%		-7.00%	0	{=FREQUENCY(C3:C202,E3:E23)}
7		5	2.09%		-6.00%	0	{=FREQUENCY(C3:C202,E3:E23)}
8		6	0.80%		-5.00%	1	{=FREQUENCY(C3:C202,E3:E23)}
9		7	0.16%		-4.00%	2	{=FREQUENCY(C3:C202,E3:E23)}
10		8	1.47%		-3.00%	4	{=FREQUENCY(C3:C202,E3:E23)}
11		9	1.16%		-2.00%	6	{=FREQUENCY(C3:C202,E3:E23)}
12		10	1.24%		-1.00%	10	{=FREQUENCY(C3:C202,E3:E23)}
13		11	1.43%		0.00%	31	{=FREQUENCY(C3:C202,E3:E23)}
14		12	2.51%		1.00%	52	{=FREQUENCY(C3:C202,E3:E23)}
15		13	1.51%		2.00%	54	{=FREQUENCY(C3:C202,E3:E23)}
16		14	-0.86%		3.00%	24	{=FREQUENCY(C3:C202,E3:E23)}
17		15	2.30%		4.00%	7	{=FREQUENCY(C3:C202,E3:E23)}
18		16	1.06%		5.00%	6	{=FREQUENCY(C3:C202,E3:E23)}
19		17	1.61%		6.00%	1	{=FREQUENCY(C3:C202,E3:E23)}
20		18	-1.36%		7.00%	0	{=FREQUENCY(C3:C202,E3:E23)}
21		19	-0.63%		8.00%	1	{=FREQUENCY(C3:C202,E3:E23)}
22		20	0.57%		9.00%	0	{=FREQUENCY(C3:C202,E3:E23)}
23		21	1.35%		10.00%	0	{=FREQUENCY(C3:C202,E3:E23)}
24		22	2.38%		Infinity	0	{=FREQUENCY(C3:C202,E3:E23)}
25		23	-2.01%				

FIGURE 21.9 Using the FREQUENCY Function

The file Ch21.9.FREQUENCY.xlsx shows an example in the context of returns data for a market-quoted asset over several periods (see Figure 21.9). (Cell G2 also contains the Sparkline form of a Column chart, created using Excel's Sparklines options within the main Insert menu.)

Note some additional points in relation to this function:

- As an array function, the whole range which is to contain the function must be selected (this range must be one cell larger than the bin range, because there could be data points larger than the upper value of the largest bin).
- The choice of the definition of the (width of) the bins will be important; if the width is too wide, the histogram will not be sufficiently detailed, whereas if it is too narrow, the histogram will look fragmented and perhaps multi-moded.
- Since the function calculates the number of data points that lie between the lower and upper bin values, one could instead create the same result using the COUNTIFS function for each bin (with two criteria: one relating to the lower bound of a particular bin and the other to its upper bound, with appropriate adjustments for the first and last bins, which have no lower or upper bound respectively). Histograms can also be created using variations of applications of the PERCENTRANK functions, but often in practice there is little if any benefit in doing so.

Figure 21.10 shows the use of the COUNTIFS function in the same context.

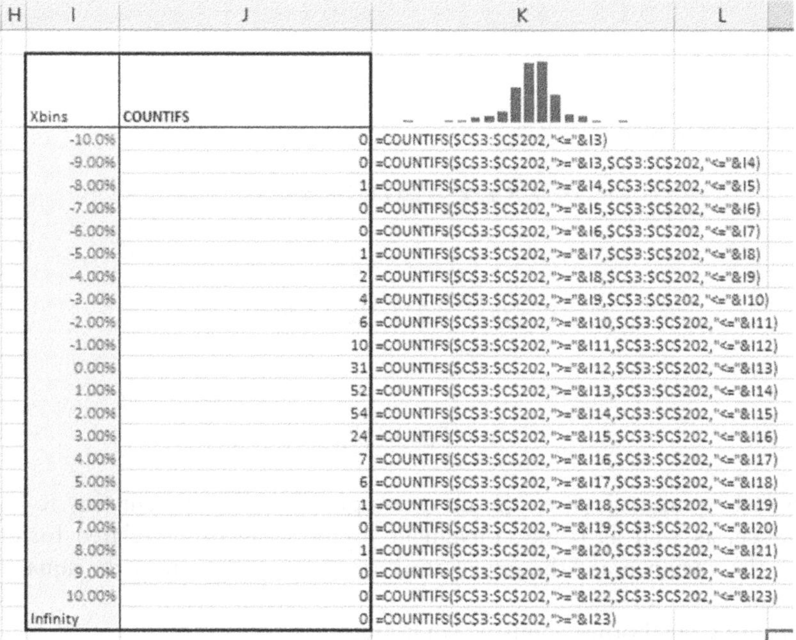

Xbins	COUNTIFS	
-10.0%	0	=COUNTIFS($C$3:$C$202,"<="&I3)
-9.00%	0	=COUNTIFS($C$3:$C$202,">="&I3,$C$3:$C$202,"<="&I4)
-8.00%	1	=COUNTIFS($C$3:$C$202,">="&I4,$C$3:$C$202,"<="&I5)
-7.00%	0	=COUNTIFS($C$3:$C$202,">="&I5,$C$3:$C$202,"<="&I6)
-6.00%	0	=COUNTIFS($C$3:$C$202,">="&I6,$C$3:$C$202,"<="&I7)
-5.00%	1	=COUNTIFS($C$3:$C$202,">="&I7,$C$3:$C$202,"<="&I8)
-4.00%	2	=COUNTIFS($C$3:$C$202,">="&I8,$C$3:$C$202,"<="&I9)
-3.00%	4	=COUNTIFS($C$3:$C$202,">="&I9,$C$3:$C$202,"<="&I10)
-2.00%	6	=COUNTIFS($C$3:$C$202,">="&I10,$C$3:$C$202,"<="&I11)
-1.00%	10	=COUNTIFS($C$3:$C$202,">="&I11,$C$3:$C$202,"<="&I12)
0.00%	31	=COUNTIFS($C$3:$C$202,">="&I12,$C$3:$C$202,"<="&I13)
1.00%	52	=COUNTIFS($C$3:$C$202,">="&I13,$C$3:$C$202,"<="&I14)
2.00%	54	=COUNTIFS($C$3:$C$202,">="&I14,$C$3:$C$202,"<="&I15)
3.00%	24	=COUNTIFS($C$3:$C$202,">="&I15,$C$3:$C$202,"<="&I16)
4.00%	7	=COUNTIFS($C$3:$C$202,">="&I16,$C$3:$C$202,"<="&I17)
5.00%	6	=COUNTIFS($C$3:$C$202,">="&I17,$C$3:$C$202,"<="&I18)
6.00%	1	=COUNTIFS($C$3:$C$202,">="&I18,$C$3:$C$202,"<="&I19)
7.00%	0	=COUNTIFS($C$3:$C$202,">="&I19,$C$3:$C$202,"<="&I20)
8.00%	1	=COUNTIFS($C$3:$C$202,">="&I20,$C$3:$C$202,"<="&I21)
9.00%	0	=COUNTIFS($C$3:$C$202,">="&I21,$C$3:$C$202,"<="&I22)
10.00%	0	=COUNTIFS($C$3:$C$202,">="&I22,$C$3:$C$202,"<="&I23)
Infinity	0	=COUNTIFS($C$3:$C$202,">="&I23)

FIGURE 21.10 Use of COUNTIFS as an Alternative to FREQUENCY

Example: Variance, Standard Deviation and Volatility

The standard deviation (σ) provides a standardised measure of the range or spread. It is a measure of the "average" deviation around the mean. All other things being equal, a distribution that has standard deviation that is larger than that of another is more spread (and has more uncertainty or risk) associated with it.

The standard deviation is calculated as the square root of the variance (V):

$$V(x) = \Sigma p_i (x_i - \mu)^2$$

and

$$\sigma = \sqrt{V} = \sqrt{\Sigma p_i (x_i - \mu)^2}$$

Here

$$\mu = \Sigma p_i x_i = E(x)$$

where the p's are the relative probability (or the frequency of occurrence) of the corresponding x-values; μ denotes the mean or mathematical expectation (Expected Value), also given by E.

One can also write the equation for variance as:

$$V = E((x - \mu)^2)$$

or

$$V = E((x - E(x))^2)$$

which can be expanded as:

$$V = E(x^2 - 2xE(x) + E(x)^2)$$

or

$$V = E(x^2) - 2E(x)E(x) + E(x)^2$$

So

$$\mathrm{V} = E(x^2) - (E(x))^2$$

This last equation is often the most computationally efficient way to calculate the variance, as well as being convenient for deriving other related formulae. It describes the variance as "the expectation of the squares minus the square of the expectation".

There are several other points worth noting:

- The standard deviation measures the square root of the average of the squared distances from the mean, which is not the same as the average deviation of the (non-squared) distances; the squaring procedure involved in calculating standard deviations slightly emphasises values that are further from the mean more than the absolute deviation does. Therefore, in some cases the absolute deviations (as calculated by the AVEDEV function) may be more pertinent as a measure of spread or risk.
- The standard deviation has the same unit as measurement as the underlying data (e.g. dollar or monetary values, time, space etc.), and so is often straightforward to interpret in a physical or intuitive sense; the variance does not have this property (e.g. in a monetary context, its unit would be dollar-squared).
- As well as being a measure of risk, the standard deviation is one of the parameters that define the Normal and Lognormal distributions (the other being the mean). These distributions are very important in financial modelling, especially relating to asset returns, stock prices and so on.
- In many financial market contexts, the standard deviation of an asset's returns (or price changes) is thought of as a core measure of risk, and is often called volatility. Other measures, such as value-at-risk, one-sided risk, semi-deviation and default probabilities are also important, depending on the context.

Generally, one is dealing with only a sample of all possible values (i.e. a subset), so that one may need to consider whether the standard deviation of the sample is representative of the standard deviation of the whole population from which the sample was drawn. In other words, any statistical measure of a sample can be considered as an estimate of that of the underlying population (rather than the true figure); the data in the sample could have been produced by another underlying (population) processes which has slightly different means or standard deviations. Thus, there are two issues that may need consideration:

- The calculation of an unbiased point estimate of the population parameters, when the data is a sample.
- The calculation of the range of possible values (confidence interval) for these parameters (since the calculations based on sample data are only an estimate of the true figure).

In this example, we show the calculations of the estimates of the variance and the standard deviation, and the associated correction factors. The formulae for the confidence intervals around the base estimates require the use of the inverse distributions of the Student (T) distribution (for the mean), and of the Chi-squared distribution (for the standard deviation), and so are covered later in the chapter.

For the calculation of the unbiased estimates:

- The average of a sample is a non-biased estimate of that of the population.
- The standard deviation of a sample is a slight underestimate of that of the population; a multiplicative correction factor of $\sqrt{\frac{n}{n-1}}$ (where n is the number of points in the sample) is required in order to provide a non-biased estimate of the population value. The function STDEV.S (or the legacy STDEV) calculate the estimated population standard deviation from sample data, and have the correction factor built in to the calculations. On the other hand, STDEV.P (or STDEVP) calculate the standard deviation on the assumption that the data is the full population (so that no correction terms are required).
- The same approach is of course required when considering the variance (using VAR.S or VAR.P), except that the correction factor is $\frac{n}{n-1}$, rather than the square root of this.
- Other statistical measures (skewness and kurtosis, see later) also require correction factors to be applied in order to create an unbiased estimate.

The file Ch21.9.VARIANCE.STDDEV.xlsx contains an example of the calculations of the variance and the standard deviation of a data set of 5 years of monthly logarithmic returns for the S&P 500 index (see Figure 21.11).

	A	B	C	D	E	F	G
1							
2		Month	Log Changes				
3			S&P		Item	Value	Formula
4		1	-1.4%		Variance	0.0013	=VAR.S(C4:C63)
5		2	-2.2%		Sqrt of Variance	3.58%	=SQRT(F4)
6		3	1.4%		Standard deviation	3.58%	=STDEV.S(C4:C63)
7		4	1.3%				

FIGURE 21.11 Variance and Standard Deviation of Returns Based on a Sample of Data

	A	B	C	D	E	F	G
1							
2		Month	Log Changes				
3			S&P		Item	Value	Formula
4		1	-1.4%		Variance	0.0013	=VAR.S(C4:C63)
5		2	-2.2%		Sqrt of Variance	3.58%	=SQRT(F4)
6		3	1.4%		Standard deviation	3.58%	=STDEV.S(C4:C63)
7		4	1.3%				
8		5	1.6%		Based on Sample Representing the Whole Population:		
9		6	3.1%		Variance	0.0013	=VAR.P(C4:C63)
10		7	2.4%		Standard deviation	3.55%	=STDEV.P(C4:C63)
11		8	2.1%		Ratios:		
12		9	0.5%		Variance	1.0169	=F4/F9
13		10	0.0%		Standard deviation	1.0084	=F6/F10
14		11	-3.1%		Cross-check		
15		12	1.2%		Sample Size, N	60	=COUNT(C4:C63)
16		13	1.1%		N/(N-1)	1.0169	=F15/(F15-1)
17		14	0.0%		Sqrt(N/(N-1))	1.0084	=SQRT(F16)

FIGURE 21.12 Reconciliation of Sample and Population Statistics

	A	B	C	D	E	F
1						
2						
3		Data		Result	Formula	
4		-1.4%		0.001	=VAR.S(B4:B63)	
5		-2.2%		3.58%	=STDEV.S(B4:B63)	
6		1.4%				
7		1.3%		0.0013	=VAR.P(B4:B63)	
8		1.6%		3.55%	=STDEV.P(B4:B63)	
9		3.1%				
10		2.4%		0.0755	=DEVSQ(B4:B63)	
11		2.1%		60	=COUNT(B4:B63)	
12		0.5%		0.0013	=D10/D11	
13		0.0%		3.55%	=SQRT(D10/D11)	
14		-3.1%				
15		1.2%		2.6%	=AVEDEV(B4:B63)	

FIGURE 21.13 Examples of the DEVSQ and AVEDEV Functions

In Figure 21.12, we show a screen-clip from the same file, showing also the figures that would apply if the sample instead represented the full population, as well as the reconciliation calculations based on the sample size.

The file Ch21.10.DeviationsGeneral.xlsx shows examples of other functions related to deviation, including the DEVSQ function (which totals the square of the deviations from the mean, so is similar to VAR.P after dividing by the total sample size, without the correction factor), as well as the AVEDEV function, which takes the average of the absolute deviations from the mean (see Figure 21.13).

Example: Skewness and Kurtosis

The coefficient of skewness (or simply skewness or skew) is a measure of the non-symmetry (or asymmetry), defined as:

$$\text{Coefficient of Skewness} = \frac{\Sigma p_i (x_i - \mu)^3}{\sigma^3}$$

The numerator represents the average "cube of the distance from the mean", and the denominator is the cube of the standard deviation–, so that skewness is a non-dimensional quantity (i.e. it is a numerical value, and does not have a unit, such as dollars, time or space).

For population data, the SKEW.P function can be used. For sample data, this function would underestimate the skewness of the population; the appropriate multiplicative correction factor to give a non-biased estimate of the population's skewness is $\frac{n^2}{(n-1)(n-2)}$. This factor is built into the SKEW function (no SKEW.S function currently exists), which therefore gives the non-biased estimate based on a sample.

Although there are some general rules of thumb to interpret skew, a precise and general interpretation is difficult because there can be exceptions in some cases. General principles include:

- A symmetric distribution will have a skewness of zero. This is always true, as each value that is larger than the mean will have an exactly offsetting value below the mean; their deviations around the mean will cancel out when raised to any odd power, such as when cubing them.
- A positive skew indicates that the tail is to the right-hand side. Broadly speaking, when the skew is above about 0.3, the non-symmetry of the distribution is visually evident when the data is displayed in a graphical (histogram or similar) format.

Kurtosis is calculated as the average fourth power of the distances from the mean (divided by the fourth power of the standard deviation, resulting in a non-dimensional quantity):

$$\text{Kurtosis} = \frac{\Sigma p_i (x_i - \mu)^4}{\sigma^4}$$

Kurtosis can be difficult to interpret, but in a sense it provides a test of the extent to which a distribution is peaked in the central area, whilst simultaneously having relatively fat tails. A normal distribution has a kurtosis of three; distributions whose kurtosis is equal to, greater or less than three are known as mesokurtic, leptokurtic or platykurtic respectively.

The Excel KURT function deducts three from the standard calculation to show only "excess" kurtosis:

$$\text{Excess Kurtosis} = \frac{\Sigma p_i (x_i - \mu)^4}{\sigma^4} - 3$$

	A	B	C	D	E
1					
2					
3		Data		Result	Formula
4		-1.4%		-0.754	=SKEW.P(B4:B63)
5		-2.2%		-0.773	=SKEW(B4:B63)
6		1.4%			
7		1.3%		1.913	=KURT(B4:B63)
8		1.6%			

FIGURE 21.14 Examples of SKEW.S and KURT Functions

As for the standard deviation and the skewness, corrections are available to estimate population kurtosis from a sample kurtosis in a non-biased way. However, these are not built into Excel at the time of writing.

The file Ch21.11.Moments.xlsx shows examples of several of these functions using the same set of data as the earlier example (5-year logarithmic returns for the S&P 500 index) (see Figure 21.14).

Example: One-sided Volatility (Semi-deviation)

As covered earlier, the STDEV-type function can be used to calculate or estimate standard deviations, and hence volatility. Such a measure is often appropriate as an indication of general risk or variation, and indeed forms the basis of much of the core standard theory and concepts in risk measurement and portfolio optimisation for financial market applications.

On the other hand, the standard deviation represents the effect of deviations around the average, whether these are favourable or unfavourable. In some risk calculations, one may wish to focus only on the unfavourable outcomes (negative or downside risk), and to not include favourable outcomes. An extreme case of such an approach is where the risk measure used is that which is based only on the worst possible outcome. A less extreme possibility is to use the semi-deviation; this is analogous to the standard deviation, except that the only outcomes that are included in the calculation are those which are unfavourable relative to the average.

At the time of writing, there is no Excel function to directly calculate the semi-deviation of a data set. Therefore, there are three main alternative approaches:

- Perform an explicit step-by-step calculation in a tabular range in Excel (i.e. calculate the average of the data set, then sum the squared deviations of each value that is either higher or lower than the average, count how many items are within each category, and finally perform the square root calculation).
- Use an array function to calculate the sum and count of the deviations above or below the average (i.e. without having to calculate the corresponding value for each individually data point explicitly).
- Create a user-defined function which calculates the value directly from the data (with all calculations occurring within the VBA code, and a parameter to indicate

	A	B	C	D	E	F	G	H
1								
2		Data		Mean	0.89%			
3		-1.4%						
4		-2.2%			Deviations below	Deviations above	Formula	
5		1.4%		Sum of squared deviations (array function)	0.0	0.0	{=SUM(IF(B3:B12>$E$2,(B3:B12-$E$2)^2,0))}	
6		1.3%		Count (array function)	4	6	{=SUM(IF(B3:B12>$E$2,1,0))}	
7		1.6%		Ratio	0.0	0.0	=F5/F6	
8		3.1%		**Square root (=Semi-dev)**	**1.98%**	**1.27%**	=SQRT(F7)	
9		2.4%						
10		2.1%						
11		0.5%						
12		0.0%						

FIGURE 21.15 Using an Array Formula to Calculate the Semi-deviation of a Data Set of Returns

whether the positive or negative deviations are to be included in the calculation). As for many other user-defined functions, this approach can help to avoid having to explicitly create tables of calculation formulae in the Excel sheet, allows a direct reference from the data set to the associated statistic and allows for more rapid adaptation of the formulae if the size of the data set changes.

The file Ch21.12.SemiDeviation.xlsx shows an example of both the explicit step-by-step calculation and the use of an array formula. The screen-clip in Figure 21.15 shows the approach using the array formula; the reader can consult the Excel file for the explicit calculation steps (the implementation of the user-defined function is covered in Chapter 33).

Note that the classical definition of semi-deviation is based on the deviation of the points from their mean (average). However, it is simple to generalise this, so that the deviation is measured with respect to any other reference figure (such as a minimum acceptable return), by using this figure within the calculations, in place of the mean.

PRACTICAL APPLICATIONS: CO-RELATIONSHIPS AND DEPENDENCIES

In both data analysis and in modelling, it is important to explore what relationships may exist between variables; an X–Y (or scatter) plot is a good starting point for such analysis, as the visual inspection aids in the development of hypotheses about possible relationships, such as:

- No apparent relationship of any form, with points scattered randomly.
- A general linear relationship but with some (as yet) unexplained (or random) variation around this. Such a relationship could be of a positive nature (an increase in the value of one variable is generally associated with an increase in the value of the other) or of a negative one. Where a relationship appears to be of a fairly linear nature, one may also choose to ask Excel to show a regression line, its equation and associated statistics.
- A more complex type of relationship, such as a U-curve, or one in which there are apparent close links between the variables in part of the range, but a looser relationship in other parts of the range.

Note that, when creating an *X–Y* scatter plot for exploratory purposes, there need not (yet) be any notion of dependent or independent variables (even if typically a variable that is considered more likely to be independent would be chosen to be placed on the *x*-axis).

Example: Scatter Plots (*X–Y* Charts) and Measuring Correlation

The file Ch21.13.Scatter.SLOPE.CORREL.xlsx shows an example of a scatter plot (Figure 21.16); some associated statistics are placed on the chart by right-clicking on any data point on the chart (to invoke the context-sensitive menu in Excel):

- The SLOPE and INTERCEPT functions are to calculate the slope of the regression line (i.e. which should in principle be the same as the values shown by the equation of the chart).
- The product or Pearson method is used to calculate the "linear" correlation, using either (or both) of the CORREL or PEARSON functions. The RSQ function calculates the square of these.
- The STDEV.S function calculates the standard deviation of each data set.
- The slope as implied by using the mathematical relationship between the correlation coefficients and the standard deviation. That is:

$$\text{Slope} = \frac{\rho_{xy}\sigma_y}{\sigma_x}$$

Of course, the slope of a line also describes the amount by which the *y*-value would move if the *x*-value changes by one unit. Therefore, the above equation shows that if the *x*-value is changed by σ_x then the *y*-value would change by an amount equal to $\rho_{xy}\sigma_y$.

Month	Log Changes S&P	Kennametal
1	-1.4%	-0.9%
2	-2.2%	-1.1%
3	1.4%	4.9%
4	1.3%	-3.7%
5	1.6%	-1.0%
6	3.1%	8.6%
7	2.4%	7.2%
8	2.1%	-1.0%
9	0.5%	-15.6%
10	0.0%	4.0%
11	-3.1%	-3.4%
12	1.2%	1.2%
13	1.1%	4.4%
14	0.0%	0.0%
15	2.5%	13.6%
16	-0.1%	-7.1%
17	3.5%	7.0%
18	-1.8%	4.1%
19	0.7%	5.0%
20	-1.1%	-1.9%
21	3.5%	3.6%
22	0.0%	4.1%
23	3.0%	-2.9%
24	-2.0%	-4.7%
25	-1.9%	-3.3%

Item	Calculation	Formula
Slope	0.9503	=SLOPE(D4:D63,C4:C63)
Intercept	0.0037	=INTERCEPT(D4:D63,C4:C63)
CORREL (between S&P, Kennametal ret	0.545	=CORREL(C4:C63,D4:D63)
PEARSON	0.545	=PEARSON(C$4:C$63,D$4:D$63)
R-Squared	0.297	=RSQ(C$4:C$63,D$4:D$63)
Square of CORREL or PEARSON	0.297	=G7^2
STDEV (for S&P monthly returns)	3.58%	=STDEV.S(C4:C63)
STDEV (for Kennametal monthly returns	6.23%	=STDEV.S(D4:D63)
Implied Slope	0.9503	=G7*G13/G12

FIGURE 21.16 Using Scatter Plots and the Relationship Between Slope and Correlation

Example: More on Correlation Coefficients and Rank Correlation

The above example showed the use of the CORREL and PEARSON functions to calculate the (linear, product or PEARSON) correlation between variables. In mathematical terms, this (ρ) is defined as:

$$\rho = \frac{\Sigma(x-\mu_x)(y-\mu_y)}{\sqrt{\Sigma(x-\mu_x)^2\,\Sigma(y-\mu_y)^2}}$$

where x and y represent the individual values of the respective data set, and μ_x represents the average (mean or expected value) of the data set X (and similarly μ_y for the Y data set).

From the formula, we can see that:

- The correlation between any two data sets can be calculated if each set has the same number of points.
- The coefficient is a non-dimensional quantity that lies between –1 and 1 (and is usually expressed as a percentage between –100% and 100%).
- Correlation captures the simultaneous movement of each variable relative to its own mean, i.e. it measures the co-relationship between two processes in the sense of whether, when observed simultaneously, they each tend to take values that are both above or both below their own means, or whether there is no relationship between the occurrence of such relative values: by considering the numerator in the above formula, it is clear that a single value, x, and its counterpart, y, will contribute positively to the correlation calculation when the two values are either both above or both below their respective means (so that the numerator is positive, being either the product of two positive or of two negative figures).
- The correlation coefficient would be unchanged if a constant were added to each item in one of the data sets, since the effect of such a constant would be removed during the calculations (as the mean of each data set is subtracted from each value).
- The correlation coefficient would be unchanged if each item in a data set were multiplied by a constant (since the effect of doing so would be equal in the numerator and the denominator).

From a modelling perspective, the existence of a (statistically significant) correlation coefficient does not imply any direct dependency between the items (in the sense of a directionality or causality of one to the other). Rather, the variation in each item may be driven by a factor that is not explicit or known, but which causes each item to vary, so that they appear to vary together. For example, a correlation would be shown between the change in the market value of two oil-derived end products; the cost of producing each would partly be determined by the oil price, but there will also be some other independent cost components, as well as other factors (beyond cost items) that affect the market price of each.

Further, a measured coefficient is generally subject to high statistical error, and so may be statistically insignificant or volatile; quite large data sets are required to reduce such error.

Although the correlation measurement used above (i.e. the linear, product or Pearson method, using CORREL or PEARSON) is the most common for general purposes, there are several other ways to define possible measures of correlation:

- The rank or Spearman method (sometimes called "non-linear" correlation), which involves replacing each value by an integer representing its position (or rank) within its own data set (i.e. when listed in ascending or descending order), and calculating the linear correlation of this set of integers. Note that this measure of correlation represents a less stringent relationship between the variables. For example, two variables whose scatter plot shows a generally increasing trend that is not a perfect straight line can have a rank correlation which is 100%. (This looser definition allows for additional flexibility in applications such as the creation and sampling of correlated multivariate distributions when using simulation techniques.) At the time of writing there is no direct Excel function to calculate a rank (Spearman) correlation; this can be done either using explicit individual steps, or an array formula or a VBA user-defined function.
- The Kendall tau coefficient. This uses the ranks of the data points, and is calculated by deriving the number of pair ranks that are concordant. That is, two points (each with an x–y co-ordinate) are considered concordant if the difference in rank of their x-values is of the same sign as the difference in rank of their y-values. Note that the calculation requires one to compare the rank of each point with that of every other point. The number of operations is therefore proportional to the square of the number of points. By contrast, for the Pearson and the rank correlation methods, the number of operations scales linearly with the number of data points, since only the deviation of each point from the mean of its own data set requires calculation.

The file Ch21.14.RankCorrel&ArrayFormula.xlsx shows an example of the calculation of the rank correlation between two data sets. Figure 21.17 shows the explicit calculation in Excel, which first involves calculation ranks of the values (Columns F and G shows the ranks, calculated from the raw data in Columns B and C), before the CORREL function is applied (cell G14). Further, the array formula in Cell C16 shows how the same calculation can be created directly from the raw data without explicitly calculating the ranked values:

$$\begin{aligned} C16 = \{&\text{CORREL(RANK.AVG(B3 : B12, B\$3 : B\$12, 1), RANK.AVG} \\ &\text{(C3 : C12, C\$3 : C\$12, 1))}\} \end{aligned}$$

	A	B	C	D	E	F	G	H
1						Explicit Calculation Steps		
2		X	Y			R(X)	R(Y)	
3		0.059	0.084			1	3	=RANK.AVG(C3,C$3:C$12,1)
4		0.339	0.061			7	1	=RANK.AVG(C4,C$3:C$12,1)
5		0.165	0.072			3	2	=RANK.AVG(C5,C$3:C$12,1)
6		0.226	0.206			4	6	=RANK.AVG(C6,C$3:C$12,1)
7		0.266	0.095			5	4	=RANK.AVG(C7,C$3:C$12,1)
8		0.095	0.153			2	5	=RANK.AVG(C8,C$3:C$12,1)
9		0.530	0.384			10	10	=RANK.AVG(C9,C$3:C$12,1)
10		0.445	0.281			8	7	=RANK.AVG(C10,C$3:C$12,1)
11		0.500	0.336			9	8	=RANK.AVG(C11,C$3:C$12,1)
12		0.318	0.336			6	9	=RANK.AVG(C12,C$3:C$12,1)
13								
14		Correl of Data	74%	=CORREL(B3:B12,C3:C12)			60%	
15								
16		Correl of Ranked Data	60%	{=CORREL(RANK.AVG(B3:B12,B$3:B$12,1),RANK.AVG(C3:C12,C$3:C$12,1))}				
17								

FIGURE 21.17 Calculation of Ranked Correlation Using Explicit Steps and an Array Formula

Example: Measuring Co-variances

The co-variance between two data sets is closely related to the correlation between them:

$$Covar(X, Y) = \Sigma(x - \mu_x)(y - \mu_y).$$

Or

$$Covar(X, Y) = \rho\sigma_x\sigma_y$$

It is clear from these formulae (and from those relating to the standard deviations) that:

- A scaling (or weighting) of all of the points in one of the data sets will result in a new data set whose covariance scales in the same way:

$$Covar(wX, Y) = \rho w\sigma_x\sigma_y$$

- The co-variance of a process with itself is simply the same as the variance (since the correlation is 100%):

$$Covar(X, X) = \sigma_x\sigma_x = V(x)$$

The function COVARIANCE.S (COVAR in earlier versions) calculates the sample covariance (i.e. an estimate of the population covariance, assuming that the data provided is only a sample of the population), and COVARIANCE.P calculates the population covariance of two data sets which represent the full population.

The file Ch21.15.CORREL.COVAR.xlsx shows examples of these functions and the reconciliation between the direct use of the COVARIANCE.S function and the indirect calculation of covariance from the correlation coefficient and the standard deviations (see Figure 21.18).

Example: Covariance Matrices, Portfolio Volatility and Volatility Time Scaling

Where there are data on more than two variables, a full correlation matrix may be calculated. Each element of this is simply the correlation between the variables that correspond to the row and column of the matrix (i.e. Row 1 of the matrix relates to the

	A	B	C	D	E	F	G	H
1								
2		Month	Log Changes					
3			S&P	Kennametal		Item	Calculation	Formula
4		1	-1.4%	-0.9%		Covariance (formula)	0.00122	=COVARIANCE.S(C$4:C$63,D$4:D$63)
5		2	-2.2%	-1.1%		Covariance (formula)	0.00120	=COVARIANCE.P(C$4:C$63,D$4:D$63)
6		3	1.4%	4.9%				
7		4	1.3%	-3.7%		CORREL (between S&P, Kennametal ret	0.545	=CORREL(C4:C63,D4:D63)
8		5	1.6%	-1.0%		STDEV (for S&P monthly returns)	3.58%	=STDEV.S(C4:C63)
9		6	3.1%	8.6%		STDEV (for Kennametal monthly returns	6.23%	=STDEV.S(D4:D63)
10		7	2.4%	7.2%		Covariance (implied)	0.00122	=G7*G8*G9
11		8	2.1%	-1.0%				
12		9	0.5%	-15.6%				

FIGURE 21.18 Calculation of the Covariance Between Two Data Sets Using Various Functions

first variable, as does Column 1 etc.) It is clear (and directly visible from the formula that defines the correlation coefficient) that:

- The diagonal elements of a correlation matrix are equal to one (or 100%), since each item is perfectly correlated with itself.
- The matrix is symmetric: the *X* and *Y* data sets have the same role and can be interchanged with each other without changing the calculated coefficient.

Similarly, one could create a covariance matrix, in which every element is equivalent to the corresponding correlation multiplied by the associated standard deviations of the variables.

A particularly important application of correlation and covariance matrices is in portfolio analysis. In particular, a portfolio made up of two assets of equal volatility will be less volatile than a "portfolio" of the same total value that consists of only one of the assets (unless the assets are perfectly correlated). This is simply because outcomes will arise in which one asset takes a higher value whilst the other takes a lower value (or vice versa), thus creating a centring (diversification) effect when the values are added together. The lower the correlation between the assets, the stronger is this effect.

Note that if a variable, *X*, is the sum of other (fundamental or underlying) processes (or assets):

$$X = Y_1 + \ldots + Y_n$$

then

$$V(X) = \sum_{i=1}^{n}\sum_{j=1}^{n} Cov(Y_i, Y_j)$$

where *Cov* represents (the definition of) the covariance between the *Y*'s. That is, the variance of the portfolio is the sum of all of the covariances between the processes.

Therefore, where a portfolio is composed from a weighted set of underlying processes (or assets):

$$X = w_1 Y_1 + \ldots + w_n Y_n$$

then

$$V(x) = \sum_{i=1}^{n}\sum_{j=1}^{n} Cov(w_i Y_i, w_j Y_j)$$

so

$$V(x) = \sum_{i=1}^{n}\sum_{j=1}^{n} w_i w_j Cov(Y_i, Y_j)$$

In practical terms, when calculating the variance (or standard deviation) of the returns of a portfolio, one may be provided with data on the returns of the underlying

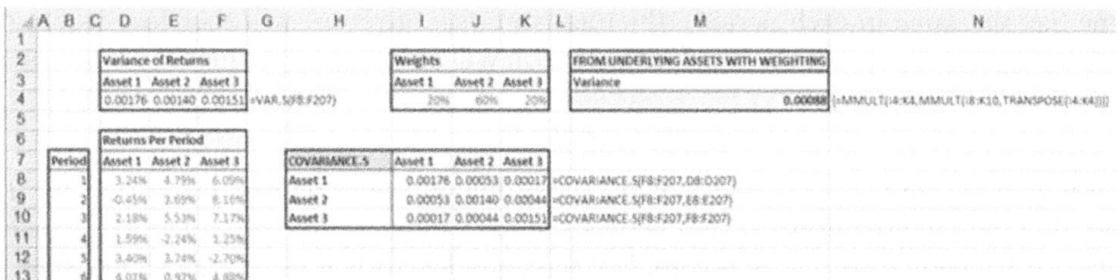

FIGURE 21.19 Portfolio Volatility Calculation Based on Data for Underlying Assets

components, not the weighted ones. For example, when holding a portfolio of several individual stocks in different proportions (e.g. a mixture of Vodafone, Apple, Amazon, Exxon, . . .), the returns data provided directly by data feeds will relate to the individual stocks. Therefore, depending on the circumstances, it may be convenient to use one or other of the above formulae.

The file Ch21.16.COVAR.PORTFOLIO.xlsx contains an example of each approach. A data set of the returns for three underlying assets is contained in Columns D:F. Figure 21.19 shows the calculations in which the returns data is taken from the underlying assets, and using portfolio weights explicitly in the (array) formula for the variance (cell M4):

$$\text{M4} = \text{MMULT(I4 : K4, MMULT(I8 : K10, TRANSPOSE(I4 : K4)))}$$

On the other hand, Figure 21.20 shows the calculation in which returns for the weighted assets (i.e. actual portfolio composition) are calculated, so that the variance (cell U4) is simply the sum of the elements of the corresponding covariance matrix:

$$\text{U4} = \text{SUM(V8 : X10)}$$

Note that, where the co-variance between the processes is zero (as would be the case for independent processes in theory for large data sets), then the variance of their sum is equal to the sum of the variances (i.e. to the sum of the co-variance of each process with itself). Thus, in the special case of a time series in which returns in each period are independent of those in other periods, the variance of the total return will be the sum of the variances of the returns in the individual periods. If these variances are constant over

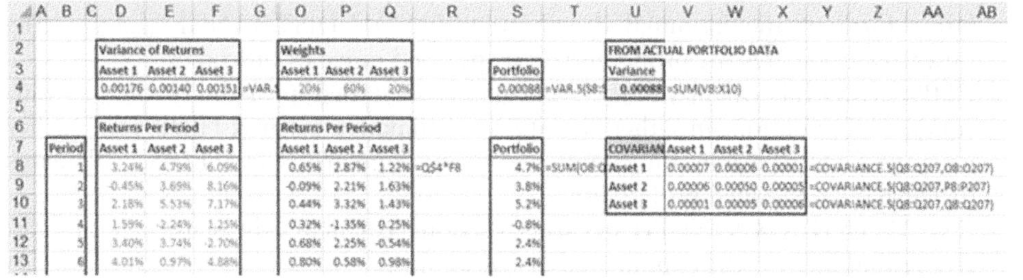

FIGURE 21.20 Portfolio Volatility Calculation Based on Data for Weighted Assets

time (i.e. the same in each period), the total variance of return will therefore increase linearly with time, so that the standard deviation will scale with the square root of time:

$$\sigma_T = \sigma\sqrt{T}$$

where σ is the standard deviation of the individual periodic return and σ_T that for T periods. One can use this to convert between annual, monthly or daily volatilities. (Such simple conversion methods do not apply if the semi-deviation is used as a risk measure.)

PRACTICAL APPLICATIONS: PROBABILITY DISTRIBUTIONS

The use of frequency (probability) distributions is essentially a way of summarising the full set of possible values for an uncertain (random or risky) process by showing the relative likelihood (or weighting) of each value. It is important to correctly distinguish the values of a process (x-axis) and the likelihood (or cumulative likelihood) associated with each value (y-axis). Thus, there are two distinct function types:

- "X-to-P" processes, in which, from a given input value, one determines the probability that a value less (or more) than this would occur (or the relative probability that the precise value would occur). Functions such as NORM.DIST (NORMDIST prior to Excel 2010) are of this form.
- "P-to-X" processes, in which the probability is an input, and one wishes to find the corresponding (percentile) value associated with that percentage. This is the same as inverting the frequency distribution. In Excel, functions such as NORM.INV (or NORMINV) are of this form. The main application areas are random sampling, hypothesis testing and the calculation confidence intervals. (The PERCENTILE-type functions are analogous, but are applied to data sets of individual or sample points, not to distribution functions.)

In this section, we provide some examples of the use of some of these distributions (a detailed presentation is beyond the scope of this text; the author's *Business Risk and Simulation Modelling in Practice* provides a detailed analysis of approximately 20 key distributions that are either directly available, or can be readily created, in Excel).

Excel's X-to-P (or standard definition) distribution functions include:

- BETA.DIST calculates the beta distribution in density or cumulative form (BETADIST in earlier versions provided only the cumulative form).
- BINOM.DIST (BINOMDIST in earlier versions) calculates the density or cumulative form of the binomial distribution; BINOM.DIST.RANGE (Excel 2013 onwards) calculates the probability of a specified range of outcomes.
- CHISQ.DIST.RT calculates the right-hand one-tailed probability of the Chi-squared distribution, in either density or cumulative form (CHIDIST in earlier versions calculated only the cumulative form). Similarly, CHISQ.DIST calculates its left-hand one-tailed probability.
- EXPON.DIST (EXPONDIST in earlier versions) calculates the density or cumulative probability for the exponential distribution.
- F.DIST.RT calculates the right-hand tail form of the F distribution in density or cumulative form (FDIST in earlier versions calculated only the cumulative form). Similarly, F.DIST calculates the left tailed form.

- GAMMA.DIST (GAMMADIST in earlier versions) calculates the gamma distribution in either cumulative or density form.
- HYPGEOM.DIST calculates the probabilities for the hypergeometric distribution in either density or cumulative form (HYPGEOMDIST in earlier versions calculated only the cumulative probability associated with a value).
- LOGNORM.DIST calculates the density or cumulative probability for Lognormal distribution based on a logarithmic parameterisation (LOGNORMDIST in earlier versions calculated only the cumulative probability).
- NEGBINOM.DIST calculates the probabilities for a negative binomial distribution in density or cumulative form (NEGBINOMDIST in earlier versions calculates only the cumulative probability).
- NORM.DIST and NORM.S.DIST (NORMDIST and NORMSDIST in earlier versions) calculate the general and the standard normal cumulative distribution respectively. PHI (Excel 2013 onwards) calculates the value of the density for a standard normal distribution GAUSS (Excel 2013 onwards) calculates 0.5 less than the standard normal cumulative distribution.
- POISSON.DIST (POISSON in earlier versions) calculates the density or cumulative form of the Poisson distribution.
- PROB uses a discrete set of values and associated probabilities to calculate the probability that a given value lies between a specified lower and upper limit (i.e. within the range specified by these bounds).
- T.DIST.2T (TDIST in earlier versions) calculates the two-tailed probability for the Student (T) distribution. Similarly, T.DIST.RT calculates the right-hand tail probability, and T.DIST calculates the left-hand probability.
- WEIBULL.DIST (WEIBULL in earlier versions) calculates the density and cumulative forms of the probability of a value associated with a Weibull distribution.

Excel's P-to-X (inverse or percentile) distribution functions that are directly available are:

- BINOM.INV (prior to Excel 2007, there is no equivalent function, i.e. "BINOMINV" did not exist but a similar function CRITBINOM was available).
- NORM.INV (or NORMINV) for general Normal distributions and NORM.S.INV or NORMSINV for the standard Normal distribution (with mean of 0 and standard deviation of 1).
- LOGNORM.INV (or LOGINV) calculates the inverse of the Lognormal cumulative distribution (based on logarithmic parameters, not the natural parameters).
- BETA.INV (or BETAINV) for the Beta distribution.
- GAMMA.INV (or GAMMAINV) for the Gamma distribution.
- T.INV.2T (TINV in earlier versions) calculates the inverse of the two-tailed T (Student) distribution. T.INV returns the left-tailed (note the syntax modification between versions).
- CHISQ.INV.RT (CHIINV in earlier versions) calculates the inverse of the right-tail for the Chi-squared distribution. CHISQ.INV calculates the inverse of the left-tail (once again, note the syntax modification).
- F.INV.RT (FINV in earlier versions) calculates the inverse of the right-tail of the F-distribution. F.INV returns the inverse of the left-tailed distribution (note the syntax modification).

Example: Likelihood of a Given Number of Successes of an Oil Exploration Process

A Bernoulli process (or distribution) is one in which there are only two possible outcomes of a trial that is conducted once (often characterised as either success/failure, or heads/tails, or 0/1). A binomial process is a generalisation, in which there may be multiple trials, each of which is independent to others, and each of which has the same probability of occurrence. Examples of binomial processes include multiple tosses of a coin, the conducting of a sequence of oil drilling activities in separate geological areas (where each drill may succeed or fail), and so on.

In such contexts, one may ask questions such as:

- What is the likelihood that there will be exactly three successes?
- What is the likelihood that there will be zero, one, two or three successes (i.e. three or less)?
- What is the likelihood that the number of successes would be between 2 and 5?

The file Ch21.17.BINOMDISTRANGE.xlsx contains examples of the BINOM.DIST and the BINOM.DIST.RANGE functions to answer such questions (see a separate worksheet for each function in the file), with screen-clips of each shown in Figure 21.21 and Figure 21.22. Note that the BINOM.DIST.RANGE function is more general, as it can produce both the density form equivalent (by setting the two number arguments to be equal) or the cumulative form (by setting the lower number argument to zero) or a range form (by appropriately choosing the lower and upper number arguments). Note also that the order of the required parameters is not the same for the two functions.

	A	B	C	D
1				
2			Binom.Dist Density	Binom.Dist Cumulative
3		Number_s (number of successes)	3	3
4		Trials (number of trials)	10	10
5		Probability_s (probability of success)	30%	30%
6		Cumulative	0	1
7		Result	26.7%	65.0%
8		Formulae in row 7	=BINOM.DIST(C3,C4,C5,C6)	=BINOM.DIST(D3,D4,D5,D6)

FIGURE 21.21 Use of the BINOM.DIST Function in Density and Cumulative Form

	A	B	C	D	E
1					
2			Binom.Dist.Range Single Point	Binom.Dist.Range Range from Lower	Binom.Dist.Range with Range
3		Trials (number of trials)	10	10	10
4		Probability_s (probability of success)	30%	30%	30%
5		Number_s (number of successes)	3	0	2
6		Number_s2 (upper number of successes)	3	3	5
7		Result	26.7%	65.0%	80.3%
8		Formulae in row 7	=BINOM.DIST.RANGE(C3,C4,C5,C6)	=BINOM.DIST.RANGE(D3,D4,D5,D6)	=BINOM.DIST.RANGE(E3,E4,E5,E6)

FIGURE 21.22 Use of the BINOM.DIST.RANGE Function in Density, Cumulative and Range Form

Example: Frequency of Outcomes Within One or Two Standard Deviations

The function NORM.S.DIST can be used to calculate both the density and cumulative form of the standard normal distribution (with mean equal to zero and standard deviation equal to one), by appropriately using the optional parameter (argument).

The file Ch21.18.NormalRanges.xlsx shows the use of the function to calculate the density curve and the cumulative probabilities for a range of values. By subtracting the cumulative probability of the point that is one standard deviation larger than the mean from the cumulative probability of the point that is one standard deviation below the mean, one can see (Cell E19) that approximately 68.27% of outcomes for a normal distribution are within the range that is one standard deviation on either side of the mean. Similarly, approximately 95.45% of outcomes are within a range that is either side of the mean by two standard deviations (Cell E23) (see Figure 21.23).

Example: Creating Random Samples from Probability Distributions

The P-to-X or inverse (percentile) functions can be used to create random samples from any distribution for which the inverse function is available. Essentially, one uses random samples drawn from a standard uniform random process (i.e. a continuous range between zero and one) to define percentages, which are then used to calculate the corresponding percentile values. Because the percentages are chosen uniformly, the resulting percentile values will occur with the correct frequency.

The file Ch21.19.NORMSINV.Sample.xlsx shows an example in which Excel's RAND() function is used to generate a random percentage probability, and the

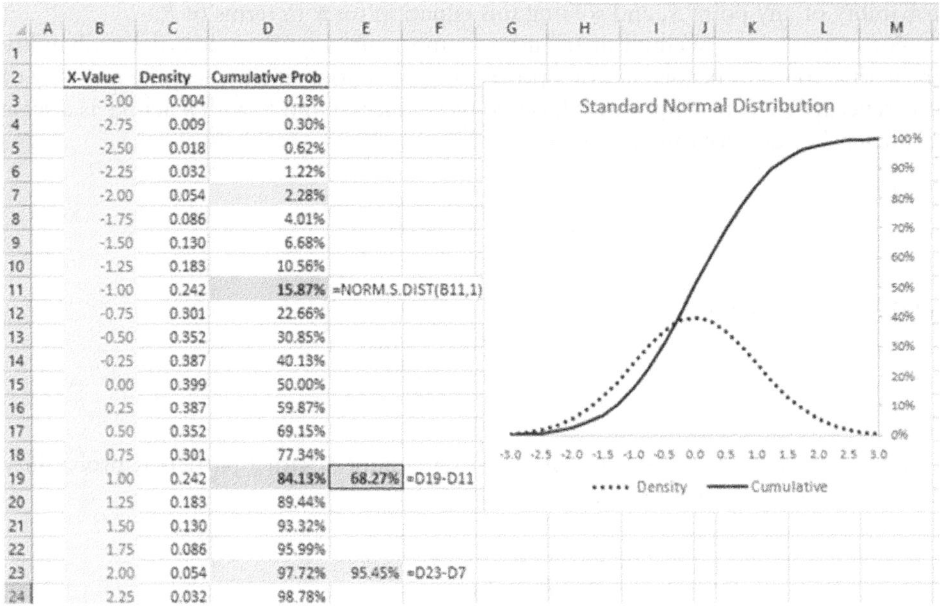

	X-Value	Density	Cumulative Prob		
3	-3.00	0.004	0.13%		
4	-2.75	0.009	0.30%		
5	-2.50	0.018	0.62%		
6	-2.25	0.032	1.22%		
7	-2.00	0.054	2.28%		
8	-1.75	0.086	4.01%		
9	-1.50	0.130	6.68%		
10	-1.25	0.183	10.56%		
11	-1.00	0.242	15.87%	=NORM.S.DIST(B11,1)	
12	-0.75	0.301	22.66%		
13	-0.50	0.352	30.85%		
14	-0.25	0.387	40.13%		
15	0.00	0.399	50.00%		
16	0.25	0.387	59.87%		
17	0.50	0.352	69.15%		
18	0.75	0.301	77.34%		
19	1.00	0.242	84.13%	68.27%	=D19-D11
20	1.25	0.183	89.44%		
21	1.50	0.130	93.32%		
22	1.75	0.086	95.99%		
23	2.00	0.054	97.72%	95.45%	=D23-D7
24	2.25	0.032	98.78%		

FIGURE 21.23 The Normal Distribution and the Frequency of Outcomes in Ranges Around the Mean

Item	Result	Formulae
Random Percentage	85.6%	=RAND()
Random Sample	1.06	=NORM.S.INV(C3)

FIGURE 21.24 Generating of Random Samples from a Standard Normal Distribution

NORM.S.INV function is used to find the value of a standard normal distribution corresponding to that cumulative probability (see Figure 21.24).

The standard normal distribution has a mean of zero and standard deviation of one; the generation of samples from other normal distributions can be achieved either by multiplying the sample from a standard normal distribution by the desired standard deviation and adding the mean, or by applying the same inversion process to the function NORM.INV (which uses the mean and standard deviation as its parameters).

Example: User-defined Inverse Functions for Random Sampling

The inverse functions provided in Excel (such as NORM.S.INV) are generally those for which the inverse process cannot be written as a simple analytic formula. For many distributions, the inversion process can in fact be performed analytically (which is perhaps one reason why Excel does not provide them as separate functions): to do so involves equating the value of P to the mathematical expression that defines the cumulative probability of any point x, and solving this equation for x in terms of P.

For example, the Weibull distribution is most often used to describe probability for the time to (first) occurrence of a process in continuous time, where the intensity of occurrence may not be constant. It has two parameters α and β, with β acting as a scale parameter. The density function is (for $x \geq 0$):

$$f(x) = \frac{\alpha x^{\alpha-1}}{\beta^{\alpha}} e^{-\left(\frac{x}{\beta}\right)^{\alpha}}$$

and the cumulative function is:

$$F(x) = 1 - e^{-\left(\frac{x}{\beta}\right)^{\alpha}}$$

By replacing the left-hand side of this latter equation with a particular probability value, P, and solving for x, we have:

$$x = \beta.\left(\mathrm{LN}\left(\frac{1}{1-P}\right)\right)^{1/\alpha}$$

so that the right-hand side is the inverse (P-to-X, or percentile) function.

	A	B	C	D
1				
2		Item	Result	Formulae
3		Random Percentage	19.9%	=RAND()
4				
5		Alpha	2	
6		Beta	2	
7		Random Sample	0.94	=C6*(LN(1/(1-C3))^(1/C5))

FIGURE 21.25 Generation of Random Samples from a Weibull Distribution

	A	B	C	D
1				
2				
3			CRITBINOM (legacy)	BINOM.INV
4		Trials (number of trials)	10	10
5		Probability_s (probability of success)	30%	30%
6		Alpha	65.0%	65.0%
7		Result	3	3
8		Formula in row 7	=CRITBINOM(C4,C5,C6)	=BINOM.INV(D4,D5,D6)

FIGURE 21.26 Inverse Function for a Binomial Process

The file Ch21.20.Weibull.Sample.xlsx shows an example of creating a random sample of a Weibull distribution (see Figure 21.25). (Within the file, one can also see a graphical representation of the cumulative Weibull distribution, formed by evaluating the formula for each of several (fixed) percentages.)

Example: Values Associated with Probabilities for a Binomial Process

A similar inversion process applies to discrete distributions (such as binomial) as it does to continuous ones, although in some cases an iterative search process must be used in order to find the appropriate value associated with a cumulated probability.

The file Ch21.21.BinomialInverseDists.xlsx shows an example of the BINOM.INV function, as well as the legacy CRITBINOM function to determine the number of outcomes associated with a cumulated probability. Figure 21.26 shows a screen-clip, from which one can see that, with a probability of (approximately) 65%, the number of successes would be three or less.

Example: Confidence Intervals for the Mean Using Student (T) and Normal Distributions

In an earlier section, we noted that the statistics calculated from a data set (such as its average and standard deviation) provide an estimate of the true (but unknown) figures of the distribution that generated the data (in other words, the distribution of the whole population). However, a distribution with a different average could also have generated the same data set, although this becomes less likely if the average of this second distribution differs significantly from the average of the data set. We also noted that the average (or mean) of a sample provides a non-biased estimate of the true mean (i.e. is an unbiased estimate, albeit nevertheless subject to uncertainty), whereas the standard deviation of a sample needs to have a correction factor applied in order to provide a non-biased (but also uncertain) estimate of the true population standard deviation.

In fact, the range of possible values (or confidence interval) of the population mean is given by:

$$\mu_s \pm t\frac{\sigma_s}{\sqrt{n}}$$

where t is the value of the T-distribution corresponding to a desired confidence percentage (in other words, after selecting the percentage, one needs to find the corresponding value of the inverse distribution) and σ_s is the unbiased (corrected) standard deviation as measured from the sample. In other words, whilst one can be (100%) sure that the true mean is between $-\infty$ and ∞, such information is not very useful for practical purposes. Rather, in order to be able to meaningfully determine a feasible range, one needs to specify a confidence level: for 95% confidence, one would determine the half-width of the corresponding T-distribution so that 95% of the area is either side of the sample mean (or 2.5% in each tail). The standard T-distribution is a symmetric distribution centred at zero, which has a single parameter, ν, known as the number of degrees of freedom (which in this case is equal to the sample size less 1). Its standard deviation is $\sqrt{\frac{\nu}{\nu-2}}$, and hence is larger than 1, but very close to 1 when ν is large (in which case the T-distribution very closely resembles a standard normal distribution; for large sample sizes, the Normal distribution is often used in place of the T-distribution).

Note that, when using Excel functions for the T-distribution, one should take care as to which version is being used: whereas T.INV returns the t-value associated with the cumulated probability (i.e. only on the left tail of the distribution), the legacy function TINV returns the value associated with the probability accumulating on both the left- and right-hand tails, as well as having a sign reversal. Thus, TINV(10%) would provide the t-value for the case where 5% of outcomes are excluded on each side of the tail, whereas this would correspond to T.INV(5%), in addition to the change of sign. In fact, the legacy TINV function corresponds to the more recent T.INV.2T function. Thus, a confidence level of (say) 95% means that 5% is excluded in total, or 2.5% from each tail. Therefore, one may use either T.INV after dividing the exclusion probability by 2, or use T.INV.2T directly applied to the exclusion probability, as well as ensuring that the signs are appropriately dealt with.

The file Ch21.22.TINV.Dists.xlsx shows examples of these, calculated at various probability values (see Figure 21.27).

The file Ch21.23.ConfInterval.Mean.xlsx contains an example of these functions in determining the confidence interval for the mean of a sample of data. Note that

Degrees of freedom
999

Cumulated Probabilty	T.INV(p)	TINV(p)	T.INT.2T
5%	-1.646	1.962	1.962
10%	-1.282	1.646	1.646
15%	-1.037	1.441	1.441
20%	-0.842	1.282	1.282
25%	-0.675	1.151	1.151
30%	-0.525	1.037	1.037
35%	-0.385	0.935	0.935
40%	-0.253	0.842	0.842
45%	-0.126	0.756	0.756
50%	0.000	0.675	0.675
55%	0.126	0.598	0.598
60%	0.253	0.525	0.525
65%	0.385	0.454	0.454
70%	0.525	0.385	0.385
75%	0.675	0.319	0.319
80%	0.842	0.253	0.253
85%	1.037	0.189	0.189
90%	1.282	0.126	0.126
95%	1.646	0.063	0.063

FIGURE 21.27 Various Forms of the Inverse Student Distribution Function in Excel

the actual data sample is not needed: the only information required is the summary statistics concerning the mean and standard deviation of the sample, the total number of data points (sample size) and the desired confidence level; from this, the required percentiles are calculated using the inverse function(s), and these (non-dimensional) figures are then scaled appropriately (see Figure 21.28).

Example: the CONFIDENCE.T and CONFIDENCE.NORM Functions

Concerning the confidence interval for the mean, Excel has two functions which allow for a more direct calculation than the one shown in the prior example; these are CONFIDENCE.T and CONFIDENCE.NORM, depending on whether one wishes to base the analysis on a T-distribution or on a normal distribution (which are very similar except for very small sample sizes, as mentioned above).

The file Ch21.24.CONFIDENCE.Mean.xlsx shows an example of these (see Figure 21.29).

	A	B	C	D
1				
2		**Sample Data**		
3		Mean of Sample	30.0	
4		StdDev of Sample	5.0	
5		Number of Data Points	1000	
6		Standard error of mean	0.16	=C$4/SQRT(C$5)
7		Degrees of Freedom	999	=C5-1
8				
9		Mean		
10				
11		Confidence Level	95.0%	
12		Exclusion probability	5.0%	=1-C11
13		t-value using "T.INV.2T"	1.96	=T.INV.2T(C12,C7)
14		Probability outside either tail	2.5%	=(1-C11)/2
15		t-value using "-T.INV"	1.96	=-T.INV(C$14,C$7)
16				
17		Lower Band Around Sample Statistic	-0.31	=-C$13*C$6
18		Upper Band Around Sample Statistic	0.31	=+C$13*C$6
19		**Lower estimate**	**29.69**	=C$3+C17
20		**Upper estimate**	**30.31**	=C$3+C18

FIGURE 21.28 Confidence Interval for the Mean Based on Sample Data

	A	B	C	D
1				
2		**Sample Data**		
3		Mean of Sample	30.0	
4		StdDev of Sample	5.0	
5		Number of Data Points	1000	
6		Standard error of mean	0.16	=C$4/SQRT(C$5)
7		Degrees of Freedom	999	=C5-1
8				
9		Mean		
10				
11		Confidence Level	95.0%	
12				
13		Width of interval using CONFIDENCE.T	0.3103	=CONFIDENCE.T(1-C11,C4,C5)
14		**Lower estimate**	**29.69**	=C$3-C13
15		**Upper estimate**	**30.31**	=C$3+C13
16				
17				
18		Width of interval using CONFIDENCE.NORM	0.3099	=CONFIDENCE.NORM(1-C11,C4,C5)

FIGURE 21.29 Confidence Interval for the Mean Using CONFIDENCE Functions

Example: Confidence Intervals for the Standard Deviation Using Chi-squared

The confidence interval for the standard deviation can be calculated by inverting the Chi-squared distribution (rather than the T-distribution, as was the case for the mean). In this case, the Chi-squared distribution has the same parameter and degrees of freedom (ν) as the T-distribution in the earlier example. However, it is a positively skewed distribution that becomes more symmetric (i.e. less skewed) as ν increases; thus, the confidence interval for the standard deviation is also positively skewed, unlike that for the mean (which is symmetric).

The file Ch21.25.ConfInterval.StdDev.xlsx contains an example (see Figure 21.30). The example uses separate distributions for the left- and right-tail probabilities, i.e. CHISQ.INV and CHISQ.INV.RT, although the legacy left-tail CHIINV function could also have been used.

Example: Confidence Interval for the Slope of Regression Line (or Beta)

Earlier in this chapter, we noted that the slope of a linear regression line is related to the standard deviations and the correlation between the two variables:

$$\text{Slope} = \frac{\rho_{xy}\sigma_y}{\sigma_x}$$

In financial market contexts, if the x-values are the periodic returns on a well-diversified market index, and the y-values are the periodic returns for some asset (such as changes

	A	B	C	D
1				
2		**Sample Data**		
3		Mean of Sample	30.0	
4		StdDev of Sample	5.0	
5		Number of Data Points	1000	
6		Standard error of mean	0.16	=C$4/SQRT(C$5)
7		Degrees of Freedom	999	=C5-1
8				
9		**StdDev**		
10				
11		Confidence Interval	95.0%	
12		Exclusion probability	5.0%	=1-C11
13		Single-sided probability	2.5%	=(1-C11)/2
14				
15		Lower Band Scaling	0.96	=SQRT(C$7/CHISQ.INV.RT(C$13,C$7))
16		Upper Band Scaling	1.05	=SQRT(C$7/CHISQ.INV(C$13,C$7))
17		**Lower estimate**	**4.79**	=C$4*C15
18		**Upper estimate**	**5.23**	=C$4*C16

FIGURE 21.30 Confidence Interval for the Standard Deviation Based on Sample Data

to a stock's price), then the slope of the regression line is known as the (empirical) beta (β) of the asset:

$$\beta_s = \frac{\rho_{sm}\sigma_s}{\sigma_m}$$

(where ρ_{sm} is the correlation coefficient between the returns of the market and that of the asset, and σ_s and σ_m represent the standard deviation of the returns of the asset and the market respectively).

Thus the beta (as the slope of the line) represents the (average) sensitivity of the returns of the asset to a movement in the market index.

The importance (for any asset) of being able to estimate its beta is because of its use in the Capital Asset Pricing Model (CAPM). This theoretical model about asset pricing is based on the idea that asset prices should adjust to a level at which the expected return is proportional to that part of the risk which is not diversifiable, i.e. to that which is correlated with the overall market of all assets. In other words, the expected return on an asset (and hence the expectations for its current price) is linearly related to its beta.

Of course, the calculation of the slope of a regression line from observed data will give only an estimate of the (true) beta. The confidence interval for the slope of a regression line (i.e. of the beta) can be calculated using formulae from classical statistics (just as earlier examples calculate confidence intervals for the population mean and standard deviation).

The file Ch21.26.Beta.ConfInterval.Explicit.xlsx shows an example of the required formulae (see Figure 21.31). The calculations involve (amongst other steps) calculating the residuals (i.e. the errors) between the actual data and the regression line at that x-value, which itself first requires that the slope and intercept of the regression line be known.

It is worth noting that (for monthly data over 5 years, i.e. 60 data points), the confidence interval for the slope is rather large. Whilst larger sample sizes for a single asset should generically increase the accuracy of the calculations, the longer the time period over which data is collected, the more likely it is that fundamental aspects of the business or the macro-economic environment have changed (so that the true sensitivity of the business to the market may have changed). Thus, the data set may not be internally

	A	B	C	D	E	F	G	H	I	J	K
1											
2		SLOPE	0.950	=SLOPE(D13:D72,C13:C72)							
3		INTERCEPT	0.37%	=INTERCEPT(D13:D72,C13:C72)							
4											
5		Degrees of Freedom	58	=COUNT(D13:D72)-2		StdDev of Residuals	5.23%	=STDEV.S(G13:G72)			
6		STDEV (S&P)	3.6%	=STDEV.S(C13:C72)		Std Dev of Beta	1.461	=G5/C6			
7		STDEV (Kennametal)	6.2%	=STDEV(D13:D72)		Standard Error of Beta	0.192	=G6/SQRT(C5)			
8		CORREL	54.5%	=CORREL(C13:C72,D13:D72)							
9		RSQ	0.297	=RSQ(C13:C72,D13:D72)							
10											
11		Month	Log Changes			Kennametal from S&P	Errors/		Confidence Intervals for Beta	T-Distribution	
12			S&P	Kennametal		Forecasted value	Residuals		Confidence level	95%	
13		1	-1.4%	-0.9%		-0.96%	0.09%		Standard Deviations Required	2.002	=T.INV.2T(1-J12,C5)
14		2	-2.2%	-1.1%		-1.73%	0.63%		Band Width	0.384	=J13*$G7
15		3	1.4%	4.9%		1.70%	3.19%		Base Figure	0.950	=$C$2
16		4	1.3%	-3.7%		1.57%	-5.28%		Lower Figure	0.566	=$C$2-J14
17		5	1.6%	-1.0%		1.93%	-2.95%		Upper Figure	1.334	=$C$2+J14
18		6	3.1%	8.6%		3.32%	5.23%				

FIGURE 21.31 Confidence Interval for the Slope (Beta) of a Regression Line by Explicit Calculation

consistent, and hence less valid. This presents one challenge to the assessment of the correct value for beta of an asset. Therefore, in practice, in order to estimate the beta of an asset (e.g. of the stock of a particular company), regression is rarely applied to the data of that asset only; rather larger sample sizes are created by using the data for several companies in an industry, in order to estimate industry betas.

PRACTICAL APPLICATIONS: MORE ON REGRESSION ANALYSIS AND FORECASTING

In addition to the foundation functionality relating to regression and forecasting covered earlier (such as X–Y scatter plots, linear regression, forecasting and confidence intervals), Excel has several other functions that provide data about the parameter values of a linear regression, confidence intervals for these values, the performance of simple multiple-regressions and the forecasting of future values based on historic trends, including:

- LINEST, which calculates the parameters of a linear trend and their error estimates.
- STEYX, which calculates the standard error of the predicted y-value for each x in a linear regression.
- LOGEST, which calculates the parameters of an exponential trend.
- TREND and GROWTH, which calculate values along a linear and exponential trend respectively. Similarly, FORECAST.LINEAR (FORECAST in versions prior to Excel 2016) calculates a future value based on existing values.
- The FORECAST.ETS-type functions. These include:
  - FORECAST.ETS, which calculates a future value based on existing (historical) values by using an exponential triple smoothing (ETS) algorithm.
  - FORECAST.ETS.CONFINT, which calculates a confidence interval for the forecast value at a specified target date.
  - FORECAST.ETS.SEASONALITY, in which Excel detects and calculates the length of a repetitive pattern within a time series.
  - FORECAST.ETS.STAT, which calculates statistical values associated with the in-built time-series forecast method.

Example: Using LINEST to Calculate Confidence Intervals for the Slope (or Beta)

LINEST is an array function that calculates not only the slope and intercept of a regression line, but also several items relating to statistical errors and to confidence intervals. In fact, the information provided by LINEST can be used to determine the confidence interval for the slope (beta) of a regression line without having to conduct any explicit forecasting of residuals (as was done in the earlier section).

The file Ch21.27.Beta.ConfInterval.LINEST.xlsx shows an example (see Figure 21.32). The function has been entered in the range H3:I7, with the range F3:G7 showing the (manually entered) labels which describe the meaning of each. The data required to conduct the confidence interval calculation is shown in the highlighted cells (H3, H4, I6) and the actual confidence interval calculation is shown in the range G13:G15 (as earlier, this requires additional assumptions about the desired confidence level, and the inversion of the T-distribution).

	A	B	C	D	E	F	G	H	I
1									
2		Month	Log Changes			LINEST Array function			
3			S&P	Kennametal		SLOPE (BETA)	INTERCEPT	0.950	0.37%
4		1	-1.4%	-0.9%		Std Error of SLOPE	Std Error of INTERCEPT	0.192	0.68%
5		2	-2.2%	-1.1%		R^2	Std Error of y estimate	0.297	5.27%
6		3	1.4%	4.9%		F-stat	Degrees of Freedom	24.539	58
7		4	1.3%	-3.7%		Regression sum of squares	Residual sum of squares	0.068	0.161
8		5	1.6%	-1.0%					
9		6	3.1%	8.6%		Confidence Intervals for Slope or Beta	T-distribution		
10		7	2.4%	7.2%		Confidence level	95%		
11		8	2.1%	-1.0%		Standard Deviations Required	2.002	=T.INV.2T(1-G10,I6)	
12		9	0.5%	-15.6%		Band Width	0.384	=G11*$H4	
13		10	0.0%	4.0%		Base Figure	0.950	=$H$3	
14		11	-3.1%	-3.4%		Lower Figure	0.566	=$H$3-G12	
15		12	1.2%	1.2%		Upper Figure	1.334	=$H$3+G12	

FIGURE 21.32 Confidence Interval for the Slope (Beta) of a Regression Line Using LINEST

	A	B	C	D	E	F	G	H	I	J	K	L	M	N
1														
2		DATA						LINEST						
3		Floor space	Offices	Entrances	Age	Value (DEPENDENT)		-702	9909	29328	48	142035	{=LINEST(F4:F14,B4:E14,TRUE,TRUE)}	
4		2610	2	2	20	333,700		85.0	2516.4	1946.9	23.1	59052.5		
5		2636	2	2	12	338,400		0.986	4720.8	#N/A	#N/A	#N/A		
6		2662	3	1.5	31	354,850		106.2	6.0	#N/A	#N/A	#N/A		
7		2688	3	2	27	352,500		9464641005	133715017	#N/A	#N/A	#N/A		
8		2714	2	3	53	326,650								
9		2740	4	2	23	397,150		PREDICTION For New Items						
10		2766	2	1.5	75	296,100		Floor space	Offices	Entrances	Age	Value		
11		2792	2	2	34	335,815		2479	2	2	45	308734	=H11*K3+I11*J3+J11*I3+K11*H3+L3	
12		2818	3	3	23	383,050								
13		2844	4	4	55	397,150								
14		2870	2	3	22	350,150								
15														

FIGURE 21.33 Using LINEST to Perform a Multiple Regression and an Associated Forecast

The STEYX function in Excel returns the standard error of the Y-estimate, which is equivalent to the value shown by the LINEST function in cell I5.

It is also worth noting that, where one is interested in the slope and intercept parameters only (and not in the other statistical measures), the last (optional) parameter of the function can be left blank; in this case, the function is entered as an array function in a single row (rather than in five rows).

Example: Using LINEST to Perform Multiple Regression

The LINEST function can also be used to perform a multiple regression (i.e. when there are several independent variables and one dependent variable). Each independent variable will have an associated slope, which describes the sensitivity of the dependent variable to a change in that independent input.

The file Ch21.28.LINEST.MultipleRegression.xlsx shows an example of the use of LINEST to derive the slope coefficients, the intercept and other relevant statistical information relating to the market values of various offices based on their characteristics (see Figure 21.33). Several points are worth noting:

- The column range into which the function is entered is extended to reflect the number of variables (i.e. there are five rows and the number of columns is equal to the total number of variables): one column is required for each of the independent variables and one for the intercept.

- The values in each cell follow the same key as shown in the prior example, simply that the first row shows the slope for each independent variable (with the last column showing the intercept), and the second row shows the standard errors of these.
- The slopes and standard errors are shown in reverse order to that in which the data on the independent variables is entered; thus, when using this data to make a prediction, one needs to take care linking the predictive calculations to the slope coefficients (as shown in the formula for cell L11).

Once again, if one is interested only in the regression slope coefficients and the intercept, then the last (optional) parameter of the LINEST function can be left blank, and the function entered in a single row (rather than in five rows).

Example: Using LOGEST to Find Exponential Fits

In a fashion analogous to LINEST, the LOGEST function can be used where one wishes to describe the relationship between variables with a curve such as:

$$y = bm^x$$

This can also be written as:

$$y = be^{x\log(m)}$$

showing that this is equivalent to an exponential curve.

In addition, one could write the relationship by:

$$log(y) = log(b) + xlog(m)$$

In this latter formulation, in which the original Y-data is transformed by taking its logarithm, the LINEST function could be applied to calculate the intercept and slope, which would be equivalent to *log*(*b*) and *log*(*m*) respectively (from which *b* and *m* can be calculated). The LOGEST function would provide these (*b* and *m*) values directly from the (non-logarithmic or untransformed) data.

The file Ch21.29.LOGEST.LINEST.xlsx shows an example in which (in the worksheet named Data) the LOGEST function is applied to data for which there appears to be an exponential relationship. Note that an exponential trend-line has also been added to the graph (by right-clicking on the data points to produce the context-sensitive menu). This also shows the value of the fitted parameters (see Figure 21.34); for the trend-line equation note that $e^{0.436} \approx 1.5466$ (i.e. as shown in cell G3).

In the same file, the worksheet named LNofData shows the result of applying the LINEST function to the natural logarithm of the data. It also shows that the reconciliation between the coefficients calculated for the slope and intercept of this linear fit are equal to the logarithms of the values calculated by using LOGEST (see Figure 21.35).

The LOGEST function can also be used for multiple independent variables, in the same way shown for LINEST to perform multiple regression, i.e. for the context where one wishes to describe the relationships by:

$$y = bm_1^{x_1} m_2^{x_2} \ldots m_n^{x_n}$$

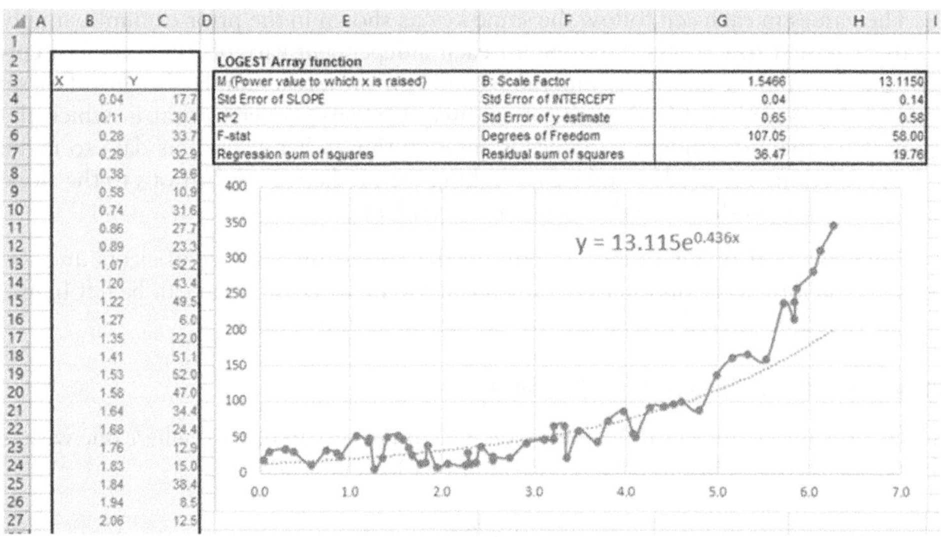

X	Y
0.04	17.7
0.11	30.4
0.28	33.7
0.29	32.9
0.38	29.6
0.58	10.9
0.74	31.6
0.86	27.7
0.89	23.3
1.07	52.2
1.20	43.4
1.22	49.5
1.27	6.0
1.35	22.0
1.41	51.1
1.53	52.0
1.58	47.0
1.64	34.4
1.68	24.4
1.76	12.9
1.83	15.0
1.84	38.4
1.94	8.5
2.06	12.5

LOGEST Array function

M (Power value to which x is raised)	B: Scale Factor	1.5466	13.1150
Std Error of SLOPE	Std Error of INTERCEPT	0.04	0.14
R^2	Std Error of y estimate	0.65	0.58
F-stat	Degrees of Freedom	107.05	58.00
Regression sum of squares	Residual sum of squares	36.47	19.76

FIGURE 21.34 Use of the LOGEST Function

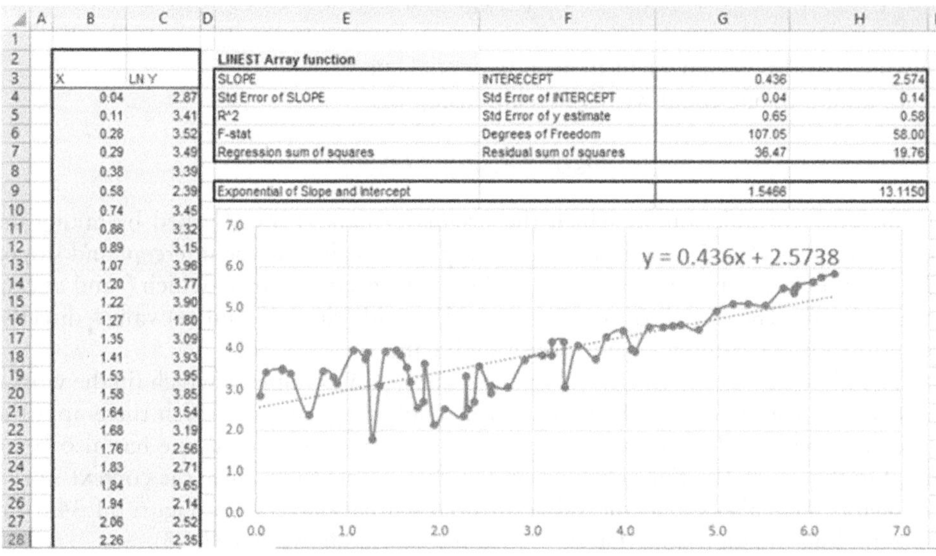

X	LN Y
0.04	2.87
0.11	3.41
0.28	3.52
0.29	3.49
0.38	3.39
0.58	2.39
0.74	3.45
0.86	3.32
0.89	3.15
1.07	3.96
1.20	3.77
1.22	3.90
1.27	1.80
1.35	3.09
1.41	3.93
1.53	3.95
1.58	3.85
1.64	3.54
1.68	3.19
1.76	2.56
1.83	2.71
1.84	3.65
1.94	2.14
2.06	2.52
2.26	2.35

LINEST Array function

SLOPE	INTERECEPT	0.436	2.574
Std Error of SLOPE	Std Error of INTERCEPT	0.04	0.14
R^2	Std Error of y estimate	0.65	0.58
F-stat	Degrees of Freedom	107.05	58.00
Regression sum of squares	Residual sum of squares	36.47	19.76
Exponential of Slope and Intercept		1.5466	13.1150

FIGURE 21.35 Comparison of LOGEST and LINEST Applied to the Logarithm of the Data

Example: Using TREND and GROWTH to Forecast Linear and Exponential Trends

The functions TREND (linear growth) and GROWTH (exponential growth) can be used to calculate (for a given x-value) a forecast of the y-value of a trend line. Of course, one would expect that the use of these functions would produce the same results as if an explicit forecast were made using the data about the slope and intercept of the trend-line:

- For the TREND function, the equivalent explicit calculations would require using SLOPE and INTERCEPT, or the equivalent values taken from the result of LINEST.
- For the GROWTH function, the explicit forecast could be done either by first calculating the logarithm of the Y-data, then applying SLOPE and INTERCEPT to this (to forecast a logarithmic *y*-value) and taking the exponent of the result. Alternatively, the required scaling parameters for the explicit forecast (*b* and *m*) can be calculated from the LOGEST function.

The file Ch21.30.TREND.GROWTH.xlsx shows an example of each approach (see Figure 21.36). By way of explanation, the X-data set is common in all cases, the Y1-data set is assumed to have essentially a linear relationship, and the Y2-data set to be essentially exponential. Both calculation approaches for forecasting are shown, i.e. using TREND applied to the logarithm of the data or GROWTH applied to the original data. Note that in the approach in which a Y2-value is forecast using the output from LOGEST, the function has been used in the single row form, in which only the regression coefficients (and not the full statistics) are given.

Example: Linear Forecasting Using FORECAST.LINEAR

The FORECAST.LINEAR function (and the legacy FORECAST function) conducts a linear forecast, and is similar to TREND, except that the order of the parameters is different.

The file Ch21.31.FORECASTLINEAR.xlsx shows an example which should be self-explanatory to a reader who has followed the discussion in the previous examples (see Figure 21.37).

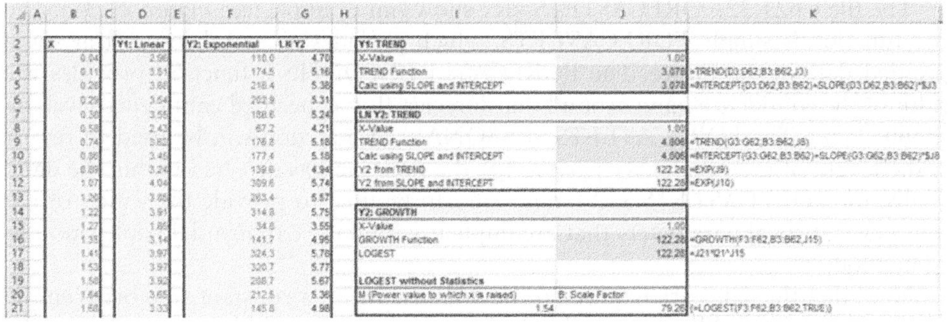

FIGURE 21.36 Use of TREND and GROWTH Functions and Comparison with Explicit Calculations

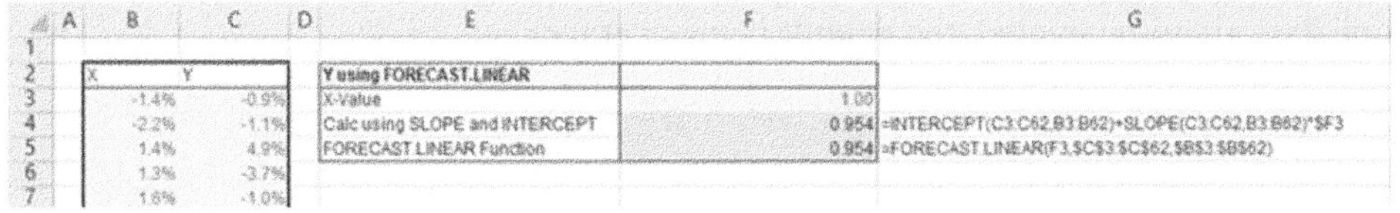

FIGURE 21.37 Use of FORECAST.LINEAR Function and Comparison with Explicit Calculations

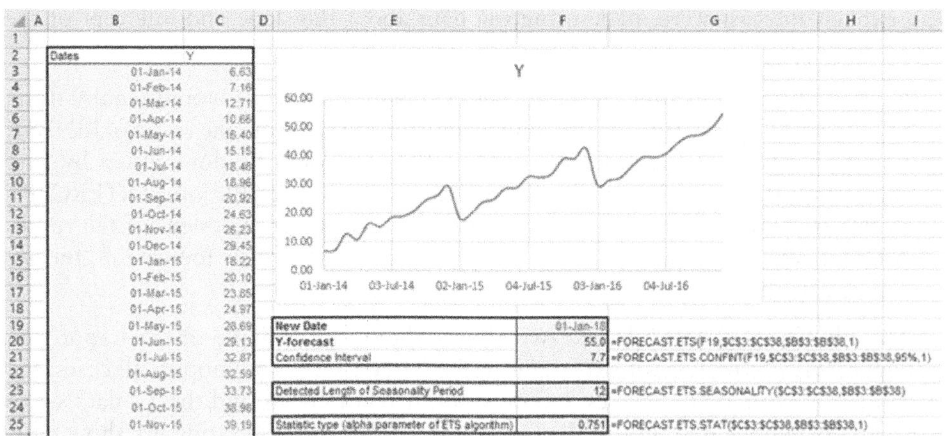

FIGURE 21.38 Example of the Use of the FORECAST.ETS Suite

Example: Forecasting Using the FORECAST.ETS Set of Functions

The suite of FORECAST.ETS-type functions provides the ability to conduct more-sophisticated forecasting of time series than the linear methods discussed earlier. The functions are based on an "exponential triple smoothing" method, which allows one to capture three major characteristics of a data set:

- A base value.
- A long-term trend.
- A potential seasonality.

The file Ch21.32.FORECASTETS.xlsx shows an example (see Figure 21.38). The core function is simply FORECAST.ETS, which provides a central forecast at some specified date in the future. The FORECAST.ETS.CONFINT function provides the width of the confidence band around that forecast (for a specified confidence level, by default 95%). The FORECAST.ETS.SEASONALITY function can be used to report on the length of the seasonality period that the function has detected within the data. Finally, the FORECAST.ETS.STAT function can be used to provide the values of the eight key statistical parameters that are implicit within the exponential triple smoothing method.

Note that the dates are required to be organised with a constant step between the time points, e.g. monthly or annually. Optional parameters include seasonality (i.e. the length of the seasonal period to be used, or 1 for seasonality to be detected automatically), data completion (i.e. 0 to treat missing data as zero, 1 to complete missing points based on the average of neighbouring points) and aggregation (i.e. how points on the same date are to be treated, the default being average).

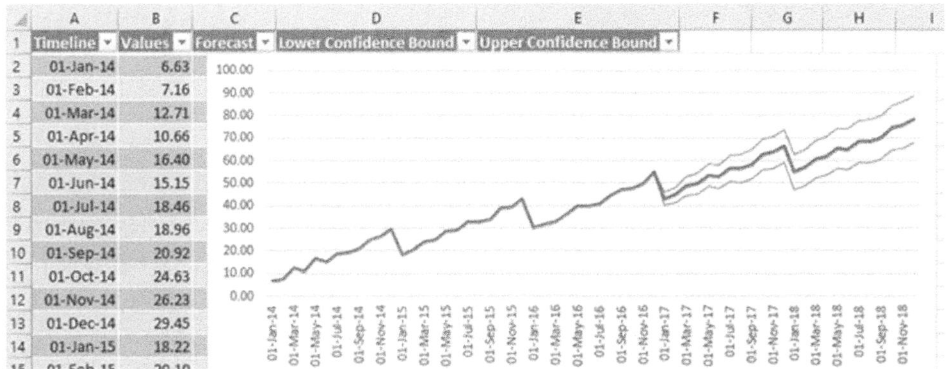

	A	B	C	D	E
1	Timeline	Values	Forecast	Lower Confidence Bound	Upper Confidence Bound
2	01-Jan-14	6.63			
3	01-Feb-14	7.16			
4	01-Mar-14	12.71			
5	01-Apr-14	10.66			
6	01-May-14	16.40			
7	01-Jun-14	15.15			
8	01-Jul-14	18.46			
9	01-Aug-14	18.96			
10	01-Sep-14	20.92			
11	01-Oct-14	24.63			
12	01-Nov-14	26.23			
13	01-Dec-14	29.45			
14	01-Jan-15	18.22			
15	01-Feb-15	20.10			

FIGURE 21.39 The Result of Using the Forecast Sheet Feature

Within this context, it is also worth mentioning another potentially useful Excel feature, which is the forecast graph; after selecting the data set of timeline and values, and choosing "Forecast Sheet" on Excel's Data tab, Excel will create a new worksheet with a forecast chart, including confidence intervals. Figure 21.39 shows the result of doing this.

CHAPTER 22

Information Functions

INTRODUCTION

This chapter covers Excel's Information functions. These generally provide information either about the content, position or format of a cell, or about the location and environment of a cell, range, worksheet or workbook:

- ISTEXT returns TRUE if its argument is text; ISNONTEXT returns TRUE if its argument is not text.
- ISNUMBER returns TRUE if its argument is a number.
- ISBLANK returns TRUE if its argument is blank.
- ISFORMULA returns TRUE if it refers to a cell that contains a formula.
- ISLOGICAL returns TRUE if its argument is a logical value.
- ISREF returns TRUE if its argument is a reference.
- ISEVEN or ISODD return TRUE if the number referred to is even or odd respectively.
- ISERROR returns TRUE if the value is any error value. ISERR returns TRUE if the value is any error value except #N/A.
- ERROR.TYPE returns a number corresponding to an error type.
- NA returns the error value #N/A.
- ISNA returns TRUE if the value is the #N/A error value.
- N returns a value converted to a number.
- TYPE indicates the data type of a value.
- CELL provides information about the formatting, location or contents of a cell.
- INFO provides information about the current operating environment.
- SHEET returns the sheet number of the referenced sheet, and SHEETS returns the number of sheets in a reference.

Note that there are other Excel functions which provide similar forms of information to some of these. For example, the functions ADDRESS, ROW, ROWS, COLUMN and COLUMNS (within Excel's Lookup & Reference category) have some characteristics in common with the CELL function; these are discussed in Chapter 25.

Practical Applications

This section provides some examples of the use of selected Information functions in data analysis and manipulation, including assessing data integrity, and providing other information.

Example: In-formula Comments Using ISTEXT, ISNUMBER or N

The ISTEXT function allows one to note or document a model by using in-formulae comments. This represents an alternative to using comments attached to cells, having the advantage that the comments can be seen when Excel is switched to its formula view (Formulas/Show Formulas). Thus, when auditing a model by inspecting its formulae, the comments are directly available.

The file Ch22.1.InCellComments.xlsx shows an example of the two approaches (when the model is displayed in formula view) (see Figure 22.1). In Cell C6, the ISTEXT function is used to provide a comment; since this function evaluates as TRUE (treated as 1 by Excel), the numerical result of the calculation is equal to the original value (12000). In Cell D6, the attached comment approach is shown, i.e. in which the comment has to be inspected separately to see its contents.

Note that the functions ISNUMBER or N could also be used in this context: for example, ISNUMBER("The comment") or N("The comment. . .") would be added to the core cell formula (rather than multiplied), as the presence of the text comment would result in each function evaluating to zero.

Example: Building a Forecast Model that Can Be Updated with Actual Reported Figures

The ISBLANK function can be used to determine whether a cell is blank (sometimes, ISBLANK embedded within a NOT function is required to determine that a cell is not blank). One application is when models are built to be updated with actuals as they become available, but to use forecast figures until the actuals are provided.

The file Ch22.2.UpdateActuals.xlsx shows an example (see Figure 22.2):

- The first part of the file (cells B2:I4) show a traditional forecasting model in which future sales are calculated based on assumptions about the value in the starting year (2016) and the growth rates in each future year. The first approach is suitable for one-off use (such as for a corporate finance transaction). However, significant rework would be needed if the model were required to be updated as data for future

	A	B	C	D
1				
2			Salaries 2017 $	
3			In-Formula Comment	Attached Comment
4		Fred	27000	27000
5		Bill	35000	35000
6		Harry	=12000*ISTEXT("Works half-time")	12000
7		Jo	43000	43000
8		Mary	57000	57000
9		Christine	45000	45000
10				

FIGURE 22.1 Use of ISTEXT to Create an In-formula Comment

	A	B	C	D	E	F	G	H	I	J
1										
2		TRADITIONAL		2016	2017	2018	2019	2020	2021	
3		SALES	Historic/Forecast	100.0	105.0	110.3	115.8	121.6	127.6	=H3*(1+I4)
4			Assumptions		5.0%	5.0%	5.0%	5.0%	5.0%	
5										
6		UPDATING		2016	2017	2018	2019	2020	2021	
7		SALES	Historic/Actuals	100.0	104.0					
8			Assumptions if No Actuals		5.0%	5.0%	5.0%	5.0%	5.0%	
9			Assumptions To Use		4.0%	5.0%	5.0%	5.0%	5.0%	=IF(ISBLANK(I7),I8,I7/H10-1)
10		SALES To Use	Growth Rate	100.0	104.0	109.2	114.7	120.4	126.4	=H10*(1+I9)

FIGURE 22.2 Use of ISBLANK to Create Forecasts that Update as Reported Data is Input

years become available (such as 2017 data at the end of that year). Of course, for a two-line model, this rework could be done very quickly, but for larger models containing many line items, the process would be cumbersome and error-prone.

- The second part of the file shows how the model may be adapted, so that the assumptions used to create the forecast depend on whether actual reported data is present, detected using the ISBLANK function. Where no reported data is present, the original forecast assumptions are used, otherwise assumptions are reset so that the resulting forecast replicates the reported figures.

Note that the =NOT(ISBLANK(G3)) combination will return a 1 in all cases where cell G3 has any content, whereas (as mentioned in Chapter 17 and Chapter 9), the use of =IF(G3,1,0) would return a 1 if cell G3 contains a non-zero number, a zero if G3 is zero and #VALUE in the case of a text entry. It is also worth noting that in such contexts, the difference between a blank cell and one containing zero in the actual field is fundamental; a blank cell means that no actual figure has yet been reported, whereas a cell containing zero means that the actual figure has been reported and that its value is zero (which is of course a valid value in many contexts, such as for the number of serious accidents that may have happened in the month).

Example: Detecting Consistency of Data in a Database

The ISBLANK functions can be used in some cases to detect inconsistency in a data set.

The file Ch22.3.ISBLANK.Consistency.xlsx (see Figure 22.3) shows an example of a set of contracts, each of which should either have both a start and end date (for existing contracts) or have both date fields as blank (for contracts currently being negotiated, for example). The ISBLANK function is used within an IF statement to detect inconsistent values, which evaluate to zero (Conditional Formatting is also used to highlight these values).

Of course, it is worth noting that other functions (such as ISNUMBER or ISTEXT) may be required in similar situations.

Example: Consistent use of "N/A" in Models

The text expression "NA" is often used within IF statements, for example to indicate that an inconsistency has arisen within the data. In general, the use of such text fields is not to be favoured (within a set of interim calculations), for subsequent calculations are likely to be more error-prone. For example, the need to begin many dependent formulae with items such as IF(G56="NA". . . . .) will add complexity, reduce transparency

Start	End	Consistency Check	Formula
1-Nov-16	31-Oct-19	1	=IF(ISBLANK(B3)=ISBLANK(C3),1,0)
1-Sep-15	31-Aug-19	1	=IF(ISBLANK(B4)=ISBLANK(C4),1,0)
1-Sep-15	31-Aug-19	1	=IF(ISBLANK(B5)=ISBLANK(C5),1,0)
1-Nov-16	31-Oct-19	1	=IF(ISBLANK(B6)=ISBLANK(C6),1,0)
1-Jan-17	31-Dec-20	1	=IF(ISBLANK(B7)=ISBLANK(C7),1,0)
1-Jul-15	30-Jun-19	1	=IF(ISBLANK(B8)=ISBLANK(C8),1,0)
1-Oct-15	30-Sep-19	1	=IF(ISBLANK(B9)=ISBLANK(C9),1,0)
	31-Oct-19	0	=IF(ISBLANK(B10)=ISBLANK(C10),1,0)
1-Jun-18	31-May-19	1	=IF(ISBLANK(B11)=ISBLANK(C11),1,0)
1-Nov-18	31-Oct-19	1	=IF(ISBLANK(B12)=ISBLANK(C12),1,0)
1-Nov-18	31-Oct-19	1	=IF(ISBLANK(B13)=ISBLANK(C13),1,0)
1-Jul-15	30-Jun-19	1	=IF(ISBLANK(B14)=ISBLANK(C14),1,0)
1-Oct-19		0	=IF(ISBLANK(B15)=ISBLANK(C15),1,0)
1-May-18	31-May-19	1	=IF(ISBLANK(B16)=ISBLANK(C16),1,0)
1-Jun-16	31-May-20	1	=IF(ISBLANK(B17)=ISBLANK(C17),1,0)

FIGURE 22.3 Use of ISBLANK to Detect Inconsistent Data Entries

and likely lead to errors (e.g. due to a misspelling or incorrect interpretation of the text field "NA", such as if it is written "#N/A").

Alternatives include:

- Using a numerical indicator (such as zero) to indicate inconsistency. This is the generally the author's preferred approach, as it retains the basic integrity of (most) models (as a set of numerical calculations), and tends to keep subsequent formulae simpler.
- Using the "=NA()" function to consistently treat such items in Excel.

The file Ch22.4.NA.Consistency.xlsx shows an example of this latter approach, comparing the use of the "NA" text field with the "=NA()" function. The latter is generally more consistent than the former in terms of delivering consistent #N/A error values when the formulae referring to the data are inapplicable. Figure 22.4 shows a screen-clip of the example.

	Using ="NA" Text Field	Using =NA() Function	Formula	Formula
Count	14	14	=COUNT(D8:D24)	=COUNT(E8:E24)
Sum	13926	#N/A	=SUM(D8:D24)	=SUM(E8:E24)
Multiplication of element	#VALUE!	#N/A	=D15*1	=E15*1

Start	End	Using ="NA" Text Field	Using =NA() Function		Formula
1-Nov-16	31-Oct-19	1094	1094	=IF(ISBLANK(B8)=ISBLANK(C8),C8-B8,"NA")	=IF(ISBLANK(B8)=ISBLANK(C8),C8-B8,NA())
1-Sep-15	31-Aug-19	1460	1460	=IF(ISBLANK(B9)=ISBLANK(C9),C9-B9,"NA")	=IF(ISBLANK(B9)=ISBLANK(C9),C9-B9,NA())
1-Sep-15	31-Aug-19	1460	1460	=IF(ISBLANK(B10)=ISBLANK(C10),C10-B10,"NA")	=IF(ISBLANK(B10)=ISBLANK(C10),C10-B10,NA())
1-Nov-16	31-Oct-19	1094	1094	=IF(ISBLANK(B11)=ISBLANK(C11),C11-B11,"NA")	=IF(ISBLANK(B11)=ISBLANK(C11),C11-B11,NA())
1-Jan-17	31-Dec-20	1460	1460	=IF(ISBLANK(B12)=ISBLANK(C12),C12-B12,"NA")	=IF(ISBLANK(B12)=ISBLANK(C12),C12-B12,NA())
1-Jul-15	30-Jun-19	1460	1460	=IF(ISBLANK(B13)=ISBLANK(C13),C13-B13,"NA")	=IF(ISBLANK(B13)=ISBLANK(C13),C13-B13,NA())
1-Oct-15	30-Sep-19	1460	1460	=IF(ISBLANK(B14)=ISBLANK(C14),C14-B14,"NA")	=IF(ISBLANK(B14)=ISBLANK(C14),C14-B14,NA())
	31-Oct-19	NA	#N/A	=IF(ISBLANK(B15)=ISBLANK(C15),C15-B15,"NA")	=IF(ISBLANK(B15)=ISBLANK(C15),C15-B15,NA())
1-Jun-18	31-May-19	364	364	=IF(ISBLANK(B16)=ISBLANK(C16),C16-B16,"NA")	=IF(ISBLANK(B16)=ISBLANK(C16),C16-B16,NA())

FIGURE 22.4 Use of the NA() Function

Example: Applications of the INFO and CELL Functions: An Overview

The INFO and CELL functions can be useful both to document models and to find out information about the current operating environment. This can be especially important in more-advanced applications, including the writing of robust VBA code.

The INFO function generally provides functionality that relate to a workbook or operating environment:

- The path of the current directory or folder. This is often important to know when writing VBA code that needs to work with all files in the same directory as the main model.
- The number of active worksheets in open workbooks.
- The cell reference of the top and left-most cell visible (as text).
- The current operating system version (as text).
- The current recalculation mode: Automatic or Manual.
- The version of Microsoft Excel being used (as text). This can be useful when writing VBA code to ensure that the latest version of Excel functionality is being used, such as in the creation of "wrapper" functions; see Chapter 33 for an example.
- The name of the operating environment: "mac" or "pcdos".

The CELL function provides information about the position, content or format of a cell or a referenced range, including:

- The full path of the file that contains the reference range (as text).
- The address (as text) of the first cell in the referenced range, or the address of the most recently changed cell in the workbook if the referenced range is omitted.
- The column number of the cell that is referenced.
- The row number of the cell that is referenced.
- Whether a cell is formatted in colour for negative values or not.
- The contents of the upper-left cell in the range that is referenced.
- The number format of the cell.
- Whether a cell is formatted with parentheses for positive or for all values.
- The label prefix of the cell, i.e. returns single quotation mark (') if the cell contains left-aligned text, double quotation mark (") if the cell contains right-aligned text etc.
- Whether a cell is locked (protected) or not.
- The type of data in a cell (e.g. returns "b" for blank if the cell is empty, "l" for label if the cell contains a text constant and "v" for value if the cell contains anything else).
- The column width of the cell (rounded to an integer), where each unit of column width is equal to the width of one character in the default font size.

The file Ch22.5.INFO&CELL.Overview.xlsx contains examples of each of these (see Figure 22.5).

Example: Creating Updating Labels that Refer to Data or Formulae

It can sometimes be useful to create labels that reference cells or ranges. For example, if a data set starts at Cell C5, one may wish to create a label such as "Data starts in C5",

INFO Function

Type	Example	Formulae
Directory	C:\Users\Michael\Documents\	=INFO(B4)
Numfile	33	=INFO(B5)
Origin	$A:$A$1	=INFO(B6)
OSVersion	Windows (32-bit) NT 10.00	=INFO(B7)
Recalc	Automatic	=INFO(B8)
Release	16.0	=INFO(B9)
System	pcdos	=INFO(B10)

CELL Function

Type	Example	Formula
Filename	C:\Users\Michael\Desktop\aaaFMPIIDraft\FM	=CELL(B14)
Address	$A$1	=CELL(B15)
Address	$B$5	=CELL(B16,$B$5:$C$6)
Col	2	=CELL(B17,$B$5:$C$6)
Row	5	=CELL(B18,$B$5:$C$6)
Color	0	=CELL(B19,$B$5:$C$6)
Contents	Numfile	=CELL(B20,$B$5:$C$6)
Format	G	=CELL(B21,$B$5:$C$6)
Parentheses	0	=CELL(B22,$B$5:$C$6)
Prefix	'	=CELL(B23,$B$5:$C$6)
Protect	1	=CELL(B24,$B$5:$C$6)
Type	l	=CELL(B25,$B$5:$C$6)
Width	31	=CELL(B26,$B$5:$C$6)

FIGURE 22.5 Overview of INFO and CELL Functions

with the label referring to the cell (so that it would update if a new row or column were introduced). Such a label can be created with a formula such as:

= "Data starts in "& CELL("address",C5)

The file Ch22.6.FormulaLabels.xlsx contains an example (see Figure 22.6).

Data For Vodafone starts in $C$5 =“Data For Vodafone starts in ”&CELL(“address”,C5)

	Daily returns		
Day	VOD	ICI	Barclays
1	1.7%	1.0%	-2.5%
2	-2.1%	1.1%	1.1%
3	0.1%	2.9%	-1.3%
4	0.0%	-1.7%	0.2%
5	-1.0%	-0.7%	-1.8%
6	1.1%	0.3%	0.9%
7	-1.3%	-3.6%	-1.9%
8	0.0%	-1.1%	-1.3%
9	1.4%	-1.7%	-0.4%
10	-2.1%	-0.8%	0.3%

FIGURE 22.6 Use of CELL Function to Create Updating Labels Referring to the Location of the Data

Example: Showing the User Which Recalculation Mode the File Is On

It may be important in some cases to clearly and explicitly let a user know what recalculation mode Excel is set to. For example, some models may need to be set to Manual calculation as they are large (or slow to recalculate for other reasons), so that recalculation may be conducted only when necessary, rather than automatically after every change is made. Of course, setting a workbook to Manual recalculation is potentially error-prone if someone were to change the input data and use the results whilst overlooking the need to recalculate the workbook. Therefore, one may wish both to explicitly show the recalculation mode as well as to highlight when it is set to Manual by using Excel's Conditional Formatting.

The file Ch22.7.RecalcInfo.xlsx contains an example in which the "Recalc" form of the INFO function is used (in practice, this would be placed somewhere that is clear to the user or within the description of the model within the Excel file itself). Conditional Formatting is used to shade the cell (yellow in the electronic file) when it shows the value of "Manual" (see Figure 22.7).

Example: Finding the Excel Version Used and Creating Backward Compatible Formulae

The use of INFO("RELEASE") will provide information about the Excel version being used; Excel 2003 is release 11, Excel 2007 release 12, Excel 2010 release 14, Excel 2013 release 15 and Excel 2016 is release 16. One example of the use of this knowledge is to create formulae that use the latest form of the functions, as available in the user's Excel version. For example, one may wish in principle for the model to use the NORM.S.INV function (see Chapter 21), but the NORMSINV function would be used for users with version 11 or earlier.

The file Ch22.8.ReleaseCompatability.xlsx contains an example (see Figure 22.8). Note that the release information resulting from using INFO("RELEASE") is a text field, but which for most purposes could be used without consequence as if it were

	A	B	C	D
1				
2		**The recalcuation of this workbook is:**	Manual	=INFO("Recalc")
3				

FIGURE 22.7 Use of CELL to Show the Recalculation Mode

	A	B	C	D
1				
2		Item	Calculation	Formula
3		Release as Text	16.0	=INFO("RELEASE")
4		Release as Value	16	=VALUE(C3)
5		Rand	0.194	=RAND()
6		Percentile of N(0,1)	-0.865	=IF(C4>=12,NORM.S.INV(C5),NORMSINV(C5))
7				

FIGURE 22.8 Use of Release Information to Create Backward Compatible Functions

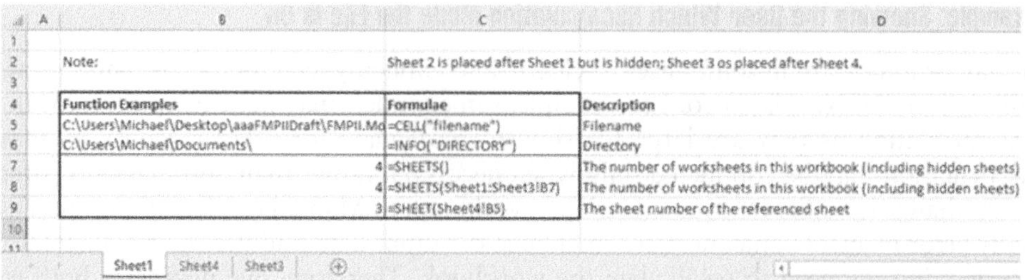

FIGURE 22.9 Integrated Example of the Use of the INFO, CELL, SHEETS and SHEET Functions

a number. However, it is generally more robust to apply the VALUE function (see Chapter 24) to turn this apparently numerical text field into its corresponding number. The formula in Cell C6 then uses one or other of the inversion functions, depending on the release version, in order to calculate the inverse (percentile) of the standard normal distribution for the percentage value generated by the RAND() function.

As discussed in Chapter 33, such functionality could be built into a VBA user-defined "wrapper" function, which would be easier to maintain (as new Excel versions become available), especially if used in several places.

Example: File Location and Structural Information Using CELL, INFO, SHEET and SHEETS

As mentioned above, the CELL and INFO functions may be used to provide the filename and directory of the current file. Other useful information can be the number of worksheets in a workbook, as well as (especially when writing VBA) the sheet number of a worksheet.

The file Ch22.9.FileDir&Sheets.xlsx shows an example of the use of the CELL and INFO functions, as well as of the SHEETS and SHEET functions (see Figure 22.9). Note that the order of the worksheets is Sheet1, Sheet2, Sheet4, Sheet3, with Sheet2 hidden. The SHEETS function shows that there are four sheets (i.e. including the hidden sheet) and the SHEET function shows that Sheet4 is the third sheet of the workbook (i.e. it also includes the hidden sheet). The SHEETS function also counts chart sheets (not just worksheets); thus, if one enters some data into the example file and presses the F11 short-cut for the insertion of a chart sheet, one will see the number of sheets increase.

CHAPTER 23

Date and Time Functions

INTRODUCTION

This chapter covers functions in Excel's Date and Time category, including:

- DATE returns the serial number of a date, corresponding to a specified year, month and day.
- DATEDIF calculates the age in a unit, i.e. number of days, months or years between two dates.
- DATEVALUE converts a date in the form of text to a serial number.
- DAY converts a number to a day of the month.
- DAYS returns the number of days between two dates.
- DAYS360 calculates the number of days between two dates based on a 360-day year.
- EDATE returns the number of the date that is the indicated number of months before or after the start date.
- EOMONTH calculates the number of the last day of the month before or after a specified number of months.
- YEAR converts a number to a year.
- MONTH converts a number to a month.
- WEEKDAY converts a number to a day of the week.
- HOUR converts a number to an hour.
- MINUTE converts a number to a minute.
- SECOND converts a number to a second.
- TODAY returns the number of today's date.
- NOW returns the number of the current date and time.
- TIME returns the number of a time.
- ISOWEEKNUM returns the number of the ISO week number of the year for a given date.
- WEEKNUM represents the week number of a date within the corresponding year.
- NETWORKDAYS returns the number of whole workdays between two dates.
- NETWORKDAYS.INTL returns the number of whole workdays between two dates using parameters to define weekends.
- TIMEVALUE converts a time in the form of text to a serial number.

- WORKDAY returns the number of the date before or after a specified number of workdays.
- WORKDAY.INTL returns the number of the date before or after a specified number of workdays using parameters to define weekends.
- YEARFRAC returns the year fraction representing the number of whole days between a start and date.

PRACTICAL APPLICATIONS

In the following, it is worth recalling that dates in Excel are numbers formatted as dates, and represent the number of days since 1 January 1900. Text fields may look like dates, but are not the same and generally do not allow direct numerical manipulation or calculations to be performed.

Example: Task Durations, Resource and Cost Estimation

The file Ch23.1.DatesAndResources.xlsx demonstrates that two dates can be subtracted to find the number of days between them. For a task that starts on a day (at the beginning of that day) and lasts until the end of another day, the total task duration is the difference between the dates plus 1 (for example, a task starting at the beginning of day 2 and lasting to the end of day 4 has a duration of 3 days). One may also use the DAYS function to calculate the task duration, if one remembers that the DAYS function captures a start-to-start (and not a start-to-end) duration, so that the result may need to be adjusted, depending on the context. The task duration can be multiplied by resource intensity requirements (such as full-time-equivalent people (FTEs) or costs per day, and so on) to calculate total resource requirements (see Figure 23.1).

Example: Keeping Track of Bookings, Reservations or Other Activities

The DATE function converts inputs corresponding to the year, month and day into a date.

The file Ch23.2.DATE.ToDate.xlsx shows an example, in which the year, month and day of each of a set of hotel reservations are entered, from which the DATE function creates the dates, and the DAYS function works out the length of stay (compared to the previous example, there is no need to add one to the result to obtain the correct figure in this context) (see Figure 23.2).

	A	B	C	D	E	F	G	H	I	J	K
1											
2			Start	Finish	Duration (in Days)		DAYS			FTEs/Day	FTEs
3			Beginning of ...	End of ...							
4		Task 1	13/12/2014	17/01/2015	36	=D4-C4+1	35	=DAYS(D4,C4)		10	360
5		Task 2	03/02/2015	07/04/2015	64	=D5-C5+1	63	=DAYS(D5,C5)		50	3200
6		Task 3	08/04/2015	28/04/2015	21	=D6-C6+1	20	=DAYS(D6,C6)		70	1470
7		Task 4	01/05/2015	16/05/2015	16	=D7-C7+1	15	=DAYS(D7,C7)		30	480
8		Task 5	17/05/2015	26/06/2015	41	=D8-C8+1	40	=DAYS(D8,C8)		10	410
9		Total			178	=SUM(E4:E8)					5920
10											

FIGURE 23.1 Use of Date Calculations and DAYS Function in Task Durations and Resource Estimation

	ARRIVAL					DEPARTURE					Length of Stay (Nights)	
	Year	Month	Day	DATE		Year	Month	Day	DATE		Using DAYS	
Person 1	2017	3	2	02/03/2017	=DATE(D4,E4,F4)	2017	3	9	09/03/2017	=DATE(I4,J4,K4)	7	=DAYS(L4,G4)
Person 2	2017	8	23	23/08/2017	=DATE(D5,E5,F5)	2017	9	6	06/09/2017	=DATE(I5,J5,K5)	14	=DAYS(L5,G5)
Person 3	2017	4	18	18/04/2017	=DATE(D6,E6,F6)	2017	4	28	28/04/2017	=DATE(I6,J6,K6)	10	=DAYS(L6,G6)

FIGURE 23.2 Using DAYS to Calculate Length of Stay of Hotel Guests

Example: Creating Precise Time Axes

The EOMONTH and EDATE functions can be used to create precise time axes. For example, EOMONTH works out the date of the month for a specified number of months after a starting date. If the starting date is set to be the beginning of a month, then the function can be used to work out full month periods to create a time axis automatically. EDATE works out the date that is a specified number of months after a starting date (e.g. 15 March is two months after 15 January). This is useful if the model periods are not aligned with the beginning of months or years. In addition, the knowledge of the exact number of days in a period may be required for detailed forecasting, such as the calculation of total production figures each quarter, when the production process runs every day or 24 hours per day.

The file Ch23.3a.DateAxis.EOMONTH.xlsx shows an example in which a quarterly axis is created using formulae based on a month-beginning start (1 January 2017) and an assumed time period of 3 months per column (the value in Cell C3 can be changed to create columns of any full-month time length: monthly, quarterly, annually or others) (see Figure 23.3). Note that the period length can also be calculated from the start and end dates (either using the difference between the dates or the DAYS function, as described earlier).

The file Ch23.3b.DateAxis.EDATE.xlsx shows a similar example using EDATE (see Figure 23.4).

Example: Calculating the Year and Month of a Date

The file Ch23.4.YearsAndMonths.xlsx shows the use of the YEAR and MONTH function to determine which year and (numerical) month correspond to a date (see Figure 23.5).

	C	D	E	F	G
Period Start	01-Jan-17	01-Apr-17	01-Jul-17	01-Oct-17	=E4+1
Months in Period	3	3	3	3	=$C3
Period End	31-Mar-17	30-Jun-17	30-Sep-17	31-Dec-17	=EOMONTH(F2,F3-1)
Days in Period	90	91	92	92	=F4-F2+1
Production Volume Tons/Day	800	805	900	950	
Production Volume	72000	73255	82800	87400	=F7*F5
Sales					
Costs....					

FIGURE 23.3 Using EOMONTH to Create a Time Axis

	A	B	C	D	E	F	G
1							
2		**Period Start**	15-Jan-17	15-Apr-17	15-Jul-17	15-Oct-17	=E4+1
3		Months in Period	3	3	3	3	=$C3
4		**Period End**	14-Apr-17	14-Jul-17	14-Oct-17	14-Jan-18	=EDATE(F2,F3)-1
5		Days in Period	90	91	92	92	=F4-F2+1
6							
7		Production Volume Tons/Day	800	805	900	950	
8		Production Volume	72000	73255	82800	87400	=F7*F5
9							
10		Sales					
11		Costs....					
12							

FIGURE 23.4 Using EDATE to Create a Time Axis

	A	B	C	D	E	F	G	H
1								
2		Date		YEAR			MONTH	
3		01/04/2015		2015	=YEAR(B3)		4	=MONTH(B3)
4								

FIGURE 23.5 Example of YEAR and MONTH Function

Example: Calculating the Quarter in Which a Date Occurs

Whilst Excel has YEAR and MONTH functions, there is (at the time of writing) no QUARTER function. If it were to exist, it would presumably have to have the flexibility to deal with the different definitions of quarters that are used around the world: the period January to March is widely considered as the first quarter, yet the British financial year ends at the beginning of April, for example.

The file Ch23.5.Quarters.xslx shows several ways to calculate the quarter of a date, after first working out its month (using MONTH), assuming that the period January to March represents quarter one. The first method uses the INT function, the second uses ROUNDUP and the third uses a lookup function based on a pre-defined table (these functions have been described earlier in the text, with the exception of the lookup functions, which are covered in Chapter 25) (see Figure 23.6).

	A	B	C	D	E	F	G	H	I	J	K	L	M	N	O	P
1																
2		Date	MONTH			QUARTER: Method 1			QUARTER: Method 2			QUARTER: Method 3			Month	Quarter
3		01/04/2015	4	=MONTH(B3)		2	=INT((C3-1)/3)+1		2	=ROUNDUP(C3/3,0)		2	=INDEX($P$3:$P$14,MA		1	1
4															2	1
5															3	1
6															4	2

FIGURE 23.6 Various Ways to Calculate the Quarter of a Given Date

Example: Creating Time-based Reports and Models from Data Sets

Given the year, month and quarter of any date, it is often possible to create reports from databases. Indeed, sometimes the most appropriate way to structure an entire model is so that it is driven from a data set, with the model essentially being a set of reports (and perhaps some further calculations based on these); this modelling approach was discussed in Chapter 5.

The file Ch23.6.DatesToModelBuild.xlsx shows an example in which a data set of items relating to the rental of a property (rental income, agent's costs, repair costs etc.) is used to create a quarterly report of revenues, total costs and profits. The date is used to calculate the year, month and quarter, from which a text key (such as "2014 Q1") is created. The report (in the range K4:M12) is created using the SUMIFS function to sum items in the data set based on the key. Finally, the profit for each quarterly period is calculated from this report (Column N) (see Figure 23.7).

Example: Finding Out on What Day of the Week You Were Born

The WEEKDAY function can be used to find which day of the week a given date falls on. Note that the default convention is for the week to start on a Sunday; if one wishes the week to start on the Monday, then the optional argument (2) can be used.

The file Ch23.7.WEEKDAY.xlsx shows an example of each approach (see Figure 23.8).

Example: Calculating the Date of the Last Friday of Every Month

The Date functions can be used in combination. For example, for detailed cash flow planning calculations, one may wish to know the exact date of the last Friday of each month (for example, as the date on which a company's payroll will be paid).

	A	B	C	D	E	F	G	H	I	J	K	L	M	N
1		Database of revenue and costs feeds summary calculation of revenue and costs, which is then used to calculate quarterly profit												
2		Items can be added at any point in the database, not only in time order												
3														
4		Date	Item	Category	Amount	Month	Year	Quarter	Year-Quarter Key		Quarter	Revenue	Cost	Profit
5		11-Mar-13	Rental Income	Revenue	1064.52	3	2013	1	2013 Q1		2013 Q1	1065	2211	**-1147**
6		11-Mar-13	Agents Fees (Mgmt)	Cost	51.10	3	2013	1	2013 Q1		2013 Q2	9000	4240	**4760**
7		11-Mar-13	Agents Fees (Rental upfront)	Cost	2160.00	3	2013	1	2013 Q1		2013 Q3	9000	3390	**5610**
8		1-Apr-13	Rental Income	Revenue	3000.00	4	2013	2	2013 Q2		2013 Q4	9000	3390	**5610**
9		1-Apr-13	Agents Fees (Mgmt)	Cost	150.00	4	2013	2	2013 Q2		2014 Q1	9000	7423	**1577**
10		1-May-13	Rental Income	Revenue	3000.00	5	2013	2	2013 Q2		2014 Q2	9000	6200	**2800**
11		1-May-13	Agents Fees (Mgmt)	Cost	150.00	5	2013	2	2013 Q2		2014 Q3	9000	6200	**2800**
12		1-Jun-13	Rental Income	Revenue	3000.00	6	2013	2	2013 Q2		2014 Q4	9000	6200	**2800**
13		1-Jun-13	Agents Fees (Mgmt)	Cost	150.00	6	2013	2	2013 Q2					

FIGURE 23.7 Creating Reports and Models from Time-based Data Sets

	A	B	C	D
1				
2		Date	WEEKDAY	
3		28 January 1974	2	=WEEKDAY(B3)
4		28 January 1974	1	=WEEKDAY(B4,2)

FIGURE 23.8 Examples of the Use of the WEEKDAY Function

Date	EOMONTH	WEEKDAY	Next Friday	EOMONTH	LastFriday
01 February 2016	29/02/2016	1	04/03/2016	31/03/2016	26/02/2016

FIGURE 23.9 Calculating the Date of the Last Friday of the Month for a Given Date

First Date	Second Date	Interval	DATEDIF		Between dates:
01-Jan-15	01-Mar-15	d	59	=DATEDIF(B3,C3,D3)	Number of days
01-Jan-16	01-Mar-16	d	60	=DATEDIF(B4,C4,D4)	Number of days
04-Jan-16	03-Mar-16	m	1	=DATEDIF(B5,C5,D5)	Complete calendar months
01-Jan-16	05-Mar-18	y	2	=DATEDIF(B6,C6,D6)	Complete calendar years
01-Jan-16	05-Mar-18	ym	2	=DATEDIF(B7,C7,D7)	Complete months, ignoring year
01-Jan-16	01-Mar-23	yd	60	=DATEDIF(B8,C8,D8)	Complete days, ignoring year
01-Jan-16	05-Mar-16	md	4	=DATEDIF(B9,C9,D9)	Complete days, ignoring month and year

FIGURE 23.10 Examples of the DATEDIF Function

The file Ch23.8.LastFridayofMonth.xlsx shows a series of calculations involving the EOMONTH and WEEKDAY functions, which calculate the date of the last Friday of the month given any input date within the month (see Figure 23.9).

Example: the DATEDIF Function and Completed Time Periods

In the previous example, we used the EOMONTH and WEEKDAY functions to work out the date of the last Friday in any month. Other similar examples involve calculating the number of months that have started since a given date (i.e. fully completed months plus the month under consideration; many contracts are such that, as soon as a month has started, the full month's payment is due). Several approaches are possible:

- Calculate the number of started months by using EDATE (rather than EOMONTH), appropriately combined with YEAR and MONTH. This exercise is left to the reader.
- Use the DATEDIF function. This computes the difference between two dates in a variety of different intervals, such as the number of years, months or days between the dates. For example, given two dates, it can provide the number of completed months (i.e. the number of started months). Although the function is potentially powerful, it is not clear (at the time of writing) to what extent it is a fully supported function (for example, although it is listed on the Microsoft Office Support website when searching for Excel Date functions, it does not appear on Excel's Date function menu).

The file Ch23.9.DATEDIF.xlsx shows examples of this function (see Figure 23.10).

CHAPTER 24

Text Functions and Functionality

INTRODUCTION

This chapter covers Excel's Text functions. These can be useful in many contexts, including facilitating the manipulation of numerical fields (such as by first turning them into text, operating on the resulting text fields and turning the new text back into a numerical field). The functions which we focus on are:

- CONCAT (and the legacy CONCATENATE) combine text from multiple ranges and/or strings. CONCAT also allows for a multiple-cell range to be concatenated into a single cell. TEXTJOIN has the additional functionality of allowing a specific delimiter to be used (equivalent to concatenation if no delimiter is defined), and to specify whether empty cells are to be ignored or not.
- VALUE converts a "numerical-looking" text field into its look-alike number. NUMBERVALUE converts text to number in a locale-independent manner, by allowing the specification of fields that define a decimal and a group separator. T returns a text argument as the same text, otherwise it returns an empty text cell.
- LEFT and RIGHT return the leftmost and rightmost characters from a text field, and MID returns a specific number of characters from the middle of a text field.
- LEN returns the number of characters in a text field.
- FIND finds one text value within another (case-sensitive). SEARCH is similar but not case-sensitive.
- REPLACE replaces *all* characters (between and specified starting and ending point) with new specified text. SUBSTITUTE replaces a *specific* character with an alternative character (by default) within the entirety of given text field, and allows a user to specify only a subset of the instances that should be substituted.
- REPT repeats text a given number of times.
- TRIM removes the 7-bit ASCII space character (code value 32) except for single spaces between words. CLEAN removes the (non-printable) 7-bit ASCII characters (code values 0 through 31).
- CHAR and UNICHAR generate the ASCII and Unicode characters for a specified code number, and CODE and UNICODE provide the code numbers for a character (or the first character in a text string).

- LOWER and UPPER convert text to lowercase and uppercase respectively. PROPER capitalises the first letter in each word of a text field, and presents the subsequent letters in each word in lower case.
- EXACT checks to see if two text values are identical.
- TEXT converts a number into text, using a specified formatting.

Other Text functions which are not explicitly covered in this text include ASC (which changes double-byte English letters within a character string to single-byte characters), DBCS (which changes single-byte English letters within a character string to double-byte characters), BAHTTEXT (which converts a number to text, using the baht currency format), PHONETIC (which extracts the phonetic characters from a text string), FIXED (which formats a number as text with a fixed number of decimals) and DOLLAR (which converts a number to text, using the $ (dollar) currency format). Functions such as LEFTB, LENB, RIGHTB, MIDB, FINDB, SEARCHB and REPLACEB are for languages which use a double-byte character set (including Japanese, Chinese and Korean).

PRACTICAL APPLICATIONS

Example: Joining Text Using CONCAT and TEXTJOIN

There are various ways to join text fields. The simplest is the "&" operator, selecting each text field individually. This is similar to the basic form of the CONCAT function, as well as the legacy CONCATENATE. The CONCAT function can also be used to join the individual elements of a multi-cell range, whereas the CONCATENTATE function cannot.

The most general and flexible approach is to use the TEXTJOIN function. This allows for individual cells or ranges to be joined, for a delimiter to be used between joined elements, and for it to be specified whether blank cells are to be ignored or not (without the possible use of a delimiter, this latter functionality would not be necessary, and the default is to ignore blank cells). When joining text fields together, it is often best to do so with a delimiter. Doing so not only allows for easier reading but also would facilitate the process to split the full resulting field (for example, if the joined result is copied to another file, and the underlying original split data becomes lost).

The file Ch24.1.TEXTJOIN.CONCAT.xlsx shows examples (see Figure 24.1). Note especially that in Cell F10 (whose formula is shown in cell G10), the TEXTJOIN

	A	B	C	D	E	F	G
1							
2		Country	Country Code	Area Code	Number	Result	Formula
3		UK	44		456789	UK44456789	=B3&C3&D3&E3
4		UK	44		456789	UK44456789	=CONCAT(B4,C4,D4,E4)
5		UK	44		456789	UK44456789	=CONCATENATE(B5,C5,D5,E5)
6		UK	44		456789	UK44456789	=CONCAT(B6:E6)
7		UK	44		456789	#VALUE!	=CONCATENATE(B7:E7)
8		UK	44		456789	UK44456789	=TEXTJOIN(,0,B8,C8,D8,E8)
9		UK	44		456789	UK44456789	=TEXTJOIN(,0,B9:E9)
10		UK	44		456789	UK-44-456789	=TEXTJOIN("-",1,B10:E10)
11		UK	44		456789	UK-44--456789	=TEXTJOIN("-",0,B11:E11)

FIGURE 24.1 Examples of the CONCAT, TEXTJOIN and Related Functions

function is set so that blanks are ignored, and hence the delimiter appears consecutively only once, whereas in Cell F11 (whose formula is shown in cell G11), blanks are not ignored, and so the delimiter appears in succession since Column D is blank.

Example: Splitting Data Using the Text-to-columns Wizard

The Text-to-Columns step-by-step (Wizard) menu on Excel's Data tab allows for a data set to be split into components on a one-off basis (i.e. without a functional or dynamic link between the original data and the result). The process consists of three steps:

- Selection of the data, and whether it is to be split into fixed-sized components or based on the presence of a delimiter.
- Defining the fixed split or type of delimiter.
- Selection of where to place the data and its formatting (the default will over-write the original data set).

The file Ch24.2.TextToColumns.xlsx shows a data set and the result of a split in which the new data is placed into a range starting in Cell C3. Figure 24.2 shows the second step of the process.

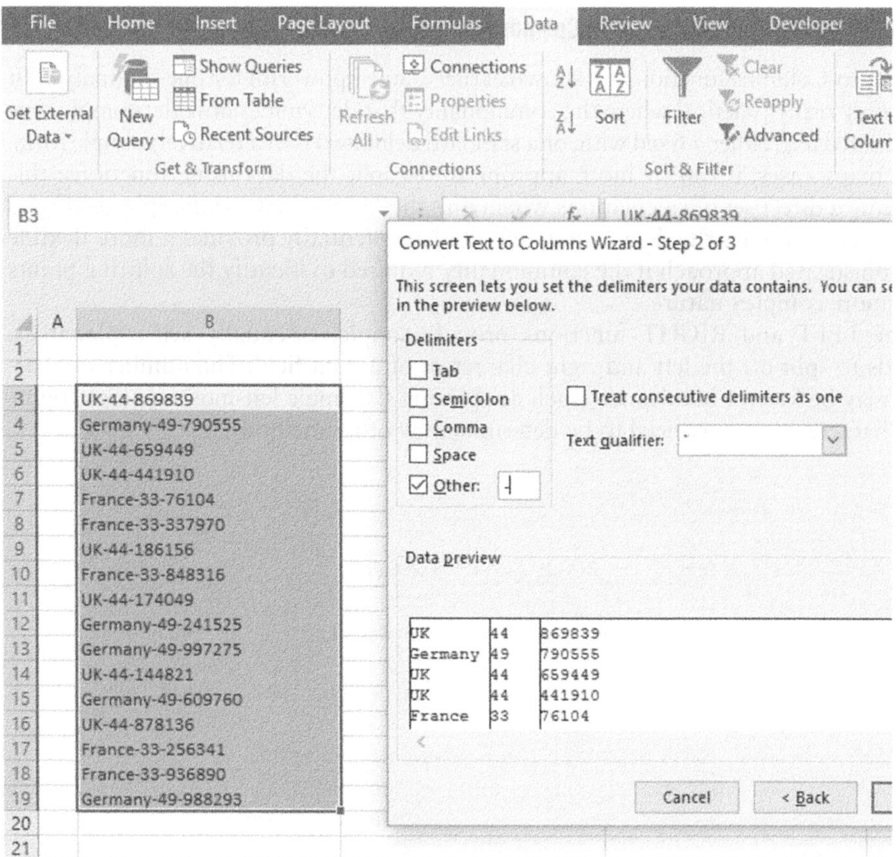

FIGURE 24.2 The Second Step of the Convert Text to Columns Wizard

Example: Converting Numerical Text to Numbers

The VALUE function turns numerical-looking text into its corresponding value. In fact, Excel often treats such (numerical-looking) text as if it were a number anyway. However, in some cases mistakes or unexpected behaviour can occur (such as when using Excel's Database functions, where the database contains numerical-looking text but the criteria being tested are written using numerical fields; see Chapter 26). Therefore, in general, it is more robust to ensure that the full transformation into a numerical field has been explicitly conducted.

The file Ch24.3.VALUE.NUMBERVALUE.xlsx shows an example (see Figure 24.3) in which the text field "23" in Cell B3 is used within a simple formula (in Cell C3), with Excel implicitly interpreting this figure as if it were a value for the purposes of the formula. Cell C4 shows that the VALUE function explicitly turns such a text field into its value (a hint that B4 is text, but C4 is a value is given by Excel's default alignment, with the text aligned left and the number aligned right). Similar comments apply to text fields that apparently look like dates (i.e. integers).

The NUMBERVALUE function is similar, but allows additional parameters for use in special applications (or language-independent treatment), in which the decimal and group separators can be explicitly defined.

Example: Dynamic Splitting Text into Components I

The Text-to-Columns functionality shown earlier is most powerful for one-off analysis. It is also only really practical where the commonality that determines how the components are delimited (e.g. either a fixed with, or a standard delimiter) is of a relatively simple form.

In many cases, it can be more appropriate to split the data using functions: this will create a direct set of calculations which link the (joined) data to the split data (and hence can be reused if the data is updated). It also potentially provides a more flexible and sophisticated approach if the commonality required to identify the splitting points is of a more complex nature.

The LEFT and RIGHT functions provide simple, essentially self-explanatory, methods to split off the left and right characters of a data field. The number of characters may be known in advance (such as splitting the single left-most or single right-most characters), or may need to be determined by other methods.

	A	B	C	D
1				
2		Text	Result	Formula
3		23	23	=B3*1
4		23	23	=VALUE(B3)
5		1987/05/13	31910	=B5*1
6		1987/05/13	31910	=VALUE(B6)
7				
8		23	23	=NUMBERVALUE(B8)
9		1987/05/13	31910	=NUMBERVALUE(B9)
10		2p500	2.5	=NUMBERVALUE(B10,"p")

FIGURE 24.3 Using the VALUE and NUMBERVALUE Functions

Loan Balance	Combined Loan-to-Income & Risk History	Loan-to-income	Formula	Risk History	Formula
49,878	E1	E	=LEFT($C3,1)	1	=VALUE(RIGHT($C3,1))
4,433	A1	A	=LEFT($C4,1)	1	=VALUE(RIGHT($C4,1))
52,774	E3	E	=LEFT($C5,1)	3	=VALUE(RIGHT($C5,1))
41,708	C3	C	=LEFT($C6,1)	3	=VALUE(RIGHT($C6,1))
89,999	G1	G	=LEFT($C7,1)	1	=VALUE(RIGHT($C7,1))
38,299	F2	F	=LEFT($C8,1)	2	=VALUE(RIGHT($C8,1))

FIGURE 24.4 Using the LEFT and RIGHT Functions

The file Ch24.4.SplitText.LEFT.RIGHT.xlsx shows an example in which the text field in Column C is split into its left- and right-most single characters, with the right-hand numerical-looking field also turned into a genuine value by using the VALUE function applied to the result of the RIGHT function (see Figure 24.4).

Also shown in the file (but not in the screen-clip) is the application of the resulting data set to create conditional summations (using SUMIFS), such as the sum of the loan balances for a particular combination of loan-to-income and risk history. The reader may verify that the SUMIFS function would still produce the correct value even if the VALUE function had not been applied.

Example: Dynamic Splitting Text into Components II

The MID function returns the part of a text string that starts at a specified point and has a specified length. It is convenient when extracting text that is in the middle of a text field.

The file Ch24.5.SplitText.MID.xlsx shows a simple application which splits a sequence of digits into its components. In this case, each component is of length 1, with the starting point at which the string is to be split given by the integers in Row 2 (see Figure 24.5). (Once again, the VALUE function has been used to ensure that the result consists of genuine numerical values.)

Example: Comparing LEFT, RIGHT, MID and LEN

The MID function is essentially a more general form of LEFT and RIGHT. If it is used where the starting point is the first character, then it is essentially almost identical to the LEFT function. It can also be made to have similar functionality to the RIGHT function, by first using LEN to determine the length of the full string, from which the starting character for the field to be extracted can be determined. For example, if one

Number	1	2	3	4	5	6	Formula
201739	2	0	1	7	3	9	=VALUE(MID($B3,H$2,1))
103401	1	0	3	4	0	1	=VALUE(MID($B4,H$2,1))
208736	2	0	8	7	3	6	=VALUE(MID($B5,H$2,1))

FIGURE 24.5 Using the MID Function to Extract Part of a Text Field

Data	Chars Reqd	LEFT	Left via MID	Chars Reqd	RIGHT	Right via MID	
201739	2	20	20	2	39	39	=MID(B3,LEN(B3)-H3+1,H3)
103401	2	10	10	2	01	01	=MID(B4,LEN(B4)-H4+1,H4)
208736	2	20	20	2	36	36	=MID(B5,LEN(B5)-H5+1,H5)

FIGURE 24.6 Comparing LEFT, RIGHT, MID and LEN

wishes to extract the right-most *N* characters, using MID instead of RIGHT, then the starting number of the character for the extraction process is given by:

$$\text{StartNum} = \text{Length } of \text{ FullString} - N + 1$$

The file Ch24.6.MID.LEFT.RIGHT.LEN.xlsx shows an example of such formulae (see Figure 24.6). (In this example, in order to keep the focus on the comparative functionality, the VALUE function has not been used.)

Example: Dynamic Splitting Text into Components III

The SEARCH function can be useful if the position(s) that describe the starting or ending character of the part of a text string are not fixed or known in advance, and need to be found.

The file Ch24.7.SplitText.SEARCH.xlsx shows an example. The SEARCH function is used to find the position of the bracket within each point of the data set (in the cells B7 downwards). The bracket is a common element of each data point whose position allows both the customer name and course length to be identified (e.g. CustA becoming A using the MID function based on two characters before the bracket, and the course length using the MID function based on the starting character one position after the bracket). From this, a summary report (such as using the COUNTIFS function to generate a summary of total courses by customer by length) can be produced (see Figure 24.7).

Customer	D	
Length	2	
Number of Courses	2	=COUNTIFS(F7:F25,C2,H7:H25,C3)

Cust & Length	SEARCH for Position of "("	Formula	Cust	Days as Text	Days as Value
CustA (1 Day)	7	=SEARCH("(",B7,1)	A	1	1
CustomerB (2 Day)	11	=SEARCH("(",B8,1)	B	2	2
CustC (1 Day)	7	=SEARCH("(",B9,1)	C	1	1
CustoD (2 Days)	8	=SEARCH("(",B10,1)	D	2	2
CustB (2 Days)	7	=SEARCH("(",B11,1)	B	2	2
CustomerB (2 Days)	11	=SEARCH("(",B12,1)	B	2	2
CustomerE (2 Days)	11	=SEARCH("(",B13,1)	E	2	2
CustF (2 Days)	7	=SEARCH("(",B14,1)	F	2	2
CustA (2 Days)	7	=SEARCH("(",B15,1)	A	2	2
CustomG (2 Days)	9	=SEARCH("(",B16,1)	G	2	2
CustA (1 Days)	7	=SEARCH("(",B17,1)	A	1	1
CustA (2 Days)	7	=SEARCH("(",B18,1)	A	2	2
CustmG (2 Days)	8	=SEARCH("(",B19,1)	G	2	2
CusA (1 Days)	6	=SEARCH("(",B20,1)	A	1	1
CustD (2 Days)	7	=SEARCH("(",B21,1)	D	2	2
CustB (3 Days)	7	=SEARCH("(",B22,1)	B	3	3

FIGURE 24.7 Using the SEARCH and MID Functions Combined

Note also that if one were to attempt to produce the same data set by splitting the data using Text-to-Columns, the process would need to be done several times for each data set, as different delimiters would be required in each case.

Example: Comparing FIND and SEARCH

The FIND and SEARCH functions are similar in concept, but FIND is case-sensitive whereas SEARCH is not; obviously, one needs to take care to ensure that the appropriate function is used, according to the circumstances.

The file Ch24.8.FIND.SEARCH.xlsx shows an example of the case-sensitivity (see Figure 24.8).

Example: the UPPER and LOWER Functions

The UPPER and LOWER functions simply turn their text arguments into upper- and lower-case respectively, and are essentially self-explanatory.

The file Ch24.9.UPPER.LOWER.xlsx shows an integrated example, which uses the SEARCH, MID and LEN functions. The overall process extracts the first letter and the remaining part of each name from the data set, recombines them so that only the names are shown, and presents the names with a starting capital and non-capitals thereafter (see Figure 24.9).

Example: the PROPER Function

The file Ch24.10.PROPER.xlsx shows how the result in the previous example could have been achieved directly with the PROPER function (see Figure 24.10). Note also that (not shown in the example) the function would capitalise the first letter in each word of a sentence (not just that of the first word, for example).

	B	D	E	G	H
2	Co./subject	Position of "S" using SEARCH	Formula	Position of "S" using FIND	Formula
3	CustA (1 Day)	3	=SEARCH("S",B3,1)	#VALUE!	=FIND("S",B3,1)
4	CustomerS (2 Day)	3	=SEARCH("S",B4,1)	9	=FIND("S",B4,1)
5	CustC (1 Day)	3	=SEARCH("S",B5,1)	#VALUE!	=FIND("S",B5,1)
6	CustoD (2 Days)	3	=SEARCH("S",B6,1)	#VALUE!	=FIND("S",B6,1)

FIGURE 24.8 Comparing the FIND and SEARCH Functions

	Name	Position of Space	First Letter using MID	UPPER	Formula	Length after Space	Remainder in LOWER	Formula	First Name Pure
3	1 amElia	2	a	A	=UPPER(D3)	6	melia	=LOWER(MID(B3,C3+2,G3-1))	Amelia
4	2 oLiVia	2	o	O	=UPPER(D4)	6	livia	=LOWER(MID(B4,C4+2,G4-1))	Olivia
5	3 emily	2	e	E	=UPPER(D5)	5	mily	=LOWER(MID(B5,C5+2,G5-1))	Emily
6	4 ava	2	a	A	=UPPER(D6)	3	va	=LOWER(MID(B6,C6+2,G6-1))	Ava
7	5 isla	2	i	I	=UPPER(D7)	4	sla	=LOWER(MID(B7,C7+2,G7-1))	Isla

FIGURE 24.9 Using the UPPER and LOWER Functions

	A	B	C	D	E	F
1						
2		Name	Postion of Space	Length after Space	First Name Pure	Formula
3		1 amElia	2	6	Amelia	=PROPER(MID(B3,C3+1,D3))
4		2 oLiVia	2	6	Olivia	=PROPER(MID(B4,C4+1,D4))
5		3 emily	2	5	Emily	=PROPER(MID(B5,C5+1,D5))
6		4 ava	2	3	Ava	=PROPER(MID(B6,C6+1,D6))

FIGURE 24.10 Example of the PROPER Function

Example: the EXACT Function

The EXACT function checks whether two texts fields are identical, including checking for blank spaces that might not be immediately visible. Of course, by design it is case-sensitive.

The file Ch24.11.EXACT.xlsx shows some examples (see Figure 24.11). The LEN function is used to illustrate that there are blank spaces in some of the fields. Note that C5 contains a trailing blank space, so that the word length is 7. This would not otherwise be visible without detailed investigation, yet the EXACT function detects the presence of a difference between B5 and C5 (as does LEN).

Example: Comparing REPLACE with SUBSTITUTE

The REPLACE and SUBSTITUTE functions are conceptually similar, but in fact provide quite distinct potential applications. The REPLACE function will, starting from a defined character, replace *all* subsequent characters (up to a specified number) with new specified text. The SUBSTITUTE function will (by default within the entirety of given text field), replace only a *specific* character with an alternative character. It also contains an optional argument to allow a user to specify only a subset of the instances which should be substituted.

The file Ch24.12.REPLACE.SUBSTITUTE.xlsx shows examples of each (see Figure 24.12). The second example using SUBSTITUTE shows the case where the optional instance parameter has been used to substitute only the second occurrence of the "." character.

Example: the REPT Function

The REPT function can be used to repeat a text field several times, and can be useful in applications such as generating visual scoreboards, dashboards or graphical displays.

The file Ch24.13.REPT.xlsx shows an example (see Figure 24.13).

	A	B	C	D	E	F	G	H
1								
2		Text1	Text2	EXACT			LEN(Text1)	LEN(Text2)
3		amelia	Amelia	FALSE	=EXACT(B3,C3)		6	6
4		Amelia	Amelia	FALSE	=EXACT(B4,C4)		7	6
5		Amelia	Amelia	FALSE	=EXACT(B5,C5)		6	7
6								

FIGURE 24.11 Use of the EXACT Function

	A	B	C	D
1				
2		Text	Result	Formula
3		1987.05.13	1987/05.13	=REPLACE(B3,5,1,"/")
4		1987.05.13	1987/13	=REPLACE(B4,5,4,"/")
5				
6		1987.05.13	1987/05/13	=SUBSTITUTE(B6,".","/")
7		1987.05.13	1987.05/13	=SUBSTITUTE(B7,".","/",2)

FIGURE 24.12 Comparing REPLACE with SUBSTITUTE

	A	B	C	D	E
1					
2		Number	Symbol	Result	Formula
3		10	✓	✓✓✓✓✓✓✓✓✓✓	=REPT(C3,B3)
4		4	×	××××	=REPT(C4,B4)
5		3	☹	☹☹☹	=REPT(C5,B5)
6					

FIGURE 24.13 Example of the REPT Function

Example: the CLEAN and TRIM Functions

The CLEAN and TRIM functions remove non-printable characters and spaces from a text field, respectively. They are especially useful in the early stages of "cleaning up" data that may have been received from other sources, such as the internet or downloads from mainframe servers.

CLEAN removes a large set of characters, i.e. those that are non-printable 7-bit ASCII characters, which correspond to code values 0 through 31. TRIM removes the space character (code value 32), except for single spaces between words. CLEAN can also remove some additional non-printable characters within the larger Unicode set.

The file Ch24.14.CLEAN.xlsx (Figure 24.14) shows an example of the CLEAN function (in Column E) being applied to text fields (in Column C), where these text

	A	B	C	D	E	F
1						
2		CodeNo	ASCII Item & Clean Text	Formula	CLEAN	Formula
3		1	▯Clean Text	=CHAR(B3)&"Clean Text"	Clean Text	=CLEAN(C3)
4		2	Clean Text	=CHAR(B4)&"Clean Text"	Clean Text	=CLEAN(C4)
5		3	▯Clean Text	=CHAR(B5)&"Clean Text"	Clean Text	=CLEAN(C5)
6		4	▯Clean Text	=CHAR(B6)&"Clean Text"	Clean Text	=CLEAN(C6)
7		5	▯Clean Text	=CHAR(B7)&"Clean Text"	Clean Text	=CLEAN(C7)
8		6	▯Clean Text	=CHAR(B8)&"Clean Text"	Clean Text	=CLEAN(C8)
9		7	▯Clean Text	=CHAR(B9)&"Clean Text"	Clean Text	=CLEAN(C9)
10		8	▯Clean Text	=CHAR(B10)&"Clean Text"	Clean Text	=CLEAN(C10)
11		9	Clean Text	=CHAR(B11)&"Clean Text"	Clean Text	=CLEAN(C11)
12		10	Clean Text	=CHAR(B12)&"Clean Text"	Clean Text	=CLEAN(C12)

FIGURE 24.14 Example Uses of the CLEAN Function I

G	H	I	J	K	L
	Unicode	Unicode Item & Clean Text	Formula	CLEAN	Formula
	127	Clean Text	=UNICHAR(H3)&"Clean Text"	Clean Text	=CLEAN(E3)
	129	Clean Text	=UNICHAR(H4)&"Clean Text"	Clean Text	=CLEAN(E4)
	141	Clean Text	=UNICHAR(H5)&"Clean Text"	Clean Text	=CLEAN(E5)
	143	Clean Text	=UNICHAR(H6)&"Clean Text"	Clean Text	=CLEAN(E6)
	144	Clean Text	=UNICHAR(H7)&"Clean Text"	Clean Text	=CLEAN(E7)
	157	Clean Text	=UNICHAR(H8)&"Clean Text"	Clean Text	=CLEAN(E8)
	160	Clean Text	=UNICHAR(H9)&"Clean Text"	Clean Text	=CLEAN(E9)

FIGURE 24.15 Example Uses of the CLEAN Function II

fields are generated from code numbers using the CHAR function. The text generated in this way (Column C) contains non-printable characters combined with the words "Clean Text", and only these words are left after the CLEAN function is applied (Column E).

In Figure 24.15, we show a screen-clip from the same file, which uses the CLEAN function to remove non-printable characters within the Unicode set.

The file Ch24.15.TRIM.xlsx (Figure 24.16) shows an example of the TRIM function to remove any leading or trailing spaces from the various text fields. The presence of such spaces can be seen from the length of each field, as shown in Column C (using the LEN function), as well as from the results of applying the LEFT and RIGHT functions in Column D and Column E. The trimmed text in Column F has no leading nor trailing spaces, and each treated field is of the same length.

Example: Updating Model Labels and Graph Titles

It is often useful to have labels that update if the model's assumptions or values change. For example, a cell may contain the text label "Net present value at 10% discount rate", where the 10% figure is an assumption contained in a cell that may be changed (say to 12%), in which case one would want the label to change (i.e. to become "Net present value at 12% discount rate"). This can be especially useful when there are different cases or sensitivities required, and most especially when several charts of these

	A	B	C	D	E	F	G	H
1								
2			LEN	1st LEFT	Last RIGHT	TRIM	Formula	LEN
3		Hello World	11	H	d	Hello World	=TRIM(B3)	11
4		Hello World	13	H		Hello World	=TRIM(B4)	11
5		Hello World	12		d	Hello World	=TRIM(B5)	11
6		Hello World	25			Hello World	=TRIM(B6)	11
7		Hello World	17			Hello World	=TRIM(B7)	11
8		Hello World	13			Hello World	=TRIM(B8)	11

FIGURE 24.16 Using the TRIM Function

cases are to be printed or presented in a report. In such cases, one may desire that the chart legends and titles change automatically as model values change.

The process for charts is in two steps:

- Create, as Excel formulae, the desired labels (legends and titles) so that they update as the data changes. This part of the process is the same as the case where no charts are to be produced, but one simply wants labels to change appropriately. This may often require the TEXT function, to format appropriately any numbers that are part of these labels. Of course, such formulae may also involve other Excel functions where necessary (e.g. Chapter 22 showed an example using the CELL function to create an updating label).
- Link these formulae to the chart labels and title. This is straightforward for legends (by editing the data source of the chart). For chart titles, one must edit the title field typing "=" within Excel's Formula Bar, point to the cell containing the required title, and press ENTER.

The file Ch24.16.TEXT.Labels&Graphs.xlsx shows an example (see Figure 24.17). Note that the second argument of the TEXT function defines the format to be used (another frequent format is to use "0.0" to show a numerical field with one decimal point, or "0" to show no decimal places, as used for the chart title). Some spaces may need to be added at appropriate places within the text fields, e.g. immediately after an opening inverted comma or before a closing one.

Example: Creating Unique Identifiers or Keys for Data Matching

In data analysis and manipulation, one is often required to match the items in two data sets in some (unique) way. Text functions, often combined with other Excel functions, can be a convenient way to do so.

The file Ch24.17.CreatingKeys.xlsx shows an example, which aims to express in a common currency (e.g. British Pounds Sterling) two data sets that are originally in

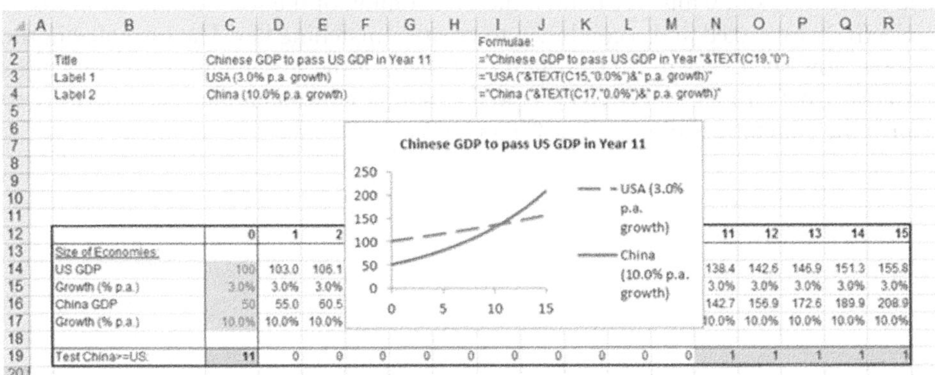

FIGURE 24.17 Updating Model Labels and Graph Titles Using TEXT to Format the Numerical Fields

Quarter	Currency	Amount (local currency)
1	Euro	32,143
3	Pound	17,203
2	Euro	16,993
2	Dollar	78,888
3	Pound	43,957
4	Dollar	25,898
1	Pound	26,856
2	Dollar	63,652
3	Dollar	29,188
4	Euro	47,153
1	Euro	51,737
2	Pound	36,332
3	Euro	33,363
1	Euro	17,635

Orig Key	**Xrate/£**
DollarQr_1	1.60
DollarQs_2	1.58
DollarQt_3	1.55
DollarQ_4	1.62
EuroQ_1	1.20
FuroQ_2	1.16
EuroQ_3	1.22
EuroQ_4	1.25
PoundQ_1	1.00
PoundQ_2	1.00
PoundQ_3	1.00
PoundQ_4	1.00

FIGURE 24.18 Two Data Sets that Can Be Linked by Creating a Common Key

their local currencies (see Figure 24.18). Since the exchange rate varies by quarter, the data in the first two columns of the first data set (Quarter and Currency) can be combined to create a key, whilst the data in the first column of the second data set needs to be selectively extracted and recombined to create a matching key. The formulae in the file show how such keys may be created (not seen on the screen-clip) using functions such as SEARCH, LEFT and RIGHT as well as simple concatenation (the procedure to perform the matching is discussed in Chapter 25).

CHAPTER 25

Lookup and Reference Functions

INTRODUCTION

This chapter discusses Lookup and Reference functions (which, for simplicity, are referred to in the subsequent text only as lookup functions). A good knowledge of these is one of the most important capabilities required to construct intermediate and advanced models.

The chapter starts with examples that relate to basic referencing processes (most of which are either essentially self-explanatory, or have already been covered earlier in the text):

- FORMULATEXT, which shows (as text) the formula in a cell.
- TRANSPOSE, which transposes an array.
- COLUMN (ROW), which returns the column (row) number of a cell or range.
- COLUMNS (ROWS), which finds the number of columns (rows) of a cell or range.
- ADDRESS, which provides a cell reference as text.
- AREAS, which shows the number of areas (separate non-contiguous ranges) in a reference.

The majority of the rest of this chapter is devoted to examples which use the other core functions in additional contexts, including combining matching and referencing processes, and the creation of dynamic ranges and flexible data structures:

- INDEX looks up the value in a specified row and column of a contiguous range (as a one- or two-dimensional matrix). The function also exists in a reference form, where it returns a reference to specified cells rather than to the value of a cell.
- CHOOSE uses one of a set of values according to an indexation number. It is especially useful (compared to other lookup functions) where the arguments are (or may need to be) in a non-contiguous range.
- MATCH finds the relative position of a specified value.
- OFFSET provides the value in a cell that is a specified number of rows and columns from a reference cell or range. It can also be used to return a range of cells (rather than an individual cell) that is a specified number of rows and columns from a reference cell or range.

- INDIRECT returns the range specified by a text string.
- HLOOKUP (VLOOKUP) searches the top row (left column) of a table for a specified value and finds the column in that row (row in that column) that contains that value. It then provides the value that is at a specified row (column) within the table.
- LOOKUP looks up values in a vector or array. In its vector form, it looks for a specified value within a one-dimensional range (of values that must be in ascending order) and returns the value from the corresponding position in another one-dimensional range.

We also briefly mention some of the functions that provide the capability to link to data sets, such as hyperlinks and related topics.

It is important to note that in many of the examples provided, there is generally no unique way to achieve a specific purpose; alternative formulations with different functions may exist. Therefore, we aim to highlight some of the criteria that can be considered when making a choice between various approaches, a topic which was also partly addressed in Chapter 9.

PRACTICAL APPLICATIONS: BASIC REFERENCING PROCESSES

Example: the ROW and COLUMN Functions

The file Ch25.1.ROW.COLUMN.xlsx provides an example of the (essentially self-explanatory) ROW and COLUMN functions (see Figure 25.1). Note that the most frequent practical use would be in the core form, in which the row or column number of a single cell is determined. However, the functions can be used as array formulae to determine the associated values for each cell of a multi-cell range. It is also worthwhile noting (for use later in this chapter) that the functions can be entered in a cell which references itself without creating a circularity (e.g. in Cell B4, the function entered is ROW(B4)).

	A	B	C	D
1				
2		Result		
3		CORE FORM		
4		4	=ROW(B4)	
5		2	=COLUMN(B5)	
6				
7		ARRAY FORMULAE		
8		4	{=ROW(B4:C5)}	
9		5	{=ROW(B4:C5)}	
10				
11		2	3	4
12		{=COLUMN(B5:D5)}	{=COLUMN(B5:D5)}	{=COLUMN(B5:D5)}

FIGURE 25.1 Single Cell and Array Formulae use of the ROW and COLUMN Functions

	A	B	C	D
1				
2		DATA		
3		22	14	21
4		11	9	11
5		2	1	7
6		14	14	19
7		5	6	18
8				
9		5	=ROWS(B3:D7)	
10		3	=COLUMNS(B3:D7)	
11				

FIGURE 25.2 Example of the ROWS and COLUMNS Function

Example: the ROWS and COLUMNS Functions

The file Ch25.2.ROWS.COLUMNS.xlsx provides an example of the ROWS and COLUMNS functions, which are also essentially self-explanatory (see Figure 25.2).

It is worth noting (for use later in this text) that, whilst ROWS(B3:D7) returns the value 5 (i.e. the number of rows in the range), in VBA the statement `Range("B3:D7").Rows` refers to the actual rows in the range (not to their number). It is the `Count` property of this set of rows that would be used to find out the number of rows in a range: `NRows= Range("B3:D7").Rows.Count`

Example: Use of the ADDRESS Function and the Comparison with CELL

The ADDRESS function returns the address of a cell in a worksheet, given specified row and column numbers. Note that in Chapter 22, we saw that the CELL function could also provide address-related (e.g. address, row, or column number) as well as other information (e.g. its format or type of contents) about a cell.

The file Ch25.3.CELL.ADDRESS.1.xlsx shows an example of the ADDRESS function and the analogous result produced using the address-form of the CELL function (see Figure 25.3).

Note (for later reference) that each function can be entered in a cell which references itself without creating a circular calculation. It is also worth noting that the CELL function has the Excel property that it is Volatile. This means that it is evaluated at every recalculation of the worksheet even when its arguments have not changed,

	A	B	C
1			
2		Result	Formula
3		$B$3	=ADDRESS(ROW(B3),COLUMN(B3))
4		$B$4	=CELL("address",B4)
5			

FIGURE 25.3 Use of ADDRESS and Comparison with CELL

	A	B	C
1	Feb		
2		Result	Formula
3		Feb!$B$3	=ADDRESS(ROW(B3),COLUMN(B3),,,$A$1)
4		Feb!$B$4	=$A$1&"!"&CELL("address",B4)
5			

FIGURE 25.4 Finding the Address of Corresponding Cells in Another Worksheet

which reduces computational efficiency. Thus, the ADDRESS function may be chosen in preference to the CELL function in some cases.

The file Ch25.4.CELL.ADDRESS.4.xlsx contains an example of the use of the ADDRESS function (see Figure 25.4). It uses the last of the function's optional arguments to find the address of a cell in another worksheet of the workbook. In other words, the ADDRESS function is providing (in Cell B3) the full address of Cell B3 of the "Feb" worksheet. A similar result can be obtaining using the address form of the CELL function by explicitly concatenating the text strings. (This approach will be important for some examples of multi-sheet models shown later in the chapter, and discussed in Chapter 6.)

PRACTICAL APPLICATIONS: FURTHER REFERENCING PROCESSES

Example: Creating Scenarios Using INDEX, OFFSET or CHOOSE

The use of scenario techniques essentially means that the values of several inputs are changed simultaneously. This is usually an extension of sensitivity analysis, which at its core involves changing the value of only one variable. Scenario techniques are useful to begin to capture a wide set of possible outcomes, and to capture dependencies between variables that are believed to exist but which are hard to represent through full mathematical relationships.

Once the scenarios have been defined with explicit data, for any given scenario, the values that are to be used can be looked up from these data sets. The use of lookup processes is an alternative to a "copy and paste" operation (in which model inputs would be manually replaced by the values for the desired scenario), with the function creating a dynamic link between the input scenarios and the model output.

The file Ch25.5.Scenarios.1.xlsx shows an example in which the CHOOSE function is used (Row 6) to pick out the values that apply to the chosen revenue scenario (see Figure 25.5). The desired scenario number is entered in Cell A6, and the references values are linked into the model's subsequent calculations (Row 10 being linked to Row 6). Note that in principle the calculations in Row 6 could instead be placed directly in Row 10. However, for large models such an approach would mean that the CHOOSE function would refer to data that is physically separated from its inputs in a more significant way, and thus be less transparent and more error-prone. Note also that the CHOOSE function requires explicit referencing of the data of each individual scenario.

	A	B	C	D	E	F	G	H	I	J
1										
2		Revenues Scenarios	2016	2017	2018	2019	2020	2021	2022	
3		Low			387	407	439	483	520	
4		Base			431	452	488	537	577	
5		High			474	497	537	591	635	
6	3	To Use			474	497	537	591	635	=CHOOSE($A6,I3,I4,I5)
7										
8		Model ... Income Statement	2016	2017	2018	2019	2020	2021	2022	
9										
10		Revenues	400	410	474	497	537	591	635	=I6
11										
12		Variable Costs	140	160	170.5	179.0	193.3	212.7	222.3	
13		% revenues	35.0%	39.0%	36.0%	36.0%	36.0%	36.0%	35.0%	
14										
15		Fixed Costs (incl. depreciation)	70	72	72.7	74.2	76.4	78.7	81.1	
16		% Growth		2.9%	1.0%	2.0%	3.0%	3.0%	3.0%	
17										
18		EBIT	190.0	178.0	230.4	244.1	267.3	299.4	331.7	
19										
20		...REST OF MODEL								

FIGURE 25.5 Use of the CHOOSE Function to Select the Relevant Scenario Data

Where the scenario data is presented in a contiguous range (such as in the above example), it can be more efficient (in terms of model building and flexibility to add a new scenario) to use the INDEX function to look up the relevant values. (Another alternative is the OFFSET function, although, as a Volatile function, it is less computationally efficient.)

The file Ch25.6.Scenarios.2.xlsx shows the scenario-selection portion of the above example, implemented using each of the CHOOSE, INDEX and OFFSET functions (see Figure 25.6). Note that the CHOOSE function explicitly refers to separate cells, the INDEX function explicitly refers to a contiguous range and the OFFSET function implicitly refers to a contiguous range (by picking out the value that is offset from the date-headers by the number of rows that is equal to the scenario number). Thus, the addition of a new scenario may be easier to achieve if the INDEX or OFFSET functions are used.

The file Ch25.7.Scenarios.3.xlsx (see Figure 25.7) shows an extension of the above scenario-selection methods, in which there are scenarios both for cost and for revenue. In principle (e.g. if the dollar signs are implemented appropriately), such scenario-selection formulae may be copied for each desired variable.

	A	B	C	D	E	F	G	H	I	J
1										
2		Revenues Scenarios	2016	2017	2018	2019	2020	2021	2022	
3		Low			387	407	439	483	520	
4		Base			431	452	488	537	577	
5		High			474	497	537	591	635	
6										
7	3	To Use: With CHOOSE			474	497	537	591	635	=CHOOSE($A7,I3,I4,I5)
8		To Use: With INDEX			474	497	537	591	635	=INDEX(I3:I5,$A7,1)
9		To Use: With OFFSET			474	497	537	591	635	=OFFSET(I2,$A7,0)

FIGURE 25.6 Use of the CHOOSE, INDEX and OFFSET Functions to Select Scenario Data

	A	B	C	D	E	F	G	H	I	J
1										
2		**Revenues Scenarios**	**2016**	**2017**	**2018**	**2019**	**2020**	**2021**	**2022**	
3		Low			387	407	439	483	520	
4		Base			431	452	488	537	577	
5		High			474	497	537	591	635	
6										
7	3	**To Use: With CHOOSE**			**474**	**497**	**537**	**591**	**635**	=CHOOSE($A7,I3,I4,I5)
8		**To Use: With INDEX**			**474**	**497**	**537**	**591**	**635**	=INDEX(I3:I5,$A7,1)
9		**To Use: With OFFSET**			**474**	**497**	**537**	**591**	**635**	=OFFSET(I2,$A7,0)
10										
11										
12		**Cost Scenarios**	**2016**	**2017**	**2018**	**2019**	**2020**	**2021**	**2022**	
13		Low			354	364	430	480	428	
14		Base			395	367	488	476	563	
15		High			385	482	505	511	527	
16										
17	3	**To Use: With CHOOSE**			**385**	**482**	**505**	**511**	**527**	=CHOOSE($A17,I13,I14,I15)
18		**To Use: With INDEX**			**385**	**482**	**505**	**511**	**527**	=INDEX(I13:I15,$A17,1)
19		**To Use: With OFFSET**			**385**	**482**	**505**	**511**	**527**	=OFFSET(I12,$A17,0)
20										
21										

FIGURE 25.7 Use of Scenarios for Multiple Model Variables

In practical cases, the scenario data may often be generated in one of two ways:

- By listing first all the revenue scenarios, and then deriving the associated cost scenarios.
- By working scenario-by-scenario (e.g. first the low, then the base, then the high scenario), determining the revenue and cost data with each.

The file Ch25.8.Scenarios.4.xlsx (see Figure 25.8) shows an example in which the structure of the scenario data follows the second of these approaches (whereas Figure 25.7 follows the first). In such a case, the use of the CHOOSE function is often the simplest and most transparent way to achieve the scenario-selection process.

Example: Charts that Can Use Multiple or Flexible Data Sources

One may also use the CHOOSE, INDEX, or OFFSET functions to pick out relevant data that is then linked to a graph, and the TEXT (or ADDRESS or other) function(s) may be used to create updating labels for specific graph elements.

	A	B	C	D	E	F	G	H	I	J
1										
2		**Scenarios**	**2016**	**2017**	**2018**	**2019**	**2020**	**2021**	**2022**	
3		**Low**								
4		Revenue			387	407	439	483	520	
5		Cost			354	364	430	480	428	
6		**Base**								
7		Revenue			431	452	488	537	577	
8		Cost			395	367	488	476	563	
9		**High**								
10		Revenue			474	497	537	591	635	
11		Cost			385	482	505	511	527	
12										
13		**To Use: With CHOOSE**	**2016**	**2017**	**2018**	**2019**	**2020**	**2021**	**2022**	
14	3	**Revenue**			**474**	**497**	**537**	**591**	**635**	=CHOOSE($A$14,I4,I7,I10)
15		**Cost**			**385**	**482**	**505**	**511**	**527**	=CHOOSE($A$14,I5,I8,I11)
16										

FIGURE 25.8 Use of Scenarios for Non-contiguous Data Sets

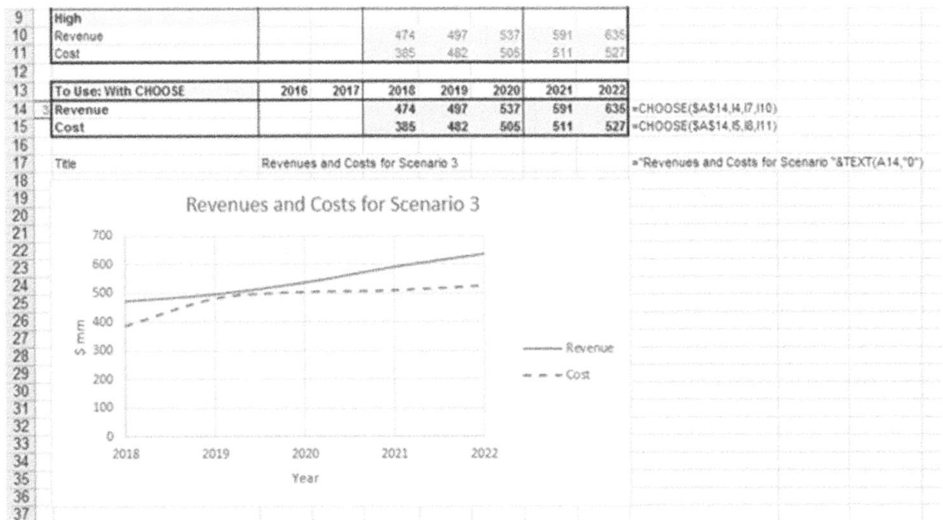

FIGURE 25.9 Scenario Approaches to Creating Graphs

The file Ch25.9.Scenarios.5.xlsx shows an example in which the data that feeds the graph, and the graph titles, are updated automatically as the scenario number is changed (see Figure 25.9).

Example: Reversing and Transposing Data Using INDEX or OFFSET

There are many situations in which one may need to reverse or transpose a data set. These include cases where time-series data has been imported from an external source, in "triangle" calculations that arise in depreciation and other similar contexts (see Chapter 18), or when using the results of the LINEST array function in a multiple regression to create predictions (since the coefficients returned by the function are in reverse order to the data sets; see Chapter 21). The INDEX and OFFSET functions can be used to create a dynamic link between an original data set (or calculations) and the reversed or transposed ones.

The file Ch25.10.ReversingTimeSeries.1.xlsx (see Figure 25.10) shows an example. The original data set is shown in Columns B and C, with Column E having been created to provide an indexation reference. The OFFSET function uses this indexation in a subtractive sense; the further down the rows the formula is copied, the less is the result offset from the original data (thus creating the reversal effect).

A similar result can be achieved using INDEX in place of OFFSET; once again, where there is a choice between the two functions, generally INDEX should tend to be favoured, because although OFFSET may have a more appealing or apparently transparent name, the fact that it is a Volatile function reduces computational effectiveness, which can be particularly important with larger data sets and models.

(Note that for simplicity of presentation of the core principles, the examples are shown with only small data sets, but in many practical cases, the number of items would of course be much larger.)

	A	B	C	D	E	F	G	H	I
1									
2		Count	15						
3							Using OFFSET		
4		Date	Adj Close				Date	Adj Close	
5		30/10/2008	4,869.30		1		10/10/2008	4,544.31	=OFFSET(C$5,C$2-E5,0)
6		29/10/2008	4,808.69		2		13/10/2008	5,062.45	=OFFSET(C$5,C$2-E6,0)
7		28/10/2008	4,823.45		3		14/10/2008	5,199.19	=OFFSET(C$5,C$2-E7,0)
8		27/10/2008	4,334.64		4		15/10/2008	4,861.63	=OFFSET(C$5,C$2-E8,0)
9		24/10/2008	4,295.67		5		16/10/2008	4,622.81	=OFFSET(C$5,C$2-E9,0)
10		23/10/2008	4,519.70		6		17/10/2008	4,781.33	=OFFSET(C$5,C$2-E10,0)
11		22/10/2008	4,571.07		7		20/10/2008	4,835.01	=OFFSET(C$5,C$2-E11,0)
12		21/10/2008	4,784.41		8		21/10/2008	4,784.41	=OFFSET(C$5,C$2-E12,0)
13		20/10/2008	4,835.01		9		22/10/2008	4,571.07	=OFFSET(C$5,C$2-E13,0)
14		17/10/2008	4,781.33		10		23/10/2008	4,519.70	=OFFSET(C$5,C$2-E14,0)
15		16/10/2008	4,622.81		11		24/10/2008	4,295.67	=OFFSET(C$5,C$2-E15,0)
16		15/10/2008	4,861.63		12		27/10/2008	4,334.64	=OFFSET(C$5,C$2-E16,0)
17		14/10/2008	5,199.19		13		28/10/2008	4,823.45	=OFFSET(C$5,C$2-E17,0)
18		13/10/2008	5,062.45		14		29/10/2008	4,808.69	=OFFSET(C$5,C$2-E18,0)
19		10/10/2008	4,544.31		15		30/10/2008	4,869.30	=OFFSET(C$5,C$2-E19,0)
20									

FIGURE 25.10 Use of OFFSET to Reverse Time-series Data

The file Ch25.11.ReversingTimeSeries.2.xlsx (see Figure 25.11) shows an implementation of the INDEX function for the same example.

Note that the indexation number created in Column E need not be explicitly placed in the worksheet (it is done so above to maximise transparency of the presentation).

	A	B	C	D	E	F	G	H	I
1									
2		Count	15						
3							Using INDEX		
4		Date	Adj Close				Date	Adj Close	
5		30/10/2008	4,869.30		1		10/10/2008	4,544.31	=INDEX(C$5:C$19,C$2-E5+1,1)
6		29/10/2008	4,808.69		2		13/10/2008	5,062.45	=INDEX(C$5:C$19,C$2-E6+1,1)
7		28/10/2008	4,823.45		3		14/10/2008	5,199.19	=INDEX(C$5:C$19,C$2-E7+1,1)
8		27/10/2008	4,334.64		4		15/10/2008	4,861.63	=INDEX(C$5:C$19,C$2-E8+1,1)
9		24/10/2008	4,295.67		5		16/10/2008	4,622.81	=INDEX(C$5:C$19,C$2-E9+1,1)
10		23/10/2008	4,519.70		6		17/10/2008	4,781.33	=INDEX(C$5:C$19,C$2-E10+1,1)
11		22/10/2008	4,571.07		7		20/10/2008	4,835.01	=INDEX(C$5:C$19,C$2-E11+1,1)
12		21/10/2008	4,784.41		8		21/10/2008	4,784.41	=INDEX(C$5:C$19,C$2-E12+1,1)
13		20/10/2008	4,835.01		9		22/10/2008	4,571.07	=INDEX(C$5:C$19,C$2-E13+1,1)
14		17/10/2008	4,781.33		10		23/10/2008	4,519.70	=INDEX(C$5:C$19,C$2-E14+1,1)
15		16/10/2008	4,622.81		11		24/10/2008	4,295.67	=INDEX(C$5:C$19,C$2-E15+1,1)
16		15/10/2008	4,861.63		12		27/10/2008	4,334.64	=INDEX(C$5:C$19,C$2-E16+1,1)
17		14/10/2008	5,199.19		13		28/10/2008	4,823.45	=INDEX(C$5:C$19,C$2-E17+1,1)
18		13/10/2008	5,062.45		14		29/10/2008	4,808.69	=INDEX(C$5:C$19,C$2-E18+1,1)
19		10/10/2008	4,544.31		15		30/10/2008	4,869.30	=INDEX(C$5:C$19,C$2-E19+1,1)
20									

FIGURE 25.11 Use of INDEX to Reverse Time-series Data

	A	B	C	D	E	F	G	H	I
1									
2		Count	15						
3							Using INDEX		
4		Date	Adj Close				Date	Adj Close	
5		30/10/2008	4,869.30				10/10/2008	4,544.31	=INDEX(C$5:C$19,C$2-(ROW(C5)-ROW(C$5)),1)
6		29/10/2008	4,808.69				13/10/2008	5,062.45	=INDEX(C$5:C$19,C$2-(ROW(C6)-ROW(C$5)),1)
7		28/10/2008	4,823.45				14/10/2008	5,199.19	=INDEX(C$5:C$19,C$2-(ROW(C7)-ROW(C$5)),1)
8		27/10/2008	4,334.64				15/10/2008	4,861.63	=INDEX(C$5:C$19,C$2-(ROW(C8)-ROW(C$5)),1)
9		24/10/2008	4,295.67				16/10/2008	4,622.81	=INDEX(C$5:C$19,C$2-(ROW(C9)-ROW(C$5)),1)
10		23/10/2008	4,519.70				17/10/2008	4,781.33	=INDEX(C$5:C$19,C$2-(ROW(C10)-ROW(C$5)),1)
11		22/10/2008	4,571.07				20/10/2008	4,835.01	=INDEX(C$5:C$19,C$2-(ROW(C11)-ROW(C$5)),1)
12		21/10/2008	4,784.41				21/10/2008	4,784.41	=INDEX(C$5:C$19,C$2-(ROW(C12)-ROW(C$5)),1)
13		20/10/2008	4,835.01				22/10/2008	4,571.07	=INDEX(C$5:C$19,C$2-(ROW(C13)-ROW(C$5)),1)
14		17/10/2008	4,781.33				23/10/2008	4,519.70	=INDEX(C$5:C$19,C$2-(ROW(C14)-ROW(C$5)),1)
15		16/10/2008	4,622.81				24/10/2008	4,295.67	=INDEX(C$5:C$19,C$2-(ROW(C15)-ROW(C$5)),1)
16		15/10/2008	4,861.63				27/10/2008	4,334.64	=INDEX(C$5:C$19,C$2-(ROW(C16)-ROW(C$5)),1)
17		14/10/2008	5,199.19				28/10/2008	4,823.45	=INDEX(C$5:C$19,C$2-(ROW(C17)-ROW(C$5)),1)
18		13/10/2008	5,062.45				29/10/2008	4,808.69	=INDEX(C$5:C$19,C$2-(ROW(C18)-ROW(C$5)),1)
19		10/10/2008	4,544.31				30/10/2008	4,869.30	=INDEX(C$5:C$19,C$2-(ROW(C19)-ROW(C$5)),1)
20									

FIGURE 25.12 Using ROW to Create an Embedded Indexation Field

Instead, the ROW function could be embedded within the formulae so that the indexation is calculated for each element (the ROWS function could also be used in place of the COUNT function in Cell C2).

The file Ch25.12.ReversingTimeSeries.3.xlsx (see Figure 25.12) shows an implementation of the INDEX function for the same example.

Concerning the transposing of data, as an alternative to the use of the TRANSPOSE array function (Chapter 18), one may use INDEX or OFFSET functions. This similar to the above, except that (to transpose row-form data to column-form), the lookup formulae are written so that as the functions are copied downwards, the lookup process moves across a row.

The file Ch25.13.TranposingWithLookup.xlsx (see Figure 25.13) shows an implementation of this (once again, using an explicit manual approach to indexation in Column B, whereas the ROW and COLUMNS or COUNT functions could be used to create the indexation, either in Column B or embedded within the functions).

	B	D	E	G	H	J	K	L	M	N	O	P	Q
2						1	2	3	4	5	6	7	8
3						100	105	110	115	120	125	130	135
5		INDEX		OFFSET									
6	1	100	=INDEX($J$3:$Q$3,1,B6)	100	=OFFSET($J$3,0,B6-1)								
7	2	105	=INDEX($J$3:$Q$3,1,B7)	105	=OFFSET($J$3,0,B7-1)								
8	3	110	=INDEX($J$3:$Q$3,1,B8)	110	=OFFSET($J$3,0,B8-1)								
9	4	115	=INDEX($J$3:$Q$3,1,B9)	115	=OFFSET($J$3,0,B9-1)								
10	5	120	=INDEX($J$3:$Q$3,1,B10)	120	=OFFSET($J$3,0,B10-1)								
11	6	125	=INDEX($J$3:$Q$3,1,B11)	125	=OFFSET($J$3,0,B11-1)								
12	7	130	=INDEX($J$3:$Q$3,1,B12)	130	=OFFSET($J$3,0,B12-1)								
13	8	135	=INDEX($J$3:$Q$3,1,B13)	135	=OFFSET($J$3,0,B13-1)								

FIGURE 25.13 Using Lookup Functions to Transpose Data

	A	B	C	D	E	F	G	H	I	J
1										
2		Period Number		1	2	3	4	5	6	
3		Volume: without shift		100	110	115	120	125	125	
4										
5		Methods to shift in time through a single delay amount i.e. spread across two future periods								
6										
7				1	2	3	4	5	6	
8		Delay is anything less than 1	0.3	70	107	114	119	124	125	=H3*$C8+I3*(1-$C8)
9		Delay in periods: whole numbers	2	0	0	100	110	115	120	=IF(AND(I$7-$C9>=1,I$7-$C9<=10),INDEX($D$3:$I$3,1,I$7-$C9),0)
10		Delay in periods: whole numbers	2	0	0	100	110	115	120	=IF(I2<=$C10,0,OFFSET(I3,0,-$C10))
11		Delay is any number	1.6	0	40	104	112	117	122	=IF(I$2<(ROUNDDOWN($C11,0)+1),0,OFFSET(I$3,0,-(ROUNDDOWN

FIGURE 25.14 Various Methods to Shift Cash Flows over Time

Example: Shifting Cash Flows or Other Items over Time

There are many circumstances in which one may wish to model the effect of a delay on production, on cash flows, or on some other quantity. In such cases, the granularity of the time axis may have an impact on the complexity of the formulae required. In the following, we discuss the following cases:

- Delays whose length is at most one model period (e.g. half a model period).
- Delays whose length is a whole number of model periods.
- Delays whose length could be any positive amount.

The file Ch25.14.TimeShiftVarious.xlsx shows an example of these (see Figure 25.14); the first can be achieved with a simple weighting formula, the second and third by use of INDEX or OFFSET functions. Other simple Excel functions (e.g. IF, AND in the second case and ROUNDDOWN in the third) are also required; the reader can consult the full formulae within the file; for cell I11, the implemented formula is:

$$= \text{IF}\ (\text{I\$2} < (\text{ROUNDDOWN}(\$\text{C11},0) + 1),\ 0,\ \text{OFFSET}\ (\text{I\$3},0,-\ (\text{ROUNDDOWN}\ (\$\text{C11},0) + 1)) * (\$\text{C11} - \text{INT}\ (\$\text{C11})) + \text{OFFSET}\ (\text{I\$3},0,-\ \text{ROUNDDOWN}\ (\$\text{C11},0)) * (1 - (\$\text{C11} - \text{INT}(\$\text{C11}))))$$

Due to their complexity, it is often better to implement them as user-defined functions in VBA (see Chapter 33).

Example: Depreciation Schedules with Triangle Calculations

The file Ch25.15.INDEX.Transpose.Depn.xlsx shows an example in which the INDEX function is used in triangle-type calculations both to transpose and to time-shift the data. The SUMPRODUCT is used to calculate the periodic depreciation (see Figure 25.15). Note that IF and AND statements are used to ensure the validity of the time period, and also that one could not robustly use an IFERROR function in this context (as the INDEX function may sometimes return the first element of a range when the indexation figure is set to zero).

	A	B	C	D	E	F	G	H	I	J	K	L
1												
2		Years		2015	2016	2017	2018	2019	2020			
3		Capex	575	100	105	120	80	50	120			
4												
5		Depreciation Schedule		1	2	3	4	5				
6		Percentage	100%	40%	30%	20%	10%	0%				
7												
8		Years	Capex	2015	2016	2017	2018	2019	2020	2021	2022	2023
9	1	2015	100	40%	30%	20%	10%					
10	2	2016	105		40%	30%	20%	10%				
11	3	2017	120			40%	30%	20%	10%			
12	4	2018	80				40%	30%	20%	10%		
13	5	2019	50					40%	30%	20%	10%	
14	6	2020	120						40%	30%	20%	10%
15												
16		Depreciation		40	72	100	99	79	91	54	29	12
17												

FIGURE 25.15 Using INDEX in a Triangle-type Depreciation Calculation

PRACTICAL APPLICATIONS: COMBINING MATCHING AND REFERENCE PROCESSES

Example: Finding the Period in Which a Condition is Met Using MATCH

It is often important to be able to identify the time period or position in a model at which a condition is met for the first time, for example:

- The first time that revenues of one product are higher than those of another.
- The first time that revenues reach the break-even point, or when those of a declining business drop below such a point.
- The date at which a producing oil field would need to be abandoned as production drops over time as the field becomes exhausted, and future NPV would be negative for the first time.
- The first time at which conditions are met which allow a loan to be refinanced at a lower rate, such as when specific covenant conditions are met.

The MATCH function is powerful in such contexts. Its general syntax is of the form:

= MATCH (ValueToFind, RowOrColRangeToLookIn, [OptionalMatchType])

Typically, it is most convenient to ensure that the lookup range contains the values of a "flag" variable, i.e. which uses an IF statement to return TRUE (or 1) when the condition is met and FALSE (or 0) otherwise. In addition, it is usually important to use the optional last argument of the function in which a match-type of zero returns the first exact match; if this is omitted, the data in the lookup range needs to be in ascending order and the largest value less than or equal to the lookup value is returned (something which is otherwise often overlooked, resulting in inconsistent values being returned).

	A	B	C	D	E	F	G	H	I	J	K	L	M	N	O	P
1																
2						2018	2019	2020	2021	2022	2023	2024	2025	2026	2027	
3		Product 1	100			103	106	109	113	116	119	123	127	130	134	=N3*(1+O4)
4		Growth (% p.a.)	3.0%			3.0%	3.0%	3.0%	3.0%	3.0%	3.0%	3.0%	3.0%	3.0%	3.0%	=$C4
5		Product 2	70			76	82	88	95	103	111	120	130	140	151	=N5*(1+O6)
6		Growth (% p.a.)	8.0%			8.0%	8.0%	8.0%	8.0%	8.0%	8.0%	8.0%	8.0%	8.0%	8.0%	=$C6
7		Test Prod2>=Prod1	8	=MATCH(1,F7:O7,0)		0	0	0	0	0	0	0	1	1	1	=IF(O5>=O3,1,0)
8																
9		Default	10	=MATCH(1,F7:O7)												
10																
11		Year of Match	2025	=INDEX(F2:O2,1,C7)												

FIGURE 25.16 Using MATCH to Find the Time at Which Revenues Reach a Target

The file Ch25.16.RevenueComp.xlsx shows an example applied to finding out when the revenue of one product will overtake that of another, according to the company's revenue growth forecasts (see Figure 25.16). Note that the range F7:O7 contains the calculations of the flag variable, and that the Cell C7 contains the MATCH function. Note also that, if the optional (last) parameter were left empty, then the function would return the position of the last match, not the first (Cell C9). Finally, it is worth reiterating that the function returns the (relative) position (or index number) at which this condition is first met, so that the value in Cell C7 is not the year number (in Row 2) but rather it shows that the match occurs in the eighth position of the data set; the actual year value can be looked up using an INDEX function (Cell C11).

Example: Finding Non-contiguous Scenario Data Using Matching Keys

Earlier in the chapter, we used the CHOOSE function to look up data for scenarios in data sets that were not contiguous, as well as using INDEX or OFFSET when the data is contiguous. Generally, these approaches are the most reliable. Nevertheless, one may encounter models in which more complex (or non-ideal) approaches have been used, and it is worthwhile to be aware of such possibilities.

The file Ch25.17.Scenarios.6.xlsx shows an example in which each scenario is uniquely defined by a text key and this is used to select the appropriate scenario data. The MATCH function finds the position of the scenario within a data set, and the INDEX function is used to look up this data (see Figure 25.17). (As mentioned in Chapter 17, the SWITCH function could also be considered here.)

Example: Creating and Finding Matching Text Fields or Keys

When manipulating data sets, including combining them or using one within the other, one may need to employ several techniques simultaneously. For example, Text functions may be used to create unique keys (as in Chapter 24) that can be matched together.

The file Ch25.18.Text.CurrencyMatch.1.xlsx shows an example (see Figure 25.18). For the first data set, Text functions are used to manipulate the underlying exchange rate data (in the range B4:C15) to create a unique key for each item (G4:G15), and a similar process is used within the main database. Finally, the position of the matching

	A	B	C	D	E	F	G	H	I	J	K
1											
2		Scenarios	KEY			2018	2019	2020	2021	2022	
3		Low									
4		Revenue	LowRevenue			387	407	439	483	520	
5		Cost	LowCost			354	364	430	480	428	
6		Base									
7		Revenue	BaseRevenue			431	452	488	537	577	
8		Cost	BaseCost			395	367	488	476	563	
9		High									
10		Revenue	HighRevenue			474	497	537	591	635	
11		Cost	HighCost			385	482	505	511	527	
12											
13		Scenarios to Use	Position			2018	2019	2020	2021	2022	
14		BaseRevenue	5	=MATCH(B14,$C$3:$C$11,0)		431	452	488	537	577	=INDEX(J$3:J$11,$C14,1)
15		BaseCost	6	=MATCH(B15,$C$3:$C$11,0)		395	367	488	476	563	=INDEX(J$3:J$11,$C15,1)
16											

FIGURE 25.17 Using MATCH to Select Data from Non-contiguous Scenarios

	A	B	C	D	E	F	G	H	I
1									
2		EXCHANGE RATE TABLE							
3		Xrate/€	Orig Key	Search for Q	LEFT	RIGHT	Key to Match		
4		1.60	DollarQr_1	7	DollarQ	1	DollarQ_1		
5		1.58	DollarQs_2	7	DollarQ	2	DollarQ_2		
6		1.55	DollarQt_3	7	DollarQ	3	DollarQ_3		
7		1.62	DollarQ_4	7	DollarQ	4	DollarQ_4		
8		1.20	EuroQ_1	5	EuroQ	1	EuroQ_1		
9		1.16	EuroQ_2	5	EuroQ	2	EuroQ_2		
10		1.22	EuroQ_3	5	EuroQ	3	EuroQ_3		
11		1.25	EuroQ_4	5	EuroQ	4	EuroQ_4		
12		1.00	PoundQ_1	6	PoundQ	1	PoundQ_1		
13		1.00	PoundQ_2	6	PoundQ	2	PoundQ_2		
14		1.00	PoundQ_3	6	PoundQ	3	PoundQ_3		
15		1.00	PoundQ_4	6	PoundQ	4	PoundQ_4		
16									
17		MAIN ("LARGE") CUSTOMER DATABASE							
18		Location	Customer no.	Quarter	Amount (loca	Currency	Key to Match	Position of Matching Item	
19		Germany	C314	1	32,143	Euro	EuroQ_1	5	=MATCH(G19,$G$4:$G$15,0)
20		London	C159	3	17,203	Pound	PoundQ_3	11	=MATCH(G20,$G$4:$G$15,0)
21		France	C265	2	16,993	Euro	EuroQ_2	6	=MATCH(G21,$G$4:$G$15,0)
22		US	C358	2	78,888	Dollar	DollarQ_2	2	=MATCH(G22,$G$4:$G$15,0)
23		London	C979	3	43,957	Pound	PoundQ_3	11	=MATCH(G23,$G$4:$G$15,0)
24		US	C323	4	25,896	Dollar	DollarQ_4	4	=MATCH(G24,$G$4:$G$15,0)
25		London	C486	1	26,858	Pound	PoundQ_1	9	=MATCH(G25,$G$4:$G$15,0)
26		London	C729	2	63,652	Dollar	DollarQ_2	2	=MATCH(G26,$G$4:$G$15,0)
27		US	C266	3	29,188	Dollar	DollarQ_3	3	=MATCH(G27,$G$4:$G$15,0)
28		Germany	C357	4	47,153	Euro	EuroQ_4	8	=MATCH(G28,$G$4:$G$15,0)
29		France	C989	1	51,737	Euro	EuroQ_1	5	=MATCH(G29,$G$4:$G$15,0)
30		London	C323	2	36,332	Pound	PoundQ_2	10	=MATCH(G30,$G$4:$G$15,0)
31		Germany	C486	3	33,363	Euro	EuroQ_3	7	=MATCH(G31,$G$4:$G$15,0)
32		Germany	C729	1	17,635	Euro	EuroQ_1	5	=MATCH(G32,$G$4:$G$15,0)
33									

FIGURE 25.18 Using Text Functions and MATCH to Find Data in Currency Database

keys is identified. (The final logical step in the analysis, in which the applicable exchange rates are looked up, is covered in the following example.)

Example: Combining INDEX with MATCH

As mentioned above, since the MATCH function finds only the relative position of an item (i.e. it returns an indexation number); this generally needs to be used as an input to a further lookup process.

The file Ch25.19.Text.CurrencyMatch.2.xlsx shows the final step in the analysis for the previous example: the INDEX function is used to look up the applicable

	H	I	J	K	L	M	N	O
16								
17								
18	Position of Matching Item			Xrate/€			Amount (€)	
19	5	=MATCH(G19,$G$4:$G$15,0)		1.20	=INDEX($B$4:$B$15,H19,1)		26786	=E19/K19
20	11	=MATCH(G20,$G$4:$G$15,0)		1.00	=INDEX($B$4:$B$15,H20,1)		17203	=E20/K20
21	6	=MATCH(G21,$G$4:$G$15,0)		1.16	=INDEX($B$4:$B$15,H21,1)		14649	=E21/K21
22	2	=MATCH(G22,$G$4:$G$15,0)		1.58	=INDEX($B$4:$B$15,H22,1)		49929	=E22/K22
23	11	=MATCH(G23,$G$4:$G$15,0)		1.00	=INDEX($B$4:$B$15,H23,1)		43957	=E23/K23
24	4	=MATCH(G24,$G$4:$G$15,0)		1.62	=INDEX($B$4:$B$15,H24,1)		15987	=E24/K24
25	9	=MATCH(G25,$G$4:$G$15,0)		1.00	=INDEX($B$4:$B$15,H25,1)		26856	=E25/K25
26	2	=MATCH(G26,$G$4:$G$15,0)		1.58	=INDEX($B$4:$B$15,H26,1)		40286	=E26/K26
27	3	=MATCH(G27,$G$4:$G$15,0)		1.55	=INDEX($B$4:$B$15,H27,1)		18831	=E27/K27
28	8	=MATCH(G28,$G$4:$G$15,0)		1.25	=INDEX($B$4:$B$15,H28,1)		37723	=E28/K28
29	5	=MATCH(G29,$G$4:$G$15,0)		1.20	=INDEX($B$4:$B$15,H29,1)		43114	=E29/K29
30	10	=MATCH(G30,$G$4:$G$15,0)		1.00	=INDEX($B$4:$B$15,H30,1)		36332	=E30/K30
31	7	=MATCH(G31,$G$4:$G$15,0)		1.22	=INDEX($B$4:$B$15,H31,1)		27347	=E31/K31
32	5	=MATCH(G32,$G$4:$G$15,0)		1.20	=INDEX($B$4:$B$15,H32,1)		14696	=E32/K32
33							413696	=SUM(N19:N32)
34								

FIGURE 25.19 Combining INDEX and MATCH Processes

exchange rates and a calculation performed to find out the total figure in Pounds Sterling (£) (see Figure 25.19).

Example: Comparing INDEX-MATCH with V- and HLOOKUP

The following examples aim to highlight that the use of INDEX-MATCH combination should almost always be preferred to the use of V- or HLOOKUP functions. This is due to reasons of flexibility, robustness, computational efficiency and superior ease of model auditing.

The file Ch25.20.VLOOKUPINDEXMATCH.1.xlsx shows an example of the use of the VLOOKUP function to provide the appropriate exchange rate data (Figure 25.20). The calculations are correct and seem to offer a sufficient solution to the situation at hand.

	A	B	C	D	E	F	G	H	I
1									
2		Currency	Xrate/£						
3		Dollar	1.60						
4		Euro	1.20						
5		Pound	1.00						
6									
7		Location	Customer no.	Date	Amount (local currency)	Currency		Xrate/£	
8		Germany	C314	Jan	32,143	Euro		1.20	=VLOOKUP(F8,$B$3:$C$5,2)
9		London	C159	Jan	17,203	Pound		1.00	=VLOOKUP(F9,$B$3:$C$5,2)
10		France	C265	Feb	16,993	Euro		1.20	=VLOOKUP(F10,$B$3:$C$5,2)
11		US	C358	Feb	78,888	Dollar		1.60	=VLOOKUP(F11,$B$3:$C$5,2)
12		London	C979	Feb	43,957	Pound		1.00	=VLOOKUP(F12,$B$3:$C$5,2)
13		US	C323	Mar	25,898	Dollar		1.60	=VLOOKUP(F13,$B$3:$C$5,2)
14		London	C486	Mar	26,856	Pound		1.00	=VLOOKUP(F14,$B$3:$C$5,2)
15		London	C729	Mar	63,652	Dollar		1.60	=VLOOKUP(F15,$B$3:$C$5,2)
16		US	C266	April	29,188	Dollar		1.60	=VLOOKUP(F16,$B$3:$C$5,2)
17		Germany	C357	April	47,153	Euro		1.20	=VLOOKUP(F17,$B$3:$C$5,2)
18		France	C989	May	51,737	Euro		1.20	=VLOOKUP(F18,$B$3:$C$5,2)
19		London	C323	June	36,332	Pound		1.00	=VLOOKUP(F19,$B$3:$C$5,2)
20		Germany	C486	July	33,363	Euro		1.20	=VLOOKUP(F20,$B$3:$C$5,2)
21		Germany	C729	August	17,635	Euro		1.20	=VLOOKUP(F21,$B$3:$C$5,2)

FIGURE 25.20 Using VLOOKUP to Find the Relevant Exchange Rate

The file Ch25.21.VLOOKUPINDEXMATCH.2.xlsx highlights that the VLOOKUP function requires values to be matched are placed on the left of the data set. This limits the flexibility in terms of repositioning data sets (copying an initial data set multiple times is an inefficient and error-prone alternative) (see Figure 25.21).

The file Ch25.22.VLOOKUPINDEXMATCH.3.xlsx highlights that the VLOOKUP function initially uses a hard-coded column number (i.e. Column 2 in this example) (see Figure 25.22). This may lead to the modeller (or another user) making inadvertent errors by adding new columns without adapting the formulae to adjust the column reference. Especially in larger databases and in those which may need to be updated at some point, such errors are frequent and often unobserved; the likelihood of being aware of errors is reduced even further if the data items have

	A	B	C	D	E	F	G	H	I
1									
2			Xrate/£	Currency					
3			1.60	Dollar					
4			1.20	Euro					
5			1.00	Pound					
6									
7		Location	Customer no.	Date	Amount (local currency)	Currency		Xrate/£	
8		Germany	C314	Jan	32,143	Euro		#N/A	=VLOOKUP(F8,$C$3:$D$5,2)
9		London	C159	Jan	17,203	Pound		#N/A	=VLOOKUP(F9,$C$3:$D$5,2)
10		France	C265	Feb	16,993	Euro		#N/A	=VLOOKUP(F10,$C$3:$D$5,2)
11		US	C358	Feb	78,888	Dollar		#N/A	=VLOOKUP(F11,$C$3:$D$5,2)
12		London	C979	Feb	43,957	Pound		#N/A	=VLOOKUP(F12,$C$3:$D$5,2)
13		US	C323	Mar	25,898	Dollar		#N/A	=VLOOKUP(F13,$C$3:$D$5,2)
14		London	C486	Mar	26,856	Pound		#N/A	=VLOOKUP(F14,$C$3:$D$5,2)
15		London	C729	Mar	63,652	Dollar		#N/A	=VLOOKUP(F15,$C$3:$D$5,2)
16		US	C266	April	29,188	Dollar		#N/A	=VLOOKUP(F16,$C$3:$D$5,2)
17		Germany	C357	April	47,153	Euro		#N/A	=VLOOKUP(F17,$C$3:$D$5,2)
18		France	C989	May	51,737	Euro		#N/A	=VLOOKUP(F18,$C$3:$D$5,2)
19		London	C323	June	36,332	Pound		#N/A	=VLOOKUP(F19,$C$3:$D$5,2)
20		Germany	C486	July	33,363	Euro		#N/A	=VLOOKUP(F20,$C$3:$D$5,2)
21		Germany	C729	August	17,635	Euro		#N/A	=VLOOKUP(F21,$C$3:$D$5,2)

FIGURE 25.21 Limitations to Data Structures When Using VLOOKUP

	A	B	C	D	E	F	G	H	I	J
1										
2		Currency		Xrate/£						
3		Dollar		1.60						
4		Euro		1.20						
5		Pound		1.00						
6										
7		Location		Customer no.	Date	Amount (local currency)	Currency		Xrate/£	
8		Germany		C314	Jan	32,143	Euro		0.00	=VLOOKUP(G8,$B$3:$D$5,2)
9		London		C159	Jan	17,203	Pound		0.00	=VLOOKUP(G9,$B$3:$D$5,2)
10		France		C265	Feb	16,993	Euro		0.00	=VLOOKUP(G10,$B$3:$D$5,2)
11		US		C358	Feb	78,888	Dollar		0.00	=VLOOKUP(G11,$B$3:$D$5,2)
12		London		C979	Feb	43,957	Pound		0.00	=VLOOKUP(G12,$B$3:$D$5,2)
13		US		C323	Mar	25,898	Dollar		0.00	=VLOOKUP(G13,$B$3:$D$5,2)
14		London		C486	Mar	26,856	Pound		0.00	=VLOOKUP(G14,$B$3:$D$5,2)
15		London		C729	Mar	63,652	Dollar		0.00	=VLOOKUP(G15,$B$3:$D$5,2)
16		US		C266	April	29,188	Dollar		0.00	=VLOOKUP(G16,$B$3:$D$5,2)
17		Germany		C357	April	47,153	Euro		0.00	=VLOOKUP(G17,$B$3:$D$5,2)
18		France		C989	May	51,737	Euro		0.00	=VLOOKUP(G18,$B$3:$D$5,2)
19		London		C323	June	36,332	Pound		0.00	=VLOOKUP(G19,$B$3:$D$5,2)
20		Germany		C486	July	33,363	Euro		0.00	=VLOOKUP(G20,$B$3:$D$5,2)
21		Germany		C729	August	17,635	Euro		0.00	=VLOOKUP(G21,$B$3:$D$5,2)
22										

FIGURE 25.22 Error-prone Nature of Hard-coded Column Numbers When Using VLOOKUP

similar values (such as columns of salary data in different periods), as errors will not be easily identifiable through the values shown being clearly wrong.

The file Ch25.23.VLOOKUPINDEXMATCH.4.xlsx shows how the above limitation of adding columns in a robust fashion can be overcome by using the MATCH function to determine the column number, so that it is no longer hard-coded (see Figure 25.23). Note that doing so means that a VLOOKUP-MATCH combination has been used to overcome one limitation, another still remains; namely, that the data set needs to be structured with the main lookup column on the left.

The file Ch25.24.VLOOKUPINDEXMATCH.5.xslx shows how the INDEX-MATCH combination can be used to create a situation in which the column data can be in any order and new columns may also be inserted without causing errors (see Figure 25.24). Note that the matching and lookup processes can be done separately (Columns G and H) or as a single embedded function (Column K).

Currency	Xrate/£
Dollar	1.60
Euro	1.20
Pound	1.00

3 =MATCH(D2,B2:D2,0)

Location	Customer no.	Date	Amount (local currency)	Currency	Xrate/£	
Germany	C314	Jan	32,143	Euro	1.20	=VLOOKUP(G8,$B$3:$D$5,I$2)
London	C159	Jan	17,203	Pound	1.00	=VLOOKUP(G9,$B$3:$D$5,I$2)
France	C265	Feb	16,993	Euro	1.20	=VLOOKUP(G10,$B$3:$D$5,I$2)
US	C358	Feb	78,888	Dollar	1.60	=VLOOKUP(G11,$B$3:$D$5,I$2)
London	C979	Feb	43,957	Pound	1.00	=VLOOKUP(G12,$B$3:$D$5,I$2)
US	C323	Mar	25,898	Dollar	1.60	=VLOOKUP(G13,$B$3:$D$5,I$2)
London	C486	Mar	26,856	Pound	1.00	=VLOOKUP(G14,$B$3:$D$5,I$2)
London	C729	Mar	63,652	Dollar	1.60	=VLOOKUP(G15,$B$3:$D$5,I$2)
US	C266	April	29,188	Dollar	1.60	=VLOOKUP(G16,$B$3:$D$5,I$2)
Germany	C357	April	47,153	Euro	1.20	=VLOOKUP(G17,$B$3:$D$5,I$2)
France	C989	May	51,737	Euro	1.20	=VLOOKUP(G18,$B$3:$D$5,I$2)
London	C323	June	36,332	Pound	1.00	=VLOOKUP(G19,$B$3:$D$5,I$2)
Germany	C486	July	33,363	Euro	1.20	=VLOOKUP(G20,$B$3:$D$5,I$2)
Germany	C729	August	17,635	Euro	1.20	=VLOOKUP(G21,$B$3:$D$5,I$2)

FIGURE 25.23 Using MATCH to Create a Flexible Column Number Within VLOOKUP

Xrate/£	Currency
1.60	Dollar
1.20	Euro
1.00	Pound

Location	Customer no.	Date	Amount (local currency)	Currency	Posn	Xrate/£	Xrate/£	
Germany	C314	Jan	32,143	Euro	2	1.20	1.20	=INDEX($B$3:$B$5,MATCH(F8,$D$3:$D$5,0),1)
London	C159	Jan	17,203	Pound	3	1.00	1.00	=INDEX($B$3:$B$5,MATCH(F9,$D$3:$D$5,0),1)
France	C265	Feb	16,993	Euro	2	1.20	1.20	=INDEX($B$3:$B$5,MATCH(F10,$D$3:$D$5,0),1)
US	C358	Feb	78,888	Dollar	1	1.60	1.60	=INDEX($B$3:$B$5,MATCH(F11,$D$3:$D$5,0),1)
London	C979	Feb	43,957	Pound	3	1.00	1.00	=INDEX($B$3:$B$5,MATCH(F12,$D$3:$D$5,0),1)
US	C323	Mar	25,898	Dollar	1	1.60	1.60	=INDEX($B$3:$B$5,MATCH(F13,$D$3:$D$5,0),1)
London	C486	Mar	26,856	Pound	3	1.00	1.00	=INDEX($B$3:$B$5,MATCH(F14,$D$3:$D$5,0),1)
London	C729	Mar	63,652	Dollar	1	1.60	1.60	=INDEX($B$3:$B$5,MATCH(F15,$D$3:$D$5,0),1)
US	C266	April	29,188	Dollar	1	1.60	1.60	=INDEX($B$3:$B$5,MATCH(F16,$D$3:$D$5,0),1)
Germany	C357	April	47,153	Euro	2	1.20	1.20	=INDEX($B$3:$B$5,MATCH(F17,$D$3:$D$5,0),1)
France	C989	May	51,737	Euro	2	1.20	1.20	=INDEX($B$3:$B$5,MATCH(F18,$D$3:$D$5,0),1)
London	C323	June	36,332	Pound	3	1.00	1.00	=INDEX($B$3:$B$5,MATCH(F19,$D$3:$D$5,0),1)
Germany	C486	July	33,363	Euro	2	1.20	1.20	=INDEX($B$3:$B$5,MATCH(F20,$D$3:$D$5,0),1)
Germany	C729	August	17,635	Euro	2	1.20	1.20	=INDEX($B$3:$B$5,MATCH(F21,$D$3:$D$5,0),1)

FIGURE 25.24 Using INDEX-MATCH in Place of VLOOKUP

In addition to the limitations on the structure of the data set and the error-prone nature of inserting columns, VLOOKUP (and similarly HLOOKUP processes) has other disadvantages:

- Where a key (on the left side of a database) is used to find the values in multiple columns, the implied matching of this key is performed each time, so that computational efficiency is reduced. By performing a single matching step (using MATCH) that is referred to by multiple separate lookup processes, the overall process is more computationally efficient.
- Models containing these functions are often difficult to audit. Partly, this is because the precedents range for any cell containing a VLOOKUP function is the entire (two-dimensional) lookup range, which is often very large. Thus, the backward tracing of potential errors often becomes extremely difficult, and the (digital) file size of the model also very large.
- The data set is hard to restructure, because it is required to be a two-dimensional contiguous range. When developing models, it is usually important to have the flexibility to move data around (for example to minimise audit path lengths by placing data reasonably close to the formulae in which it is used). Moreover, many models have one axis which is logically dominant (such as a time axis in traditional models, or the list of unique identifiers in database models); in such cases a one-dimensional approach to look up processes is often preferable, more flexible and more robust.

The file Ch25.25.VLOOKUPINDEXMATCH.6.xlsx provides an example where each VLOOKUP function is implicitly matching the scenario key (rather than a single match being conducted for each key, followed by the process to look up the values, as shown earlier); as noted above, the looking up of the same scenario multiple times will reduce computational efficiency (recalculation speed) (see Figure 25.25).

Figure 25.26 and 25.27 show simple examples of the dependents- and precedents-tracing processes, showing that every cell in the lookup range is a precedent to every VLOOKUP function that refers to that range.

The file Ch25.26.VLOOKUPINDEXMATCH.7.xlsx shows an implementation of the alternative, which first creates a cell containing the MATCH function to find the relevant row in which data should be taken from (Cell A8), and the INDEX function is driven from individual columns of data. The dependency structure is much clearer and more computationally efficient (see Figure 25.28).

	A	B	C	D	E	F	G	H	I
1									
2		Revenue Scenari	2018	2019	2020	2021	2022		
3		A	387	407	439	483	520		
4		B	431	452	488	537	577		
5		C	474	497	537	591	635		
6									
7		Scenarios to Use	2018	2019	2020	2021	2022		
8		B	431	452	488	537	577	=VLOOKUP($B8,$B$3:$G$5,G$7-$C$7+2)	
9									

FIGURE 25.25 Computation Inefficiency of VLOOKUP When Multiple Items are Looked Up Requiring the Same Underlying Key

	A	B	C	D	E	F	G	H
1								
2		Revenue Scenari	2018	2019	2020	2021	2022	
3		A	387	407	439	483	520	
4		B	431	452	488	537	577	
5		C	474	497	537	591	635	
6								
7		Scenarios to Use	2018	2019	2020	2021	2022	
8		B	431	452	488	537	577	=VLOOKUP($B8,$B$3:$G$5,G$7-$C$7+2)

FIGURE 25.26 Dependency Tracing when VLOOKUP Functions are Used

	A	B	C	D	E	F	G	H
1								
2		Revenue Scenari	2018	2019	2020	2021	2022	
3		A	387	407	439	483	520	
4		B	431	452	488	537	577	
5		C	474	497	537	591	635	
6								
7		Scenarios to Use	2018	2019	2020	2021	2022	
8		B	431	452	488	537	577	=VLOOKUP($B8,$B$3:$G$5,G$7-$C$7+2)
9								

FIGURE 25.27 Precedents Tracing when VLOOKUP Functions are Used

	A	B	C	D	E	F	G	H
1								
2		Revenue Scenari	2018	2019	2020	2021	2022	
3		A	387	407	439	483	520	
4		B	431	452	488	537	577	
5		C	474	497	537	591	635	
6								
7		Scenarios to Use	2018	2019	2020	2021	2022	
8	2	B	431	452	488	537	577	=INDEX(G$3:G$4,$A8,1)
9								

FIGURE 25.28 Greater Transparency and Computational Efficiency of an INDEX/MATCH Approach

Note that although a MATCH function could be embedded within each INDEX function, where the same matching item (i.e. scenario B corresponding to column 2) is used to drive multiple lookup processes (i.e. the functions in Cell C8:G8), it is more computationally efficient to have the MATCH function explicitly in a single cell, so that only a single matching process for each item would happen.

Although the above examples have been shown with reference to the VLOOKUP function, analogous comments apply to HLOOKUP, and so we discuss this with only one specific example.

The file Ch25.27.HLOOKUPINDEXMATCH.8.xlsx shows an example of the error-prone nature of HLOOKUP if new rows are added. Figure 25.29 shows an initial set of formulae which correctly pick out the value of the cost field, and Figure 25.30

	A	B	C	D	E	F	G	H
1								
2			2018	2019	2020	2021	2022	
3		Costs	800	840	882	926	972	
4		Capex	100	105	110	116	122	
5								
6			2018	2019	2020	2021	2022	
7		Costs	800	840	882	926	972	=HLOOKUP(G$6,$B$2:$G$4,2)
8								

FIGURE 25.29 Use of HLOOKUP to Select Values from a Table

9								
10								
11			2018	2019	2020	2021	2022	
12		Revenues	1000	1050	1103	1158	1216	
13		Costs	800	840	882	926	972	
14		Capex	100	105	110	116	122	
15								
16			2018	2019	2020	2021	2022	
17		Costs	1000	1050	1103	1158	1216	=HLOOKUP(G$16,$B$11:$G$14,2)
18								

FIGURE 25.30 Potential Errors when a Row is Inserted Within the HLOOKUP Range

shows how the use of a hard-coded row number would lead to an error if a row were inserted without also manually adjusting the row number (i.e. resulting in Row 17 showing revenue data instead of the cost information).

Example: Comparing INDEX-MATCH with LOOKUP

The LOOKUP function exists in two forms: the vector form and the array form. Although the Excel Help menu recommends using VLOOKUP or HLOOKUP in place of the array form, the author generally recommends using the INDEX-MATCH approach in place of these! In fact, the vector form is similar to the INDEX-MATCH approach: the function looks for a specified value within a one-dimensional range (of values that must be in ascending order) and returns the value from the corresponding position in another one-dimensional range (if the specified value cannot be found in the first lookup range, matches the largest value that is less than or equal to the specified value; the function returns #N/A where the specified value is smaller than all values in the lookup vector).

The file Ch25.28.LOOKUPINDEXMATCH.xlsx contains an example similar to those above, in which the currency name is first looked up in one field (E3:E5) which provides the position of the relevant currency amount in the other field (C3:C5) (see Figure 25.31).

In summary, the best approach overall would seem to be to use the INDEX-MATCH approach in essentially all cases where VLOOKUP (or HLOOKUP) may otherwise be considered, and even in cases where the vector form of the LOOKUP

	A	B	C	D	E	F	G	H	I
1									
2			Xrate/£		Currency				
3			1.60		Dollar				
4			1.20		Euro				
5			1.00		Pound				
6									
7		Location	Customer no.	Date	Amount (local currency)	Currency		Xrate/£	
8		Germany	C314	Jan	32,143	Euro		1.20	=LOOKUP(F8,$E$3:$E$5,$C$3:$C$5)
9		London	C159	Jan	17,203	Pound		1.00	=LOOKUP(F9,$E$3:$E$5,$C$3:$C$5)
10		France	C265	Feb	16,993	Euro		1.20	=LOOKUP(F10,$E$3:$E$5,$C$3:$C$5)
11		US	C358	Feb	78,888	Dollar		=LOOKUP(F	=LOOKUP(F11,$E$3:$E$5,$C$3:$C$5)
12		London	C979	Feb	43,957	Pound		1.00	=LOOKUP(F12,$E$3:$E$5,$C$3:$C$5)
13		US	C323	Mar	25,898	Dollar		1.60	=LOOKUP(F13,$E$3:$E$5,$C$3:$C$5)
14		London	C486	Mar	26,856	Pound		1.00	=LOOKUP(F14,$E$3:$E$5,$C$3:$C$5)
15		London	C729	Mar	63,652	Dollar		1.60	=LOOKUP(F15,$E$3:$E$5,$C$3:$C$5)
16		US	C266	April	29,188	Dollar		1.60	=LOOKUP(F16,$E$3:$E$5,$C$3:$C$5)
17		Germany	C357	April	47,153	Euro		1.20	=LOOKUP(F17,$E$3:$E$5,$C$3:$C$5)
18		France	C989	May	51,737	Euro		1.20	=LOOKUP(F18,$E$3:$E$5,$C$3:$C$5)
19		London	C323	June	36,332	Pound		1.00	=LOOKUP(F19,$E$3:$E$5,$C$3:$C$5)
20		Germany	C486	July	33,363	Euro		1.20	=LOOKUP(F20,$E$3:$E$5,$C$3:$C$5)
21		Germany	C729	August	17,635	Euro		1.20	=LOOKUP(F21,$E$3:$E$5,$C$3:$C$5)

FIGURE 25.31 Using the Vector Form of the LOOKUP Function as an Alternative to INDEX-MATCH

function could be used. The VLOOKUP (and HLOOKUP) functions create a lack of flexibility, are error-prone, are difficult to audit and are often computationally inefficient. Of course, in simple models (e.g. those containing two columns of data with the lookup values placed in the left column) the use of VLOOKUP would be slightly quicker to implement than the INDEX-MATCH approach. However, it so often arises that initial models are subsequently developed or added to, so that an inappropriate function choice quickly becomes embedded in a larger model and is hard to rectify without significant rework.

The INDEX-MATCH approach is also slightly preferable to the vector form of the LOOKUP function: first, the explicit separation of a single matching step is more efficient where the results are to be used in several subsequent lookup processes (rather than implicitly conducting an embedded match within each). Second, it provides a consistent (and parsimonious) approach to modelling. Third, the LOOKUP function seems to be treated by Microsoft as a legacy function.

Example: Finding the Closest Matching Value Using Array and Other Function Combinations

The lookup functions may be used to find the closest value within a data set that matches an inputted value, by combining the use of several Excel functions. In addition, an approach using array formulae may be considered.

The file Ch25.29.ClosestinList.xlsx shows an example (see Figure 25.32). The requirement is for the user to type a value into Cell C20, with the function sequence determining the value in the list (cells C3:C8) that is closest to this. The calculations on the right-hand side (Columns E rightwards) are the explicit calculation steps, in which the absolute difference between each data point and the input value is calculated (Column F) and the minimum of these is then found (cell I2), the position of this within the data set is found (cell I3) and the value looked up (cell I4). The equivalent

	A	B	C	D	E	F	G	H	I	J
1										
2			Data		Diff	ABS		Min	24	=MIN(F3:F18)
3			472		319	319		Position	9	=MATCH(I2,F3:F18,0)
4			359		206	206		Value	177	=INDEX(C3:C18,I3,1)
5			117		-36	36				
6			715		562	562				
7			757		604	604				
8			364		211	211				
9			801		648	648				
10			691		538	538				
11			177		24	24				
12			865		712	712				
13			953		800	800				
14			806		653	653				
15			757		604	604				
16			637		484	484				
17			792		639	639				
18			744		591	591				
19										
20		Value	153							
21		Closest in list	177	{=INDEX(C3:C18,MATCH(MIN(ABS(C3:C18-C$20)),ABS(C3:C18-C$20),0),1)}						
22		Closest in list	177	{=OFFSET(C2,MATCH(MIN(ABS(C3:C18-C$20)),ABS(C3:C18-C$20),0),0)}						

FIGURE 25.32 Finding Closest Matching Values Using Lookup and Array Formula

calculations can be performed directly as an array formula (without having to create Columns E rightwards), as shown in Cell C21. (Cell C22 shows a variation for reference, in which OFFSET is used to perform the final lookup stage.)

PRACTICAL APPLICATIONS: MORE ON THE OFFSET FUNCTION AND DYNAMIC RANGES

The OFFSET function can be particularly useful to create formulae that refer to ranges which are flexible, in the sense that either the size or location adjusts based on inputs or calculations. In the following examples, we show three main variations:

- Where the referenced range is a cell and the returned reference is a cell.
- Where the referenced range is a range and the returned reference is a range (without using the optional height and width arguments of the function).
- Where the referenced range is a cell and the returned reference is a range (by using the optional height and width arguments of the function).

Note that the INDEX function also exists in a reference form (rather than the array form used earlier in the chapter), and as such can often be used to perform operations similar to some of those shown here. However, we find that the use of such a form is typically less flexible and less transparent than other formulations, so it is not discussed further in this text.

Example: Flexible Ranges Using OFFSET (I)

A simple example of the use of OFFSET to create dynamic ranges is to sum a range from one point to another. For example, one may wish to sum the values along a row between two cells whose location may vary (e.g. where the starting and ending cells are either model inputs or are determined from calculations.)

The file Ch25.30.DynamicRange.SumColumn.1.xlsx shows an example in which the user defines which part of a series of cash flows are to be included in the summation,

	A	B	C	D	E	F	G	H	I	J	K	L	M
1													
2				1	2	3	4	5	6	7	8	9	10
3		Cash Flow/Model Results		-100	-50	-5	542	583	538	541	537	598	581
4													
5		Sum	3339	=SUM(OFFSET(D3,0,C6-1,1,C7-C6+1))									
6		Start Period	4										
7		Finish Period	9										

FIGURE 25.33 Using OFFSET to Sum Between User-defined Cells

by providing the starting and end period as inputs (see Figure 25.33). The formula in Cell C7 is:

$$= \text{SUM}\,(\text{OFFSET}\,(\text{D3}, 0, \text{C6} - 1, 1, \text{C7} - \text{C6} + 1))$$

In this formula, the last two arguments of the OFFSET function (which are optional function arguments) are used to create a range of height one and width six, starting from the fourth cell in the range D3:M3 (i.e. based on the user-defined inputs in cells C6 and C7).

The file Ch25.31.DynamicRange.SumColumn.2.xlsx shows an extension of this in which the starting point for the summation is determined from the calculations in the model, specifically to sum the cash flows in the six-year range starting from the point at which the first positive cash flow is detected (calculated by the array function in Cell C6). Thus, in a real-life model in which the cash flows in Row 3 are determined through calculations based on other inputs, the starting point for the summation would move dynamically as input values were changed (see Figure 25.34). Note that similar calculations could be done to sum the range backwards from a starting point; this might be required in tax calculations where only a certain number of prior years of tax losses can be carried forward.

Example: Flexible Ranges Using OFFSET (II)

Another simple example of creating flexible range using OFFSET is a formula which sums the items in the rows above it, in such a way that if a row is introduced, the summation would still be correct.

The file Ch25.32.DynamicRange.SumRowsAbove.xlsx shows an example (see Figure 25.35). Note that this example is of a legacy nature in Excel. In older versions, the introduction of a new row between the last item and the sum formula (i.e. between the Row 10 and 11 as shown) would have resulted in a SUM formula (shown initially

	A	B	C	D	E	F	G	H	I	J	K	L	M	N
1														
2				1	2	3	4	5	6	7	8	9	10	
3		Cash Flow/Model Results		-100	-50	-5	542	583	538	541	537	598	581	
4														
5		Sum	3339	=SUM(OFFSET(D3,0,C6-1,1,C7-C6+1))										
6		Start Period	4	{=MATCH(1,IF(D3:M3>0,1,0),0)}										
7		Finish Period	9	=C6+5										

FIGURE 25.34 Using OFFSET to Sum Between Calculated Cells

	A	B	C	D	E	F	G	H	I
1									
2			Standard			Using OFFSET			
3		Item 1	10			10			
4		Item 2	10			10			
5		Item 3	10			10			
6		Item 4	10			10			
7		Item 5	10			10			
8		Item 6	10			10			
9		Item 7	10			10			
10		Item 8	10			10			
11		**Total**	**80**	=SUM(C3:C10)		**80**	=SUM(F3:OFFSET(F11,-1,0))		

FIGURE 25.35 Using OFFSET to Sum Rows Above

in Cell C11, but which would then be in Cell C12) that would not include this new row. On the other hand, the formula in F11 automatically sums the items until the row immediately above the formula, and so will adapt automatically. Note that recent versions of Excel will automatically adjust the summation formula (C11) by extending its range when a row is inserted and a value entered.

Example: Flexible Ranges Using OFFSET (III)

Whereas the above examples using OFFSET focused on changing the size of a referenced range, other uses relate to changing the data set that is being referred to. One application is in the calculation of correlation matrices in which there are several variables, or for which the data of an additional variable may be added at some future point. When using reference formulae, such as CORREL(Range1, Range2), where Range1 and Range2 are direct input ranges, the formula created in an initial cell cannot be copied to the rest of the correlation matrix (since it is not possible to create a single formula with the correct $ structure (for absolute cell referencing) that can be copied in both the row and column directions). On the other hand, the OFFSET function can be used to create a single formula in which the ranges adapt automatically, and can therefore be copied to the full range of the matrix. Except for very small matrices (such as 2x2 or 3x3) this saves time and ensures that subsequent additions to the data set can also be rapidly incorporated.

The file Ch25.33.DynamicRange.Correl.xlsx shows an example (see Figure 25.36). Note that the formulae using the OFFSET function themselves create ranges (and not values). Therefore, they must be embedded within another function (and cannot be placed explicitly in an Excel cell). Thus, the formula in Cell F9 is:

= CORREL (OFFSET ($C$17 : $C$77,0,F$8 – 1), OFFSET ($C$17 : $C$77,0,$B9 – 1))

Example: Flexible Ranges Using OFFSET (IV)

The file Ch25.34.DynamicRange.Languages.xlsx shows a final example of the use of the OFFSET function to translate Excel functions from one language to another.

	A	B	C	D	E	F	G	H	I	J
1										
2			1	2	3	4				
3		1	100%	24%	9%	60%	=CORREL(F17:F77,C17:C77)			
4		2	24%	100%	34%	69%				
5		3	9%	34%	100%	53%				
6		4	60%	69%	53%	100%				
7										
8			1	2	3	4				
9		1	100%	24%	9%	60%	=CORREL(OFFSET($C$17:$C$77,0,F$8-1),OFFSET($C$17:$C$77,0,$B9-1))			
10		2	24%	100%	34%	69%				
11		3	9%	34%	100%	53%				
12		4	60%	69%	53%	100%				
13										
14										
15		DATA	Daily returns							
16		Day	Asset 1	Asset 2	Asset 3	Asset 4				
17		1	1.7%	1.0%	-2.5%	-0.9%				
18		2	-2.1%	1.1%	1.1%	-0.5%				
19		3	0.1%	2.9%	-1.3%	1.1%				
20		4	0.0%	-1.7%	0.2%	-0.2%				
21		5	-1.0%	-0.7%	-1.8%	-2.1%				
22		6	1.1%	0.3%	0.9%	1.7%				
23		7	-1.3%	-3.6%	-1.9%	-4.4%				
24		8	0.0%	-1.1%	-1.3%	-1.3%				
25		9	1.4%	-1.7%	-0.4%	-1.2%				
26		10	-2.1%	-0.8%	0.3%	-1.7%				

FIGURE 25.36 Creation of a Correlation Matrix Using a Single Formula

	A	B	C	D	E	F	G
1							
2		Using VLOOKUP			Using MATCH, then INDEX		
3							
4		English	German		English	German	
5		COUNTA	ANZAHL2		COUNTA	ANZAHL2	
6			=VLOOKUP(B5,B9:C377,2)			=INDEX(E10:E377,MATCH(E5,F10:F377,0),1)	
7							
8							
9		English	German		German	English	
10		ABS	ABS		ABS	ABS	
11		ACCRINT	AUFGELZINS		AUFGELZINS	ACCRINT	
12		ACCRINTM	AUFGELZINSF		AUFGELZINSF	ACCRINTM	
13		ACOS	ARCCOS		ARCCOS	ACOS	
14		ACOSH	ARCCOSHYP		ARCCOSHYP	ACOSH	
15		ADDRESS	ADRESSE		ADRESSE	ADDRESS	
16		AMORDEGI	AMORDEGRK		AMORDEGRK	AMORDEGRC	
17		AMORLINC	AMORLINEARK		AMORLINEAR	AMORLINC	
18		AND	UND		UND	AND	
19		AREAS	BEREICHE		BEREICHE	AREAS	
20		ASC	ASC		ASC	ASC	

FIGURE 25.37 Translation Between Two Fixed Languages

As a starting point for the discussion, Figure 25.37 shows the possible use of the VLOOKUP function if one is translating from a language that is always on the leftmost column of the data set. As discussed earlier, the INDEX-MATCH approach provides more flexibility irrespective of how the data is laid out. However, these examples are

H	I	J	K	L	M	N
Using MATCH then OFFSET						
Starting Language	Function	Ending Language	Translated Functio			
German	ANZAHL2	English	COUNTA			
2	60	1	=OFFSET(H9,I6,J6-1)			
=MATCH(H5,H9:L9,0)	=MATCH(I5,OFFSET(H:	=MATCH(J5,H9:L9,0)				
English	German	French	Spanish	Italian		
ABS	ABS	ABS	ABS	ASS		
ACCRINT	AUFGELZINS	INTERET.ACC	INT.ACUM	INT.MATURATO.PER		
ACCRINTM	AUFGELZINSF	INTERET.ACC.MAT	INT.ACUM.V	INT.MATURATO.SCAD		
ACOS	ARCCOS	ACOS	ACOS	ARCCOS		
ACOSH	ARCCOSHYP	ACOSH	ACOSH	ARCCOSH		
ADDRESS	ADRESSE	ADRESSE	DIRECCION	INDIRIZZO		

FIGURE 25.38 Translation Between Any Two Languages

based on the idea that the two languages are both fixed and that the translation is in a known order (i.e. English to German in these examples).

In Figure 25.38, we show an example from the same file, in which the translation can be done from any language to any other. In this case the MATCH function is used to determine the relative column position of each language within the data set (e.g. German is the second column). A key formula is that in cell I6 (showing the value 60), which is:

$$= \text{MATCH}\ (\text{I5}, \text{OFFSET}\ (\text{H10} : \text{H377}, 0, \text{H6} - 1), 0)$$

In this formula, the position of the word to be translated (here: Anzahl2) is looked up within a column range, which is itself determined as that which is offset from the first column of the data set in accordance with the language in which this word exists.

PRACTICAL APPLICATIONS: THE INDIRECT FUNCTION AND FLEXIBLE WORKBOOK OR DATA STRUCTURES

Example: Simple Examples of Using INDIRECT to Refer to Cells and Other Worksheets

Where a text field can be interpreted by Excel as the address of a cell or range of cells, the INDIRECT function can be used to find the values in that cell or range. For example, the statement:

= INDIRECT (“C2”)

would refer to Cell C2, as if one had used the direct cell reference formula:

= C2

	A	B	C	D	E	F
1						
2		Revenue	100			
3						
4					100	=C2
5					100	=INDIRECT("C2")

FIGURE 25.39 Basic Application of the INDIRECT Function

The file Ch25.35.INDIRECT.Basic.xlsx shows some examples of these. Figure 25.39 shows a simple example in which the value in Cell C2 is required in later parts of the model (Column E).

In Figure 25.40, we show an extended example, in which the cell reference C2 is either hard-coded (Cell E6) or is determined using various forms of the ADDRESS or CELL function.

In Figure 25.41, we show a further example, in which the data is taken from another worksheet, using both a direct reference to the cell in the other worksheet and an indirect one.

Finally, Figure 25.42 shows an example of the function being applied where the input text field identifies a range, rather than a single cell.

These approaches are used in practice in the next examples.

	E	F
6	C2	
7	100	=INDIRECT(E6)
8	$C$2	=ADDRESS(2,3)
9	100	=INDIRECT(E8)
10	$C$2	=ADDRESS(ROW(C2),COLUMN(C2))
11	100	=INDIRECT(E10)
12	$C$2	=CELL("address",C2)
13	100	=INDIRECT(E12)

FIGURE 25.40 Combining INDIRECT with ADDRESS or CELL Functions

	E	F
15	100	=Data!C2
16	100	=INDIRECT("Data"&"!"&"C2")

FIGURE 25.41 Direct and Indirect Referencing of Data on Another Worksheet

	C	E	F
18	100	200	=SUM(INDIRECT("C18:C19"))
19	100		

FIGURE 25.42 Use of a Text Argument as a Range Within the INDIRECT Function

Example: Incorporating Data from Multiple Worksheet Models and Flexible Scenario Modelling

One of the most powerful applications of the use of the INDIRECT function is to create "data-driven" models, in which there are several worksheets containing underlying data, and in which the user specifies the worksheet that data is to be taken from. The function is used to refer to the values on the specified worksheet. Such an approach allows new data worksheets to be added (or old ones deleted) with minimal effort or adjustment, as long as the data worksheets have a common structure.

An important specific application of this approach is in scenario modelling, where the number of scenarios is not known in advance. If the number is fixed (say, three or five), then separate data worksheets for each scenario could be built in the model, and the data selected using a direct cell reference approach (such as with the CHOOSE or INDEX function). Where the number of scenarios is not known, then this multi-sheet approach allows a scenario sheet to be added (or deleted).

The file Ch25.36.INDIRECT.DataSheetSelection.xlsx contains an example of this. Note that there are four underlying data worksheets in the original model, as well as a data selection worksheet (named Intermediate). The user defines which worksheet the data is to be taken from (by entering its name in Cell A1 of the Intermediate worksheet). The formulae in the Intermediate worksheet each find the reference of their own cell, before the INDIRECT function is used to find the value in a cell with the same reference but in the selected data worksheet (see Figure 25.43). (For illustrative purposes, both CELL and ADDRESS have been used.)

Note that:

- In general, in a real-life model, the Intermediate worksheet will itself be used to make a (direct) link to (or "feed") a model worksheet. The model worksheet does not then need to have the same structure as the Intermediate worksheet, nor as the data worksheets. The use of this intermediate step (i.e. bringing data indirectly from the data sheets to an Intermediate worksheet and from there to a model sheet) allows one to ensure a strict consistency between the cell structure of the Intermediate worksheet and those of the underlying data worksheets; this is required in order to have a simple and robust indirect referencing process.
- Although it is important generally that the data worksheets have a similar structure to each other, in some more complex practical cases, the data worksheets may also contain calculations which are specific to each one (and different from worksheet to worksheet). However, providing there is a summary area in each sheet which has a structure that is common to the other data worksheets, then the above approach can still be used.

	A	B	C	D
1	Jan			
2		Revenue	100	=INDIRECT($A$1&"!"&CELL("address",C2))
3		Cost	70	=INDIRECT(ADDRESS(ROW(C3),COLUMN(C3),,,$A$1))
4				

FIGURE 25.43 Using INDIRECT to Incorporate Data from a Specified Sheet

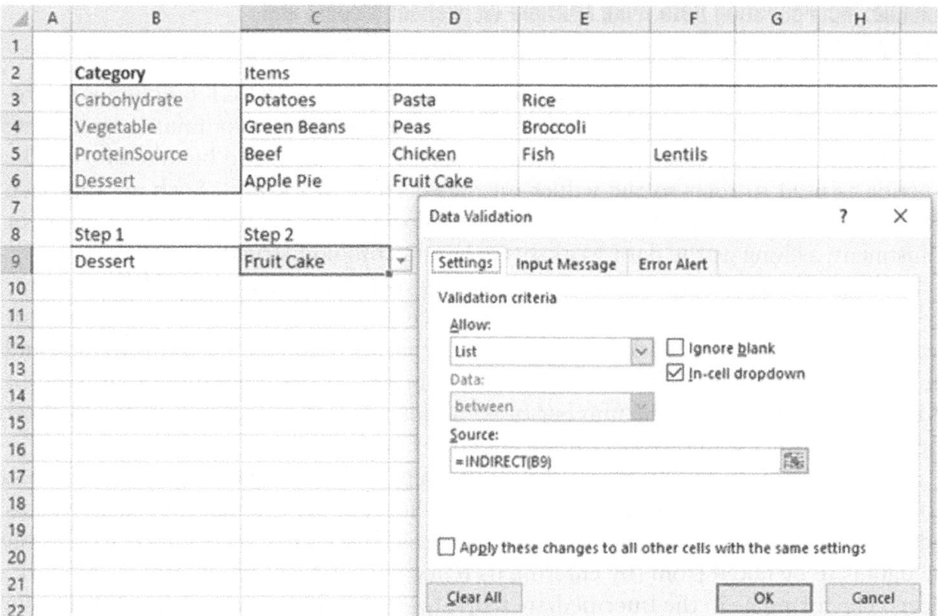

FIGURE 25.44 Sequential Drop-downs Using INDIRECT

These topics are closely related to the data-driven modelling approaches that were discussed in detail in Chapter 5 and Chapter 6.

Example: Other Uses of INDIRECT – Cascading Drop-down Lists

There are of course many possible uses of the INDIRECT function other than those above.

The file Ch25.37.INDIRECT.DataValidation.SequentialDropDowns.xlsx contains an example of context-sensitive drop-down lists (or cascading menus). The user first selects a main category of food, after which the INDIRECT function is used to create a new drop-down, which lists only the relevant items within the chosen category (see Figure 25.44). Note that this is achieved using the category names as Excel Named Ranges which each refer to the list of items within that category (e.g. ProteinSource is the range C5:F5), and using the INDIRECT function within a Data Validation list (for Cell C9), so that the list refers only to items in that category.

PRACTICAL EXAMPLES: USE OF HYPERLINKS TO NAVIGATE A MODEL, AND OTHER LINKS TO DATA SETS

In this section, we briefly mention some functions that can be used to provide links to data sets:

- HYPERLINK creates a short-cut or jump that can be used to insert a hyperlink in a document as a function. The link may be either a named range within the Excel

	A	B
1	Area of Model Where Data Starts	
2		
529		
530		
531	Data Start Area	=HYPERLINK(DataAreaStart,"Data Start Area")
532	Data Start Area	#N/A

FIGURE 25.45 Comparison and Use of HYPERLINK Function or Insert/Hyperlink Menu

file, or more generally a link to a document stored on a network server, an intranet or the Internet. The function has an optional parameter so that the displayed link may also be given a "friendly name". This is similar in overall concept to the use of the Insert/Hyperlink operation, except that this latter operation results in a direct link (rather than a function which returns a link).

- GETPIVOTDATA returns data stored in a PivotTable report.
- RTD retrieves real-time data from a program that supports COM automation.

Example: Model Navigation Using Named Ranges and Hyperlinks

The file Ch25.38.Hyperlinks.NamedRanges.xlsx shows an example of the use of both the HYPERLINK function and of a hyperlink inserted using the Insert/Hyperlink operation, in each case to reference a part of the model (Cell A1) defined with a named range (DataAreaStart) (see Figure 25.45).

CHAPTER 26

Filters, Database Functions and PivotTables

INTRODUCTION

This chapter discusses several Excel functions and functionalities that can assist in the analysis of data sets, including:

- Filter and Advanced Filters, which present or extract a filtered data set whose elements meet specific criteria.
- Database functions, which return calculations of the values in a database that meet certain criteria (without explicitly extracting the relevant data points), and whose results are live-linked to the data set. Although equivalent calculations can generally be conducted with regular Excel functions (such as SUMIFS or MAXIFS), the Database functions allow the identity of the criteria to be more rapidly changed. As functions, they generally require that errors or other specific values within the data set are corrected or explicitly dealt with through new criteria, to eliminate them from the calculation process.
- PivotTables, which create summary reports by category and cross-tabulations. Although not live-linked to the data set (so need refreshing if the data changes), PivotTables allow for very rapid reports to be created, for the identity of the criteria to be changed, and for rapid "drill-downs" or more detailed analysis of the data to be conducted very quickly. They also allow for errors or other specific values in the underlying data to be ignored (or filtered out) when applying the criteria or filters.

The chapter does not deal with the linking of Excel to external data sets, such as an Access database or SQL servers, or other options that are contained on the Data tab; such techniques are outside the scope of this text.

ISSUES COMMON TO WORKING WITH SETS OF DATA

Cleaning and Manipulating Source Data

In practice one will often have to manipulate or clean initial data before it can be used for analysis and reporting purposes. There are many techniques that may need to be applied in such cases, including:

- Splitting items into separate components using the Data/Text-to-Columns functionality or Excel functions (such as Text functions, see Chapter 23).
- Recombining or joining items based on finding (or creating) keys in one set that uniquely match with keys in another (see Chapter 23, Chapter 24 and Chapter 25 for many of the underlying techniques frequently required).
- Reversing or transposing data, using either Copy and Paste/PasteSpecial or functions (e.g. array or lookup functions, see Chapter 18 and Chapter 25).
- Identifying spelling mistakes or unclear identifiers. For example, it may be that a country name (such as Italy) is listed with multiple identifiers (such as Italy, Italie, Italia, Repubblica Italiana, or simply It). Similarly, there may be blanks or other unwanted items in the data set. Most of these can be identified by application of a Filter, followed by the inspection of the drop-down menu, which will list the unique values. Alternatively, the full column of data can be copied to a separate field and techniques such as Data/Remove Duplicates and/or a Data/Sort applied. One can also use Excel's Conditional Formatting options to highlight certain values, such as errors, duplicates, positive or negative items etc.
- Correcting spelling mistakes or unclear identifiers. This can be done either manually when there are only a few entries, or using operations such as Find/Replace.
- Deleting unwanted items. Some items, such as blank rows or entries that are not relevant for any analysis, may need to be deleted. This can be done manually if there are only a few items, or using Filters if there are more (see example below). In more extensive cases, the process can be largely automated using macros (see Chapter 32). An alternative to deleting unwanted items is to extract them; this may be achieved using the Advanced Filter functionality (see below).
- To identify the unique list of items within a category (such as country names and customers), or a unique list of combined items (such as unique country–customer combinations). Once again, the Data/Remove Duplicates functionality can be helpful in this respect.

Static or Dynamic Queries

In general when analysing data sets, one has two generic approaches to creating summary reports:

- Those which are fully live-linked to the data as well as to the criteria, i.e. as functions. The use of Database functions (or perhaps of regular Excel functions such as SUMIFS or MAXIFS) falls into this category, and is generally more appropriate where:
  - The structure of a data set is essentially fixed and well understood, with little exploratory ("drill-down") analysis required.

  - The data values will be regularly updated, so that a dynamic calculation will automatically update with little or no rework.
  - The identities of the criteria used are relatively stable and simple.
  - The data contain few errors or, where errors are present, they can be easily (ideally automatically) identified, eliminated or handled appropriately.
  - The reports form an interim step in a modelling process, with the results used to perform further calculations, and it is desired (from a modelling perspective) to have a full dynamic link from the underlying data through to the model results.
- Those which are numerical summaries of the data, but which are not fully live-linked. The use of Filters and PivotTables falls into this category. Such approaches are often appropriate where one intends to explore relationships between items, conduct drill-down analysis, change the criteria that are used to present a report, or otherwise alter the presentation of reports (e.g. change row into column presentations).

Creation of New Fields or Complex Filters?

When performing complex database queries (based on multiple underlying criteria or on unusual criteria), one has a choice as to whether to apply such criteria at the reporting level only (whilst leaving the data set unchanged), or whether to add a new calculated field to the data set, with such a field being used to identify whether the more complex set of criteria has been met (e.g. by producing a flag field that is 0 or 1, accordingly). This latter approach is often simpler and more transparent than creating a complex criteria combination at the query level. Of course, it increases the size of the data set, so that where many such combinations are required, it can be more efficient (or only possible) to build them within the reporting structure instead.

In some cases, a combined approach may be necessary. For example, if one of the criteria for a query were the length of the country name, or the third letter of the name, then it would likely be necessary to create a new field (e.g. using the LEN or MID functions) to create this field explicitly in the database.

Excel Databases and Tables

An Excel database is a contiguous range of cells in which each row contains data relating to properties of an item (e.g. date of birth, address, telephone number of people), with a set of column headers that identify the properties. The column structure of a database differentiates it from general Excel data sets, in which formulae may be applied to either rows or columns.

Note also that it is generally important for the field names (headers) to be in a single cell, and for a structured approach to be used to create them (especially for larger databases). The frequent approach in which categories and sub-categories are used to define headers using two or more rows is not generally the most appropriate approach. Rather, field headers will need to be in a single row. For example, instead of having one "header" row and a "sub-header" row beneath it, the headers and sub-header fields can be combined in a structured way. This is illustrated in Figure 26.1, in which the range B2:I3 contains the (inappropriate) two-row approach, and in Figure 26.2, where the range B3:I3 contains the adapted single-row approach.

	A	B	C	D	E	F	G	H	I
1									
2		Name		Compensation 2016			Compensation 2017		
3		First	Last	Salary	Bonus	Pension	Salary	Bonus	Pension
4		data	data	data	data	data	data	data	data
5		data	data	data	data	data	data	data	data
6		data	data	data	data	data	data	data	data
7		data	data	data	data	data	data	data	data
8		data	data	data	data	data	data	data	data
9		data	data	data	data	data	data	data	data
10		data	data	data	data	data	data	data	data
11		data	data	data	data	data	data	data	data
12		data	data	data	data	data	data	data	data
13		data	data	data	data	data	data	data	data

FIGURE 26.1 Multiple Row Field Identifiers – To Be Avoided When Using Databases and Tables

	A	B	C	D	E	F	G	H	I
1									
2									
3		Name.First	Name.Last	Comp.Salary.2016	Comp.Bonus.2016	Comp.Pension.2016	Comp.Salary.2017	Comp.Bonus.2017	Comp.Pension.2017
4		data	data	data	data	data	data	data	data
5		data	data	data	data	data	data	data	data
6		data	data	data	data	data	data	data	data
7		data	data	data	data	data	data	data	data
8		data	data	data	data	data	data	data	data
9		data	data	data	data	data	data	data	data
10		data	data	data	data	data	data	data	data
11		data	data	data	data	data	data	data	data
12		data	data	data	data	data	data	data	data
13		data	data	data	data	data	data	data	data

FIGURE 26.2 Single Row Field Identifiers – To Be Preferred When Using Databases and Tables

An Excel Table is a database that has been explicitly defined as a Table, using any of:

- Insert/Table.
- Home/Format as Table.
- The short-cut Ctrl+T (or Ctrl+L).

During the process of creating a Table, there is a possibility to explicitly define a name for it; otherwise Excel will automatically assign one (such as Table1).

The key properties (and benefits) of Tables are:

- Data extension when a new data row is added in a contiguous row at the bottom of the data set. Any formula that refers to the table (using the Table-related functions and syntax) will automatically adapt to include the new data.
- Formulae extension when a formula is introduced into the first data cell of a new column; the formula is automatically copied down to all rows as soon as it is entered.
- Alternate-row colour formatting (by default) for ease of reading.
- The default naming based on a numerical index can facilitate the automation of some procedures when using VBA macros.

(Once a Table has been defined, it can be converted back to a range by right-clicking on it and using Table Tools/Convert to Range, or by using the Convert-to-Range button on the Design tab that appears when selecting any point in the table.)

Automation Using Macros

In many real-life applications, the techniques in this chapter (and general techniques in data manipulation and analysis) become much more effective when automated with VBA macros. For example:

- Although an individual (manually activated) filter can be applied to remove items with properties (such as blanks), a VBA routine that removes a specified item at the click of a button can be more effective when such repeated operations are required.
- To automate the process (at the click of a button) of producing a list of unique items for a field name (e.g. by automating the two manual steps of copying the data and removing duplicates).
- To explicitly extract many individual subsets of the data and place each one in a new worksheet or workbook.
- To perform multiple queries using Database functions for a set of criteria whose structure is changing (as calculated blanks or fields are not truly blank).
- Some databases may be generated using a single bank of formulae that is copied to individual cells by use of macros. The copying process may be done in stages, after each of which formula are replaced with values, to reduce memory space and computational intensity.

Examples of these techniques are discussed in Chapter 32.

PRACTICAL APPLICATIONS: FILTERS

Example: Applying Filters and Inspecting Data for Errors or Possible Corrections

Filters can be applied by simply selecting any cell in the database range and clicking on the Data/Filter icon. Note that when doing so it is important to ensure that the field headers are included (or the top row will by default be treated as containing the headers).

Further, one should define the data set within a single isolated range with (apart from the headers) no adjoining labels, and have no completely blank rows or columns within the intended data set. In this case, the default data set will be the Current Region of the selected point, i.e. the maximum-sized rectangular region defined by following all paths of contiguity from the original point. In practical terms, all rows above and below are included up to the point at which a first blank row is encountered (and similarly for columns), so that it is important to ensure that there are no blank rows in the data set, and that there are no additional labels immediately below the data set or above the field headings (and similarly in the column direction). Note that the Current Region of the selected point can rapidly be seen by using the shortcut Ctrl+Shift+*.

The file Ch26.1.DaysLateAnalysis.Initial.xlsx shows an example of a filter applied to a data set. Note that drop-down menus are automatically added to the headers, with these drop-downs providing sorting options as well as field-sensitive filtering options. The list of filtering options for a given field (e.g. for the Country field) provides the ability to quickly inspect for errors (e.g. spelling errors, or negative numbers in contexts where all numbers should be positive, as well as see whether blank items are present). Figure 26.3 shows an example of the initial data set, and Figure 26.4 shows the results of applying, within the Country field, the filters to select only the blanks or incorrect spelling of the country Italy.

Note that potential disadvantages of this standard filter approach are that:

- The criteria used to filter the data set are embedded within the drop-down menus and are therefore not explicit unless one inspects the filters.
- For data sets with many columns, it is not always easy to see which filters have been applied.

	A	B	C	D	E
1					
2					
3					
4		Customer	Country	Amount £	Due Date
5		Cust02	UK	12232	20-Mar-17
6		Cust06	Italy	4749	16-Mar-17
7		Cust07	Italy	7282	12-Apr-17
8		Cust03	Italy	12759	14-Jun-17
9		Cust10	UK	12334	24-May-17
10			Italy	4283	24-Mar-17
11		Cust06	Germany	7992	5-May-17
12		Cust06	Italy	13202	
13		Cust04	Germany	12684	4-Jun-17
14		Cust10	UK	11862	13-Jun-17
15		Cust10	Ita	13630	21-May-17
16		Cust07	UK	14593	20-Jan-17
17		Cust07		4394	4-May-17
18		Cust09	Italy	15712	8-Apr-17
19		Cust10	UK	6503	28-Mar-17
20		Cust05	France		8-Apr-17
21		Cust02	Germany	9274	17-Jun-17
22		Cust05	Italy	7919	27-Jun-17
23		Cust05	Italy	6402	14-Jun-17
24		Cust04	France	9100	6-Jun-17
25		Cust08	Spain	14120	2-Jul-17
26		Cust06	Spain	8889	8-Jun-17
27		Cust04	France	9547	1-Jun-17
28		Cust10	UK	14001	13-Jun-17
29		Cust01	Spain	4486	27-Apr-17
30		Cust05	Germany	9832	18-Apr-17
31		Cust08	Spain	9022	14-Apr-17

FIGURE 26.3 Part of an Initial Data Set Before Correcting for Spelling Mistakes or Blanks

	A	B	C	D	E
1					
2					
3					
4		Customer	Country	Amount £	Due Date
15		Cust10	Ita	13630	21-May-17
17		Cust07		4394	4-May-17
34		Cust10	Italia	7250	13-May-17
61		Cust06		15842	1-Jul-17
105					

FIGURE 26.4 Data Filtered to Show Only Incorrect or Blank Entries Within the Country Field

	A	B	C	D	E
1					
2					
3					
4		Customer	Country	Amount £	Due Date
15		Cust10	Ita	13630	21-May-17
17		Cust07		4394	4-May-17
34		Cust10	Italia	7250	13-May-17
61		Cust06		15842	1-Jul-17
105					
106				1042744	=SUM(D5:D104)
107				41116	=SUBTOTAL(9,D5:D104)
108				41116	=SUBTOTAL(109,D5:D104)

FIGURE 26.5 Functions Applied to a Filtered Data Set

An easy way to remove all filters is with the short-cut Alt-D-F-S.

Note that one needs to take extra care when applying most Excel functions to a filtered data set, as the results may be unexpected or not intuitive. For example, for most regular Excel functions (e.g. SUM, COUNT), the result is the same whether the data is visible or not and whether it is filtered or not. On the other hand, the SUBTOTAL function has options to include or ignore hidden data (see Chapter 17), but these options may have unexpected effects when the data is filtered. Once a filter is applied, a row that is hidden (either before or after the application of the filter) is treated as if it were filtered out (rather than being not filtered out but simply hidden).

Figure 26.5 shows the functions applied to a filtered data set, and Figure 13.6 shows the same, except that one of the rows has been hidden. Within each case, the SUBTOTAL function returns the same result, which is that based on the visible data, so that the function options regarding hidden data seem to have no effect in Figure 26.6. The reader can verify in Excel file that with filters removed, the hiding of a row will lead to the two SUBTOTAL functions giving different results.

Thus, it is generally advisable not to apply Excel functions to filtered data. Rather, the use of Database functions or other approaches in which criteria are made explicit within the functions (such as using SUMIFS) are to be preferred.

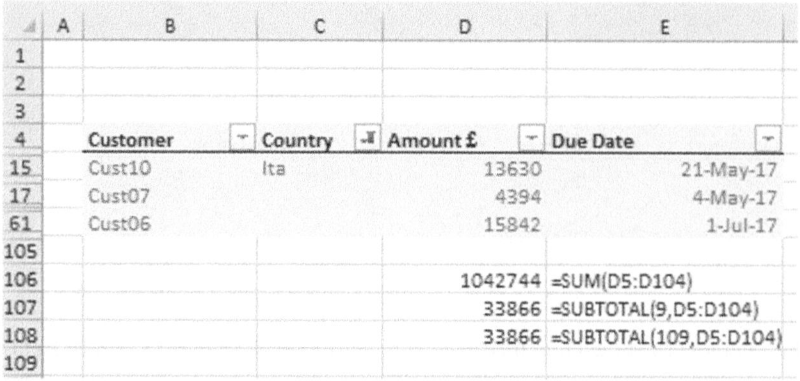

	A	B	C	D	E
1					
2					
3					
4		Customer	Country	Amount £	Due Date
15		Cust10	Ita	13630	21-May-17
17		Cust07		4394	4-May-17
61		Cust06		15842	1-Jul-17
105					
106				1042744	=SUM(D5:D104)
107				33866	=SUBTOTAL(9,D5:D104)
108				33866	=SUBTOTAL(109,D5:D104)
109					

FIGURE 26.6 Functions Applied to a Filtered Data Set with a Hidden Row

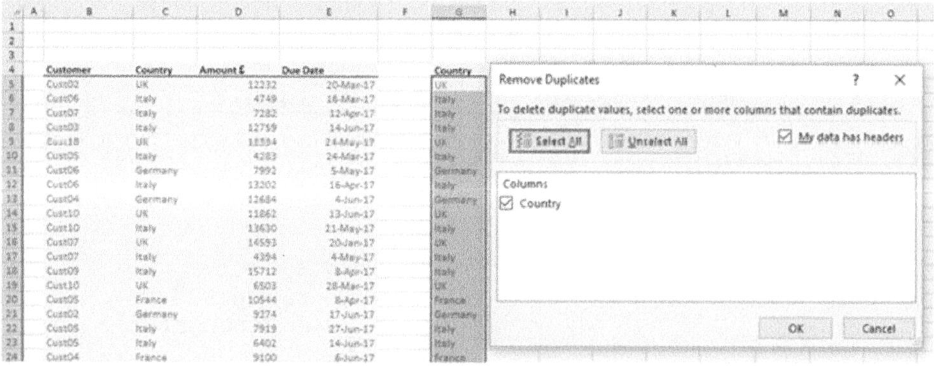

FIGURE 26.7 Applying Remove Duplicates to Copied Data

Example: Identification of Unique Items and Unique Combinations

In order to analyse a data set, one may also need to identify the unique list of items within a category (such as country names and customers), or a unique list of combined items (such as unique country-customer combinations). The use of Excel's Remove Duplicates (on the Data tab) is an important functionality in this respect, enabling one to generate the actual list of unique items.

The file Ch26.2.DaysLateAnalysis.UniqueItems.xlsx shows an example. In the first step, one copies all the data in the relevant common (such as the country names) to another area not contiguous with the data set (perhaps using the short-cut Ctrl+Shift+↓ to select the data). The Remove Duplicates menu is then used to create a list of unique items (taking care as to whether the header field has been copied or not). Figure 26.7 shows the initial steps of this process, applying the Remove Duplicates to the copied set of Country data, with the result shown in Figure 26.8.

The identification of unique combinations can be done in one of two ways:

- Creating a text field which combines (joins or concatenates) these items (as discussed in Chapter 12), and use Remove Duplicates on the field of combined items.
- Using the Remove Duplicate menu applied to the copied data set of the two fields.

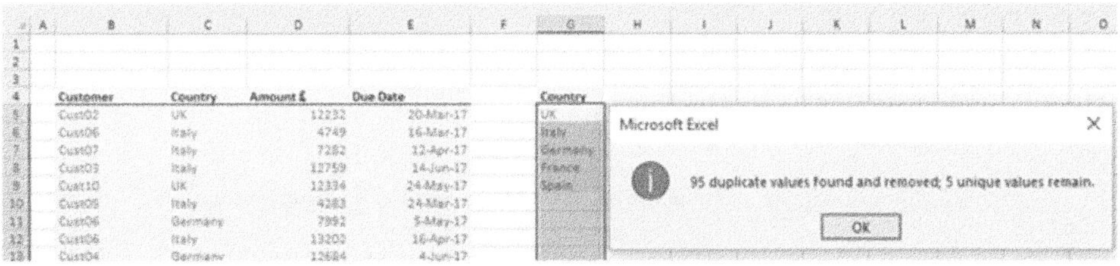

FIGURE 26.8 Unique Items Resulting from Application of Remove Duplicates

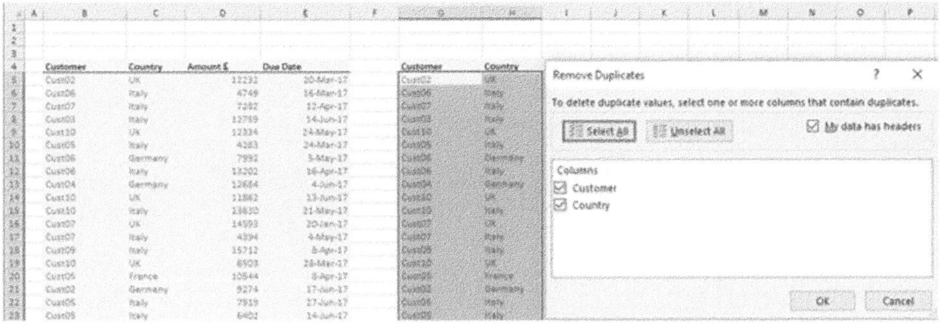

FIGURE 26.9 Application of Remove Duplicates to Identify All Unique Combinations

The file Ch26.3.DaysLateAnalysis.UniqueCombinations.xlsx shows the results of using the second approach. Figure 26.9 shows the initial steps in its application (i.e. the copying of the relevant data sets and application of the Remove Duplicated menu). Note that if working with a larger data set (such as if the whole data set had been copied so that the columns for the date or amount would not be relevant for the definition of unique items), the check-boxes that show within the Remove Duplicates dialog for these items would simply be left unticked. Figure 26.10 shows the result of the process.

Example: Using Filters to Remove Blanks or Other Specified Items

When cleaning or tidying data sets, one may wish to simply delete some rows, including:

- Where data is incomplete.
- Where there are errors.
- Where other specific items are not relevant or desired (such as all entries for the country Italy).
- Where there are blank rows.

As noted above, the use of the short-cut Ctrl+Shift+* to select the data would not select anything below the first blank row, so that if the presence of blank rows within the data set is possible, this shortcut should not be used; rather, the data set should be selected explicitly in its entirety before applying filters.

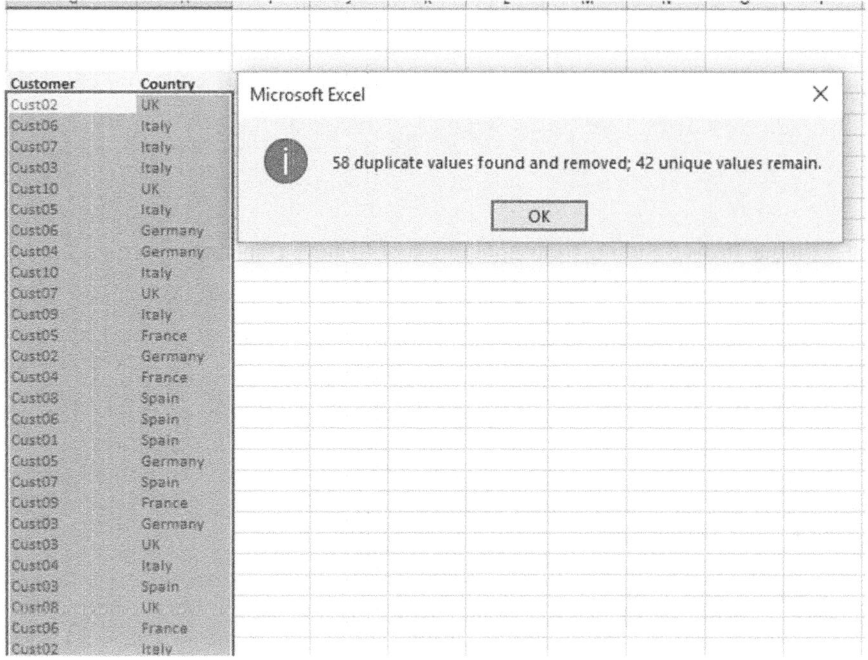

FIGURE 26.10 Unique Combinations Resulting from Application of Remove Duplicates

The file Ch26.4.DaysLateAnalysis.DeleteUsingFilter.xlsx shows an example. The main steps in are:

- Apply a filter to identify and select the items that one wishes to delete (generally, it is worth keeping a copy of the original data set, in case mistakes arise during some part of the process and steps need to be redone).
- Select the full range of filtered rows (this can be done in the usual way, as if selecting a contiguous range of cells, even if the cells are in fact not contiguous).
- Delete these rows in the usual way (i.e. using Home/Delete Cells or right-clicking to obtain the context-sensitive menu).
- Remove the filters.

Let us assume that it is desired to remove all records for which the Country field is either blank or applies to Italy (which are assumed to both be regarded as irrelevant for all subsequent analysis purposes). Figure 26.11 shows the part of the process which has filtered the data, and has selected the filter rows in preparation for their deletion. Figure 26.12 shows the result when these rows have been deleted and the filters removed, thus giving the cleaned data set.

Note that this process can be automated relatively easily with VBA macros. For example, when the macro is run, the user could be asked to click on a specific cell which contains the identifier of the items to be deleted within that field (e.g. a blank cell, or a cell containing the word Italy), with the macro taking care of all other steps behind the scenes. In this way, data sets can be rapidly cleaned: the copying, filtering and removal of filters is embedded as part of the overall process, and one can run such a process many times very quickly.

	A	B	C	D	E	F
1						
2						
3						
4		Customer	Country	Amount £	Due Date	
6		Cust06	Italy	4749	16-Mar-17	
7		Cust07	Italy	7282	12-Apr-17	
8		Cust03	Italy	12759	14-Jun-17	
9		Cust10		12334	24-May-17	
10		Cust05	Italy	4283	24-Mar-17	
12		Cust06	Italy	13202	16-Apr-17	
13		Cust04		12684	4-Jun-17	
15		Cust10	Italy	13630	21-May-17	
16		Cust07		14593	20-Jan-17	
17		Cust07	Italy	4394	4-May-17	
18		Cust09	Italy	15712	8-Apr-17	
21		Cust02		9274	17-Jun-17	
22		Cust05	Italy	7919	27-Jun-17	
23		Cust05	Italy	6402	14-Jun-17	
34		Cust10	Italy	7250	13-May-17	
40		Cust04	Italy	7768	31-May-17	
41		Cust05	Italy	11381	15-Apr-17	
45		Cust02	Italy	4449	14-Jul-17	
47		Cust10	Italy	11433	4-Jul-17	
55		Cust08	Italy	4876	10-May-17	
57		Cust05	Italy	14322	25-May-17	
61		Cust06	Italy	15842	1-Jul-17	
65		Cust10	Italy	13334	15-May-17	
69		Cust07	Italy	13911	13-Jul-17	
71		Cust10	Italy	14647	15-Aug-17	
74		Cust05	Italy	11079	31-Jul-17	
78		Cust05	Italy	4711	26-May-17	
91		Cust08	Italy	9057	29-Aug-17	
103		Cust06	Italy	8726	3-Sep-17	
105						

FIGURE 26.11 Filtering and Selecting of Rows Which Are Desired to be Deleted

Example: Extraction of Data Using Filters

In some cases, one may wish to use filters to extract items rather than to delete them. In such a case, the initial part of the process can be performed as above (up to that shown in Figure 26.11), whereas the latter part would involve copying the data to a new range, rather than deleting it. This is in principle a very straightforward and standard operation if basic Excel elements are respected (such as ensuring that any copy operation does not overwrite the original data). Note that Excel will replace any calculated items with their values to ensure integrity of the process.

Example: Adding Criteria Calculations to the Data Set

Although Excel provides several in-built options regarding filters, it is often more convenient to add a new criterion to the data set.

The file Ch26.5.DaysLateAnalysis.NewCriteria.xlsx shows an example in which it is desired to identify and delete all rows in which two or more field elements are blank. A new column has been added which uses the COUNTBLANK function to

	A	B	C	D	E
1					
2					
3					
4		Customer	Country	Amount £	Due Date
5		Cust02	UK	12232	20-Mar-17
6		Cust06	Germany	7992	5-May-17
7		Cust10	UK	11862	13-Jun-17
8		Cust10	UK	6503	28-Mar-17
9		Cust05	France	10544	8-Apr-17
10		Cust04	France	9100	6-Jun-17
11		Cust08	Spain	14120	2-Jul-17
12		Cust06	Spain	8889	8-Jun-17
13		Cust04	France	9547	1-Jun-17
14		Cust10	UK	14001	13-Jun-17
15		Cust01	Spain	4486	27-Apr-17
16		Cust05	Germany	9832	18-Apr-17
17		Cust08	Spain	9022	14-Apr-17
18		Cust02	Germany	14290	1-Jun-17
19		Cust07	Spain	10007	29-May-17
20		Cust09	France	15080	7-Apr-17
21		Cust03	Germany	9373	3-May-17
22		Cust07	UK	9006	26-Apr-17
23		Cust03	UK	8302	17-May-17
24		Cust03	Germany	10855	30-Jun-17

FIGURE 26.12 Result of Deleting Specified Rows

calculate the number of blanks fields (see Figure 26.13). For simplicity of presentation, Conditional Formatting has been applied to highlight those cells where the identified number of blanks in the row is equal to the threshold figure (defined in Cell F2). In other words, it identifies the rows that may be desired to be deleted. Note that (since the original data set in the example was not explicitly defined as an Excel table), once this column is added, the Data/Filter menu will need to be reapplied to ensure that a filter is included in the new column. The same procedure(s) as in the above examples can then be used to simply filter out and delete (or copy) these rows.

Example: Use of Tables

Generally, it is preferable to define the data set as an Excel Table. Note that one needs to take care to ensure that, if an original data set contains blank rows, then the Table range needs to be extended to include all data (as the Insert/Table operation will have selected only the Current Region of a data point by default).

The file Ch26.6.DaysLateAnalysis.Table1.xlsx shows an example of the process to create a Table (see Figure 26.14), noting that the default range would have been only up to Row 15 (as Row 16 is blank), so that the range was manually extended to include the rows up to Row 104.

	A	B	C	D	E	F
1						
2					Threshold	2
3						
4		Customer	Country	Amount £	Due Date	No. of Blan
5		Cust02	UK	12232	20-Mar-17	0
6		Cust06	Italy	4749	16-Mar-17	0
7		Cust07		7282	12-Apr-17	1
8		Cust03	Italy	12759	14-Jun-17	0
9		Cust10		12334		2
10		Cust05	Italy	4283	24-Mar-17	0
11			Germany	7992	5-May-17	1
12		Cust06	Italy		16-Apr-17	1
13		Cust04	Germany	12684	4-Jun-17	0
14		Cust10	UK	11862	13-Jun-17	0
15		Cust10	Italy	13630		1
16						4
17		Cust07	Italy	4394	4-May-17	0
18		Cust09		15712	8-Apr-17	1

FIGURE 26.13 Addition of a New Field to Capture Specific or Complex Criteria

	A	B	C	D	E
1					
2					
3					
4		Customer	Country	Amount £	Due Date
5		Cust02	UK	12232	20-Mar-17
6		Cust06	Italy	4749	16-Mar-17
7		Cust07		7282	12-Apr-17
8		Cust03	Italy	12759	14-Jun-17
9		Cust10		12334	
10		Cust05	Italy	4283	24-Mar-17
11			Germany	7992	5-May-17
12		Cust06	Italy		16-Apr-17
13		Cust04	Germany	12684	4-Jun-17
14		Cust10	UK	11862	13-Jun-17
15		Cust10	Italy	13630	
16					
17		Cust07	Italy	4394	4-May-17
18		Cust09		15712	8-Apr-17
19		Cust10	UK	6503	28-Mar-17

Create Table ? X
Where is the data for your table?
$B$4:$E$104
☑ My table has headers
OK Cancel

FIGURE 26.14 Defining the Data Range for a Table

Once defined as a Table, any (contiguous) new contiguous rows or columns that are added will automatically become part of the Table. In addition, a formula entered in the first data cell of a field will be copied to all rows of the table. Indeed, the simple making of entry in such a cell (such as in Cell F5 of the original, non-extended, Table) will result in a new column being added automatically. Figure 26.15 shows the same process as above (in which the COUNTBLANK function is used as a new field), when applied to a Table.

	A	B	C	D	E	F
1						
2						
3						
4		Customer	Country	Amount £	Due Date	No. of Bl ks
5		Cust02	UK	12232	20-Mar-17	0
6		Cust06	Italy	4749	16-Mar-17	0
7		Cust07		7282	12-Apr-17	1
8		Cust03	Italy	12759	14-Jun-17	0
9		Cust10		12334		2
10		Cust05	Italy	4283	24-Mar-17	0
11			Germany	7992	5-May-17	1
12		Cust06	Italy		16-Apr-17	1
13		Cust04	Germany	12684	4-Jun-17	0
14		Cust10	UK	11862	13-Jun-17	0
15		Cust10	Italy	13630		1
16						4
17		Cust07	Italy	4394	4-May-17	0
18		Cust09		15712	8-Apr-17	1
19		Cust10	UK	6503	28-Mar-17	0

FIGURE 26.15 Addition of a New Column to a Table

Note that the syntax of the formula in every cell within the Table range of column F is the same (and is not row-dependent):

= COUNTBLANK(Table 1[@[Customer] : [Due Date]])

If one were to change the formula, such as to count the blanks from different points, then the deletion of the original field name (as shown Figure 26.16) will produce a drop-down menu of field names that can be chosen instead to build the required formula.

Note also that, when using a Table, one can create formulae using the Header Names that the Table generates, such as:

= SUM(Table 1[Amount £])

Finally, note also that when one has selected a cell within the Table, the Table Tools Design Tab appears. This contains icons to Remove Duplicates and to create a PivotTable summary. The tab also allows one to rename the Table, although experience

	A	B	C	D	E	F	G
1							
2							
3							
4		Customer	Country	Amount £	Due Date	No. of Bl ks	
5		Cust02	UK	12232	20-Mar-17	(Table1[[C	
6		Cust06	Italy	4749	16-Mar-17	0	
7		Cust07		7282	12-Apr-17	1	
8		Cust03	Italy	12759	14-Jun-17	0	
9		Cust10		12334		2	
10		Cust05	Italy	4283	24-Mar-17	0	
11			Germany	7992	5-May-17	1	
12		Cust06	Italy		16-Apr-17	1	

COUNTBLANK(range)

- Customer
- Country
- Amount £
- Due Date
- No. of Blanks
- #All
- #Data
- #Headers
- #Totals
- @ - This Row

FIGURE 26.16 Modification of Formulae Using the Header Names Generated Within the Table

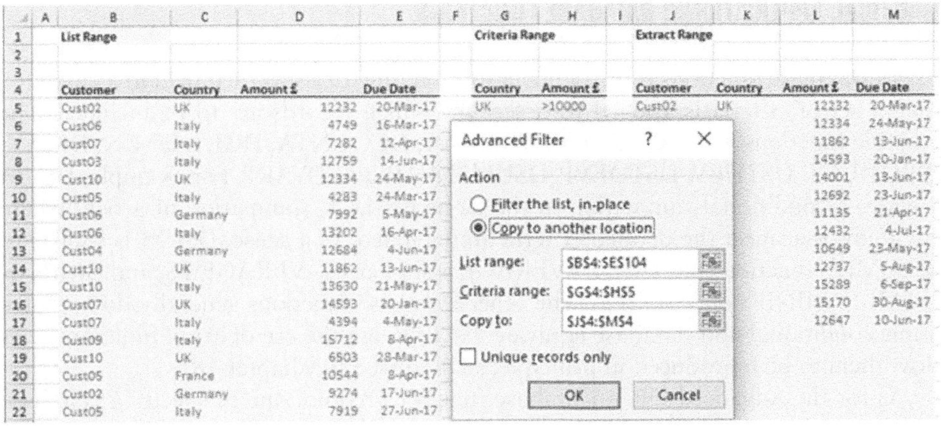

FIGURE 26.17 Example of the Implementation of An Advanced Filter

suggests that this process is best done when the Table is first created, and not once formulae have been built that refer to the name.

Example: Extraction of Data Using Advanced Filters

In some earlier examples, we used the filtering process embedded within the drop-down menus both to delete unwanted data and to extract data that may be wanted for separate analysis. In practice, such approaches are generally most appropriate only for the deletion of data, whereas the extraction of wanted items to another range is more effectively implemented using the Data/Advanced Filter tool.

The file Ch26.7.DaysLateAnalysis.ExtractCriteriaRange.xlsx shows an example (see Figure 26.17). Note that there is a separate range to define the criteria for the extraction and another range in which to copy the extracted data (this latter range is optional; as per the dialog box, the list can otherwise be filtered in place, so that the original full data set would simply be filtered as if done with a drop-down menu).

Note that:

- The Criteria range consists of some headers and at least one row below that which is contiguous with the headers. When multiple items are entered in a (non-header) row, are treated as representing "And" criterion. If additional non-header rows are used, each row is treated as an "Or" criterion (i.e. the results of the criteria on one row are added to those of the criteria on another); a frequent mistake is to include a blank row within the criteria range, which means that all elements would be included in the extraction or filter process.
- The header fields used in the Criteria range need to be identical to those of the main data set. If they are spelled even slightly differently, the process will not work as needed.
- For the Extract range, the headers are important only for cosmetic purposes; the extracted data set will be placed in the file in the same order as in the original data set, even if headers are not present in the Extract range. Of course, in practice, it is by far the most convenient to define the Extract range as that which contains a copy of the field headers (as in our example).

PRACTICAL APPLICATIONS: DATABASE FUNCTIONS

Excel's Database functions return calculations relating to a specified field in a database, when a set of criteria is applied to determine which records are to be included. The available functions are DAVERAGE, DCOUNT, DCOUNTA, DGET, DMIN, DMAX, DPRODUCT, DSTDEV, DSTDEVP, DSUM, DVAR and DVARP. For example, DSUM provides a conditional summation in the database, i.e. a summation of a field where only items that meet the defined criteria are included. In a sense, DSUM is similar to the SUMIFS function (similarly, DAVERAGE is similar to AVERAGEIFS, and DMIN or DMAX to MINIFS or MAXIFS). The other Database functions generally do not have simple conditional non-database equivalents (although the use of array functions does allow them to be reproduced in principle, as discussed in Chapter 18).

As for the Advanced Filter, Database functions require one to specify a Database (which may have been defined as an Excel Table), a Criteria Range (headers and at least one row, with additional contiguous rows representing OR criteria) and a field on which the conditional calculations are to be conducted.

Database functions and their non-database equivalents provide calculations which are dynamic or live-linked to the data set (in contrast to PivotTables). Each has advantages over the other:

- Non-database functions have the advantage that they work irrespective of whether the data is laid out in row or column form, and that they can be copied into contiguous rows (so that the functions can provide a set of values that relate to queries that involve different values of the same underlying criteria type, e.g. the sum of all items in the last month, or in the last two months etc.)
- Database functions require the data to be in column format. Their advantages include that they allow for the identity of the criteria to be changed very quickly: by entering values in the appropriate area of the criteria range, different criteria (not just different values for the same criteria) are being used. For example, one may wish to calculate the sum of all items in the last month, and then the sum of all items worth over £10,000, or all items relating to a specific country, and so on. When using the non-database equivalent (SUMIFS in this example), one would have to edit the function for each new query, to ensure that it is referencing the correct ranges in the data set and also in the criteria range. Note also that Database functions require the use of field header names (as do PivotTables), whereas non-database functions refer to the data set directly, with headers and labels being cosmetic items (as for most other Excel functions).

Example: Calculating Conditional Sums and Maxima Using DSUM and DMAX

The file Ch26.8.DaysLateAnalysis.DatabaseFunctions1.xlsx contains an example. Figure 26.18 shows part of a data set (which has been defined as a Table, and given the name DataSet1) as well as the additional parameter information required to use the Database functions, i.e. the name of the field which is to be analysed (in this case the field "Amount £") and the Criteria Range (cells I4:L5). Figure 26.19 shows the implementation of some of the functions.

	A	B	C	D	E	F	G	H	I	J	K	L	M
1		Database					Field		Criteria				
2													
3													
4		Customer	Country	Amount £	Due Date		Amount £		Customer	Country	Amount £	Due Date	
5		Cust02	UK	12232	20-Mar-17					UK	>£10000		
6		Cust06	Italy	4749	16-Mar-17								
7		Cust07	Italy	7282	12-Apr-17								
8		Cust03	Italy	12759	14-Jun-17								
9		Cust10	UK	12334	24-May-17								

FIGURE 26.18 Database and Parameters Required to Use Database Functions

M	N	O	P	Q	R	S	T	U
	Dfunctions							
	DCOUNT	DSUM	DMIN	DMAX				
	13	167773	10649	15289	=DMAX(DataSet1[#All],$G$4,$I$4:$L$5)			

FIGURE 26.19 Implementation of Selected Database Functions

Example: Implementing a Between Query

If one wishes to implement a between-type query (e.g. sum all items whose amounts are between £5000 and £10,000), the simplest way is usually to extend the Criteria Range by adding a column and applying two tests to the same criteria field; this is analogous to the procedure when using a SUMIFS function, as discussed earlier in the text. (An alternative is to implement two separate queries and take the difference between them.)

The file Ch26.9.DaysLateAnalysis.DatabaseFunctions2.xlsx contains an example, which is essentially self-explanatory; Figure 26.20 shows the extended Criteria Range that could be used in this case.

Example: Implementing Multiple Queries

When using Database functions, the Criteria Range consists of field headings and one or more contiguous rows below this. Thus, if a second set of criteria were required, a new Criteria Range would be needed, and if many such sets of criteria were required, there would be several such ranges, so that the space taken up in the workbook could

G	H	I	J	K	L	M
Field		Criteria				
Amount £		Customer	Country	Amount £	Amount £	Due Date
			UK	>£5000	<=£10000	

FIGURE 26.20 Criteria Range Extended by a Column to Implement a Between Query

Alignment Number

=IF(ISBLANK(INDEX(J$13:J$24,$H5,1)),"",INDEX(J$13:J$24,$H5,1))

G	H	I	J	K	L	M	O	P	Q	R
Field		Criteria					Dfunctions			
Amount £		Customer	Country	Amount £	Amount £	Due Date	DCOUNT	DSUM	DMIN	DMAX
	3		=IF(ISBLANK		<=£10000		0	0	0	0
		Customer	Country	Amount £	Amount £	Due Date	DCOUNT	DSUM	DMIN	DMAX
			UK		<=£10000		10	72974	5096	9006
							PASTED VALUES OF RESULTS:			
		Customer	Country	Amount £	Amount £	Due Date	DCOUNT	DSUM	DMIN	DMAX
	1				<=£10000		43	304157	4095	9942
	2				>£10000		57	749131	10007	15851
	3		UK		<=£10000		10	72974	5096	9006
	4		UK	>£5000	<=£10000					
	5		Germany		<=£10000					
	6		Germany	>£5000	<=£10000					
	7		Italy		<=£10000					
	8		Italy	>£5000	<=£10000					
	9		France		<=£10000					
	10		France	>£5000	<=£10000					
	11		Spain		<=£10000					
	12		Spain	>£5000	<=£10000					

FIGURE 26.21 Database Functions Do Not Treat Calculated Blanks as True Blanks

become quite large (i.e. each Criteria Range would require at least three rows of Excel – the header, the criteria values and a blank row before the next Criteria Range).

An alternative is to have a single Criteria Range, and to place in sequence the set of values to be used for each query within this range, each time also recording the results of the query (as if doing a sensitivity analysis). Unfortunately, such a process cannot in general be simplified by using lookup functions to place the data within the criteria range: if the criteria range contains functions which return blank cells, then the Database functions do not consider such calculated blanks as being the same as if the cell containing the same criteria value were truly empty.

Thus, in practice, such a process needs to be done either manually or automated using VBA macros (see Chapter 32), because the copying in Excel (or assigning in VBA) of a blank cell into the Criteria Range leads to its value being treated as genuinely empty.

The file Ch26.10.DaysLateAnalysis.DatabaseFunctions3.xlsx shows examples of these. Figure 26.21 shows that the Database functions will return zero (cells O5:R5) when a lookup process is used to find the desired value to be used in the criteria range, even when the additional step is built, in that when blanks within the input ranges are referred to, the return values are also set to blank, not as zeros; see the Formula Bar. Since calculated blanks within the Criteria Range are not treated as if they were simple empty cells, no matching records are found. However, when the queries are pasted individually into the Criteria Range (for demonstration purposes, a new range has been set up in cells I8:M9), no such issue arises. One can repeat the process to copy the individual queries and each time paste the results into a storage range; in the Figure, the first three criteria sets have been completed, with the results pasted in cells O13:O15). Clearly, such a process can be automated using a VBA macro, as discussed in Chapter 32.

PRACTICAL APPLICATIONS: PIVOTTABLES

PivotTables can be used to produce cross-tabulation reports which summarise aspects of a database by category. Their main advantages include:

- They allow to create reports very rapidly, for the identity of the criteria to be changed, and for "drill-downs" or more detailed analysis of the data to be conducted easily and quickly.
- The presentation of the report can easily be changed, e.g. switching rows and columns or reporting an average instead of a total. Further, additional filters and "slicers" can be added or removed, which can allow for very rapid exploration and analysis.
- They also allow for errors or other specific values in the underlying data to be ignored (or filtered out) when applying the criteria or filters.
- PivotCharts are easy to create from a PivotTable.
- They are supported by VBA, so that one can record macros based on actions applied to a PivotTable, and adapt these as required.

Despite their power, PivotTables have some properties which can be potential disadvantages:

- They are not live-linked to the data set, so need refreshing if the data changes. (This is because they use a "cache" of the original data. In fact, multiple PivotTables can be created using the same underlying data, and this should ideally be done by copying the first PivotTable to ensure that the same cached data is used and so not diminish computation efficiency when dealing with large data sets.)
- They will "break", and will need to be rebuilt, if field headings change. For example, a PivotTable based on a field heading "2016 Salaries" would need to be rebuilt if – during an annual update process – the field header changed to "2017 Salaries". This contrasts with regular (non-database) Excel functions (which are linked only to the data, with the field labels being essentially cosmetic), and to Database functions (which if implemented correctly do not break if field headings change, or at least require only minimal re-work). Thus, they may not be the most effective reporting methods for complex queries that will regularly be updated.
- Since the structure of the PivotTable (e.g. row–column layout, number of rows etc.) depends on the underlying data, it is generally not appropriate to use these as an interim calculation step (i.e. Excel formulae should generally avoid referencing cells in a PivotTable). PivotTables are thus best used both for general exploratory analysis, and as a form of final report.

Example: Exploring Summary Values of Data Sets

The file Ch26.11.DaysLateAnalysis.PivotTable1.xlsx shows an example of a simple PivotTable. The underlying database has been defined as an Excel Table called DataSet1 (although doing so is not necessary to create a PivotTable). The PivotTable was

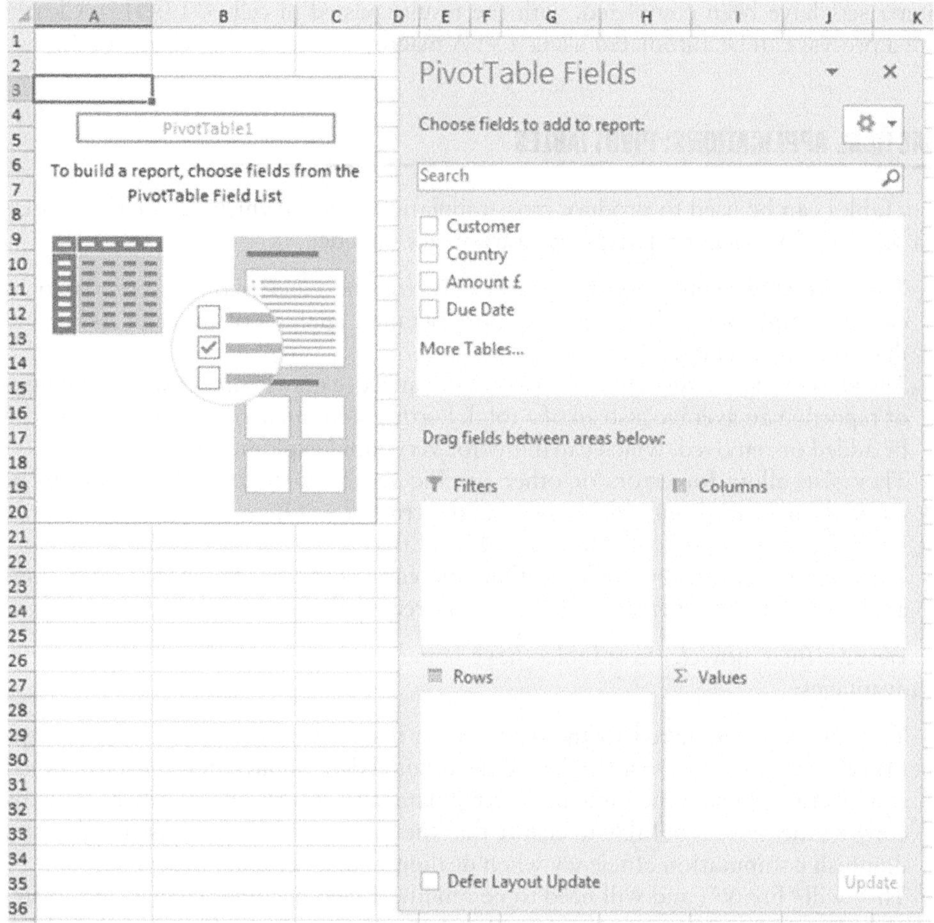

FIGURE 26.22 Foundation Structure of a PivotTable

created by selecting any cell in the database and using Insert/PivotTable, and then filling in the data or choices required by the dialog box. When doing so, one may in general choose to place the PivotTable on a new worksheet to keep the data separate from the analysis, and to allow adaptation of the data set (insertion of new rows) without potentially causing conflicts. Figure 26.22 shows the foundation structure that is created automatically.

Thereafter, the user can select field names using the check boxes and drag these to the Rows, Columns, Values or Filters areas, as desired. Figure 26.23 shows an example report which summarises the figures by country and customer.

Note that the report would simply be transposed if the items row–column structure of the country and customer were switched.

Figure 26.24 shows how one may choose to use a filter approach to present the results. In this example, the Country field was moved from the Columns are to the

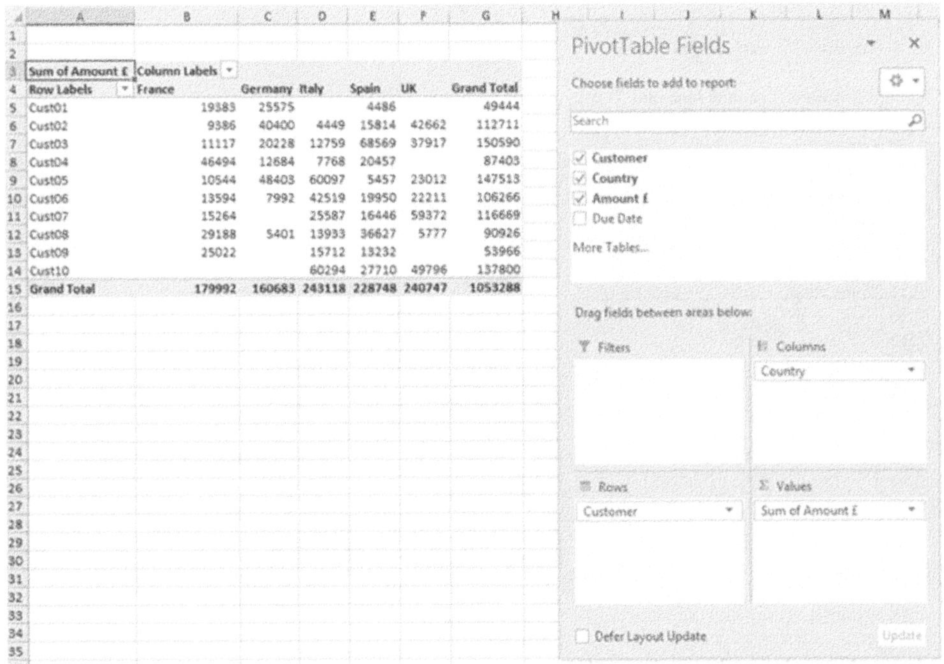

Sum of Amount £	Column Labels					
Row Labels	France	Germany	Italy	Spain	UK	Grand Total
Cust01	19383	25575		4486		49444
Cust02	9386	40400	4449	15814	42662	112711
Cust03	11117	20228	12759	68569	37917	150590
Cust04	46494	12684	7768	20457		87403
Cust05	10544	48403	60097	5457	23012	147513
Cust06	13594	7992	42519	19950	22211	106266
Cust07	15264		25587	16446	59372	116669
Cust08	29188	5401	13933	36627	5777	90926
Cust09	25022		15712	13232		53966
Cust10			60294	27710	49796	137800
Grand Total	179992	160683	243118	228748	240747	1053288

FIGURE 26.23 Creation of PivotTable Row–column and Reporting Structure

Filters area with the result that a new filter appeared in Row 1; this has been applied to show only the data relating to Germany.

Some additional important points include:

- Items can be re-ordered within the presentation using the Sort options, or manually by either right-clicking on an item and using the context-sensitive (Move) menu, or by simply clicking on the border of the cell containing the label and dragging this cell to the desired location.
- The PivotTable Tools/Analyze tab provides a wide range of options, including the use of the Field Settings to display calculations other than the sum totals, as well as the use of customised calculations.
- A second PivotTable (based on the same data cache) can be created either by using the More Tables option in the PivotTable Fields dialog, or by choosing Entire PivotTable within the Select option on the PivotTable Tools/Analyze tab, and then using a standard Copy/Paste operation. A PivotTable can be deleted by the same selection process and then using Excel's regular Clear Contents menu.

Figure 26.25 shows an example in which some of these points have been implemented: a second PivotTable has been inserted, a Filter is used in place of a column structure, and the order of the countries has been manually changed. Note that the PivotTable Fields dialog appears only once but is specific to the PivotTable that is active.

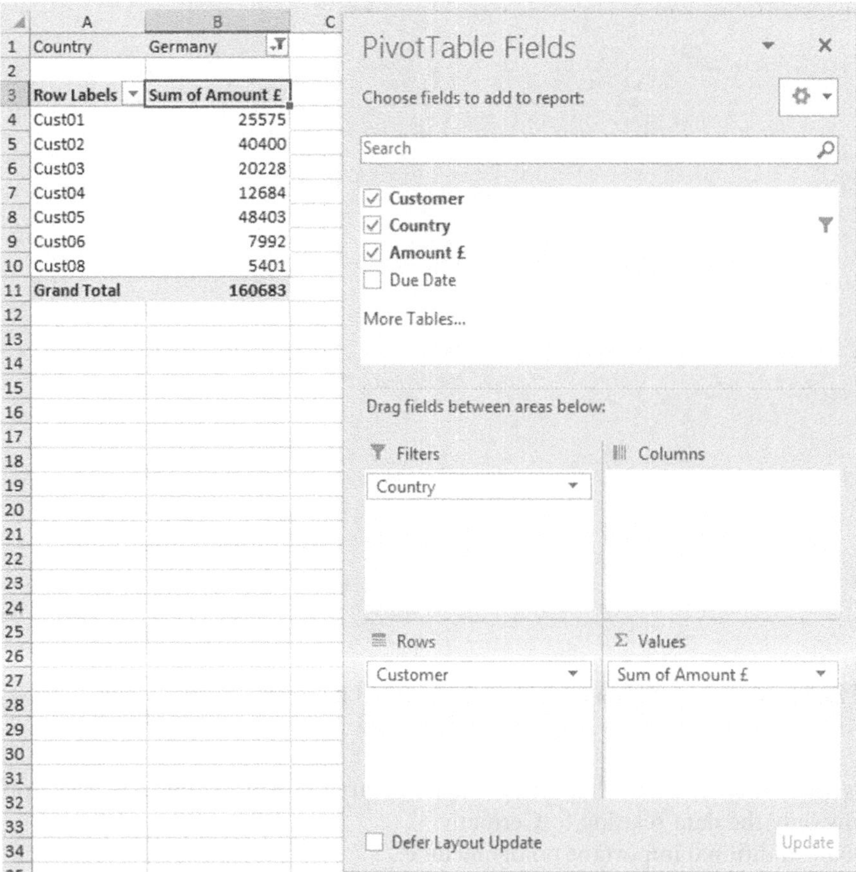

FIGURE 26.24 Basic Use of a Filter

Example: Exploring Underlying Elements of the Summary Items

An important feature of PivotTables is the ability to rapidly see the individual items that make up the summarised figure, i.e. to list the relevant detailed individual records in the underlying database. One can create such a list either by:

- Double-clicking on the cell in the PivotTable.
- Right-clicking and using Show Details.

Figure 26.26 shows the result of applying this process to Cell B23 (summary data for France) in the above example (shown in the DrillDown worksheet of the example file).

Example: Adding Slicers

In their basic form, Slicers are rather like Filters, but simply provide an enhanced visual display, as well as more flexibility to rapidly experiment with options.

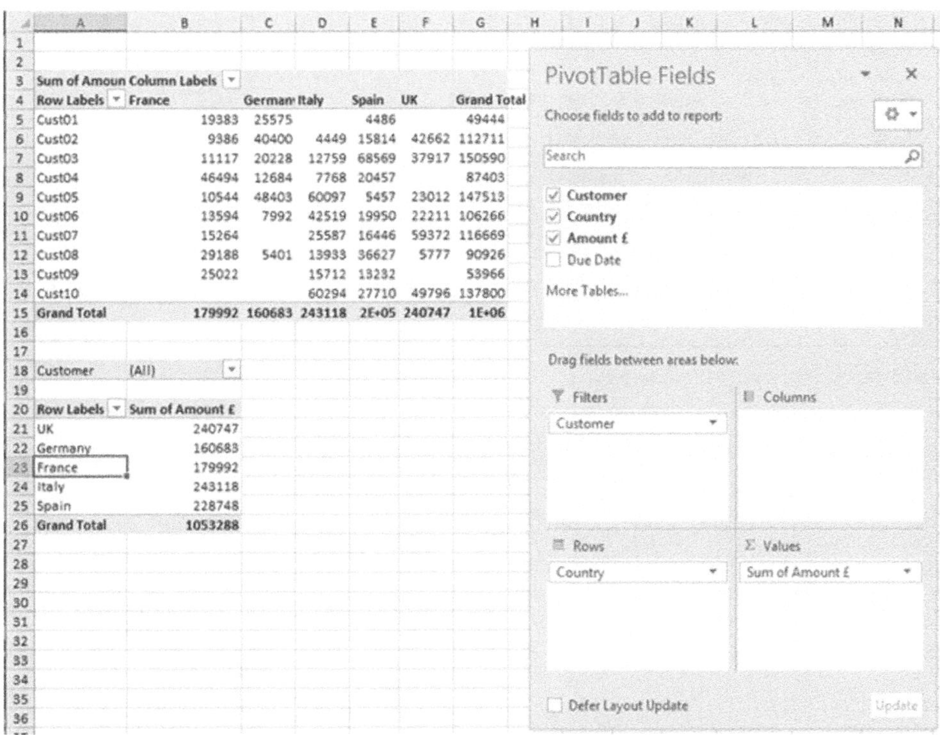

Sum of Amoun Column Labels
Row Labels France Germany Italy Spain UK Grand Total
Cust01 19383 25575 4486 49444
Cust02 9386 40400 4449 15814 42662 112711
Cust03 11117 20228 12759 68569 37917 150590
Cust04 46494 12684 7768 20457 87403
Cust05 10544 48403 60097 5457 23012 147513
Cust06 13594 7992 42519 19950 22211 106266
Cust07 15264 25587 16446 59372 116669
Cust08 29188 5401 13933 36627 5777 90926
Cust09 25022 15712 13232 53966
Cust10 60294 27710 49796 137800
Grand Total 179992 160683 243118 2E+05 240747 1E+06
Customer (All)
Row Labels Sum of Amount £
UK 240747
Germany 160683
France 179992
Italy 243118
Spain 228748
Grand Total 1053288
PivotTable Fields
Choose fields to add to report:
Search
Customer
Country
Amount £
Due Date
More Tables...
Drag fields between areas below:
Filters
Columns
Customer
Rows
Values
Country
Sum of Amount £
Defer Layout Update
Update

FIGURE 26.25 Representation of Report Based on a Copied PivotTable

	A	B	C	D
1	Customer	Country	Amount £	Due Date
2	Cust03	France	11117	07/08/2017
3	Cust02	France	9386	23/07/2017
4	Cust08	France	13337	22/07/2017
5	Cust07	France	15264	29/05/2017
6	Cust04	France	8548	04/06/2017
7	Cust09	France	9942	01/08/2017
8	Cust04	France	12790	04/07/2017
9	Cust01	France	5853	05/07/2017
10	Cust04	France	6509	16/05/2017
11	Cust01	France	13530	17/06/2017
12	Cust08	France	15851	14/07/2017
13	Cust06	France	13594	23/05/2017
14	Cust09	France	15080	07/04/2017
15	Cust04	France	9547	01/06/2017
16	Cust04	France	9100	06/06/2017
17	Cust05	France	10544	08/04/2017
18				

FIGURE 26.26 Example of Results of Drill-down of An Item in a PivotTable

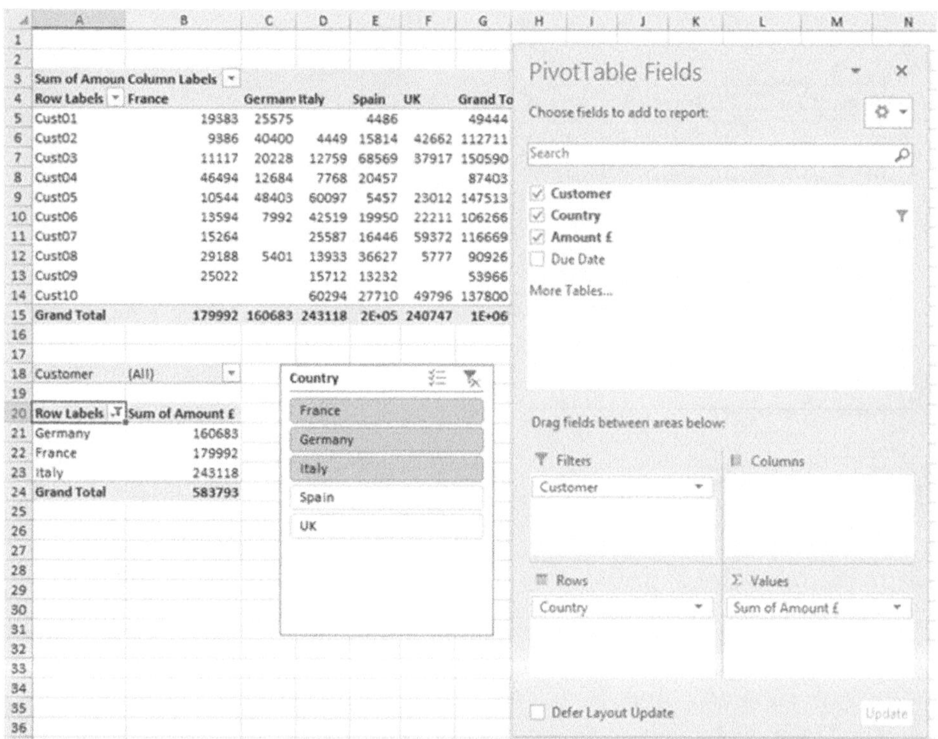

FIGURE 26.27 Use of a Single Slicer

Slicers can be created using the menu on the PivotTable Tools/Analyze tab. Figure 26.27 shows an example of adding a Slicer on the Country field of the second PivotTable, and then showing the summary results for the selected set of countries (holding the Ctrl key to select multiple items).

In Figure 26.28, we show the result of including a second Slicer (based on Customer), in which all items for the second Slicer are selected. Figure 26.29 shows the result of using the second Slicer to report only the items that relate to the customer Cust01; one sees that the Country slicer adjusts to show that such a customer is not present in Italy. This highlights one of the main advantages of slicers over filter approaches (i.e. reflecting correctly the interactions between subsets of the data).

Example: Timeline Slicers

Timeline Slicers are simply a special form of slicer that can be used (inserted using the PivotTable Tools/Analyze tab) when a date field is to be analysed. Rather than have to adapt the data (such as by using the MONTH or YEAR functions), the slicers automatically provide options to analyse the data according to different levels of time granularity. Figure 26.30 shows the result of inserting a TimeLine Slicer (in which the full Customer list is used), with the drop-down menu of the slicer set to the "Months" option.

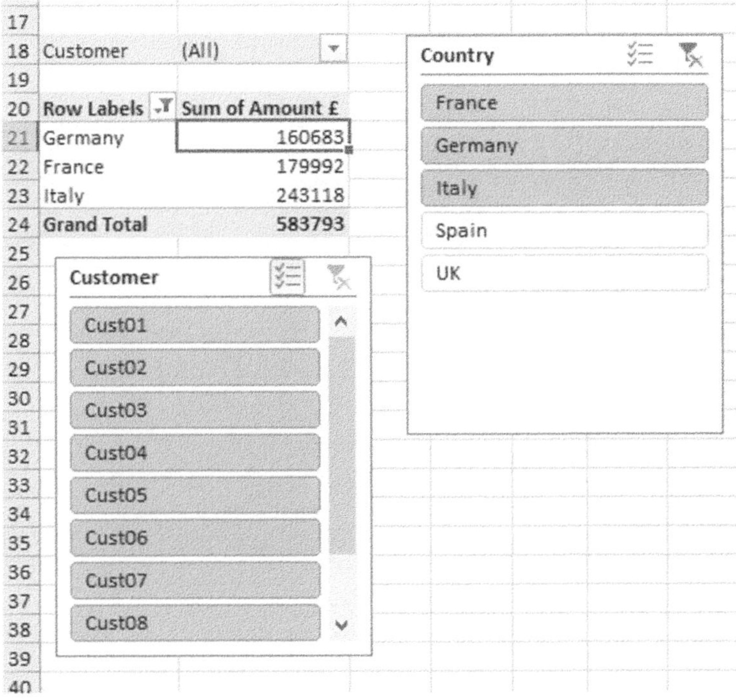

FIGURE 26.28 Inclusion of a Second Slicer

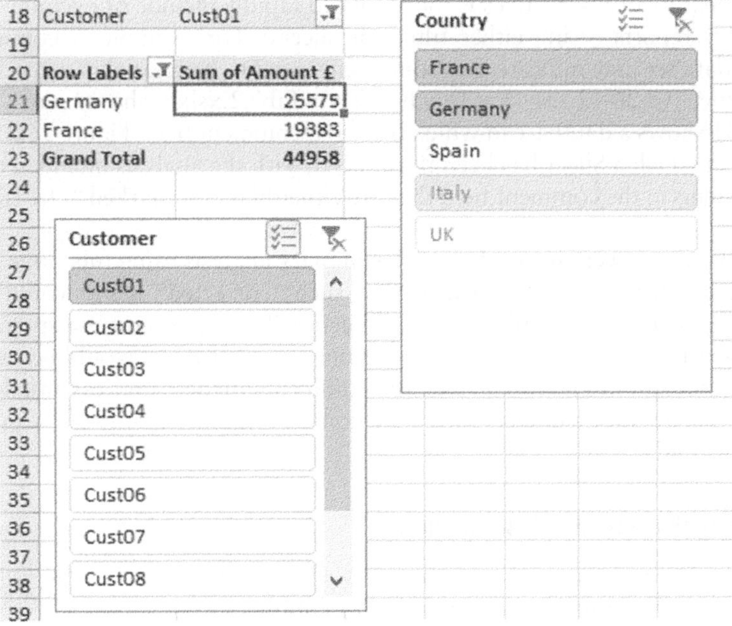

FIGURE 26.29 Interactions Between the Slicers

FIGURE 26.30 Use of a TimeLine Slicer

Example: Generating Reports Which Ignore Errors or Other Specified Items

One useful feature of PivotTables is the ability to rapidly include or exclude data from the summary reports (using either filters or slicers). For example, a comment field within the data set may indicate that some items need to be treated in a special way.

The file Ch26.12.DaysLateAnalysis.PivotTable2.xslx shows an example. Figure 26.31 shows a database in which there is a comment field. Figure 26.32 shows a PivotTable in which a Slicer has been introduced, with the analysis intended to include only those items in the comment field that are either blank or marked "OK" or marked "Checked".

Note that if one were to conduct such summary analysis using functions (database or non-database), the bespoke treatment of such "corrected" items would be much more cumbersome: for example, one would generally need to create a special field in the database that acts as a criterion to determine whether items would be included or not in the calculation. However, since the comments made could essentially be anything, it could be quite cumbersome, time-consuming and error-prone to create the applicable formulae.

Example: Using the GETPIVOTDATA Functions

One can obtain (or lookup) a value in any visible PivotTable using the GETPIVOTDATA function. The function has a number of parameters:

- The name of the data field (enclosed in quotation marks).

Customer	Country	Amount £	Due Date	Comments
Cust02	UK	12232	20-Mar-17	OK
Cust06	Italy	4749	16-Mar-17	exclude until have checked with Bob
Cust07	Italy	7282	12-Apr-17	OK
Cust03	Italy	12759	14-Jun-17	OK
Cust10	UK	12334	24-May-17	OK
Cust05	Italy	4283	24-Mar-17	Should be left out
Cust06	Germany	7992	5-May-17	OK
Cust06	Italy	13202	16-Apr-17	
Cust04	Germany	12684	4-Jun-17	Checked 31 August
Cust10	UK	11862	13-Jun-17	
Cust10	Italy	13630	21-May-17	unsure if data is correct
Cust07	UK	14593	20-Jan-17	
Cust07	Italy	4394	4-May-17	
Cust09	Italy	15712	8-Apr-17	
Cust10	UK	6503	28-Mar-17	
Cust05	France	10544	8-Apr-17	
Cust02	Germany	9274	17-Jun-17	

FIGURE 26.31 Data Set with a Comment Field

Sum of Amount £	Column Labels					
Row Labels	France	Germany	Italy	Spain	UK	Grand Total
Cust01	19383	25575		4486		49444
Cust02	9386	40400	4449	15814	42662	112711
Cust03	11117	20228	12759	68569	37917	150590
Cust04	46494	12684	7768	20457		87403
Cust05	10544	48403	55814	5457	23012	143230
Cust06	13594	7992	37770	19950	22211	101517
Cust07	15264		25587	16446	59372	116669
Cust08	29188	5401	13933	36627	5777	90926
Cust09	25022		15712	13232		53966
Cust10			46664	27710	49796	124170
Grand Total	179992	160683	220456	228748	240747	1030626

Comments
Checked 31 August
exclude until have checke...
OK
Should be left out
unsure if data is correct
(blank)

FIGURE 26.32 Using Slicers to Exclude Specific Commented Items

Customer	Cust06	
Result	106266	=GETPIVOTDATA("Amount £",$B$12,B3,C3)

Customer	Cust06	
Country	Italy	
Result	42519	=GETPIVOTDATA("Amount £",$B$12,B7,C7,B8,C8)

Sum of Amount £	Column Labels					
Row Labels	France	Germany	Italy	Spain	UK	Grand Total
Cust01	19383	25575		4486		49444
Cust02	9386	40400	4449	15814	42662	112711
Cust03	11117	20228	12759	68569	37917	150590
Cust04	46494	12684	7768	20457		87403
Cust05	10544	48403	60097	5457	23012	147513
Cust06	13594	7992	42519	19950	22211	106266
Cust07	15264		25587	16446	59372	116669
Cust08	29188	5401	13933	36627	5777	90926
Cust09	25022		15712	13232		53966
Cust10			60294	27710	49796	137800
Grand Total	179992	160683	243118	228748	240747	1053288

FIGURE 26.33 Use of the GETPIVOTDATA Function

- The Pivot_table argument, which must provide a reference to any cell in the PivotTable from which data is desired to be retrieved (or a range of cells, or a named range).
- The field and item names: these are optional arguments, and there could be several, depending on the granularity and number of variables in the PivotTable.

The file Ch26.13.DaysLateAnalysis.PivotTable3.xslx contains an example, shown in Figure 26.33.

Since the data must already be visible, one might ask as to the benefit of this. One case where it may be useful is if there are many large PivotTables, but one wishes only selected data from them. In such cases, it may be that functions such as SUMIFS would be more appropriate (which may often be the case, unless the filter and slicer functionality is required simultaneously).

Example: Creating PivotCharts

Once a PivotTable has been created, a PivotChart can also be added using the PivotChart icon on the Analyze tab of the PivotTable Tools. The two objects are then inherently linked: the application of a filter on one will adjust the corresponding filter on the other, and the insertion of a slicer will affect both.

The file Ch26.14.DaysLateAnalysis.PivotTable4.xslx contains an example. Figure 26.34 shows a PivotChart in which a country filter is applied, and the column

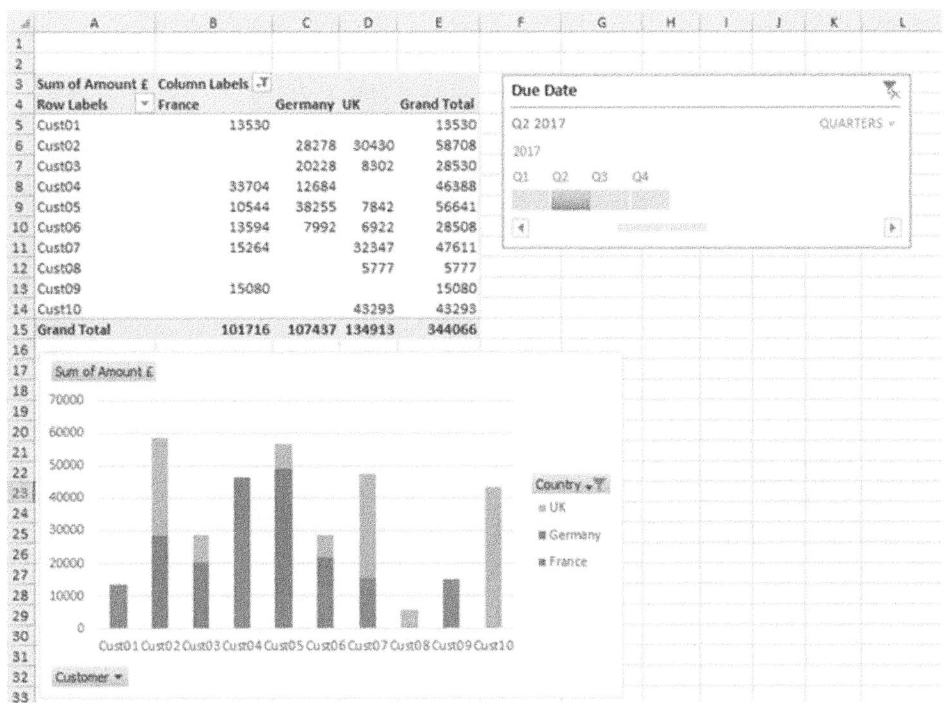

Sum of Amount £	Column Labels			
Row Labels	France	Germany	UK	Grand Total
Cust01	13530			13530
Cust02		28278	30430	58708
Cust03		20228	8302	28530
Cust04	33704	12684		46388
Cust05	10544	38255	7842	56641
Cust06	13594	7992	6922	28508
Cust07	15264		32347	47611
Cust08			5777	5777
Cust09	15080			15080
Cust10			43293	43293
Grand Total	101716	107437	134913	344066

FIGURE 26.34 Example of a Pivot Chart and Alignment of Filters with Its PivotTable

format of the PivotTable adjusts automatically. The Timeline slicer that has been inserted for the PivotTable also affects the display shown on the chart.

Example: Using the Excel Data Model to Link Tables

Where one wishes to produce reports based on multiple databases or tables, it may be cumbersome to have to consolidate them together into a single database. Excel's Data Model allows for PivotTable analysis of multiple data sets by linking them through relationships (of course, one would still need to have, or to create, some form of identifier or key that enables the matching process to take place through the relationship, but the cumbersome and memory-intensive lookup functions can often be avoided).

The file Ch26.15.DataModel.xlsx shows an example. Figure 26.35 shows three data sets that have been defined as Excel Tables, with the first providing a complete list of unique identifiers for each customer, the second providing information on revenues and dates, and the third providing cost information.

To create a PivotTable report that uses information from these tables (without explicitly joining them into a single data set), the following steps are necessary:

- Define each data set as an Excel Table (see earlier).
- On the Data tab, use the Connections icon to add each Table in turn to the DataModel. This is done by using the drop-down from the Add menu to find

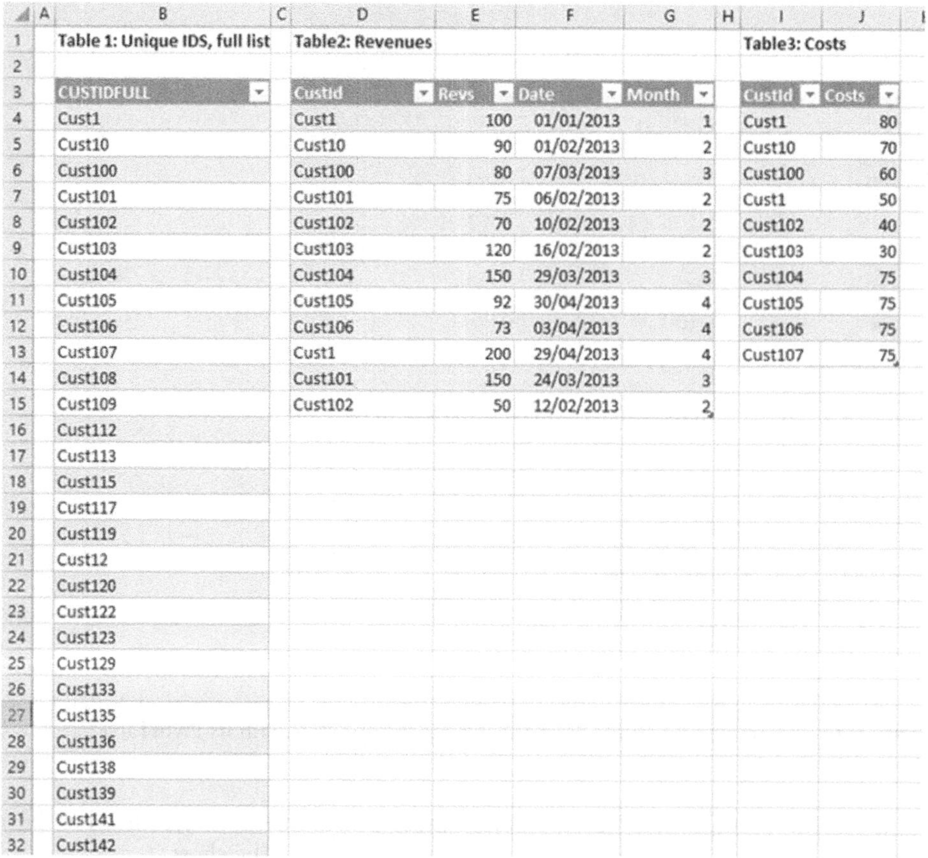

	A	B	C	D	E	F	G	H	I	J
1		Table 1: Unique IDS, full list		Table2: Revenues					Table3: Costs	
2										
3		CUSTIDFULL		CustId	Revs	Date	Month		CustId	Costs
4		Cust1		Cust1	100	01/01/2013	1		Cust1	80
5		Cust10		Cust10	90	01/02/2013	2		Cust10	70
6		Cust100		Cust100	80	07/03/2013	3		Cust100	60
7		Cust101		Cust101	75	06/02/2013	2		Cust1	50
8		Cust102		Cust102	70	10/02/2013	2		Cust102	40
9		Cust103		Cust103	120	16/02/2013	2		Cust103	30
10		Cust104		Cust104	150	29/03/2013	3		Cust104	75
11		Cust105		Cust105	92	30/04/2013	4		Cust105	75
12		Cust106		Cust106	73	03/04/2013	4		Cust106	75
13		Cust107		Cust1	200	29/04/2013	4		Cust107	75
14		Cust108		Cust101	150	24/03/2013	3			
15		Cust109		Cust102	50	12/02/2013	2			
16		Cust112								
17		Cust113								
18		Cust115								
19		Cust117								
20		Cust119								
21		Cust12								
22		Cust120								
23		Cust122								
24		Cust123								
25		Cust129								
26		Cust133								
27		Cust135								
28		Cust136								
29		Cust138								
30		Cust139								
31		Cust141								
32		Cust142								

FIGURE 26.35 Data Sets Used for PowerView Example

Workbook Connections ? ×

Name

ThisWorkbookDataModel

Add...

Remove

FIGURE 26.36 Adding a New Workbook Connection I

AddtotheDataModel (see Figure 26.36), and selecting the Tables tab. When complete, the list of connections will be shown as in Figure 26.37.

- Define the relationships using Data/Relationships/New. In this example, the CUSTIDFULL field from the first table acts as the Primary Key (see Figure 26.38).
- Finally, create the PivotTable by using Insert/PivotTable. When doing so, one will need to check the "Use an external data source" within the dialog box, and choose "Tables in Workbook Data Model". Figure 26.39 shows an example report.

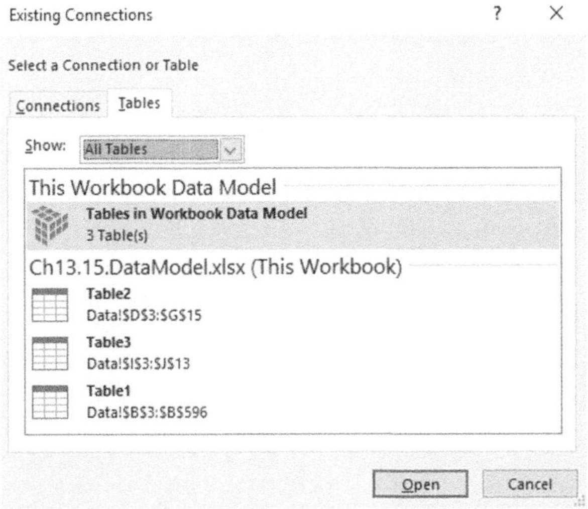

Existing Connections ? ×

Select a Connection or Table

Connections Tables

Show: All Tables

This Workbook Data Model

Tables in Workbook Data Model
3 Table(s)

Ch13.15.DataModel.xlsx (This Workbook)

Table2
Data!$D$3:$G$15

Table3
Data!$I$3:$J$13

Table1
Data!$B$3:$B$596

Open Cancel

FIGURE 26.37 Completed List of Connections

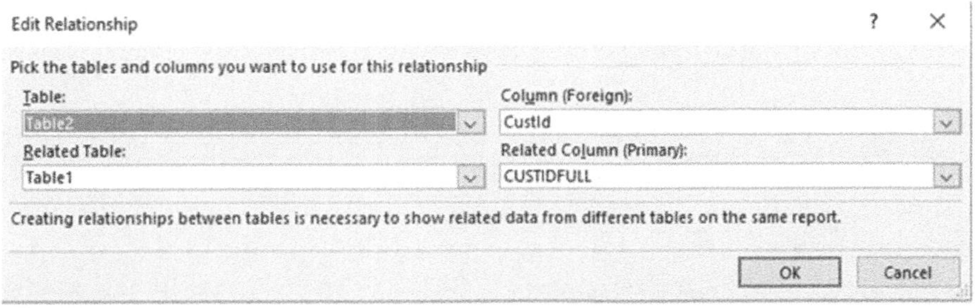

Edit Relationship ? ×

Pick the tables and columns you want to use for this relationship

Table: Table2

Column (Foreign): CustId

Related Table: Table1

Related Column (Primary): CUSTIDFULL

Creating relationships between tables is necessary to show related data from different tables on the same report.

OK Cancel

FIGURE 26.38 Defining Relationships Between the Tables

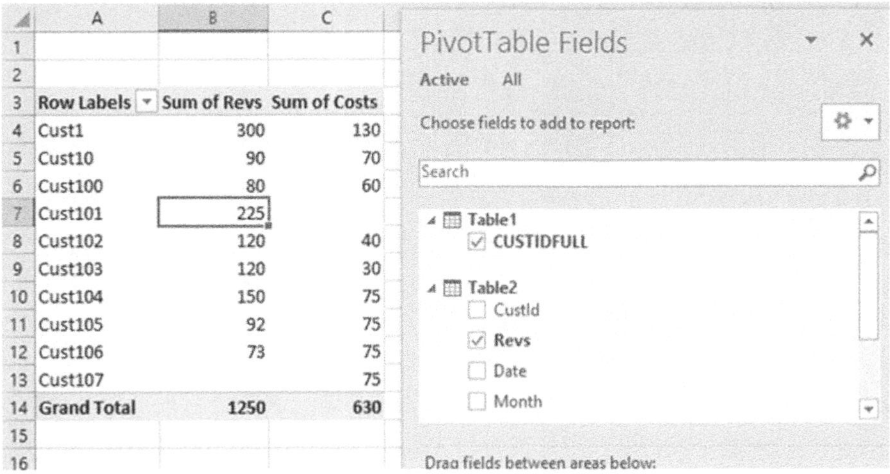

	A	B	C
1			
2			
3	Row Labels	Sum of Revs	Sum of Costs
4	Cust1	300	130
5	Cust10	90	70
6	Cust100	80	60
7	Cust101	225	
8	Cust102	120	40
9	Cust103	120	30
10	Cust104	150	75
11	Cust105	92	75
12	Cust106	73	75
13	Cust107		75
14	Grand Total	1250	630
15			
16			

PivotTable Fields

Active All

Choose fields to add to report:

Search

Table1
☑ CUSTIDFULL

Table2
☐ CustId
☑ Revs
☐ Date
☐ Month

Drag fields between areas below:

FIGURE 26.39 PivotTable Report Based on the DataModel

CHAPTER 27

Selected Short-cuts and Other Features

INTRODUCTION

This chapter presents a list of the key short-cuts that the author has found to be the most useful. Most of these are self-evident once they have been practised several times, so that only a few screen-clips are shown to demonstrate specific examples. The mastering of short-cuts can improve efficiency and speed of working. Therefore, each modeller should develop a good familiarity with those short-cuts that will be most relevant to them, and have a general understanding of the wider set available should they be useful in specific circumstances. It is worth noting that some of the short-cuts become particularly relevant when recording VBA code, as they allow to capture the code for operations that would not otherwise be evident. There are of course short-cuts available in Excel that are not covered in this chapter, and the reader may conduct his or her own research in this regard, perhaps using the list in this chapter as an initial check-list. The chapter also briefly mentions some of the Excel KeyTips, as well as some other potentially useful tools, such as Sparklines and the Camera.

KEY SHORT-CUTS AND THEIR USES

The key short-cuts we cover are structured into their main categories of application:

- Entering and modifying data and formulae.
- Formatting.
- Auditing, navigation and other items.

Note that, on a UK keyboard, some of these short-cuts (such as Ctrl+&) would require one to use the Shift key to access the relevant symbol (such as &); in such cases the Shift is not considered as part of the short-cut.

Entering and Modifying Data and Formulae

Core short-cuts for copying values and formulae, and correcting entries, include:

- Ctrl+C to copy a cell or range, Ctrl+X to cut, Ctrl+V to paste.
- Ctrl+Z to undo.
- When editing a formula in the Formula Bar, F4 implements absolute cell references (e.g. place a $ before a row reference); repeated pressing enables one to cycle through all possible combinations ($ before row and columns, and removal of $). The ease of applying the short-cut may lead to the creation of "over-dollared" formulae, i.e. ones in which the $ symbol is inserted before both the row and column references, whether only one or the other is required; this will typically result in formulae that cannot be correctly copied to elsewhere in the model.
- A formula (as well as its cell formatting) can be copied from a single cell into a range by using Ctrl+C (to initiate the copy procedure) and then, with this cell selected, either:
  - Pressing Shift and simultaneously selecting the last cell of the range in which the formula is desired to be copied, followed by Ctrl+V.
  - Pressing F8 and (following its release) selecting the last cell of the range in which the formula is desired to be copied, followed by Ctrl+V.
  - Using Ctrl+Shift+Arrow to select the range from the current cell to end of range in the direction of the arrow, followed by Ctrl+V.
- A formula (but not its formatting) can be copied from a single cell into a range by creating the formula in the first cell of the range, then using any of the techniques mentioned above to select the range in which the formula is to be copied, and then – working in the Formula Bar – entering Ctrl+Enter (or Ctrl+Shift+Enter for an array formula). This is particularly useful when modifying models which are already partially built and formatted, as it does not replace the formats that have been set in the cells to be overwritten. Figure 27.1 shows an example, just prior to using Ctrl+Enter, i.e. the formula has been created in the Formula Bar and the range has been selected.
- A formula can be copied down all the "relevant" rows in a column by double-clicking on bottom right of cell; the number of rows that are copied into will be determined by the rows in the Current Region of that cell (i.e. in the simplest case, to the point where the adjacent column also has content).
- Ctrl+' (apostrophe) can be used to recreate the contents of the cell directly above (rather than copying formula which would then generally alter the cell references within it). One case where this is useful is where one wishes to split a compound formula into its components, showing each component on a separate line. One can initially repeat the formula in the rows below, and delete the unnecessary components to isolate the individual elements. This will often be quicker and more robust than re-typing the individual components. As a trivial illustrative example, the individual components within a formula such as:

  = SUM('Finance Revenue'!P21,'Licence Fee'!P21,'Subscription Fee'!P21)

could be isolated in separate cells before being summed.

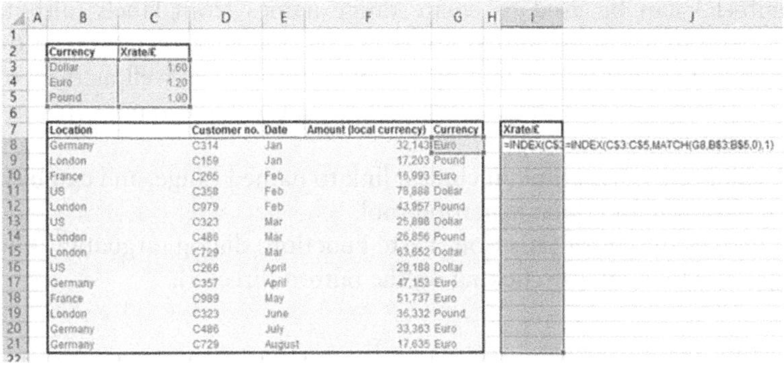

FIGURE 27.1 Copying a Formula Without Altering Preset Formatting

When creating formula, the following are worth noting:

- After first typing a valid function name (e.g. such as "MATCH"):
  - Ctrl+Shift+A shows the argument names and parentheses required for a function, and places these within the Formula Bar; an example is shown in Figure 27.2.
  - Ctrl+A invokes the Insert Function dialog, allowing for the function's parameters to be connected to cells more easily.
- Defining and using named ranges:
  - When creating formulae that require referencing ranges that have been named, pressing F3 when in the Formula Bar will provide a menu of the names that can be used (i.e. of workbook and worksheet-scoped names). Figure 27.3 shows an example of a formula being built by pressing F3 to show the list of named areas (and selecting them as relevant).
  - Ctrl+F3 can be used to invoke the Name Manager to define a named range.

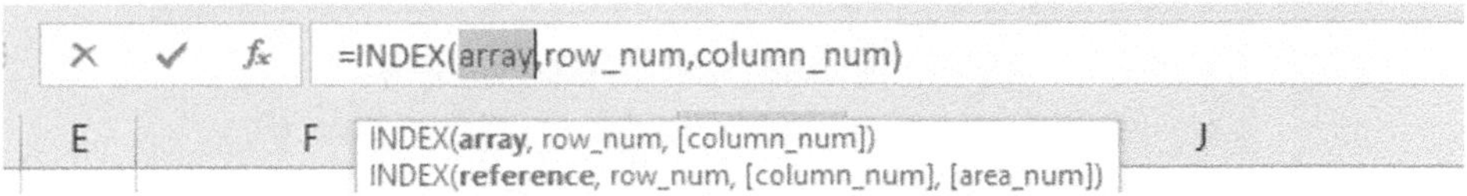

FIGURE 27.2 Invoking Function Parameters Within the Formula Bar Using Ctrl+Shift+A

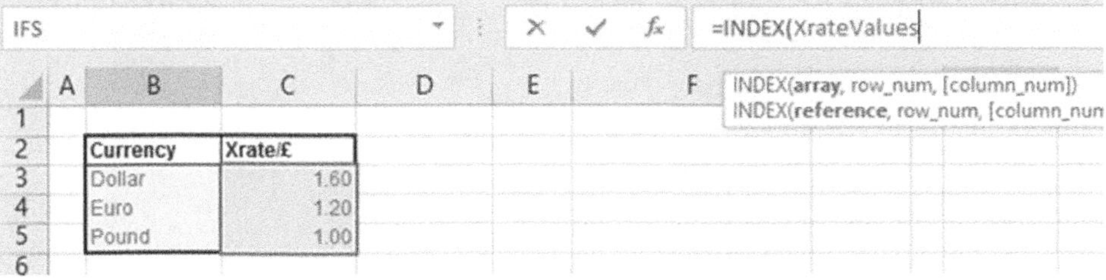

FIGURE 27.3 Building a Formula by Invoking the List of Named Ranges

  - Ctrl+Shift+F3 can be used to create range names from labels (although the author generally recommends to not do so; taking time to reflect on the most appropriate structure and hierarchy of named ranges, as well as their scope, is usually very important, and an automatic naming will often not generate such a set of names).
  - Ctrl+K will insert a hyperlink, include a link to named range, and can be a useful model navigation and documentation tool.
- Shift+F3 invokes the Insert Function (Paste Function) dialog (arguably, doing so is not any quicker than simply clicking on the button directly).

Formatting

The use of appropriate formatting can dramatically enhance transparency of a model, by highlighting the flow. Unfortunately, poor formatting is a key weakness of many models. Partly, this is due to a lack of discipline and time. Therefore, the knowledge and use of a few key format-related short-cuts can help to rapidly improve a model (even as the underlying calculations are unchanged). Key elements in this respect are:

- Using Ctrl+* (or Ctrl+Shift+Space) to select the Current Region of a cell (i.e. to select a range of cells that may require formatting in similar ways or have a border placed around them) (see Figure 27.4) for an example in which the Current Region of a cell (D13) is selected in this way.
- Ctrl+1 to display the main Format Cells menu.
- To work with the text in cells or ranges:
  - Crtl+2 (or Ctrl+B) to apply or remove bold formatting.
  - Ctrl+3 (or Ctrl+I) to apply or remove italic formatting.
  - Ctrl+4 (or Ctrl+U) to apply or remove underlining.

	A	B	C	D	E	F
1						
2		Location	Customer no.	Date	Amount	Currency
3		Germany	C314	Jan	32,143	Euro
4		London	C159	Jan	17,203	Pound
5		France	C265	Feb	16,993	Euro
6		US	C358	Feb	78,888	Dollar
7		London	C979	Feb	43,957	Pound
8		US	C323	Mar	25,898	Dollar
9		London	C486	Mar	26,856	Pound
10		London	C729	Mar	63,652	Dollar
11		US	C266	April	29,188	Dollar
12		Germany	C357	April	47,153	Euro
13		France	C989	May	51,737	Euro
14		London	C323	June	36,332	Pound
15		Germany	C486	July	33,363	Euro
16		Germany	C729	August	17,635	Euro
17						

FIGURE 27.4 Selecting the Current Region of a Cell (Cell D13)

- The rapid placing of borders around ranges can be facilitated by:
  - Ctrl+& to place borders.
  - Ctrl+ _ to remove borders.
- The Format Painter (on the Home tab) can be used to copy the format of one cell or range to another (double-clicking on the icon will keep it active, so that it can be applied to multiple ranges in sequence, until it is deactivated by a single click).
- Alt+Enter to insert a line break in a cell when typing labels.
- Ctrl+Enter to copy a formula into a range without disturbing existing formats (see above).
- Ctrl+T or Ctrl+L can be used to create an Excel Table from a range (this is more than a pure formatting operation, as discussed in Chapter 26).

Auditing, Navigation and Other Items

The rapid auditing of a model can be facilitated by use of a variety of short-cuts, including:

- Ctrl+' (left quotation mark) to show formulae (equivalent to Formulas/Show Formulas), which can be used to:
  - Search for hidden model inputs.
  - Look for inconsistent formulae across a range.
- Dependency tracing:
  - Ctrl+[selects those cells (on any worksheet) which are the direct precedents of a formula(e) (see Figure 27.5).
  - Ctrl+Shift+{ selects those cells (on the same worksheet as the formula(e)) which are either direct or indirect precedents (i.e. the backward calculation steps).
  - Ctrl+] select those cells (on any worksheet) which are the direct dependents of a formula(e).
  - Ctrl+Shift+} selects those cells (on the same worksheet as the formula(e)) which are either direct or indirect dependents (i.e. the forward calculation steps).
- When using the Formulas/Trace Precedents or Trace Dependents, double-clicking on the dependency arrows will move one to the corresponding place.
- Shift+F5 (or Ctrl+F) to find a specified item. Once this is done, Shift+F4 can be used to find the next occurrence of that element (rather than having to re-invoke the full Find menu and specifying the item again).

	A	B	C	D	E	F	G	H	I
1									
2		Currency	Xrate/£						
3		Dollar	1.60						
4		Euro	1.20						
5		Pound	1.00						
6									
7		Location		Customer no.	Date	Amount (local currency)	Currency		Xrate/£
8		Germany		C314	Jan	32,143	Euro		1.20

FIGURE 27.5 Use of Short-cuts to Trace Precedents (of cell I8)

- F5 (or Ctrl+G) to go to a cell, range or named range. When using this, the Special option can be used to find formulae, constants, blanks. Thus, model inputs (when in stand-alone cells in same worksheet) may be found using F5/Special, selecting Constants (not Formula), and under Formula selecting Numbers (similarly for text fields). The "Last cell" option of the Special menu is also useful, especially for the recording of the syntax required when automating the manipulation of data sets with VBA (see Figure 27.6).
- F1 invokes the Help menu.
- F2 inspects or edits a formula in the cell (rather than in the Formula Bar, which typically requires more eye movement when frequently moving one's attention between the worksheet and the Formula Bar).
- Working with comments:
  - Shift+F2 inserts a comment into the active cell.
  - Ctrl+Shift+O (the letter O) select all cells with comments (e.g. so that they can all be found and read, or alternatively all deleted simultaneously).
- F3 will provide a list of named ranges that are valid in the worksheet (i.e. those of workbook and worksheet-scoped names). Generating such a list can not only be useful for auditing and documentation, but also when writing VBA code; the copying into VBA (as the code is being written) of the list of names can help to ensure the correct spelling within the code.
- F7 checks spelling.
- F9 recalculates all open workbooks.
- Alt+F8 shows the list of macros in the workbook.
- Alt+F11 takes one to the VBA Editor.
- F11 inserts a chart sheet.
- Further aspects of moving around the worksheet:
  - Home to move to Column A within the same row.
  - Ctrl+Home to move to Cell A1.
  - Ctrl+Shift+Home to extend the selection to Cell A1.
  - Ctrl+Arrow moves to the first non-blank cell in the row or column.

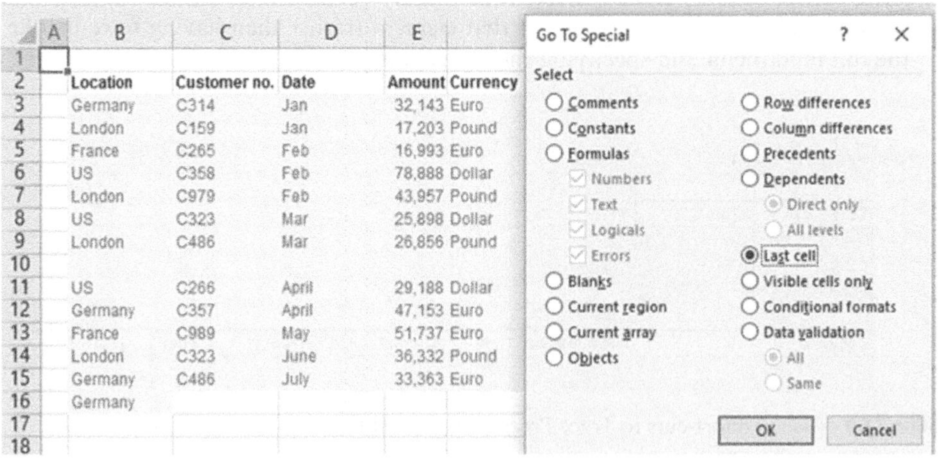

	A	B	C	D	E	
1						
2		Location	Customer no.	Date	Amount	Currency
3		Germany	C314	Jan	32,143	Euro
4		London	C159	Jan	17,203	Pound
5		France	C265	Feb	16,993	Euro
6		US	C358	Feb	78,888	Dollar
7		London	C979	Feb	43,957	Pound
8		US	C323	Mar	25,898	Dollar
9		London	C486	Mar	26,856	Pound
10						
11		US	C266	April	29,188	Dollar
12		Germany	C357	April	47,153	Euro
13		France	C989	May	51,737	Euro
14		London	C323	June	36,332	Pound
15		Germany	C486	July	33,363	Euro
16		Germany				
17						
18						

FIGURE 27.6 Finding the Last Cell in the Used Range

- Ctrl+Shift+Arrow extends selection to the last nonblank cell in the column or row.
- Shift+Arrow extends the selection of cells by one cell.
- Ctrl+Shift+End extends the selection to the last used cell on the worksheet.

- Ctrl+F1 toggles to hide/unhide Excel's detailed menu items, retaining the menu tab names and Formula Bar. Ctrl+Shift+F1 toggles so that the Excel's menu items and tabs become hidden/unhidden. These can be useful for improving the display of a file, for example when presenting to a group.

Excel KeyTips

Excel KeyTips are activated by using the Alt key, resulting in a display of letters that may be typed to access many parts of the Excel menu. Some examples of important KeyTips include:

- Alt-M-H to display formulae (equivalent to Ctrl+').
- Alt-M-P to trace precedents.
- Alt-M-D to trace dependents.
- Alt-A-V for the data validation menu.
- Alt-D-F-S to clear all data filters.
- Alt-H-V-V to paste values (Alt-E-S-V also works).

(The "–" indicates that the keys are used separately in sequence, in contrast to the traditional short-cuts, where the "+" indicates that the keys are to be used simultaneously.)

The accessing of KeyTips is generally a simple and self-evident visual operation; this contrasts with the more traditional short-cuts, whose existence is not self-evident *per se*. Thus, the reader can simply experiment, and find those that may be most useful in their own areas of application.

OTHER USEFUL EXCEL TOOLS AND FEATURES

Sparklines

Sparklines (Excel 2010 onwards) can be used to display a series of data in a single cell (rather like a thumbnail graph). There are three forms: line, column and win/loss charts. They can be created by activating the worksheet in which the sparklines are to be displayed, using Insert/Sparklines and selecting the relevant data. (The data range may be on a different worksheet to that in which the sparklines are displayed; if the sparklines are to be on the same sheet as the data, one can select the data first and use Insert/Sparklines afterwards.)

The Camera Tool

The Camera tool can be used to create a live picture of another part of the workbook. This allows one to create a summary report area without having to make a formulae reference to the data, and to easily consolidate several areas in a single place. (The live picture updates as the source areas in the workbook change.)

The tool can be added to the Quick Access Toolbar by using Excel Options/Quick Access Toolbar and under "Choose Commands From" selecting "Commands not in the Ribbon" (on the drop-down menu) and double-clicking on the Camera icon. Once added in this way, it can be used by selecting the Excel range that one wish to take a picture of, clicking on the Camera icon in the QAT, and drawing the rectangle in the area that one wishes the picture to be.

In fact, a similar result can also be achieved using a Linked Picture (without explicitly accessing the Camera tool): one simply selects the required source range and copies it (using Ctrl+C), then clicks on the on the range in Excel where the picture is desired to be placed, followed by using Home/Paste/Other Paste Options/LinkedPicture.

PART Six

Foundations of VBA and Macros

CHAPTER 28

Getting Started

INTRODUCTION

This chapter describes some core elements of Excel's Visual Basic for Applications (VBA). A good familiarity with this is essential for anyone wishing to progress beyond basic level financial modelling applications. The text focuses on the topics that we consider to be the most important. We aim to enable the reader who is a beginner with VBA to rapidly become familiar with core operations and to be able to write and use some simple, yet practical and robust code. In particular, we focus on subroutines and user-defined functions: subroutines consist of sequences of tasks or processes, whereas user-defined functions perform bespoke calculations that may not be available as Excel functions. Other areas of VBA, such as user forms and class modules, are not covered in this text. In this way, we hope to have created a text that is accessible for the beginner whilst still being of high value when applied to many real-life modelling situations.

This chapter attempts to present only those concepts which are essential to getting started and to demonstrate the core concepts; topics concerning the writing of more general and robust code are covered later in the text. The first section of this chapter provides an overview of the main uses of VBA. The second section presents some core building blocks and key operations.

Note that in this Part of the text, we use the term "Excel" (or "pure Excel") to refer to the traditional part of Excel where no VBA is involved (i.e. consisting of the workbook, worksheet grid, functions, and so on). Also, whereas the term "macro" is often used to refer to VBA, we will generally use to refer to subroutines or other procedures (and not for user-defined functions, for example).

MAIN USES OF VBA

The main uses of VBA can be summarised as:

- Automating tasks.
- Creating user-defined functions.
- Detecting and reacting to Excel or model events.

- Enhancing or managing the user interface.
- Developing generalised applications.

This section provides a brief description of each, with much of the rest of the text devoted to the first two topics.

Task Automation

Tasks that need to be repeated (in similar form) many times can be automated to enhance efficiency. Typical areas include:

- Manipulation of data sets. This could include operations to clean underlying data or to consolidate data together.
- Database queries and extraction. This includes where database queries need to be run multiple times, especially in cases where the use of multiple database criteria ranges would be inconvenient.
- Resolving circular references through iteration.
- Running scenarios. Especially in cases where a model contains a circular reference that is resolved using a macro, the running of multiple scenarios will generally also require a macro.
- Running simulations. The use of (Monte Carlo) simulation is a generalisation of scenario modelling, in which many scenarios are generated automatically using random sampling of probability distributions.
- Running Excel's GoalSeek or Solver several times.

Creating User-defined Functions

User-defined (or user-created) functions can be very powerful in many circumstances. Here, we simply note that the main advantages that may be achieved include to perform calculations that are cumbersome to create and modify in Excel, to reduce the size of the model interface in Excel, to increase flexibility in the structure of a model, and to create easily reuseable logic and more transparency in the calculations. Later in this chapter, we provide a simple introductory example. More detailed coverage and further practical examples are provided in Chapter 33.

Detecting and Reacting to Model Events

In some contexts, it is required to detect changes that happen to, or within, a workbook, and to respond to these in some way. This could include:

- Automatically running a macro whenever the workbook is opened, if data is changed, or if some other workbook event has happened, including:
  - Ensuring that the user is always automatically taken to the main model (or some other) worksheet when the workbook is opened.
  - Showing a Disclaimer statement when the workbook is opened.
  - Finding the cell whose value was changed most recently.
  - (Automatically) running a macro when any cell in the input range is changed.
- Highlighting the row and column of any cell whenever one double-clicks on it.

Enhancing or Managing the User Interface

VBA can be used to enhance the user interface. The simplest types of interactions are message boxes (`MsgBox`) and input boxes (`InputBox`). More sophisticated examples include user forms (`UserForm`), which can take input from a user in a structured process, ensure the integrity of the input data or create a database with the inputted data.

Application Development

The Excel-VBA environment is surprisingly powerful and flexible for the development of "full blown" applications. These may integrate various capabilities, such as enhancing the user interface, accessing data in other applications (such as Access), manipulating data, performing calculations and generating reports and charts.

It is also fairly easy to produce add-ins, especially for code that is frequently used or is required to be accessed from a number of workbooks. This can be shared easily, and also password-protected.

Whilst the systematic creation and use of add-ins is beyond the scope of this text, it is worth noting that that they can be created simply by saving the original workbook with an .xlam file extension when using Excel's Save As feature.

CORE OPERATIONS

In this section, we cover the basic elements relating to the main areas of generating and running VBA code:

- Showing the Developer tab on Excel's toolbar.
- Accessing the Visual Basic Editor.
- Recording macros.
- Writing code and adapting recorded code.
- Running code.
- Creating code by writing rather than recording it.

Adding the Developer Tab to Excel's Toolbar

To work with VBA, it is usually most convenient to have Excel's Developer tab shown (which is usually not the case in Excel's default shipping). This can be achieved under the Excel Options menu, although the precise way to do it is specific to the version. Figure 28.1 shows the process of invoking the Developer tab in Excel 2016, and Figure 28.2 shows the resulting Excel toolbar.

The Visual Basic Editor

The Visual Basic Editor (VBE) is required to write or modify code. It can be accessed using the Visual Basic button on the Developer tab (or the short-cut Alt+F11). By default, the `Project Explorer` and the `Properties` windows should be displayed within the VBE; if not, they are accessible under the VBE `View` menu (see Figure 28.3).

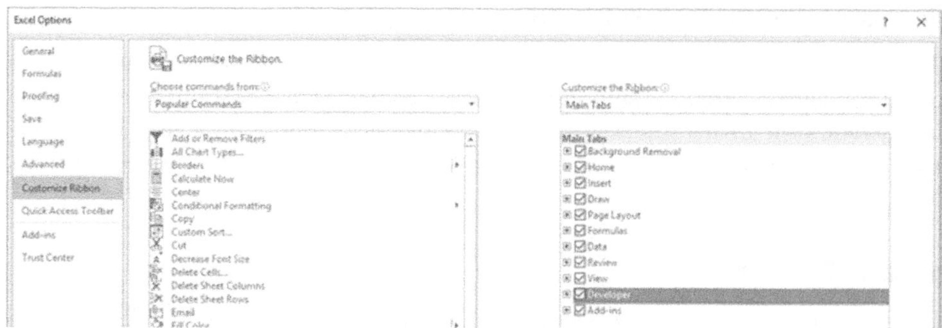

FIGURE 28.1 Invoking the Developer Tab

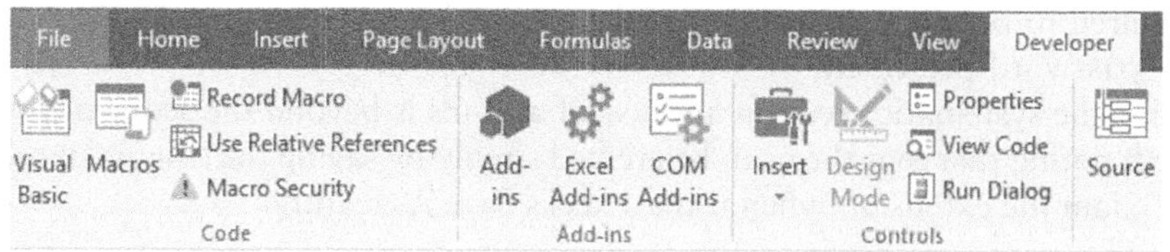

FIGURE 28.2 The Developer Tab

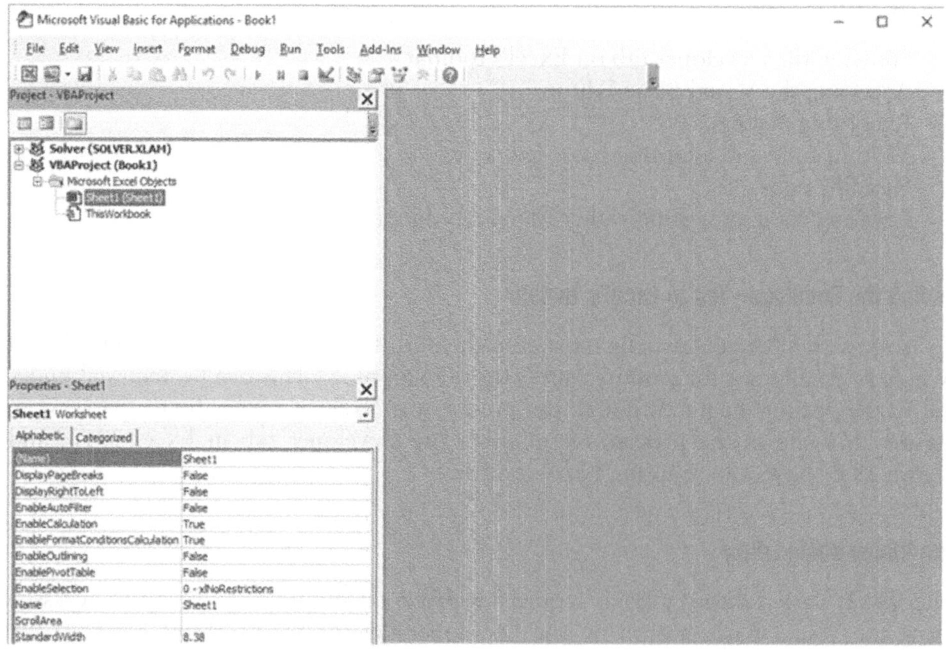

FIGURE 28.3 Core Elements of the Visual Basic Editor

The `Project` Window shows a list of open workbooks in the user's environment, and so will be different for each user and vary from one working session to another.

Note that it is often convenient to use a vertically split screen simply by resizing each of the Excel and the VBE windows, and arranging them side by side.

Recording Macros

The recording of macros is the process whereby one instructs Excel to capture a record of all changes made to the Excel environment as one is working. The recording process can be carried out by using the Record Macro button on the Developer tab to start the process (see Figure 28.2) and then using the Stop Recording Macro button (which shows only once the recording process has started) when finished.

Some points to bear in mind are:

- Before recording, it is advisable to practise the exact sequence of operations that will be used. This helps to eliminate the recording of unnecessary processes (such as the selection of the wrong worksheet tabs or menu items).
- There is an option (toward the beginning of the recording process) to give the macro a name, and assign a short-cut key, and a description. However, these are generally unnecessary, as the recording process typically should only be used only to provide information about the correct syntax to be used for a specific operation, with this syntax used (or copied and adapted) in new code that is written directly.
- Another option is to store a macro in a Personal Macro Workbook, which will create a file within Excel's XLStart folder that is always loaded when Excel starts. This approach is not used within this text as it is not appropriate where the macro (sub-routine or user-defined function) is required as an integral part of the model (which may therefore need to be shared with, or sent to, others). However, for some application areas which may be required to be performed by a model builder, but not necessarily be an inherent part of a specific model (such as some aspects of data manipulation), their use may be appropriate.
- It generally makes sense to place the workbook on Manual recalculation (under File/Options/Formulas) before the macro is recorded. This will help one to focus on making explicit the stages at which a recalculation instruction is required within the code (such as when pressing F9 would be required when on Manual recalculation). Doing so will help to ensure that the macro works in all environments (i.e. independently of whether the calculation settings are on Manual or on Automatic). An alternative approach is to switch to Manual recalculation as the first step in the recording process.
- Do not forget to stop recording as the desired steps have been completed; this is a common mistake!

Figure 28.4 shows the VBE and displays the code that results from recording a macro as a Copy/Paste operation is conducted (in which Cell A1 is copied to Cell A4).

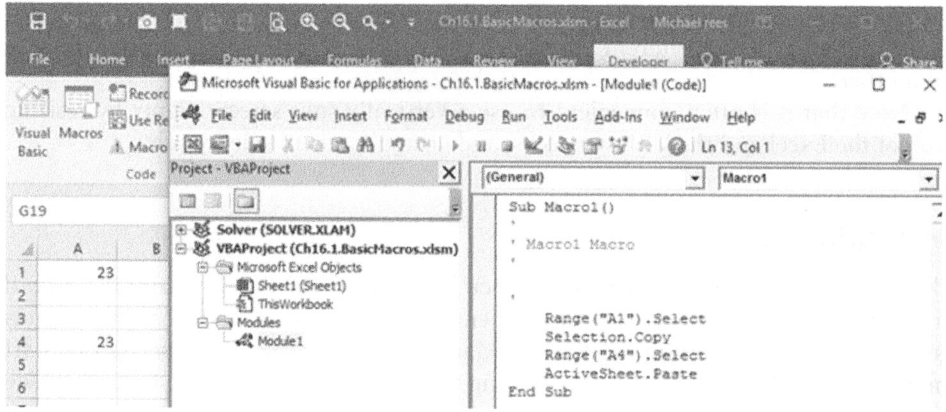

FIGURE 28.4 Recording A Copy/Paste Operation

Typical Adaptations Required When Using Recorded Code

Although many beginners start by recording code (and indeed often use such code in their final models), generally it is rare that code created by recording is sufficiently general, efficient or robust. Typically, recorded code would need adaptation, such as:

- Increasing the generality of application:
  - Replacing fixed cell references, either with named ranges or with code which determines the correct range (such as where the data starts, or refers to a data range with a size that is determined by the data set).
  - Using a loop to repeat similar operations (note that a loop cannot be recorded).
  - Adding conditional statements (these can also not be recorded).
  - Adding a forced recalculation of Excel; code which has been recorded whilst Excel's calculation mode is set on (its default) Automatic will not explicitly have captured that Excel may have recalculated during the process. To ensure that the code works correctly with other settings (such as Manual), it may be necessary to force an explicit recalculation of Excel at specific points.
- Improving efficiency:
  - Replacing operations that involve selecting ranges (such as Copy/Paste) with more direct statements (such as assignment on the values from one range to the other); this will generally result in code which is much more efficient and quicker to execute. Similarly, direct approaches to identify or reference worksheets will typically be more efficient than the conducting of an Excel operation to select such objects.
  - Removing or modifying steps that may be unnecessary, but which appeared in the recording (such as formatting operations).

Thus, the main (most valid) reason for recording code is as a means to facilitate the finding of the correct syntax for specialised operations (such as capturing the VBA-equivalent of Excel short-cuts, refreshing a PivotTable, running GoalSeek or Solver, and so on). In other words, the results of the recording are used to provide insight into a functionality, from which the specifically relevant instructions are derived.

Note also that many aspects of VBA simply cannot be recorded, and so must be written: these include loops, conditional statements (and many other aspects of controlling execution) and using functions.

Writing Code

As a rule, to have robust and effective VBA code, one will need to write most of it from scratch (or copy and adapt it from somewhere else), complemented by occasionally referring to and adapting recorded code.

As shown in Figure 28.4, where code is generated by recording Excel operations, a code module will be inserted automatically (and if one already exists, new recorded code will be placed within that). However, when writing code from scratch, it will be necessary to ensure that there is a code module available within the appropriate workbook (`Project`); this can be achieved by selecting the workbook name within the `Project Window` and using `Insert/Module`.

Some core points are worth noting in this respect:

- The `ThisWorkbook` and `Sheet` are "object modules" and are reserved for procedures relating to workbook and worksheet events, and should not be used to place general purpose code. For example, the `ThisWorkbook` module can be used to write code that will execute whenever the workbook is opened (see later for an example). `Class Module` and `UserForm` module possibilities are also beyond the scope of this text.
- Within a code module, one will need to define whether one is writing a subroutine or a function:
  - A subroutine can be created by typing the words `Sub` followed by a name (such as `Sub FirstCode()`); the words `End Sub` appear automatically. The empty brackets after the name indicate that the subroutine has no parameters associated with it. Many subroutines are task sequences which do not require arguments, although some may (the code in Figure 28.4 shows a similar example).
  - A function can be created by typing `Function` followed by a name and argument list in brackets; the words `End Function` will appear automatically.
- Where several procedures are to be written, these can either be included within the same module or in a new module. If several procedures have been created in a module, the drop-down list in the `Procedure` box can be used to rapidly move between them. One may choose to split the code across several modules in order both to increase transparency and to ease navigation. For example, subroutines could be placed in one (or several modules) and functions in another. In such cases, it can be useful to give an appropriate name to each module by using the `Name` box within the `Properties` window.
- The name of the procedures within a module (subroutine or functions) can be chosen to be essentially anything (subject to a few restrictions, such as not containing any spaces, not using reserved words and so on; see later for more details).
- The code will be saved whenever the workbook is saved as an .xlsm file (a .xlsx file may not contain code).

The code window should also appear once the module is inserted; if not, `View/Code` can be used to display it. The code within any module can be made visible by double-clicking on the name of the module.

When writing code, some points to bear in mind are:

- Comment lines are simply notes that have no effect when the code is run. A comment starts with an apostrophe, and may either be on a stand-alone line or be placed on a code line (after the code). Comment lines are shown automatically in green; the recorded macro in Figure 28.4 contains some comment lines that were automatically inserted.
- A line of code or a comment can be continued (on another line), by the use of SPACE followed by UNDERSCORE at the end of the line that is to be continued.
- Indentation can be used to make the code visually more attractive. The Tab key can be used to indent code, and Shift+Tab to un-indent. The `Tools/Options/Editor` menu in VBE can be used to alter the tab width (when using several levels of indenting, the default tab width of four spaces is often too wide).
- When in the `Code` window, the typing of a full stop after an object will result in a drop-down menu appearing, which presents the available list of menu items relating to that object. For example, by typing `Range("A1").` one sees the menu items that are relevant to a range, such as `Range("A1").Activate` to make A1 the active cell, `Range("A1").ClearContents` to clear the contents of Cell A1, and `Range("A1").Value` to refer to its value (the value is also the default property of a range, so `Range("A1")` would be interpreted as referring to the value).

Running Code

Before running any VBA macros, it is important to realise that in general there is no undo feature. Thus, code which alters the Excel worksheet in some way (such as overwriting existing data or formulae) can cause problems if it has not been checked first. Therefore, before running any code, it is often worthwhile to keep a back-up of the file, or at least to check before saving the file that the macro has not produced any errors.

Macros (or sub-routines) can be run in several ways:

- When in VBE, with the cursor placed within the code of the subroutine to be run, press F5 (or `Run/Run Sub`). A macro can also be called from another macro, so that, in more complex situations, embedded or sequential structures can be created in order to modularise the code into smaller components.
- When in Excel's Developer tab, using the Macros button to select the macro and then choosing Run. The short-cut Alt+F8 can also be used (from anywhere in Excel) to invoke the Macros command.
- Within Excel, by clicking on any object which has had a macro assigned to it. Such an object may be created in any standard way in Excel (such as using the Insert menu to create a TextBox, a Chart or other shape or graphic), with right-clicking on the shape used to invoke the Assign Macro menu. Alternatively, the Insert/FormControls command on the Developer tab can be used to create a button or other control, in which case the macro-assignment process is invoked automatically. (ActiveX controls should not generally be used.) Objects such as text boxes and buttons can of course be renamed, resized and repositioned as desired (e.g. by right-clicking to edit). It is important to label them clearly to ensure that macros are not run by accident. Therefore, it should be made clear to the user in some way that clicking on the shape will run a macro (e.g. by labelling the shape); if this is

not clear, then the macro may be run unintentionally, which may not be desirable. For example, assigning to a chart a macro that is needed to update the chart data would seem sensible, whereas if the macro performs some other operation (not related to the chart), then it would probably be better to use a separate button.
- From the Customize menu on the Quick Access Toolbar, choose More Commands, then Macros (in place of the default Popular Commands), select the macro name, and choose Add. One can then use the Modify menu to use a symbol to represent the macro. Since this will change the general Excel interface and create an icon that will have an effect only when the workbook that contains the macro is active, it is probably worthwhile doing only for procedures that are to be used in a variety of workbooks, such as some of those in the Personal Macro Workbook (which we do not use in this text; see earlier).
- From a `User Form`.

Debugging Techniques

Before running code completely, it is usually worth running some simple checks:

- Using the `Debug/Compile` menu will often find basic errors of syntax or consistency.
- Stepping through the code line-by-line, by using the F8 key (or `Debug/Step Into`). This will often highlight the location of fundamental errors that prevent complete code execution. When stepping through, a few points are worth bearing in mind:
  - The code line that is about to run (but has not yet done so) will appear in yellow.
  - Placing the cursor over a variable will show its value at that point in the code execution.
  - Ctrl+F8 or `Debug/Run to Cursor` can be used to run from the beginning to the position of the cursor; this can be useful if one believes that the code up to that point is working and one wishes to double-check by running it.
  - One can set a breakpoint in the code by clicking on the side-bar, or placing the cursor at the desired code line and pressing F9, or using `Debug/Toggle Breakpoint`. The code can then be run to the breakpoint by using F5 (assuming it is error-free up to that point) and thereafter using F8 to step through the subsequent lines individually.
  - A simple message box (e.g. `MsgBox x`) can be used to return the value of a variable at that line in the code. It can be commented out (using an apostrophe) or deleted when no longer needed.
- When running the code, the `Run/Break` and `Run/Reset` buttons can be used to halt code execution and break out, such as if one is caught in a long or endless loop (Excel's Task Manager can be used as a last resort).
- The VBA `Help` menu can be accessed from the toolbar or using F1 from within VBE.

Whilst the use of these step-through and break-point techniques is usually sufficient for simple code, other debugging and robust code-writing techniques may be required or recommended in general practical examples. The later chapters in this Part (especially Chapter 31) cover these in detail.

Note that the fact that code can perform operations without crashing is not the same as the code being free of errors or of meeting its functionality requirements! This is the same as in Excel, where the fact that a formula calculates without returning an error message does not mean that the model is correct. In addition, as a general rule, the types of possible errors that can occur in VBA are usually more varied and potentially subtler than in Excel.

SIMPLE EXAMPLES

This section provides some simple examples of code which illustrate many of the points covered earlier in the chapter. We show examples of:

- Taking a value from an Excel cell and using it in VBA code.
- Using named Excel ranges to make the communication between Excel and VBA more robust.
- Placing a value from VBA code into an Excel range.
- Replacing a Copy/Paste operation with an assignment statement.
- Creating a simple user-defined function.

When running code in the example files, it will be necessary to enable the macros in them. This can be done either on an individual basis (in response to the security warnings that are likely to appear), or by temporarily enabling all macros using the Macro Settings within the Trust Centre options (on the Excel Options menu), or by setting the folder containing the files as a trusted location using the Add Trusted Locations option.

Example: Using Excel Cell Values in VBA

The file Ch28.1.ExcelToVBA.1.xlsm contains an example of code which reads the values from two Excel cells into VBA, multiplies them, and displays the result to the user in a MessageBox (see Figure 28.5).

The code used is:

```
Sub MRTakeNumberFromExcel()
i &equals; Range("C2")
j &equals; Range("C3").Value
k &equals; i * j
MsgBox k
End Sub
```

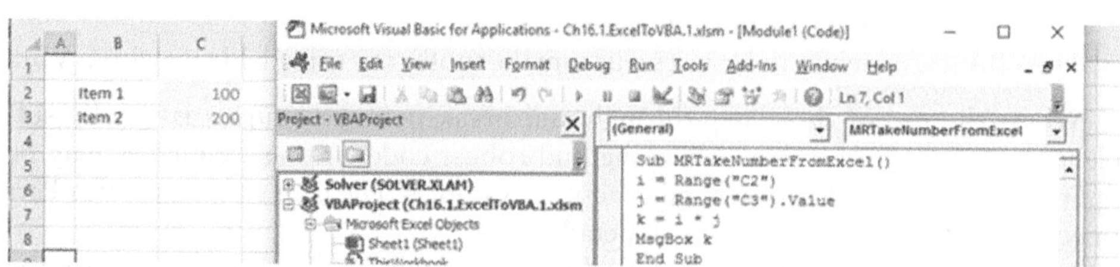

FIGURE 28.5 Simple Example of Using Values from Excel in VBA

Note the following:

- The Excel cell ranges are referred to in a way which uses cell references as text fields (i.e. `Range("C2")`, not `Range(C2)`). Therefore, such text fields would not adjust automatically if a row were introduced at the top of the worksheet, and the code would not work as anticipated; this is one reason why the use of named ranges for Excel cells will be more robust (see later).
- The = sign is not a statement of mathematical equality; rather it is an operation which assigns the item on the right to the item on the left. This is similar to other computing languages, and indeed also to Excel, where (for example) when working in Cell B5, the typing of =B2 will assign the contents of B2 into B5.
- The default property within VBA of a single Excel cell is its value. Therefore, the `.Value` statement used in the second assignment operation is not required here. However, it is generally more robust and transparent to explicitly state which property of a cell is required (e.g. its format, text colour or font size), since VBA code can be used to conduct operations based on many properties of cells and ranges.
- Where the range referred to is a multi-cell range, the `.Value` property would generally be necessary for the code to execute correctly.

Figure 28.6 shows the results of running this code, displaying a message box (`MsgBox`) of the result.

Example: Using Named Excel Ranges for Robustness and Flexibility

To make the above procedure more robust, it would help if the Excel cell ranges were given names. This would allow the individual cells to be moved elsewhere (or a new row inserted above them, or columns before them) without affecting the results.

Figure 28.7 shows the names that are given in this example using Excel's Formula/Name Manager menu.

The VBA code can then be adapted as follows:

```
Sub MRTakeNumberFromExcel()
i &equals; Range("Item1")
j &equals; Range("Item2").Value
k &equals; i * j
MsgBox k
End Sub
```

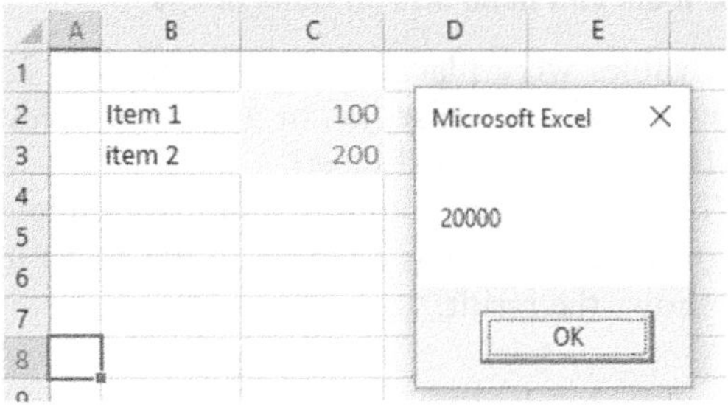

FIGURE 28.6 Results of Running Some Simple Code, with the Message Box Displayed

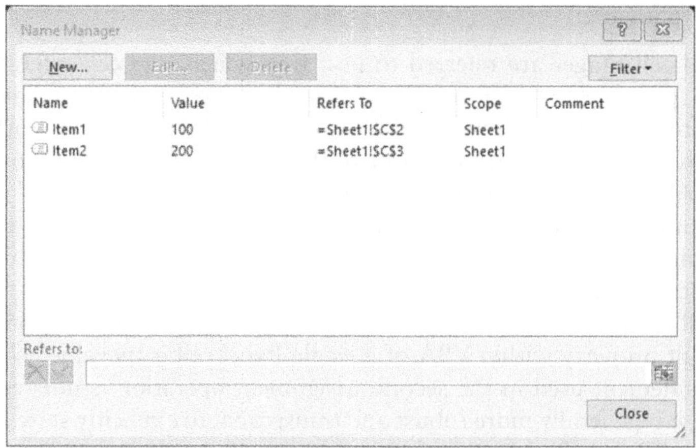

FIGURE 28.7 Creating Named Ranges in Excel

Note that:

- If the name of a range is modified in the Excel workbook, then it will also need to be changed in the VBA code. The link is not automatic, as the VBA code encloses the name in parenthesis, as for a text field. (Once again, this contrast to Excel formulae, where the name used is modified automatically.)
- In auditing a model that contains VBA code, it is advisable to inspect any VBA code before changing the Excel part of the model in any way (introducing rows, columns, changing named ranges or other operations could all create unintended changes).
- It can be useful to use the F3 short-cut key to create a list of Excel named ranges, which can then be copied into VBA code to avoid spelling mistakes. (Chapter 30 shows an example of a macro which can be used to list all the named ranges within a workbook, as an alternative.)

Once these changes are made to the code, new rows and columns could be introduced into Excel, as desired, and the code should run correctly.

The file Ch28.2.ExcelToVBA.2.xlsm is provided so that the reader can experiment with this.

Example: Placing a Value from VBA Code into an Excel Range

In the above example, values were placed from code into an Excel worksheet. The process can be used in the opposite sense (i.e. in which variables that are used in the code take their values from an Excel worksheet).

The file Ch28.3.VBAtoExcel.xlsm contains a simple example; the number 100 is assigned to the value of the cell that has been given the Excel named range ValItem (Cell C2); Figure 28.8 shows the result.

```
Sub MRAssignl()
Range("ValItem").Value &equals; 100
End Sub
```

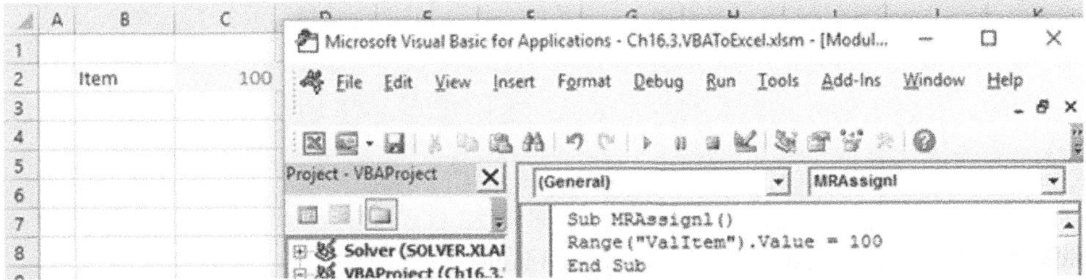

FIGURE 28.8 Result of Running a Simple Macro to Assign Values from VBA into Excel

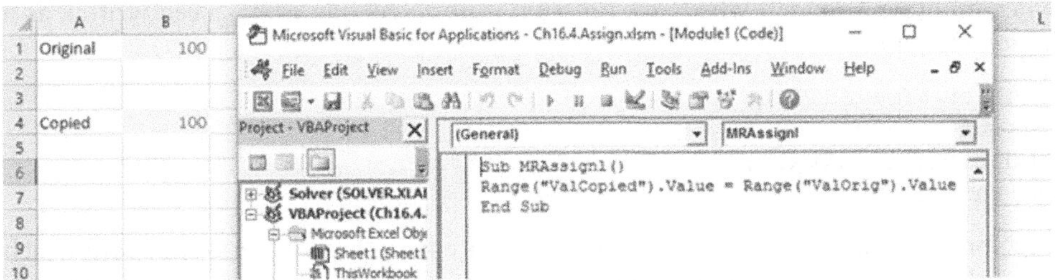

FIGURE 28.9 Results of Assignment Operation Instead of Copy/Paste

Example: Replacing Copy/Paste with an Assignment

As a rule, it will be much more computationally efficient to use assignment operations instead of Copy/Paste. The difference in speed between the two becomes much clearer when the operations are performed many times in sequence.

The file Ch28.4.Assign.xlsm shows an example of how assignment can be used to place the value of one cell (named range) into another without explicitly selecting the cells, or using a Copy/Paste operation (see Figure 28.9).

```
Sub MRAssignl()
Range("ValCopied").Value &equals; Range("ValOrig").Value
End Sub
```

Example: A Simple User-defined Function

Functions are distinguished from subroutines in that they can only provide a result in an Excel cell or range (for array functions). As for Excel functions, the link between a function's parameters and the result of the calculations is "live". By contrast, subroutines can perform procedures (including returning a value into an Excel cell), but are not live linked to the input assumptions, so need to be re-run if the value of these assumptions were to change.

The file Ch28.5.UDFSimple.xlsm shows a simple example (see Figure 28.10). Note that user-created functions can be accessed in Excel by direct typing (provided they have the default scope of `Public`), or by using the Formula/Insert Function menu (where they will be listed under the user-defined category). To facilitate the direct

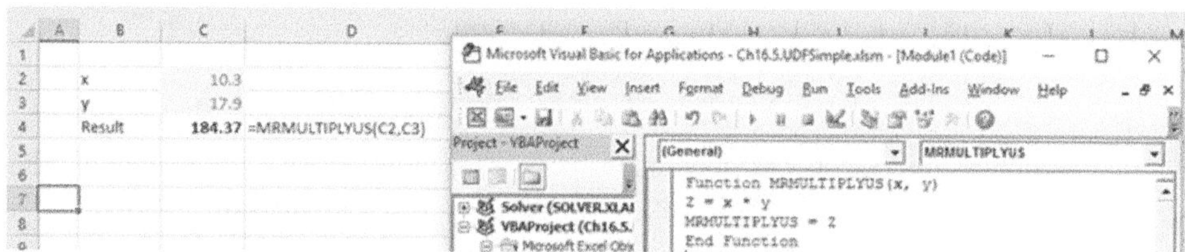

FIGURE 28.10 Simple Example of a User-defined Function

typing approach, the author generally names all his functions so that the first two letters are those of his initials (i.e. MR. . .); such nomenclature also helps to identify (when auditing a model) whether a function is an Excel one or has been written as a bespoke function.

```
Function MRMULTIPLYUS(x, y)
Z &equals; x * y
MRMULTIPLYUS &equals; Z
End Function
```

Note that the code must contain a return statement (before `End Function`) which explicitly assigns the value of the calculation to the function's value (a frequent error is to omit the return statement when writing the initial code).

Of course, as is the case when using other VBA procedures, user-defined functions have the disadvantage that the model may be less transparent to users who are not familiar with them. Their use can nevertheless be a powerful tool in the right circumstances, as discussed in more detail in Chapter 33.

Example: Displaying a Message when a Workbook is Opened

A simple example of event-driven code is that of automatically displaying a message whenever a workbook is opened. The key point is that a specific subroutine using the reserved word `Workbook_Open()` must be placed within the `ThisWorkbook` code module.

The file Ch28.6.WorkbookOpenDisclaimer.xlsm contains a simple example. Figure 28.11 shows a screen-clip. Note that in this example, the worksheet in Excel that contains the disclaimer is named "Disclaimer", and has been given the code name `ModelDisclaimer` in VBA. Thus, the code activates that worksheet and then displays a message box to the user (the message box could also display the text of the disclaimer, as an additional option or as an alternative).

```
Sub Workbook_Open()
With ThisWorkbook
  ModelDisclaimer.Activate
  MsgBox ("Please read the disclaimer in the Disclaimer worksheet")
  'MsgBox ("...or you could write the Disclaimer text here ...")
End With
End Sub
```

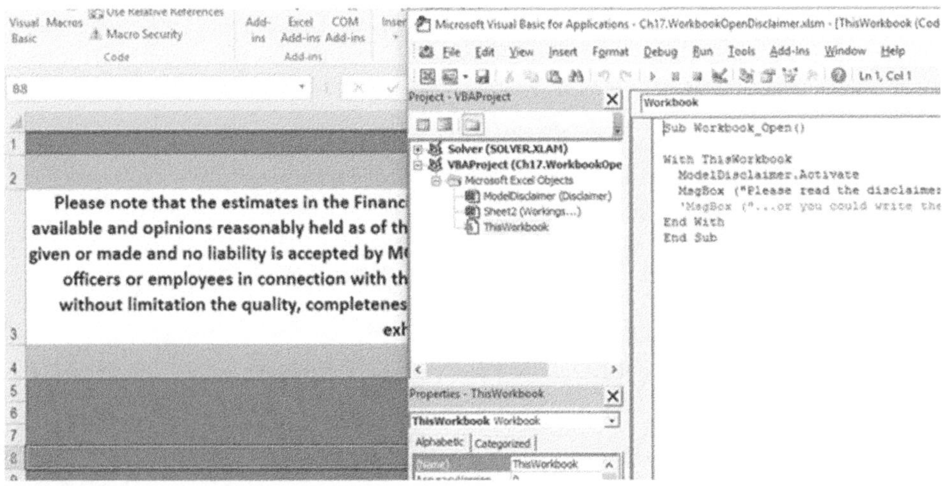

FIGURE 28.11 Displaying a Message when a Workbook is Opened

Note also that procedures can be run whenever a workbook is closed using the subroutine `Workbook_Close`, which is also a reserved word that must be placed in the `ThisWorkbook` code module.

```
Sub Workbook_Close()
'Write code to run here
End Sub
```

CHAPTER 29

Working with Objects and Ranges

INTRODUCTION

This chapter introduces the structure of objects within the Excel environment. We focus on those that are key in general financial modelling, especially:

- Referring to ranges of cells.
- Using collections of objects and hierarchies of objects.

OVERVIEW OF THE OBJECT MODEL

For many modellers, the subject of Excel objects is not one that would seem to be of immediate relevance: first, many traditional Excel models are based on arithmetic operations and functions, with objects apparently having no real role. Second, simple VBA code can be recorded or written without there appearing to be any need to refer to objects specifically. However, knowledge of the principles of Excel objects is very important to be able to write clear, flexible and robust code, as well as to access the wide set of applications that the Excel/VBA object environment allows, so that one can develop (or audit) a wider set of modelling applications.

Objects, Properties, Methods and Events

In many ways, the logic used in the Excel/VBA environment is similar to that of natural language:

- Objects are analogous to nouns. They are essentially the parts of Excel that can be seen, including cells, ranges, rows, columns, workbooks, worksheets, charts, PivotTables, text boxes, cell comment boxes, shapes, and so on.
- Properties are analogous to adjectives, describing some aspect of an object, of which there are generally several. For example, properties of a book include its author, title, number of pages, weight, and so on, whereas those of an Excel cell may include its value, or its type of formatting.

- Methods are analogous to verbs (e.g. a book could be opened, closed, read, put on the bookshelf, bought or sold).
- Events are like methods, but where the action is triggered by the system (such as when a workbook is opened, the value in a worksheet is changed, and so on).

The objects, properties, methods and events are of course specific to those that are relevant to the Excel/VBA environment (and do not have the full richness and complexity of natural language). As a set of instructions to be carried out by a computer, the syntax of VBA is more concise and precise than that of natural languages: for example, rather than "Would you mind washing the dishes, please?", the code would be analogous to "dishes.wash". In addition, whilst in natural language it is generally clear from the context which dishes are being referred to (our dirty ones, rather than the neighbours' clean ones), such contextual issues are not necessarily uniquely defined when considered from a computer's perspective. To write robust code, it would generally necessary (or better) to specify such issues very precisely and unambiguously.

As in natural language, the properties of an object may result in another object: for example, the "screen property" of a computer is also an object (i.e. the screen). Similarly, in VBA, `Range("A2:B5").Rows` refers to the rows of that range (i.e. Rows 2, 3, 4 and 5), and `Range("A2:B5").Rows.Count` would use the `Count` method to count the number of rows (i.e. four). Other methods associated with range objects include `Activate`, `ClearContents`, `ClearFormats`, `Copy`, `PasteSpecial` and `Select`.

Note that one specific object is `Application`, which represents the entire application (i.e. Excel in this case).

Object Hierarchies and Collections

Within Excel/VBA, objects can exist in Collections as well as in Hierarchies.

Examples of Collections include:

- `Workbooks` is the set of all open workbooks.
- `Worksheets` is the set of worksheets in the specified or active workbook (the `Sheets` object includes both worksheets and chart sheets).
- `ChartObjects` is the set of charts in the specified or active worksheet. `Charts` is the set of chart sheets in the specified or active workbook, not the set of charts.
- `Names` is the set of named ranges in the specified or active workbook.
- `PivotTables` is the set of all PivotTables in the specified or active worksheet.
- `WorksheetFunction` is a top-level object, whose properties are the individual Excel functions.

This gives rise to hierarchies of objects. Thus, using the fact that Worksheets is a member of the Workbook object:

- `Workbooks("Model.xlsm").Worksheets("Data1")` refers to the indicated worksheet (i.e. Data1) in the Model workbook.
- `Workbooks("Model.xlsm").Worksheets.Add` is part of the syntax required to add a new worksheet to the Model workbook.

Note that when working in VBA, typing "." after an object collection invokes VBA to provide a drop-down list of methods and properties that can be applied at that point.

The use of collections can allow certain operations to be conducted easily that might otherwise appear to be complex or time-consuming (see later examples).

Using Set. . .=. . . .

The use of the `Set` statement is of fundamental importance when working with Excel objects. For example, in the last chapter, we used basic code lines from such as:

```
i = Range("C2")
j = Range("C3").Value
```

On reflection, it becomes clear that the first line of code is unclear or ambiguous: the role of the variable `i` in the code is to take a value, whereas C2 is a cell (not just a value) that has several properties; its value, font size, colour, other formatting aspects, and so on. Therefore, the first line is trying to assign a multi-faceted object to a single number. This is inherently inconsistent, and indeed one may wonder as to why the code can execute at all (the reason being that the default property of a range object is its value). The second line of this code is clearer, because it explicitly works with the `Value` property of the range and assigns only this to the variable `j`.

The `Set` statement can be used not only to overcome this ambiguity, and is in fact generally necessary, especially when the left-hand side of an "=" statement is an object. For example:

- `Set DataRange=Range("A1:A100")`
- `Set Rng = ActiveSheet.UsedRange`

The failure to include `Set` is a common error, resulting in an error message, such as `Object variable not set (Error 91)` when one runs the code.

Using the With. . .End With Construct

The `With...End With` construct allows one to specify an object and to conduct several operations with that object using syntax that is more concise. Thus, one could write:

```
With Range("A1").Font
   .Name = "Calibri"
   .Size = 10
   .Color = -16776961
End With
```

The construct can be embedded within others, such as:

```
With Application.ThisWorkbook
 With Range("A1")
  With .Font
    .Name = "Calibri"
    .Size = 10
    .Color = -16776961
  End With
 End With
End With
```

The main uses in practice are:

- To increase speed of writing code that refers to the same object multiple times.
- To facilitate the use of full referencing, by making it less cumbersome to implement.
- To make the code more transparent by emphasising which object is being worked with.

Finding Alternatives to the Selection or Activation of Ranges and Objects

Typically, the code that results from recording processes contains steps in which cells, ranges or objects are selected (or activated). On the other hand, often the ultimate operation needed does not require such selection or activation processes. It is almost always much more computationally efficient and much quicker to run code that is written to eliminate the explicit selection or activation of objects (which is often, although not always, possible). In some cases, such as when working with charts or PivotTables, it may be necessary to activate objects before some operations can be performed on them, but it is generally worth trying to test if such activation is truly necessary.

For example, the recording of code to clear the range A1:E8 would give:

```
Range("A1:E8").Select
    Selection.ClearContents
```

whereas the direct equivalent would be

```
Range("A1:E8").ClearContents
```

(The word `Selection` is worksheet-specific and is a word reserved by VBA to refer to the last range that was last selected on that worksheet.)

Similarly, the use (but not the selection) of syntaxes such as `xlCellTypeLastCell`, `CurrentRegion` or `UsedRange` (discussed later in this chapter) are typically more efficient than the results of recording Excel operations such as Ctrl+Shift+RightArrow, which might give code such as:

```
Range(Selection, Selection.End(xlDown)).Select
Range(Selection, Selection.End(xlToRight)).Select
```

WORKING WITH RANGE OBJECTS: SOME KEY ELEMENTS

This section focuses on key elements of working with ranges (range objects).

Basic Syntax Possibilities and Using Named Ranges

There are many ways to refer to Excel range objects:

- `Range("B2")` refers to a single cell.
- `Range("B2:C10")` refers to the range consisting of cells B2 to C10.
- `Range("B2", "C10")` also refers to the range consisting of cells B2 to C10.

Named Ranges and Named Variables

As mentioned earlier, within VBA code, it is almost always preferable to use named ranges instead of direct cell references. As well as being more robust if the worksheet structure were to change (new rows or columns added), their use generally creates more transparency.

There are several situations that arise, which affect the appropriate point at which a name should be assigned to a range:

- Where the size and location of the ranges are fixed, one can define the names in the Excel workbook (using Excel's Formulas/Name Manager menu) as the model is being built (or as the VBA code is being written). A range defined in this way would be referred to in the code using inverted commas (e.g. `Range ("PriceInput")` or `Range("NumberofTimestoRunLoop")`, and so on). When auditing such code, to find out which range is being referred to by the name, one could use either the Excel Name Manager, or VBA's `Immediate` window (see later).
- Where the size or location of the range is determined only when the code is run, the name would be defined within the VBA code, such as:

```
Set dRange = ......
```

The right-hand side of the `Set` statement would refer to the (variable-sized) range that is determined at run time from the data set (perhaps using some of the techniques below, such as `CurrentRegion`, `UsedRange` and so on). The left-hand side creates an object variable that corresponds to that range. When referring to such a range within the code, one can then directly use the variable name (i.e. not the inverted comma format), such as:

```
NRows=dRange.Rows.Count
```

- One could also use theAddmethod within VBA to create an Excel name as the code is run (for both fixed- and variable-sized ranges). For example, to create a new name that refers to cells A1:B100 on the worksheet Sheet1, one could use:

```
Names.Add Name:="DataRange", RefersTo:="=Sheet1!$a$1:$B$100"
```

When doing so, one would need to ensure that the name does not already exist (for example, by attaching an indexation number to it that is tracked and incremented each time a name is added). Often, this approach is therefore not as useful or as convenient as the other approaches.

The CurrentRegion Property

The `CurrentRegion` property of a cell or range is the largest two-dimensional range that results from including within it all cells which are contiguous with some other cell of the region. That is, it is the range (surrounded by empty cells or the physical limits of Excel) that would be found if one started at any cell within the range, and included every non-empty cell which is contiguous to it, and then all non-empty cells contiguous to these, and so on, until there are no further new cells to include.

If one were not aware of the syntax, one could establish it by recording a macro, using either:

- The F5 (GoTo)/Special/Current region menu sequence.
- The short-cut Ctrl+* (Ctrl+Shift+8).

Note that the recording process will generally result in the range being selected, creating code such as:

```
Selection.CurrentRegion.Select
```

whereas it will generally be more efficient not to select objects (but to use only the `CurrentRegion` part of the syntax in the later code).

The xlCellTypeLastCell Property

One can locate the last cell that contains data or formatting by using either:

- The F5 (GoTo)/Special/Last cell menu sequence.
- The short-cut Ctrl+End.

Once again, the macro that results from the recording process will generally select the last cell, such as:

```
Sub Macro4()
    Range("A1").Select
    Selection.SpecialCells(xlCellTypeLastCell).Select
End Sub
```

However, for practical purposes, one would need to extract the relevant code elements without explicitly selecting any cells:

```
With Range("A1")
  Set lcell = .SpecialCells(xlCellTypeLastCell)
End With
```

after which further operations may be conducted, such as:

```
NRows = lcell.CurrentRegion.Rows.Count
```

Thus, in principle, if it were known (due to structural reasons) that all the data on a worksheet were in a single contiguous range, then a code line such as:

```
With Range("A1")
Set dRange=.SpecialCells(xlCellTypeLastCell).CurrentRegion
End With
```

would create an object variable that represents the full data set (including any headers).

Note that the last cell may be blank if the formatting or contents of that cell have been altered during a working session (e.g. content inserted and then deleted). Thus, when using this to identify a data range, one may have to take care as to whether such operations are conducted within the code, and adapt the code accordingly.

Worksheet Names and Code Names

In general, one may need to state which worksheet (and perhaps which workbook) is desired to be referred to during the run of the code. For example, a statement such as `Range("A1")` does not make clear on which worksheet the range is. Worksheets can be referred to either:

- Using their names as defined by the model builder when working in Excel (or using the Excel defaults, such as Sheet1 etc). The VBA code would be, for example:

```
With Worksheets("Sheet1")
...
End With
```

- Using the VBA code name for the sheet. Within the VBE window a worksheet can be given a name by first selecting it within the `Project` window, and changing its associated name within the `Properties` window. This code name can be different to the Excel name, so that the use of the code name will mean that the code will still work even if the worksheet name in Excel is changed:

```
With DataSheet
...
End With
```

The UsedRange Property

The `UsedRange` is a property of a worksheet that defines its used range (this may include blank rows and columns where these have been used in some form, including the addition and subsequent deletion of content).

The syntax requires a worksheet to have been specified, such as:

When using Excel worksheet names:

```
With Worksheets("Sheet1")
Set dRange = .UsedRange
End With
```

or when using code sheet names:

```
With DataSheet
Set dRange = .UsedRange
End With
```

One can easily see the `UsedRange` by running code such as:

```
With DataSheet
.UsedRange.Select
End With
```

This can be used in an analogous way to the `xlCellTypeLastCell` property, with the advantage this it unifies multiple non-contiguous ranges.

Note also that some (perhaps expected) range definitions do not exist in VBA (e.g. `CurrentRange`, `ActiveRegion` or `ActiveRange` do not exist).

The Cells Property

The `Cells` property creates a range defined relative to the starting point of another range. It can be used in many contexts:

To operate on all the cells in a worksheet. For example:

```
With Worksheets("Sheet1").Cells
.ClearContents
End With
```

or

```
With Worksheets("Sheet1").Cells
 With.Font
  .Name = "CourierNew"
  .Size = 10
 End With
End With
```

- To operate on cells defined relative to the starting point of a worksheet. For example, to place the value 400 in Cell C5, i.e. the 5th row and 3rd column of the worksheet

```
With Worksheets("Sheet1").Cells(5, 3)
.Value=400
End With
```

- To operate on cells defined relative to another range. For example, to place the value 500 into the cell that is 5 rows and 3 columns removed from Cell B2 (i.e. into Cell D6), one could write:

```
With Worksheets("Sheet1").Range("B2").Cells(5, 3)
.Value=500
End With
```

Note that the following statement refers to Cell C7, being the cell that is the 5th row and 3rd column of the range that starts at Cell A3:

```
Worksheets("Sheet1").Range("A3:B10").Cells(5, 3)
```

- To specify a range of cells on a worksheet, such as the range A1:C5:

```
With Worksheets("Sheet1")
Range(.Cells(1, 1), .Cells(5, 3)).Value=800
End With
```

- To find the first cell in the `UsedRange` of a worksheet:

```
With Worksheets("Sheet1").UsedRange
Set dstart = .Cells(1, 1)
End With
```

`Cells` can also be used in the context of the cell number in the worksheet or relative to a starting cell (from left to right and then top to bottom), such as `Cells(1)`, `Cells(2)`. In particular, this can be used to find the starting point of a range (i.e. `Cells(1)`). However, there is a risk of lack of compatibility and errors when using this property more widely, since code may have been originally written in Excel 2003 (which had 256 columns): `Cells(257)` would correspond to Cell A2 in Excel 2003 but to cell `IW1` in Excel 2007.

The Offset Property

The `Offset` property of a range is conceptually similar to Excel's OFFSET function. However, there are a number of differences:

- It is a property of a range, not a function.
- Its reference range is external to it (not an integral part or parameter of the function).
- There are no optional height and width arguments.

Examples of its use include:

- `Range("A1").Offset(2, 0)` refers to Cell A3, being offset by two rows and no columns from Cell A1.
- `Range("A1:B5").Offset(1,2)` is the range C2:D6, i.e. that which is offset by one row and two columns from the reference range.

To a large extent, `Offset` is an alternative to `Cells`, so that they are interchangeable. In many cases, `Offset` may be more intuitive than `Cells` (just as, with Excel functions, OFFSET is often more intuitive than INDEX). In Excel, the OFFSET function is Volatile, and so is to be avoided unless no real alternative is available (see Chapter 5 and Chapter 26). However, no such restriction exists in VBA, so that the use of `Offset` or `Cells` is often just a case of personal preference (the author generally has the habit of using `Offset`).

The Union Method

The `Union` method unites several ranges. Thus, `Union(Range("B2"), Range("C10"))` refers only to the cells B2 and C10, whereas `Range("B2", "C10")` would refer to the full range B2:C10.

The following sets the values and the font formats of non-contiguous cells:

```
Set uRange = Union(Range("A1"), Range("B7"), Range("C5"))
With uRange
.Value = 500
 With .Font
  .Name = "Arial"
  .Size = 18
 End With
End With
```

InputBox and MsgBox

The `InputBox` and `MsgBox` can be used to communicate basic information to and from a user, including to take simple numerical information that could be used within the code (such as which scenario number is to be run, or the number of times to run a recalculation loop in a simulation model). In the code below, the first input box code line will provide a message but the user input is not stored, whereas the second input box code line will store the user's input in the variable x, and the message box will display this stored value:

```
Sub MRTakeInput1()
InputBox "Type a Number"
x = InputBox("Sorry, retype it")
MsgBox x
End Sub
```

Application.InputBox

In many applications, it can be important for the user to input a cell reference (not simply a number). For example, one may wish to point to the first cell of a data set, so that the code can then detect the full set of data that is contiguous with the cell (and which may form the definition of the data that is to be manipulated). In this case, the input cell reference would be an object variable, so that the `Set` statement is required, with the `Type` argument used to indicate that the input provided is a cell reference (by use of the value 8):

```
Set dInputCell = Application.InputBox("Select Any Cell within Data Range", Type:=8)
```

One can then define the data range as being (for example) the current region associated with that input cell:

```
Set dFullRange = dInputCell.CurrentRegion
```

and one can find the first cell of that range using:

```
Set dStartCell=dFullRange.Cells(1,1)
```

Defining Multi-cell Ranges

Where possible, it is usually more efficient (i.e. the code will run more quickly) to work with multi-cell ranges, rather than the individual cells within the range. For example, to place the same value in all cells of the range A1:C5, code such as the following could be used:

```
With Worksheets("Sheet1")
Set dRange1=Range(.Cells(1, 1), .Cells(5, 3))
dRange1.value=100
End With
```

Similarly, to place the same value in the range A12:C16, the following could be used:

```
With Worksheets("Sheet1").Range("A12")
Set DRange1 = Range(.Offset(0, 0), .Offset(4, 2))
dRange1.Value = 200
End With
```

Using Target to React to Worksheet Events

The word `Target` is a reserved word in VBA that is used to refer to a range that has been just changed by the user (not by an Excel recalculation). It can be used to react to events that occur within a worksheet (so that a macro is run as such events occur). The code containing this word must be placed in the code module of the worksheet in

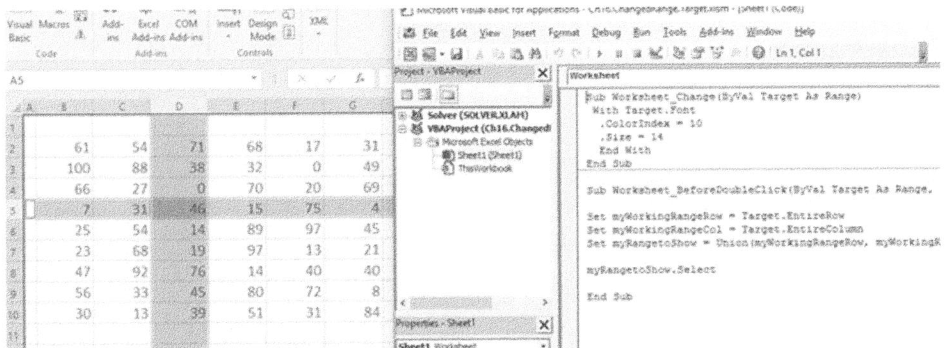

FIGURE 29.1 Highlighting the Row and Column of a Chosen Cell

which one wishes to detect such changes (not in a general code module), and also use the `Worksheet_Change` subroutine (which is reserved syntax for code that is to run when such worksheet events occur).

As an example, the following code will ensure that any changes made to the sheet (such as the entry of data, formulae or text) will be displayed in green and with a font size of 14.

```
Sub Worksheet_Change(ByVal Target As Range)
 With Target.Font
  .ColorIndex = 10
  .Size = 14
  End With
End Sub
```

Similarly, the following code would ensure that the entire row and entire column of a cell is highlighted when one double-clicks on it (see Figure 29.1):

```
Sub Worksheet_BeforeDoubleClick(ByVal Target As Range, Cancel
As Boolean)
 Set myWorkingRangeRow = Target.EntireRow
 Set myWorkingRangeCol = Target.EntireColumn
 Set myRangetoShow = Union(myWorkingRangeRow, myWorkingRangeCol)
myRangetoShow.Select
End Sub
```

Using Target to React to Workbook Events

In order to detect and react to changes anywhere in the workbook, one can use the `Workbook_SheetChange` subroutine, which must be placed in the `ThisWorkbook` module, for example:

```
Sub Workbook_SheetChange(ByVal Sh As Object, ByVal Target As Range)
 str = "You just changed cell " & Target.Address & " of " & Sh.Name
& " to " & Target.Value
 MsgBox str
End Sub
```

CHAPTER 30

Controlling Execution

INTRODUCTION

This chapter describes the key elements relating to the defining and controlling of the steps for the code to follow as it runs. We cover a range of topics including the core syntax and commands, and provide some selected examples of these.

CORE TOPICS IN OVERVIEW

Input Boxes and Message Boxes

The use of the `InputBox`, `MsgBox` and `Application.InputBox` were mentioned in the last chapter, and so are not addressed further here in detail. However, it is worth noting that the use of these approaches means that code execution is halted until some feedback is provided by the user, which can be inconvenient in cases where one wishes to complete code to run automatically and without intervention.

For. . .Next Loops

The use of a `For...Next` loop is the most basic and important approach to automate repetitive operations involving calculations. The core syntax is typically of a form such as:

```
For i = 1 To 1000
...Code to be executed (that involves i)
Next i
```

or

```
For i = 1 To Range("NLoops")
...Code to be executed (that involves i)
Next i
```

These create a looping process in which an indexation variable `i` starts with the value 1 and is incremented by the default of 1 each time that a step of the loop is executed (and hence takes the values 1, 2, ... in sequence).

Some basic points to note are:

- The `Next` statement is required to define at what point to start to repeat the operation within the loop, rather than moving to the code steps that are intended to be run after the loop.
- The `i` after the `Next` statement is optional, but its inclusion renders the code easier to read and so is less error-prone. Especially where there are multiple or embedded loops, the "closing" of the loops in this way is important.
- The code within the loop will (almost) always depend in the value of the indexation number `i` in some way.
- The indexation variable (here: `i`) could essentially be given any (valid, non-reserved) name. Of course, it is recommended and common practice for the name of a variable to provide some indication as to the nature of the variable, so that names such as `i` or `iCount` and so on are frequently used for integers (as are `j, k, l, m` and `n`), with `x`, `y`, `z` often being used for variables that can take any value.

In some cases, increments other than 1 are needed, for example:

- `For i = 1 To 1000 Step 2` will loop through the values for `i` of 1, 3, 5, 7, . . . , 999.
- `For i = 1000 To 1 Step -1` will loop through values 1000, 999, 998, . . . 1.

For Each. . . In. . .Next

A `For Each...In...Next` loop can be used to automate the repetition of operations by working through the items in an object collection (rather than through a set if integers or a structured indexation set when using a `For...Next` loop). A typical syntax would be:

```
For Each mySheet in Worksheets
...Code to be executed (that involves mySheet)
Next mySheet
```

Note that the name `mySheet` in the above is simply an indexation variable, and one which would (generally) be used within the loop to specify the object on which the operation is to be performed (such as `mySheet.Delete`); once again, the name is essentially arbitrary (within the constraints of name validity, such as no spaces, and no reserved words). Of course, it makes sense from a transparency perspective to use a name that indicates the nature of the object within that context.

The uses of this type of loop include:

- To delete specific worksheets in a workbook, such as those whose name starts with a specific word or another identifier.
- To reformat all charts (`ChartObjects`) in a workbook.
- To make a list of the names of all worksheets in a workbook.

It is also worth noting that the items in the object collection are worked through in their implicit numerical order (even if such an order is not immediately obvious to a modeller or user), just as a `For...Next` loop uses a positive step of one by default. For example, code such as:

```
For Each nm in Names
MyStrName = Range(nm).Name.Name
Next nm
```

would work through the names of the named ranges in a workbook. Note that the word `Name` is required twice in the above code: since `Names` refers to the collection of named ranges, `Names.Name` refers to a specific name object (which has several properties, including its name) and so `Names.Name.Name` refers to the name.

If. . .Then

The `If...Then` statement is essentially self-explanatory, creating the situation where the code conducts different operations depending on some condition. The simplest form is essentially:

```
If ConditionTest Then
... first possible set of instructions
Else
... second set of instructions
End If
```

Note that there are cases in which an operation is required to be conducted only when a condition is met, with no operation required when the condition is not met. In such cases, one may consider leaving out the `Else` statement. However, it is generally more transparent to state explicitly that no operation is required; this can be achieved by using the `Else` statement but with a simple comment line afterwards.

Where there are multiple conditions to be tested, the `ElseIf` statement can be used, before a single `Else`:

```
If ConditionTest-1 Then
... first possible set of instructions
ElseIf ConditionTest-2 Then
... second possible set of instructions
ElseIf ConditionTest-n Then
... nth possible set of instructions
Else
... final possible set of instructions
End If
```

Select Case. . .End Select

This can be used to execute one of a set of statements depending on the result of a test. In a sense, it is an alternative to an `If...Then` statement, being more transparent in some cases (such as when running scenarios), simply because it is often visually easier to identify in the code which case is to apply in specific circumstances. A typical syntax is:

```
ScNo = InputBox("Enter Scenario Number")
Select Case ScNo
Case 1 To 3
... Apply the relevant operation (e.g. lookup function based on ScNo)
Case 4, 5
... Apply the relevant operation (e.g. lookup function based on ScNo)
Case 6 To 10
... Apply the relevant operation (e.g. lookup function based on ScNo)
Case Else
MsgBox "INVALID CASE NUMBER: RERUN AND CHECK YOUR ENTRY"
End Select
```

GoTo

The GoTo statement may also be used to determine branching that is to apply as the result of the evaluation of a condition (such as If...Then or Case condition) or with an On Error statement to branch to an error-handling procedure (see later).

As an example, in the following, where a user has provided an invalid entry into the InputBox, the Case Else statement will be applied, resulting in the code using the GoTo command to return to the scenario input code line at the beginning of the Select Case statement.

```
  TrySelectCaseAgain:
ScNo = InputBox("Enter Scenario Number")
Select Case ScNo
Case 1 To 3
'...Apply the relevant operation (e.g. lookup function based on ScNo)
Case 4, 5
'...Apply the relevant operation (e.g. lookup function based on ScNo)
Case 6 To 10
'...Apply the relevant operation (e.g. lookup function
based on ScNo)
Case Else
  GoTo TrySelectCaseAgain
End Select
```

Note that the key syntax is the use of a (valid, but essentially arbitrary) name after the GoTo statement, and the use of that name (followed by colon) to indicate the place in the code at which one wishes to return (without the colon, an error message would arrive as one would be effectively creating a variable without specifying any operation to be conducted on it, so the code line would be incomplete).

Do...While/Until...Loop

The Do...Loop structure is useful when one wishes to repeat aspects of code execution an indefinite number of times, until a condition is satisfied.

Note that:

- The structure is typically used with one (but not both) of either the While statement or the Until statement. The first continues looping whilst a condition is still true, whilst the latter loops until the condition is met for the first time.
- The While (or the Until) conditional statements can be used at either the beginning or the end of the loop, depending on whether one wishes for the loop's operations to be conducted at least once or not: that is, the two generic structures with the While form are:

```
Do While ConditionToCheck
... Operation to run ....
Loop
```

and

```
Do
... Operation to run ...
Loop While ConditionToCheck
```

(The use of `Until` also has two analogous generic structures.)

An additional, and similar, structure is the `While...Wend` construct (although it is sometimes regarded as less flexible and clear than the others):

```
WhileConditionToCheck ... Operation to run ....
Wend
```

One important example of these is in the resolution of circular references, as discussed in Chapter 10.

Note that when using such looping structures (including with the use of `GoTo` for correcting input data in the previous example), there could be a possibility that the condition is never met, irrespective of how many times the loop is run. Therefore, such loops may also need to include an indexation number which increments at each iteration of the loop, and which exits the procedure if a preset number of iterations of the loop is exceeded (using the `Exit Sub` statement at the appropriate point in the code).

Calculation and Calculate

An important topic is that of the recalculation of Excel as a macro is running. There are two main objectives:

- To ensure that correct numerical values result during code execution. A macro that has been written or recorded in an environment in which Excel's calculation options are set Automatic (under File/Options/Formulas) may implicitly rely on Excel having (automatically) recalculated at the required times. Such a macro may give incorrect results if run when the calculation options are set to Manual, because the recalculations will not occur. Some techniques that can be used to reduce the chance of such cases arising (by forcing a focus during the process as to when recalculations are required) are:
  - Switch the Excel calculation settings to Manual, before the recording process.
  - Switch the Excel calculation settings to Manual as the first step of the recording process.
  - Write and/or test the macro when the calculations are set to Manual.
- To optimise computational time, conducting (as far as possible) only those calculations that are necessary. This is a highly non-trivial topic: of course, the recalculation of a workbook during code execution increases computational time taken, so that ideally one should only recalculate when it is necessary. However, it can be rather subtle to determine whether a recalculation is necessary or not, partly because – when Excel is set to Automatic calculation – some actions that trigger recalculation may not initially be expected to do so (such as entering new data, deleting or inserting a row, renaming a worksheet, hiding or unhiding rows, some filtering actions, creating or modifying named ranges, and so on). Further, only

specific parts of a model may in theory be required to be updated as a macro is run. For example, some parts may require recalculation only toward the beginning or end of a macro (or set of macros), whereas other items may need to be calculated at each step of a loop.

Workbook recalculation settings can be applied from within the code (e.g. at the start and at the end) using the following syntaxes (which could be established by recording a macro as one selects the calculation settings):

- Application.Calculation = xlManual for manual recalculation.
- Application.Calculation = xlSemiautomatic for automatic recalculation, with the exception of DataTables.
- Application.Calculation = xlAutomatic for automatic recalculation, including DataTables.
- Application.Iteration = True for using iterative calculations to resolve any circular references.

As mentioned above, in many cases it can make sense to create macros which by default place a workbook on Manual recalculation at the beginning and then only calculate when necessary. On the other hand, there is a risk when doing so that some necessary recalculation steps are overlooked.

When one wishes to control calculation during the run of code, the possibilities are:

- `Calculate` or `Application.Calculate` (recording of F9 short-cut). This invokes Excel's "smart" recalculation engine, which calculates only items that have changed since the last recalculation, Volatile functions and conditional formats, and items dependent on others, or which are otherwise flagged as needing recalculation (sometimes known as "dirty" items). It calculates these items for all open workbooks and would update DataTables as required if the Automatic Except Tables (`xlSemiautomatic`) setting has been used for a workbook.
- `Application.CalculateFull` (recording of Ctrl+Alt+F9 short-cut). This forces a recalculation of all formulas in all open workbooks, including all DataTables.
- `Application.CalculateFullRebuild` (recording the Shift+Ctrl+Alt+F9). This forces a complete rebuild of all dependencies and a full calculation of the workbook.

In many practical cases, it is usually sufficient to simply use the `Application.Calculate` statement at the appropriate places in the code (such as when new data is brought in or generated etc.). This is a quick recalculation approach, because in most cases only part of the input data or a few formulae change between calculations. (Note that the word "Calculate" is shown in Excel's Status Bar if a higher-level build is required (such as a full rebuild), or if the model contains a circular reference.)

Some additional points to bear in mind concerning the recalculation and optimisation of the run time are:

- If one is unsure whether a recalculation is necessary, it will generally be better to favour using too many recalculations, rather than too few.
- Most of the benefit in terms of improving computational speed generally results from making a few key changes to the code; the achievement of a perfect optimisation may not be a sensible objective (if computation speed is of genuine

fundamental importance, one may need to work outside the Excel/VBA environment, and to use pre-compiled code, not code that compiles at run time, as is the case with VBA).

- The overall run time is often highly influenced by the underlying design and structure of the model, as well as the VBA code. For example:
  - The inappropriate use of lookup functions (such as VLOOKUP) or the use of Volatile functions (such as OFFSET and INDIRECT) can slow down a model significantly.
  - Within the VBA code, the use of Copy/Paste operations (and the selection of objects in general) will be much less efficient than the use of assignment statements (or the direct manipulation of objects without selecting them explicitly).
  - The use of VBA arrays rather than Excel cells or ranges to store data (see later) or intermediate calculations may be a more efficient way to generate optimised run time. It allows one a clearer view of when Excel recalculates or needs to do so. Excel will not recalculate during the conducting of operations that involve purely the values in the arrays (whereas equivalent operations conducted on tables of data in Excel ranges may force a recalculation each time that a data point in the range is changed).
  - In principle, one can structure models according to which parts need recalculation at the same time, so that different parts of the model can be recalculated only when absolutely necessary (individual worksheets or ranges). This would be a requirement if one were to aim to achieve maximal computational efficiency, although in some cases, even small changes in a model can make a difference.

Where one wishes to ensure that the calculation of specific worksheets is switched off as the code is running, one can use code such as:

```
With AnalysisSheet
  .EnableCalculation = False
End With
```

In such cases, toward the end of the code run, the recalculation of such as worksheet would then need to be reset and performed:

```
With AnalysisSheet
  .EnableCalculation = True
  .Calculate
End With
```

(i.e. the first would be used toward the beginning of the overall code, and the second toward the end).

Similarly, individual ranges can be calculated using the `Range.Calculate` method. In other words:

- `Application.Calculate` calculates all open workbooks.
- `Worksheets("Sheet1").Calculate` calculates only the specified sheet.
- `Worksheets("Sheet1").Rows(2).Calculate` calculates only the specified range (the specified row).

Dependents and volatile cells which are outside the range are ignored.

Screen Updating

One simple way to speed up code execution (by roughly 30% in many cases) is to switch off the automated updating of the Excel display as the code is running. This can be done by using (toward the beginning of the code):

```
Application.ScreenUpdating = False
```

and (toward the end of the code):

```
Application.ScreenUpdating = True
```

The main disadvantage is that having visibility of the display can sometimes help in debugging, or help one to see the progress of code execution, and it is sometimes simply comforting to see the actions being performed. Thus, this technique may be most applicable at the later stages of code development, after testing is essentially complete.

Measuring Run Time

In principle, the time required to run code can be measured by using the VBA `Timer` function, which is expressed in seconds (its has no arguments so its parenthesis can be omitted or left empty). The code would generically read as:

```
Starttime = Timer()
```

. . . Conduct calculations or operations

```
Endtime = Timer()
RunTime = Endtime - Starttime
```

It is of course worth bearing in mind that:

- The `Timer` function is based on elapsed time since midnight, and so would be misleading if the code were run over this threshold. The more general `Time` function could be used in its place, but is slightly less convenient in that it provides the current system time in days, so generally needs to be converted to express the value in seconds (by the appropriate multiplication).
- If other applications are running at the same time or the computer is involved in other processing activities in the background (e.g. virus checking), then these will affect the run time; it is not easy to determine to what extent this plays a role in an individual run. Nevertheless, the overall run time (especially when measured several times) can provide a good indication as to the effectiveness of potential measures to improve overall speed and efficiency.
- If a step-through approach is used to check that such code is working, it will not return values that are representative of what would happen if the code were to be run, as the elapsed time will of course include that taken to step through the code.

The total run time should also be shown on Excel's StatusBar, using:

```
Application.StatusBar="RunTime " & Round(RunTime, 2) & " Seconds "
```

Displaying Alerts

In some cases, messages that display warnings in Excel must be disabled for the code execution to continue as desired. For example, an attempt to instruct Excel to delete a worksheet typically leads to a prompted warning that the operation is not reversible, and one needs to (manually) confirm that one indeed intends to continue with the instruction. The equivalent in VBA would also lead to the suspension of code execution at that point.

The default warnings can be switched off by using:

```
Application.DisplayAlerts = False
```

Of course in general it is beneficial to have such warnings active, and once they have been disabled in a section of code for a specific reason, they typically will need to be switched on again at the end of that section of code using:

```
Application.DisplayAlerts = True
```

Accessing Excel Worksheet Functions

VBA has several built-in functions which can be used in the code. For example, `Sqr` returns the square root of its argument (equivalent to Excel's SQRT), `Log` gives the natural logarithm (equivalent to Excel's LN) and `Rnd` returns a uniformly distributed random number between 0 and 1 (equivalent to Excel's RAND).

Some key points about these functions are:

- A list of the available VBA functions can be seen by typing `VBA.` in the `Code` window. When doing so, it will be seen that the number of arithmetic operations is very limited when compared with Excel. For example, although there is an extensive range of functions to manipulate text (such as `Left`, `Mid`, `IsEmpty`), the basic arithmetic operations corresponding to Excel's SUM, MIN and MAX functions do not exist (the specific list of mathematical and financial functions available can be accessed by typing `VBA.Math.` and `VBA.Financial.`).
- A list of all worksheet functions that are available in VBA can be seen by typing `WorksheetFunction.` in the code window. These can be implemented within VBA by typing `WorkSheetFunction.Sum( )`, and so on. It is also often convenient to create a worksheet function object variable, so that individual functions can be more efficiently accessed from it:

```
Set wsf=Application.WorksheetFunction
Set wsfSum=wsf.Sum
Set wsfCount=wsf.Count
...
```

- For those worksheet functions which use the "dot" notation in Excel, such as many of the statistics functions in Excel 2010 onwards, an underscore is required when these are accessed within VBA (e.g. `WorksheetFunction.StDev_S)`.
- Where VBA and Excel functions for the same calculation both exist (including `Sqr, Rnd, Log )`, the VBA functions must be used.

Executing Procedures Within Procedures

When code becomes large, it is useful to structure it into separate procedures, with each having a limited and clear functionality. This will require that subroutines and functions in the same module, same workbook or other workbooks are used.

When using several procedures, one will need to take care that the scope of each is appropriate. The scope of a procedure defines its availability for use by another procedure. Subroutines and functions can have one of two scopes:

- `Public`. When used in general code modules, such procedures are available within the project (workbook), as well as to any other project that references it. `Public` is the default scope for procedures (except for event procedures, which are `Private` by default), so most procedures do not need an explicit definition as `Public`.
- `Private`. The declaration of a procedure as `Private` (e.g. using `Private Sub NameofSub()`) would mean that it is available only to other procedures in the same module of the workbook, and not to the whole workbook or to other modules within it. A subroutine declared as `Private` will not display in Excel's Macro dialog box (other procedures that will not show in this dialog are those that require arguments, and those contained in add-ins). Similarly, a function declared as `Private` (e.g. using `Private MyFunction(arg1, arg2)`) will not be accessible from Excel, and also available only within its own VBA code module. The `Option Private Module` statement can be used at the beginning of a module to make all procedures in a module `Private`.

Subroutines and functions which are `Public` can be executed from the Excel workbook in which they are contained using the methods earlier in this text (e.g. use of the Macro dialog or the Formula/Insert Function menu).

When executing procedures from other procedures in the same workbook, the following possibilities exist:

- Subroutines which are `Public` can be executed (as can `Private` subroutines in the same module) by:
  - Using the `Run` method, typing the name in inverted commas followed by the parameter list (not enclosed in brackets), e.g. `Run "SubName", arg1, arg2`.
  - Using the `Call` statement, typing any required arguments in brackets, e.g. `Call SubName(arg1, arg2)`. The `Call` statement can be omitted if the argument list is not enclosed in brackets, e.g. `SubName arg1, arg2`. The use of the `Call` statement is arguably preferable as it is a more explicit statement that control is being transferred to another procedure.
- Functions which are `Public` (or `Private` in the same module) can also be accessed in the above ways, although generally one is interested in knowing the return value of a function, so that alternatives or variants of these methods are used:
  - Using a variable to represent the value returned by the function (e.g. `ValueToUse=MyFunction(arg1, arg2)`).
  - Using the `Run` method, enclosing the procedure name and arguments in brackets (e.g. `ValueToUse=Run("MyFunction", arg1, arg2)`).

When executing `Public` procedures in another workbook (whether from Excel or from VBA code), a reference needs to be created to the procedure either by:

- Preceding the name of the procedure with the name of the workbook in which it resides and using the `Run` method or the return value method (e.g. `Run "Book2.xlsm!SubName"` or `x=Book2.xlsm!MyFunction(arg1,arg2)`.
- Creating a reference to the second workbook, using `Tools/References` in the VBE. In this case, the procedure can be accessed without preceding it with the workbook name, and the referenced workbook does not need to be open.

When passing arguments between procedures, one may also need to be careful with respect to whether this is done on a `ByRef` or `ByVal` basis, as discussed in Chapter 31.

Accessing Add-ins

When using add-ins (such as Solver), one first needs to make a reference within VBE to the add-in. This can be achieved using `Tools/References,` checking (tick-selecting) the relevant box; if the add-in box is not visible, it should be verified that the add-in has been loaded (by using the Excel Options menu, and under Options/Add-ins/Manage: Excel Add-ins, selecting Go).

PRACTICAL APPLICATIONS

This section shows some simple examples of the main building blocks described earlier in the chapter. More complete and powerful applications are discussed in later chapters.

Example: Numerical Looping

A frequently required technique is to work through individual elements of a range and write a different value in each cell. Figure 30.1 shows the code and the results of running it, where the objective is to write the integers from 1 to 10, and their squares, in two adjacent columns in Excel. Several points are worth pointing out:

- From the `Project` window, one can see that the name of the worksheet in the workbook is "30.1", whereas the code name is `Sheet1`; this code name has been used to refer to the worksheet, rather than using Worksheets("30.1"), so that the code would still work if the worksheet name were changed in the workbook.
- The `With...End With` statement is used to ensure that all operations are conducted with respect to the Cell A1 of the specified worksheet.
- The `Offset` property of the range is used to move down the rows and across the columns; the loop indexation `i` is used to represent the number of rows to offset, and the column offsets (of 0 and 1) are hard-coded. The `Cells` property could have been used in its place.

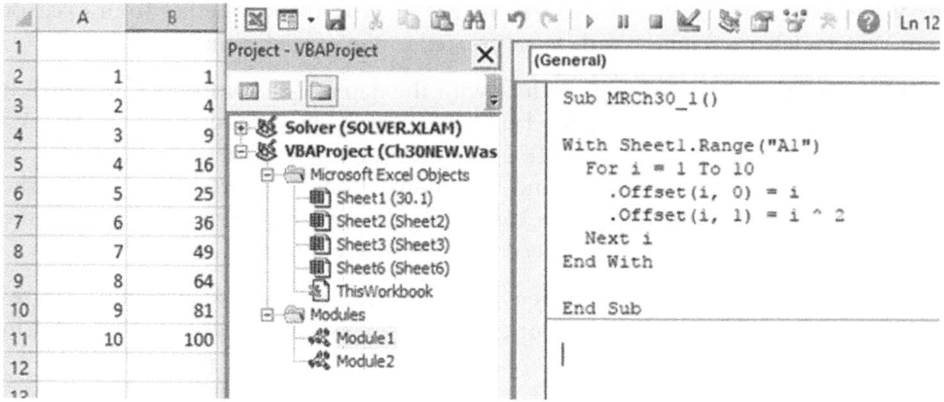

FIGURE 30.1 Example of Code for a `For...Next` Loop

Example: Listing the Names of All Worksheets in a Workbook

A list of all the names of the worksheets in a workbook can be created by using code shown below, noting the following points:

- The `For Each...Next` construct is used to loop through the collection of worksheets in the workbook (known as `Worksheets`).
- The `iCount` variable is used as an indexation to ensure that the worknames are written under the other in Column D of the worksheet with the worksheet whose sheet code name is Sheet1. The variable is incremented by 1 at each pass through the loop.

```
iCount = 0
For Each ws In Worksheets
  With Sheet1.Range("D1")
    .Offset(iCount, 0) = ws.Name
  End With
  iCount = iCount + 1
Next ws
```

The individual items in collections can be accessed using code such as `Workbooks.Item(3)` or simply `Workbooks(3)`. Such a technique may also be used to access individual elements of a range (for example `Range("DataSet")(i)` corresponds to `Range("DataSet").Cells(i, 1).Value`). However, in the context of object collections (such as `Worksheets`), one generally does not initially know how many items there are in the collection, so that this is frequently not the most appropriate way to refer to such items, unless the total number is first determined:

```
With ThisWorkbook
  N = Worksheets.Count
End With
```

Example: Adding a New Worksheet to a Workbook

The `Worksheets` collection can also be used to add a worksheet to the active workbook and to name this new worksheet. For example, if the worksheet is to contain results of some calculations, then it could be added as soon as the macro execution starts, using:

```
Worksheets.Add.Name = "Results"
```

One could also generalise the process, so that multiple Results worksheets can be added and named in accordance with the number of worksheets that are already in the workbook:

```
With ThisWorkbook
  N = Worksheets.Count
  Worksheets.Add.Name = "Results" & N
End With
```

The code could also be broken down into the separate steps of adding a new sheet and then renaming it:

```
With ThisWorkbook
  N = Worksheets.Count
  Set Sheetnew = Worksheets.Add
  Sheetnew.Name = "Results" & N
End With
```

Note that these code lines attach a number to the name of the Results worksheets that depends on the number of worksheets in the workbook, not according to the number of Results worksheets that already exist (so that the first Results sheet may receive a name such as Results3). To name the sheet according to the number of Results sheets only, one would need to count these: for example, a variable (such as `iCount` in the example above) could be used (initialised at 0, and incremented every time a new Results sheet is added). Alternatively, a `For Each` loop could be used to work through all worksheets in a workbook and count how many of them start with the word "Results", i.e. by checking (for example) that the first seven letters of the name are "Results" (and incrementing a similar `iCount` variable if so). Although the former approach is computationally more efficient, in general both approaches may be required: the latter may be used to establish the initial value of the variable `iCount`, as the code may already contain Results worksheets, but once this initial value is established, it need be incremented only when a new Results worksheets is added (or deleted).

Example: Deleting Specific Worksheets from a Workbook

Worksheets can be deleted from a workbook using VBA code, but of course one would generally wish to switch off the display of the Excel alerts (as mentioned earlier). Also, one would wish only to delete specific worksheets, not all of them. The following code deletes all worksheets whose Excel name starts with the word "Results". It uses the (VBA) `Left` function (and the `Name` property) to find the first seven characters of each worksheet name, and the VBA `UCase` function (equivalent to Excel's UPPER) to transform these characters into upper case for the comparison process (to ensure that all such worksheets are identified independently of the case of the spelling, whether lower-, upper- or mixed-case).

```
Application.DisplayAlerts = False
With ThisWorkbook
For Each ws In Worksheets
If UCase(Left(ws.Name, 7)) = "RESULTS" Then ws.Delete
Next ws
End With
Application.DisplayAlerts = True
```

Example: Refreshing PivotTables, Modifying Charts and Working Through Other Object Collections

The use of object collections can also be powerful to modify or manipulate other types of Excel objects. For example, the list of PivotTables (i.e. PivotTable objects) in a worksheet can be identified using:

```
Worksheets("NameofWorksheet").PivotTables
```

This can form the basis for other operations, such as:

```
NPvtTbls= Worksheets("SummarySheet").PivotTables.Count
```

In order to refresh (one or all) PivotTables, it would be most convenient to record the process of refreshing one (in order to establish the base syntax) and to adapt this as required. The resulting code may look like:

```
 For Each pt In ActiveSheet.PivotTables
    pt.RefreshTable
 Next pt
```

If one wanted to refresh specific PivotTables only, the code may look like:

```
For Each pt In ActiveSheet.PivotTables
 Select Case pt.Name
    Case "PivotTable1", "PivotTable3", "PivotTable6"
          pt.RefreshTable
     Case Else
       ' Do Nothing
   End Select
Next pt
```

For PivotTables that are spread across multiple worksheets, one may also loop through each worksheet in the workbook and refresh the PivotTables in each worksheet as one is doing so:

```
For Each ws In ActiveWorkbook.Worksheets
  For Each pt In ws.PivotTables
            pt.RefreshTable
  Next pt
Next ws
```

Of course, similar concepts apply to other object collections, with the properties and methods used being specific to those objects. For example, one could create a list of all named ranges in a workbook (as well as being able to see their scope and address) using code such as:

```
With ThisWorkbook
With Sheet1
icount = 0
For Each nm In Names
  With Range("A1")
    .Offset(icount, 0) = nm.Name
    .Offset(icount, 1) = nm.RefersToRange.Address
    icount = icount + 1
  End With
Next nm
End With
End With
```

When working with charts, the `ChartObjects` collection can be used to perform operations on all charts (NB: `Charts` is the collection of chart sheets, not that of embedded charts.) For example, the following code would work through all charts and move the legend to the bottom (once again, a macro that performed the operation once was recorded, and adapted to work within a loop):

```
For Each ws In Worksheets
 For Each co In ws.ChartObjects
   co.Activate
    With ActiveChart
      .SetElement (msoElementLegendBottom)
    End With
Next co
Next ws
```

(Note that, within the code, the charts need to be activated for this operation to work.)

Similarly, one could delete all comments in a workbook, working with the `Comments` collection.

CHAPTER 31

Writing Robust Code

INTRODUCTION

This chapter addresses some key topics involved in writing code that is robust in the sense that it:

- Is fairly general and useable in a reasonably wide set of similar circumstances.
- Is transparent and clear.
- Is reasonably computationally efficient.
- Is free from errors, at least when applied to its core uses, and its limits of validity are documented.

KEY PRINCIPLES

The remainder of this chapter covers a range of topics that help to ensure that code is robust.

From the Specific to the General

Typically, it can be helpful to start the code-writing process by first creating some simple code that works in a specific circumstance, and to generalise it so that it is more flexible and applies to a wider range of situations. Examples of the approaches to generalise code typically include:

- Adapting recorded code so that it works in a wider range of cases, beyond the specific case and environment in which it was recorded.
- Ensuring that the code still works if the input data is changed in some way, such as where there are more (or less) rows of data than in the original context, or where the position of the data within the Excel worksheet is different.
- Detecting whether time-series data that are input from another source have the date-axis in ascending or descending order, and running the appropriate code to ensure the correct treatment in each case.

- Building error-checking or error-handling procedures, for example as to whether the input data is consistent with requirements (such as being numerical values rather than text).
- Adding looping structures so that operations are performed several times, not just once.
- Adding conditional statements or user-defined functions (since these cannot be recorded).
- Taking input values from a user at run time, rather than assuming that the values are fixed.

As the code is generalised, it should be tested, and its functionality and limitations should also be noted (e.g. by using comments).

Adapting Recorded Code for Robustness

In Chapter 28, we discussed that the main reason for recording code is to facilitate the finding of the correct syntax for specialised operations, even as much of the rest of the code would need to be adapted (for example, by using named ranges in place of cell references, the addition of loops or conditional statements, the use of assignment rather than copy/paste operations, and so on).

Event Code

As noted earlier in the text, it is important that code is placed within the appropriate modules. The `Workbook` and `Sheet` modules should be used only for event-driven code, with general code placed in other modules.

Comments and Indented Text

The use of comments is important from a transparency perspective, especially as code becomes more complex. It allows one to document the purpose of key areas, as well as any restrictions that may limit is applicability. Comment lines are simply notes that have no effect when the code is run. A comment line starts with an apostrophe and may reside on a code line. Some points to consider when creating comments and deciding on their content include:

- Comments should describe the aim and functionality of the key lines (especially the more complex ones).
- Comments can be useful to state what is out of the scope or where the code has other limitations that the user may need to be aware of. For example, code may have been written that would work only if the data were arranged in contiguous cells in a column, or if certain inputs need to be set within the code by the user, rather than taken from the worksheet etc. No code can be perfectly flexible and robust, but the use of comments about code limitations also signals that the developer has tested the code, so that it is likely to be more robust.
- Generally, it is better to over-comment rather than under-comment; if, after a break of a few days, the code writer is not quickly able to see what the code does, then it is probably not commented sufficiently.

- Code that is desired to be retained for possible use later can be commented out (by adding an apostrophe before it) and copied or commented back in (by deleting the apostrophe) when needed. This can be useful for checking and debugging code, where `MsgBox` and `Debug.Print` statements can be commented in and out as needed.
- Where it is desired to ensure that a user receives adequate warning about some key aspects of the code, these can be placed in comments, although a more powerful method can be to use event code to make such text appear as the workbook opens.

The use of indented text is also an important tool to make the code visually more attractive. A few points are worthy of note here:

- The Tab key can be used to indent code, and Shift+Tab to un-indent.
- The `Tools/Options/Editor` menu in VBE can be used to alter the tab width (when using several levels of indenting, the default tab width of four spaces is often too wide).

Modular Code

Generally, it is useful to break larger code into separate structures, and to use (or call) each piece of code in sequence from a master procedure. This allows for separate testing and easier sharing or transportability of code from one application (or workbook) to another.

Blocks of code which have closely interrelated functionality may be placed in the same module, whilst separate modules may be used for code with different natures or functionalities. For example, user-defined functions may be in one code module and subroutines in another (there may also be separate modules for each of a category of user-defined functions and for each category of subroutine, and so on).

When modularising code, some additional points are worth bearing in mind:

- The names of the modules can be set within the `Properties` window, so that they can be given meaningful names, i.e. according to their functionality.
- One may need to take care to ensure that procedures are available to a procedure in another module, by appropriate use of the `Public` and `Private` declarations (as discussed in Chapter 30).
- When passing arguments (variables) between procedures, it will be important to ensure that these are passed correctly, either using `ByRef` or `ByVal`, as appropriate (see below).

Passing Arguments ByVal or ByRef

When procedures with arguments are called from other procedures, it is important to remember that the default method for passing arguments in VBA is by reference (`ByRef`). This means that the memory address of the argument is passed. If the second procedure changes the value of its arguments within the procedure, then this new value will apply to the value of the variable in the original procedure. The solution to this is to place the `ByVal` specification in the called procedure before the argument to be called.

The following describes an example. In the code for the following two subroutines, the first has its arguments passed using the default method (`ByRef`), whereas the second explicitly uses the `ByVal` method.

```
Sub Sub1(y)
y = y + 2
End Sub

Sub Sub2(ByVal y)
y = y + 2
End Sub
```

When the first subroutine is called, for example using:

```
x = 0.5
Call Sub1(x)
```

then the value of x will change to 2.5, and be used as such within the subsequent code.

On the other hand, when using:

```
x = 0.5
Call Sub2(x)
```

then the value of x will remain as 0.5 after the subroutine call.

The same comments apply to functions: the first function below has its arguments passed using the default method (`ByRef`), whilst the second explicitly uses `ByVal`:

```
Function Fn1(y)
y = y + 2
Fn1 = y
End Function

Function Fn2(ByVal y)
y = y + 2
Fn2 = y
End Function
```

If these functions are called using:

```
x = 0.5
Z = Fn1(x)
```

and

```
x = 0.5
Z = Fn2(x)
```

then in both cases the value of `Z` after the function call will be 2.5, but the value of `x` in the subsequent code will have changed to 2.5 in the first case, but remain as 0.5 in the second.

These properties can be seen in Figure 31.1, which results from running the code below.

```
Sub CallingRoutine()
```

```
x = 0.5
Range("B2") = x
  Call Sub1(x)
Range("D2") = x

x = 0.5
Range("B3") = x
  Call Sub2(x)
Range("D3") = x

x = 0.5
Range("B6") = x
  Z = Fn1(x)
Range("C6") = Z
Range("D6") = x

x = 0.5
Range("B7") = x
  Z = Fn2(x)
Range("C7") = Z
Range("D7") = x

End Sub
```

If one obtains unexpected results when running or stepping-through the code, it is worth considering whether such issues are playing a role.

Full Referencing

In a statement such as `Range("A1")`, it is not directly clear in which worksheet (nor which workbook) the desired range is to be found. If the code does not explicitly specify the workbook or worksheet, VBA's default is to use the active one. The idea of full referencing is to make explicit which workbook, worksheet or object is desired to be referred to.

In simpler financial modelling applications, the lack of full referencing may not cause problems: for example, the code may need to refer only to the same workbook, and perhaps even only to a single sheet within it, or it may need to refer only to predefined workbook-scoped named ranges. In such cases, the default object-referencing methods are often sufficient, even if they are not in accordance with best practices (just as a very small but poorly laid out Excel model may be sufficiently transparent and computationally correct).

	A	B	C	D
1	**SUBS**	x Before		x After
2	Routine 1	0.5		2.5
3	Routine 2	0.5		0.5
4				
5	**FUNCTIONS**	x Before	z	x After
6	Function 1	0.5	2.5	2.5
7	Function 2	0.5	2.5	0.5
8				

FIGURE 31.1 Results of Passing Arguments `ByRef` and `ByVal`

On the other hand, in more complex cases, it will be important to clearly and explicitly define which object is to be referenced for each operation. In particular, if code appears to be operating on unexpected ranges or objects, then a lack of full (or correct) referencing is an important area to investigate.

The manipulation of multiple data sets is a typical example: one may need to work with multiple worksheets or workbooks (such as consolidating the data from several sources together), and in such cases an unclear referencing (or one that relies on default behaviour) may be wrong or not sufficiently robust.

The `With...End With` construct (see Chapter 29) is especially convenient to facilitate the systematic implementation of full referencing, whose syntax can otherwise be cumbersome, or time-consuming to implement (and hence not used).

For example, instead of writing

```
x = ThisWorkbook.Worksheets("Sheet1").Range("A1").Value
y = ThisWorkbook.Worksheets("Sheet1").Range("A2").Value
z = ThisWorkbook.Worksheets("Sheet1").Range("A3").Value
```

one may write

```
With ThisWorkbook.Worksheets("Sheet1")
x = .Range("A1").Value
y = .Range("A2").Value
z = .Range("A3").Value
End With
```

Variations of its syntax include:

```
With ThisWorkbook
' Many code lines
End With
```

or similarly:

```
With ThisWorkbook
With Sheet1
' Many code lines
End With
End With
```

The `Set` statement (see Chapter 29) can also aid this requirement, for example:

```
Set wb=ThisWorkbook
With wb
' Many code lines
End With
```

The genuine full referencing of objects often also requires referring to the Excel application object, by using `Application`:

```
With Application.Workbooks("Book1.xlsx").Worksheets("Sheet1")
' Many code lines
End With
```

The use of `ActiveSheet` and `ActiveWorkbook` are often of relevance, even as these are the defaults.

Using Worksheet Code Numbers

Generally, it is more robust to refer to worksheets by using their code names, rather than the names in the Excel workbook (whose spelling or names may be changed by a user inadvertently, unaware that the names are also used within some code).

A worksheet can be given a new code name by first selecting it within the `Project` window and changing its associated name within the `Properties` window. Thus, one may refer to a worksheet as (for example) `ModelSheet` and not `Worksheets("Model")`.

Where the worksheet structure within a workbook is not altered as the code runs, the code name approach is preferable, due to its increased robustness. However, if the code adds worksheets as it is running (or other structural changes are made), the use of code names can be problematic: although the code name can be found using the `.CodeName` property of a worksheet, VBA does not permit the changing of a worksheet's code name from the VBA code itself (and the use of the `.CodeName` property on the left-hand side of an assignment statement will generate an error message and code execution will stop). Thus, traditional Excel worksheet names will need to be used to add worksheets during code execution. Thus, the following code will add a new Results worksheet, and give it a specified name in Excel, with the code name assigned automatically:

```
With ThisWorkbook
  N = Worksheets.Count
  Set Sheetnew = Worksheets.Add
  Sheetnew.Name = "Results" & N
  MsgBox Sheetnew.CodeName
End With
```

Therefore, in cases where the VBA code may add or delete worksheets as it runs, one would have to generally use the Excel worksheet names within the VBA code, rather than worksheet code names.

Assignment Statements, and Manipulating Objects Rather Than Selecting or Activating Them

In Excel, the first step to work with an object (such as a cell, range, chart, PivotTable, comment, text box etc.) is generally to activate or select it. As a result, code that arises through the recording of a macro often contains steps in which objects are activated or selected, after which the main operation is performed (e.g. change the colour, clear the contents etc.).

In VBA, both these steps may be able to be conducted differently, and more efficiently: one can often specify or identify the object by means other than selecting or activating it in Excel, and the equivalent operation (e.g. copy/paste) may be able to be conducted in other ways (such as the use of an assignment statement). Where such alternatives exist, the result is usually a process which is almost always much more computationally efficient (and quicker to run) than code in which selection or activation are used. For example, as discussed in Chapter 29, one can clear the contents of a range without first explicitly selecting it:

```
Range("A1:E8").ClearContents
```

A particularly important case is the use of assignment statements in place of Copy/Paste operations. For example, the following code was written by first recording a macro of a Copy/Paste operation and then adding the loop in order to copy (say 100 times) the value in Cell A1 into the range of rows starting at Cell B5:

```
Range("A1").Select
    Selection.Copy

For i = 1 To 100
    Range("B5").Offset(i - 1, 0).Select
    ActiveSheet.Paste
Next i
```

The equivalent using an assignment statement, would be:

```
x = Range("A1").Value
For i = 1 To 100
  Range("C5").Offset(i - 1, 0).Value = x
Next i
```

In the author's test of this code (using the `Timer` function), the first took approximately 200 times longer to run than the assignment approach.

Working with Ranges Instead of Individual Cells

With reference to the above example, one can improve the run time of each approach (Copy/Paste or assignment) by using a single range statement, rather than a loop, e.g.

```
Range("A1").Select
    Selection.Copy
    Range("B5:B1004").Select
    ActiveSheet.Paste
```

and

```
x = Range("A1").Value
    Range("C5:C1004").Value = x
```

In each case, the code runs much quicker when using a single range rather than a loop. The assignment statement is still approximately 10 times quicker (in the author's tests) than the use of the adapted Copy/Paste operation.

Data Types and Variable Declaration

The data type of a variable describes its nature (and specifically represents the type of storage space that will be used for it when the code runs). Whilst it is not necessary for the code-writer to specify the data types of the variables, doing so generally will have several advantages:

- The code will run more quickly.
- The code will generally be more robust. If variables are not declared, any errors (e.g. mistyped variable names) may not be obvious, so the code is more likely to contain hidden errors, and to be harder to debug.
- It will help to avoid name-conflict errors.

The default data type (i.e. where unspecified) is Variant, in which case the storage space associated with the variable is allocated when the code runs. Where it is desired to specify the data types, the following are the most frequently required:

- `Integer`. These range from −32,768 to +32,767.
- `Long`. These are integers that range between −2^31 and 2^31−1. The use of `Long` is very often preferable to `Integer` (which may be too limiting for some purposes, such as the number of times to recalculate a simulation model).
- `Object`. These are objects in the `Excel Object Model`, such as `Range`, and also include `Collections`, such as `Names`, and `Comments`.
- `Single`. These are values in the approximate range 10^−45 to 10^38 (both positive and negative).
- `Double`. These are values in the approximate range 10^−324 to 10^308 (both positive and negative).
- `String`. These are variable-length strings. `String *` can be used length for fixed-length strings.

Other data types include Boolean (which can be either `True` or `False`), Byte (unsigned, eight-bit numbers in the range zero to 255), Currency, Date (which allows dates from AD 100, unlike pure Excel which allows dates from AD 1900) and `Type` (which is a user-defined type, and is beyond the scope of this text).

The following points are worthy of note:

- The `Dim` statement (e.g. `Dim NDataPts As Long`) is used to declare a variable, that is, to specify its existence and data type.
- When declaring variables of the same type, one must use a separate `As` clause for each variable (e.g. `Dim i As Long, j As Long` is acceptable, but `Dim i, j As Long` is not).
- The declarations are placed in the code according to the scope of a variable. Often for many initial applications, variables will have procedure-level scope (and so should be declared at the beginning of the procedure).
- Type-declaration characters exist for legacy reasons, e.g. `Single` is represented by `!`, `Double` by #, `Integer` by %, `Long` by `&`, and `String` by $ etc. It is useful to be aware of them when reviewing code, but arguably preferable to avoid their use when developing new code.
- The code writer can be forced to declare all variables by placing the `Option Explicit` statement at the top of the code module. This can either be typed directly on the code window or made an automatic part of all code windows by checking the `Require Variable Declaration` box under `Tools/Options/Editor` tab of the VBE menu.

Choice of Names

For very short pieces of code (such as 3–5 lines), the functionality of the code and the role of each variable within it is usually clear. In such cases, arguably little attention needs to be given to the choice of names. For larger pieces of code (including several short pieces in a modular structure), a good choice of the names can help to create transparency and reduce errors. The following are some guidelines when choosing names of ranges, variables and procedures:

- Names should be clear and reasonably descriptive. For example, one may use `i_loopcount` for an integer variable that serves to count a loop. It is useful to

employ naming rules (such as that any variables beginning with the letters `i`, `j` or `k` are `Integer` or `Long`, and that any variable beginning with the letters `v`, `x`, `y` or `z` are `Double`, and so on). The `DefType` statement (which only affects the module in which the code resides) can also be useful to do this efficiently: for example, the declaration statement becomes: `DefInt i-k`, `DefLng i-k`, `DefDbl v-z` and so on.
- Names should be kept as short as possible subject to their role being clear (even short code which contains long variable names can be tiresome to read and therefore less transparent.)
- There are some constraints on the choice of names, but they usually pose little difficulty.
  - There must be no blank spaces, and no `&` symbol within the name (underscores are acceptable and indeed frequently used).
  - Reserved words (e.g. "return") may not be used.
  - Care must be taken so that names do not unintentionally refer to cell references (such as DCF, NPV, ALL, DEL, Q1, Q2 etc.).
  - Names are not case sensitive.

Working with Arrays in VBA

VBA arrays can be used to store items in a data set (of the same type, such as all `Double`). There are several uses, including:

- To read data from Excel ranges into VBA arrays before conducting operations on the data within VBA, and then returning the results to Excel.
- To act as a store of data that is generated directly in VBA. For example, in simulation models, one may first generate all random numbers or samples within a VBA array before using them in the main Excel simulation model, or to conduct statistical analysis on the results.
- As interim repositories of calculations, analogous to tables of calculations in Excel. For example, when user-defined functions are written in an array form (where the function's output extends over a multi-cell Excel range), then the individual cell values for the function are generally best calculated as a VBA array, before being returned to Excel.

As an example, the following code creates a user-defined function that sums the integers from 1 to an input number, N. It places the individual integer values in an array, which is summed using the Excel worksheet function SUM.

```
Option Explicit
Option Base 1
Function MRSum1ToN(ByVal N)
Dim i As Long
Dim DataSet() As Double
ReDim DataSet(1 To N) As Double
For i = 1 To N
DataSet(i) = i
Next i
MRSum1ToN = WorksheetFunction.Sum(DataSet)
End Function
```

This example demonstrates some important points, including that:

- The declaration of an array is similar to the declaration of other variables, but also includes its size and dimensions, such as:

```
Dim myArray(1 to 1000) As Double
```

- The VBA default is for the first element of an array to have the index number zero. This can be desirable in some cases, for example where the elements of the array are used to represent the values of an asset in a time series, it may provide clarity if the current value were represented by `AssetValue(0)`, with `AssetValue(1)` denoting the value in period one, and so on. Where it is desired to ensure that arrays always start with a specific index number (generally 0 or 1), one can explicitly state this by placing statements such as `Option Base 0` or `Option Base 1` at the beginning of any code (before the subroutines), as shown in the example above.
- In many cases the required size may not be known until the code is run (for example, where the array will be populated with a data set whose size may vary). In such cases, the `ReDim` statement (see the example above) can be used to redefine the dimensions of an array once it is known (doing so will erase the values currently held in the array; if these values need to be kept, then the statement `ReDim Preserve` can be used).

Arrays can also be multi-dimensional (e.g. store daily values of the prices of various stocks), with the maximum allowed number of dimensions allowed being 60. A two-dimensional array could be declared with a statement such as:

```
Dim ResultsArray(1 to 1000, 1 to 1000) As Double
```

Since the items in an array must all be of the same data type, a multi-dimensional array could not in general be used to store the elements of a database (where for example some columns would contain values and others would contain text). Such a situation could be dealt with by having a separate one-dimensional array for each database column or by creating a user-defined data type or classes (this is beyond the scope of this text, but may crudely be thought of as being rather like a one-dimensional array, but where each element has multiple information attached to it).

Understanding Error Codes: An Introduction

Error codes in VBA have a number attached to them. The full list of VBA error codes can be seen by searching for `trappable errors` within VBA `Help`. For each error there can be many causes; a selection of the most frequent errors and their typical causes includes:

- `Invalid procedure call or argument (Error 5)`: An argument exceeds the range of permitted values.
- `Subscript out of range (Error 9)`: An array has not been dimensioned using the `Dim` or `ReDim` statements.
- `Type mismatch (Error 13)`: A variable or "property is not of the correct type.
- `Object variable not set (Error 91)`: Omission of the `Set` statement.

- `Object doesn't support this property or method (Error 438)`: A method or property was specified that does not exist for the object.
- The error code `1004` occurs when an error results from Excel rather than VBA, but has its effect within the Code.

In general, errors of the above nature will correspond to unintentional errors that will cause code execution to stop.

FURTHER APPROACHES TO TESTING, DEBUGGING AND ERROR-HANDLING

The use of step-through and break-point techniques discussed in Chapter 29 is usually sufficient to debug simple code. In this section, we cover some more advanced techniques that are useful when debugging larger blocks of code (as well as functions):

General Techniques

Some additional techniques that are useful in general include:

- Using the `Debug` menu within VBE (or the associated short-cuts) to:
  - `Step Over` (Shift +F8) procedures that do not contain errors (e.g. called subroutines that have already been checked); the short-cut can be used.
  - `Step Out` (Ctrl+ Shift +F8) to run the rest of a called subroutine (e.g. if one has stepped into a called subroutine or that one knows is working, or if a user-defined function is called at each step of a loop in a sub-routine).
  - Clear or toggle breakpoints.
- Using the `View/Locals` window to show the values of all variables in a subroutine during a run, allowing the values of many variables to be checked simultaneously.
- Using the `View/Watch Window` to:
  - Monitor the values of a variables as one steps through the code (right-click on the variable and use `Add Watch`).
  - Replace the current value of a variable with any desired value (for variables that are on the left sign of an assignment statement), i.e. the value shown in the `Watch Window` can simply be typed over with another value that will be used in the subsequent code steps.
- Using `View/Immediate Window`. This provides immediate results for statements typed in, and can be used to see the values of variables not explicitly set up within a `Watch Window`, such as when only a one-off analysis of the value is likely to be needed:
  - The `?` or `Debug.Print` expressions can be used within the window to evaluate the expression (such as `? x` or `Debug.Print x` or `? Range("NCalcs").Address` or `? Range("C3").Value`). Such expressions can also be placed within the code, in which case the evaluation of the expression is shown in the `Immediate` window when the code executes at that point.
  - A procedure can be executed immediately by entering the procedure name in this window.
- Using `View/CallStack` (Ctrl+L) to show the list of procedures that were executed to arrive at the current point.

Debugging Functions

The debugging of functions is generally more complicated and cumbersome than that of subroutines, because functions with arguments will not by default allow their code to be stepped through or break-points to be set.

On the other hand, functions do have the advantage of being live-linked to their input parameters, which allows the use of sensitivity analysis to test the robustness of a function once it seems to be working in principle. Therefore, the first step in creating robust functions often aims simply to create the function so that it at least provides a result (rather than failing to execute, and returning an error message). In this respect, some simple techniques are often useful:

- Placing a simple return statement at specific points of the code. For example, if the function is not executing (and only returning error messages), once could place a code line such as `MyFunction=1` early on in the code (immediately followed by the `Exit Function`). If the function's code is working up to the point at which these statements are placed, the function will provide a return value into Excel. These code lines can then be moved to later in the code, until the lines at which errors are produced are identified. (The return and exit statements can be deleted in turn as the code is corrected.)
- The function can be called from a subroutine, so that it can be stepped-through. For example:

```
Sub DebugbyCallingFunction()
Dummy=FntoDebug(12, 5)
MsgBox Dummy
End Sub

Function FntoDebug(x, y)
'... lots of code ...
FntoDebug = calculated value from the code
End Function
```

Where the function input parameters are to be Excel ranges, one can use these within the calling subroutine, such as:

```
Sub DebugbyCallingFunction()
Dummy=FntoDebug(Range("A1"), Range("A2"))
MsgBox Dummy
End Sub
```

The Function may need to be defined as one which is `Volatile`, by using `Application.Volatile` immediately after the function name.

Note that stepping through a function will often lead at some point to other macros being run or called. If these are working correctly, they can be stepped over using the methods outlined earlier, such as `Step Over` (Shift+F8), or simply running to various break points and then stepping through.

As for other calculations in Excel, functions can also be checked by using them with a wide set of input values (i.e. performing a sensitivity analysis of the results of the function), to ensure that the calculations are robust, and to detect further potential errors or limitations.

Implementing Error-handling Procedures

When using code written by oneself, it is likely that one will input data that is appropriate for the context and as required by the code (for example, one is likely to input an integer for a scenario number). On the other hand, another user may provide inputs that could either cause an error, or stop code execution, or lead to unexpected behaviour. Therefore, one may wish to write code that both checks the validity of the input assumptions and manages the process, so that the code execution branches in accordance with valid or invalid inputs.

VBA functions such as `IsObject`, `IsEmpty`, `IsMissing`, `IsNull`, `IsNumeric`, `IsDate`, and so on can be used to check the nature of the parameters that are input or passed to a subroutine or function. When dealing with potential errors, it is also important to ensure that all possible cases are handled (sometimes the `Select Case...Case Else...End Select` construct is useful, with `Case Else` used to treat invalid entries).

There can be cases where errors are acceptable, so that it is not desired for the code to stop executing even when an error is detected. The `On Error` statement is useful in this respect, providing instructions as to what to do in case of an error (so that execution is not stopped by default):

- `On Error Resume Next` can be used so that code will continue execution. This would be used in cases where the occurrence of an error at that point would not be regarded as important (an example might be if an object collection were empty, or if code which is written to highlight a precedent cell may by default return an error for cells with no precedents, even if such a situation (e.g. for numerical inputs) may be of no real concern).
- `On Error` can be combined with a `GoTo` statement to jump to another part of the code (designated by a label) within the same subroutine. In this case, the `Exit Sub` statement may be required to ensure that the code associated with the label runs only where relevant.
- `On Error GoTo 0` (or `On Error Resume 0`) can be used to restore VBA's normal error handling for the subsequent code.

For example:

```
... earlier part of code ...
On Error Resume Next
... code to be executed even if error detected
On Error Resume 0
... any code here is subject to VBA's normal error handling ...
```

and

```
... earlier part of code ...
        On Error GoTo ErrorLabel
... code to be executed even if no error
Exit Sub
ErrorLabel:
MsgBox "There was an error somewhere"
```

CHAPTER 32

Manipulation and Analysis of Data Sets with VBA

INTRODUCTION

This chapter focuses on the use of VBA in the manipulation and analysis of data sets. In fact, almost all of the necessary techniques used here have already been mentioned earlier; to some extent this chapter represents the integration and consolidation of these within the specific context of data analysis.

PRACTICAL APPLICATIONS

The examples in this section include:

- Working out the size of a given data range.
- Defining the data set at run time, based on user input.
- Defining the data set at run time by automatically detecting its position.
- Reversing the rows and/or columns of a data set (either into a new range, or in place).
- Automation of general Excel functionalities.
- Automation of processes to clean data sets, such as deleting rows containing blanks.
- Automation of the use of filters to clean, delete or extract specific items.
- Automation of Database function queries.
- Consolidation of several data sets that reside in different worksheets or workbooks.

Example: Working Out the Size of a Range

One of the most compelling reasons to use VBA to manipulate or analyse data sets (rather than build the corresponding operations using Excel functions and functionality) is that VBA can detect the size of a data set, and conduct its operations accordingly.

Day	Asset 1	Asset 2	Asset 3	Asset 4	Asset 5
1	100.0	100.0	100.0	100.0	100.0
2	100.0	98.9	99.6	99.6	100.8
3	101.7	98.0	99.9	99.7	102.1
4	103.1	96.5	100.6	100.2	104.7
5	104.2	97.3	99.1	101.9	107.0
6	103.7	96.2	100.9	102.5	106.0
7	104.9	97.0	101.8	103.0	109.0
8	104.3	95.3	103.8	101.6	108.3
9	104.1	94.3	104.1	100.2	106.7
10	105.0	95.3	104.0	100.3	107.8
11	107.3	97.4	102.3	102.3	108.1

FIGURE 32.1 Using `CurrentRegion` to Detect the Size of a Range

By contrast, if the size of a data set changes, then Excel functions that refer to this data would generally need to be adapted as well as copied to additional cells (unless dynamic ranges or Excel Tables are used, as discussed earlier in the text). As mentioned in Chapter 29, the use of the `CurrentRegion` property of a cell or range is one very important tool in this respect.

The file Ch32.1.Current.Region.xlsm contains an example (see Figure 32.1). In the file, Cell B2 has been given the Excel named range DataSetStart, and it is assumed that any new rows or columns that are added to the data set will be contiguous with existing data. The worksheet containing the data has been given the VBA code name DataSheet, so that in this example, we assume that there is only one such worksheet.

The screen-clip shows the effect of running the following code, which selects the entire data range.

```
Sub MRSelectData
With DataSheet
 Range("DataSetStart").CurrentRegion.Select
End With
End Sub
```

Note that in practice (as mentioned earlier), it is usually best to conduct directly the operation that is desired without selecting ranges. Thus, code such as the following could be used to directly define the data set (as an object variable called `DataSet`):

```
Sub MRDefineData1()
 Set DataSet = Range("DataSetStart").CurrentRegion
End Sub
```

Generally, the number of rows and columns in the data set would wish to be known, which could be established by code such as:

```
Set DataSet = Range("DataSetStart").CurrentRegion
 NRows = DataSet.Rows.Count
 NCols = DataSet.Columns.Count
```

Example: Defining the Data Set at Run Time Based on User Input

In many cases, one may not wish to have to pre-define an Excel cell or named range within a data set, but instead to have the user identify the starting (or any other) cell of the data, assuming a contiguous data set. As mentioned in Chapter 29, an `Application.InputBox` can be used take a cell reference from the user at run time, for example:

```
Set dInputCell = Application.InputBox("Select Any Cell within Data Range", Type:=8)
```

One can then define the data range as being (for example) the current region associated with that particular input cell:

```
Set DataSet = dInputCell.CurrentRegion
```

The file Ch32.2.InputBoxCellRef.xlsm contains an example of this, and Figure 32.2 shows the part of the process step where a user may identify any cell within the data range as an input cell, from which the full data range is established:

```
Sub MRCountDataRowsCols()
 Set dInputCell = Application.InputBox("Select Any Cell within Data Range", Type:=8)
 Set DataSet = dInputCell.CurrentRegion
 NRows = DataSet.Rows.Count
 NCols = DataSet.Columns.Count
 End Sub
```

Example: Working Out the Position of a Data Set Automatically

Of course, asking the user to be involved in defining the data set may not be desirable or may limit one's ability to automate the identification of multiple data sets (for example, that are each contained in a separate worksheet). Thus, one may wish to automate the process of inspecting a worksheet to detect the data range. Important tools in this respect are those that detect the used range and the last cell that is used in a worksheet.

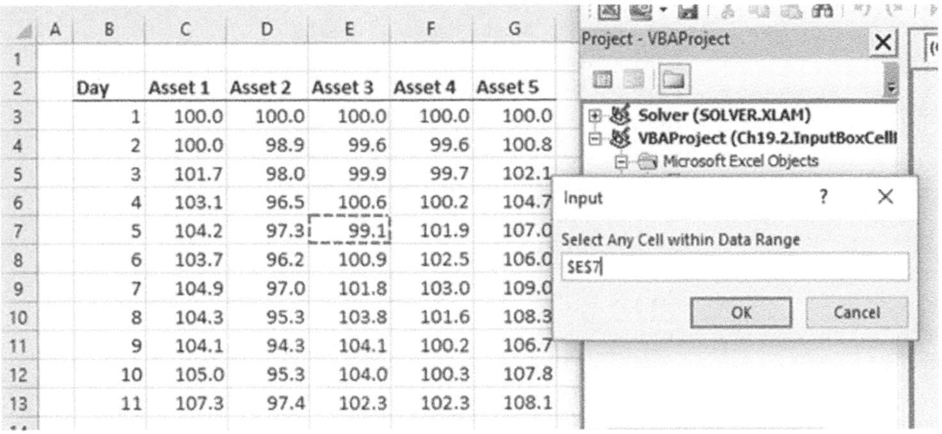

FIGURE 32.2 Taking User Input About the Location of a Cell or Data Point

The file Ch32.3.DataSizeGeneral.xlsm contains the code described below, and an example data set on which it can be tested. The used range on a worksheet can be determined with code such as:

```
With DataSheet
 Set dRange = .UsedRange
End With
```

In applications where there are multiple worksheets, some of which may need to be deleted or added during code execution, most frequently the worksheet names would be Excel worksheet names, rather than code names. (For example, the worksheets may have been inserted automatically though the running of other procedures, and not have code names attached to them, as described in Chapter 31.) In this case, the code would be of the form:

```
With Worksheets("Results1")
 Set dRange = .UsedRange
End With
```

The first cell of the used range could be set using:

```
Set dstart = .UsedRange.Cells(1, 1)
```

Similarly, the code syntax .UsedRange.Address can be used to find the address of the data set and report it using a message box when the code is run (see Figure 32.3).

Once the full data set is defined, its row and columns can be counted, so that the last cell of the data set would be given by:

```
NRows = DataSet.Rows.Count
NCols = DataSet.Columns.Count
Set LastCell = DataStart.Cells(NRows, NCols)
```

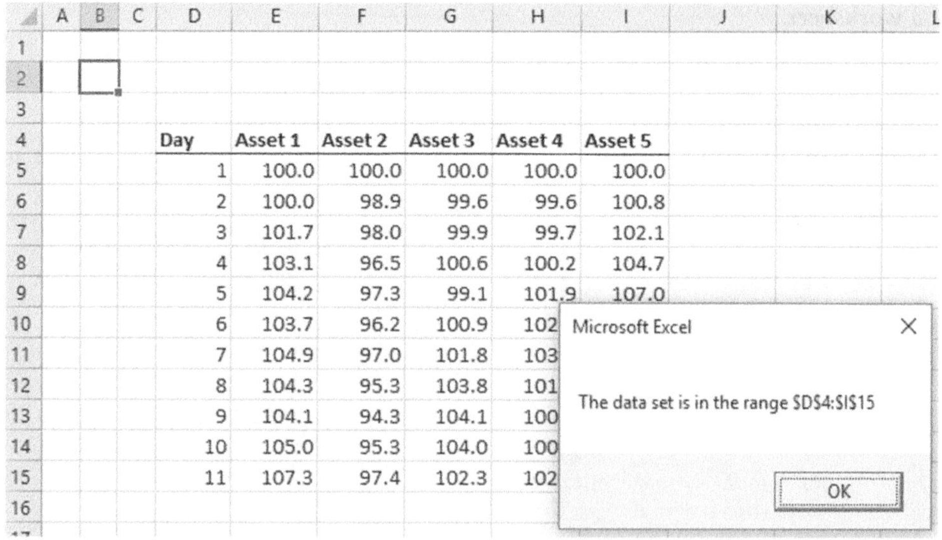

Day	Asset 1	Asset 2	Asset 3	Asset 4	Asset 5
1	100.0	100.0	100.0	100.0	100.0
2	100.0	98.9	99.6	99.6	100.8
3	101.7	98.0	99.9	99.7	102.1
4	103.1	96.5	100.6	100.2	104.7
5	104.2	97.3	99.1	101.9	107.0
6	103.7	96.2	100.9	102	
7	104.9	97.0	101.8	103	
8	104.3	95.3	103.8	101	
9	104.1	94.3	104.1	100	
10	105.0	95.3	104.0	100	
11	107.3	97.4	102.3	102	

Microsoft Excel

The data set is in the range $D$4:$I$15

OK

FIGURE 32.3 Finding the Full Range of any Single Contiguous Data Set

Alternatively, the last cell could be identified using the code discussed in Chapter 29, arising from recording a macro as Excel's GoTo/Special operation is conducted:

```
With Worksheets("Data").Range("A1")
  Set lcell = .SpecialCells(xlCellTypeLastCell)
End With
```

Example: Reversing Rows (or Columns) of Data I: Placement in a New Range

The techniques to detect the location and size of data sets are generally a precursor to subsequent operations. A simple example could be the need to reverse the order of all the rows (and/or columns), such as for a data set of time series.

The file Ch32.4.ReverseAllRowsExceptHeaders.xlsm contains the code which uses the methods above to detect and define a data set of contiguous data, and then reverses all its rows, except for the header. The new data is placed one column to the right of the original data, and the headers are copied across (Figure 32.4 shows the result of running the code):

```
Sub ReverseDataRows()
With Worksheets("Data")
 Set DataStart = .UsedRange.Cells(1, 1)
 Set DataSet = DataStart.CurrentRegion
 NRows = DataSet.Rows.Count
 NCols = DataSet.Columns.Count
  With DataStart.Cells(1, 1)
   For j = 1 To NCols
    For i = 2 To NRows
     .Offset(NRows - i + 1, NCols + j).Value = .Offset(i - 1, j - 1).Value
    Next i
     'copy the label across
     .Offset(0, NCols + j).Value = .Offset(0, j - 1).Value
  Next j
  End With
End With
End Sub
```

	A	B	C	D	E	F	G	H	I	J
1										
2		Date	Type	Description	Amount		Date	Type	Description	Amount
3		16/09/2016	TFR	Payroll	1259.41		29/09/2016	DEB	Bank fee	0.35
4		16/09/2016	DEB	Bus	36.60		29/09/2016	DEB	Train	12.79
5		20/09/2016	DEB	Train	22.00		28/09/2016	DEB	Bus	7.40
6		20/09/2016	DEB	Train	50.00		28/09/2016	DEB	Bank fee	0.20
7		22/09/2016	DEB	Food	10.30		27/09/2016	DEB	Book	11.20
8		22/09/2016	DEB	Drink	11.40		27/09/2016	DEB	Book	6.99
9		23/09/2016	DEB	Food	10.41		26/09/2016	DEB	Train	11.60
10		23/09/2016	DEB	Food	20.00		23/09/2016	DEB	Food	20.00
11		26/09/2016	DEB	Train	11.60		23/09/2016	DEB	Food	10.41
12		27/09/2016	DEB	Book	6.99		22/09/2016	DEB	Drink	11.40
13		27/09/2016	DEB	Book	11.20		22/09/2016	DEB	Food	10.30
14		28/09/2016	DEB	Bank fee	0.20		20/09/2016	DEB	Train	50.00
15		28/09/2016	DEB	Bus	7.40		20/09/2016	DEB	Train	22.00
16		29/09/2016	DEB	Train	12.79		16/09/2016	DEB	Bus	36.60
17		29/09/2016	DEB	Bank fee	0.35		16/09/2016	TFR	Payroll	1259.41
18										

FIGURE 32.4 Reversing Data and Placing the Results Next to the Original Data

(Note that the code has been written to leave a column gap between the original and the reversed data. This ensures that the `CurrentRegion` of `.UsedRange.Cells(1,1)` refers only to the original data set.)

In more general cases, one may wish also to reverse the column order of the data. This is possible by a straightforward adaptation, in which the indexation number on the left-hand side of each assignment statement (i.e. those for the value and for the labels) is modified, by replacing `NCols + j` with `2 * NCols + 1 - j`. This results in the columns being worked in reverse order; this code is also included in the example file.

Example: Reversing Rows (or Columns) of Data II: In Place

One can also manipulate data "in-place", rather than writing the results to a separate range. A simple way to do this is to read the original data into a VBA array as an intermediate step, and then read the results from the array back into Excel (thereby overwriting the original data range).

The file Ch32.5.ReverseInPlaceArray.xlsm contains an example, using the following code:

```
Sub ReverseDataRowsArray()
Dim aData()
With Worksheets("Data")
 Set DataStart = .UsedRange.Cells(1, 1)
 Set DataSet = DataStart.CurrentRegion

 'Set dpoint = Application.InputBox(prompt:="Select a cell in the data range", Type:=8)
 'Set DataSet = dpoint.CurrentRegion

 NRows = DataSet.Rows.Count
 Ncols = DataSet.Columns.Count

 ReDim aData(1 To NRows, 1 To Ncols)

  With DataStart.Cells(1, 1)
  ' //// READ INTO THE ARRAY
   For j = 1 To Ncols
    For i = 2 To NRows
     aData(i, j) = .Offset(i - 1, j - 1).Value
    Next i
    Next j
  ' //// WRITE FROM THE ARRAY
  For j = 1 To Ncols
    For i = 2 To NRows
     .Offset(i - 1, j - 1).Value = aData(NRows + 2 - i, j)
    Next i
    Next j
  End With
End With
End Sub
```

Note that the step in the earlier code in which the header is copied is no longer necessary in this example, as the data remains in place and the columns are not reversed.

Example: Automation of Other Data-related Excel Procedures

One can automate many standard Excel operations by adapting the macros that result from recording operations, often using some of the range-identification techniques above when doing so. These could include:

- Clearing ranges.
- Removing duplicates.
- Applying Find/Replace.
- GoTo/Special Cells (e.g. selection of blanks, dependents, precedents etc.).
- Sorting.
- Refreshing PivotTables.
- Inserting SUBTOTAL functions using the Wizard.
- Inserting a Table of Contents with Hyperlinks to each worksheet.
- Using Filters and Advanced Filters.

Examples of some of these have been provided earlier in the text. Here, and later in this chapter, we discuss a few more.

The file Ch32.6.ClearContentsNotHeaders.xlsm shows an example (containing the following code) that uses the `ClearContents` method to clear an entire data range, except for the first row (which is assumed to contain heads that wish to be retained):

```
Sub DeleteDataExceptHeaders()
With Worksheets("Data")
 Set DataStart = .UsedRange.Cells(1, 1)
 Set DataSet = DataStart.CurrentRegion
 NRows = DataSet.Rows.Count
 NCols = DataSet.Columns.Count
 With DataStart
 Set RangeToClear = Range(.Offset(1, 0), .Offset(NRows - 1, NCols - 1))
 RangeToClear.ClearContents
 End With
End With
End Sub
```

(In practice, some additional code lines or error-handling procedures may be added to deal with the case that no data is present, i.e. only headers for example, such as would be the case if the code were run twice in succession.)

The file Ch32.7.FindSpecialCells.xslm contains another similar example; this shades in yellow all precedents of a selected cell. To achieve this, two macros were recorded, combined and adapted: the first uses GoTo/Special to find the precedents of a selected cell or range, and the second shades a selected range with the colour yellow. The code also has an error-handling procedure which overrides the warning message that would appear if the cell or range has no precedents (and a button has been set up in the file, so that the macro could be used repeatedly and easily in a larger model).

```
Sub ColorAllPrecedentsYellow()
On Error GoTo myMessage
 Selection.Precedents.Select
  With Selection.Interior
    .Color = 65535
  End With
  Exit Sub
myMessage:   MsgBox "no precedents found"
End Sub
```

Example: Deleting Rows Containing Blank Cells

One can select all blank cells within an already selected range by using the GoTo/Special (F5 short-cut) functionality in Excel. When this is recorded as a macro, one has syntax of the form:

```
Selection.SpecialCells(xlCellTypeBlanks).Select
```

This is easily adapted to create code which will delete all rows in a selection that contains blank cells (and with the addition of an error-handler to avoid an error message if there are no blank cells in the selection):

```
Sub DeleteRowsinSelection_IfAnyCellBlank()
On Error Resume Next 'for case that no blank cells are found
Set MyArea = Selection.SpecialCells(xlCellTypeBlanks)
Set rngToDelete = MyArea.EntireRow
rngToDelete.Delete
End Sub
```

The file Ch32.8.DaysLateAnalysis.DeleteRows1.xlsm contains an example. Figure 32.5 shows a selected data set, and Figure 32.6 shows the result of running the above code.

	A	B	C	D	E	F
1						
2						
3						
4		Customer	Country	Amount £	Due Date	
5		Cust02	UK	12232	20-Mar-17	
6		Cust06	Italy	4749	16-Mar-17	
7		Cust07	Italy	7282	12-Apr-17	
8		Cust03	Italy	12759	14-Jun-17	
9		Cust10	UK	12334	24-May-17	
10			Italy	4283	24-Mar-17	
11		Cust06	Germany	7992	5-May-17	
12		Cust06	Italy	13202		
13		Cust04	Germany	12684	4-Jun-17	
14		Cust10	UK	11862	13-Jun-17	
15		Cust10	Ita	13630	21-May-17	
16		Cust07	UK	14593	20-Jan-17	
17		Cust07		4394	4-May-17	
18		Cust09	Italy	15712	8-Apr-17	
19		Cust10	UK	6503	28-Mar-17	
20		Cust05	France		8-Apr-17	
21		Cust02	Germany	9274	17-Jun-17	
22		Cust05	Italy	7919	27-Jun-17	
23		Cust05	Italy	6402	14-Jun-17	
24						
25		Cust08	Spain	14120	2-Jul-17	
26		Cust06	Spain	8889	8-Jun-17	
27		Cust04	France	9547	1-Jun-17	
28		Cust10	UK	14001	13-Jun-17	
29		Cust01	Spain	4486	27-Apr-17	
30		Cust05	Germany	9832	18-Apr-17	
31		Cust08	Spain	9022	14-Apr-17	

FIGURE 32.5 A Selected Data Set Before the Delete Blank Rows Code is Run

	A	B	C	D	E
1					
2					
3					
4		Customer	Country	Amount £	Due Date
5		Cust02	UK	12232	20-Mar-17
6		Cust06	Italy	4749	16-Mar-17
7		Cust07	Italy	7282	12-Apr-17
8		Cust03	Italy	12759	14-Jun-17
9		Cust10	UK	12334	24-May-17
10		Cust06	Germany	7992	5-May-17
11		Cust04	Germany	12684	4-Jun-17
12		Cust10	UK	11862	13-Jun-17
13		Cust10	Ita	13630	21-May-17
14		Cust07	UK	14593	20-Jan-17
15		Cust09	Italy	15712	8-Apr-17
16		Cust10	UK	6503	28-Mar-17
17		Cust02	Germany	9274	17-Jun-17
18		Cust05	Italy	7919	27-Jun-17
19		Cust05	Italy	6402	14-Jun-17
20		Cust08	Spain	14120	2-Jul-17
21		Cust06	Spain	8889	8-Jun-17
22		Cust04	France	9547	1-Jun-17
23		Cust10	UK	14001	13-Jun-17
24		Cust01	Spain	4486	27-Apr-17
25		Cust05	Germany	9832	18-Apr-17
26		Cust08	Spain	9022	14-Apr-17
27		Cust02	Germany	14290	1-Jun-17
28		Cust07	Spain	10007	29-May-17
29		Cust10	Italia	7250	13-May-17
30		Cust09	France	15080	7-Apr-17
31		Cust03	Germany	9373	3-May-17

FIGURE 32.6 The Data Set After the Delete Blank Rows Code Has Run

Example: Deleting Blank Rows

In the above example, the range in which rows were to be deleted was pre-selected by the user. A more automated procedure would be to invoke the `.UsedRange` property of a worksheet. When doing this, one needs to take into account that the simultaneous deletion of multiple rows may not be permissible, and that when a single row is deleted, those that are below it are moved up in Excel; as a result, one needs to work backwards from the bottom of the range to delete the blank rows.

The file Ch32.9.DaysLateAnalysis.DeleteRows2.xlsm contains an example of this, using the following code:

```
With ActiveSheet
  NRows = .UsedRange.Rows.Count
  For i = NRows To 1 Step -1 ' need to work backwards else may get empty rows
    Set myRow = Rows(i).EntireRow
     NUsedCells = Application.WorksheetFunction.CountA(myRow)
      If NUsedCells = 0 Then
        myRow.Delete
          Else
      End If
  Next i
```

	A	B	C	D	E
1					
2					
3					
4		Customer	Country	Amount £	Due Date
5		Cust02	UK	12232	20-Mar-17
6		Cust06	Italy	4749	16-Mar-17
7					
8		Cust03	Italy	12759	14-Jun-17
9		Cust10	UK	12334	24-May-17
10			Italy	4283	24-Mar-17
11		Cust06	Germany	7992	5-May-17
12		Cust06	Italy	13202	
13		Cust04	Germany	12684	4-Jun-17
14					
15		Cust10	Ita	13630	21-May-17
16		Cust07	UK	14593	20-Jan-17
17		Cust07		4394	4-May-17
18		Cust09	Italy	15712	8-Apr-17
19					
20		Cust05	France		8-Apr-17
21		Cust02	Germany	9274	17-Jun-17
22		Cust05	Italy	7919	27-Jun-17
23		Cust05	Italy	6402	14-Jun-17
24					
25		Cust08	Spain	14120	2-Jul-17
26		Cust06	Spain	8889	8-Jun-17
27		Cust04	France	9547	1-Jun-17

FIGURE 32.7 Deleting All Blank Rows in the Used Range: Before

Figure 32.7 shows an original data set to which this is applied, and Figure 32.8 shows the result. Note that blank rows at the top of the worksheet were removed, but also that rows in which not all cells are blank are not deleted.

The above two examples could be used in sequence to remove all rows which are either blank, or for which one of the data entries is blank (even if the row is not entirely blank).

Example: Automating the Use of Filters to Remove Blanks or Other Specified Items

In some cases, the items that one may wish to remove when cleaning or tidying a data set may not be those containing blanks, but those that have some other form of identifier (including blanks as one case). In Chapter 26, we showed the use of Excel's Data/Filter and Data/Advanced Filter to perform such operations on a one-off basis. It is relatively straightforward to record and appropriately adapt a macro of such operations. Recall that the main steps in the process that would initially be recorded are:

- Applying a filter to identify and select the items that one wishes to delete.
- Selecting the full range of filtered rows.

	A	B	C	D	E
1		Customer	Country	Amount £	Due Date
2		Cust02	UK	12232	20-Mar-17
3		Cust06	Italy	4749	16-Mar-17
4		Cust03	Italy	12759	14-Jun-17
5		Cust10	UK	12334	24-May-17
6			Italy	4283	24-Mar-17
7		Cust06	Germany	7992	5-May-17
8		Cust06	Italy	13202	
9		Cust04	Germany	12684	4-Jun-17
10		Cust10	Ita	13630	21-May-17
11		Cust07	UK	14593	20-Jan-17
12		Cust07		4394	4-May-17
13		Cust09	Italy	15712	8-Apr-17
14		Cust05	France		8-Apr-17
15		Cust02	Germany	9274	17-Jun-17
16		Cust05	Italy	7919	27-Jun-17
17		Cust05	Italy	6402	14-Jun-17
18		Cust08	Spain	14120	2-Jul-17
19		Cust06	Spain	8889	8-Jun-17
20		Cust04	France	9547	1-Jun-17
21		Cust10	UK	14001	13-Jun-17

FIGURE 32.8 Deleting All Blank Rows in the Used Range: After

- Deleting these rows in the usual way (i.e. using Home/Delete Cells or right-clicking to obtain the context-sensitive menu).
- Removing the filters.

The file Ch32.10.DaysLateAnalysis.DeleteUsingFilter.xlsm contains an example. Figure 32.9 shows an original data set (assumed to be contiguous for the moment). One could then record the above steps, for example where one removes either blanks or the entries associated with Italy (from the Country field). If one initially records the

	A	B	C	D	E	F
1						
2						
3						
4		Customer	Country	Amount £	Due Date	
5		Cust02	UK	12232	20-Mar-17	
6		Cust06	Italy	4749	16-Mar-17	
7		Cust07	Italy	7282	12-Apr-17	
8		Cust03	Italy	12759	14-Jun-17	
9		Cust10		12334	24-May-17	
10		Cust05	Italy	4283	24-Mar-17	
11		Cust06	Germany	7992	5-May-17	
12		Cust06	Italy	13202	16-Apr-17	
13		Cust04		12684	4-Jun-17	

FIGURE 32.9 Original Data Set Before Application of the Procedure

above steps, except for the deletion process (i.e. those of selecting the data set, applying a filter and then removing the filter), one would have code such as:

```
Sub Macro1()
 Range("B4").Select
 Selection.CurrentRegion.Select
 Selection.AutoFilter

 ActiveSheet.Range("$B$4:$E$104").AutoFilter Field:=2, Criteria1:="="
 ActiveSheet.Range("$B$4:$E$104").AutoFilter Field:=2, Criteria1:="Italy"

 ActiveSheet.ShowAllData
End Sub
```

Note that for reference purposes regarding the syntax, when recording the code, the filter on the Country field was first applied to blanks and then applied to Italy.

When developing a more general macro, one would likely wish to include additional elements such as:

- Specifying the value of the field that is of interest for deletion (e.g. blank rows or those associated with Italy), including ensuring that the filter is applied to the correct column Field. For example, one may instead wish to delete all blanks or all entries associated with Cust07 in the Customer field.
- Deleting the filtered rows, except for the headings.

The following points about the sample code below are worth noting:

- The `Application.InputBox` is used to take a cell reference from the user, whose contents identifies the item that define the items to be deleted.
- With reference to this cell, the field column number associated within this identifier is calculated (i.e. equivalent to `Field:=2`) in the above example, noting that this column field number is its relative position within the data set.
- The filter is then applied, and a range created that contains all filtered data, except for the header.
- In practice, one may wish to switch on/off the screen updating (see Chapter 30), especially if such operations were to be further automated within a large loop that deletes a large set of records, according to pre-defined identifiers (this is not shown within the text of the code for simplicity of presentation).

```
Sub MRWrittenFilter()
 Set CelltoSearch = Application.InputBox("Click on cell containing
the identifier data to delete", Type:=8)
  With CelltoSearch
     idItemtoDelete = .Text
     Set DataAll = .CurrentRegion
     icolN = .Column - DataAll.Cells(1, 1).Column + 1
  End With

  DataAll.AutoFilter Field:=icolN, Criteria1:=idItemtoDelete

  Set DataAll = DataAll.CurrentRegion.Offset(1, 0)
  DataAll.EntireRow.Delete

  ActiveSheet.ShowAllData
End Sub
```

The code could be modified so that it works for non-contiguous ranges of data (using `.UsedRange` rather than `.CurrentRegion`). In this case, one would generally first delete all rows that are completely blank (using the method outlined in the earlier example), before deleting filtered rows according to the user input (as shown in the earlier part of this example). Thus, one could have two separate subroutines that are each called from a master routine; the following code is also contained within the file:

```
Sub MRClearBlankRowsANDIdRows()
Call MRDeleteBlankRows
Call MRDeleteIdRows
End Sub

Sub MRDeleteBlankRows()
'/// DELETE ALL COMPLETELY BLANK ROWS
With ActiveSheet
  Set DataAll = .UsedRange
  NRows = DataAll.Rows.Count
  For i = NRows To 1 Step -1
    Set myRow = Rows(i).EntireRow
     NUsedCells = Application.WorksheetFunction.CountA(myRow)
      If NUsedCells = 0 Then
        myRow.Delete
          Else
      End If
  Next i
End With
End Sub

Sub MRDeleteIdRows()
'/// DELETE BASED ON USER INPUT
With ActiveSheet
  Set DataAll = .UsedRange
  Set CelltoSearch = Application.InputBox("Click on cell containing
the identifier data to delete", Type:=8)
  With CelltoSearch
     idItemtoDelete = .Text
     icolN = .Column - DataAll.Cells(1, 1).Column + 1
  End With
  DataAll.AutoFilter Field:=icolN, Criterial:=idItemtoDelete
  Set DataAll = DataAll.CurrentRegion.Offset(1, 0)
  DataAll.EntireRow.Delete
  ActiveSheet.ShowAllData
End With
End Sub
```

Finally, note that there are many possible variations and generalisations of the above that would be possible, such as:

- Removing items based on multiple identifiers, by specifying these identifiers within a range and then working through all elements of that range (rather than using a user input box for each item).

- Copying the items to a separate area (such as a new worksheet that is automatically added using the techniques discussed earlier) before deleting the records from the main data set, thus creating two data sets (i.e. a main clean data set, and another containing the items that have been excluded). In practice, the data set of excluded items may define a set of items for which the data records need further manual investigation, before reinclusion in the main data set.
- Extracting or deleting items based on a Criteria Range and Advanced Filters.

The experimentation with such generalisations is left to the reader.

Example: Performing Multiple Database Queries

We noted in Chapter 26 that, when trying to perform multiple queries using Database functions one was not able to use functions within the Criteria Range (to perform a lookup process), since blanks that are calculated within the Criteria Range are not treated as genuinely empty cells. The alternative was the repeated Copy/Paste/Value-type operations; clearly, these can be automated using VBA macros (using assignment statements within a Loop).

The file Ch32.11.DaysLateAnalysis.DatabaseFunctions3.MultiQuery.xlsm contains an example. Figure 32.10 shows a screen-clip of the criteria ranges and the results ranges (the database is in the left-hand columns of the file, not shown in the clip). The basic procedure (as indicated by the arrows) is to assign, into the Criteria Range, the values of the various queries that are to be run, to recalculate the Database functions, and to assign the results to storage area. To facilitate the writing and robustness of the code, the various header fields have been given named ranges within the Excel file (e.g. CritToTestHeader refers to the header of the range that list the set of criteria to be tested, and CritHeader refers to the header for the criteria range for the Database functions.)

The code to do this is:

```
Sub MRMultiQueries()
Dim i As Long, N As Long
With DataSheet
N = Range("CritToTestHeader").CurrentRegion.Rows.Count
N = N - 1
For i = 1 To N
 Range("CritHeader").Offset(1, 0).Value = _
      Range("CritToTestHeader").Offset(i, 0).Value
 Calculate
 Range("ResultStoreHeader").Offset(i, 0).Value = _
 Range("Result").Offset(1, 0).Value
Next i
End With
```

In a more general application, one would likely wish to clear the results range (but not its headers) at the beginning of the code run, using techniques discussed earlier; this is left as an exercise for the interested reader.

F	G	H	I	J	K	L	M	N	O	P	Q	R	S
	Field		Criteria						Dfunctions				
	Amount £		Customer	Country	Amount £	Amount £	Due Date		DCOUNT	DSUM	DMIN	DMAX	
				Spain	>£5000	<=£10000			5	35265	5457	9022	
			Customer	Country	Amount £	Amount £	Due Date		DCOUNT	DSUM	DMIN	DMAX	
						<=£10000			43	304157	4095	9942	
						>£10000			57	749131	10007	15851	
				UK		<=£10000			10	72974	5096	9006	
				UK	>£5000	<=£10000			10	72974	5096	9006	
				Germany		<=£10000			6	46586	4714	9832	
				Germany	>£5000	<=£10000			5	41872	5401	9832	
				Italy		<=£10000			13	81866	4283	9057	
				Italy	>£5000	<=£10000			7	54404	6402	9057	
				France		<=£10000			7	58885	5853	9942	
				France	>£5000	<=£10000			7	58885	5853	9942	
				Spain		<=£10000			7	43846	4095	9022	
				Spain	>£5000	<=£10000			5	35265	5457	9022	

FIGURE 32.10 Results of Running a Set of Queries of Different Structures

Example: Consolidating Data Sets That Are Split Across Various Worksheets or Workbooks

A useful application is the consolidation of data from several worksheets. In this example, we assume that the data that needs to be consolidated resides on worksheets whose Excel names each start with a similar identifier (such as Data.Field1, Data.Field2, with the identifier being the word Data in this case). Further, we assume that the column structure of the data set in each of these worksheets is the same (i.e. the database fields are the same in each data set, even as the number of row entries may be different, and perhaps the placement within each Excel data sheet may be different).

The file Ch32.12.DataConsol.xlsm contains an example. Figure 32.11 shows the worksheet structure of the file, which is intended to capture the more generic case in which:

- There are multiple separate data worksheets.
- A macro is used to consolidate these into a single data set (in the ConsolData worksheet).
- The final model is built by using queries to this database (such as using SUMIFS functions) as well as other specific required calculations.

Figure 32.12 shows an example of the data set for Asset1, and Figure 32.13 shows the final consolidated data set.

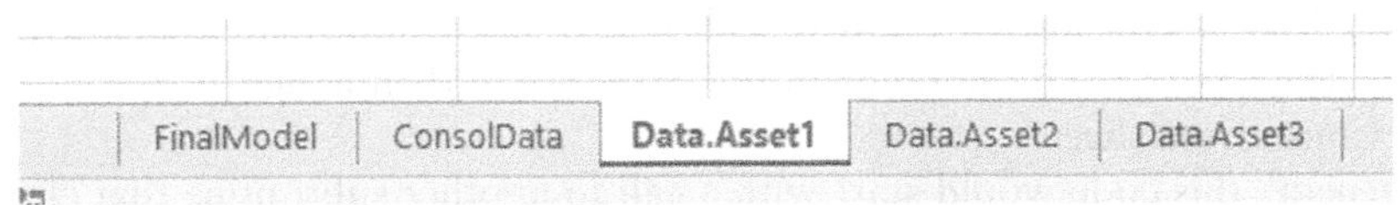

FIGURE 32.11 Generic Model Worksheet Structure

	A	B	C	D	E
1					
2		Field Name	Year	Capex $mm	Production BOEmm
3		Asset1	2012	100	0
4		Asset1	2013	250	0
5		Asset1	2014	50	0
6		Asset1	2015	0	0
7		Asset1	2016	0	0
8		Asset1	2017	0	10
9		Asset1	2018	0	25
10		Asset1	2019	0	20
11		Asset1	2020	0	20
12		Asset1	2021	0	20
13		Asset1	2022	0	20
14		Asset1	2023	0	20
15		Asset1	2024	0	20
16		Asset1	2025	0	20
17		Asset1	2026	0	20
18		Asset1	2027	0	20
19		Asset1	2028	0	20
20					
21					

FIGURE 32.12 Example Data Set

The following macro is contained within the file, and will consolidate the data sets together. The code works through the collection of worksheets in the workbook, and checks each worksheet's name to detect if it is a data sheet (as discussed earlier in this text):

- Where a data sheet is detected, it is activated and the size of the used range on that sheet is determined (the number of columns and the total number of points). The code implicitly assumes that the first row of the data contains headers that do not need copying (in fact, to make this code slightly simpler, we assume that the headers are already placed within the ConsolData worksheet). It then defines a range that contains all data except the headers, and counts the number of rows in this range.
- The ConsolData sheet is then activated and the number of rows that are already used in this range is counted (for example, when copying the second data set, one should not overwrite the data copied from the first data set). A new range is created whose size is the same as required to copy the data set that is currently being worked on, and whose position is such that it starts immediately below existing data. The values from the range in the data set are then assigned to the range in the ConsolData sheet.
- In general, this code would start with a call to another subroutine that clears out all data in the ConsolData sheet (apart from the headers). For clarity of presentation, this step has been left out of the code below, but its implementation simply requires using techniques covered earlier in the text.

	A	B	C	D	E	F
1						
2		Field Name	Year	Capex $mm	Production BOEmm	
3		Asset1	2012	100	0	
4		Asset1	2013	250	0	
5		Asset1	2014	50	0	
6		Asset1	2015	0	0	
7		Asset1	2016	0	0	
8		Asset1	2017	0	10	
9		Asset1	2018	0	25	
10		Asset1	2019	0	20	
11		Asset1	2020	0	20	
12		Asset1	2021	0	20	
13		Asset1	2022	0	20	
14		Asset1	2023	0	20	
15		Asset1	2024	0	20	
16		Asset1	2025	0	20	
17		Asset1	2026	0	20	
18		Asset1	2027	0	20	
19		Asset1	2028	0	20	
20		Asset2	2015	75	0	
21		Asset2	2016	100	0	
22		Asset2	2017	0	8	
23		Asset2	2018	0	8	
24		Asset2	2019	0	8	
25		Asset2	2020	0	8	
26		Asset2	2021	0	8	
27		Asset2	2022	0	8	
28		Asset2	2023	0	8	
29		Asset3	2013	50	0	
30		Asset3	2014	75	0	
31		Asset3	2015	50	0	
32		Asset3	2016	25	5	
33		Asset3	2017	10	10	

FIGURE 32.13 Final Consolidated Data

```
Sub MRConsolFieldSheets()
With ThisWorkbook
For Each ws In Worksheets
 If UCase(Left(ws.Name, 4)) = "DATA" Then
  ws.Activate
  With ActiveSheet.UsedRange
   NCols = .Columns.Count 'number of columns in the user range
   NPts = .Count ' total number of cells in the used range
   Set startcelldata = .Cells(NCols + 1) ' 1st cell of second row
   Set endcelldata = .Cells(NPts)
   Set rngToCopyFrom = Range(startcelldata, endcelldata)
   NRowsCopyFrom = rngToCopyFrom.Rows.Count
  End With

  ConsolDataSheet.Activate
```

```
    With ConsolDataSheet
     Set firstcell = .UsedRange.Cells(1)
     Set fulldata = firstcell.CurrentRegion
     NRowsExisting = fulldata.Rows.Count
     Set firstcellofPasteRange = firstcell.Offset(NRowsExisting, 0)
     Set endcellofPasteRange = firstcellofPasteRange.Offset
 (NRowsCopyFrom - 1, NCols - 1)
     Set rngTocopyTo = Range(firstcellofPasteRange, endcellofPasteRange)
    End With

    rngTocopyTo.Value = rngToCopyFrom.Value

    Else ' worksheet is not a DATA sheet
    'do nothing
    End If
Next ws
End With
End Sub
```

Note that similar code can be written when the data sets are distributed across several workbooks that are contained in a separate data folder. Most of the principles of the code would be similar to above, although some additional techniques and syntaxes may be necessary, including:

- Being able to locate automatically the folder containing the data sets. Assuming that such a folders is called DataSets and is contained within a larger folder that includes the main workbook, this could be achieved with code such as:

```
strThisWkbPath = ThisWorkbook.Path
strDataFolder = strThisWkbPath & "\" & "DataSets"
```

- Opening each workbook in turn, with code such as:

```
Workbooks.Open (strWkbToOpen)
```

- Closing each workbook once the relevant data has been copied (or assigned), with code such as:

```
Workbooks(strFileNoExt).Close SaveChanges:=False
```

(Doing so is left as an exercise for the interested reader.)

CHAPTER 33

User-defined Functions

INTRODUCTION

This chapter focuses on the application of user-defined functions ("udfs"). The first section summarises the potential benefits of using udfs. The second section recaps some main points about their syntax and implementation. The third section provides examples, especially of those which may have their application in general financial modelling contexts: these include "wrapper" functions (that include several Excel or VBA functionalities together within an overall function), and those that capture calculation processes that do not exist as Excel functions, including some statistical measures.

BENEFITS OF CREATING USER-DEFINED FUNCTIONS

Functions are distinguished from subroutines in that they can provide a result only into an Excel cell (or into a range, for array functions), and that they create a live-link between the function's parameters and the results in Excel.

User-defined functions can be very powerful in many circumstances, including:

- To reduce the size of models in which there are otherwise large tables of intermediate calculations (where only the result is of explicit interest, rather than the individual steps).
- To perform calculations that are cumbersome to create in Excel.
- To increase flexibility in model structure. A udf can allow for a more rapid adaptation of the model as new data is added. For example, many sequences of Excel calculations are linked to specific input ranges, and as new data is added, the size or location of the ranges referred to by these functions may need to change. On the other hand, a udf can be written that can detect the size of the data range, and dynamically adjust the calculations within its code, rather than (in Excel) having to adjust or copy the formulae to refer to the new data.
- To increase flexibility in complex calculations. For example, where a cell (or range) would be referenced multiple times within an Excel formula, a udf allows it to

be referred to only once. Similarly, the correction of formulae in Excel can be cumbersome if they have been used in several places (since the corrected formulae needs to be copied to all places in which the original one is used, and this can be time-consuming and error-prone); the code for a corresponding udf would need to be corrected only once.

- To create reuseable logic. It can be especially cumbersome and error-prone to copy formulae, especially those that are complex, or refer to cells that are not adjacent to the formula, or require repeated reference to the same cells. On the other hand, the VBA code for the function can be copied very easily, and linked to the relevant cells in a new model.
- To create transparently named calculations. In Excel, large tables of calculations can be hard to follow, partly as such calculations have no explicit name. However, the equivalent calculations conducted as a udf can be given a (function) name, creating more transparency.
- To create "wrapper" functions. These are usually defined by small pieces of code which "wrap" existing Excel or VBA functions into a new function, without a great deal of underlying new calculations. They are useful to increase robustness or access within Excel some functions that are available by default only in VBA. For example, one may wish for the Excel model to always use the most recent Excel function version (such as the latest form of the statistics functions) or use the functionality of VBA functions such as `Val`, `StrReverse` or `Split`.

SYNTAX AND IMPLEMENTATION

Some general points (that were mostly mentioned earlier) about udfs are worth recapping:

- They can be accessed in Excel by direct typing (provided they have the default scope of `Public`) or by using the Formula/Insert Function menu (where they will be listed under the user-defined category). A function which is only needed within the VBA code itself (and not within Excel) may be declared as `Private`, and will not be accessible in this way.
- To facilitate the insert of udfs by direct typing, the author generally uses names that start with his initials (i.e. MR. . .). This also facilitates the auditing of models, as udfs can be easily identified.
- The author's approach is usually to place udfs within VBA code that is part of the main workbook. However, where such functions are in other workbooks (or in add-ins), they can be accessed by preceding the function name by the name of the workbook in which it resides or by creating an appropriate reference to the workbook or add-in.
- Sometimes, a udf will need to be defined as a Volatile function, by using the statement `Application.Volatile` (or `Application.Volatile True`) at the beginning of the code. (Recall that a Volatile function is one that recalculates at every recalculation of Excel, even when the values of its arguments have not changed since the last recalculation.)
- They may exist as array functions, in which case they are entered in Excel using Ctrl+Shift+ENTER, just as for Excel array functions.

- A description may be added to a function by activating the workbook containing it, displaying the Macro dialog box in Excel on the Developer tab, typing the function name into the box, clicking the Options button and entering the description. Functions may be assigned to categories (other than the user-defined category), but doing so may often arguably result in less transparency, and so is not covered further here.
- They may have parameters (arguments) which are optional; as for Excel functions, such parameters must be the last parameters of the function.
- When documenting a model which contains udfs in several places, it can be useful to include an additional separate worksheet that demonstrates its underlying calculations (i.e. by replicating the same calculations in Excel for a specific case and with separate input assumptions that the user may change or experiment with).

PRACTICAL APPLICATIONS

In this section, we provide general examples of such functions, including:

- "Wrapper" functions, e.g.:
  - That allow one to access (in Excel) functions that originally exist only in VBA.
  - That detect the Excel version used, and use the latest available Excel function in that version.
  - That replicate the IFERROR function, in a way that can be used with any Excel version (e.g. with Excel 2003).
- General functions, such as:
  - Those that replace general tables of calculations with a summary value (e.g. when using sequences of formulae, or when summing the absolute values of all cells in a range, to facilitate detection of errors).
  - The rapid creation of time axes.
  - Creation of functions which replace triangle-type Excel calculation ranges.
  - Creating functions which use the Excel sheet name as an input.
- Statistical functions that do not exist in Excel, such as:
  - The rank correlation between two data sets.
  - The standard deviation, skew and kurtosis of a data set where both the values and the probabilities of each value is given.
  - The semi-deviation of a data set.

User-defined functions can be valuable in many other financial modelling contexts, including:

- To create functions that sample from various probability distributions, and/or to create correlated random sampling between several variables.
- In portfolio optimisation, to calculate the optimum mean-variance portfolio of a set of assets (with given expected returns and standard deviations of returns, and no constraints on the weights).
- The value of a European call or put option using the Black–Scholes formula, or of a European or American call or put option using a binomial tree (or when using a finite difference method).
- The implied volatility of an option using Newton-Raphson iteration.

Selected examples of some of these are discussed later.

Example: Accessing VBA Functions for Data Manipulation: Val, StrReverse and Split

VBA contains several functions which can perform operations that are not available with Excel functions. By using these in VBA to return in Excel the output of a udf, one can easily access these. Some of these have application to the manipulation of data, including:

- `Val`. This reads a string until the first point at which a character cannot be recognised as a number. Thus, it could be applied to separate the components of a string in which the first part is a number and the second part is text, even when there is no explicit identifiable delimiter at the transition between the two.
- `StrReverse`. This reverses the characters of a string.
- `Split`. This splits a string into components according to a specified delimiter (assumed to be a blank if omitted), and can also be used to extract only that portion of a string that is placed after a number of occurrences of a delimiter.

The file Ch33.1.Val.StrReverse.Split.VBAFunctions.xlsm contains examples of these being called from udfs, so that their functionality can be accessed in Excel. Note that, of course, any such udf will have parameters that include all the required parameters of the underlying VBA function.

Figure 33.1 and Figure 33.2. show the use of `Val` and `StrReverse` to create corresponding functions accessible from Excel, based on the code (that is contained within the file):

```
Function MRSTRREVERSEVBA(Txt)
MRSTRREVERSEVBA = StrReverse(Txt)
End Function

Function MRVALVBA(Txt)
MRVALVBA = Val(Txt)
End Function
```

	A	B	C	D
1				
2		String	Result	
3		55OakAvenue	55	=MRVALVBA(B3)
4		37YearsOld	37	=MRVALVBA(B4)
5		25Dec2016Christmas	25	=MRVALVBA(B5)
6		1Jan2017NewYear	1	=MRVALVBA(B6)
7		12	12	=MRVALVBA(B7)
8				

FIGURE 33.1 Using VBA's Val to Create a User-defined Function

	A	B	C	D
1				
2		String	Result	
3		?sihTdaeRuoYnaC	CanYouReadThis?	=MRSTRREVERSEVBA(B3)
4				

FIGURE 33.2 Using VBA's StrReverse to Create a User-defined Function

	A	B	C	D	E	F	G	H	I	J	K	L	M
1													
2		String	Delim	N (At most)	Result								
3		12-AB-3&!-CDE-5&G7-8-9B	-	4	12	AB	3&!	CDE-5&G7-8-9B					{=MRSPLITINTON(B3,C3,D3)}
4		12-AB-3&!-CDE-5&G7-8-9B	-	6	12	AB	3&!	CDE					{=MRSPLITINTON(B4,C4,D4)}
5		12-AB-3&!-CDE-5&G7-8-9B	-	6	12	AB	3&!	CDE	5&G7	8-9B			{=MRSPLITINTON(B5,C5,D5)}
6		12-AB-3&!-CDE-5&G7-8-9B	-	8	12	AB	3&!	CDE	5&G7	8	9B	#N/A	{=MRSPLITINTON(B6,C6,D6)}

FIGURE 33.3 Using VBA's Split to Create a User-defined Array Function

	A	B	C	D	E	F
1						
2		String	Delim	Extract Between Nth and (N+1)th	Result	
3		12-AB-3&!-CDE-5&G7-8-9B	-	2	3&!	=MREXTRACTAFTERNTH(B3,C3,D3)
4		12-AB-3&!-CDE-5&G7-8-9B	-	4	5&G7	=MREXTRACTAFTERNTH(B4,C4,D4)
5		12-AB-3&!-CDE-5&G7-8-9B	&	2	G7-8-9B	=MREXTRACTAFTERNTH(B5,C5,D5)

FIGURE 33.4 Using VBA's Split to Create a User-defined Function to Extract Part of a String

Figure 33.3 shows the use of `Split` to create an array function that is accessible in Excel. In this example, the new function splits the string at each delimiter, into at most the specified number of components. (Note in the various examples that if the size of the range to which the function is entered is too small, then some of the split text will be missing (as in row 4), whereas if it is unnecessarily large, one will simply have an #N/A message.) The code used is:

```
Function MRSPLITINTON(Txt, Delim, N)
MRSPLITINTON = Split(Txt, Delim, N)
End Function
```

Figure 33.4 shows the use of `Split` to create a function that extracts the part of a string that exists after a specified number of occurrences of a delimiter (e.g. after the fourth occurrence of the delimiter); this functionality does not exist directly in Excel, where one can search only for the first occurrence of a delimiter in order to split a string. The code is:

```
Function MREXTRACTAFTERNTH(Txt, Delim, N)
MREXTRACTAFTERNTH = Split(Txt, Delim)(N)
End Function
```

The VBA `Date` function is another example of where a wrapper may be useful, in accessing dates before 1900.

Example: A Wrapper to Access the Latest Excel Function Version

As discussed in Chapter 21, several new Excel functions have been introduced in recent versions, which generally represent some technical improvement over existing (legacy) functions. For example, in Excel 2010, the NORM.S.INV function was introduced as an improvement to the legacy NORMSINV function. Thus, one may wish to build a model in which the latest version of a function is used, whilst retaining backward compatibility. Further, one may wish to be able to update the calculations behind such a function (for example, if Excel introduces a further improvement with a modified function name) without having to modify the Excel worksheet in which they are used.

The `Application.Version` property can be used to find the version of Excel that is being used (as a text field that can be converted to its corresponding value):

```
nVersion = Val(Application.Version)
```

(Note that Excel 2003 is version 11, Excel 2007 is version 12, Excel 2010 is version 14, Excel 2013 is version 15 and Excel 2016 is version 16.)

These can be wrapped into a udf that uses one function or an alternative function, according to the Excel version being used:

```
Function MRNORMSINV(Probability)
Set wsf = Application.WorksheetFunction
nVersion = Val(Application.Version)
Select Case nVersion
 Case Is <= 12
  xValofPToX = wsf.NormSInv(Probability)
 Case Else
   xValofPToX = wsf.Norm_S_Inv(Probability)
 End Select
MRNORMSINV = xValofPToX
End Function
```

Note that we chose to use the `Select Case` syntax (rather than `If...Then`), as this would allow for easier adaptation of the code if additional forms of the function were introduced into later versions of Excel (the udf entered in Excel would not need to be modified, only the code that defines the udf).

The file Ch33.2.Wrapper.NormSInv.xlsm contains this code, with example results shown in Figure 33.5.

Example: Replication of IFERROR for Compatibility with Excel 2003

To create compatibility with models built in versions later than Excel 2003, one may wish to replace a function with its Excel 2003 equivalent. For example, in a model built with many IFERROR functions, one way to achieve this would be to create a user-defined function:

```
Function IF2003ERROR(Calc, AltValue)
If IsError(Calc) Then
 IF2003ERROR = AltValue
Else
 IF2003ERROR = Calc
End If
End Function
```

One could then use Excel's Find/Replace to replace the words IFERROR with IF2003ERROR and the model will work in Excel 2003. (The choice of the name of the function also allows one to remove it by performing the replacement in the reverse sense.) This is left as an exercise for the interested reader.

	A	B	C	D
1				
2		Percentage	Using VBA Wrapper	
3		5.0%	-1.64	=MRNORMSINV(B3)
4		10.0%	-1.28	=MRNORMSINV(B4)
5		50.0%	0.00	=MRNORMSINV(B5)
6		90.0%	1.28	=MRNORMSINV(B6)
7		95.0%	1.64	=MRNORMSINV(B7)

FIGURE 33.5 Wrapper Function to Use the Latest Excel Function Version

	A	B	C	D	E	F	G	H	I	J
1										
2		Sum of Values	0.00	=SUM(D6:M8)						
3		Sum of Absolute Values	4.64	=MRSumAbsValues(D6:G7)						
4										
5		Consolidate Error-Checks		1	2	3	4	5	6	7
6		Eorr check 1		3.8	0.9	0.0	0.0	0.0	0.0	0.0
7		Eorr check 2		0.0	0.0	0.0	0.0	0.0	0.0	0.0
8		Eorr check 3		-3.8	-0.9	0.0	0.0	0.0	0.0	0.0
9										

FIGURE 33.6 Example of a Consolidated Error Check Using a User-defined Function

Example: Sum of Absolute Errors

When building error checks, one may have several cells which should each evaluate to zero (i.e. when there are no errors). In a large model, such cells may initially be present at many separate places. It can therefore be helpful to create a single consolidated (and contiguous) range whose cells directly refer to the original error checks. Further, it may be most convenient to create a single figure which summarises these in order to be able to quickly check whether an issue has arisen in any of the underlying error checks. To avoid cases where the summing of such individual elements could result in two errors cancelling out (due to one being positive and the other negative), one may wish to sum the absolute values of each. A udf can be created to do this.

The file Ch33.3.SumAbsValues.xlsm contains the following code, which returns the sum of the absolute values of the cells in a contiguous range of data, with example results shown in Figure 33.6:

```
Function MRSumAbsValues(Data)
 With Data.Cells(1, 1)
  MRSumAbsValues = 0
   For i = 1 To Data.Rows.Count
    For j = 1 To Data.Columns.Count
     MRSumAbsValues = MRSumAbsValues + Abs(.Offset(i - 1, j - 1))
    Next j
   Next i
 End With
 MRSumAbsValues = MRSumAbsValues
End Function
```

Note that alternative methods (using Excel only) are possible. For example, one could create another range, which references every cell in the consolidated range and uses the ABS function when doing so, and then sums the cells in this new range. An alternative method is to use an array formula, in which the ABS function is embedded within the SUM function. (One could also use the ABS function in the initial (underlying) error-checking calculations; however, it is easy to forget to do so when building the formulae, and further, if an error is detected, it can be convenient to be able to see the sign of the error.)

Example: Replacing General Excel Calculation Tables or Ranges

In the above example, we demonstrated a udf to reduce the visual size of a model by eliminating large tables of calculations in Excel. Of course, this makes sense when it is only the final results of the calculation that are of explicit interest, and not the intermediate calculations. In this example, a udf is implemented which replicates the result of a sequence of calculations in which only the final result is of interest.

The file Ch33.4.MonthCount.xlsm shows a set of calculations in Excel that work out the number of months between any two dates, including any months that are started (thus, if the start date and end date were the same, there is one started month). The Excel calculation involves consideration of the differences between the dates using the YEAR, MONTH and EDATE functions; when broken into individual steps, this would take 4–5 Excel cells. Note that the results of the individual steps are of no real interest other than when developing or checking the logic of the method used. Therefore, such steps could instead be captured in a udf, which directly returns the result. Figure 33.7 shows an example of the detailed calculation steps, and the resulting udf, based on the following code:

```
Function MRStartedMonthCount(StartDate, EndDate)
Set wsf = WorksheetFunction
YearDiff = Year(EndDate) - Year(StartDate)
MonthDiff = Month(EndDate) - Month(StartDate)

InitialDiff = 12 * YearDiff + MonthDiff
If (EndDate >= wsf.EDate(StartDate, InitialDiff)) Then
ICorrectionFactor = 1
Else
ICorrectionFactor = 0
End If
MRStartedMonthCount = InitialDiff + ICorrectionFactor
End Function
```

Example: Using Application.Caller to Generate a Time Axis as an Array Function

The `Application.Caller` object can be used when one needs to know (within the VBA code) something about the Excel process that has invoked the code. For example, one may wish to know the address of the cell in which the function has been placed, or to know the size of the range in which a udf array function has been entered (e.g. the number of rows and columns).

	A	B	C	D
1				
2		Start of	25 February 2010	
3		End of	5 March 2012	
4				
5		Year Diff	2	=YEAR(C3)-YEAR(C2)
6		Month Diff	1	=MONTH(C3)-MONTH(C2)
7		Initial Diff	25	=12*C5+C6
8		Correction	0	=IF(C3>=EDATE(C2,C7),1,0)
9		Result	25	=C7+C8
10				
11		UDF (replicates Ex	25	=MRStartedMonthCount(C2,C3)

FIGURE 33.7 A User-defined Function to Replace Calculation Ranges

	A	B	C	D	E	F	G	H	I	J	K	L	M
1													
2		2018	2019	2020	2021	2022	2023	2024	2025	2026	2027	2028	
3													

FIGURE 33.8 Example of Application.Caller with User-defined Array Functions

The file Ch33.5.ApplicationCaller.DateRange.xlsm contains an example of a function which is entered in a single row range, and which counts the number of columns in the range of the calling function (see Figure 33.8). Cell B2 contains the value for the initial year number, with the function simply entered as an array function into a row range, using the fixed increment of one.

```
Function MRDatesinRange(iFirst As Integer, Increment As Integer)
Dim Storage() As Double
NCols = Application.Caller.Columns.Count
ReDim Storage(1 To NCols)
For i = 1 To NCols
Storage(i) = iFirst + Increment *i
Next i
MRDatesinRange = Storage
End Function
```

Note that:

- The `Application.Caller` object is used to determine the number of columns of the range in which the calling procedure (i.e. the udf) is entered; this information is needed to define the number of loops required.
- Since the function being created is an array function, the values that would be returned to the individual cells in the Excel range are stored in a VBA array (in this case, `Storage`) before being assigned to the function's value in the return statement.

	A	B	C	D
1				
2		Number	5	
3				
4		**Individual Functions**		
5		Sum Of Integers	15	=MRSum1ToN(C2)
6		Sum of Squares	55	=MRSum1ToNSQR(C2)
7		Sum of Cubes	225	=MRSum1ToNCUBE(C2)

FIGURE 33.9 Individual User-defined Functions

Example: User-defined Array Functions in Rows and Columns

The previous example showed a udf which was entered into a row range of Excel. In fact, this is the default form of an array function in Excel. Where the function would always be used only in a row, this may be acceptable. However, functions may often need to return values into a column range. The `Application.Caller` object can be used to detect whether the function's input range has only one row or only one column, and the code can be adapted appropriately to ensure that the function will return the correct figures when entered as an array function in a column. (If the appropriate adaptation is not performed, the column's values will be the single value corresponding to that in the first position of the array.)

The file Ch33.6.ArrayFunction.RowsColumns.xlsm contains an example. Initially, there are three separate functions which, for a given integer input (N), return the value of the sum of the integers from 1 to N, the sum of the squares, and the sum of the cubes, respectively (see Figure 33.9), using the following code:

```
Function MRSum1ToN(ByVal N)
Dim i As Long
Dim DataSet() As Double
ReDim DataSet(1 To N) As Double
For i = 1 To N
DataSet(i) = i
Next i
MRSum1ToN = WorksheetFunction.Sum(DataSet)
End Function

Function MRSum1ToNSQR(ByVal N)
Dim i As Long
Dim DataSet() As Double
ReDim DataSet(1 To N) As Double
For i = 1 To N
DataSet(i) = i ^ 2
Next i
MRSum1ToNSQR = WorksheetFunction.Sum(DataSet)
End Function

Function MRSum1ToNCUBE(ByVal N)
Dim i As Long
Dim DataSet() As Double
ReDim DataSet(1 To N) As Double
```

```
For i = 1 To N
DataSet(i) = i ^ 3
Next i
MRSum1ToNCUBE = WorksheetFunction.Sum(DataSet)
End Function
```

The following array function could instead be used, in which the three elements of the VBA array are populated by calls to each of the above individual functions:

```
Function MRSum1ToNPOWERS3ArrayROW(ByVal N)
Dim tot(1 To 3) As Double
tot(1) = MRSum1ToN(N)
tot(2) = MRSum1ToNSQR(N)
tot(3) = MRSum1ToNCUBE(N)
MRSum1ToNPOWERS3ArrayROW = tot
End Function
```

(Note again that, since the function being created is an array function the values are stored in a VBA array (`tot`) before being assigned to the function's value in the final return statement.)

Figure 33.10 shows the effect of implementing this function in both a row and a column range of Excel, demonstrating that the values are correct only when the function is entered in a row, with the column values all showing the same single figure.

To adapt the function, the initial results must be transposed, and the `Application.Caller` object can be used to detect whether the input range has only one row or only one column, and hence identify when transposition is required (i.e. when called from a function that is placed in a range with only one column). Figure 33.11 shows that the function then works correctly, whether entered in a row or in a column.

10	ARRAY FUNCTION DEFAULT FORM: VALID FOR FUNCTIONS PLACED IN A ROW				
11					
12	Array Function in Row	Sum Of Integers	Sum of Squares	Sum of Cubes	
13		15	55	225	
14		{=MRSum1ToNPOWERS3ArrayROW({	{=MRSum1ToNPOWERS3ArrayROW({	{=MRSum1ToNPOWERS3ArrayROW(C2)}	
15					
16	Array Function in Column				
17	Sum Of Integers	15	{=MRSum1ToNPOWERS3ArrayROW(C2)}		
18	Sum of Squares	15	{=MRSum1ToNPOWERS3ArrayROW(C2)}		
19	Sum of Cubes	15	{=MRSum1ToNPOWERS3ArrayROW(C2)}		

FIGURE 33.10 An Array Function Valid Only in the Row Form

21	ARRAY FUNCTION ADAPTED FORM: VALID FOR FUNCTIONS PLACED IN A ROW OR IN A COLUMN			
22				
23	Array Function in Row	Sum Of Integers	Sum of Squares	Sum of Cubes
24		15	55	225
25		{=MRSum1ToNPOWERS3Array(C2)}	{=MRSum1ToNPOWERS3Array(C2)}	{=MRSum1ToNPOWERS3Array(C2)}
26				
27	Array Function in Column			
28	Sum Of Integers	15	{=MRSum1ToNPOWERS3Array(C2)}	
29	Sum of Squares	55	{=MRSum1ToNPOWERS3Array(C2)}	
30	Sum of Cubes	225	{=MRSum1ToNPOWERS3Array(C2)}	
31				

FIGURE 33.11 Adapted Array Function that Can Be Entered in Row or Column Form

The code is as follows:

```
Function MRSum1ToNPOWERS3Array(ByVal N)
Dim tot(1 To 3) As Double
Dim nRows As Long, nCols As Long
Dim AC As Object
tot(1) = MRSum1ToN(N)
tot(2) = MRSum1ToNSQR(N)
tot(3) = MRSum1ToNCUBE(N)
Set AC = Application.Caller
nRows = AC.Rows.Count
nCols = AC.Columns.Count
If WorksheetFunction.And(nRows > 1, nCols > 1) Then
  MRSum1ToNPOWERS3Array = "Too many rows and columns"
  Exit Function
Else
  If nRows = 1 Then
    MRSum1ToNPOWERS3Array = tot
    Exit Function
  Else
    MRSum1ToNPOWERS3Array = WorksheetFunction.Transpose(tot)
    Exit Function
  End If
End If
End Function
```

Example: Replacing Larger Sets of Excel Calculations: Depreciation Triangles

As mentioned earlier, by being able to conduct intermediate calculations "behind the scenes", udfs can reduce the visual size of some Excel models. This allows the interface to be focused on the important elements, creating more transparency. In addition to the size-reduction effect, udfs can help to create more flexibility, particularly if the size of the model or of its input data changes.

In Chapter 18, we described triangle-type calculations relating to the depreciation of a capital expenditure profile and a generic depreciation schedule. Figure 33.12 shows an example of such calculations: Row 3 and Row 6 contain the basic input data (which in general may themselves be the result of calculations), with Rows 9–19 showing the triangle calculations. Note that, if the time-frame of the model were extended then the triangle would need to be adjusted, by adding a new row and a new column and modifying and copying the formulae. Were a model to have several such triangles, or have a more granular time axis (so that the triangle would become very large), the process of modifying the model would become very cumbersome, time-consuming and error-prone.

Since one is typically interested only in the yearly depreciation totals (and not the components of that total), one can use a udf to replicate the calculations within the VBA code: the results of such a function are shown on row 22, i.e. in a single row. This would clearly both save space in a model, and be much more flexible: if a new column is added to the time axis, the reference range of the function needs to be altered and the function simply re-entered.

Years		2018	2019	2020	2021	2022	2023	2024	2025	2026	2027
Capex		250	200	50	50	50	75	100	125	150	150

Generic Periods		1	2	3	4	5
Depreciation Schedule	100%	30%	25%	20%	15%	10%

Excel for Specific Depreciation Schedule		2015	2016	2017	2018	2019	2020	2021	2022	2023	2024
2018	250	30%	25%	20%	15%	10%					
2019	200		30%	25%	20%	15%	10%				
2020	50			30%	25%	20%	15%	10%			
2021	50				30%	25%	20%	15%	10%		
2022	50					30%	25%	20%	15%	10%	
2023	75						30%	25%	20%	15%	10%
2024	100							25%	20%	15%	10%
2025	125								20%	15%	10%
2026	150									15%	10%
2027	150										10%
Total		75.0	122.5	115.0	105.0	92.5	72.5	66.3	72.5	72.5	60.0

UDF for Specific Depreciation Schedule		2015	2016	2017	2018	2019	2020	2021	2022	2023	2024
Total		75.0	122.5	115.0	105.0	92.5	72.5	71.3	90.0	112.5	130.0

FIGURE 33.12 Creating a User-defined Functions for Triangle-type Calculations

Note that such a function could have wide applicability in financial modelling and business planning: one can generalise its use by simply considering that the capex field be re-interpreted as representing any set of items (each of which has an effect during several future time periods) and that depreciation be re-interpreted as the generic effect of each project from the data of initiation. For example:

- The first (capex) field could be considered to be the number of new projects started in a year, whilst the second (generic depreciation) could be considered as the profile of revenues generated by each project.
- The first field could represent the number of insurance policies sold in a particular month, and the second could represent the monthly insurance premiums received and/or the average losses incurred during the period of validity of the policy.

The determination of the code for such a function can be derived by writing the corresponding algebraic formulae which define the total depreciation in a particular year, based on the indexation number of the capex and depreciation arrays. This is left as an exercise for the reader.

Example: Sheet Reference Functions

User-defined functions which are written so that a worksheet name is an input parameter can be useful. Such functions would in some ways be analogous to Excel formulae based on using the INDIRECT function (Chapter 25). However, the use of udfs allows for the creation of a much clearer syntax (such as avoiding providing the same input cell reference multiple times), as well as more flexibility. It allows the embedding of other functions within the created function. For example, one of the author's functions combines the above depreciation (time re-allocation) example with a worksheet reference approach.

The file Ch33.7.SheetRef.xlsm shows two simple examples, with the following code:

```
Function MRGetDataInAddress(SheetName As String, CellAddress As String)
MRGetDataInAddress = Worksheets(SheetName).Range(CellAddress).Value
End Function

Function MRGetDataInSameCell(SheetName As String)
CellAddress = Application.Caller.Address
MRGetDataInSameCell = Worksheets(SheetName).Range(CellAddress).Value
End Function
```

The first function takes as its input an Excel worksheet name and a cell address (as a text field), and returns the value from that worksheet and that cell address. The second function takes an Excel worksheet name as its input and returns the value from that worksheet for the cell whose address is the same as the cell address from which the function was called. This latter approach could be used to create multi-datasheet models, in which new data sheets can be added or deleted without having to alter formulae because of (not having) formula links directly to the data sheets (in a similar way to some examples in Chapter 25)

Figure 33.13 shows the results of the implementation of these functions. Note that the function in Cell D3 returns the value from Cell D7 of the worksheet Data1 (which is not shown in the screen-clip), since "D7" is specified as a text string (in Cell C), On the other hand, the function in Cell D7 (of the calling worksheet, as shown in the screen-clip) returns the value from the same cell (i.e. D7) of the worksheet Data1; the requirement to refer to the same cell address as that of the calling function is embedded within the function's logic, and so it does not need to be specified as a function argument.

Of course, one can add more richness or capability to such functions. For example, Figure 33.14 shows a function which conducts a conditional calculation (using SUMIF,

	A	B	C	D	E
1					
2		Sheet	Cell Ref	Result	
3		Data1	D7	96.04	=MRGetDataInAddress(B3,C3)
4		Data2	$C$4	239.90	=MRGetDataInAddress(B4,C4)
5					
6		Sheet		Result	
7		Data1		96.04	=MRGetDataInSameCell($B$7)

FIGURE 33.13 Examples of User-defined Functions with Worksheet Names as Inputs

	A	B	C	D
1				
2		Sheet	Data2	
3		Row1Id.CriteriaId	Asset2	
4		CriteriaValue	240.0	
5		Row1CalcId	Asset3	
6		ValIfError	999	
7		Type (1 or missing=SumIf, 2=CountIf, 3=AverageIF)	1	
8		Value	982.0	=MRSumIfColFinderRow1(C2,C3,C4,C5,C6,C7)

FIGURE 33.14 Functions with Worksheet Names as Inputs and Additional Calculation Capability

COUNTIF or AVERAGEIF, as specified) relating to data on a specified worksheet (assuming that the field headers are in the first row of each data sheet). The function looks in the specified data sheet (Data2 in the example) for two field headers (Asset 2 and Asset 3 in this example) and sums up (or applies the other conditional calculations to) the values for Asset3 (in this example), conditional on the value of Asset2 being 240 (in this example). The function's optional argument (`itype`) is used to specify which conditional calculation is to be conducted, defaulting to SUMIF if omitted.

The code is as follows:

```
Function MRSumIfColFinderRow1(SheetName As String, Row1CritId,
CritVal, Row1CalcId, ValueIfError, Optional iType As Integer)

On Error GoTo ErrorValue
Set wsf = WorksheetFunction
With Worksheets(SheetName)
 Set SearchRange = .Range("1:1")
 ColNoToSum = wsf.Match(Row1CalcId, SearchRange, 0)
 Set RangeToSum = .Range("A:A").Offset(0, ColNoToSum - 1)

 ColNoForCritCheck = wsf.Match(Row1CritId, SearchRange, 0)
 Set RangeToCheck = .Range("A:A").Offset(0, ColNoForCritCheck - 1)
End With

Select Case iType
 Case 1
  MRSumIfColFinderRow1 = wsf.SumIf(RangeToCheck, CritVal, RangeToSum)
 Case 2
  MRSumIfColFinderRow1 = wsf.CountIf(RangeToCheck, CritVal)
 Case 3
  MRSumIfColFinderRow1 = wsf.AverageIf(RangeToCheck, CritVal,
RangeToSum)
 Case Other
  MRSumIfColFinderRow1 = wsf.SumIf(RangeToCheck, CritVal, RangeToSum)
End Select
Exit Function
ErrorValue:
  MRSumIfColFinderRow1 = ValueIfError
End Function
```

Example: Statistical Moments when Frequencies Are Known

In Chapter 21, we discussed the Excel functions that can calculate the key statistical "moments" of a data set, i.e. the average, standard deviation, skewness and kurtosis. However, the data set that is required as an input to those functions generally consists of a full list of individual data points, with no explicit information about their probabilities or frequencies; implicitly each point is treated as being of equal likelihood. (The exception is when using SUMPRODUCT to calculate the mean by multiplying values by probabilities and summing these.) It is straightforward to create a user-defined function which calculates such statistical moments, using the mathematical formulae for them that were presented in Chapter 21.

	A	B	C	D
1				
2			Population Moments	
3		Mean	58.00	{=mrmoments(B9:B18,C9:C18)}
4		StdDev	31.35	{=mrmoments(B9:B18,C9:C18)}
5		Skew	0.36	{=mrmoments(B9:B18,C9:C18)}
6		Kurtosis	2.53	{=mrmoments(B9:B18,C9:C18)}
7				
8		Xs	Ps	
9		10	20%	
10		20	5%	
11		30	5%	
12		40	10%	
13		50	50%	
14		60	10%	
15		70	5%	
16		80	10%	
17		90	20%	
18		120	15%	
19				

FIGURE 33.15 Array Function for the Probability-weighted Moments of a Data Set

The file Ch33.8.Moments.xlsm contains an array function that calculates the four moments. It first calculates the average (mean), with the other three being determined based on their deviations from this. Figure 33.15 contains a screen-clip of the results of the following code:

```
Function MRMoments(X As Range, probs As Range)
Dim SumP As Double
Dim i As Integer, N As Integer
Dim nRows As Long, nCols As Long
Dim AC As Object
Dim Calcs(1 To 4) As Double

N = probs.Count

SumP = 0
 For i = 1 To 4
  Calcs(i) = 0
 Next i
 For i = 1 To N
  SumP = SumP + probs(i)
 Next i

 For i = 1 To N
  Calcs(1) = Calcs(1) + X(i) * probs(i)
 Next i

  Calcs(1) = Calcs(1) / SumP
```

```
 For i = 1 To N
  Calcs(2) = Calcs(2) + ((X(i) - Calcs(1)) ^ 2) * probs(i)
  Calcs(3) = Calcs(3) + ((X(i) - Calcs(1)) ^ 3) * probs(i)
  Calcs(4) = Calcs(4) + ((X(i) - Calcs(1)) ^ 4) * probs(i)
 Next i

  Calcs(2) = Calcs(2) / SumP
  Calcs(3) = Calcs(3) / SumP
  Calcs(4) = Calcs(4) / SumP

  Calcs(1) = Calcs(1)
  Calcs(2) = Sqr(Calcs(2))
  Calcs(3) = Calcs(3) / (Calcs(2) ^ 3)
  Calcs(4) = Calcs(4) / (Calcs(2) ^ 4)

Set AC = Application.Caller
nRows = AC.Rows.Count
nCols = AC.Columns.Count

If WorksheetFunction.And(nRows > 1, nCols > 1) Then
  MRMoments = "Too many rows and columns"
  Exit Function
Else
  If nRows = 1 Then
    MRMoments = Calcs
    Exit Function
  Else
    MRMoments = WorksheetFunction.Transpose(Calcs) ' to place
in a column
    Exit Function
  End If
End If

End Function
```

(The above formulae are those relating to what applies when the data set represents the whole population, rather than a sample.)

Example: Rank Order Correlation

As covered in Chapter 21, Excel does not have a function to calculate the (Spearman) rank correlation between two data sets. However, it can be calculated by first determining the rank of each item within its own data set (using RANK.AVG, for example) and then calculating the (Pearson) correlation between the set of ranked items (using the CORREL or PEARSON functions). Of course, if the size of the data sets is large and likely to change regularly, then the extra tabular space requirements in Excel, as well as the cumbersome process to adapt and copy the formulae, can be inconvenient. On the other hand, it is straightforward to implement a user-defined function which simply replicates the corresponding process in Excel.

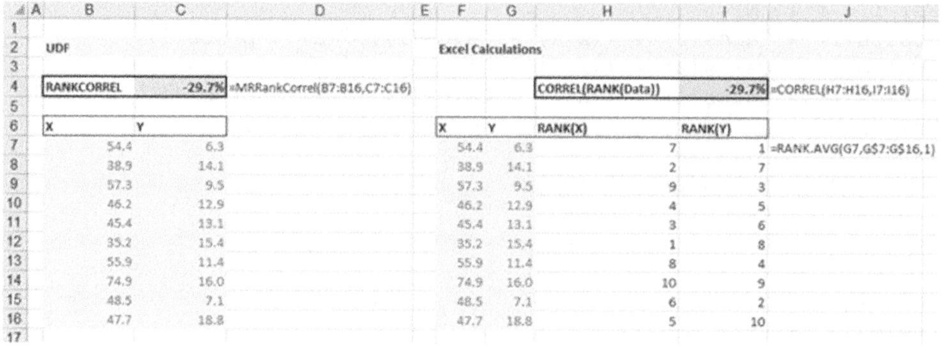

	A	B	C	D	E	F	G	H	I	J
1										
2		UDF				Excel Calculations				
3										
4		RANKCORREL	-29.7%	=MRRankCorrel(B7:B16,C7:C16)				CORREL(RANK(Data))	-29.7%	=CORREL(H7:H16,I7:I16)
5										
6		X	Y			X	Y	RANK(X)	RANK(Y)	
7		54.4	6.3			54.4	6.3	7	1	=RANK.AVG(G7,G$7:G$16,1)
8		38.9	14.1			38.9	14.1	2	7	
9		57.3	9.5			57.3	9.5	9	3	
10		46.2	12.9			46.2	12.9	4	5	
11		45.4	13.1			45.4	13.1	3	6	
12		35.2	15.4			35.2	15.4	1	8	
13		55.9	11.4			55.9	11.4	8	4	
14		74.9	16.0			74.9	16.0	10	9	
15		48.5	7.1			48.5	7.1	6	2	
16		47.7	18.8			47.7	18.8	5	10	
17										

FIGURE 33.16 Rank Correlation Using a User-defined Function

The file Ch33.9.RankCorrel.xlsm contains an example, with the code shown below. The screen-clip in Figure 33.16 shows the user-defined function that directly links to the data set, as well as the explicit calculations that would be required if using only Excel.

```
Function MRRankCorrel(X As Range, Y As Range)
Dim i As Long, NxlVersion As Long
Dim RX() As Double, RY() As Double 'use to store the rank
Dim wsf As WorksheetFunction

Set wsf = Application.WorksheetFunction

If X.Count <> Y.Count Then
  MsgBox "Ranges are not of same size-please redefine"
  MRRankCorrel = "Function Error"
Exit Function
End If

ReDim RX(1 To X.Count)
ReDim RY(1 To X.Count)

NxlVersion = Val(Application.Version)

Select Case NxlVersion
Case NxlVersion <= 12
  For i = 1 To X.Count
    RX(i) = wsf.Rank(X(i), X, 1)
    RY(i) = wsf.Rank(Y(i), Y, 1)
  Next i
Case Else
  For i = 1 To X.Count
    RX(i) = wsf.Rank_Avg(X(i), X, 1)
    RY(i) = wsf.Rank_Avg(Y(i), Y, 1)
  Next i
End Select

  MRRankCorrel = wsf.Correl(RX, RY)
End Function
```

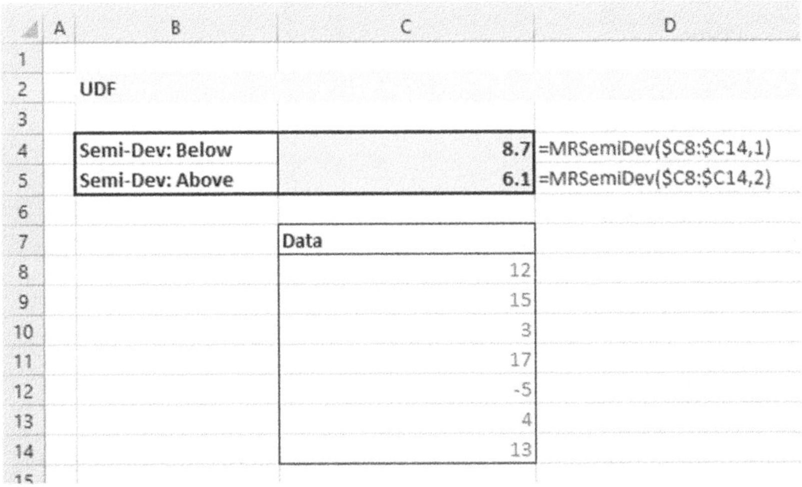

	A	B	C	D
1				
2		UDF		
3				
4		Semi-Dev: Below	8.7	=MRSemiDev($C8:$C14,1)
5		Semi-Dev: Above	6.1	=MRSemiDev($C8:$C14,2)
6				
7			Data	
8			12	
9			15	
10			3	
11			17	
12			-5	
13			4	
14			13	

FIGURE 33.17 Semi-deviation Using a User-defined Function

A similar approach could be used to create a udf for Kendall's Tau (see Chapter 21); this is left as an exercise for the interested reader.

Example: Semi-deviation of a Data Set

As covered in Chapter 21, the semi-deviation of a data set is a useful measure of one-sided risk (e.g. downside risk), in comparison to the standard deviation, which is a two-sided measure. It is calculated as the square root of the average of the squared deviations from the mean (values exactly equal to the mean are traditionally excluded from the calculation, i.e. when counting the number of relevant deviations to be used in the denominator when calculating the average).

The file Ch33.10.SemiDeviation.xlsm contains a udf for the calculation of the semi-deviation with respect to the mean. The function contains an optional parameter (`iType`) to be used to specify whether the deviation below or above the mean is required, with deviations below as the default method. Figure 33.17 shows the udf returning the result based on a direct link to the data set. The file also contains the explicit calculations that would be required if using only Excel (Columns F through J, not shown in the screen-clip). The code is:

```
Function MRSemiDev(Data, Optional iType As Integer)
Dim n As Long, ncount As Long, i As Long
Dim sum As Single, mean As Single
ncount = 0
mean = 0
sum = 0
n = Data.Count
mean = Application.WorksheetFunction.Average(Data)

If IsMissing(iType) Then
  iType = 1
```

```
  Else
  iType = iType
 End If

If iType = 1 Then
 For i = 1 To n
  If Data(i) < mean Then
  ncount = ncount + 1
  sum = sum + (Data(i) - mean) ^ 2
  Else
  End If
 Next i
Else
 For i = 1 To n
  If Data(i) > mean Then
  ncount = ncount + 1
  sum = sum + (Data(i) - mean) ^ 2
  Else
  End If
  Next i
End If
MRSemiDev = Sqr(sum / ncount)
End Function
```

(Note that it is a straightforward modification to the code to instead calculate the semi-deviation with respect to another specified value, which would be added to the function's parameter set, either as a required argument or as an optional one.)

Index

ABS 229, 232–3, 235, 480
absolute cell referencing restrictions 96
absolute/variation base-case considerations, sensitivity analysis 27–8, 31–2
access methods, udfs 474–5
accessing data manipulation VBA functions example, udfs 475, 476–7
accessing the latest Excel function version example, udfs 475, 477–8, 490
ACCRINT 255
ACCRINTM 255
ACOS 229, 240–1
`Activate` 404, 414, 439, 448, 471–2
`ActiveRange` 419
`ActiveSheet` 402, 415, 446, 463–4, 466–8
`ActiveWorkbook` 446
ActiveX 404
activity-based costing 220–2
`Add` 417, 437, 452
`Add Watch` 452
add-ins 4, 144, 156, 163–70, 175–6, 180–5, 194–7, 206–10, 399–400, 435, 474
addition, transparency/flexibility/efficiency choices 105–7
ADDRESS 115, 299, 325, 327–8, 330–1, 350–2, 486
Advanced Filter 356, 369, 370, 461, 464–5, 468
AGGREGATE 114–15, 204, 210–12, 214, 227–8
alerts, VBA 433, 437–8
algebraic (mathematical) manipulations 119, 121–2, 128, 130–1, 133, 140–1, 222–5, 485

Alt key 73, 361, 391, 392, 393, 399–400, 404, 430
Alt+Enter 73, 391
Alt+F8 392, 404
Alt+F11 392, 399–400
ambiguity of the modelling process, challenges 10
American options 475
analysis layers, data layers 37–9
analysis roles, decision-making 16
AND 83, 106–7, 110, 111, 147, 201, 202–3, 228, 251, 334–5
annuities 92, 243
`Application` 127–8, 172–6, 195–6, 414, 422, 446, 463, 467, 478–84, 489–91
`Application.Calculate` 127–8, 172–6, 195–6, 430–1, 468
`Application.CalculateFull` 430–1
`Application.CalculateFullRebuild` 430–1
`Application.Caller` 480–6, 489
`Application.DisplayAlerts` 433, 438
`Application.InputBox` 422, 425, 457, 460, 466–7
`Application.ScreenUpdating` 432
`Application.Version` 478, 490
`Application.Volatile` 453, 474–5
`Application.WorksheetFunction` 463, 467, 478, 480, 482–4, 489–91
Apply Names 86
ARABIC 229, 241
arbitrage-free valuation methods 17
AREAS 325
arguments, VBA 443–5, 451, 453
arithmetic 105–14, 201–16, 229–41, 413, 486–7
array formulae 217–18, 225–8, 276–7, 326–7, 344–5, 480
arrays 115, 159–60, 204–28, 258–67, 272–80, 326–7, 333–4, 344–5, 389–90, 409–10, 448–51, 460, 473–92

arrays (*Continued*)
advantages/disadvantages 218
declarations 451
definitions 217–18, 451
errors 218, 451–2
Excel 217–28, 326–7, 450–1, 460, 473, 480–4
implementation methods 217–18
practical applications 115, 218–28, 258–64, 276–7, 333–4, 344–5
udfs 115, 272–3, 276, 473–4, 477, 480–4, 488–92
VBA 409–10, 448, 450–1, 460, 473, 477–8, 480–4, 488–92
ASC 314
ASCII 313, 321
ASIN 229, 239–41
asset prices 231–2, 239, 266–7, 278–80, 289–90
Assign Macro 404
assignment operations, VBA 409, 447–8
ATAN 229, 240–1
audit paths 59, 62–9, 79–80, 106–7, 116, 143–51, 341
audits 15, 47–77, 79–81, 97–8, 106–7, 116, 125, 133–4, 141–51, 341, 387–93, 474
documentation 143–4
key short-cuts 387, 391–3
model auditors 59–62, 79–80, 143–51
pure audits 143–4, 145, 147
`AutoFilter` 466–8
Automatic calculation method 124–5, 148, 157–9, 305, 401–2, 425–6, 429–31, 455
Automatic Except Tables 430
automatic position determination example 457–9
automating filters to remove blanks or other items example 464–8
automation, VBA 359, 364–5, 372, 392, 397–8, 455, 461, 464–8
AVEDEV 265, 268, 270
AVERAGE 53–4, 90, 106, 114–15, 129–30, 139, 201, 206, 210, 214, 257–60, 491
AVERAGEA 201, 206, 257
AVERAGEIF 112–13, 201, 206–7, 257, 259, 370, 487
AVERAGEIFS 113, 201, 206–7, 257, 370

backward compatibility 477–8
backward thought processes, modelling 4–6, 18–19, 26–30, 149–50, 163–70, 185
bad models 15, 60, 79–80, 85, 89–90
BAHTEXT 314
balance sheets 48, 87, 107–9
bar charts (histograms) 264–7, 271
BASE 229, 241
base case models 85, 159
best practices 4, 13–21, 47–77, 79–86, 91–103, 143–51, 173, 445, 473–4
BETA 195, 280, 281, 292, 290, 291–3
BETA.DIST 280
BETAINV 281
BETA.INV 281
between-type queries, databases 371
biases 4, 11–13, 189–90, 193, 269, 272, 286
BINOM 195
BINOM.DIST 280, 282
BINOMDIST 280
BINOM.DIST.RANGE 282
binomial distributions 195, 280–2
binomial trees 103, 182, 237–8, 475
BINOM.INV 281, 285
black swans 9
black-box models 21
Black-Scholes options pricing formula 17, 90, 165, 167, 182, 475
blank cells 68, 80–2, 111–12, 201–5, 299, 300–2, 363–5, 372, 461–8
bold, optimal formatting guidelines 71–3, 390–1
bonds 243, 248, 252–4
bonuses 118, 121–31, 235
border combinations 71–3, 84, 144, 390–1

brackets, custom formatting 75–6
break points 97, 125–31, 133–4, 138–40, 141, 151, 405–6, 452
breakeven analysis 164–6, 173–5
broken circular path method, circular references 125–31, 133–4, 138–40, 141, 148
budgets 7, 83–4
building of models 3–6, 12–21, 57–151, 158, 191–4, 232–3, 390–1
Business Risk and Simulation Modelling in Practice Using Excel, VBA and @RISK 187, 191, 194, 239, 280
buy or lease decisions, IRR/NPV uses 248–51
`ByRef` 443–5
`ByVal` 443–5, 450–1

Calculate 124–5, 429–31
`Calculate` 127–8, 172–6, 195–6, 430–1, 468
Calculation Option 124–5, 429–31
calculations 5–10, 26–40, 50–116, 123–51, 158–76, 190–7, 230–41, 272–3, 305, 344–5, 429–31, 468, 473–92
  break points 97, 125–31, 133–4, 138–40, 141, 151
  building methods 79, 91–103
  choosing Excel functions for transparency/flexibility/efficiency 105–16, 218
  duplicate calculations 96–7, 101, 146, 461
  errors 10, 79, 84, 91–103
  formatting 39, 70–6, 98
  identification needs 69–76, 191–4
  recalculations 305, 401–2, 421–2, 429–31
  repeated calculations restrictions 96–7, 101, 146
  separating the data layer 37–9, 40
  speed factors 140–1, 429–31
  tests 79, 91–103
  transparency 59–77, 105–16, 145–6, 218, 474
`Call` 434–5, 444–5, 451
call options 475
`Caller` 480–6, 489
Camera 387, 393–4
Capital Asset Pricing Model (CAPM) 290–1
capital expenditures 48, 69, 83, 131, 209, 218–19, 239–41, 251–2, 335, 469–72, 485
capital gains tax 165, 167–8, 175–6
capitalisation, optimal formatting guidelines 71–3
carry-forward balances, balance sheets 87
cascading drop-down lists, INDIRECT 352
`Case` 427, 428, 438–9, 454, 478, 487, 490
cash 5, 34–5, 40, 48, 87, 92–3, 100, 109, 118–20, 128–31
cash flow statements 48, 87, 109, 131
cash flows 5, 34–48, 92–3, 100, 118–20, 129–41, 164–70, 179–82, 201–16, 243–55, 334, 345–9
CEILING.MATH 229, 235
CELL 115, 299, 303–4, 306, 323, 327–8, 350–2
cells, absolute cell referencing restrictions 96
`Cells` 175–6, 420–2, 435–6, 458, 459–60, 466, 471–2, 479
central-values statistical functions, position/ranking/central-values practical applications 258–64
CHAR 313, 321–2
`ChartObjects` 414–15, 426–7, 439
Charts 144, 148, 306, 392
checks 40, 70, 79, 80, 84, 86, 91–2, 97–103, 146, 151
CHIDIST 280
CHIINV 281, 289
CHISQ.DIST.RT 280
CHISQ.INV 281, 289
CHISQ.INV.RT 281, 289
choice (exclusion) and consolidation (inclusion) information-usage processes, multiple worksheets 52–6
CHOOSE 52, 97, 115, 116, 159, 161, 173, 325, 328–31, 351
choosing Excel functions for transparency/flexibility/efficiency 105–16, 218
Circle Invalid Data 101
circular references 6, 49, 80, 85, 117–43, 148, 156, 171–6, 326, 398, 429
  avoidance considerations 117, 120–1, 131–2, 133–7, 141
  background 80, 85, 117, 118–22, 125–41, 148
  calculation speed factors 132, 140–1
  convergent circularities 134–7
  definition 117, 118–19
  divergent circularities 134–5, 138
  floating circularities 134–7, 141
  iterative techniques 120, 122–31, 133–41, 148–9
  resolving methods 119–41, 429
circularities 117–41, 156, 171–6, 326
class modules 397
`ClassModule` 403
CLEAN 313, 321–2
Clear Contents 159, 375, 461
Clear Print Area 91
`ClearContents` 404, 414, 416, 420, 447–8, 461
`ClearFormats` 414
clinical trials 236
closed-form approaches 191
co-relationships and dependencies 273–80
CODE 313
code basics 399, 402–11, 413–23, 425–39, 441–54, 456–72, 474–92

code basics (*Continued*)
comments 404, 439, 442–3
control of execution methods 425–39
data types 448–51
debugging 405–6, 452–4
error codes 451–2
modular approaches 443–4
name choices 449–50
recording code 399–400, 401–3, 416, 418, 429–31, 441–2, 447, 459, 461
robust code 441–54
running code 404–5, 407
writing code 403–4, 413, 416, 435–9, 441–54, 456–72, 474–92
`Code` 404
cognitive biases 11
collections, objects 414–15, 438–9, 449
colour-coding uses 19, 39, 70–2, 84, 98–9, 159, 461
COLUMN 299, 325, 326–8
COLUMN (ROW) 325
COLUMN (ROWS) 325
COLUMNS 299, 327, 333
`Columns` 456–9, 461, 467, 471–2, 479, 481, 489
COMBIN 229, 237–8, 257
comments 59, 76–7, 84, 106, 144, 148–9, 300–6, 381, 392, 404, 439, 442–3, 449
commodities 39
common keys 323–4, 336–7
communications, modelling benefits 9, 16–17, 21, 421–2
complexity issues 15–19, 35, 41–9, 59–66, 79–93, 108–9, 133–4, 145, 192, 301–2, 351–8, 367
CONCAT 313, 314–15
CONCATENATE 313, 314–15
conditional formatting 70–6, 98–101, 144, 149–50, 301–2, 305, 356, 366, 390–1
conditional logic 91–3, 442
conditional maxima/minima 226–8
Conditional Sum Wizard 206, 210–13, 461
confidence intervals 269–70, 285–97
CONFIDENCE.NORM 287–8
CONFIDENCE.T 287–8
confidential data 50
Connection 383–5
`ConsolDataSheet` 469–72
Consolidation, choice (exclusion) and consolidation (inclusion) information-usage processes 52–6
consolidation of data sets across multiple workbooks/worksheets example 469–72
constant level of repayments required 246–8
constants 39, 149–50, 392
construction projects 10, 26–30, 34
contextual assumptions 34–5
Continental Formatting 75
contingencies 189
continuous time 10, 232, 263, 284–5
control of execution methods, VBA 425–39, 466
controllability/non-controllability of input processes 177, 178–82, 184–5, 188, 192–3
convergent circularities 134–7
conversion factors 39, 70, 240–1, 255, 314, 476–7
Convert-to-Range 359
`Copy` 414, 448
Copy/Paste 127, 375, 401–9, 431, 442, 447–8, 468
copying uses 63–6, 94–6, 122–7, 146–56, 375, 387–92, 401–9, 431, 441–2, 447–8, 459–60, 468, 474
core competencies 15–21
core themes, modelling 1–21
corrections/handling of errors 79, 84, 91, 100–3, 119–23, 128, 138, 145–51, 212–15, 359–62, 373, 380, 451–4, 461–2, 474–5, 487
CORREL 274, 275–80, 290, 347–8, 489–91
correlations 190, 262, 273–80, 289–90, 347–8, 475, 489–91
COS 229, 240–1
costs 5, 10, 26–33, 41–9, 60–2, 83–9, 92, 118, 158, 164–76, 196–222, 308, 384–5
COUNT 53–4, 106, 114–15, 201, 205–6, 210, 214, 257, 258–60, 270, 290, 302, 333, 361–3
COUNTA 81, 201, 204, 205, 210, 214, 257, 348–9
COUNTBLANK 201, 205, 257, 365–8
`Count` 327, 414, 417–18, 433, 436–7, 438, 447, 456, 459–63, 467–8, 471–2, 479, 481, 488–91
COUNTIF 100–1, 113, 201, 205, 257, 487
COUNTIFS 113, 201, 257, 259–60, 266–7, 318
COUP. . . 255
COVAR 277–80
COVARIANCE.P 277–80
COVARIANCE.S 277–80

Create Formulae 87, 389
CRITBINOM 281, 285
Criteria Range 369, 370–3, 468
cross-tabulation reports 373–85
CrystalBall 196
Ctrl+& 73, 387, 391
Ctrl+_ 73, 391
Ctrl key short-cuts, basics 73–5, 86, 91, 96, 102, 149, 217–18, 306, 358, 359, 363, 387–94, 399, 416–18, 474
Ctrl+1 73, 390
Ctrl+2 (or B) 73, 390
Ctrl+3 (or I) 73, 390
Ctrl+4 (or U) 73, 390
Ctrl+A 389
Ctrl+Alt+F9 430
Ctrl+apostrophe 388, 391
Ctrl+Arrow 392
Ctrl+C 388, 394
Ctrl+End 418
Ctrl+Enter 73, 388, 391
Ctrl+F 391
Ctrl+F1 393
Ctrl+G 392
Ctrl+Home 392
Ctrl+K 390
Ctrl+L 391, 452
Ctrl+Shift+A 389
Ctrl+Shift+Arrow 388, 393, 416
Ctrl+Shift+End 393
Ctrl+Shift+Enter 388, 474
Ctrl+Shift+F1 393
Ctrl+Shift+F3 390
Ctrl+Shift+F8 452
Ctrl+Shift+Home 392
Ctrl+Shift+O 392
Ctrl+Shift+RightArrow 416
Ctrl+Shift+Space 73, 390, 418
Ctrl+T 391
Ctrl+V 388
Ctrl+X 388
Ctrl+Z 388
cultural issues 16
CUMIPMT 246–8
CUMPRINC 246–8
currencies 39, 323–4, 336–9
Current Region 73, 366–8, 390–1, 416
`CurrentRegion` 416, 417–19, 422, 456–7, 459–61, 466–8
custom formatting 72, 75–6, 144
cut-and-paste uses 86–7, 106, 126–7, 147, 151, 356, 375–6, 388–93, 401–9, 431, 442–8, 468

daisy chains 96–7
data compactness 41–2
data insufficiencies, modelling challenges 12–13
data layers, analysis layers 37–9
Data Model, PivotTables 383–5
data ranges 39–40, 455–9, 461–72, 473–92
data requirements, modelling benefits 9, 16, 20, 26
data sets, background 9, 39, 40, 70–7, 80, 86, 91–2, 97–103, 226–8, 326, 331–4, 352–3, 355–85, 398, 455–77, 487–92
data sheets 50–2, 66, 469–72
data structures 20, 35, 47, 145, 149, 349–52, 356–85
Data Table 140–1, 143–4, 151, 155, 156–61, 172, 366–8, 430–1
data tables 115, 140–1, 143–4, 151, 155, 156–61, 172, 366–8, 456
data types, VBA 448–51
Data Validation, input value restrictions 100–1, 144
Data/Filter 144, 148, 355–9, 393, 464–5
Data/Advanced Filter 356, 369, 370, 461, 464–5, 468
Data/Consolidation feature 52, 54–6
Data/Filter 359–69
Data/Remove Duplicates 356, 362–3, 368–9, 461
Data/Sort 356, 461
Database 43–5, 370–3, 468–9
databases 4, 20, 37–45, 71–2, 82, 114, 204, 355–9, 370–3, 398, 468–9
  definition 357–8
  practical applications 370–3, 468–9
`DataSet` 456–60, 482–4
`DataSheet` 419, 456, 458–9, 468–9
`DataStart` 458–61
DataTables 38
DATE 307
`Date` 477
DATEDIF 307, 312
dates 74–6, 115, 307–12, 480
DATEVALUE 307
DAVERAGE 370
DAY 307

DAYS 307, 308–9
days late analysis 360–73, 380–2, 462–8
DAYS360 307
DCF 450
DCOUNT 370, 372, 469
DCOUNTA 370
DDB 250–1
debt-equity ratios 118
`Debug` 405, 452
`Debug/Compile` 405
`Debug/Run` 405
`Debug/StepInto` 405
`Debug/ToggleBreakpoint` 405, 452
debugging, VBA 405–6, 426, 452–4
DECIMAL 229, 241
decimals, basic formatting 72
decision errors, modelling 10, 13
decision trees 5–6, 185
decision-chance-decision structures 183–4
decision-making 3–4, 7–13, 16–17, 70–1, 76, 133, 144–5, 155–61, 179–86, 189–97
decision-support stage of modelling 3, 4, 12, 16–17, 25–6, 30, 144, 145, 155
default probabilities 268
default settings, Excel 123–5, 148
Define Name 86
`DefType` 450
DEGREES 229, 239–41
`Delete` 426, 437–8, 462–4, 467–9
Delete Cells 364–6, 462, 465
deleting blank cell rows example 462–4
deleting blank rows example 463–4
`Delim` 477
demand-curve modelling 33, 160–1
dependencies 26–30, 151, 160–1, 169–70, 192–4, 257, 273–80, 328–30, 341–4, 391–3, 461
depreciation 48, 69, 70, 158, 161, 209, 218–19, 243, 249, 250–2, 334–5, 484–5
  background 218–19, 250–2, 334–5, 484–5
derivatives 17, 90, 103, 165, 167, 475
design of models 3, 4–6, 11–56, 60–80, 84, 91–103, 116, 143–51, 155, 191–4, 390–1
  background 25–35, 37–45, 47–56, 62, 83, 334
detail/aggregation levels, modelling 5–6, 26–9, 30–1, 40–1, 45
Developer 399–401, 404, 475
DEVSQ 265, 270
DGET 370
diagonal audit paths, complexity issues 62–6, 145
`Dim` 449, 450–1, 468–9, 481–4, 488–91
direct cell references 43
DISC 255
Disclaimer 102, 398–9, 410–11
discounting 17, 83, 92, 118, 165, 179–82, 244–55
discrete time 10
dispersion measures 258, 264–73
`DisplayAlerts` 433, 438
#DIV/0! 138, 228
divergent circularities 134–5, 138
diversified markets 289–90
dividends 48, 131
division, transparency/flexibility/efficiency choices 105–7
DMAX 204, 370–1, 372, 469
DMIN 204, 370, 372
documentation 59, 76–7, 84, 91, 102–3, 133, 143–8, 303–4, 441–3, 475
DOLLAR 314
DOLLARDE 255
DOLLARDFR 255
`Double` 449, 450–1, 481–4, 488–90
double-byte character sets 314
double-clicks 149, 388, 391–2, 423
`Do...While/Until...Loop` 128, 428–9
DPRODUCT 370
'drill-downs', PivotTables 355, 356–7, 373–85
drop-down lists 352, 414–15
DSTDEV 370
DSTDEVP 370
DSUM 114, 370–2, 469
duplicate calculations 96–7, 101, 146, 461
DURATION, background 252–4
DVAR 370
DVARP 370
dynamic queries 356–7
dynamic splitting 316–19

EBIT 158, 160–1, 166, 174
EDATE 307, 309, 480–1
Edit Comment 76
Edit Links 148
`Editor` 404, 443, 449
EFFECT 255

effectiveness 80
efficiencies 80, 105–16, 132, 140–4, 149–56, 164, 218, 341–2, 387, 402–4, 416, 429–30, 441–54
  background 105–16, 140–1, 218, 402–4, 429–31, 441–54
Einstein, Albert 19
Eisenhower, Dwight D. 8
`Else...` 128, 427, 428, 438–9, 454, 463, 467, 471–2, 478, 480–4, 489–92
`ElseIf` 427
embedded (compound) functions 82–3, 91–6, 108–11, 129, 143–9, 215, 225–6, 243, 480, 485–6
embedded IF statements 108, 109–11, 116, 215, 225, 243
Enable Iterative Calculation 124–5
`End...` 127–8, 403, 406–23, 427–9, 431, 435–9, 444–7, 456–7, 463, 466–8, 471–2, 478, 480–4
`End Function` 403, 410, 453, 476–92
`End If` 427, 463, 467, 472, 478, 480–4, 489–92
`End Select` 427, 428, 438, 478, 487, 490
`End Sub` 127–8, 403, 406–11, 418, 422–3, 429, 444–5, 456–62, 466–8, 472
`End With` 410–11, 415–23, 431, 436–9, 446–7, 456–61, 466–8, 471–2, 479, 487
Enter key short-cuts 73, 217–18, 323, 387, 388, 391, 474
`EntireColumn` 423, 462–7
`EntireRow` 423, 462–7
entropy, systems 60
EOMONTH 307, 309, 312
equilibrium, circularity concepts 117–19, 122, 132–3
Error Alert 101
error-checks 40, 70, 79–86, 91–2, 97–103, 146–51, 156–8, 212–15, 232–3, 243–4, 251, 301–2, 442, 451–4, 479–90
  building 98–100, 102–3, 146, 149–51, 158, 232–3, 442
  colour-coding uses 98–9
  corrections/handling 79, 84, 91, 100–3, 119–23, 128, 138, 145, 149–51, 212–15, 359–62, 373, 380, 451–4, 461–2, 474–5, 487
  definition 97–8
  detection methods 40, 70, 79, 80, 84, 86, 91–103, 145, 149–51, 156–7, 301–2, 359–62, 451–2, 479–80, 487, 490
  formatting 98–9
  optional aspects 97–8
errors 73–4, 107, 112–15, 146, 149–51, 211–12, 228, 301–2, 359–62, 404–6, 415, 420–1, 429–30, 441–54, 479–80
  arrays 218, 451–2
  codes 451–2
  correlations 275–6
  Excel 73–4, 107, 112, 115, 146, 149–51, 211–12, 228, 301–2, 359–62, 406, 429–30, 452, 479–80
  filters 359–62
  linked workbooks 47
  multiple worksheets 49, 81, 85, 93–6
  PivotTables 380–1
  sensitivity testing 91–3, 156–7
  types 9–10, 13, 79–85, 91–103, 112, 115, 118–19, 128, 132, 138–41
  VBA 404–6, 415, 420–1, 429–30, 441–50, 451–4, 479–80
European options 17, 90, 165, 167, 475
EXACT 314, 320
Excel 20, 73–5, 85, 86, 91, 96, 102, 149, 199–394, 399–400, 421, 433, 475, 477–8, 490
  see also individual topics
  2003 421, 475, 478–9
  2007 85, 215, 305, 421, 478
  2010 257, 305, 393, 433, 477–8
  2013 305
  2016 305, 399–400, 478
  arithmetic 105–14, 201–16, 413, 486–7
  arrays 217–28, 326–7, 450–1, 460, 473, 480–4
  databases 43–5, 355–9, 370–3, 468
  date and time functions 115, 307–12, 480
  Developer 399–401, 404, 475
  filters 355–69, 461
  financial functions 243–55
  function types 105–16, 201–16, 217–28, 229–41, 243–55, 257–97, 299–306, 307–12, 313–24, 325–53, 433, 455, 461–72, 480–92
  information functions! 82, 299–306

Excel (*Continued*)
key short-cuts 73–5, 86, 91, 96, 102, 149, 217–18, 306, 358–63, 387–94, 399, 401–8, 416, 418, 430, 452, 474
logical operations 106–14, 201–16
lookup functions 116, 144, 146–8, 150, 156, 160, 161, 173–6, 215–16, 225, 299, 325–53, 485–6
mathematical functions 105–14, 201–16, 229–41
PivotTables 38, 44–5, 144, 148, 353, 355–9, 368–9, 370, 373–85, 414–15, 461
Save As 399
short forms of functions 111–12, 202–16
Sparklines 266–7, 387, 393
speed factors 140–1, 429–31
statistical functions 257–97, 475, 487–92
Status Bar 124–5, 148, 430–1, 432
Task Manager 405
VBA 171–6, 406–11, 413–23, 429–39, 461–72, 473–92
version information 85, 215, 257, 305–6, 393, 399–400, 421, 433, 475, 477–8, 490
Excel Help 343, 392
Excel Key Tips 387, 393
exchange rates 39, 323–4, 336–9
exclusion, choice (exclusion) and consolidation (inclusion) information-usage processes 52–6
`Exit Function` 453, 484, 487, 489–90
`Exit Sub` 429, 454, 461
EXP 229–32, 238, 295
expected values (EVs) 258–60
EXPON.DIST 280
EXPONDIST 280
extended ranges 102–3
external data sources 39–40

F1 392, 393, 405
F2 392
F3 86, 89, 390, 392, 408
F4 96, 388
F5 (Go To) Special 70, 72, 149–50, 391–2, 404, 418, 462–4
F7 392
F8 388, 392, 404, 405, 452, 453
F9 83, 124–5, 134, 157, 158–9, 392, 401, 430
F11 306, 392
FACT 229, 237–8
'fallacy. . .' biases 190
FALSE 112, 202–3, 320, 335–6
false formulae 65, 71, 72
false negatives/positives, modelling challenges 11
`False` 431–3, 472
FDIST 280
F.DIST.RT 280
field names 357–8, 370, 373–6
file location information 306
filters 144, 148, 355–69, 370, 375–6, 383, 393, 455, 461, 464–8
financial functions 243–55
financial instruments 39
Financial Modelling in Practice (author) 25
financial statement modelling 5–6, 17, 48–9, 69, 87, 117–19, 131–2, 201–16
financial year 234
FIND 88, 90, 148, 149–51, 313, 314, 319, 356
Find & Select 149–50
Find/Replace 356, 461, 478–9
finding first positive item in a list 225–6
finding periods in which conditions met using MATCH 33–56
finite difference methods 475
FINV 281
F.INV 281
F.INV.RT 281
FIXED 314
fixed assets 69, 250–2, 334–5
fixed costs 5, 158, 161, 165–70, 172–6
flag fields 97
flexibility requirements 16–35, 79–80, 86–7, 91–2, 105–16, 144, 345–9, 407–8, 442, 473–92
floating circularities 134–7, 141
FLOOR.MATH 229, 235
`Font` 420
fonts, optimal formatting guidelines 71–3
`For. . .` 127–8, 172–6, 195–6, 425–7, 436–9, 450–1, 459–64, 468, 479, 481–4, 488–92
`For Each. . .In. . .Next` 426–7, 436–7, 438–9
`For. . .Next` 127–8, 172–6, 195–6, 425–7, 436, 450–1, 459–63, 468, 479, 481–92
FORECAST 291, 295–7
forecast models 18, 39, 68–9, 72, 257, 273–80, 289–90, 291–7, 300–1
Forecast Sheet 297

FORECAST.ETS 291, 296
FORECAST.ETS.CONFINT 291, 296
FORECAST.ETS.SEASONALITY 291, 296
FORECAST.ETS.STAT 291, 296
FORECAST.LINEAR 291, 295–6
Format Cells 102, 390–1
Format Painter 73, 391
formatting
  background 59, 60–2, 69–76, 84, 98–9, 144–50, 159, 224, 314, 387–91, 413–14, 461
  basic approaches 71–2, 75–6, 98–9, 144
  key short-cuts 73, 387, 390–1
FormControls 404
Formula Bar 53–4, 83, 86, 94, 96, 217–18, 323, 372, 388–9, 392–3
Formula View 77
formula-dominated situations 20, 26, 37–45
formulae approaches 34–45, 53–92, 97–116, 143–51, 164–70, 217–18, 225–8, 303–4, 387–9, 473–4
  background 37–45, 67–9, 79–87, 91–103, 105–16, 134–5, 146–51, 387–9, 391
Formulas 86, 92–3, 97, 124–5, 148–9, 151, 392, 401, 407–9, 417, 429–31
FORMULATEXT 325
forward-calculation processes, modelling 5–6, 26–30, 149–50, 163
Fraction 224
FREQUENCY 217, 259–60, 264–7
frozen panes 147–8
full referencing, VBA 445–6
full stops 404
full-time-equivalent people (FTEs) 308
`Function` 403, 410, 444, 450–1, 453, 476–92
FV 244–6, 248
FVSCHEDULE 231, 244–5

GAMMA 195
GAMMA.DIST 281
GAMMADIST 281
GAMMA.INV 281
GAMMAINV 281
GAUSS 281
GDP statistics 323
general overview of the model 146, 147–51
generic numbers 12–13
GEOMEAN 258, 260–1
GETPIVOTDATA 380–2
Go To 70, 72, 90, 149–50
Go To Special 70, 72, 149–50, 391–2, 459, 461, 462–4
GoalSeek 156, 157, 163–70, 171, 172, 173–6, 247, 398, 402
good models 15–35, 47–56, 60–77, 79–84, 91–103, 143–51, 390–1, 413–14, 441–54, 473–4
`GoTo` 428–9, 454, 459, 461, 487
granularity of the time axis 30–1, 83, 334
graphical output displays 194, 330–2, 393–4
GROWTH 291, 294–5
growth rates 29, 38, 68–9, 92–3, 158, 160, 161, 208–9, 243–55, 291, 294–5

HARMEAN 258, 260–1
Help 343, 392
`Help` VBA menu 405, 451
heuristics 186
hidden inputs 82, 209–14, 306, 393
hidden worksheets 82, 147–8, 209–14, 306, 393
Hide 101–2
hierarchies, objects 414–15
HLOOKUP 85, 116, 146–7, 326, 338–44
Home 364–6, 391, 392, 394
Home/Delete Cells 364–6, 465
horizontal/vertical guidelines, audit paths 62–6, 145
HOUR 307
HYPERLINK 352–3
hyperlinks 76–7, 326, 352–3, 390, 461
HYPGEOMDIST 281
HYPGEOM.DIST 281

IF 17, 82–100, 107–16, 133, 190, 195, 201–3, 213–15, 225–8, 232–3, 251, 301–2, 334–5, 480–4
  embedded IF statements 108, 109–11, 116, 215, 225, 243
  MIN/MAX alternatives 107–9
  practical applications 107–14, 202–3, 213–15, 225–8, 232–3, 251, 301–2
IF2003ERROR 478–9
IFERROR 84, 100, 201, 212–15, 243, 334–5, 475, 478–9
`If...Then` 128, 427, 428, 463, 467, 471–2, 478, 480–4, 489–92
`Immediate` 417, 452
imperfect tests 11, 80

implementation errors, modelling 10, 13
implementation stage of modelling 4, 16, 17–18, 39, 80, 86, 144, 146–51, 157
implied volatilities 165, 167, 475
IN 257
'in-place' manipulations 460
income statements 48, 87, 118, 158, 174–6
inconsistent formulae within a range, mistakes 83–4, 85
incorrect ranges, mistakes 80–2
indented text, VBA 442–3
INDEX 29, 93–4, 110–11, 115–16, 161, 325, 328–45, 348, 356, 389
INDIRECT 52, 90, 115, 116, 160, 326, 349–52, 431, 485–6
influencing-factors/relationships benefits of modelling 7–8, 20
INFO 115, 299, 303–6
information functions 82, 299–306
Input Message 101
input value restrictions, Data Validation 100–1, 144
`InputBox` 399, 421–2, 425, 428, 457, 460, 466–7
inputs
  controllability/non-controllability of input processes 177, 178–82, 184–5, 188, 192–3
  formatting 70–6, 159
  hidden input mistakes 82
  identification needs 69–76, 191–4, 461
Insert Function 389, 409–10, 474–5
Insert/Hyperlink Menu 353
`Insert/Module` 403
Insert/PivotTable 374
Insert/Table 358–9
insight-generation benefits of modelling 7, 8, 9, 12–13
insurance policies 485
INT 229, 233–4, 310
`Integer` 449, 450, 487, 488–91
integers, sum of the integers from 1 to N 222–5
INTERCEPT 170, 273, 274, 290, 292, 294–5
interest rate calculations 34, 83, 85, 118, 121–2, 128–41, 166, 243–55
intermediate worksheets 50–6, 351–2, 473
internal rate of return 100, 165, 166
INTRATE 255
intuition 8–9, 11–12, 76, 133, 186
INV 195
`Invalid procedure call or argument (Error 5)` 451
inverse of a matrix 222–5
inverse square root law 193
investment valuations 243
IPMT 246–8
IRR 100, 165, 166, 248–51, 252
ISBLANK 68, 111–12, 203, 299, 300–2, 372
`IsDate` 454
`IsEmpty` 454
ISERROR 215, 299
ISEVEN 299
ISFORMULA 299
ISLOGICAL 299
`IsMissing` 454
ISNA 299
ISNONTEXT 299
`IsNull` 454
ISNUMBER 76, 77, 111–12, 203, 299–300, 301
`IsNumeric` 454
`IsObject` 454
ISODD 299
ISOWEEKNUM 307
ISREF 299
ISTEXT 38–9, 76, 77, 111–12, 203, 299–300, 301
italics, optimal formatting guidelines 71–3, 144, 390–1
Iteration 430
iterations/recalculations required, simulations 193–6
iterative techniques, circular references 120, 122–31, 133–41, 148–9

Kendall tau coefficient 276
key short-cuts, basics 73–5, 86, 91, 96, 102, 149, 217–18, 306, 358–63, 387–94, 399, 401–8, 416, 418, 430, 452, 474
Key Tips 387, 393
KURT 265, 272–3
kurtosis measures 265, 271–3, 475, 487–9

labels 61–2, 82, 144, 148, 159, 303–4, 322–3, 373, 404–5
LARGE 214, 227–8, 258, 260–2, 263–4
`LastCell` 458–9
lattice methods 185
launch dates, portfolio projects 179–82
layouts, good models 20, 143–4, 145
least-squares (regression) method 169, 170

LEFT 313, 314, 316–18, 324
LEN 313, 314, 317–18, 320, 357
leptokurtic distributions 271–3
LINEST 170, 217, 291–5
Linked Picture 394
linked workbooks 47–8, 50, 68, 146–7, 148
LN 229–32, 237–8, 433
loans 30, 82–3, 100, 107–9, 165, 212–15, 246–51, 335–6
localised inputs, uses 64–6
Locked 102
Log 433
logarithmic curves 169, 170, 195, 237–8, 294–5
LOGEST 291, 293–5
logic flows 6, 16, 40, 68–9, 79–80, 89–96, 119, 133–4, 143–51, 171–6, 184, 191–2
Logical 212
logical operations 106–14, 201–16
LOGINV 281
LOGNORM 195
LOGNORM.DIST 281
LOGNORMDIST 281
LOGNORM.INV 281
Long 449, 450, 468, 482, 488–91
LOOKUP 326, 343–4
lookup functions 85, 91–6, 110–11, 116, 144–61, 173–9, 215–17, 225, 299, 323–56, 485–6
  overview of core functions 325–6
  practical applications 326–53, 485–6
Loop 128, 428–9, 468
Los Alamos National Laboratory 187
LOWER 314, 319

Macaulay duration 253
Macro Settings 406, 475
macro-economic forecasts 161
macros 4, 18, 51–6, 80–5, 120–47, 156–7, 164, 171–6, 185, 196, 239, 260, 358–9, 364, 373, 392, 395–492
  definition 127, 359, 397, 404
  recording 399–400, 401–3, 416, 418, 429–31, 441–2, 447, 459, 461
Manage Rules/New Rule 73, 149–50
Manual calculation method 124–5, 126–7, 148, 157, 305, 401–2, 429–31
MATCH 29, 93–4, 100, 110–11, 116, 147, 161, 325, 335–46, 348–9, 389
  background 29, 93–4, 325, 335–45, 389
  practical applications 335–45, 346, 348–9, 389
matching 324
Math&Trig category 217, 229, 257
mathematics 105–14, 119, 121–2, 128, 130–3, 140–1, 201–17, 219–25, 229–41
matrix algebra 185
matrix calculations 217, 221, 222–5, 278–80
matrix multiplications 219–22
MAX 17, 88–9, 106–9, 133, 147, 190, 201–4, 210–14, 225, 228, 232–3, 243, 257, 261–2, 433
MAXA 81, 204, 257
MAXIF 225–6, 257
MAXIFS 201, 204, 225–6, 259, 355, 356, 370
MDETERM 222
MDURATION, background 253–4
mean values 11, 33, 258–61, 271–3, 285–91, 475, 488–9, 491–2
mean-variance portfolios 475
MEDIAN 214, 258–64
mesokurtic distributions 271–3
MID 94–6, 313, 314, 317–18, 357
MIN 17, 106–9, 133–7, 147, 179–82, 190, 201–4, 210, 214, 225–33, 243, 257, 261–2, 345, 433
MINA 81, 204, 257
MINIFS 201, 204, 257, 259, 370
MINUTE 307
MINVERSE 217, 221, 222, 224–5
MIRR 250
mirror worksheets, linked workbooks 48, 50, 68, 146–7
mistakes 79–103, 112–23, 132, 138–45, 151, 243–8, 299, 356, 360, 451–2
  examples 80–5
  general causes 79–80
mixed formulas 37–8, 40, 82, 143–5, 148
MMULT 209, 219–22, 279–80
MOD 229, 236
MODE 214, 258–64
Model 151
model assumptions, definition 34
model events, VBA 398–9, 423, 442
'model as you read' principle 68–9
modelling
  see also building. . .; design. . .; *individual topics*; robust. . .

modelling (*Continued*)
background 1–35, 41–5, 59, 60–2, 79–80, 143–55, 163–70, 185, 189–92, 269, 397
bad models 15, 60, 79–80, 85, 89–90
benefits 7–9, 16–21
best practices 4, 13–21, 47–77, 79–86, 91–103, 143–51, 173, 445, 473–4
challenges 4, 7, 8–13, 189–90, 191–2, 269
critique 4–6, 7, 8–13, 15–21, 43–5, 143–51
definition 3–4, 8
detail/aggregation levels 5–6, 26–9, 30–1, 40–1, 45
documentation 59, 76–7, 84, 91, 102–3, 133, 143–4, 147, 441, 442–3, 475
good models 15–35, 47–56, 60–77, 79–84, 91–103, 143–51, 390–1, 413–14, 441–54, 473–4
granularity of the time axis 30–1, 83, 334
influencing-factors/relationships benefits of modelling 7–8, 20
insight-generation benefits of modelling 7, 8, 9, 12–13
multiple worksheets 20, 47–56, 62, 81, 85, 87, 93–6
numerical-information benefits of modelling 7–8, 13
objectives 3, 16–17, 26, 143–51, 184–5
passwords 50, 102, 147–8
rebuilds/restructurings to improve the model 86–9, 96, 120, 139, 145–51, 430–1
reviews 12, 59–62, 143–51
sensitivity and flexibility requirements 25–35
simplicity 16, 19, 20–1, 41, 59, 60–2
stages 3–4, 9–10, 15–16, 25, 79–80, 144, 155
updates 15–25, 39–41, 47–8, 84–5, 97–8, 108, 130–1, 144–51, 429–32, 441–3, 466, 473–4
validity issues 4, 10, 18–19, 21, 34–5, 40, 88, 92–3, 132–3, 141, 143–51, 393, 441–2
ModelRisk 196
MODE.MULT 258, 259–60
MODE.SNGL 257, 258–64
modified duration 253–4
modular approaches 49–50, 63–6, 67, 443–4
moments 11, 33, 210, 214, 258–65, 267–73, 283–4, 285–91, 475, 487–9
Monte Carlo Simulation (MCS) 180–1, 187–91, 398
MONTH 307, 309–10, 312, 480–1
More Commands 405
More Options 102
mortgages 243, 246–8
motivational/political biases 11
'MR. . .' names, udfs 474
MROUND 229, 235
`MsgBox` 399, 405, 406–7, 410–11, 421–2, 423, 425, 427, 447, 453–4
multi-cell ranges, VBA 407, 422, 450–1
Multi-sheet ("3-dimensional") formulae 52, 53–4, 68, 148–9
multi-sheet workbooks 20, 68
multiple queries, databases 371–2, 468–9
multiple regressions 292–4
multiple worksheets 20, 47–56, 62, 81, 85–7, 93–6, 143–51, 351–2, 458–9, 469–72
background 47–56, 62–6, 81, 85–7, 143–8, 351–2, 391–3, 458–9, 469–72
best practices 49–56, 63–6, 81, 145
errors 49, 81, 85, 93–6
INDIRECT uses 351–2
passwords 50, 147–8
multiplication, transparency/flexibility/efficiency choices 105–7

N 299
#N/A 92, 137, 259–60, 299, 301–2
NA function 302–3
`Name` 403, 437–8, 449
Name Box 86, 90–1
name choices, code basics 449–50
Name Manager 86, 90, 148, 389–90, 407–8, 417
named ranges 48, 77–91, 140–8, 151, 173–6, 352–3, 389–92, 407–9, 416–23, 436, 449–57
advantages/disadvantages 86–91
best practices 85–6
hyperlinks 353, 390
key short-cuts 389–90, 392, 408
linked workbooks 48, 68
mechanics and implementation 86
mistakes 80–2, 85, 86–90, 151
`Names` 414–15, 449
natural logarithms 229–32
navigation uses, key short-cuts 387, 391–3
negative numbers, formatting 75
NEGBINOM.DIST 281
NEGBINOMDIST 281
net asset values 48

net income 118, 121–2, 126
net present value (NPV) 83, 88–9, 106, 160, 165, 179–82, 185, 248–51, 335, 450
NETWORKDAYS 307
NETWORKDAYS.INTL 307
new fields 357
Newton-Raphson iteration 475
Next 127–8, 172–6, 195–6, 425–7, 436, 438–9, 450–1, 454, 459–63, 468, 471–2, 479, 481–4, 488–92
NOMINAL 255
non-contiguous scenario data, MATCH 336–7
non-linear curve fitting methods 165, 169–70
non-transparent assumptions, mistakes 82
NORM 195, 257, 281
normal distributions 271–3, 280–91
NORM.DIST 257, 280, 281
NORMDIST 280, 281
NORM.DIST 281
NORM.INV 280, 281, 284
NORMINV 280, 281
NORMSDIST 281
NORM.S.DIST 281, 283
NORMSINV 281, 283–4, 305–6, 477–8
NORM.S.INV 281, 283–4, 477–8
NOT 111, 201, 202–3, 300–1
NOW 115, 307
NPER 246–8
NPV 83, 88–9, 106, 165, 179–82, 185, 248–51, 335, 450
nuclear weapons 187
#NULL! 86
#NUM! 100, 138–41, 213
NUMBERVALUE 313, 316
numerical assumptions 34–5
numerical field alternatives, text fields 112
numerical-information benefits of modelling 7–8, 13

Object 415, 449, 488
Object doesn't support this property or method (Error 438) 452
Object variable not set (Error 91) 415, 451–2
objectives-driven benefits, good models 16, 26, 143–51
objects 403, 404, 413–23, 438–9, 445–8, 449
ODDFPRICE 255
ODDFYIELD 252
ODDLPRICE 255
ODDLYIELD 252
OFFSET 40, 90, 115, 116, 325, 328–34, 336, 345–9, 421, 431
  inefficiencies 115, 116
  practical applications 115, 116, 328–34, 336, 345–9
Offset 172–6, 195–6, 421, 422, 435–6, 439, 448, 459–61, 467–8, 479, 487
oil 183–4, 275, 282, 335–6
On Error... 454, 461–2, 487
one-sided risk 268
one-way data tables 157–61
operating profits 69
optimisation 4–9, 21, 33, 62–9, 80, 140, 149–56, 163–70, 175–94, 222, 232, 398
  background 62–9, 169–70, 177–86, 188, 222, 232
  curve fitting methods 169–70
  logic flows 68–9, 149
  objectives 184–5
  portfolios 222, 272–3, 475
  practical examples 179–82, 185
  tools 184–6, 232
Option Base 451
Option Explicit 449, 450–1
options 17, 90, 103, 165, 167, 475, 102, 124–5, 399, 401, 406, 429–31, 475
OR 106–7, 111, 147, 201, 202–3, 370
organisational behaviour 13
outputs 59–77, 143–51, 155–61, 163–70, 171–6, 177–86, 190–7, 328–32, 355–85, 393–4, 399
  formatting 70–6, 159
  identification needs 69–76, 191–4
  types 71, 143–51, 190
over-dollared formulae 96
overconfidence, mistakes 80

'P-to-X' processes, probability distributions 280–5
Page Layout 77, 91
Page Setup 77
Palisade's Evolver 184
passwords 50, 102, 144, 147–8
Paste List 86
Paste Names 86
PasteSpecial 356, 414
payroll costs 26–30, 31, 32, 35, 311–12
PDURATION 254–5
PEARSON 274, 275–7, 489
percentage variations 28–30, 31, 32, 45

PERCENTILE 214, 258, 262–4, 265, 280
PERCENTILE.EXC 258, 262–4
PERCENTILE.INC 258, 262–4
PERCENTRANK.EXC 258, 263–4, 266–7
PERCENTRANK.INC 258, 263–4, 266–7
performance indicators 190
PERMUT 257
Personal Macro Workbook 401, 405
pharmaceuticals 183
PHI 281
PHONETIC 314
physicians 201–16
PI 229, 239–41
PivotCharts 382–3
`PivotTables` 438–9
PivotTables 38, 44–5, 144, 148, 353, 355–9, 368–9, 370, 373–85, 402, 414–15, 438–9, 461
  advantages/disadvantages 373–4
  background 355–9, 368, 370, 373–85, 402, 414–15, 438–9, 461
  errors 380–1
  practical applications 373–85
planning 23–56
platykurtic distributions 271–3
PMT 82–3, 165, 246–8
POISSON 281
POISSON.DIST 281
politics 11, 189
Popular Commands 405
portfolios 179–82, 185, 209, 222–5, 272–3, 277–80, 289–90, 475
position statistical functions, practical applications 258–64
positive numbers, formatting 75
POWER 229, 236–7
PowerView 384
PPMT 100, 212–15, 246–8
precedents 149–50, 341–4, 391–3, 461
presentation (reporting) layers 37–9, 50–2
PRICE. . . 255
prices 5, 26–30, 32, 33–5, 47–8, 60–2, 89, 160–1, 172–6, 178–9, 184
printing 48, 77, 91, 452
`Private` 434–5, 443, 474–5
PROB 281
`Probability` 478
probability distributions 33, 181, 188, 191–7, 207–8, 237–9, 257, 264–73, 280–91, 475, 487–9
  background 271–3, 280–91, 475, 487–9
  practical applications 280–91
  types 280–1
PROBE 257
problem-solving skills 16, 17, 21
`Procedure` 403–4
procedures executed within procedures, VBA 434–5, 443, 451
processes/tools to audit/validate implementations 146–51
PRODUCT 106, 201, 207–9, 210, 214
product designs 8–9
productivity 161, 169
profits 34, 40–1, 60–2, 69, 87–9, 118, 121, 158, 160–1, 164–70, 172–6, 190
`Project` 400–2, 403, 419, 435–6
`Project Explorer` 399–400
project finance 201
project rejections 13
`Project Window` 403
PROPER 314, 319–20
`Properties` 399–400, 403–4, 407, 414, 419, 443, 447
Protect Sheet 102
Protect Workbook 102
protected cells/ranges/worksheets/workbooks 84, 101–3, 143–4, 147–8, 209–11, 214
Protection 102
`Public` 409–10, 434–5, 443, 474–5
pure audits 143–4, 145, 147
put options 475
PV 244–6, 248, 254

quadratic curve fitting methods 165, 169–70
qualitative approaches 3–5, 8, 25, 191
quantitative approaches 3–4, 5, 8, 12, 25, 191–2
quarter of a given date 310
QUARTILE 214, 258
QUARTILE.EXC 258
QUARTILE.INC 258
Quick Access Toolbar (QAT) 394, 405

RAND 115, 194–7, 238–40, 257, 283–5, 433
random numbers 33, 115, 156, 180–2, 187–8, 193–7, 238–9, 283–4, 450–1
Range 86–97
range objects, VBA 413, 416–23, 445–6, 448
`Range.Calculate` 431
`Range` 86, 127–8, 172–6, 195–6, 327, 402, 404, 406–9, 414–23, 425–7, 436, 445–6, 447–9, 456, 459, 461, 466–8, 471–2, 486–90

RANK 262–3, 264, 276–80
RANK.AVG 258, 262–3, 264, 489–91
RANK.EQ 257, 258, 261–3, 264
ranking statistical functions, practical applications 258, 260–4, 275–7
rapid 'drill-downs', PivotTables 355, 356–7, 373–85
RATE 255
rationality 11–12, 20–1, 25
ratios 118, 231
read-only workbooks 102
real options, definition 184
rebuilds/restructurings to improve the model 86–9, 96, 120, 139, 145–51, 430–1
recalculations 193–6, 305, 401–2, 421–2, 429–31
recalculations of Excel when a macro is running 429–31
RECEIVED 255
recombining trees 237–8
Record Macro 401
recording, macros 399–400, 401–3, 416, 418, 429–31, 441–2, 447, 459, 461
recovery trails 147
ReDim 450–1, 481, 482, 490
redundant names 90
#REF! 90, 150
reference functions 325–53, 485–7
References 175, 217, 325–53, 435, 485–6
Refers To 90
RefersToRange 439
refinancing conditions 30
regression, background 170, 274, 289, 290
regression analysis 169, 170, 257, 273–80, 289–90, 291–7
RELEASE 305–6
Remove Duplicates 356, 362–3, 368–9, 461
removing blanks/items, filters 363–5, 464–8
repeated calculations, restrictions 96–7, 101, 146
REPLACE 88, 151, 313, 314, 320–1, 356
reports 37–9, 50–2, 311, 355–85, 399
REPT 313, 320–1
Require Variable Declaration 449
residual values, depreciation 251–2, 484–5
resource forecasting 220–2
ResultsArray 451
Resume 454, 462–4
return values 82–3, 112, 230–2, 243–55, 266–80, 290, 299–306, 409–10, 453, 475
reusable model logic 63–6, 159, 441–2, 474
revenues 5, 29–49, 60–9, 83–92, 108–11, 121–2, 160–76, 184, 201–22, 335–6, 384–5
reversing/transposing data 331–4, 356, 455, 459–60
Review 76, 102, 147
Reviewing Toolbar 76
reviews 12, 59–62, 143–51
RIGHT 313, 314, 316–18, 324
right-clicks 404, 465
@RISK 181–2, 185, 194
risk identification 191–2
risk management 189–90, 191
risk mapping 191–2
risk mitigation 8–9, 188, 191–2
risk modelling 8–19, 181–2, 185, 187–97, 268–9, 272–3, 290, 491–2
  benefits 189–90
  beta 290, 291–3
  Capital Asset Pricing Model (CAPM) 290–1
  definition 182, 188
  key steps 191–4
  @RISK 181–2, 185, 194
  simulation contrasts 188
risk-neutral valuation methods 17, 222
risk-tolerances 183
RiskOptimizer 185
RiskSolver 196
Rnd 433
robust models 4–9, 21, 48–9, 79–103, 116, 134–5, 143–51, 197, 303–4, 334, 341–2, 402–17, 441–54, 474
ROMAN 229, 241
ROUND 229, 233–4
ROUNDDOWN 229, 233–4, 334
ROUNDUP 229, 310
ROW 299, 326–8, 333
ROWS 299, 327
Rows 327, 414, 417–18, 456–64, 467–8, 471–2, 479, 489
RRI 254–5
RSQ 274, 290
RTD 353
Run 434–5
run-time measurements, VBA 432–3
Run/Break 405
Run/Reset 405
Run/Run Sub 404–5
running code, VBA 404–5, 407

S&P 500 index 269–70
sales 5, 18–19, 26–30, 68–9, 161, 164–70, 172–6, 184
Save As 102, 399
`SaveChanges` 472
saved work 147
scatter-plots (X-Y charts) 190, 273–5, 291
scenario analysis 8–21, 32–40, 91–3, 149, 155, 160–1, 171–86, 239, 328–36, 341, 351–2, 421–7
  core techniques 155, 160–1, 172–6
  definition 32–3, 160–1, 188–9
  limitations 188–9
  practical applications 160–1, 172–6, 328–30, 336, 341, 351–2
Scenarios Manager 161
scope of model validity 4, 10, 88
screen updating, VBA 432, 466
SEARCH 93–6, 313, 314, 318–19, 324
SECOND 307
`Select` 90, 414, 416, 418, 427, 428, 438, 448, 456, 462–4, 466–8
`Select Case...End Select` 427, 428, 438, 454, 478, 487, 490
`Selection` 402, 416, 418, 448, 461, 462–4, 466
self-regulating systems, circularities 117–19, 132–3
self-validating models 144
semi-deviation (one-sided volatility) 265, 268, 272–3, 280, 475, 491–2
  definition 272–3, 491
sensitivity analysis 4–19, 25–38, 55–6, 91–3, 127, 140–9, 151–63, 171–86, 232, 328–30
  absolute/variation base-case considerations 27–8, 31–2
  background 25–35, 155–61, 172–9, 188–9
  circular references problems 127, 132, 140–1
  core techniques 155–61, 172–6
  detail/aggregation levels 5–6, 26–9, 30–1
  error detection methods 91–3, 145, 156–7
  limitations 188–9
  overview of techniques 155
  practical applications 158, 160–1, 172–6, 328–30
  scenario analysis 32–3, 91–3, 149, 160–1, 328–30
  VBA 156, 171–6
sensitivity-analysis thinking (SAT) 25–35
sensitivity-driven model designs 4
separation of data/analysis/presentation layers 37–9, 40
`Set` 415–23, 433, 437, 446–7, 450–2, 456–72, 478–80, 484, 487–90
Set Print Area 91
setting-to-zero approach, GoalSeek/Solver tips 163–4
shape practical applications, statistical functions 264–73
share prices 189
SHEET 77, 299, 306
`Sheet` 403, 408, 419, 423, 442
SHEETS 299, 306
Shift 387, 388, 390, 392–3, 404, 430, 442, 452, 474
Shift+Arrow 393
Shift+Ctrl+Alt+F9 430
Shift+F2 392
Shift+F3 390
Shift+F5 391
Shift+F8 452
Shift+Tab 404, 443
short forms of functions 111–12, 202–16
short-cuts *see* key short-cuts
Show All Comments 76
Show Details 376
Show Formulas 148, 149–50, 391
Show icon 75, 76
`ShowAllData` 466–8
SIGN 229, 232–3, 235
simplicity, good models 16, 19, 20–1, 41, 59, 60–2, 145
simulations 11, 21, 33, 160, 177–86, 187–97, 398, 450–1
  definition 177–8, 182, 185, 187–8, 190–1
  Excel 194–7
  Monte Carlo Simulation (MCS) 180–1, 187–91, 398
  origins 187–8
  practical applications 179–82, 185, 190–1
  risk modelling contrasts 188
  VBA 33, 187, 194–7, 398, 450–1
SINE 229, 239–41
`Single` 449, 491
single main formulae worksheet and several data and local analysis worksheets (type III) models 50–2, 55, 66
single main formulae worksheet and several data worksheets (type II) models 50–2

single worksheet (type I) models, best practice examples 50–2, 160
size limitations, structural issues 102–3
SKEW 264–5, 271–3
skewness measures 264–5, 271–3, 475, 487–9
SKEW.P 271–3
SKEW.S 271–3
skills 16, 17–18, 21
slicers, PivotTables 376–80
SLN 250–1
SLOPE 170, 274, 289, 290, 291–5
SMALL 214, 227–8, 258, 261–2
Solver 33, 156, 163–76, 180–2, 184–5, 247, 398, 402, 436, 457
  definition 163–4
  limitations and tips 163–4
sorting 257, 258, 260–2, 356, 461
SPACE 86, 404
spaces, formatting guidelines 75–6
Sparklines 266–7, 387, 393
Spearman Rank Correlation 262, 275–7, 475, 489–91
`SpecialCells` 462–4
specific-to-the-general code writing guidelines 441–2
specification (model) errors, modelling 9–10, 13, 119, 120–1
specification stage of modelling 3–4, 9–10, 13, 33, 117, 120–1, 144, 148
spelling mistakes 356, 360, 392, 408
`Split` 474, 476–7
splitting considerations, embedded (compound) functions 94–6
splitting data 315, 316–17, 356, 476–7
spread practical applications, statistical functions 264–73
SQL 355
`Sqr` 433
SQRT 229, 236–7, 269–70, 288, 289, 290, 433
SQRTPI 229, 241
stages of modelling 3–4, 9–10, 15–16, 25, 144, 155
standard deviations 33, 210, 214, 265, 267–73, 283–4, 475, 487–9, 491
standard error 291
STANDARDIZE 265
start date limitations 18–19, 34–5, 92–3
static queries 356–7
Statistical category 257
statistical functions 112–13, 169–70, 190, 195, 201, 206–7, 257–97, 475, 487–92
statistics 190–4, 201–16, 217, 257–97, 487–92
Status Bar 124–5, 148, 430–1, 432
STDEV 210, 214, 265, 269–71, 272, 290
STDEVA 265
STDEVP 210, 214, 265, 269–71
STDEV.P 265, 269–71
STDEVPA 265
STDEV.S 257, 265, 269–71, 274, 277, 290
`Step` 426, 452–3, 463
STEYX 291
stochastic optimisation 185, 189
Stop Recording Macro 401
`Storage` 481
`String` 449, 476, 486
`StrReverse` 474, 476–7
structural biases 11
structural issues 8–30, 37–80, 85–91, 102–3, 117–44, 159–60, 182–3, 306, 349–85, 415–23
Student T distributions 281, 285–92
`Sub` 403–11, 418, 422–3, 436, 444–5, 454–7, 459–61, 466–8, 471–2
sub-optimal choice of functions, mistakes 80
sub-optimal solution sufficiencies, optimisation 186
subroutines 397, 403–11, 434–5, 443–5, 452–3
`Subscript out of range (Error 9)` 451
SUBSTITUTE 313, 320–1
substitution processes 95–6
SUBTOTAL 114–15, 201, 209–13, 214, 361, 461
subtraction, transparency/flexibility/efficiency choices 105–7
SUM 67, 81, 88–98, 105–9, 113–15, 118, 147, 201, 206–14, 230–3, 258–60, 279–80, 302, 346–51, 361, 368, 388, 433, 450–1, 480
sum of absolute errors example, udfs 475, 479–80
sum of the integers from 1 to N 222–5
sum of squares 170, 482–4
SUMIF 112–13, 116, 201, 206–7, 257, 486–7

SUMIFS 29, 38–45, 53–6, 82, 97–9, 112–16, 201–7, 311, 317, 355–6, 361, 370–1, 382, 469–72
summary calculations, logic flows 69, 71
summary figures 43, 92–3, 113–14, 373–6
SUMPRODUCT 83, 106, 112, 201, 202–3, 209, 218–20, 222, 253–4, 258–60, 265, 334–5, 487–9
sunk costs 13
SWITCH 161, 201, 215–16, 336
SYD 250–1
systems concepts 60, 117–19

T 313
Tab key 404, 443
Table 40, 90, 94, 358–9, 366–9, 373–4, 383–5, 391
Table of Contents, hyperlinks 461
Table Tools Design Tab 368–9
TAN 229, 240–1
`Target` 422–3
task durations 308
tax 34–5, 48, 82, 92, 108–9, 118, 165, 166, 167–8, 175–6
tax-loss carry-forwards 35
TBILLEQ 255
TBILLPRICE 255
TBILLYIELD 252
TDIST 281
T.DIST 281
T.DIST.2T 281
T.DIST.RT 281
template sheets 52
tests 11, 15–16, 57, 79–80, 91–103, 146, 151, 429–30, 442–3, 448, 452–4
TEXT 38–9, 93–4, 314, 323, 330–1
text fields 37–9, 71, 81–3, 100–1, 112, 202–5, 215–16, 308, 336–7, 406–7, 442–9, 476–7
text functions 38–9, 93–6, 313–24
Text-to-Columns Wizard 315, 356
TextBox 404
TEXTJOIN 313, 314–15
This Worksheet 149–50
`ThisWorkbook` 403, 410–11, 423, 471–2
TIME 307
  date and time functions 115, 307–12, 480
time axis 29–31, 39–50, 83–7, 309–12, 334, 341–2, 431–2, 475, 480–5
time dependences 42
time-based reports 311
'time-bomb' models 80
time-scaling, volatilities 277–80
time-series models 5–6, 225–6, 331–4, 441–2
time-shifting mechanisms 34–5, 39, 85, 248, 334
`Timer` 432, 448
TIMEVALUE 307
timing alterations 34–5
TINV 281, 286–91
T.INV 281, 286–91
T.INV.2T 281, 286, 288, 292
TODAY 115, 307
Tools 102, 175, 375–9
Tools/Analyze 375–9
`Tools` 404, 435, 443, 449
`Tools/References` 435
Trace Dependents 149–50, 341–2
Trace Precedents 149–50, 341–4, 391–3
tracking methods, changes 147
traditional models *see* formula-dominated situations
transfer areas 64–6, 96–7
translations 347–8
transparency 9–21, 33–9, 48, 59–116, 133–4, 144–51, 164, 218, 301–2, 341–5, 390–1, 410, 416, 441–54, 474
  background 59–77, 84, 105–16, 145–6, 150–1, 218, 390–1, 474
  core elements of transparent models 61–9
  enhancement methods 59–77, 84, 145, 150–1, 218, 390
  good models 20–1, 33, 48, 60–77, 84, 116, 145, 390–1, 441–54, 474
  meta-principle 62
TRANSPOSE 209, 217, 218–22, 251, 279–80, 325, 333–4
`trappable errors` 451–2
Treasury bills 252, 255
trees 5–6, 103, 182, 185, 237–8
TREND 291, 294–5
triangle calculations 334–5, 475, 484–5
TRIM 313, 321–2
TRIMMEAN 258, 260–1
TRUE 83, 101, 112, 175, 202–3, 292, 299–306, 335–6
`True` 431–3, 474
TRUNC 229, 233–4
Trust Centre 406
two-way data tables 157–61
TYPE 299
`Type mismatch (Error 13)` 451
`Type` 422

U-shaped curves, optimisation 184–5
`UCase` 438, 471–2
udfs *see* user-defined functions
uncertainties 8–13, 18–19, 33, 70–1, 178–86, 187–97
underlinings 71–3, 390–1
UNDERSCORE 404
UNICHAR 313, 322
UNICODE 313
`Union` 421, 423
unique combinations/items, data sets 362–3
unique identifiers 323–4, 336–7, 362–3
unknown unknowns 9, 11
Unprotect Workbook 147
`Until` 128, 428–9
unused calculations, restrictions 96–7
updates 15–25, 39–48, 84–5, 97–8, 108, 130–1, 144–51, 429–32, 441–3, 473–4
UPPER 314, 319, 438
Use in Formula 86
`UsedRange` 415, 416, 417, 419–20, 457–65, 467, 471–2
user forms 397, 399, 403, 405
user-defined functions (udfs) 19–21, 52–6, 94, 103, 115, 144, 194, 218, 265, 272–3, 284–5, 397–8, 409–10, 442, 473–92
  see also individual topics; Visual Basic for Applications
  access methods 474–5
  background 94, 115, 276, 303, 397, 398, 473–92
  benefits 473–4
  code basics 474–92
  definition 397, 398, 473–4
  general functions 475, 479–87
  implementation methods 273, 474–5
  limitations 410
  practical applications 475–92
  simple example 409–10
  syntax 474–5
  'wrapper' functions 303, 473, 475–9
user-friendly modelling 16, 20–1, 144, 150–1, 163–4
user-interface enhancement/management uses, VBA 399, 421–2, 425, 455, 457, 466, 467
`UserForm` 399, 403, 405

`Val` 474, 476–8
Validation 87–9, 100–1
validity issues 4, 10, 18–21, 34–5, 40, 88–93, 132–3, 141–51, 393, 441–2
valuations 17, 90, 103, 165, 167, 182, 208–9, 222, 290, 475
VALUE 87–9, 93–6, 111–12, 201–3, 218, 301, 313–18, 468
value-added decision-support guide 4, 8, 12, 25–6, 30, 76–7, 98–9, 144–5, 155, 191
value-added error-checks 98–9
value-at-risk 268
`Value` 127–8, 195–6, 406–9, 415, 420, 422, 446, 448, 459–60, 486–7
VAR 210, 214, 265, 269–71
VARA 265
variable costs 5, 26–30, 31, 32, 48–9, 158, 161, 165–70, 174–6
variables 26–41, 45, 70–6, 178–82, 183–6, 187–97, 448–9, 451
  declarations 448–9, 451
  detail/aggregation levels 30–1, 40–1, 45
variance 265, 267–71, 277–80, 475
`Variant` 449
VARP 210, 265
VAR.P 265, 269–71
VARPA 265
VAR.S 265, 269–71
VBA *see* Visual Basic for Applications
VBA Project 102
VDB 250–2
version information, Excel 85, 215, 257, 305–6, 393, 399–400, 421, 433, 475, 477–8, 490
vertical/horizontal guidelines, audit paths 62–6, 145
View 147
`View menu` 399–400, 452–3
`View/CallStack` 452
`View/Code` 403
`View/Locals` 452
`View/Watch Window` 452
Visual Basic for Applications (VBA) 171–6, 395–492
  see also code basics; *individual topics*; user-defined functions
  automation 359, 364–5, 372, 392, 397–8, 425–6, 455, 461, 464–8
  control of execution methods 425–39, 466
  core operations 171–6, 397, 399–411
  data sets' manipulation/analysis 398, 455–72, 476–7
  efficiencies 402–4, 416, 429–31, 441–54
  Excel 171–6, 406–11, 413–23, 429–39, 461–72, 473–92
  getting started 397–411

Visual Basic (*Continued*)
objects 403, 404, 413–23, 438–9, 445–8
overview of the main uses 397–9
practical applications 172–6, 406–11, 435–9, 455–72, 475–92
range objects 413, 416–23, 445–6, 448
robust code 441–54
`Set` 415–23, 433, 437, 446–7, 450–2, 456–72, 478–80, 484, 487–90
simple examples 406–11
speed factors 140–1, 429–31
`UsedRange` 415, 416, 417, 419–20, 458–63, 467, 471–2
Visual Basic Editor 147, 175, 392, 399–400, 443, 449
visual influence diagrams, Excel limitations 20
visual inspections 148–9
VLOOKUP 85, 93–4, 116, 146–7, 326, 338–44, 348
`Volatile` 453, 474–5
volatile functions 115–16, 327–8, 430–1, 474–5
volatilities 165, 167, 185, 267–71, 272–3, 277–80, 475, 491–2
Voltaire 8
volumes 5, 18–19, 26–35, 40–5, 60–2, 160–1, 164–70, 172–6, 184

Watch Window 92–3, 151, 452
websites 39–40, 76–7, 326, 352–3, 390, 461
WEEKDAY 307, 311, 312
WEEKNUM 307
WEIBULL 281
Weibull distributions 281, 284–5
WEIBULL.DIST 281
weighted averages 258–60
`Wend` 429
what if? analysis 155, 157, 161, 163–70
What-If-Analysis 157, 161, 163–70
`With...` 410–11, 415–23, 431–9, 446, 447, 456–61, 466, 468, 471–2, 479, 487
workbook structures 37–9, 47–56, 62–8, 84–6, 101–3, 143–8, 209–14, 371–2, 393–4, 400–39, 445–6, 469–75
`Workbook_Close` 411
`Workbook_Open` 410
`Workbooks` 414–15, 442, 446, 472
`Workbooks.Close` 472
`Workbook_SheetChange` 423
`Workbooks.Open` 472
WORKDAY 308
WORKDAY.INTL 308
working capital 81
working processes, modelling benefits 9
worksheets 47–56, 63–6, 82–6, 101–3, 143–51, 160, 209–14, 349–52, 391–3, 414–22, 433–49, 458, 485–7
`Worksheet_Change` 423
`WorksheetFunction` 414–15, 433, 467, 478, 480, 482–4, 489–91
`Worksheets` 414–15, 419, 420, 422–3, 426–7, 437, 438–9, 446, 486–7
'wrapper' functions 303, 473, 475–9
writing code, VBA 403–4, 413, 416, 435–9, 441–54, 456–72, 474–92

'X-to-P' processes, probability distributions 280–1
XIRR 250
`xlCellTypeLastCell` 416, 418, 419
`xlSemiautomatic` 430
XLStart 401
XNPV 250

YEAR 307, 309–10, 312, 480–1
YEARFRAC 308
YIELD 252–4
YIELDDISC 252
YIELDMAT 252
yields 243, 248, 252–4

Printed and bound by CPI Group (UK) Ltd, Croydon, CR0 4YY

23/04/2025

14660950-0004